THE JOSSEY-BASS
READER ON
GENDER IN EDUCATION

○

Foreword by

Susan M. Bailey

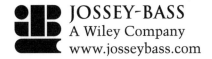

JOSSEY-BASS
A Wiley Company
www.josseybass.com

Published by

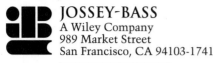 **JOSSEY-BASS**
A Wiley Company
989 Market Street
San Francisco, CA 94103-1741

www.josseybass.com

Jossey-Bass books and products are available through most bookstores. To contact Jossey-Bass directly, call (888) 378-2537, fax to (800) 605-2665, or visit our website at www.josseybass.com.

Substantial discounts on bulk quantities of Jossey-Bass books are available to corporations, professional associations, and other organizations. For details and discount information, contact the special sales department at Jossey-Bass.

We at Jossey-Bass strive to use the most environmentally sensitive paper stocks available to us. Our publications are printed on acid-free recycled stock whenever possible, and our paper always meets or exceeds minimum GPO and EPA requirements.

Project Editor: Elisa Rassen
Acquiring Editor: Lesley Iura
Senior Production Editor: Pamela Berkman

Marketing Manager: Currie McLaughlin
Permissions Editor: Veronica Oliva
Cover Designer and Interior Designer: Bruce Lundquist

Library of Congress Cataloging-in-Publication Data

The Jossey-Bass reader on gender in education.
        p. cm.—(The Jossey-Bass education series)
    Includes bibliographical references.
    ISBN 0-7879-6074-8
    1. Sex differences in education—United States. 2. Sex discrimination in education—United States. 3. Educational equalization —United States.
    I. Title: Jossey-Bass reader on gender. II. Jossey-Bass Inc. III. Title.
    IV. Jossey-Bass education series.
    LC212.92 .J67 2002

    306.43—dc21   2002001145

PB Printing   10 9 8 7 6 5 4 3 2 1

The Jossey-Bass
Education Series

CONTENTS

Sources   xi
About the Authors   xv
Acknowledgments   xix
Foreword   xxi
Susan M. Bailey

INTRODUCTION
The History of Gender Issues in Education

1. "Too Strong for a Woman"—The Five Words
   That Created Title IX   2
   Bernice R. Sandler
2. Feminists Discover the Hidden Injuries of Coeducation   12
   David Tyack and Elisabeth Hansot

PART ONE
Female and Male Identity

3. Images of Relationship   51
   Carol Gilligan
4. Real Boys: The Truths Behind the Myths   88
   William Pollack
5. Where It All Begins: The Biology of Boyhood   101
   Michael Gurian
6. Do Girls and Boys Have Different Cultures?   125
   Barrie Thorne

PART TWO
Negotiating the Classroom

7. Thorns Among Roses: The Struggle of Young Boys
   in Early Education   153
   Dan Kindlon and Michael Thompson

8. The Miseducation of Boys   182
   Myra Sadker and David Sadker
9. The Madgirl in the Classroom   204
   Lyn Mikel Brown
10. How Girls Negotiate School   243
    Research for Action
    (American Association of University Women)

                        PART THREE
               Gender Equity in the Curriculum
   ──

11. Course-Taking Patterns   277
    American Association of University Women
12. Breaking the Barriers: The Critical Middle School Years   301
    Beatriz Chu Clewell
13. Misreading Masculinity: Speculations on the
    Great Gender Gap in Writing   314
    Thomas Newkirk
14. Girls and Design: Exploring the Question of
    Technological Imagination   329
    Margaret Honey, Babette Moeller, Cornelia Brunner,
    Dorothy Bennett, Peggy Clements, and Jan Hawkins
15. Educational Software and Games: Rethinking the
    "Girls' Game"   345
    American Association of University Women
16. The Evaded Curriculum   361
    American Association of University Women
17. Sexuality, Schooling, and Adolescent Females:
    The Missing Discourse of Desire   375
    Michelle Fine

                         PART FOUR
                    Violence in Schools
   ──

18. Bullying as Sexual Harassment in Elementary Schools   409
    Nan Stein
19. How Early Vulnerability Becomes Bad Behavior:
    Hurt Little Boys Become Aggressive Big Boys   429
    James Garbarino

20. Striking Back: Sexual Harassment at Weston 459
    Peggy Orenstein
21. Boys to Men: Questions of Violence 476
    Harvard Education Letter

PART FIVE

The Interaction of Gender, Race, and Class

22. Diversity in Girls' Experiences: Feeling Good
    About Who You Are 497
    Sumru Erkut, Jacqueline P. Fields, Rachel Sing, and Fern Marx
23. School Rules 510
    Janie Ward
24. Characteristics of Communities Affecting
    Participation/Success 543
    Angela Ginorio and Michelle Huston
25. Naughty by Nature 584
    Ann Arnett Ferguson
26. Examining Women's Progress in the Sciences
    from the Perspective of Diversity 609
    Beatriz Chu Clewell and Angela B. Ginorio

PART SIX

Single Sex Versus Coeducation

27. Single-Sex Education in Grades K–12:
    What Does the Research Tell Us? 647
    Pamela Haag
28. Single-Sex vs. Coeducational Schools 677
    Valerie Lee
29. Why Johnny Can't, Like, Read and Write 700
    Christina Hoff Sommers
30. What's Sex Got to Do with It? Simplistic Questions,
    Complex Answers 722
    Patricia B. Campbell and Ellen Wahl
31. Anita Hill Is a Boy: Tales from a Gender-Fair Classroom 734
    Peggy Orenstein

SOURCES

CHAPTER ONE

Bernice R. Sandler. "Too Strong for a Woman." *Equity & Excellence in Education: The University of Massachusetts School of Education Journal,* April 2000, 33(1).

CHAPTER TWO

David Tyack and Elisabeth Hansot. *Learning Together: A History of Coeducation in American Public Schools.* New York: Russell Sage Foundation, 1992.

CHAPTER THREE

Carol Gilligan. *In a Different Voice: Psychological Theory and Women's Development.* Cambridge, Massachusetts: Harvard University Press, 1982.

CHAPTER FOUR

William Pollack. *Real Boys: Rescuing Our Sons from the Myths of Boyhood.* New York: Henry Holt and Company, 1998.

CHAPTER FIVE

Michael Gurian. *The Wonder of Boys: What Parents, Mentors and Educators Can Do to Shape Boys into Exceptional Men.* New York: Jeremy P. Tarcher/Putnam, 1996.

CHAPTER SIX

Barrie Thorne. *Gender Play: Girls and Boys in School.* New Brunswick, New Jersey: Rutgers University Press, 1993.

CHAPTER SEVEN

Dan Kindlon and Michael Thompson. *Raising Cain: Protecting the Emotional Life of Boys.* New York: Ballantine Books, 1999.

CHAPTER EIGHT

Myra Sadker and David Sadker. *Failing at Fairness: How Our Schools Cheat Girls.* New York: Simon & Schuster, 1994.

CHAPTER NINE
Lyn Mikel Brown. *Raising Their Voices: The Politics of Girls' Anger.* Cambridge, Massachusetts: Harvard University Press, 1998.

CHAPTER TEN
Research for Action, Inc. *Girls in the Middle: Working to Succeed in School.* Washington, D.C.: American Association of University Women Educational Foundation, 1996.

CHAPTER ELEVEN
American Institutes for Research. *Gender Gaps: Where Schools Still Fail Our Children.* Washington, D.C.: American Association of University Women Educational Foundation, 1998.

CHAPTER TWELVE
Beatriz Chu Clewell, Bernice Taylor Anderson, and Margaret E. Thorpe. *Breaking the Barriers: Helping Female and Minority Students Succeed in Mathematics and Science.* San Francisco: Jossey-Bass Publishers, 1992.

CHAPTER THIRTEEN
Thomas Newkirk. "Misreading Masculinity: Speculations on the Great Gender Gap in Writing." *Language Arts,* March 2000, 77(4).

CHAPTER FOURTEEN
Margaret Honey, Babette Moeller, Cornelia Brunner, Dorothy Bennett, Peggy Clements, and Jan Hawkins. "Girls and Design: Exploring the Question of Technological Imagination." *Bank Street College of Education Technology Report,* #17.

CHAPTER FIFTEEN
AAUW Educational Foundation Commission on Technology, Gender, and Teacher Education. *Tech-Savvy: Educating Girls in the New Computer Age.* Washington, D.C.: American Association of University Women Educational Foundation, 2000.

CHAPTER SIXTEEN
Wellesley College Center for Research on Women. *How Schools Shortchange Girls: The AAUW Report.* New York: Marlowe & Company, 1995.

CHAPTER SEVENTEEN
Lois Weis and Michelle Fine, editors. *Beyond Silenced Voices: Class, Race, and Gender in United States Schools.* New York: State University of New York Press, 1993.

CHAPTER EIGHTEEN
Nan Stein. *Classrooms and Courtrooms: Facing Sexual Harassment in K–12 Schools*. New York: Teachers College Press, 1999.

CHAPTER NINETEEN
James Garbarino. *Lost Boys: Why Our Sons Turn Violent and How We Can Save Them*. New York: The Free Press, 1999.

CHAPTER TWENTY
Peggy Orenstein. *SchoolGirls: Young Women, Self-Esteem, and the Confidence Gap*. New York: Doubleday, 1994.

CHAPTER TWENTY-ONE
Carol Gilligan, James Garbarino, James Gilligan, and Michael Thompson. "Boys to Men: Questions of Violence." *Harvard Education Letter,* July/August 1999.

CHAPTER TWENTY-TWO
Bonnie J. Ross Leadbeater and Niobe Way, editors. *Urban Girls: Resisting Stereotypes, Creating Identities*. New York: New York University Press, 1996.

CHAPTER TWENTY-THREE
Janie Victoria Ward. *The Skin We're In: Teaching Our Children to Be: Emotionally Strong, Socially Smart, Spiritually Connected*. New York: The Free Press, 2000.

CHAPTER TWENTY-FOUR
Angela Ginorio and Michelle Huston. *Si, Se Puede! Yes, We Can: Latinas in School*. Washington, D.C.: American Association of University Women Educational Foundation, 2001.

CHAPTER TWENTY-FIVE
Ann Arnett Ferguson. *Bad Boys: Public Schools in the Making of Black Masculinity*. Ann Arbor, Michigan: University of Michigan Press, 2000.

CHAPTER TWENTY-SIX
Cinda-Sue Davis, Angela B. Ginorio, Carol S. Hollenshead, Barbara B. Lazarus, Paula M. Rayman, and Associates. *The Equity Equation: Fostering the Advancement of Women in the Sciences, Mathematics, and Engineering*. San Francisco: Jossey-Bass Publishers, 1996.

CHAPTER TWENTY-SEVEN
American Association of University Women Educational Foundation. *Separated by Sex: A Critical Look at Single-Sex Education for*

Girls. Washington, D.C.: American Association of University
Women Educational Foundation, 1998.

CHAPTER TWENTY-EIGHT

Anthony S. Bryk, Valerie E. Lee, and Peter B. Holland. *Catholic Schools
and the Common Good*. Cambridge, Massachusetts: Harvard University Press, 1993.

CHAPTER TWENTY-NINE

Christina Hoff Sommers. *The War Against Boys: How Misguided Feminism Is Harming Our Young Men*. New York: Simon & Schuster, 2000.

CHAPTER THIRTY

American Association of University Women Educational Foundation. *Separated by Sex: A Critical Look at Single-Sex Education for Girls*. Washington, D.C.: American Association of University Women Educational Foundation, 1998.

CHAPTER THIRTY-ONE

Peggy Orenstein. *SchoolGirls: Young Women, Self-Esteem, and the Confidence Gap*. New York: Doubleday, 1994.

ABOUT THE AUTHORS

Susan McGee Bailey is the executive director of the Wellesley Centers for Women at Wellesley College, which includes the Center for Research on Women and the Stone Center. She is also professor of women's studies and education at Wellesley College. Susan has a B.A. from Wellesley College and an M.A. and Ph.D. in social science educational research from the University of Michigan. She held a postdoctoral fellowship in public health from Johns Hopkins University. She was principal author of *The AAUW Report: How Schools Shortchange Girls* and has directed several projects focused on improving opportunities for women and girls in science and mathematics.

Lyn Mikel Brown is associate professor of education and human development and women's studies at Colby College. She is coauthor of *Meeting at the Crossroads: Women's Psychology and Girls' Development.*

Patricia B. Campbell is president and director of Campbell-Kibler Associates, an educational consulting firm.

Beatriz Chu Clewell is principal research associate for the Education Policy Center at the Urban Institute, a nonpartisan economic and social policy research organization, in Washington, D.C.

Cinda-Sue Davis is Director of the University of Michigan Women in Science and Engineering Program of the Center for the Education of Women.

Sumru Erkut, Ph.D., is the Associate Director and Senior Research Scientist at the Center for Research on Women at Wellesley College.

Ann Arnett Ferguson is assistant professor of African American studies and women's studies at Smith College.

Jacqueline P. Fields, Ph.D., works at the Center for Research on Women at Wellesley College.

Michelle Fine is professor of the social/personality/psychology program at the Graduate School and University Center of the City University of New York. She is coauthor of *Becoming Gentlemen.*

James Garbarino is codirector of the Family Life Development Center and professor of human development at Cornell University.

Carol Gilligan is the Patricia Albjerg Graham Professor of Gender Studies at the Harvard Graduate School of Education. She is the author of *Between Voice and Silence: Women and Girls, Race and Relationship.*

Angela Ginorio is associate professor of women's studies and adjunct associate professor in the departments of psychology and American ethnic studies at the University of Washington in Seattle.

Michael Gurian is a social philosopher, family therapist, educator, and author of fourteen books. He is cofounder of the Gurian Institute, an educational training organization.

Pamela Haag is a senior research associate with the American Association of University Women's Educational Foundation.

Elisabeth Hansot is senior lecturer of political science at Stanford University.

Michelle Huston is research coordinator for the Northwest Center for Research on Women in Seattle.

Dan Kindlon is a clinical and research psychologist specializing in the behavioral problems of children and adolescents. He holds joint assistant professorships in the psychiatry department of the Harvard Medical School and the department of maternal and child health at the Harvard School of Public Health.

Valerie Lee is associate professor of education at the University of Michigan and a reseacher for the Consortium of Chicago School Research.

Fern Marx, M.H.S., is Senior Research Scientist at the Center for Research on Women at Wellesley College. She also leads projects about welfare; non-traditional age college students; and child, adolescent, and young adult development.

Thomas Newkirk is a professor of English at the University of New Hampshire, where he directs the summer Institutes in Writing. His most recent book is *The Performance of Self in Student Writing*.

Peggy Orenstein was formerly managing editor of *Mother Jones* magazine and was a founding editor of the award-winning *7 Days* magazine. She has served on the editorial staffs of *Manhattan, Inc.* and *Esquire*, and her work has appeared in such publications as the *New York Times Magazine*, *Vogue*, *Glamour*, the *New Yorker*, *New York Woman*, and *Mirabella*.

William Pollack is director of the Center for Men and Young Men and director of continuing education (psychology) at McLean Hospital. He is also an assistant clinical professor of psychology in the department of psychiatry at Harvard Medical School and a founding member and fellow of the Society for the Psychological Study of Men and Masculinity of the American Psychological Association.

David Sadker is a professor at the American University and has served as a teacher educator for three decades.

Myra Sadker (1943–1995) served as a professor and Dean of the School of Education at the American University for over twenty years.

Bernice Sandler is senior scholar of the Women's Research and Educational Institute and is adjunct associate professor at MCP Hahnemann School of Medicine.

Rachel Sing, M.Ed., teaches at the Graduate School of Education, Harvard University, MA.

Christina Hoff Sommers is the W. H. Brady Fellow at the American Enterprise Institute in Washington, D.C. Formerly, she served as a professor of philosophy at Clark University.

Nan Stein is senior researcher and project director of the Wellesley College Center for Research on Women.

Michael Thompson is a consultant, author, and child and family psychologist practicing in Cambridge, Massachusetts. He is also a member of the faculty of the New Heads Institute run by the National Association of Independent Schools.

Barrie Thorne is professor of sociology and women's studies at the University of California at Berkeley. She is also codirector of the Center for Working Families and coeditor of *Childhood: A Global Journal of Child Research*.

David Tyack is Vida Jacks Professor of History and Education at Stanford University.

Ellen Wahl has served as senior scientist at the Center for Children and Technology at the Educational Development Center.

Janie Ward is associate professor of education and human services at Simmons College in Boston. She is also project director for the Alliance on Gender, Culture and School Practice at Harvard Graduate School of Education.

Lois Weis is Professor and Associate Dean in the Graduate School of Education at the State University of New York at Buffalo. She is also Past President of the American Educational Studies Association.

ACKNOWLEDGMENTS

The Jossey-Bass Education Team would like to thank Susan McGee Bailey, Craig P. Flood, Jan Perry Evenstad, John P. Gaa, Pamela Haag, and Brewster Ely for their valuable contribution to this volume. Their advice and consultation helped make this Reader more interesting, comprehensive, and balanced.

Special thanks are due to Elisa Rassen, who managed all aspects of this project from beginning to end. Her editorial acumen, organizational skills, writing ability, and passion for the subject turned a vision into reality.

FOREWORD

Susan M. Bailey

DESPITE TWO CENTURIES OF DEBATE and significant federal and state legislation, gender remains a controversial topic in U.S. education. The past decade has been marked by heated discussions in which sound bites often carry the day and K–12 education frequently appears as a zero sum game—if girls win, boys must lose, and vice versa.

The Jossey-Bass Reader on Gender in Education provides a much-needed antidote to this oversimplification. The thirty-one articles and book chapters that follow represent a range of opinions, perspectives, and approaches to the topic of gender equity. Taken together they dispel any notion of quick fixes or exclusively one-sided disadvantage. Many reading the selections may be left with more questions than answers. But everyone will gain a clearer understanding of the complexities inherent in discussions of education and gender. The book is valuable for anyone interested in education and educational policy. Teachers, administrators, policy makers, parents, and academics will all find the selections provocative and informative.

The volume begins with an historic overview of the 1960s through the 1980s, a period during which women and girls made significant progress in education. With the passage of Title IX in 1972, legal barriers to equal access tumbled, even though enforcement of the law often lagged behind the letter of the legislation. But as the 1990s opened, the journey toward gender equitable education—first begun in the earliest years of the nation with the question of whether public funds should be used to educate girls—continued to be a series of torturous hairpin turns rather than a long, but basically straight, path.

The American Association of University Women (AAUW) published *How Schools Shortchange Girls* in early 1992. No sooner had the headlining-grabbing title focused attention on girls than concern for boys arose. Soon, helping girls was equated with somehow hurting boys, as the media rushed to present the "two sides" of the issue. There was little focus on the stated thesis of the report that "by studying what happens to girls in school we gain valuable insights about what has to change in order for each student, every girl and every boy to do as well as she or he can." The challenge the report posed was to "help girls *and* boys acquire both the relational and the competitive skills needed for full participation in the workforce, the family and community."[1]

The Reader goes on to chronicle the debates of the 1990s. The selections reflect major differences about the nature and the origin of gender differences as well as about the most effective ways of addressing them. Each of the six major sections in the volume covers an aspect of the debate. Part One, Female and Male Identity, focuses on the nature versus nurture debate. Part Two, Negotiating the Classroom, presents a range of views on classroom interactions. Some chapters outline the way boys are at a disadvantage in today's classrooms; others detail the problems girls face. In sum, the authors present a strong case for gender equitable approaches that can help *both* sexes.

Gender Equity in the Curriculum is the focus of Part Three. This section looks at the time-honored measures of equity, the differential achievement, and course-taking patterns of boys and girls. It also contains perspectives on sexuality and socioemotional development that point out how ignoring these issues undercuts academic achievement. What this section does not address, except in passing, is the content of academic materials and coursework. Little has been written on this topic in the past decade by gender equity advocates. This is perhaps in part because earlier work resulted in some significant changes in curricular materials. It may also reflect the move toward national standards and statewide testing that has left little room for curricular change, expansion, or enhancement.

Part Four, Violence in Schools, addresses concerns that have claimed headlines during the 1990s—physical violence and sexual harassment and bullying. These issues are not as new as the expanded media coverage suggests, but the coverage itself is an example of how changing societal sensitivities reveal new aspects of old patterns. For example, within a few months in the early 1990s, sexual harassment went from rarely mentioned to front-page news. Anita Hill testified in the Clarence Thomas hearings in the fall of 1991. *How Schools Shortchange Girls* was released in February of 1992 with a short section on sexual harassment covering the limited research then available. Two weeks later, the U.S. Supreme Court ruled unanimously that school districts were financially liable if they failed to provide an educational environment that was free from sex discrimination and sexual harassment.[2] Suddenly, sexual harassment in schools was "hot." Research and debate followed. The articles in this section reflect key findings and perspectives that emerged.

The articles in Part Five, The Interaction of Gender, Race, and Class, challenge the idea that all students, or all girls, or all poor children, or all children from a particular racial or ethnic group are "the same." The authors use various methodologies but all focus on how to better understand the complexities and the realities of children's lives in school. These are areas that have gained visibility during the past decade, as researchers worked to challenge and refute a one-dimensional view of difference and disadvantage. A future edition of this Reader will hopefully include work focusing on another critical variable—disability, and the particular ways gender influences the education of students with special needs.

The final section of the book looks at single sex versus coeducation, an apt finale as these chapters bring the discussion of gender and education to another hairpin turn and within viewing distance of the debate as stated in the late nineteenth century. Then, as now, the questions centered on whether the education of girls and boys should be separate *and* different, separate *but* the same, together *and* the same, or together *but* different.[3]

The Future

Preparing young people for citizenship in a democracy has always been a central mission of public education in the United States. The tragic and horrifying events of September 11, 2001, require renewed attention to this fundamental goal. Our future as a free society depends on active and informed citizens who value the principles of human rights and justice contained in our Constitution. By definition, education for citizenship must be gender equitable education; an education in which every voice is heard and each girl and boy has an equally wide range of educational opportunities and life choices. Furthermore, it is no longer possible to consider educating students for effective citizenship without helping them to acquire a global awareness and sensitivity. As they learn more about other nations and cultures, both girls and boys need to learn of the work women do around the globe to protect the environment and secure peace. UN Secretary General Kofi Annan has said, "For generations, women have served as peace educators, both in their families and in their societies. They have proved instrumental in building bridges rather than walls."[4] The primary victims of the world's armed conflicts today are women and children. But women are rarely at the negotiating table or in visible leadership positions. Whether in the Middle East, Africa, Latin America, Eastern Europe, or Northern Ireland, women have worked successfully to promote peace, but most of this work has been behind the scenes and much of it is unknown to students and their teachers.

Twenty-first century girls and boys must grow up valuing and learning not only from men's accomplishments but also from women's. This is the challenge for educators in the century ahead. It is the next turn on the road to gender equitable education.

NOTES

1. Wellesley College Center for Research on Women (1995), *The AAUW Report: How Schools Shortchange Girls,* New York, Marlowe and Company, pp. 4–5.

2. Franklin v. Gwinnett County (GA) Public Schools, 111 S. CT. 1028 (1992).

3. See, for example, Chapter Two, "Why Educate Girls" in Tyack and Hanson, *Learning Together, A History of Coeducation in American Public Schools,* New Haven, Yale University Press, 1990, pp. 28–45.

4. Kofi Annan, October 2000, Remarks to the UN Security Council as quoted in Hunt and Posa, "Women Waging Peace," *Foreign Policy Magazine,* 2001.

INTRODUCTION

THE HISTORY OF GENDER ISSUES IN EDUCATION

IN 1969, WHEN UNIVERSITY OF MARYLAND teacher Bernice R. Sandler was passed over for promotion for being "too strong for a woman," sex discrimination was already illegal under the Civil Rights Act. However, educational institutions were specifically excluded from this act. Throughout K–12 education and higher education, sexual discrimination was rampant, infiltrating every aspect of school life, from hiring practices to curriculum content to funding for athletic teams.

The passage of Title IX in 1972, which Sandler details in her piece " 'Too Strong for a Woman'—The Five Words That Created Title IX," was a landmark event in the history of gender issues in education. Crucial to understanding its impact on schools today, however, is an appreciation of the history of women's education in America as well as an examination of how Title IX was, and was not, enacted and enforced in the following years. In "Feminists Discover the Hidden Injuries of Co-education," David Tyack and Elisabeth Hansot take an in-depth look at both the history and the aftermath of Title IX, illuminating the issues that set the stage for the passage of the ground-breaking law and the ways that it both solved and created new problems for women in education.

It is impossible to fully appreciate or understand today's raging debates over gender issues in education without first taking into account the path that led us here. Only an exploration of the struggle for gender equality over the last thirty years can begin to illuminate what education was, what it is now, and what we hope it will be.

"TOO STRONG FOR A WOMAN"

THE FIVE WORDS THAT
CREATED TITLE IX

Bernice R. Sandler

THE YEAR WAS 1969. I had been teaching part-time at the University of Maryland for several years during the time I worked on my doctorate and shortly after I finished it. There were seven openings in the department and I had just asked a faculty member, a friend of mine, why I was not even considered for any of the openings. It was not my qualifications; they were excellent. "But let's face it," he said, "You come on *too strong for a woman*."

My reaction? I went home and cried. I had no idea that this rejection would not only change my life but would change the lives of millions of women and girls because it led ultimately to the passage of Title IX, the law that prohibits sex discrimination in educational institutions receiving federal dollars. Instead, I bemoaned the fact that I had spoken out at staff meetings with suggestions for improving procedures. I lamented the times that I had discussed teaching and professional issues with faculty members. I regretted my participation in classes as a graduate student. In short, I accepted the assessment that I was "too strong for a woman."

It was my then husband who helped me understand what the words "too strong *for a woman*" meant. He labeled the department's behavior as "sex discrimination"—a label that started me thinking. Was this really a question of my being "too strong"? After all there were many strong men in the department. Yet the label of "sex discrimination" was a new one for me, and initially I was not ready to apply it to my not getting the position at Maryland. Like many women at that time, I was somewhat ambivalent about the women's movement and halfway believed the press descriptions of its supporters as "abrasive," "man-hating," "radical," and "unfeminine." Surely I was not like that.

In the next few months I had two more similar rejections. A research executive who interviewed me for a position spent nearly an hour explaining to me why he would not hire women because they stayed at home when their children were sick. (That my children were in high school was deemed irrelevant.) Then an employment agency counselor looked at my resume and told me that I was "not really a professional" but "just a housewife who went back to school."

Although later, in retrospect, I would discover other instances of sex discrimination in my life, at that point I had not consciously noticed it. Yet here were three incidents within a short period which I could not rationalize away. I began to think about the ramifications of discrimination and the burgeoning women's movement and started to explore how the law treated sex discrimination. Knowing that sex discrimination was immoral, I assumed it would also be illegal.

But this *was* 1969. Although sex discrimination was indeed illegal in certain circumstances, I quickly discovered that *none* of the laws prohibiting discrimination covered sex discrimination *in education*. Title VII of the Civil Rights Act, which prohibited discrimination in employment on the basis of race, color, religion, national origin, and sex, excluded "educational institutions in their educational activities"—meaning faculty and administrators were exempt. Title VI of the same act prohibited discrimination on the basis of race, color, and national origin in federally assisted programs, but did not cover sex discrimination. Thus students were not protected against sex discrimination. The Equal Pay Act prohibited discrimination in salaries on the basis of sex but exempted all professional and administrative employees, including faculty. The Fourteenth Amendment to the Constitution assures all persons "equal protection of the laws," but at that time no case concerning discrimination against women in education had ever been decided in favor of women by the Supreme Court.

I began to read more about the civil rights movement to see what Blacks had done to break down segregated school systems and employment discrimination, with the hope of learning what might be applicable to women's issues. The breakthrough occurred when I was reading a report of the U.S. Commission on Civil Rights which examined the impact of antidiscrimination laws on race discrimination. The report described a presidential Executive Order prohibiting federal contractors from discrimination in employment on the basis of race, color, religion, and national origin. There was a footnote, and being an academic, I quickly turned to the back of the report to read it. It stated that Executive Order 11246 had been amended by President Johnson, effective October 13, 1968, to include discrimination based on sex.

Even though I was alone, I shrieked aloud with my discovery: I had made the connection that, since most universities and colleges had federal contracts, they were forbidden from discriminating in employment on the basis of sex. Yes, there was a legal route to combat sex discrimination even though few people knew it at the time.

I called the Office of Federal Contract Compliance at the Department of Labor to be certain that sex discrimination was covered by the Executive Order. I was immediately connected to the director, Vincent Macaluso, who had been waiting for someone to use the Executive Order in regard to sex discrimination. We met, and together we planned the first complaint against universities and colleges and the strategies to bring about enforcement of the Executive Order.

Two months later under the auspices of the Women's Equity Action League (WEAL) I began what was soon to become a national campaign to end discrimination in education and which eventually culminated in the passage of Title IX. On January 31, 1970, WEAL filed a historic class action complaint against all universities and colleges in the country with specific charges against the University of Maryland. The charges were filed with the U.S. Department of Labor under Executive Order 11246, as amended, and asked for an immediate compliance review of all institutions holding federal contracts. Because these were administrative charges filed with a federal agency rather than a lawsuit filed in court, it was not necessary for me to be an attorney. There were no special forms to fill out. Individuals did not need to be named; the charges were filed on behalf of all women in higher education. Thus, the complaint did not name me or describe the incident in which I was involved.

Until that time the Executive Order had been used almost exclusively in cases concerning blue-collar workers, and although the Order had covered sex discrimination since October 1968, there had been virtually no enforcement by the government until WEAL began its campaign.

The WEAL complaint charged "an industry-wide pattern" of discrimination against women in the academic community and asked for an investigation in the following areas: admission quotas to undergraduate and graduate schools, financial assistance, hiring practices, promotions, and salary differentials.

At Macaluso's advice, I put together about 80 pages of documentation to accompany the complaint. He pointed out that a large appendix to the complaint was important; even if no one read it, they would assume that the many pages confirmed the charges. I included some articles and the limited data available, including a study of women faculty at the University of Chicago written by Jo Freeman, then a graduate student in sociology, and a study of women faculty at Columbia University by the Columbia Women's Liberation group. I also included similar data I had gathered at the University of Maryland, posing as a researcher. I underlined key passages in the document with a thick pen to catch the attention of anyone leafing through the materials.

In those days copy machines were a rarity. With the help of a friend at the Ford Foundation, 200 copies of the 80-page complaint were photocopied and sent to the press and others. Macaluso had suggested that copies of the complaint and appendix also be sent to selected members of Congress, along with a handwritten note requesting that they write the Secretary of Labor asking him to enforce his own regulations governing the Executive Order, to investigate educational institutions holding federal contracts to ensure that there was no sex discrimination, and to keep the member informed of the progress of the investigations. Within a few weeks, more than 20 members of Congress had contacted the Secretary of Labor.

In the next few months, the limited press coverage about WEAL's filing began to electrify women throughout the academic community, particularly when they realized I could file charges against their institution without naming them. Many women faculty contacted me, sometimes with personal stories of discrimination but almost always with a concern about the overall problem of discrimination in their institution in general. In order for me to file a complaint against their institution under the Executive Order, I would ask the women to gather information, especially about the number and rank of men compared to women in a few selected departments. I then compared this information to data about the "availability of women," usually the number and percentage of women doctorates in those fields. The result was striking: many departments had no women at all, even though women often obtained as many as 25 percent of the doctorates in those fields. The pattern was clear: the higher the rank, the fewer the women. The more prestigious the field, the department, or institution, the fewer the women. In the administrative ranks, women were a rarity; at that time even many women's colleges were headed by men. I used to quip that, were it not for the Catholic sisters who headed their own women's colleges, the number of whooping cranes would exceed the number of women who were college presidents.

With the exception of the first charge, which was filed by the president of WEAL, I filed the others as chair of WEAL's Action Committee for Federal Contract Compliance in Education (I was the entire committee). During the next two years, I filed charges against approximately 250 institutions. Another 100 or so were filed by other individuals and organizations such as the National Organization for Women (NOW). Among the institutions charged by WEAL were the University of Wisconsin, the University of Minnesota, Columbia University, the University of Chicago, and the entire state university and college systems of California, New Jersey, and Florida.

But simply filing charges would not be enough to get the federal government to begin enforcing the Executive Order. As women provided me with information and I filed against their institutions, I asked them to write their representatives in the House and Senate and encourage others to do the same. The women were to ask their representatives to contact the Secretary of Labor and the Secretary of Health, Education and Welfare (HEW), requesting that they enforce the Executive Order and keep the congressperson informed about the investigations. In addition to putting congressional pressure on the two departments, the letter-writing campaign was aimed at sensitizing congressional staff about sex discrimination in education. At one point we generated so much mail that HEW had to assign a full-time person only to handle the congressional letters. More than 300 congressional letters were received by the Department of Labor in a short period of time.

On March 9, 1970, Representative Martha Griffiths (MI), who was on WEAL's national advisory board, gave the first speech in the U.S. Congress on discrimination against women in education, based in large measure on the information I gave her. She criticized the government for not enforcing its own regulations with regard to sex discrimination in universities and colleges. Her speech, the barrage of congressional letters to the secretaries of Labor and Health, Education and Welfare, and the numerous meetings that women's organizations such as WEAL and NOW had with the departments of Labor and HEW paid off. Three weeks later, the first contract compliance investigation began at Harvard University. In June 1970, the Department of Labor issued its long awaited Sex Discrimination Guidelines for federal contractors and HEW issued a memorandum to all field personnel to routinely include sex discrimination in all contract compliance investigations. HEW also hired its first female compliance investigator.

But something else was happening in the months following the initial complaints. Representative Edith Green (OR) (also a member of WEAL's national advisory board) had long been aware of sex discrimination in higher education, and she was in a unique position to shape new legislation. She had been urged to hold hearings by Phineas Indritz (a congressional staff member who "dabbled" in civil rights issues), but she was hesitant to do so because there was little data available and apparently no constituency whom she could count on to testify.

It was a time when there were virtually no books and only a few articles that addressed the issue of discrimination against women in education. No conferences had been held to examine the issue. There was little research or data, and barely a handful of unnoticed women's studies courses. There were no campus commissions on the status of women, and only a few institutions had even begun to examine the status of women on their campus. Women's caucuses in the disciplinary organizations were just beginning to develop. The issue of sex discrimination in education was so new that I received many letters from women and men asking me if it was true that such discrimination existed, and if so, could I send them proof.

With all the WEAL filings I sent to her, Rep. Green now had information about sex discrimination in higher education. Because I knew almost everyone who was actively working to end sex discrimination in education, I was able to provide Rep. Green with a list of people who could testify and provide the information needed to justify new legislation to prohibit sex discrimination. She agreed to draft legislation and to hold hearings.

The first congressional hearings on the education and employment of women were held by Rep. Green in June and July of 1970. This was the official beginning of the bill that eventually became Title IX. The original bill, part of a larger measure on higher education, proposed to amend Title VII of the Civil Rights Act to cover employees in educational institutions, Title VI to cover sex discrimination in federally assisted programs, and the Equal Pay Act to cover executives, administrators, and professionals.

I supplied the names of women (and some men) who would be willing to testify as well as the names of relevant organizations. I also testified. Because the original bill covered employment in general, there was a wide array of testimony documenting discrimination in employment, the professions, civil service, want ads, and education. No one from the official world of higher education testified, although they were invited to do so. A representative of the American Council in Education told the subcommittee counsel, "There was no sex discrimination in higher education," and even if it did exist, it wasn't "a problem." Apparently, Rep. Green's bill was not seen as being of much interest to, or having any major implications for, educational institutions.

There were seven days of hearings. Except for Rep. Green, who was in attendance throughout the hearings, only a few subcommittee members made short token appearances. Federal officials testified that they supported the aim of the bill but not the bill "in its present form"—a euphemism for opposition. Women employed in educational institutions across the country testified in support of the bill and provided data. Representative Shirley Chisholm (NY) (another WEAL national advisory board member) testified that during her entire political history, her sex had been "a far greater handicap than [her] skin pigmentation." Other African American women and female members of Congress also testified in support of the bill. Much of the testimony dealt with the employment of women both in and outside of higher education; there was some testimony (but not much) about female students, mainly focusing on admissions and counseling. When the hearings were finished, I was asked by Rep. Green to join the subcommittee staff to put together the written record of the hearings. (Thus I became the first person ever appointed to the staff of a congressional committee to work specifically in the area of women's rights.)

The seven days of hearings resulted in a two-volume set of nearly 1,300 pages. Because there was so little written about women in employment and education, I appended numerous documents. This appendix material, which represented a sizable portion of the information on women available at the time, included 14 studies of women at colleges and universities. As a result, the hearing record became a solid source of information about women for some time to come.

Usually only a few hundred copies of hearings are printed, but Rep. Green received permission to print 6,000 copies. She sent a copy with a note to every member of Congress. I drew up a list for her to send copies to prominent organizations and individuals in higher education, and the press.

The widespread distribution of the hearings, the charges against institutions, and the letters sent to Congress by women from all over the country set the stage for support of legislation to end sex discrimination in education. The hearings probably did more than anything else to make sex discrimination in education a legitimate issue. When administrators or faculty members would deny the existence of sex discrimination in academe, women (and men) could point out that this was not a frivolous issue and that Congress itself has held *days* of hearings on this important subject. Thus the hearings, as well as the continuing filings of charges against institutions under the Executive Order, gave women throughout academe hope and courage to become advocates for women and change within their institution. Higher education itself, even before the passage of Title IX, began to acknowledge that there was some validity to the issue, and numerous institutions appointed committees to study the problem and develop recommendations for their campuses.

At some point after the hearings, higher education began to recognize that the bill might affect their institutions. Officials from Harvard, Princeton, Yale, and Dartmouth were concerned that they might have to admit women in equal numbers. (The first three institutions had recently admitted women but had strict quotas restricting their numbers to about 30 percent; Dartmouth was planning to admit women in the near future.) These institutions lobbied successfully for an exemption in the bill for private undergraduate admissions, claiming that different sex ratios were best for learning and that individual institutions knew what the best ratios were. Of course there was no data to support these allegations, but these institutions and their alumni in Congress were powerful. The amendment stood, although Rep. Green made sure that once students of both sexes were admitted to an institution there could be no discrimination against them. The amendment also meant private men's and women's colleges would not be prohibited from remaining single-sex institutions. There was no opposition to this provision. The service academies were also exempted. An exemption for admission to publicly supported single-sex undergraduate institutions was also added to the bill.

The bill was ably managed in the Senate by Senator Birch Bayh (IN), who was also a member of WEAL's national advisory board. However, by the time the bill reached the Senate, several new issues were raised, such as how the bill would affect single sex groups such as fraternities and sororities, Boy Scouts and Girl Scouts, and single sex youth conferences sponsored by the American Legion (Boys State, Boys Nation, Girls State, and Girls Nation). The issue of educational institutions holding beauty pageants with scholarships going to the winners was also a stumbling block, as well as father-son and mother-daughter school sponsored activities. Sen. Bayh carefully crafted an amendment to the bill exempting college sororities and fraternities, certain single sex youth service groups, most campus beauty contests, and father-son/mother-daughter events.

Because colleges and universities had only a rudimentary understanding of the problem of discrimination at the time, the higher education community apparently believed it had taken care of what they saw as the major impacts of the bill—undergraduate admissions. They were not aware that the bill would have covered athletics. By the time the bill was ready for passage, however, it was clear to Rep. Green, to myself, and to a few others that the bill would indeed cover athletics. We were beginning to understand that Title IX would open up opportunities for girls and women to participate in sports, although we did not fully appreciate just what that would mean. Higher education did not lobby for or against the bill, and because it was attached to a higher education measure, the elementary and secondary education community also was largely unaware of the bill.

Also unnoticed in Rep. Green's bill was an amendment to the Equal Pay Act, which opened up coverage to administrators, professionals, and executives. Because the wording of the amendment was artfully crafted by Morag Simchak (a WEAL member who worked at the Department of Labor)—it was phrased as a technical amendment—it was difficult to realize, from a quick reading of the bill, what it did. As a result, the Department of Labor, which has enforcement responsibility for the Equal Pay Act, was unaware until after passage that their jurisdiction was to be significantly expanded.

As the bill drew close to passage, a group of women (including myself) who represented women's organizations met with Rep. Green to offer our lobbying services. She informed us that it would be better if we did not lobby because there was no opposition to the bill, and the less that people knew about the bill, the better its chances were for passage. We were skeptical, but she was absolutely right.

In the spring of 1972, two years after the hearings, a portion of Rep. Green's original bill became law when Title VII of the Civil Rights Act was amended by Congress in a separate action to cover all employees in educational institutions. Initially, Rep. Green had also sought to amend Title VI of the Civil Rights Act (prohibiting discrimination on the basis of race, color, and national origin in all federally funded activities) to include sex discrimination. However, at the urging of African American leaders and others, who were worried that opening Title VI for amendment could weaken its coverage, she proposed a separate and new title, which became Title IX. In its final form, Title IX was identical to that of Title VI, except that it was restricted to educational activities, contained additional exemptions, and included the amendment to the Equal Pay Act. On June 23, 1972, Title IX of the Education Amendments of 1972 was passed by the Congress and on July 1 was signed into law by President Richard Nixon. The historic passage of Title IX was hardly noticed. I remember one or two sentences in the Washington papers.

It would be another three years before the regulation for Title IX would be issued, and yet another year before it would take effect. By then, higher education and the country understood that Title IX was going to change the landscape of higher education forever.

The entire WEAL campaign had cost only a few hundred dollars in postage, but hours and hours of time from women in academe who patiently and painstakingly gathered and analyzed data about men and women in their institutions, pressed their representatives and senators for action, organized together, and became advocates for change. They are the true unsung heroes of this story. They took enormous risks. Many did not have tenure and as a result of their activities never received it and were lost to the higher educational community. Some became lawyers or found other successful careers; a few went on welfare.

It was the words "too strong for a woman" that turned me into a feminist, although I did not know it at the time. I have often wondered what would have happened if I had been considered for a position at Maryland. I might still be a part-time faculty member. Title IX, or something like it, would eventually have been enacted, but probably in a weaker version with more exemptions because of subsequent backlash.

For myself, I had no idea what I was getting into. I had no legal, political, or organizing experience and had no idea that the political and legal action I began would force open the issue of sex discrimination on campus. I was extraordinarily naïve; I believed that if we passed Title IX it would only take a year or two for all the inequities based on sex to be eliminated. After two years, I upped my estimate to five years, then to ten, then to twenty five, until I finally realized that we were trying to change very strong patterns of behavior and belief, and that changes would take more than my lifetime to accomplish.

The struggle for educational equity is by no means over, despite the enormous progress that has been made. As women look to the future with greater understanding of the politics of change, their mood is best expressed by a paraphrase of a famous biblical quotation, written by Mary Chagnon:

> And they shall beat their pots and pans into printing presses,
> And weave their cloth into protest banners,
> Nations of women shall lift up their voices with other women,
> Neither shall they accept discrimination anymore.

Because of Title IX, the campus has changed irretrievably, and the world of higher education, and the nation, will never again be the same.

2

FEMINISTS DISCOVER THE HIDDEN INJURIES OF COEDUCATION

David Tyack and Elisabeth Hansot

BY THE SECOND DECADE of the twentieth century a few feminists were dreaming of a world in which traditional gender distinctions would wither away as a result of truly identical coeducation. One of these visionaries, a New York teacher named Henrietta Rodman, argued in 1915 that "coeducation is one of the essentials of civilization. This mixing makes the girls brave and resourceful and the boys courteous and helpful." Boys might play with dolls and dishes if they wanted, and "girls would not be told that they can't play vigorous games because they must keep their dresses clean and they must be ladylike." The cultural division into masculine and feminine was artificial, she said: "there is no quality good in one sex that is not good in the other." True coeducation could lead to a world in which women and men would have equal opportunity in all aspects of life.[1]

Another radical feminist, Crystal Eastman, argued in 1920 that the passage of the Nineteenth Amendment granting women the vote was only the beginning of women's liberation. She defined the task ahead in this way: "how to arrange the world so that women can be human beings, with a chance to exercise their infinitely varied gifts in infinitely varied ways, instead of being destined by the accident of their sex to one field of activity—housework and child-raising." Such a project would require "a revolution in the early training of both boys and girls. It must be womanly as well as manly to earn your own living, to stand on your own feet. And it must be manly as well as womanly to know how to cook and sew and clean and take care of yourself in the ordinary exigencies of life. I need not add that the second part of this revolution will be more passionately resisted than the first."[2]

Rodman and Eastman won few converts to their point of view in their day. They wanted a transformation—a thorough blending—of the traditional roles of men and women. Their pleas fell mostly on deaf ears in a period when many educational reformers wanted more, not less, gender differentiation in schools and when advocates of woman's rights often stress the female virtues. But their vision of coeducation would be reborn a half-century later. Under the scrutiny of the new feminists, the coeducational school that had supposedly served girls rather well suddenly seemed rife with bias. The word *sexist*, applied to schools with increasing frequency in the 1970s, symbolized a major new departure in thinking about equality of the sexes in public education.[3]

The starting point for these later feminists who fought to reform coeducational schools was not education itself; rather, it was the unequal station and opportunities of adult women in the economic, political, and social life of the nation. They believed that if adult women lacked power and opportunities, the schools had played a large part in their subordination. The quest for gender justice in education grew out of and drew much of its energy, strategies, and agenda from the broader women's liberation movement of the 1960s and 1970s.[4]

Again, as during the Progressive Era, a familiar pattern of reform emerged in efforts to change gender practices and policies in the schools; broad objective and ideological changes in gender patterns in the society as a whole prompted activists to generate an agenda for education reform, and in turn educators institutionalized the changes in differing degrees.

A major reason for the impact of the new feminist movement, as William H. Chafe has observed, was the congruence of its program with major social trends. At a time when about half of all married women were employed in the paid labor force, the attitude that women's place was in the home was becoming implausible. Well-publicized reports showed that women college graduates earned less than men who had only completed elementary school. In a period of postponed marriages and declining birthrates, more women were seeking fulfillment through careers, yet they found themselves blocked by males who were entrenched at the top levels in business corporations, the media, and the prestigious professions. Working-class women found themselves shunted to low-paying, sex-segregated jobs. Women active in politics and government were regularly excluded from the arenas where policy was made and from positions of power and influence.[5]

But it was not only in the labor market or public life that women experienced frustration. Many homemakers found that Betty Friedan's best-selling book, *The Feminine Mystique* (1963), expressed their own unnamed discontent. In 1963 Brigid Brophy published an article in the *Saturday Evening Post* entitled "Women Are Prisoners of Their Sex." Women, she wrote, may feel free, "but in reality women in the western, industrialized world today are like the animals in a modern zoo. There are no bars. It appears that cages have been abolished. Yet in practice women are still kept in place just as firmly as the animals are kept in their enclosures. The barriers which keep them in now are invisible."[6]

Ninety percent of housewives surveyed by Gallup in 1962 "did not want their daughters to lead the same type of life they had led. They hoped their daughters would get more education and marry later." As the Gallup poll response indicated, attitudes toward women's roles in the home and in the workplace were already changing before the women's liberation movement gathered momentum in the late 1960s and 1970s. The transformation of women's attitudes owed quite as much to their everyday experience as to the ideological impact of feminism, for their attitudes showed the biggest changes before the media began publicizing feminism.[7]

The women's movement of the 1960s and 1970s might be construed, says Kathleen M. Dalton, as an "equity earthquake." It constituted a sudden realignment of beliefs and values along a social fault line to match major changes in the objective conditions of women's lives. The women's movement gave voice and direction to new attitudes already half-formed, a public language in which women could describe their individual situations. Thus, when feminists redefined women's grievances as a public issue rather than as a person problem, they found in some quarters a ready audience. And sexual discrimination in schools became one of their prime targets.[8]

If the Progressive Era was the time of the "boy problem," the 1970s was the decade of the "girl problem" (although some feminists also addressed issues of gender justice for males). By sex equity in education, they understood the elimination of sex bias and a reduction of sex stereotyping. Whereas opponents of coeducation in the nineteenth century had claimed that high schools were too virile to fit the girls, and the champions of masculinity had claimed that schools feminized the boys, the new feminist activists reversed the charge: public education made the girls too feminine and the boys too masculine. They argued that schools perpetuated male dominance and female subordination because boys and girls did not really learn the same things in coeducational schools. In the process, unequal schooling contributed to the asymmetrical distribution of power, income, and prestige among adult women and men.[9]

This reformulation of sex discrimination derived from a new conviction that schools could not be considered to be favoring girls over boys or even to be observing gender-neutral policies if their women graduates fared so poorly in adult life. Unconsciously or deliberately, schools played a part in the subordination of women. It was the job of feminist researchers to document and remedy the hidden inequities that blocked women's access to the same opportunities that men enjoyed. The education press shows a sharply rising number of publications on women's issues after 1969.[10]

Opposition to feminist reform in education took many forms, ranging from mild foot-dragging to active resistance. One common reaction was incredulity: Was there really a problem for girls? Most educators from 1930 to the early 1960s did not believe there was a serious problem of sex bias in coeducational classrooms. They regarded boys and girls as largely interchangeable parts for institutional purposes. In theory, the public school was gender-blind, just as it was thought to be class-blind.

When educational researchers and policy advocates of this period did detect a gap between the ideal and the reality of gender-blind schooling, they usually focused on boys. Males, they claimed, did not get a fair shake. What was their evidence of discrimination? Their case would have been a familiar one to educators of the early twentieth century. Boys, researchers reported, were held back in grade far more often than girls and outnumbered them in remedial classes in reading. Boys performed about the same as or better than girls on standardized achievement tests but earned lower grades. They were much more likely to present discipline problems or be referred to special classes or child-guidance clinics for learning or behavioral disorders. Women teachers, said some latter-day writers on the "boy problem," scolded boys more and tried to make them conform to a female regime. In the process, they produced either rebels or feminized males. Critics accused textbook writers of feminizing the curriculum and called for stories in school readers that would appeal more to male interests (they showed that girls would be willing to read "boys' " stories, but not vice versa). In the 1960s scholars like Patricia Cayo Sexton and Daniel Levine argued that a "feminized" school especially hurt male blacks and Hispanics.[11]

Opposition to the feminist educational agenda also came from people to whom "sex-stereotyping" seemed natural and desirable. Unlike racial discrimination, which had been written into law and conscious policy, much educational discrimination against girls and women was unconscious and thus invisible to people—both educators and the general public. What was the problem, they asked, if boys behaved like boys and girls like girls? The task of the school was to teach both sexes the same subjects in the same manner, and was this not what was happening? In 1972 *Nation's Schools* polled school administrators on this question:

> Recent studies report that many elementary-school textbooks present a "biased" and negative view of girls and women, i.e., girls generally portrayed as "passive and emotional," while boys are depicted as "aggressive and logical." Do you think this type of sex bias exists in curriculum materials?[12]

Only 16 percent answered *yes* and 84 percent answered *no*. A California schoolman described the whole idea as "hogwash," while a Virginia administrator declared sex discrimination "just a figment of some feminist's frustrated imagination."

To some public educators, the requirements of antidiscrimination statutes like Title IX and litigation about sex bias were simply bothersome and costly distractions from their real business—proper education, not some new kind of social engineering. Racism was a more obvious target than sexism, and skeptical officials in the Office of Civil Rights (OCR) needed steady prodding to enforce the laws against gender discrimination. Under the Reagan administration, believers in the God-given traditional gender order sought to derail the feminist campaign.

Convinced of the hidden injuries of coeducation, educational activists in the women's movement had several tasks: convincing people that there was a problem by documenting gender discrimination; devising legal and policy remedies; following up on implementation; and raising the consciousness of educators about bias in everyday activities that they took for granted.[13]

Like many other social movements, the women's movement was itself a massive educational agency and intellectual forum. By a variety of means—publications, demonstrations, legislation, litigation, consciousness-raising groups, guerrilla theater, activist research, and media attention—it sought to change minds. Reforming schools was only one of the feminists' goals and the coeducational public school only one of many forms of education they analyzed. Dialogue within the feminist movement assured constant recasting of issues; movement members were hardly rigid or uniform in their beliefs. Thus, it is not surprising that in the 1980s a new group of feminist theorists would question the diagnoses and solutions of the liberal feminists of the 1970s. Although the women's movement had historically represented a varied constituency and promoted a changing agenda, the attack on the hidden injuries of the coeducational public school represented a new departure in the long history of American education and of women's search for equal rights.[14]

Defining and Explaining Sexism in Education

The movement for women's liberation owed much of its inspiration and its legal and educational strategies to the civil rights movement. Feminism was not an isolated venture but part of a broader array of social movements that swept the nation in the 1960s. Like their nineteenth-century predecessors, many of whom had been abolitionists, a number of the leaders of the modern women's movement had taken part in the campaign to secure equality for blacks. That crusade had demonstrated that discriminatory attitudes and practices could be exposed and that the status quo could change.[15]

In many respects, sexual discrimination differed from racial bias in education. There were crucial distinctions in the way the law was used to oppress or liberate blacks and white women, for example. In the South and in some parts of the North, racial segregation in the school system and unequal resources for schooling resulted from clearly racist laws and deliberate public policy. Like the disenfranchisement of blacks, legalized educational inequality buttressed racial caste, and what law had helped to create, it could also undo, however difficult the process. But law and conscious policy had not been major contributors to sex inequity in public education. At the time of the *Brown v. Board of Education of Topeka* decision attacking racial discrimination in education, nearly all American schools were desegregated by sex, except for a few peripheral courses and activities. Statutes and district regulations of the Progressive Era that distinguished between the sexes in coeducational public schools were few in number and could trace their origins as reforms, not discrimination. These regulations became ready targets for a statute like Title IX that banned single-sex classes in vocational subjects, for example.[16]

In other ways, however, race was similar to sex. Beyond the bias built into law and clear policy, blacks also faced a more amorphous and less conscious kind of discrimination, which became labeled "institutional racism." Blacks found that civil rights laws did not dismantle many of the attitudinal, economic, and institutional hurdles they faced. In public education, civil rights groups targeted a number of forms of institutional racism: the omission of blacks and the use of negative stereotypes of African-Americans in textbooks; biased behavior of teachers toward people of color, arguably all the more potent in its impact when unconscious; the use of racially unfair tests; bias in counseling; the failure to appoint and advance black employees; and the tracking of blacks into slow lanes or dead-end vocational programs that blocked them from further education or white-collar jobs.[17]

The concept of sexism owed much to this discovery of institutional racism. In a 1970 article called "Woman as Nigger," which popularized the term "sexism," Gayle Rubin wrote that "people are more sophisticated about blacks than they are about women: black history courses do not have to begin by convincing people that blacks are not in fact genetically better suited to dancing than to learning." As we have said, sexism in public schools was not nearly as visible to most people as racism. Many educators thought gender distinctions natural and hence regarded sex stereotyping as a non-issue. They saw gender differences but not discrimination. Teachers who equated bias with conscious unfairness or dislike resented the accusation of "sexism"—it was an article of faith with most teachers that they should be and were fair in their dealings with students.[18]

Many educators who agreed that blacks were not well served by schools did not see any significant academic or social disabilities for girls. Differences of academic achievement by sex sometimes favored boys, sometimes girls; they were relatively slight—ranging from about 1 to 5 percent; and they were much smaller than racial or class differences. Gender cuts across all social classes, but disproportionate numbers of blacks were poor. Discrimination against blacks, therefore, was compounded by class bias. In addition, girls seemed to fit well into schools and were less often perceived to be educationally disadvantaged than were boys.[19]

The concept of institutional sexism caught on rapidly among feminists, however, for it defined the silent, subtle character of sex conditioning and the broad scope of the battle for sex equity. Feminist researchers on institutional sexism labored to expose the schools' hidden curriculum, in part to convince educators and parents that sex bias was a reality. The growth of women's studies programs and local consciousness-raising groups fueled the effort to document and remedy discrimination. Some investigators were based in universities, but much research was a grassroots effort on the part of teachers in elementary and high schools, NOW chapters in places like New York City, feminist writers and librarians, and parents and students. These groups found many disturbing signs of institutional sexism, systematic patterns of bias against females:[20]

○ Textbooks proved to be riddled with bias. Investigators found that stories had many more male than female characters and illustrations; that history books ignored, distorted, or trivialized the role of women; that texts portrayed occupations in sex-stereotyped ways; and that even mathematics and science texts showed a consistent male bias.[21]

○ Studies of classroom interactions between teachers and students revealed that instructors typically paid more attention to boys, criticizing them disproportionately but also rewarding them more for active thinking. Teachers often reinforced sex stereotyping of social behavior and aspirations.[22]

○ Counselors often held sex-stereotyped notions of what courses or careers were appropriate for males and females; the tests they employed also were sex-typed.[23]

○ Sports and extracurricular activities reinforced the image of boys as active, aggressive, and enterprising and of girls as passive or oriented to personal relationships rather than public activity. Funds spent on boys' athletics were grossly disproportionate to those available for girls' sports.[24]

○ Teacher educators and the textbooks they wrote showed little awareness of the ways in which teachers perpetuated sex bias.[25]

○ Although girls started out ahead of boys in their academic performance, by the end of high school boys had caught up with and were surpassing girls in subjects like mathematics and science. By the college years there were great disparities between men and women in enrollments in fields like engineering and science.[26]

○ Since administrators were overwhelmingly male, pupils learned that men ran things. Subtle and overt forms of discrimination barred women from positions of influence in education even though they constituted two-thirds of all teachers. Men dominated the governance of education, vastly outnumbering women on school boards.[27]

Feminist researchers generally focused on three occasionally overlapping concepts to explain the origins of discriminatory policies: (1) patriarchy, which encompassed the whole of society as the unit of analysis and described universal male domination; (2) sex-role stereotyping, which stressed the individual's internalization of cultural gender roles; and (3) institutional sexism, which addressed the inequalities built into institutional structures and policies.

The patriarchal interpretation asserted that male domination characterized society as a whole. In this view, schools, like all other institutions, revealed a pattern of discrimination against women: men set educational policy and preempted the administration of schools; they determined what knowledge was considered most important; and their values permeated instruction. To dislodge patriarchy would require nothing less than a revolution in attitudes and a profound redistribution of power.[28]

Another approach that had greater currency in educational analysis—the sex-role socialization model—focused on how girls and boys were taught different gender roles. One reason for the popularity of this interpretation may be that psychological thinking has dominated educational research in fields like developmental psychology and in programs like compensatory education. It could also accommodate the peculiarly American self-help therapies, such as assertiveness training for women or Dale Carnegie's strategies for winning friends. Advocates of this position typically took a hierarchical view of sex-role socialization, according to which adults such as parents or teachers inculcated the stereotypes in the child. Underlying this approach was an individualist and pluralist ideal: that all pupils, if given the right help, could realize all their potential in a world in which people were no longer handicapped by faulty gender socialization.[29]

If the patriarchal interpretation took all of society as the unit of analysis and the sex-role socialization model focused on the individual, the institutional approach highlighted the school as intermediary between society and the individual. The tendency to shift responsibility onto the schools had been witnessed before in educational reform movements. Educators of the Progressive Era did not explain the poorer academic performance and higher dropout rates of boys in terms of boys' deficiencies but instead claimed that the school had become a feminized environment ill suited to boys. Activists in the black liberation movement attacked the notion that innate racial differences could account for black students' educational problems, arguing instead that the school was a white, middle-class institution that failed to meet the needs of black students. Likewise, feminists who developed the idea of institutional sexism treated the school itself as a key source of gender inequities, both in education and in the larger society.[30]

Why, in such diverse circumstances, did the blame fall on the institution? Part of the answer to this question lies in the increased prominence of schools as institutions. In the nineteenth century, when the common school was more informal and occasional, educators and citizens usually attributed students' educational failings to the individuals' lack of character, not to defects in the schools. As bureaucratized educational systems began to occupy more of students' lives and have greater impact on their chances in future life, some reformers came to view the school as a quasi-independent and powerful agency in its own right. It became reasonable, then, to talk of institutional racism or institutional sexism.[31]

Advocates of the institutional model of reform sought to change discriminatory policies or procedures imbedded in institutional structures and cultures. They attacked biased institutional practices through demands for policies explicitly requiring open enrollment for both sexes, equal funding, and affirmative action. This approach relied less on changing individual consciousness or behavior and more on changing the institutional rules of the game.[32]

As feminists gained momentum in their campaign against sexism in public education, they expressed optimism about the possibility of change as well as anger at the inequities they had discovered. Public schools seemed a logical target for reform. As public institutions, schools were expected to be more egalitarian than private organizations. In rhetoric at least, educators had espoused an ideology of equal opportunity that could be used to prick their consciences. For over a century the public had regarded schools as an appropriate domain for women, who constituted over two-thirds of all teachers. If these teachers could be alerted to the ways in which they were shortchanging the girls in their classes, they might be able to counteract the hidden injuries of coeducation. The civil rights movement had demonstrated that legislatures and courts, when pressed by protest groups, could alter some racist practices in public education. The feminist agenda was taking shape.

Strategies of Educational Reform

Just as they used different explanations of sexual inequities in the schools, feminists used different approaches to reform, ranging from national legislation to local consciousness raising. "Like its nineteenth-century counterpart," wrote activist Florence Howe, "the new feminism is a teaching movement. In addition to leaflets, pamphlets, magazines, newspapers, and a few books, the consciousness-raising group has made an important impact on our lives and has begun to be felt in classrooms." Howe pointed out that in colleges and universities feminism was an unswelling of change "*from the ground up*"; the number of women's studies courses increased, for example, from about 64 in 1970 to more than 1,200 in 1973. By contrast, she wrote, the "pattern of change . . . in public education is *from the top down*," through legislation and activities in national educational organizations. What was needed in public schools was also an unleashing of the same kinds of energy that had begun to transform women teachers' and students' experience in higher education.[33]

The political-legal strategies used by feminist organizations like NOW to eliminate sex bias in the schools resembled those of an earlier reform movement in education run by women: the campaign by the Women's Christian Temperance Union (WCTU) to require instruction in temperance. The WCTU was organized on the national, state, and local levels. This federated structure offered distinct advantages in enacting and policing legislation, for the national organization could shape policy and influence the federal government, state affiliates could lobby their legislatures, and local chapters could monitor and enforce laws. Such a three-pronged strategy offered special advantages in changing so decentralized and vast an enterprise as public education. While statutes provided leverage for reform, they were hardly self-enforcing. Community pressure persuaded local officials to enforce the laws.[34]

Working on these three levels, the WCTU achieved remarkable success. By the early twentieth century all the states had passed laws mandating "scientific temperance instruction" in the public schools, and Congress had done so for the District of Columbia and the Territories. Not content simply with passing laws, the WCTU asked its local branches to ensure that the statutes were obeyed. Furthermore, it created model curricular units, successfully pressured publishers to alter textbooks, and trained teachers in proper methods of temperance instruction (this special training was sometimes required by law). By working both from the top down and from the bottom up, the WCTU succeeded in making temperance instruction the one subject that was universally mandated in all American public schools. The General Federation of Women's Clubs used similar techniques to install home economics in American schools.[35]

Although the goals of feminists who belonged to organizations like NOW in the 1960s and 1970s differed from those of their predecessors in the temperance movement, their methods were similar. They pressed for legislation at the federal and state levels but realized they would have to lobby local leaders in order to see these laws implemented. Liberals in the legislatures might be willing to pass symbolic statutes in order to satisfy feminist activists, but bureaucrats charged with enforcement often dragged their feet. Male-dominated governments and school districts were likely to ignore sex discrimination in the schools unless pressured and closely monitored.[36]

But even if successful, the political-legal strategy of reform could only touch the tip of the iceberg of institutional sexism in public education. It might make coeducation more egalitarian by attacking sex-separate vocational schools and classes, separate physical education programs and sports, or employment policies that discriminated against women. But these changes did not reach the subtler forms of sexism, such as biased textbooks and sex-stereotyped ways of teaching. More profound reforms would require the same strategies that the WCTU had employed: training teachers, rewriting curricular materials, and grass-roots campaigns to arouse the public.

Activists in the feminist movement worked to write sex equity into leg-islation like the Equal Pay Bill of 1963 and Title VII of the Civil Rights Act of 1964. Such laws, however, were no stronger than their enforce-ment; in the beginning, some members of the Equal Employment Oppor-tunity Commission regarded the sex provision of the Civil Rights Act of 1964 as a joke, deeming their real business to be promoting racial equal-ity. The EEOC's neglect of women's issues impelled liberal feminists to work through NOW and other action groups, such as the Women's Equity Action League (WEAL), in order to publicize inequalities, bring sex-equity suits, lobby officials, testify at congressional hearings, and press for legis-lation. At its second national conference in 1967, NOW drew up a women's bill of rights that included this demand: "Equal and unsegre-gated education."[37]

Liberal feminists were in effect affirming the importance of truly iden-tical coeducation and arguing at the same time that it did not exist. Their major legal tool in implementing equal coeducation was Title IX of the 1972 Education Amendments. Its controlling provision read as follows: "No person in the United States shall, on the basis of sex, be excluded from participation in, be denied the benefits of, or be subjected to dis-crimination under any education program or activity receiving Federal financial assistance." Since all but a tiny handful of public elementary and secondary schools were already coeducational, the law covered practically all students in public education. Despite its sweeping language, Title IX aroused little interest or controversy as it passed through Congress, which was being buffeted at the time by the storm over court-ordered racial bus-ing. The bill was thin on particulars, beyond the threat of cutting off fed-eral funds to schools that did not comply.[38]

Title IX can be interpreted as a symbolic gesture on the part of a Con-gress that delegated to the administrative branch the crucial task of devis-ing regulations and modes of enforcement. Ann N. Costain argues that it was a typical strategy at the time for the "Congress to pass legislation responding to the grievances of [a disadvantaged] group, then for the bureaucracy to delay implementation of this legislation for prolonged peri-ods of time. This has the effect of forcing the group to fight its most

difficult political battles in bureaucratic settings, out of the public eye."
The history of implementation of Title IX corroborates Costain's analysis and illuminates the strategies of the pressure groups that emerged on
both sides of the campaign against sex discrimination.[39]

Passed by a Democratic Congress, the statute languished in the Repub-
lican administrations of Presidents Richard Nixon and Gerald Ford. "To
get Title IX regulations was like pulling teeth with your fingers," complained Senator Birch Bayh, who was a key ally of feminists. The Department of Health, Education and Welfare (HEW), charged with devising
regulations, stalled for two years before finally issuing a tentative version
in 1974 for congressional and public comment. This delay gave constituencies on both sides the chance to mobilize their forces.[40]

The lobby for strong enforcement of Title IX—called the Educational
Task Force—was composed largely of sympathetic educational organizations and feminist research, legal, and political action groups. The most
vocal opponents were representatives of college sports who feared that
sex equity in athletics would endanger that citadel of masculinity, football. Costain reports that HEW officials were "not willing to view women
or the Task Force as a constituency," whereas football coaches won easy
access to President Ford's White House. Within Congress a number of
conservatives tried to kill the regulations on affirmative action, the griev-
ance process, integrated physical education programs, and revenue-
producing sports. But by gaining the support of black congressmen concerned about the potential for a similar gutting of civil rights provisions,
the women's lobby managed to save the Title IX regulations proposed by
HEW. They finally went into effect three years after passage of the bill.[41]

Although the regulations for Title IX that were finally approved in
1975 did not contain all the provisions sought by feminists, they did provide a legal basis for making public elementary and secondary coeducation more identical for both sexes. They required every school system to
evaluate its policies and alter them if they did not comply with the rules.
Every district was to appoint a Title IX officer responsible for coordinating compliance and hearing complaints about sex discrimination. With
some exceptions, regulations outlawed separate-sex classes in health,
physical education, and vocational subjects as well as banning sex-
segregated vocational programs and schools. The regulations outlined the
general principle of equal treatment of boys and girls in athletics but
exempted contact sports and shaded the mandate of sex equality in sports
by ambiguous language that would later provide grist for lawyers. They
banned discriminatory counseling and sex-biased guidance tests and materials. Districts were enjoined not to discriminate by sex in employment

and compensation or to treat students or employees differently according to marital status or pregnancy.[42]

Rough legal tools were now available to combat explicit sex bias in public education of the sort that existed on the periphery of the system and to attack sexual discrimination in employment. Legal action against even obvious forms of sex bias was "stalled at the start," however. A report on enforcement by NOW's Project on Equal Education Rights (PEER) in 1977 told a depressing story: federal implementation of Title IX in public elementary and secondary schools was "indifferent, inept, ignorant of the law itself, or bogged down in red tape." The HEW civil rights office, the report claimed, had failed to publicize the law adequately, clarify disputed points in the regulations, train staff, conduct thorough investigations into non-complying districts, and resolve complaints within a reasonable period of time. As one insider put it, "it's not respectable to work on Title IX in the agency."[43]

PEER pointed out that most of the cases, by their nature, required prompt resolution, for justice delayed was often justice denied for students who were passing rapidly through school. The cases illuminate the kinds of discrimination practiced in local districts. Parents of girls in Louisiana complained in 1974 that their daughters in an all-girls high school could not take the Latin and advanced mathematics courses offered in the boys' school; in 1977 their case was still pending. A mother in Massachusetts wrote that her daughter had been denied access to a shop class; when HEW got around to calling her, the family had moved. When a NOW chapter in Pennsylvania asserted that three districts were disobeying Title IX, HEW took twenty-two months to reply and reported two years later that it had lost the original report. A NOW member in that community observed: "When we first filed the complaint, the school people were really nervous. Today, when you talk to someone in the school district, they just smile. They know nothing is going to happen."[44]

Other investigations by agencies inside and outside the federal government largely confirmed PEER's dismal account of enforcement in the early years of Title IX, although the record improved during the Carter administration. Despite a court order in 1977 stemming from a feminist suit against HEW for failing to enforce the law, the Civil Rights Commission reported in 1980 that the agency was still a Bermuda Triangle of unresolved complaints and that it was laggard in making compliance reviews in school districts. Although feminists, like blacks, had resorted to the federal government to secure rights not honored at the local level, both groups knew that reform from the top down could easily be stymied by a reluctant or inefficient bureaucracy. Despite the fact that some districts openly challenged Title IX, the federal government never imposed the ultimate sanction, the cutting off of federal funds. Indeed, in the case of *Grove City College v. Bell* in 1984, the U.S. Supreme Court, following the lead of the Reagan administration's brief, narrowed the coverage of Title IX to particular programs that discriminated, not to institutions as a whole, thereby further limiting whatever fiscal threat remained. Feminists united with other equity advocates to pass the Civil Rights Restoration Act in 1988 to undo some of the damage of *Grove*.[45]

Under the administration of President Ronald Reagan, feminist programs suffered not only the indifference or inefficiency of the federal bureaucracy but also direct attacks. A prime target was the Women's Educational Equity Act (WEEA). In 1974 Congress had passed this act to establish model educational programs to combat sex bias. Although a small program—its funding never exceeded $10 million—through demonstration projects it provided state and local education agencies with services that had previously been lacking in the implementation of Title IX. WEEA took the lead, for example, in developing programs to open scientific and technological courses and careers to girls and women, counteract sex stereotypes in vocational education, eliminate the barriers that kept women from administrative positions, and create sex-fair programs in physical education and athletics. It constituted the only action arm of a federal government that had otherwise taken a passive stance toward the implementation of Title IX. As such, it became a lightning rod for opponents of the feminist agenda.[46]

Conservative publications attacked WEEA as "an important resource for the practice of feminist policies and politics" and as a "money machine for a network of openly radical feminist groups." President Reagan first tried to abolish the agency and when that failed, to withhold funds. When this maneuver also failed, his Education Department tried another tack: appointing as field readers for WEEA-sponsored projects a number of people, some associated with Phyllis Schlafly's Eagle Forum, who were unsympathetic to feminist goals. One of these field readers wrote this appraisal of a grant proposal: "Do not see the need for project. Most girls and boys go into field because it is way parents bring them up and mostly they are born with certain desires." The director of WEEA was reassigned to another job, and a pro-feminist advisory council for WEEA was replaced by Reagan-appointed members who promptly fired the executive director and hired as her successor a member of Eagle Forum who had opposed appropriations for WEEA.[47]

Conservatives in Congress also assaulted the campaign against sex discrimination in education. In 1979 and again in 1981, senators introduced a Family Protection Act that was designed, in the words of Senator Paul Laxalt, to "withhold funds to any program that teaches children values that contradict demonstrated community beliefs or to buy any textbooks that denigrate, diminish, or deny the historically understood role differences between the sexes." These bills also left to the states or local districts "the right, with parental consultation, to limit or prohibit intermingling of the sexes in sports or other school-related activities, free of Federal interference." Promoted by the Moral Majority and applauded by *Conservative Digest,* the Family Protection Act shows that anti-feminists, too, tried to use the power of the federal government to serve their aims. Although this campaign was unsuccessful except in symbolic terms, it demonstrated that in some quarters anti-feminism was a potent cause.[48]

Fearful that the federal government was undermining the quest for sex equity, feminist activists turned to state governments for support in their attack on sex bias in the schools. In 1987 Phyllis W. Cheng reported that a total of twelve states (all but one of them in the North) had adopted comprehensive laws on sex equity similar to Title IX, nineteen had adopted fragmented statutes, and nineteen had passed no legislation on the subject (of these, fourteen were in the South). The timing of the state Title IX laws was revealing: Only one was passed before the federal statute; four were enacted during the period of ferment over the federal regulations from 1972 to 1975; none appeared in the period from 1976 to 1980 when feminists were focusing on federal implementation of the new regulations; and seven, or over half, were adopted during the Reagan years, when feminists had reason to believe that the federal government was sabotaging their work.[49]

The new laws generally covered the same guarantees as the regulations of the federal Title IX, but half of them also banned sex discrimination in instructional materials such as textbooks. As in the case of the federal government, no state ever cut off funding because of non-compliance. Although the states that passed Title IX laws did demonstrate more sex-fair practices in the schools after enactment than before, it is obviously hard to disentangle the effects of federal and state laws or to assess the impact of changes that had little to do with the laws. Some states made rapid progress because influential and committed state educational officers or sex-equity coordinators worked in tandem with women's lobbies that monitored local districts.[50]

As in the case of the WCTU and local enforcement of temperance instruction, women's groups worked hard in local districts to publicize and correct sex discrimination. In community after community, feminists created grassroots coalitions to educate the educators about the federal and state laws and compel compliance. "The key to enforcement is community pressure," said an activist in the Iowa state department of education. "That is the only viable vehicle for enforcing the law." The key to success in such efforts, wrote PEER in a report on these campaigns, was to "set limited, concrete goals," build "a broad base of public support," and publicize "findings to the widest possible audience."[51]

The South, which had passed no sex-equity laws and was generally traditional in gender values, offered a somewhat unlikely case in point. In 1975 Winnifred Green, who had worked to end racial segregation as a worker for the American Friends Service Committee, shifted her attention to gender bias. She recruited volunteers to monitor violations of Title IX in twenty-one communities in six southern states. In a region already in turmoil over racial desegregation, the monitors encountered much hostility. In Arkansas a superintendent declared: "We'll comply the last minute of the last day." When Green had collected a massive array of Title IX violations, she presented a complaint to the regional offices of the OCR in Atlanta and Dallas. The media broadcast her report, and this publicity galvanized the Atlanta OCR into action (pp. 10–12).

The federal courts came into play as well. A number of communities had responded to racial integration by establishing separate-sex high schools as a way of keeping black boys and white girls apart. As a result, girls found that they did not have access to advanced science, math, and language courses. A federal judge ended this policy, arguing that sex-segregation "results in a similar if not equivalent injury to school children as would occur if a racially segregated school system were imposed" (p. 12).

In Iowa, a state senator, Joann Orr, started another sex-equity campaign when she invited members of women's groups to a meeting to discuss enactment of a state law on sex bias. The women left the meeting determined to document the problems by monitoring their own communities. These women's groups—the League of Women Voters, the American Association of University Women, the PTA, NOW, and others—provided networks for recruiting volunteers. A PEER staff member from Washington, D.C., came to train the local monitors and provided press releases on Title IX to local media. The volunteers collected reports on twenty-three districts and provided documentation and publicity that helped persuade legislators to pass a sex-discrimination bill (pp. 16–18).

The volunteers also worked with local educators. In Pella, Iowa, activists interviewed the superintendent, teachers, and counselors, helping them analyze textbooks and their own practices. They believed that such an approach was more productive in a small town than confrontation. The superintendent, apprehensive at first, said "all in all it was a positive experience. And the people doing the monitoring were local. It wasn't like it was someone from outside the community." One volunteer wrote: "Teachers came to realize that the texts were, in fact, sex biased. . . . The long-range impact of our study will be through changing the consciousness of teachers." Some people might think the feminist concerns were silly, she said, but in the face of local pressure they stopped criticizing so loudly (pp. 16–18).

A campaign to monitor sex equality in twelve Michigan school districts illustrates how national organizations, state and local women's groups, the media, school districts, foundations, and local volunteers interacted. In 1977a director from PEER, Elizabeth Giese, began by going from community to community, speaking to local groups, working through organizational newsletters, collaring volunteers at meetings, and meeting with local media people to explain sex equity. Foundations and corporations supported the effort. Giese urged local monitors to secure endorsements from local organizations and to take a cooperative approach, assuming that educators wanted equitable schools (pp. 32–34).

Detroit, facing a huge deficit and a desegregation order for a school population that was 87 percent minority, proved to be "a special challenge," Giese wrote. "You want to talk about the equality of their program . . . and they wonder if they'll have a program." Less than a third of the staff and only 13 percent of the students had ever heard of Title IX. Over two-thirds of the district's vocational classes were sex-segregated. "We don't have a problem with sex discrimination in my class," observed an aerospace teacher, "because we don't have any girls." Despite such obstacles, a PEER official and her blue-ribbon advisory board moved ahead, wrote a report that was distributed across the system, and won the endorsement of eighteen community groups. The strategy was one used in many other communities: documenting problems, creating community awareness, and generating pressure to change. "Because educators are busy people involved in running regular school programs," wrote PEER, "they tend to overlook suggestions for change unless there is evidence of widespread community support for them. That is why an organized campaign is important" (pp. 34–35, 37).

What Happened in the Schools?

Case studies of local campaigns, like those of the WEEA projects, were often success stories of Title IX implementation, while individual complaints to HEW, litigation, and compliance reviews by federal or state agencies told of failures to carry out the law. More difficult to assess is the degree to which approximately sixteen thousand local school districts actually complied with the mandate to make coeducation more identical for both sexes. In such a vast, decentralized system local attitudes toward gender mattered; both community expectations and school cultures differed greatly by region, by size of community, and by social class.

As in past attempts to reform gender relationships in the schools, policy talk and practice often diverged. Some changes were easier to make than others; some reforms were largely symbolic, others practical. And amid the campaigns in the past generation to root out sex inequities or to restore a partly mythical traditional order of sex differentiation, both feminists and their foes sometimes lost sight of the substantial gender parities built long ago into the structure of instruction in coeducational classrooms.

School districts responded in a variety of ways to Title IX and to the broader feminist campaign against institutional sexism. Some sought to meet the spirit as well as the letter of the law by addressing the subtler as well as the more obvious forms of institutional sexism. Most complied at least with the letter of the law—for example, by abolishing the sex-labeling of courses and by expanding sports programs for girls. Some districts remained ignorant of the requirements of Title IX or openly defied it.

Part of the difficulty in evaluating the effects of Title IX and programs like WEEA arises, as Rita Bornstein observes, from the ambiguity of the criteria used to determine compliance or success. Such diffuse goals "were both confusing and liberating. Confusing in that they provided few clear, specific guidelines for action; liberating because their very unclarity invited creative local definitions." Complicating this story still further is the fact that feminists themselves came to disagree about whether a gender-neutral approach—one that sought to expose girls and boys to identical coeducation—was preferable to a gender-sensitive strategy that recognized differences between males and females and attempted to honor feminine values and cognitive and behavioral styles.[52]

Another problem in assessing implementation is an absence of statistics on gender practices. Federal and state records on implementation are so spotty and incomplete that PEER found as late as the 1980s that it had to rely in part on data collected independently by private agencies.[53]

A sense of fair play and social justice motivated many school officials to comply with Title IX regulations. Compliance usually cost money—as in upgrading girls' athletics—and did not increase resources, because funds for sex desegregation in local districts were minuscule. The negative incentives for compliance were perhaps more compelling: a fear of bad publicity resulting from local or state monitoring of practices; the threat of state or federal investigations of complaints; and the prospect of costly and time-consuming lawsuits. Although not many Title IX cases entered the courts, the fear of litigation probably induced many administrators to comply, for potential lawsuits cast a long shadow on school districts. By the end of the 1970s all but the most uninformed or recalcitrant districts had probably implemented, at least in a formal way, the most explicit regulations of Title IX. But the gap between token and full compliance was enormous.[54]

The results of the campaign for sex equity were summed up in the title of a 1981 report prepared by the National Advisory Council on Women's Educational Programs: *Title IX: The Half Full, Half Empty Glass.* If complaints and lawsuits constituted the half-empty glass, the success stories in the report balanced the image:

- A man teaching auto mechanics in Kingstree, South Carolina, concluded that "the three girls in my first year class are doing just as well as the boys."

- A teacher in Kansas recalled that "if I went back to before '79, . . . we had boy lines and girl lines, . . . boy bubblers [drinking fountains] and girl bubblers. . . . If a boy would drink out of a girls' bubbler, goodness sakes! . . . segregation doesn't solve a problem. You solve a problem through integration."

- A student in Louisiana said of her drafting teacher: "He has really helped me a lot to see what I can do now and later. He understands the female students can make a career based on skills learned in his class."

- A parent who served as a Title IX monitor said: "It is exciting to realize that individuals who care about equity and work toward that can truly make a change. . . . My daughter, in her first year of junior high school, is becoming an effective community advocate who knows her rights, the rights of others, and stands up for what she believes."[55]

The complaints and the successes convey the human side of the search for sex equity, but statistics, hard as they are to find, illuminate concrete institutional changes. Certain parts of the Title IX regulations lent themselves to statistical analysis: for example, data on girls' participation in athletics, on the number of girls in nontraditional vocational education courses or programs, and on the hiring of women administrators.[56]

In the federal government, state capitols, local districts, and the courts, the quest for sex-fair athletics initially aroused controversy and continued to generate debate and legal tangles. Sports had great symbolic importance in gender psychology and politics and had mobilized the public's interest in and support for public education. In the Progressive Era, school leaders welcomed competitive football and baseball because they made the high school seem virile. The prospect—rare, as it turned out—of girls playing on boys' teams aroused fears of a female invasion of a traditionally masculine domain. The panicky response of male administrators to boys with long hair or earrings—and the large number of cases involving the length of boys' hair but not girls'—suggests that many schoolmen were still anxious about the "feminization" of male students (in Salem, Alabama, the high-school principal suspended three boys for wearing earrings, complaining that "I feel that young men should dress like young men and young ladies should dress like young ladies").[57]

The inequalities between boys' and girls' athletics at the time of the passage of Title IX were blatant. The ratio of expenditures for girls' sports in comparison to boys' ranged from 1:8 to 1:450 in eight communities. In two states, public schools spent no funds on girls' sports, while in Minneapolis the district spent more on one football team than on all girls' sports in the eleven city high schools. Public opinion supported greater equality of athletic opportunity for girls, however, and the decade after Title IX was a time of rapid progress. In 1974 the Gallup poll found that 88 percent of all respondents and 89 percent of high-school juniors and seniors agreed that girls and boys should "have equal financial support for their athletic activities." In this case, "equal" typically meant separate: girls played on their own teams, and this practice generally did not disrupt the boys' programs. In 1971 girls constituted only 7 percent of all interscholastic athletes, but by 1980–81 the ratio of girls had increased to nearly 36 percent. The proportion of female athletes varied widely between states, ranging from 54 percent in Iowa to 24 percent in Alabama.[58]

During the 1970s there was a fivefold increase in high-school girls' participation in competitive sports. While this was a major gain—one that paralleled the greater recognition of women athletes in the society as a whole—boys' programs continued to be better funded and girls continued to be limited to fewer sports and to be excluded from contact sports. Women physical educators also raised important questions about whether the earlier philosophy of women's sports, which stressed participation and cooperation over commercialized competition among the star athletes, might be lost if girls' athletics were to become assimilated to male sports.[59]

Coeducational physical education—especially in the elementary school—aroused less resistance than the apparent threat posed by full coeducation to the male domains of contact sports and interscholastic athletics, yet it raised a number of questions about the nature of equity. In supposedly mixed classes resegregation often took place when students engaged in contact sports. Certain activities deemed appropriate to women—such as modern dance—were sometimes dropped from the co-educational physical education curriculum because they were not considered virile enough for the boys. As physical education departments became sexually integrated, women athletic directors and coaches were often replaced by men. By 1983–84, only 17 percent of coaches in senior high schools were women. The analogy with racial desegregation in the South is striking: there, as white and black schools were merged, large numbers of black principals lost their jobs to whites.[60]

Sports might be regarded as peripheral to the main academic purpose of the public schools, but their symbolic value propelled them into the limelight during the Title IX controversy. Similarly, relatively few students entered the elective vocational education programs, but the direct connection between such practical training and sex-typed jobs made sex bias and sex segregation in vocational education one of the primary targets of feminists. Activists argued that inadequate job training was one of the major reasons for the low status of women in the labor market. Similar reasoning lay behind the sex-equity provisions in the 1976 amendments to the Vocational Education Act (P.O. 94–482). Because advocates of vocational education had justified their programs as a way to prepare students for the adult workforce, it was natural to assume that changes in vocational training could improve the lot of women in the workforce.[61]

That connection between school training and a sex-stratified work force also made more than token compliance with the law difficult, however. In theory, enrollment in occupational programs was voluntary, but many factors influenced and constrained the choices of students, including the attitudes of fellow students, the advice of school staff and parents, interactions with teachers, and perceptions of opportunity after graduation. A school system might declare that all occupational classes were open to both sexes and still find that boys and girls continued to choose sex-typed programs. Only in required classes in subjects like home economics and shop could school systems prescribe mixing by sex, but these were usually regarded not as specific job preparation but rather as general education for all students.[62]

Before Title IX, prevocational and vocational classes were highly sex-segregated. In the middle grades of many school systems, boys and girls were separated in required home economics and shop classes. Another form of segregation was the separate-sex vocational school. New York City, for example, had thirteen schools for boys only and five for girls. The male schools offered a far wider range of courses, most of which led to higher-paying jobs than programs for girls. Separate vocational schools for girls mostly prepared them for work in the home or low-paying female jobs. In Boston, graduates of the girls' trade school could expect to earn 47 percent less than graduates of the boys' school. Title IX regulations banned such sex-segregated vocational schools and required integration of courses such as shop and home economics that had been limited to one sex.[63]

In comprehensive coeducational high schools that offered vocational programs and courses as electives, sex segregation was also widespread, either as a result of deliberate policy—as in the case of boys-only welding classes—or as a result of student choice (constrained, of course, by sex stereotyping). In 1972–73, 79 percent of all girls in vocational classes were enrolled in homemaking or office-business training programs. Eighty-eight percent of students in technical courses in high schools and 86 percent in trades-industry courses were boys. It was clearly not enough to declare—as required by Title IX—that all classes were open to girls and boys alike; active efforts were needed to recruit students for courses that were non-traditional for their sex and to institute sex-fair methods of teaching. When Congress attached sex-equity amendments to its funding of vocational education in 1976, it required states to appoint full-time sex-equity coordinators in their vocational departments and provided them with a list of duties explicitly designed to lessen sex segregation and discrimination.[64]

What were the results of these attempts to achieve sex equity in occupational training? There were improvements in some fields between 1972 and 1979: female enrollments in agriculture programs went from 5.3 percent to 19.2 percent and in technical programs from 9.7 percent to 17.5 percent; male enrollments in certain home economics specialties increased somewhat during those years. But a survey conducted in 1979 disclosed that almost half of vocational programs enrolled students of one sex only and that only 8.5 percent of students in apprenticeship programs were women. A 1980 study found that over 90 percent of students training to be nursing assistants and secretaries were women and between 94 and 96 percent of students in carpentry, auto mechanics, welding, and small-engine repair were men. Almost 70 percent of women were preparing for occupations that paid below-average wages. PEER reported that in 1982–83 only 13 percent of women were enrolled in non-traditional vocational programs—those previously defined as for men only—almost one percentage point lower than the 1978–79 school year figure. Clearly, severe problems persisted in the effort to make occupational training sex-fair. Despite some programs that attempted to redress the bias of vocational training, students were often reluctant to enter fields that were non-traditional for their sex. In general, enrollments reflected the sex segregation of the work force.[65]

Table 2.1. Women in Various Administrative Positions (Estimated).

	1972–73 (%)	1983–84 (%)
Superintendent	0.1	6.8
High School Principal	1.4	6.1
Junior High School Principal	2.9	10.2
Elementary School Principal	19.6	26.5

Sources: *Andrew Fishel and Janice Pottker, "Women in Educational Governance: A Statistical Portrait," in Janice Pottker and Andrew Fishel, eds.,* Sex Bias in the Schools: The Research Evidence *(Rutherford, N.J.: Farleigh Dickinson University Press, 1977), p. 511; "The PEER Report Card: Update on Women and Girls in America's Schools—A State-by-State Survey,"* PEER Policy Paper, no. 4, Autumn 1985, charts 3, 5–7.

Women have been historically underrepresented in the administration of public schools. Attempts to remedy this in equality directly challenged the dominant position of men and thus aroused opposition (usually not explicit but powerful nonetheless). Title IX and several other statutes and executive orders prohibited sex discrimination in employment, and securing more leadership positions has been a key item on the feminist education agenda. As table 2.1 indicates, the progress made in promoting women between 1972–73 and 1983–84 was mixed at best for a system in which women continued to constitute about two-thirds of all teachers. Data on the sex of school administrators are only approximate, for agencies that normally gather all sorts of statistics on them have been laggard in recording both sex and ethnicity. The greatest growth in the percentage of women administrators appears to have taken place in the 1980s, in part because women have entered administrative training programs in much greater numbers than before and in part because activists have worked hard to clear the obstacles in their path.[66]

Efforts to dislodge sex bias in physical education and athletics, vocational education, and the hiring of administrators to fulfill the requirements of Title IX produced mixed results. Certain kinds of mandates were clear and demanded institutional responses—that is, they called for definite changes in policy, regardless of the commitments and values of individual educators and students. It became illegal, for example, to limit courses to one sex only or to limit job descriptions to one sex, as in notices for administrative positions. Even in such cases, resistant staff might evade the intent of the law: for example, teachers might resegregate a coeducational class by assigning different activities to the two sexes, or school boards might tap the "old boy" network to screen candidates for an administrative position.

But even when the new policies were clear and enforced, and hence formal discrimination was absent, there was considerable leeway for differential gender practices that could be attributed to individual choice. A district could open a nursing-assistant class to boys and a carpentry class to girls, but strong pressures from parents, peers, and some school staff often kept all but the most intrepid students from making unorthodox choices. When student and public opinion was in line with new opportunities—as in the case of girls' sports—rapid change occurred. Boys' and girls' athletics, in which participation was voluntary, may have become more equal in funding and public support, but they continued to be segregated as a rule. But when men's traditional dominance was directly challenged, as in administrative hiring practices, changes in the law did not erase, though they did erode, the many informal barriers blocking women from leadership positions.

Feminists seeking to bring about change in sixteen thousand decentralized school districts have relied on a complex mix of federal and state legislation, model projects, and federated pressure groups operating at each level, including local communities. But one major target of feminist reform in education was not so decentralized and hard to reach: the large corporations that produced textbooks for the vast education market. Here reformers did not have to police thousands of local districts or change the choices of millions of students. Publishers, sensitive to negative publicity that might hurt sales, responded to charges of sex bias by changing their products, at least in token ways. They knew, also, that several states had passed laws prohibiting the use of sex-stereotyped curricular materials. A number of states and publishers issued guidelines for non-sexist language. Five large states went beyond proscribing sex-stereotyping in textbooks to require social studies classes to include women's experience and contributions to American history. Publishers who did not adapt their textbooks faced the loss of lucrative markets. In any case, feminists on the editorial staffs of the publishing companies were committed to producing non-sexist books.[67]

Changes in the textbooks, unlike reforms in sports or vocational education, went to the core of the educational process: what millions of students learned in regular classrooms. The feminists' initial research on textbooks reported a deeply ingrained male bias: they found, among other things, highly unequal representation of the sexes in text and illustrations, blatant sex stereotyping, and generic use of male pronouns. Many companies adopted guidelines to eliminate these obvious forms of bias. Feminist educators welcomed these improvements but feared that textbook reform might stop at the surface of the problem. Cleaning up the pronouns, adding a few token women, and eliminating the more obvious forms of sex stereotyping—these were only the beginning of a much more thorough rethinking of the curriculum that feminists advocated.[68]

Since textbooks constituted the chief source of academic knowledge in public schools, they became the focus of a debate over what the common understanding of the world should be. Much of the reconceptualization of women's experience was related to the rapid growth of women's studies programs. In higher education, women's studies courses burgeoned in the 1970s. Researchers in fields like history and literature not only made invisible women visible but questioned the male canon of what should be taught and male paradigms of explanation.[69]

In 1986 Mary Kay Tetreault indicated what a feminist analysis might entail when she appraised a dozen high-school texts published between 1979 and 1982. Janice Trecker's earlier study of U.S. history textbooks of the 1960s revealed that they largely excluded women, in part because their experience was not directly relevant to the chief topics of traditional male history: politics, wars, and diplomacy. Tetreault found that although women were no longer invisible in the later textbooks, they still were far less prominent than men. She estimated that only about 5 percent of the prose and from 30 to 58 percent of the pictures described women. All the books discussed and illustrated a similar cast of famous women, especially those who most easily blended into political history, such as presidents' wives.[70]

This "contributionist" stance, though similar in tone to the early treatment of minorities in textbooks, was accompanied by the appearance of a new theme in the more recent books: the oppression of women (the limitation of their legal and political rights) and their efforts to liberate themselves. Some texts discussed women's participation in the paid labor force. But by and large, the texts stopped there in their treatment of women's experience, even though the illustrations offered more opportunity to analyze the everyday lives of women. Tetreault concluded that the "textbooks *have changed* since Trecker's analysis," but women were included mostly as contributors to major events of traditional (male) history or as the complements in oversimplified, dualistic (male versus female, public versus private) treatments of social issues. What was lacking was a new conceptualization that reflected the new questions and findings of feminist history—and, more generally, the social history of groups excluded from traditional textbooks—and did not simply shoehorn women into the existing frameworks of interpretation.[71]

To provide an accurate picture of the past, Tetreault argued, textbook authors should "pay attention to the content of women's everyday lives by including women's reproductive work within the home—childbearing, childrearing, and housework. Textbooks must document women's efforts to break out of their traditional sphere of the home in a way that uses women's activities, not men's, as the measure of historical significance." Tetreault's recommendations were aimed at creating a curriculum that would legitimate women's experience as different from but of equal importance to men's.[72]

On the other side, conservatives complained that feminist revision of textbooks had gone too far and that textbooks no longer promoted traditional sex roles. One of these critics, Paul C. Vitz, analyzed stories used in basal readers from the third through the sixth grade in Texas and California. "By far the most noticeable ideological position in the readers is a feminist one," he concluded. Striking for their absence were stories celebrating romance, marriage, or motherhood, and stories or pictures showing girls with dolls. Instead, he found many stories in which heroines acted like and outshone boys: the new girl on the block who wins at "King of the Hill"; a girl in a dog sled race who turns back to help a boy but wins the race nonetheless; and a princess who agrees to marry a dragon-prince "only if her new kingdom has lots of dragons in it for her to slay and lots of drawbridges for her to fix."[73]

An oblique corroboration of Vitz came from a feminist sociologist, Mary Jo Neitz, who argued that students resisted feminist analysis in women's studies classes that stressed "persistent, structural inequality of men and women in our society." Part of the reason, according to her, was that young women believed their education had been on the whole a sex-fair enterprise and had "experienced much of their schooling through reformed textbooks." In the sanitized world of the textbooks students picked up the message that "the unequal position of women has largely been ameliorated."[74]

As Vitz's attack suggests, publishers and public-school educators in the 1980s have been caught in a crossfire of opinion about gender lessons in textbooks. Fundamentalists have protested in court against reversals of traditional sex roles in textbooks, which corrupt their children and violate their religious convictions; in a highly publicized Tennessee case, they objected to a story in which a girl read to a boy while he was cooking. Some advocates of academic freedom argued that guidelines on sex equity constituted censorship. Whether changes in textbooks represented progress, regress, or inept cosmetic responses, then, depended on the eye of the beholder.[75]

NOTES

1. Rodman quotes in George MacAdam, "Feminist Apartment House to Solve Baby Problem," *New York Times,* January 24, 1915, pt. 5, p. 9, in June Sochen, ed., *The New Feminism in Twentieth-Century America* (Lexington, Mass.: D.C. Heath, 1971), 56.

2. Crystal Eastman, "Now We Can Begin," *The Liberator* 3(1920): 23–24, as quoted in Sochen, ed., *New Feminism,* 65–66. For an analysis of this broader kind of feminism, which had little influence until recently in education, see Nancy F. Cott, *The Grounding of Modern Feminism* (New Haven: Yale University Press, 1987).

3. Nancy Frazier and Myra Sadker, *Sexism in School and Society* (New York: Harper & Row, 1973). On p. 2 they quote a definition of "sexism" by Kathleen Shortridge: "(1) A belief that the human sexes have a distinctive make-up that determines their respective lives, usually involving the idea that one sex is superior and has the right to rule the other; (2) a policy of enforcing such asserted right; (3) a system of government and society based upon it." The term "sexism," derived from "racism," was used by Prof. Margaret Feldman during the fall of 1968 and gained currency at a conference on women at Cornell in 1969; letter from Dr. Feldman to David Tyack, January 29, 1989.

4. Caroline Bird, *Born Female: The High Cost of Keeping Women Down* (New York: Pocket Books, 1971); Terry Saario, Carol Nagy Jacklin, and Carol Tittle, "Sex-Role Stereotyping in the Public Schools," *Harvard Educational Review* 43(1973): 386–418.

5. William Chafe, *Women and Equality: Changing Patterns in American Culture* (New York: Oxford University Press, 1977), chap. 5; Kirsten Amundsen, *The Silenced Majority* (Englewood Cliffs, N.J.: Prentice-Hall, 1971), 70, 78–80.

6. Betty Friedan, *The Feminine Mystique* (New York: Dell, 1963); Brigid Brophy, "Women Are Prisoners of Their Sex," *Saturday Evening Post,* November 2, 1963, p. 10; David M. Potter, "American Women and the American Character" (written in 1962), in Don E. Fehrenbacher, ed., *History and American Society: Essays of David M. Potter* (New York: Oxford University Press, 1973), 277–303.

7. Barbara Sinclair Deckard, *The Women's Movement: Political, Socioeconomic and Psychological Issues* (New York: Harper & Row, 1979), 341; Therese L. Baker, "Changes in the Educational and Career Plans of American High School Senior Women in the Past Quarter-Century: A Comparative Cohort Study of National Samples of Women Seniors in 1960, 1972,

and 1980" (unpublished manuscript, Department of Sociology, DePaul University, tables 1 and 3); Karen Oppenheim Mason, John L. Czaja, and Sara Arber, "Change in U.S. Women's Sex-Role Attitudes, 1964–1974," *American Sociological Review* 41(1976): 589, 573–96.

8. Kathleen M. Dalton, *A Portrait of a School: Coeducation at Andover* (Andover, Mass.: Phillips Academy, 1986), 1.

9. Janice Pottker and Andrew Fishel, eds., *Sex Bias in the Schools: The Research Evidence* (Rutherford, N.J.: Farleigh Dickinson University Press, 1977).

10. Ellen Carol DuBois et al., *Feminist Scholarship: Kindling in the Groves of Academe* (Urbana: University of Illinois Press, 1985) analyzes feminist scholarship in education and other fields; the authors point out (pp. 175–77) that there was not much feminist scholarship in mainstream research journals in education, but there were many articles after 1969 in policy-oriented and practitioner journals, a number of which devoted special issues to feminist scholarship.

11. Walter B. Waetgen and Jean D. Grambs, "Sex Differences: A Case of Educational Evasion?" *Teachers College Record* 65(1963): 261–71; E. S. Carter, "How Valid Are Marks Assigned by Teachers?" *Journal of Educational Psychology* 43(1952): 218–28; Earl H. Hansen, "Do Boys Get a Square Deal in School?" *Education* 79(1959): 597–98; Jean Stockhard, "Sex Differences in Behavior, Learning Problems, and Attitudes" in Jean Stockhard et al., *Sex Equity in Education* (New York: Academic Press, 1980), chap. 2; Jerome Kagan, "The Child's Sex-role Classification of School Objects," *Child Development* 35(1964): 1051–56; Daniel Levine, "Coeducation—A Contributing Factor in Miseducation of the Disadvantaged," *Phi Delta Kappan* 46(1964): 126–28; Gary L. Peltier, "Sex Differences in the School: Problem and Proposed Solution," *Phi Delta Kappan* 50(1968): 182–85; Patricia Cayo Sexton, *The Feminized Male: Classrooms, White Collars, and the Decline of Manliness* (New York: Random House, 1969); F. C. Ellenburg, "Elementary Teachers: Male or Female?" *Journal of Teacher Education* 26(1975): 329–34. For a recent call for male teachers for inner-city schools, see Spencer H. Holland, "A Radical Approach to Educating Young Black Males," *Education Week,* March 28, 1987.

12. "Schoolbook Sex Bias," *Nation's Schools* 91(1972), as reprinted in Pottker and Fishel, *Sex Bias,* 529–30.

13. Frazier and Sadker, *Sexism;* in her introduction to the book Florence Howe discusses the gap between rapid progress in instituting women's studies in higher education and the slower pace of feminist changes in the public schools. One of the earliest and most perceptive articles linking sex stereo-

typing in schools with gender stratification was Alice S. Rossi, "Equality Between the Sexes: An Immodest Proposal," in Robert Jay Lifton, ed., *The Woman in America* (Boston: Beacon Press, 1967; reprint of *Daedalus,* Spring 1964), 88–143.

14. Jo Freeman, ed., *Social Movements of the Sixties and Seventies* (New York: Longman, 1983); Florence Howe, *The Myths of Coeducation: Selected Essays, 1964–1983* (Bloomington: Indiana University Press, 1984).

15. Flexner, *Century of Struggle,* chaps. 4–6; Chafe, *Women and Equality,* chaps. 3–4; Jo Freeman, "The Women's Liberation Movement: Its Origins, Structure, Activities, and Ideas," in Jo Freeman, ed., *Women: A Feminist Perspective* (Palo Alto, Calif.: Mayfield Publishing, 1984), 543–56.

16. David Tyack, Thomas James, and Aaron Benavot, *Law and the Shaping of Public Schools, 1785–1954* (Madison: University of Wisconsin Press, 1987), chap. 5, epilogue.

17. E. R. Feagin and Clairece Booher Feagin, *Discrimination American Style: Institutional Racism and Sexism* (Englewood Cliffs, N.J.: Prentice-Hall, 1978), chaps. 1–2, 5.

18. Gayle Rubin, "Woman as Nigger," *Argus,* March 28–April 11, 1970, as quoted in Amundsen, *Silenced Majority,* 44.

19. For data on school performance by sex, see Marcia C. Linn and Anne C. Petersen, "Facts and Assumptions about the Nature of Sex Differences," in Susan S. Klein, ed., *Handbook for Achieving Sex Equity through Education* (Baltimore: Johns Hopkins Press, 1985), 53–90; for analyses of the relation between class and gender, see Stephen Walker and Len Barton, eds., *Gender, Class, and Education* (New York: Falmer Press, 1983).

20. For an example of one local investigation into sexist practices in schools, see Education Committee, New York Chapter of NOW, *Report on Sex Bias in the Public Schools,* 4th ed. (New York: NOW, 1977). For a handbook aimed at educators, see Myra Pollack Sadker and David Miller Sadker, *Sex Equity Handbook for Schools* (New York: Longman, 1982).

21. Marjorie U'Ren, "The Image of Women in Textbooks," in Vivian Gornick and Barbara Moran, eds., *Woman in Sexist Society* (New York: Basic Books, 1971), 218–25; Janice Pottker, "Psychological and Occupational Sex Stereotypes in Elementary School Readers," and Janice Law Trecker, "Women in U.S. History High-School Textbooks," in Pottker and Fishel, eds., *Sex Bias,* 111–162; Women on Words and Images, "Look, Jane, Look: See Sex Stereotypes," in Judith Stacey, Susan Bereaud, and Joan Daniels, eds., *And Jill Came Tumbling After: Sexism in American Education* (New York: Dell, 1974), 159–77.

22. Pauline Sears and David Feldman, "Teacher Interaction with Boys and Girls," *National Elementary Principal* 46(1966): 30–35; Betty Levy and Judith Stacey, "Sexism in the Elementary School: A Backward and Forward Look," *Phi Delta Kappan* 55(1973): 105–23; Raphaela Best, *We've All Got Scars: What Boys and Girls Learn in Elementary School* (Bloomington: University of Indiana Press, 1983); Jere Brophy, "Interactions of Male and Female Students with Male and Female Teachers," in Louise Cherry Wilkinson and Cera B. Marrett, *Gender Influences in Classroom Interaction* (New York: Academic Press, 1985), 115–42.

23. John J. Pietrofesa and Nancy K. Scholsberg, "Counselor Bias and the Female Occupational Role," and Carol Kehr Tittle, Karen McCarthy, and Jane Faggen Steckler, "Women and Educational Testing," in Pottker and Fishel, eds., *Sex Bias,* 217–220, 256–74.

24. Celeste Ulrich, "She Can Play as Good as Any Boy," *Phi Delta Kappan* 60(1973): 113–17.

25. David Sadker and Myra Sadker, "The Treatment of Sex Equity in Teacher Education," in Klein, ed., *Handbook for Achieving Sex Equity,* 145–62.

26. Marcia C. Linn and Anne C. Petersen, "Facts and Assumptions about the Nature of Sex Differences," and Elizabeth K. Stage et al., "Increasing the Participation and Achievement of Girls and Women in Mathematics, Science, and Engineering," in Klein, ed., *Handbook for Achieving Sex Equity,* 53–90, 237–58; Elizabeth Fennema, "Girls, Women, and Mathematics," in Elizabeth Fennema, ed., *Women and Education: Equity or Equality* (Berkeley: McCutchan, 1984), 137–65.

27. Suzanne S. Taylor, "Educational Leadership: A Male Domain?" *Phi Delta Kappan* 70(1973): 124–28; Catherine Dillon Lyon and Terry N. Saario, "Women in Public Education: Sexual Discrimination in Promotions," *Phi Delta Kappan* 60(1973): 120–23; Suzanne Estler, "Women as Leaders in Public Education," *Signs* 1(1975): 363–86; Andrew Fishel and Janice Pottker, "Women in Educational Governance: A Statistical Portrait," in Pottker and Fishel, eds., *Sex Bias,* 505–13.

28. Dale Spender, *Invisible Women: The Schooling Scandal* (London: Writers and Readers Publishing Cooperative Society, 1982); Dale Spender, *Men's Studies Modified: The Impact of Feminism on the Academic Disciplines* (Oxford: Pergamon, 1981), chap. 11. For a discussion of the patriarchal paradigm, see Joan Scott, "Is Gender a Useful Category of Historical Analysis?" *American Historical Review* 91(1986): 1053–75.

29. The 1970s produced a plethora of self-help books for women. On problems with the sex-role socialization model, see R. W. Connell, "Theorising Gender,"

Sociology 19(1985): 260–72; Judith Stacey and Barrie Thorne, "The Missing Feminist Revolution in Sociology," *Social Problems* 32(1985): 301–16.

30. William Ryan, *Blaming the Victim* (New York: Pantheon, 1971); Larry Cuban and David Tyack, "Mismatch: Schools and Children Who Don't Fit Them" in Henry Levin, ed., *Accelerated Schools,* 1993.

31. From her analysis of descriptions of nineteenth-century classrooms, Barbara Jean Finkelstein concludes that "teachers treated academic failure, not as a reflection of their own inabilities as instructors, but as evidence of the students' personal and moral recalcitrance"; see Barbara Jean Finkelstein, "Governing the Young: Teacher Behavior in American Primary Schools, 1820–1880: A Documentary History" (Ed.D. diss., Teachers College, Columbia University, 1970), 134–35.

32. This institutional approach was more a reform strategy than an articulated mode of analysis of gender; for a discussion of the latter, see Elisabeth Hansot and David Tyack, "Gender in American Public Schools: Thinking Institutionally," *Signs* 13(1988): 741–60.

33. Florence Howe, "Introduction: The Teacher and the Women's Movement," in Frazier and Sadker, *Sexism,* xi, xiii, xv, xi–xv. An example of combining models of explanation and strategies for change is Stockhard et al., *Sex Equity in Education.*

34. Tyack, James, and Benavot, *Law and the Shaping of Public Schools,* chap. 6.

35. Ibid. Even without the vote, women had access to decision-makers (the President of the General Federation of Women's Clubs, for example, was the wife of the U.S. senator who pushed to include home economics in Smith-Hughes), and clubwomen were skilled in networking and lobbying at different levels of the federated political system; see Jane Bernard Powers, "The 'Girl Question' in Education: Vocational Training for Young Women in the Progressive Era" (Ph.D. diss., Stanford University, 1986), chaps. 6, 8.

36. For a general analysis of strategies and action, see Nancy E. McGlen and Karen O'Connor, "An Analysis of the U.S. Women's Rights Movements: Rights as a Public Good," *Women and Politics* 1(1986): 65–85. For a summary of national politics, see Andrew Fishel and Janice Pottker, *National Politics and Sex Discrimination in Education* (Lexington, Mass.: Lexington Books, 1977).

37. NOW bill of rights in Deckard, *Women's Movement,* 348, and see also 342–49.

38. Title IX, Education Amendments of 1972, Public Law 92–318, 92d Cong., S. 659, June 23, 1972; Andrew Fishel and Janice Pottker, "Sex Bias in Sec-

ondary Schools," in Pottker and Fishel, eds., *Sex Bias,* 92; Anne N. Costain, "Eliminating Sex Discrimination in Education: Lobbying for Implementation of Title IX," *Policy Studies Journal* 7(Winter 1978): 189–95; Fishel and Pottker, *National Politics;* U.S. Congress, House Committee on Education, *Discrimination against Women: Hearings before the Special Subcommittee on Education of the Committee on Education and Labor on Section 805 of H.R. 16098,* pt. 1, 91st Cong., 2d sess., 1970, and pt. 2, 91st Cong., 2d sess., 1971; United States Commission on Civil Rights, *Enforcing Title IX* (Washington, D.C.: CCR, October, 1980).

39. Costain, "Lobbying for Implementation of Title IX," 189, 189–95.

40. Bayh quoted in Project on Equal Education Rights, NOW Legal Defense and Education Fund, *Stalled at the Start: Government Action on Sex Bias in the Schools* (Washington, D.C.: PEER, 1977), 33–35.

41. Costain, "Lobbying for Implementation of Title IX," 189–95.

42. Title IX regulations reprinted in U.S. Commission on Civil Rights, *Enforcing Title IX,* 63–70.

43. PEER, *Stalled at the Start,* 38, 5, 33–39. An internal report in the U.S. Office of Education noted that the office itself was doing a bad job of appointing women to professional positions; Commissioner's Task Force on the Impact of Office of Education Programs on Women, *A Look at Women in Education: Issues and Answers for HEW* (Washington, D.C.: Photocopied Report, November 1972). PEER reviewed 858 complaints of sex discrimination filed with the HEW civil rights investigators by private citizens from June 1972 to October 1976. The largest number, 564, alleged bias in employment, followed in order by athletics, access to classes, procedural regulations, student rules, and then a miscellaneous set of grievances. PEER found that HEW had resolved only 7 percent of these cases within six months and that only one in five had been resolved by 1976 (complaints still on the docket in 1976 had been at HEW for an average of 16 months).

44. PEER, *Stalled at the Start,* 21, 21–25; Appendix E.

45. U.S. Commission on Civil Rights, *Enforcing Title IX;* Order, *Adams v. Califano,* Civ. No. 3095–70, and *Weal v. Califano,* Civ. No. 74–1720 D.D.C., filed December 29, 1977 (commonly referred to as the *Adams* case and order); General Accounting Office, Report no. HRD-77–78, March 30, 1977; *Grove City College v. Bell* (1984) 465 U.S. 104 S. Ct. 1211 No. 82–792; Nancy Duff Campbell et al., *Sex Discrimination in Education: Legal Rights and Remedies* (Washington, D.C.: National Women's Law Center, 1983).

46. Patricia A. Schmuck et al., "Administrative Strategies for Institutionalizing Sex Equity in Education and the Role of Government," in Klein, ed., *Handbook for Achieving Sex Equity,* 96–100; Citizens Council on Women's Education, *Catching Up: A Review of the Women's Educational Equity Act Program* (Washington, D.C.: National Coalition for Women and Girls in Education, 1984).

47. Theresa Cusick, *A Clash of Ideologies: The Reagan Administration Versus the Women's Educational Equity Act* (Washington, D.C.: PEER, 1983); PEER, "The New Women's Educational Equity Act: Still Alive and Making a Difference," *PEER Policy Paper,* no. 3, Spring 1985; Citizens Council on Women's Education, *Catching Up,* 2, 39.

48. Paul Laxalt, *Family Protection Act* (27 September 1979, *Congressional Record,* 96th Cong., 1st sess., 125, pt. 20:26435–36); "Protecting the American Family," *Conservative Digest* 5(1979): 31–32; S. 1378, 97th Cong., 1st sess., June 17, 1981.

49. Phyllis W. Cheng, "The Second Wave: State Title IX Laws and the New Federalism" (unpublished paper presented at AERA Convention, Washington, D.C., April 22, 1987—a report on the Project on State Title IX Laws sponsored by WEEA), 10–12, 21.

50. Ibid., 14–15, 19; Susan Bailey and Rebecca Smith, *Policies for the Future: State Policies, Regulations, and Resources Related to the Achievement of Educational Equity for Females and Males* (Washington, D.C.: Resource Center for Sex Equity, Council of Chief State School Officers, 1982).

51. PEER, *Campaigns for Equal Education* (Washington, D.C.: PEER, 1982), 16, 5. The passages quoted in the paragraphs that follow derive from the same source and will be identified by page references in the text only.

52. Rita Bornstein, "Ambiguity as Opportunity and Constraint: Evolution of a Federal Sex Equity Education Program," *Educational Evaluation and Policy Analysis* 7(1985): 103, 99–114. For an evaluation of the project in Miami that Bornstein discusses, see B. E. Stake et al., *Evaluation of the National Sex Equity Demonstration Project, Final Report* (Urbana: Center for Instructional Research and Instructional Evaluation, University of Illinois, 1983).

53. National Advisory Council on Women's Educational Programs, *Title IX: The Half Full, Half Empty Glass* (Washington, D.C.: GPO, 1981); PEER, "The PEER Report Card: Update on Women and Girls in America's Schools—A State-by-State Survey," *PEER Policy Paper,* no. 4, Autumn 1985, 1–4.

54. Glen Harvey and Leslie F. Hergert, "Strategies for Achieving Sex Equity in Education," *Theory into Practice* 25(Autumn 1986): 295, 290–99; Kath-

leen B. Boundy, "Sex Inequities in Education," *Clearinghouse Review* 14(February 1981): 1048–56, esp. 1052–53, and Campbell et al., *Sex Discrimination,* chaps. 1–3 (chapter 6 indicates grounds for action other than Title IX). In a survey of 1,631 cases dealing with students in state courts from 1976 to 1981, researchers found 14 cases involving sex discrimination, 10 of which concerned sports—as opposed to 765 involving the education of the handicapped, for example; see Thomas B. Marvell, Armand Galfo, and John Rockwell, *Court Selection: Student Litigation in State and Federal Courts* (Williamsburg, Va.: National Center for State Law Courts, 1982), 52–53.

55. National Advisory Council on Women's Educational Programs, *Title IX,* 9, 15, 20, 16.

56. PEER, "PEER Report Card."

57. Alabama principal quoted in *Los Angeles Times,* January 9, 1986, p. 16; Janice C. Wendt and John M. Carley, "Resistance to Title IX in Physical Education: Legal, Institutional, and Individual," *Journal of Physical Education, Recreation, and Dance* 54(1983): 54–59; David Monahan, "The Failure of Coed Sports," *Psychology Today* 17(March 1983): 58–63; Michael Brown, "Hair, the Constitution, and the Public Schools," *Journal of Law and Education* 1(1972): 371–82.

58. Fishel and Pottker, "Sex Bias in Secondary Schools," 97–103; George H. Gallup, "Participation in Sports by Girls," in Pottker and Fishel, eds., *Sex Bias,* 531; National Advisory Council on Women's Educational Programs, *Title IX,* 41; "PEER Report Card," 2, charts 1 and 2.

59. "Should Interscholastic Athletics Be Provided for High School Girls and College Women?" *Journal of Health, Physical Education and Recreation* 33(May 1962): 7–8; Julia M. Brown, "Women in Physical Education: The Dribble Index of Liberation," in Joan I. Roberts, ed., *Beyond Intellectual Sexism: A New Reality* (New York: David McKay, 1976), 365–80; Cheryl M. Fields, "Title IX at X," Ann Uhlir, "The Wolf Is Our Shepherd: Shall We Not Fear?" and Jay J. Coakley and Marcia Westkott, "Opening Doors for Women in Sport: An Alternative to Old Strategies," in D. Stanley Eitzen, ed., *Sport in Contemporary Society: An Anthology* (New York: St. Martin's Press, 1984), 368–73, 374–84, 385–400.

60. Patricia L. Geadelmann, with Judy Bishoff, Mary Hoferek, and Dorothy B. McKnight, "Sex Equity in Physical Education and Athletics," in Klein, ed., *Handbook for Achieving Sex Equity,* 319–37; "PEER Report Card," 2; National Advisory Council on Women's Educational Programs, *Title IX,*

40–42; Brown, "Women in Physical Education"; Uhlir, "The Wolf Is Our Shepherd"; Coakley and Westkott, "Opening Doors for Women in Sport."

61. Helen S. Farmer and Joan Seliger Signey, with Barbara A. Bitters and Martine G. Brizius, "Sex Equity in Career and Vocational Education," in Klein, ed., *Handbook for Achieving Sex Equity,* 338–59.

62. Ruth S. Barnhart, "Children's Sex-typed Views of Traditional Occupational Roles," *School Counselor* 31(November 1983): 167–70; Geraldine Jonçich Clifford, " 'Marry, Stich, Die or Do Worse': Educating Women for Work," in Harvey Kantor and David B. Tyack, eds., *Work, Youth, and Schooling: Historical Perspectives on Vocationalism in American Education* (Stanford: Stanford University Press, 1982), 233–68.

63. Fishel and Pottker, "Sex Bias in Secondary Schools," 94–96; Farmer et al., "Sex Equity."

64. Donna Mertens, "Federal Policy for Sex Equity in Vocational Education," *Educational Evaluation and Policy Analysis* 6(1984): 401–9; Fishel and Pottker, "Sex Bias in Secondary Schools," 94–96.

65. Mertens, "Federal Policy for Sex Equity," 405–6; Farmer et al., "Sex Equity," 342–43; "PEER Report Card," 3, chart 15; Learita Garfield-Scott and Paul LeMahieu, "Targeting Nontraditional Students; A Study of Change Process in Vocational Education," *Vocational Guidance Quarterly* 33(December 1984): 157–68.

66. On the problem of obtaining adequate statistics and some additional estimates of numbers of women administrators in the years between 1972 and 1984, see Effie H. Jones and Xenia P. Montenegro, *Recent Trends in the Representation of Women and Minorities in School Administration and Problems in Documentation* (Arlington, Va.: Office of Minority Affairs, American Association of School Administrators, 1982); Charol Shakeshaft, "Strategies for Overcoming the Barriers to Women in Educational Administration," in Klein, ed., *Handbook for Achieving Sex Equity,* 124–44. Jacqueline Clement (*Sex Bias in School Leadership* [Evanston, Ill.: Integrated Education, 1976]) speaks of a "conspiracy of silence" on gender statistics in administration. William Gerritz, Julia Koppich, and James Guthrie, *Preparing California School Leaders: An Analysis of Supply, Demand, and Training* (Berkeley, Calif.: PACE, 1984); articles on "Women in Administration," *Phi Delta Kappan* 67(1985): 281–301. Sakre Kennington Edson, in *Pushing the Limits: The Female Administrative Aspirant* (Albany: State University of New York Press, 1988) reports fewer women superintendents in 1984–85 (3 percent) than the PEER report card cited in table 16.

67. Bailey and Smith, *Policies for the Future,* 75–76. On the tendency of publishers to respond to criticism, see Frances Fitzgerald, *America Revised* (Boston: Little, Brown, 1979). Like textbook publishers, corporations that produced tests, which had come under severe criticism for bias, faced similar legal and commercial pressures to change. Title IX banned the use of separate-sex tests for appraisal purposes. The Strong Vocational Interest Blank, which had been issued in separate blue and pink versions, for example, was remade into a uniform integrated format. For continuing problems in testing, see Esther E. Diamond and Carol Kehr Tittle, "Sex Equity in Testing," in Klein, ed., *Handbook for Achieving Sex Equity,* 167–88.

68. See, for example, Women on Words and Images, "Sex Stereotypes."

69. On the impact of feminist research and women's studies programs on conceptualizations of women's experience, see Howe, *Myths of Coeducation;* Peggy McIntosh and Elizabeth Kamarck Minnich, "Varieties of Women's Studies," *Women's Studies International Forum* 7(No. 3, 1984): 139–48.

70. Mary Kay Tetreault, "Thinking about Women: The Case of United States History Textbooks," *The History Teacher* 19(February 1986): 211–62.

71. Ibid.; Tetreault, "The Journey from Male-Defined to Gender-Balanced Education," *Theory into Practice* 25(Autumn 1986): 230.

72. Tetreault, "Thinking about Women"; Tetreault, "Gender-Balanced Education"; Maxine Greene, *Landscapes of Learning* (New York: Teachers College Press, 1978), chaps. 15–17.

73. Paul C. Vitz, "Religion and Traditional Values in Public School Textbooks," *The Public Interest* 84(Summer 1986): 88–89.

74. Mary Jo Neitz, "Resistance to Feminist Analysis," *Teaching Sociology* 12(April 1985): 339, 346–47, 339–53.

75. Kathryn P. Scott and Candace Garrett Schau, "Sex Equity," 226. On the question of censorship, see the exchange between Robert B. Moore and Lee Burgess in *English Journal* 70(September 1981): 14–19. On the influence of advocacy groups over textbook publishers, and the generally cosmetic and partial responses the publishers make, see Fitzgerald, *America Revised,* and Harriet Tyson-Bernstein, *A Conspiracy of Good Intentions: America's Textbook Fiasco* (Washington, D.C.: Council for Basic Education, 1988), 17–18.

PART ONE

FEMALE AND MALE IDENTITY

THROUGHOUT THE STRUGGLE for gender equity, both inside and outside of the field of education, much of the focus has centered around the idea that women are equal to men in every way. More recently, however, a different question has become increasingly prominent: simply because women are *equal to* men, does that mean they are *the same as* men? Many people today want to know if girls and boys are born with vastly different personalities, interests, and learning styles, or if our society instills these differences by emphasizing different values, expectations, and characteristics in its male and female children. Or, on the other hand, are girls and boys really not so unlike each other after all?

In this section, four authors try to answer these complicated and hotly debated questions. Both Carol Gilligan and William Pollack contend that our society, rather than biology, creates distinct cultures divided along gender lines. In "Images of Relationship," an excerpt from her seminal work, *In a Different Voice,* Gilligan uses interviews with girls and boys to demonstrate how their unique points of view on relationships create dramatic differences in their approach to problems. Pollack, in "Real Boys: The Truths Behind the Myths," focuses his attention on young boys, arguing against the "myth" of an inevitable testosterone-induced aggression and other rigid male stereotyping.

Author Michael Gurian presents the opposite end of the spectrum in "Where It All Begins: The Biology of Boyhood," asserting that biology, not society, has created two genders that are inherently different. From the effects of testosterone to the way the left and right brains interact, Gurian argues for a "nature" over "nurture" approach.

Amidst these strongly conflicting opinions, Barrie Thorne steps back in order to question the debate itself: are boys and girls really so different? In "Do Girls and Boys Have Different Cultures?" she uses her observations of children in classrooms and on the playground to make the case that there is far more variety and difference within each gender group than there is between them.

While a clear answer to the complex question of male and female identity is unlikely to emerge, each of these pieces represents a crucial element in the ongoing discussion.

3

IMAGES OF RELATIONSHIP

Carol Gilligan

IN 1914, WITH HIS ESSAY "On Narcissism," Freud swallows his distaste at the thought of "abandoning observation for barren theoretical controversy" and extends his map of the psychological domain. Tracing the developing of the capacity to love, which he equates with maturity and psychic health, he locates its origins in the contrast between love for the mother and love for the self. But in thus dividing the world of love into narcissism and "object" relationships, he finds that while men's development becomes clearer, women's becomes increasingly opaque. The problem arises because the contrast between mother and self yields two different images of relationships. Relying on the imagery of men's lives in charting the course of human growth, Freud is unable to trace in women the development of relationships, morality, or a clear sense of self. This difficulty in fitting the logic of his theory to women's experience leads him in the end to set women apart, marking their relationships, like their sexual life, as "a 'dark continent' for psychology" (1926, p. 212).

Thus the problem of interpretation that shadows the understanding of women's development arises from the differences observed in their experience of relationships. To Freud, though living surrounded by women and otherwise seeing so much and so well, women's relationships seemed increasingly mysterious, difficult to discern, and hard to describe. While this mystery indicates how theory can blind observation, it also suggests that development in women is masked by a particular conception of human relationships. Since the imagery of relationships shapes the narrative of human development, the inclusion of women, by changing that imagery, implies a change in the entire account.

The shift in imagery that creates the problem in interpreting women's development is elucidated by the moral judgments of two eleven-year-old children, a boy and a girl, who see, in the same dilemma, two very different moral problems. While current theory brightly illuminates the line and the logic of the boy's thought, it casts scant light on that of the girl. The choice of a girl whose moral judgments elude existing categories of developmental assessment is meant to highlight the issue of interpretation rather than to exemplify sex differences per se. Adding a new line of interpretation, based on the imagery of the girl's thought, makes it possible not only to see development where previously development was not discerned but also to consider differences in the understanding of relationships without scaling these differences from better to worse.

The two children were in the same sixth-grade class at school and were participants in the rights and responsibilities study, designed to explore different conceptions of morality and self. The sample selected for this study was chosen to focus the variables of gender and age while maximizing developmental potential by holding constant, at a high level, the factors of intelligence, education, and social class that have been associated with moral development, at least as measured by existing scales. The two children in question, Amy and Jake, were both bright and articulate and, at least in their eleven-year-old aspirations, resisted easy categories of sex-role stereotyping, since Amy aspired to become a scientist while Jake preferred English to math. Yet their moral judgments seem initially to confirm familiar notions about differences between the sexes, suggesting that the edge girls have on moral development during the early school years gives way at puberty with the ascendance of formal logical thought in boys.

The dilemma that these eleven-year-olds were asked to resolve was one in the series devised by Kohlberg to measure moral development in adolescence by presenting a conflict between moral norms and exploring the logic of its resolution. In this particular dilemma, a man named Heinz considers whether or not to steal a drug which he cannot afford to buy in order to save the life of his wife. In the standard format of Kohlberg's interviewing procedure, the description of the dilemma itself—Heinz's predicament, the wife's disease, the druggist's refusal to lower his price— is followed by the question, "Should Heinz steal the drug?" The reasons for and against stealing are then explored through a series of questions that vary and extend the parameters of the dilemma in a way designed to reveal the underlying structure of moral thought.

Jake, at eleven, is clear from the outset that Heinz should steal the drug. Constructing the dilemma, as Kohlberg did, as a conflict between the values of property and life, he discerns the logical priority of life and uses that logic to justify his choice:

> For one thing, a human life is worth more than money, and if the druggist only makes $1,000, he is still going to live, but if Heinz doesn't steal the drug, his wife is going to die. (*Why is life worth more than money?*) Because the druggist can get a thousand dollars later from rich people with cancer, but Heinz can't get his wife again. (*Why not?*) Because people are all different and so you couldn't get Heinz's wife again.

Asked whether Heinz should steal the drug if he does not love his wife, Jake replies that he should, saying that not only is there "a difference between hating and killing," but also, if Heinz were caught, "the judge would probably think it was the right thing to do." Asked about the fact that, in stealing, Heinz would be breaking the law, he says that "the laws have mistakes, and you can't go writing up a law for everything that you can imagine."

Thus, while taking the law into account and recognizing its function in maintaining social order (the judge, Jake says, "should give Heinz the lightest possible sentence"), he also sees the law as man-made and therefore subject to error and change. Yet his judgment that Heinz should steal the drug, like his view of the law as having mistakes, rests on the assumption of agreement, a societal consensus around moral values that allows one to know and expect others to recognize what is "the right thing to do."

Fascinated by the power of logic, this eleven-year-old boy locates truth in math, which, he says, is "the only thing that is totally logical." Considering the moral dilemma to be "sort of like a math problem with humans," he sets it up as an equation and proceeds to work out the solution. Since his solution is rationally derived, he assumes that anyone following reason would arrive at the same conclusion and thus that a judge would also consider stealing to be the right thing for Heinz to do. Yet he is also aware of the limits of logic. Asked whether there is a right answer to moral problems, Jake replies that "there can only be right and wrong in judgment," since the parameters of action are variable and complex. Illustrating how actions undertaken with the best of intentions can eventuate in the most disastrous of consequences, he says, "like if you give an old lady your seat on the trolley, if you are in a trolley crash and that seat goes through the window, it might be that reason that the old lady dies."

Theories of developmental psychology illuminate well the position of this child, standing at the juncture of childhood and adolescence, at what Piaget describes as the pinnacle of childhood intelligence, and beginning through thought to discover a wider universe of possibility. The moment of preadolescence is caught by the conjunction of formal operational thought with a description of self still anchored in the factual parameters of his childhood world—his age, his town, his father's occupation, the substance of his likes, dislikes, and beliefs. Yet as his self-description radiates the self-confidence of a child who has arrived, in Erikson's terms, at a favorable balance of industry over inferiority—competent, sure of himself, and knowing well the rules of the game—so his emergent capacity for formal thought, his ability to think about thinking and to reason things out in a logical way, frees him from dependence on authority and allows him to find solutions to problems by himself.

This emergent autonomy follows the trajectory that Kohlberg's six stages of moral development trace, a three-level progression from an egocentric understanding of fairness based on individual need (stages one and two), to a conception of fairness anchored in the shared conventions of societal agreement (stages three and four), and finally to a principled understanding of fairness that rests on the free-standing logic of equality and reciprocity (stages five and six). While this boy's judgments at eleven are scored as conventional on Kohlberg's scale, a mixture of stages three and four, his ability to bring deductive logic to bear on the solution of moral dilemmas, to differentiate morality from law, and to see how laws can be considered to have mistakes points toward the principled conception of justice that Kohlberg equates with moral maturity.

In contrast, Amy's response to the dilemma conveys a very different impression, an image of development stunted by a failure of logic, an inability to think for herself. Asked if Heinz should steal the drug, she replies in a way that seems evasive and unsure:

> Well, I don't think so. I think there might be other ways besides stealing it, like if he could borrow the money or make a loan or something, but he really shouldn't steal the drug—but his wife shouldn't die either.

Asked why he should not steal the drug, she considers neither property nor law but rather the effect that theft could have on the relationship between Heinz and his wife:

If he stole the drug, he might save his wife then, but if he did, he might have to go to jail, and then his wife might get sicker again, and he couldn't get more of the drug, and it might not be good. So, they should really just talk it out and find some other way to make the money.

Seeing in the dilemma not a math problem with humans but a narrative of relationships that extends over time, Amy envisions the wife's continuing need for her husband and the husband's continuing concern for his wife and seeks to respond to the druggist's need in a way that would sustain rather than sever connection. Just as she ties the wife's survival to the preservation of relationships, so she considers the value of the wife's life in a context of relationships, saying that it would be wrong to let her die because, "if she died, it hurts a lot of people and it hurts her." Since Amy's moral judgment is grounded in the belief that, "if somebody has something that would keep somebody alive, then it's not right not to give it to them," she considers the problem in the dilemma to arise not from the druggist's assertion of rights but from his failure of response.

As the interviewer proceeds with the series of questions that follow from Kohlberg's construction of the dilemma, Amy's answers remain essentially unchanged, the various probes serving neither to elucidate nor to modify her initial response. Whether or not Heinz loves his wife, he still shouldn't steal or let her die; if it were a stranger dying instead, Amy says that "if the stranger didn't have anybody near or anyone she knew," then Heinz should try to save her life, but he should not steal the drug. But as the interviewer conveys through the repetition of questions that the answers she gave were not heard or not right, Amy's confidence begins to diminish, and her replies become more constrained and unsure. Asked again why Heinz should not steal the drug, she simply repeats, "Because it's not right." Asked again to explain why, she states again that theft would not be a good solution, adding lamely, "if he took it, he might not know how to give it to his wife, and so his wife might still die." Failing to see the dilemma as a self-contained problem in moral logic, she does not discern the internal structure of its resolution; as she constructs the problem differently herself, Kohlberg's conception completely evades her.

Instead, seeing a world comprised of relationships rather than of people standing alone, a world that coheres through human connection rather than through systems of rules, she finds the puzzle in the dilemma to lie in the failure of the druggist to respond to the wife. Saying that "it is not right for someone to die when their life could be saved," she assumes that if the druggist were to see the consequences of his refusal to lower his price, he would realize that "he should just give it to the wife and then have the husband pay back the money later." Thus she considers the solution to the dilemma to lie in making the wife's condition more salient to the druggist or, that failing, in appealing to others who are in a position to help.

Just as Jake is confident the judge would agree that stealing is the right thing for Heinz to do, so Amy is confident that, "if Heinz and the druggist had talked it out long enough, they could reach something besides stealing." As he considers the law to "have mistakes," so she sees this drama as a mistake, believing that "the world should just share things more and then people wouldn't have to steal." Both children thus recognize the need for agreement but see it as mediated in different ways—he impersonally through systems of logic and law, she personally through communication in relationship. Just as he relies on the conventions of logic to deduce the solution to this dilemma, assuming these conventions to be shared, so she relies on a process of communication, assuming connection and believing that her voice will be heard. Yet while his assumptions about agreement are confirmed by the convergence in logic between his answers and the questions posed, her assumptions are belied by the failure of communication, the interviewer's inability to understand her response.

Although the frustration of the interview with Amy is apparent in the repetition of questions and its ultimate circularity, the problem of interpretation is focused by the assessment of her response. When considered in the light of Kohlberg's definition of the stages and sequence of moral development, her moral judgments appear to be a full stage lower in maturity than those of the boy. Scored as a mixture of stages two and three, her responses seem to reveal a feeling of powerlessness in the world, an inability to think systematically about the concepts of morality or law, a reluctance to challenge authority or to examine the logic of received moral truths, a failure even to conceive of acting directly to save a life or to consider that such action, if taken, could possibly have an effect. As her reliance on relationships seems to reveal a continuing dependence and vulnerability, so her belief in communication as the mode through which to resolve moral dilemmas appears naïve and cognitively immature.

Yet Amy's description of herself conveys a markedly different impression. Once again, the hallmarks of the preadolescent child depict a child secure in her sense of herself, confident in the substance of her beliefs, and sure of her ability to do something of value in the world. Describing herself at eleven as "growing and changing," she says that she "sees some things differently now, just because I know myself really well now, and I know a lot more about the world." Yet the world she knows is a different world from that refracted by Kohlberg's construction of Heinz's dilemma. Her world is a world of relationships and psychological truths where an awareness of the connection between people gives rise to a recognition of responsibility for one another, a perception of the need for response. Seen in this light, her understanding of morality as arising from the recognition of relationship, her belief in communication as the mode of conflict resolution, and her conviction that the solution to the dilemma will follow from its compelling representation seem far from naïve or cognitively immature. Instead, Amy's judgments contain the insights central to an ethic of care, just as Jake's judgments reflect the logic of the justice approach. Her incipient awareness of the "method of truth," the central tenet of nonviolent conflict resolution, and her belief in the restorative activity of care, lead her to see the actors in the dilemma arrayed not as opponents in a contest of rights but as members of a network of relationships on whose continuation they all depend. Consequently her solution to the dilemma lies in activating the network by communication, securing the inclusion of the wife by strengthening rather than severing connections.

But the different logic of Amy's response calls attention to the interpretation of the interview itself. Conceived as an interrogation, it appears instead as a dialogue, which takes on moral dimensions of its own, pertaining to the interviewer's uses of power and to the manifestations of respect. With this shift in the conception of the interview, it immediately becomes clear that the interviewer's problem in understanding Amy's response stems from the fact that Amy is answering a different question from the one the interviewer thought had been posed. Amy is considering not *whether* Heinz should act in this situation ("*should* Heinz steal the drug?") but rather *how* Heinz should act in response to his awareness of his wife's need ("Should Heinz *steal* the drug?"). The interviewer takes the mode of action for granted, presuming it to be a matter of fact; Amy assumes the necessity for action and considers what form it should take. In the interviewer's failure to imagine a response not dreamt of in Kohlberg's moral philosophy lies the failure to hear Amy's question and to see the logic in her response, to discern that what appears, from one perspective, to be an evasion of the dilemma signifies in other terms a recognition of the problem and a search for a more adequate solution.

Thus in Heinz's dilemma these two children see two very different moral problems—Jake a conflict between life and property that can be resolved by logical deduction, Amy a fracture of human relationship that must be mended with its own thread. Asking different questions that arise from different conceptions of the moral domain, the children arrive at answers that fundamentally diverge, and the arrangement of these answers as successive stages on a scale of increasing moral maturity calibrated by the logic of the boy's response misses the different truth revealed in the judgment of the girl. To the question, "What does he see that she does not?" Kohlberg's theory provides a ready response, manifest in the scoring of Jake's judgments a full stage higher than Amy's in moral maturity; to the question, "What does she see that he does not?" Kohlberg's theory has nothing to say. Since most of her responses fall through the sieve of Kohlberg's scoring system, her responses appear from his perspective to lie outside the moral domain.

Yet just as Jake reveals a sophisticated understanding of the logic of justification, so Amy is equally sophisticated in her understanding of the nature of choice. Recognizing that "if both the roads went in totally separate ways, if you pick one, you'll never know what would happen if you went the other way," she explains that "that's the chance you have to take, and like I said, it's just really a guess." To illustrate her point "in a simple way," she describes her choice to spend the summer at camp:

> I will never know what would have happened if I had stayed here, and
> if something goes wrong at camp, I'll never know if I stayed here if it
> would have been better. There's really no way around it because there's
> no way you can do both at once, so you've got to decide, but you'll
> never know.

In this way, these two eleven-year-old children, both highly intelligent and perceptive about life, though in different ways, display different modes of moral understanding, different ways of thinking about conflict and choice. In resolving Heinz's dilemma, Jake relies on theft to avoid confrontation and turns to the law to mediate the dispute. Transposing a hierarchy of power into a hierarchy of values, he defuses a potentially explosive conflict between people by casting it as an impersonal conflict of claims. In this way, he abstracts the moral problem from the interpersonal situation, finding in the logic of fairness an objective way to decide who will win the dispute. But this hierarchical ordering, with its imagery of winning and losing and the potential for violence which it contains, gives way in Amy's construction of the dilemma to a network of connection, a web of relationships that is sustained by a process of communication. With this shift, the moral problem changes from one of unfair domination, the imposition of property over life, to one of unnecessary exclusion, the failure of the druggist to respond to the wife.

This shift in the formulation of the moral problem and the concomitant change in the imagery of relationships appear in the responses of two eight-year-old children, Jeffrey and Karen, asked to describe a situation in which they were not sure what was the right thing to do:

Jeffrey	*Karen*
When I really want to go to my friends and my mother is cleaning the cellar, I think about my friends, and then I think about my mother, and then I think about the right thing to do. (*But how do you know it's the right thing to do?*) Because some things go before other things.	I have a lot of friends, and I can't always play with all of them, so everybody's going to have to take a turn, because they're all my friends. But like if someone's all alone, I'll play with them. (*What kinds of things do you think about when you are trying to make that decision?*) Um, someone all alone, loneliness.

While Jeffrey sets up a hierarchical ordering to resolve a conflict between desire and duty, Karen describes a network of relationships that includes all of her friends. Both children deal with the issues of exclusion and priority created by choice, but while Jeffrey thinks about what goes first, Karen focuses on who is left out.

The contrasting images of hierarchy and network in children's thinking about moral conflict and choice illuminate two views of morality which are complementary rather than sequential or opposed. But this construction of differences goes against the bias of developmental theory toward ordering differences in a hierarchical mode. The correspondence between the order of developmental theory and the structure of the boys' thought contrasts with the disparity between existing theory and the structure manifest in the thought of the girls. Yet in neither comparison does one child's judgment appear as a precursor of the other's position. Thus, questions arise concerning the relation between these perspectives: what is the significance of this difference, and how do these two modes of thinking connect? These questions are elucidated by considering the relationship between the eleven-year-old children's understanding of morality and their descriptions of themselves:

Jake	*Amy*

(How would you describe yourself to yourself?)

Perfect. That's my conceited side. What do you want—any way that I choose to describe myself?

You mean my character? *(What do you think?)* Well, I don't know. I'd describe myself as, well, what do you mean?

(If you had to describe the person you are in a way that you yourself would know it was you, what would you say?)

I'd start off with eleven years old. Jake [last name]. I'd have to add that I live in [town], because that is a big part of me, and also that my father is a doctor, because I think that does change me a little bit, and that I don't believe in crime, except for when your name is Heinz; that I think school is boring, because I think that kind of changes your character a little bit. I don't sort of know how to describe myself, because I don't know how to read my personality. *(If you had to describe the way you actually would describe yourself, what would you say?)* I like corny jokes. I don't really like to get down to work, but I can do all the stuff in school. Every single problem that I have seen in school I have been able to do, except for ones that take knowledge, and after I do the reading, I have been able to do them, but sometimes I don't want to waste my time on easy homework. And also I'm crazy about sports. I think, unlike a lot of people, that the world still has hope. . . . Most people that I know I like, and I have the good life, pretty much as good as any I have seen, and I am tall for my age.

Well, I'd say that I was someone who likes school and studying, and that's what I want to do with my life. I want to be some kind of a scientist or something, and I want to do things, and I want to help people. And I think that's what kind of person I am, or what kind of person I try to be. And that's probably how I'd describe myself. And I want to do something to help other people. *(Why is that?)* Well, because I think that this world has a lot of problems, and I think that everybody should try to help somebody else in some way, and the way I'm choosing is through science.

In the voice of the eleven-year-old boy, a familiar form of self-definition appears, resonating to the inscription of the young Stephen Daedalus in his geography book: "himself, his name and where he was," and echoing the descriptions that appear in *Our Town*, laying out across the coordinates of time and space a hierarchical order in which to define one's place. Describing himself as distinct by locating his particular position in the world, Jake sets himself apart from that world by his abilities, his beliefs, and his height. Although Amy also enumerates her likes, her wants, and her beliefs, she locates herself in relation to the world, describing herself through actions that bring her into connection with others, elaborating ties through her ability to provide help. To Jake's ideal of perfection, against which he measures the worth of himself, Amy counterposes an ideal of care, against which she measures the worth of her activity. While she places herself in relation to the world and chooses to help others through science, he places the world in relation to himself as it defines his character, his position, and the quality of his life.

The contrast between a self defined through separation and a self delineated through connection, between a self measured against an abstract ideal of perfection and a self assessed through particular activities of care, becomes clearer and the implications of this contrast extend by considering the different ways these children resolve a conflict between responsibility to others and responsibility to self. The question about responsibility followed a dilemma posed by a woman's conflict between her commitments to work and to family relationships. While the details of this conflict color the text of Amy's response, Jake abstracts the problem of responsibility from the context in which it appears, replacing the themes of intimate relationship with his own imagery of explosive connection:

Jake	*Amy*
(When responsibility to oneself and responsibility to others conflict, how should one choose?)	
You go about one-fourth to the others and three-fourths to yourself.	Well, it really depends on the situation. If you have a responsibility with somebody else, then you should keep it to a certain extent, but to the extent that it is really going to hurt you or stop you from doing something that you really, really want, then I think maybe you should put yourself first. But if it is your responsibility

Jake (cont.)

Amy (cont.)

to somebody really close to you, you've just got to decide in that situation which is more important, yourself or that person, and like I said, it really depends on what kind of person you are and how you feel about the other person or persons involved.

(Why?)

Because the most important thing in your decision should be yourself, don't let yourself be guided totally by other people, but you have to take them into consideration. So, if what you want to do is blow yourself up with an atom bomb, you should maybe blow yourself up with a hand grenade because you are thinking about your neighbors who would die also.

Well, like some people put themselves and things for themselves before they put other people, and some people really care about other people. Like, I don't think your job is as important as somebody that you really love, like your husband or your parents or a very close friend. Somebody that you really care for—or if it's just your responsibility to your job or somebody that you barely know, then maybe you go first— but if it's somebody that you really love and love as much or even more than you love yourself, you've got to decide what you really love more, that person, or that thing, or yourself. *(And how do you do that?)* Well, you've got to think about it, and you've got to think about both sides, and you've got to think which would be better for everybody or better for yourself, which is more important, and which will make everybody happier. Like if the other people can get somebody else to do it, whatever it is, or don't really need you specifically, maybe it's better to do what you want, because the other people will be just fine with somebody

Jake (cont.)

Amy (cont.)

else so they'll still be happy, and then you'll be happy too because you'll do what you want.

(What does responsibility mean?)

It means pretty much thinking of others when I do something, and like if I want to throw a rock, not throwing it at a window, because I thought of the people who would have to pay for that window, not doing it just for yourself, because you have to live with other people and live with your community, and if you do something that hurts them all, a lot of people will end up suffering, and that is sort of the wrong thing to do.

That other people are counting on you to do something, and you can't just decide, "Well, I'd rather do this or that." *(Are there other kinds of responsibility?)* Well, to yourself. If something looks really fun but you might hurt yourself doing it because you don't really know how to do it and your friends say, "Well, come on, you can do it, don't worry," if you're really scared to do it, it's your responsibility to yourself that if you think you might hurt yourself, you shouldn't do it, because you have to take care of yourself and that's your responsibility to yourself.

Again Jake constructs the dilemma as a mathematical equation, deriving a formula that guides the solution: one-fourth to others, three-fourths to yourself. Beginning with his responsibility to himself, a responsibility that he takes for granted, he then considers the extent to which he is responsible to others as well. Proceeding from a premise of separation but recognizing that "you have to live with other people," he seeks rules to limit interference and thus to minimize hurt. Responsibility in his construction pertains to a limitation of action, a restraint of aggression, guided by the recognition that his actions can have effects on others, just as theirs can interfere with him. Thus rules, by limiting interference, make life in community safe, protecting autonomy through reciprocity, extending the same consideration to others and self.

To the question about conflicting responsibilities, Amy again responds contextually rather than categorically, saying "it depends" and indicating how choice would be affected by variations in character and circumstance. Proceeding from a premise of connection, that "if you have a responsibility *with* somebody else, you should keep it," she then considers the extent to which she has a responsibility to herself. Exploring the parameters of separation, she imagines situations where, by doing what you want, you would avoid hurting yourself or where, in doing so, you would not thereby diminish the happiness of others. To her, responsibility signifies response, an extension rather than a limitation of action. Thus it connotes an act of care rather than the restraint of aggression. Again seeking the solution that would be most inclusive of everyone's needs, she strives to resolve the dilemma in a way that "will make everybody happier." Since Jake is concerned with limiting interference, while Amy focuses on the need for response, for him the limiting condition is, "Don't let yourself be guided totally by others," but for her it arises when "other people are counting on you," in which case "you can't just decide, 'Well, I'd rather do this or that.' " The interplay between these responses is clear in that she, assuming connection, begins to explore the parameters of separation, while he, assuming separation, begins to explore the parameters of connection. But the primacy of separation or connection leads to different images of self and of relationships.

Most striking among these differences is the imagery of violence in the boy's response, depicting a world of dangerous confrontation and explosive connection, where she sees a world of care and protection, a life lived with others whom "you may love as much or even more than you love yourself." Since the conception of morality reflects the understanding of social relationships, this difference in the imagery of relationships gives rise to a change in the moral injunction itself. To Jake, responsibility means *not doing* what he wants because he is thinking of others; to Amy, it means *doing* what others are counting on her to do regardless of what she herself wants. Both children are concerned with avoiding hurt but construe the problem in different ways—he seeing hurt to arise from the expression of aggression, she from a failure of response.

If the trajectory of development were drawn through either of these children's responses, it would trace a correspondingly different path. For Jake, development would entail coming to see the other as equal to the self and the discovery that equality provides a way of making connection safe. For Amy, development would follow the inclusion of herself in an expanding network of connection and the discovery that separation can be protective and need not entail isolation. In view of these different paths of development and particularly of the different ways in which the experiences of separation and connection are aligned with the voice of the self, the representation of the boy's development as the single line of adolescent growth for both sexes creates a continual problem when it comes to interpreting the development of the girl.

Since development has been premised on separation and told as a narrative of failed relationships—of pre-Oedipal attachments, Oedipal fantasies, preadolescent chumships, and adolescent loves—relationships that stand out against a background of separation, only successively to erupt and give way to an increasingly emphatic individuation, the development of girls appears problematic because of the continuity of relationships in their lives. Freud attributes the turning inward of girls at puberty to an intensification of primary narcissism, signifying a failure of love or "object" relationships. But if this turning inward is construed against a background of continuing connection, it signals a new responsiveness to the self, an expansion of care rather than a failure of relationship. In this way girls, seen not to fit the categories of relationships derived from male experience, call attention to the assumptions about relationships that have informed the account of human development by replacing the imagery of explosive connection with images of dangerous separation.

The significance of this shift is revealed by a study of the images of violence that appear in stories written by college students to pictures on the TAT, a study reporting statistically significant sex differences in the places where violence is seen and in the substance of violent fantasies as well. The themes of separation and connection are central to the study, conducted by Susan Pollak and myself and based on an analysis of stories, written prior to the study, by students as a class exercise in a psychology course on motivation (Pollak and Gilligan, 1982). The study began with Pollak's observation of seemingly bizarre imagery of violence in men's stories about a picture of what appeared to be a tranquil scene, a couple sitting on a bench by a river next to a low bridge. In response to this picture, more than 21 percent of the eighty-eight men in the class had written stories containing incidents of violence—homicide, suicide, stabbing, kidnapping, or rape. In contrast, none of the fifty women in the class had projected violence into this scene.

This observation of violence in men's stories about intimacy appeared to us as a possible corollary to Horner's (1968) report of imagery of violence in women's stories about competitive success. Horner, exemplifying her category of "bizarre or violent imagery" in depicting women's anticipation of negative consequences following success, cites a story that portrays a jubilant Anne, at the top of her medical school class, physically beaten and maimed for life by her jealous classmates. The corollary observation of violent imagery in men's fantasies of intimate relationships is illustrated by a story written by one of the men in the class to the picture of the river-bench scene:

Nick saw his life pass before his eyes. He could feel the cold pene-
trating ever deeper into his body. How long had it been since he had
fallen through the ice—thirty seconds, a minute? It wouldn't take long
for him to succumb to the chilling grip of the mid-February Charles
River. What a fool he had been to accept the challenge of his room-
mate Sam to cross the frozen river. He knew all along that Sam hated
him. Hated him for being rich and especially hated him for being
engaged to Mary, Sam's childhood sweetheart. But Nick never realized until now that Mary also hated him and really loved Sam. Yet
there they were, the two of them, calmly sitting on a bench in the
riverbend, watching Nick drown. They'd probably soon be married,
and they'd probably finance it with the life insurance policy for which
Mary was the beneficiary.

Calling attention to the eye of the observer in noting where danger is
seen, Pollak and I wondered whether men and women perceive danger in
different situations and construe danger in different ways. Following the
initial observation of violence in men's stories about intimacy, we set out
to discover whether there were sex differences in the distribution of violent fantasies across situations of achievement and affiliation and whether
violence was differentially associated by males and females with intimacy
and competitive success. The findings of the resulting images of violence
study corroborate previous reports of sex differences in aggression (Terman and Tyler, 1954; Whiting and Pope, 1973; Maccoby and Jacklin,
1974) by revealing a far greater incidence of violence in stories written by
men. Of the eighty-eight men in the motivation class, 51 percent wrote at
least one story containing images of violence, in comparison to 20 percent of the fifty women in the class, and no woman wrote more than one
story in which violence appeared. But the study also revealed sex differences in the distribution and substance of violent fantasies, indicating a
difference between the way in which men and women tend to imagine
relationships.

Four of the six pictures that comprised the test were chosen for the purposes of this analysis since they provided clear illustrations of achievement
and affiliation situations. Two of the pictures show a man and a woman
in close personal affiliation—the couple on the bench in the river scene,
and two trapeze artists grasping each other's wrists, the man hanging by
his knees from the trapeze and the woman in mid-air. Two pictures show
people at work in impersonal achievement situations—a man sitting alone
at his desk in a high-rise office building, and two women, dressed in white
coats, working in a laboratory, the woman in the background watching

while the woman in the foreground handles the test tubes. The study centered on a comparison between the stories written about these two sets of pictures.

The men in the class, considered as a group, projected more violence into situations of personal affiliation than they did into impersonal situations of achievement. Twenty-five percent of the men wrote violent stories only to the pictures of affiliation, 19 percent to pictures of both affiliation and achievement, and 7 percent only to pictures of achievement. In contrast, the women saw more violence in impersonal situations of achievement than in situations of affiliation; 16 percent of the women wrote violent stories to the achievement pictures and 6 percent to the pictures of affiliation.

As the story about Nick, written by a man, illustrates the association of danger with intimacy, so the story about Miss Hegstead, written by a woman, exemplifies the projection of violence into situations of achievement and the association of danger with competitive success:

> Another boring day in the lab and that mean bitchy Miss Hegstead always breathing down the students' backs. Miss Hegstead has been at Needham Country High School for 40 years and every chemistry class is the same. She is watching Jane Smith, the model student in the class. She always goes over to Jane and comments to the other students that Jane is always doing the experiment right and Jane is the only student who really works hard, etc. Little does Miss Hegstead know that Jane is making some arsenic to put in her afternoon coffee.

If aggression is conceived as a response to the perception of danger, the findings of the images of violence study suggest that men and women may perceive danger in different social situations and construe danger in different ways—men seeing danger more often in close personal affiliation than in achievement and construing danger to arise from intimacy, women perceiving danger in impersonal achievement situations and construing danger to result from competitive success. The danger men describe in their stories of intimacy is a danger of entrapment or betrayal, being caught in a smothering relationship or humiliated by rejection and deceit. In contrast, the danger women portray in their tales of achievement is a danger of isolation, a fear that in standing out or being set apart by success, they will be left alone. In the story of Miss Hegstead, the only apparent cause of the violence is Jane's being singled out as the best student and thus set apart from her classmates. She retaliates by making arsenic to put in the teacher's afternoon coffee, yet all Miss Hegstead did was to praise Jane for her good work.

As people are brought closer together in the pictures, the images of violence in the men's stories increase, while as people are set further apart, the violence in the women's stories increases. The women in the class projected violence most frequently into the picture of the man at his desk (the only picture portraying a person alone), while the men in the class most often saw violence in the scene of the acrobats on the trapeze (the only picture in which people touched). Thus, it appears that men and women may experience attachment and separation in different ways and that each sex perceives a danger which the other does not see—men in connection, women in separation.

But since the women's perception of danger departs from the usual mode of expectation, the acrobats seeming to be in far greater danger than the man at his desk, their perception calls into question the usual mode of interpretation. Sex differences in aggression are usually interpreted by taking the male response as the norm, so that the absence of aggression in women is identified as the problem to be explained. However, the disparate location of violence in the stories written by women and men raises the question as to why women see the acrobats as safe.

The answer comes from the analysis of the stories about the trapeze. Although the picture of acrobats shows them performing high in the air without a net, 22 percent of the women in the study added nets in the stories they wrote. In contrast, only 6 percent of the men imagined the presence of a net, while 40 percent either explicitly mentioned the absence of a net or implied its absence by describing one or both acrobats as plummeting to their deaths. Thus, the women saw the scene on the trapeze as safe because, by providing nets, they had made it safe, protecting the lives of the acrobats in the event of a fall. Yet failing to imagine the presence of nets in the scene on the trapeze, men, interpreting women's responses, readily attribute the absence of violence in women's stories to a denial of danger or to a repression of aggression (May, 1981) rather than to the activities of care through which the women make the acrobats safe. As women imagine the activities through which relationships are woven and connection sustained, the world of intimacy—which appears as mysterious and dangerous to men—comes instead to appear increasingly coherent and safe.

If aggression is tied, as women perceive, to the fracture of human connection, then the activities of care, as their fantasies suggest, are the activities that make the social world safe, by avoiding isolation and preventing aggression rather than by seeking rules to limit its extent. In this light, aggression appears no longer as an unruly impulse that must be contained but rather as a signal of a fracture of connection, the sign of a failure of relationship. From this perspective, the prevalence of violence in men's fantasies, denoting a world where danger is everywhere seen, signifies a problem in making connection, causing relationships to erupt and turning separation into a dangerous isolation. Reversing the usual mode of interpretation, in which the absence of aggression in women is tied to a problem with separation, makes it possible to see the prevalence of violence in men's stories, its odd location in the context of intimate relationships, and its association with betrayal and deceit as indicative of a problem with connection that leads relationships to become dangerous and safety to appear in separation. Then rule-bound competitive achievement situations, which for women threaten the web of connection, for men provide a mode of connection that establishes clear boundaries and limits aggression, and thus appears comparatively safe.

A story written by one of the women about the acrobats on the trapeze illustrates these themes, calling into question the usual opposition of achievement and affiliation by portraying the continuation of the relationship as the predicate for success:

> These are two Flying Gypsies, and they are auditioning for the big job with the Ringling Brothers Circus. They are the last team to try out for the job, and they are doing very well. They have grace and style, but they use a safety net which some teams do not use. The owners say that they'll hire them if they forfeit the net, but the Gypsies decide that they would rather live longer and turn down the job than take risks like that. They know the act will be ruined if either got hurt and see no sense in taking the risk.

For the Gypsies in the story, it is not the big job with the circus that is of paramount importance but rather the well-being of the two people involved. Anticipating negative consequences from a success attained at the risk of their lives, they forfeit the job rather than the net, protecting their lives but also their act, which "would be ruined if either got hurt."

While women thus try to change the rules in order to preserve relationships, men, in abiding by these rules, depict relationships as easily replaced. Projecting most violence into this scene, they write stories about infidelity and betrayal that end with the male acrobat dropping the woman, presumably replacing the relationship and going on with the act:

> The woman trapeze artist is married to the best friend of the male who has just discovered (before the show) that she has been unfaithful to his

friend (her husband). He confronted her with this knowledge and told
her to tell her husband but she refused. Not having the courage to confront him himself, the trapeze artist creates an accident while 100 feet
above ground, letting the woman slip out of his grasp in mid-flight. She
is killed in the incident but he feels no guilt, believing that he has
rectified the situation.

The prevalence of violence in male fantasy, like the explosive imagery
in the moral judgment of the eleven-year-old boy and the representation
of theft as the way to resolve a dispute, is consonant with the view of
aggression as endemic in human relationships. But these male fantasies
and images also reveal a world where connection is fragmented and communication fails, where betrayal threatens because there seems to be no
way of knowing the truth. Asked if he ever thinks about whether or not
things are real, eleven-year-old Jake says that he wonders a lot about
whether people are telling the truth, about "what people say, like one of
my friends says, 'Oh yeah, he said that,' and sometimes I think, 'Is he
actually saying the truth?' " Considering truth to lie in math and certainty
to reside in logic, he can see "no guidelines" for establishing truth in English class or in personal relationships.

Thus, although aggression has been construed as instinctual and separation has been thought necessary for its constraint, the violence in male
fantasy seems rather to arise from a problem in communication and an
absence of knowledge about human relationships. But as eleven-year-old
Amy sets out to build connection where Kohlberg assumes it will fail, and
women in their fantasies create nets of safety where men depict annihila-
tion, the voices of women comment on the problem of aggression that
both sexes face, locating the problem in the isolation of self and in the
hierarchical construction of human relationships.

Freud, returning in *Civilization and Its Discontents* (1930) to the
themes of culture and morality that had preoccupied him as a youth,
begins by addressing the standard of measurement, the notion of "what
is of true value in life" (p. 64). Referring to a letter from Romain Rolland,
who wrote that what is of ultimate comfort to man is a "sensation of
'eternity,' " an "oceanic" feeling, Freud, while honoring his friend, rejects
this feeling as an illusion, since he cannot "discover this oceanic feeling in
myself." Describing this feeling of "an indissoluble bond, of being one
with the external world as a whole," he explains that, "from my own
experience I could not convince myself of the primary nature of such a
feeling. But this gives me no right to deny that it does not in fact occur in
other people. The only question is whether it is being correctly inter-

preted." Yet raising the question of interpretation, Freud immediately dispels the problem he posed, rejecting the primacy of a feeling of connection on the grounds that "it fits in so badly with the fabric of our psychology." On this basis, he subjects the feeling to a "psychoanalytic—that is, a genetic explanation," deriving the feeling of connection from a more primary feeling of separation (p. 65).

The argument Freud builds centers on the "feeling of our self, of our own ego," which "appears to us as something autonomous and unitary, marked off distinctly from everything else." While he then immediately points out that "such an appearance is deceptive," the deception he sees lies not in the failure to recognize the connection between self and other, but in the failure to see the ego's connection to the unconscious id, "for which it serves as a kind of facade." Turning to the genetic explanation, he traces the feeling of fusion back to the infant's failure to distinguish his ego from the external world as the source of sensation. This distinction arises through the experience of frustration when external sources of sensations evade the infant, "most of all, his mother's breast—and only reappear as a result of his screaming for help" (pp. 65–67). In this screaming for help, Freud sees the birth of the self, the separation of ego from object that leads sensation to be located inside the self while others become objects of gratification.

This disengagement of self from the world outside, however, initiates not only the process of differentiation but also the search for autonomy, the wish to gain control over the sources and objects of pleasure in order to shore up the possibilities for happiness against the risk of disappointment and loss. Thus connection—associated by Freud with "infantile helplessness" and "limitless narcissism," will illusion and the denial of danger—gives way to separation. Consequently, assertion, linked to aggression, becomes the basis for relationships. In this way, a primary separation, arising from disappointment and fueled by rage, creates a self whose relations with others or "objects" must then be protected by rules, a morality that contains this explosive potential and adjusts "the mutual relationships of human beings in the family, the state and the society" (p. 86).

Yet there is an intimation on Freud's part of a sensibility different from his own, of a mental state different from that upon which he premises his psychology, the "single exception" to the "primary mutual hostility of human beings," to the "aggressiveness" that "forms the basis of every relation of affection and love among people," and this exception is located in women's experience, in "the mother's relation to her male child" (p. 113). Once again women appear as the exception to the rule of relationships, by demonstrating a love not admixed with anger, a love arising neither from separation nor from a feeling of being at one with the external world as a whole, but rather from a feeling of connection, a primary bond between other and self. But this love of the mother cannot, Freud says, be shared by the son, who would thus "make himself dependent in a most dangerous way on a portion of the external world, namely his chosen love-object, and expose himself to extreme suffering if he should be rejected by that object or lose it through unfaithfulness or death" (p. 101).

Although Freud, claiming that "we are never so defenceless against suffering as when we love" (p. 82), pursues the line of defense as it leads through anger and conscience to civilization and guilt, the more interesting question would seem to be why the mother is willing to take the risk. Since for her love also creates the possibility of disappointment and loss, the answer would seem to lie in a different experience of connection and a different mode of response. Throughout Freud's work women remain the exception to his portrayal of relationships, and they sound a continuing theme, of an experience of love which, however described—as narcissistic or as hostile to civilization—does not appear to have separation and aggression at its base. In this alternate light, the self appears neither stranded in isolation screaming for help nor lost in fusion with the entire world as a whole, but bound in an indissoluble mode of relationship that is observably different but hard to describe.

Demonstrating a continuing sense of connection in the face of separation and loss, women illuminate an experience of self that, however disparate from Freud's account, speaks directly to the problem of aggression which in the end he confronts, the problem of "how to get rid of the greatest hinderance to civilization," aggressiveness and the defences against it that "cause as much unhappiness as aggression itself" (pp. 142–143). In considering this problem, Freud begins to envision its solution in a more primary sense of connection, not an oceanic feeling but an "altruistic urge" that leads to a mode of relationships with others anchored in the "wish for union" with them. While describing the urge toward union with others as antagonistic to individual development (p. 141), Freud intimates a line of development missing from his previous account, a line that leads not through aggression to separation but through differentiation to interdependence. In calling this urge "altruistic," Freud alludes to a different moral conception, arising not to limit aggression but to sustain connection.

Thus alongside the drama Freud creates between happiness and culture in which morality plays the central part, transforming the danger of love into the discomfort of civilization—a drama that darkly illuminates the role of "love in the origin of conscience and the fatal inevitability of the sense of guilt" (p. 132)—another scenario begins to emerge. In this changed light, connection, rather than seeming an illusion or taking on an explosive or transcendental cast, appears as a primary feature of both individual psychology and civilized life. Since "the human individual takes part in the course of the development of mankind at the same time as he pursues his own path in life" (p. 141), separation suddenly begins to appear as illusory as connection formerly had seemed. Yet to incorporate this sense of connection into the fabric of his psychology would change, as Freud sees, not only the coloration of the instinctual life but also the representation of self and the portrayal of relationships.

The "male pattern" of fantasy that Robert May (1980) identifies as "Pride" in his studies of sex differences in projective imagination leads from enhancement to deprivation and continues the story that Freud has told of an initial fracture of connection leading through the experience of separation to an irreparable loss, a glorious achievement followed by a disastrous fall. But the pattern of female fantasy May designates as "Caring" traces a path which remains largely unexplored, a narrative of deprivation followed by enhancement in which connection, though leading through separation, is in the end maintained or restored. Illuminating life as a web rather than a succession of relationships, women portray autonomy rather than attachment as the illusory and dangerous quest. In this way, women's development points toward a different history of human attachment, stressing continuity and change in configuration, rather than replacement and separation, elucidating a different response to loss, and changing the metaphor of growth.

Jean Baker Miller (1976), enumerating the problems that arise when all affiliations are cast in the mould of dominance and subordination, suggests that "the parameters of the female's development are not the same as the male's and that the same terms do not apply" (p. 86). She finds in psychology no language to describe the structuring of women's sense of self, "organized around being able to make and then to maintain affiliations and relationships" (p. 83). But she sees in this psychic structuring the potential for "more advanced, more affiliative ways of living—less wedded to the dangerous ways of the present," since the sense of self is tied not to a belief in the efficacy of aggression but to a recognition of the need for connection (p. 86). Thus envisioning the potential for a more creative and cooperative mode of life, Miller calls not only for social equality but also for a new language in psychology that would separate the description of care and connection from the vocabulary of inequality and oppression, and she sees this new language as originating in women's experience of relationships.

In the absence of this language, the problem of interpretation that impedes psychologists' understanding of women's experience is mirrored by the problem created for women by the failure to represent their experience or by the distortion in its representation. When the interconnections of the web are dissolved by the hierarchical ordering of relationships, when nets are portrayed as dangerous entrapments, impeding flight rather than protecting against fall, women come to question whether what they have been exists and whether what they know from their own experience is true. These questions are raised not as abstract philosophical speculations about the nature of reality and truth but as personal doubts that invade women's sense of themselves, compromising their ability to act on their own perceptions and thus their willingness to take responsibility for what they do. This issue becomes central in women's development during the adolescent years, when thought becomes reflective and the problem of interpretation thus enters the stream of development itself.

The two eleven-year-old children, asked to describe their experiences of moral conflict and choice, presage the themes of male and female adolescent development by recounting in one sense the same story but telling it from very different perspectives. Both children describe a situation in school where they confronted a decision of whether or not to tell. For Jake, this dilemma arose when he decided to take action against injustice and seek the enforcement of rules to protect a friend who was being "unfairly" beaten up and hurt. Having gone with his friend to inform the principal of these events, he then wonders whether or not to tell another friend that the principal was told. Since this friend only beat up the other in response to provocation, not telling would subject him to reprisals that would in his case be unjust.

In describing his dilemma, Jake focuses on whether or not it would be right in this instance to violate his standard of trying "to practice what I preach," in this case of keeping his word that no one would know that the principal was told. The quandary hinges on whether or not he can construe his action in telling as fair, whether his various activities of care for the two friends with whom he is involved can be reconciled with the standards of his moral belief. If he can match his action to his standard of justice, then he will not feel "ashamed" and will be "willing to own up" to what he has done; otherwise, he says, he will have to admit to himself and his friends that he has made a mistake.

Amy's dilemma stems from the fact that she saw one friend take a book that belonged to another. Construing the problem as a conflict in loyalties, an issue of responsiveness in relationship, she wonders whether to risk hurting one friend in responding to the hurt of another. Her question is how to act, given what she has seen and knows, since in her construction, not telling as well as telling constitutes a response. As Jake considers violating his standards and going back on his word, compromising his principles out of loyalty to a friend, Amy considers stepping apart from a friendship to assert a standard in which she believes, a standard of sharing and care, of protecting people from hurt. But given this standard, she thinks about the extent to which either friend will be hurt and focuses on the parameters of the situation in order to assess what the likely consequences of her action will be. Just as Jake wonders whether in acting out of friendship he will violate his personal integrity, so Amy worries whether in asserting her beliefs, she will hurt a friend.

In describing her thinking about what to do, Amy recreates the inner dialogue of voices to which she attends—a dialogue that includes the voices of others and also the voice of herself:

> Nobody will ever know I saw, and nobody will hold it against me, but then you start sitting there thinking about it and think that somebody will always know—you'll always know that you never told, and it makes me feel really bad because my friend is sitting there. "Has anybody seen my book? Where is it? Help! I need my book for next class. Help! It's not here. Where is it?" And I think if you know that, it is more important to tell, and you know you're not really tattling or anything, because it's better, you know, to tell.

Just as her awareness of the other's cry for help makes the failure to tell a failure to care, so telling is not tattling when placed in *this* context of relationships. But this contextual mode of analysis leads interpretation readily to shift, since a change in the context of relationships would turn her act of care into an act of betrayal.

In this way, realizing that others may not know what she has seen and heard and recognizing how easily her action can be misconstrued, Amy wonders if it would be better to say nothing or at least not to tell that she told. Thus if the secrets of male adolescence revolve around the harboring of continuing attachments that cannot be represented in the logic of fairness, the secrets of the female adolescent pertain to the silencing of her own voice, a silencing enforced by the wish not to hurt others but also by the fear that, in speaking, her voice will not be heard.

With this silence, the imagery of the Persephone myth returns, charting the mysterious disappearance of the female self in adolescence by mapping an underground world kept secret because it is branded by others as selfish and wrong. When the experience of self and the understanding of morality change with the growth of reflective thought in adolescence, questions about identity and morality converge on the issue of interpretation. As the eleven-year-old girl's question of whether or not to listen to herself extends across the span of adolescence, the difficulty experienced by psychologists in listening to women is compounded by women's difficulty in listening to themselves. This difficulty is evident in a young woman's account of her crisis of identity and moral belief—a crisis that centers on her struggle to disentangle her voice from the voices of others and to find a language that represents her experience of relationships and her sense of herself.

Claire, a participant in the college student study, was interviewed first as a senior in college and then again at the age of twenty-seven. When asked, as a senior, how she would describe herself to herself, she answers "confused," saying that she "should be able to say, 'Well, I'm such and such,' " but instead she finds herself "more unsure now than I think I have ever been." Aware that "people see me in a certain way," she has come to find these images contradictory and constraining, "kind of found myself being pushed, being caught in the middle: I should be a good mother and daughter; I should be, as a college woman, aggressive and high-powered and career-oriented." Yet as the feeling of being caught in the middle has turned, in her senior year, into a sense of being constrained to act, of "being pushed to start making decisions for myself," she has "come to realize that all these various roles just aren't exactly right." Thus she concludes:

> I am not necessarily the type of girlfriend I should be or that I've been perceived as, and I'm not necessarily the type of daughter that I've been perceived as. You grow up to find yourself in the way other people see you, and it's very hard, all of a sudden, to start separating this and start realizing that really nobody else can make these decisions.

Faced as a senior with the need to make a choice about what to do the following year, she attempts to separate her perception of herself from the perceptions of others, to see herself directly rather than in reflection through others' eyes:

> For a long time, I was seeing myself as other people wanted to see me. I mean, it really appealed to my boyfriend to have a wife who was a professor of English, and I was kind of pushing it back in my mind that I didn't want to do this; I really felt maybe this is what I really wanted to do. I started seeing all the positive sides of it because I was seeing it through his eyes, and then, suddenly, I kind of

realized, I can't do this anymore. And I can't, you know, I've got
to stop this and see myself as I want to see *it,* and then I realized that
no, this is very stuffy, and this world of academia isn't necessarily
right for me, even though I would be the ideal wife in that situation.
So then I am naturally faced with what is right for me, and it's very
hard, because at the same time, I'm faced with a feeling that I can't
grow up.

Thus, as her way of looking at herself becomes more direct, the moral
question correspondingly shifts from what is "right" to what is "right for
me." Yet in facing that challenge, she immediately draws back as she
encounters the feeling "that I can't grow up."

Caught by the interviewer's request for self-description at a time when
she is resisting "categorizing or classifying myself," she finds it "hard to
start defining what I'm in the process of undefining," the self that, in the
past, would "try to push my feelings under the rug" so as not to create
any "repercussions." Describing herself as "loving," she is caught between
the two contexts in which that term now applies: an underground world
that sets her "apart from others, apart from their definitions of me," and
a world of connections that sets her apart from herself. In trying to
explain her sense of herself as at once separate and connected, she encounters a problem with "terminology" when trying to convey a new understanding of both self and relationship:

> I'm trying to tell you two things. I'm trying to be myself alone, apart
> from others, apart from their definitions of me, and yet at the same time
> I'm doing just the opposite, trying to be with or relate to—whatever
> the terminology is—I don't think they are mutually exclusive.

In this way she ties a new sense of separation to a new experience of connection, a way of being with others that allows her also to be with herself.

Reaching for an image that would convey this uncharted sense of connection but unable to find one herself, she seizes on one offered by a
friend, the character of Gudrun in D. H. Lawrence's *Women in Love.* The
image of Gudrun evokes for Claire her sense of being "childish" and
"untamed," responsive to the sensuality both in nature and in herself. This
connection to the world of "sensual enjoyment" represents the "artistic
and bohemian" side of herself and contrasts with the view of herself as
"ladylike and well brought-up." Yet the image of Gudrun, despite its evocation of a different form of connection, is in the end morally problematic for her because it implies being "uncaring of others."

Again Claire is caught, but in a different way, not between the contradictory expectations of others but between a responsiveness to others and to herself. Sensing that these modes of response "aren't mutually exclusive," she examines the moral judgment that in the past kept them apart. Formerly, she considered "a moral way of looking" to be one that focused on "responsibility to others"; now she has come to question what seemed in the past a self-evident truth, that "in doing what's right for others, you're doing what's right for yourself." She has, she says, "reached the point where I don't think I can be any good to anyone unless I know who I am."

In the process of seeking to "discover what's me," she has begun to "get rid of all these labels and things I just don't see on my own," to separate her perceptions from her former mode of interpretation and to look more directly at others as well as herself. Thus, she has come to observe "faults" in her mother, whom she perceives as endlessly giving, "because she doesn't care if she hurts herself in doing it. She doesn't realize—well, she does realize, that in hurting herself, she hurts people very close to her." Measured against a standard of care, Claire's ideal of self-sacrifice gives way to a vision of "a family where everyone is encouraged to become an individual and at the same time everybody helps others and receives help from them."

Bringing this perspective to Heinz's dilemma, Claire identifies the same moral problem as the eleven-year-old Amy, focusing not on the conflict of rights but on the failure of response. Claire believes that Heinz should steal the drug ("His wife's life was much more important than anything. He should have done anything to save her life"), but she counters the rights construction with her own interpretation. Although the druggist "had a right, I mean he had the legal right, I also think he had the moral obligation to show compassion in this case. I don't think he had the right to refuse." In tying the necessity for Heinz's action to the fact that "the wife needed him at this point to do it; she couldn't have done it, and it's up to him to do for her what she needs," Claire elaborates the same concept of responsibility that was articulated by Amy. They both equate responsibility with the need for response that arises from the recognition that others are counting on you and that you are in a position to help.

Whether Heinz loves his wife or not is irrelevant to Claire's decision, not because life has priority over affection, but because his wife "is another human being who needs help." Thus the moral injunction to act stems not from Heinz's feelings about his wife but from his awareness of her need, an awareness mediated not by identification but by a process of communication. Just as Claire considers the druggist morally responsible for his refusal, so she ties morality to the awareness of connection, defining the moral person as one who, in acting, "seriously considers the consequences to everybody involved." Therefore, she criticizes her mother for "neglecting her responsibility to herself" at the same time that she criticizes herself for neglecting her responsibility to others.

Although Claire's judgments of Heinz's dilemma for the most part do not fit the categories of Kohlberg's scale, her understanding of the law and her ability to articulate its function in a systematic way earn her a moral maturity score of stage four. Five years later, when she is interviewed at the age of twenty-seven, this score is called into question because she subsumes the law to the considerations of responsibility that informed her thinking about the druggist, Heinz, and his wife. Judging the law now in terms of whom it protects, she extends her ethic of responsibility to a broader vision of societal connection. But the disparity between this vision and the justice conception causes her score on Kohlberg's scale to regress.

During the time when Claire's moral judgments appeared to regress, her moral crisis was resolved. Having taken Kohlberg's course, she suspected that what she had experienced as growth was no progress in his terms. Thus, when she received the letter asking if she would be willing to be interviewed again, she thought:

> My god, what if I have regressed. It seems to me that at one stage of my life, I would have been able to answer these dilemmas with a lot more surety and said, "Yes, this is absolutely right and this is absolutely wrong." And I am just sinking deeper and deeper into the mire of uncertainty. I am not sure if that is good or bad at this point, but I think there has been, in that sense, a direction.

Contrasting an absolute standard of judgment with her own experience of the complexity of moral choice, she introduces the question of direction, the interpretation of her own development.

The question of interpretation recurs throughout the text of her interview at age twenty-seven when, married and about to start medical school, she reflects on her experience of crisis and describes the changes in her life and thought. Speaking of the present, she says that "things have fallen into place," but immediately corrects her phrasing since "that sounds like somebody else put them together, and that's not what happened." The problem of interpretation, however, centers on describing the mode of connection. The connection itself is apparent in Claire's description of herself which she says, "sounds sort of strange," as she characterizes herself as "maternal, with all its connotations." Envisioning herself "as a physician, as a mother," she says that "it's hard for me to think about myself without thinking about other people around me that I am giving to." Like Amy, Claire ties her experience of self to activities of care and connection. Joining the image of her mother with that of herself, she sees herself as a maternal physician, as preparing, like Amy, to become a scientist who takes care of the world.

In describing the resolution of a crisis that extended over a period of years, she retraces her steps in order to explain her discovery of "a direction underlying it all." The crisis began in her sophomore year in college:

> For an entire weekend I didn't get out of bed because there was no reason to. I just couldn't bring myself to get out of bed. I didn't know what I would do if I got out of bed, but more of my sophomore year was like that. I didn't know what I was doing, what the reason for doing anything was. Nothing seemed to connect together.

Tying her despair to her sense of disconnection, she casts about for a word or image to fit the experience:

> It wasn't a turning point in that, when I got out of bed, everything was right again. That didn't happen. It wasn't a great epiphany or anything like that. It just sticks out in my mind, even though at the time it didn't seem like a powerful experience. It did not seem like anything was happening to me. No. It seems like it was a very powerful experience. It was real.

In measuring her own experience against existing metaphors of crisis and change, she begins to conclude that nothing had happened, or that what happened was not powerful or real. She did not hit rock bottom, nor did she experience an epiphany or "ultimate despair":

> I didn't lie in bed and think my life is so totally worthless. It wasn't that. It wasn't like profound unhappiness. It was just nothing. Maybe that is the ultimate despair, but you don't feel it at the time. I guess that sticks out as one thing because it was so devoid of feeling. Another thing was the extreme bitterness and extreme hatred I felt toward [a relative] who abandoned the family. I mean it was just the opposite; it was so intense.

Finding, in both the absence of feeling and in the presence of hatred, no way to connect with others, she interprets her experience of despair as arising from the sense of disconnection that ensued, in part, from the failure of family relationships.

The feeling of disconnection from others leads Claire to struggle to see herself as "worthwhile," as worthy of her own care and thus as justified in acting on her own behalf. As she describes the process through which she came to risk doing what she wanted to do, she indicates how in this process her conception of morality changed. Whereas she used to define the good person as "the person who does the most good for others," now she ties morality to the understanding that arises from the experience of relationship, since she considers the capacity "to understand what someone else is experiencing" as the prerequisite for moral response.

Impatient now with Heinz's dilemma, she structures it starkly as a contrast between the wife's life and the druggist's greed, seeing in the druggist's preoccupation with profit a failure of understanding as well as of response. Life is worth more than money because "everybody has the right to life." But then she shifts her perspective, saying, "I'm not sure I should phrase it that way." In her rephrasing, she replaces the hierarchy of rights with a web of relationships. Through this replacement, she challenges the premise of separation underlying the notion of rights and articulates a "guiding principle of connection." Perceiving relationships as primary rather than as derived from separation, considering the interdependence of people's lives, she envisions "the way things are" and "the way things should be" as a web of interconnection where "everybody belongs to it and you all come from it." Against this conception of social reality, the druggist's claim stands in fundamental contradiction. Seeing life as dependent on connection, as sustained by activities of care, as based on a bond of attachment rather than a contract of agreement, she believes that Heinz should steal the drug, whether or not he loves his wife, "by virtue of the fact that they are both there." Although a person may not like someone else, "you have to love someone else, because you are inseparable from them. In a way it's like loving your right hand; it is part of you. That other person is part of that giant collection of everybody." Thus she articulates an ethic of responsibility that stems from an awareness of interconnection: "The stranger is still another person belonging to that group, people you are connected to by virtue of being another person."

Claire describes morality as "the constant tension between being part of something larger and a sort of self-contained entity," and she sees the ability to live with that tension as the source of moral character and strength. This tension is at the center of the moral dilemmas she has faced which were conflicts of responsibility that pertained to an issue of truth and turned on the recognition of relationship. The problem of truth became apparent to her when, after college, she worked as a counselor in an abortion clinic and was told that, if a woman wanted to see what was evacuated from her uterus, she should be told, "You can't see anything now. It just looks like jelly at this point." Since this description clashed with the moral turmoil Claire felt while working at the clinic, she decided that she "had to face up to what was going on." Thus, she decided to look at a fetus evacuated in a late abortion, and in doing so, she came to the realization that:

> I just couldn't kid myself anymore and say there was nothing in the uterus, just a tiny speck. This is not true, and I knew it wasn't true, but I sort of had to see it. And yet at the same time I knew that's what was going on. I also believed that it was right; it should have happened. But I couldn't say, "Well, this is right and this is wrong." I was just constantly torn.

When she measured the world by eye and relied on her perceptions in defining what was happening and what was true, the absolutes of moral judgment dissolved. As a result, she was "constantly torn" and mired in uncertainty with respect to the issue of abortion, but she was also able to act in a more responsible way:

> I struggled with it a whole lot. Finally, I just had to reconcile myself—I really do believe this, but it is not an easy thing that you can say without emotions and maybe regret—that, yes, life is sacred, but the quality of life is also important, and it has to be the determining thing in this particular case. The quality of that mother's life, the quality of an unborn child's life—I have seen too many pictures of babies in trash cans and that sort of thing, and it is so easy to say, "Well, either/or," and it just isn't like that. And I had to be able to say, "Yes, this is killing, there is no way around it, but I am willing to accept that, but I am willing to go ahead with it, and it's hard." I don't think I can explain it. I don't think I can really verbalize the justification.

Claire's inability to articulate her moral position stems in part from the fact that hers is a contextual judgment, bound to the particulars of time and place, contingent always on "that mother" and that "unborn child" and thus resisting a categorical formulation. To her, the possibilities of imagination outstrip the capacity for generalization. But this sense of being unable to verbalize or explain the rationale for her participation in abortion counseling, an inability that could reflect the inadequacy of her moral thought, could also reflect the fact that she finds in the world no validation of the position she is trying to convey, a position that is neither pro-life nor pro-choice but based on a recognition of the continuing connection between the life of the mother and the life of the child.

Thus Claire casts the dilemma not as a contest of rights but as a problem of relationships, centering on a question of responsibility which in the end must be faced. If attachment cannot be sustained, abortion may be the better solution, but in either case morality lies in recognizing connection, taking responsibility for the abortion decision or taking responsibility for the care of the child. Although there are times when "killing like that is necessary, it shouldn't become too easy," as it does "if it is removed from you. If the fetus is just jelly, that is removed from you. Southeast Asia is further removed from you." Thus morality and the preservation of life are contingent on sustaining connection, seeing the consequences of action by keeping the web of relationships intact, "not allowing somebody else to do the killing for you without taking the responsibility." Again an absolute judgment yields to the complexity of relationships. The fact that life is sustained by connection leads her to affirm the "sacred tie" of life rather than "the sacredness of life at all costs," and to articulate an ethic of responsibility while remaining cognizant of the issue of rights.

The problem of truth also arose for Claire when a friend asked her to write a peer recommendation for a job, creating a dilemma similar to the one that Amy described. While Amy wondered whether "to keep friendship or keep justice," though in the end the question became one of responding to others and thus keeping peace with herself, the matter of honesty was from the beginning at the center of Claire's concern: "How could I be honest and at the same time do her justice?" But the issue of justice was an issue of responsibility, arising from the recognition that her actions in forming the friendship had set up a chain of expectations, leading her friend to believe that she could count on Claire for help. Claire, realizing that she "really didn't like" her friend and that their value systems were "very different," also recognized the reality of the relationship and the impossibility of being both honest and fair. The question of what to do hinged on a judgment of the relative hurt her actions would cause, to the friend and to the people whose lives would be affected if the friend succeeded in getting the job. Deciding that in this situation, writing the letter was the better solution, she realized the dilemma could have been avoided by "being a little more honest with her from day one."

With the question of honesty, Claire comes in the end to the drama of "Mr. Right" and "Mr. Wrong," a drama that joins the various themes of relationship, responsibility, and interpretation by personalizing the question of moral truth rather than objectifying the issue of personal relationships. Mr. Right, like Anne in Horner's story, was at the top of his medical school class and "hated not to have all his Sunday to study," given his wish to stay at the top. Consequently, on Saturday nights he would return to sleep on his own bed, leaving Claire feeling not only alone and abandoned but also "selfish" and "wrong":

> What is wrong with me that I want more? There is obviously something. I am a terribly selfish person, and I never really faced the fact that there was something obviously wrong with the relationship.

As a result of this experience, she began to suspect that Mr. Right was not "right for me." But unwilling to end the relationship, she turned instead to Mr. Wrong:

> By senior year, it just blew, but instead of saying, "I am asserting myself, I am not going to stand for this any longer," I had this very sordid affair behind his back and then threw it up to him. And not only threw it up to him, but went to him in tears and confessed, which felt wonderful, but it was all sort of subconsciously calculated to hurt him.

Claire first describes the conflict or the dilemma as a disparity between judgment and action, given her "very strict kind of in a funny way monogamous feelings," but then adds that the real conflict was between two images of herself, "this virginal pure thing and this other side of myself that was sort of starting to blossom." The problem arose because she "was not able to make a decision at that point of what I wanted to do." Stranded between two images of herself, she was caught between two worlds of relationship:

> I was not willing to give up the first relationship because it represented a lot of things. This was Mr. Right to everybody else but me who knew better. And the other guy, who clearly was, in contrast, Mr. Wrong, sort of represented that same sort of animal thing to me at that time, and I wasn't able to give that up either.

As she began to confront the disparity within her perception of herself, she also began "to see that moral standards imposed by somebody else aren't necessarily right for me." Thus, as Mr. Right turned out not to be right, so Mr. Wrong was not so wrong.

Focusing on her actions that revealed the unresolved conflict within herself, she says that "the two people involved in that conflict were myself and myself." As she explores the inner division, she explores the world of relationships as well, identifying her unwillingness to "take responsibility for my actions" as having perpetuated a cycle of hurt:

> That was part of the whole problem with the relationship, my not taking responsibility for my part of it. It was also, I think, sort of designed to hurt him as deeply as he hurt me, even though I had never taken the responsibility for having him stop hurting me. I never said, "You stay here this Saturday or else this is the end of the relationship." Only two or three years later did I realize what was going on.

Claire, looking back on the dilemma of Mr. Right and Mr. Wrong, locates the problem not only in her failure to assert herself but also in "not understanding that I *should* be asserting myself." But the act of assertion is an act not of aggression but rather of communication. By telling Mr. Right the truth about herself, she would not only have prevented aggression but also have provided an opportunity for response. As the "I" who spoke clearly at eleven becomes in adolescence "confused," so the resolution of that confusion occurs through the discovery that responsiveness to self and responsiveness to others are connected rather than opposed.

Describing the people whom she admires—her mother for being "as giving as she is," her husband who "lives by what he believes"—Claire envisions for herself a life of integrity centered on activities of care. This vision is illuminated by the actions of a woman physician who, seeing the loneliness of an old woman in the hospital, "would go out and buy her a root beer float and sit at her bedside just so there would be somebody there for her." The ideal of care is thus an activity of relationship, of seeing and responding to need, taking care of the world by sustaining the web of connection so that no one is left alone.

While the truths of psychological theory have blinded psychologists to the truth of women's experience, that experience illuminates a world which psychologists have found hard to trace, a territory where violence is rare and relationships appear safe. The reason women's experience has been so difficult to decipher or even discern is that a shift in the imagery of relationships gives rise to a problem of interpretation. The images of hierarchy and web, drawn from the texts of men's and women's fantasies and thoughts, convey different ways of structuring relationships and are associated with different views of morality and self. But these images create a problem in understanding because each distorts the other's representation. As the top of the hierarchy becomes the edge of the web and as the center of a network of connection becomes the middle of a hierarchical progression, each image marks as dangerous the place which the other defines as safe. Thus the images of hierarchy and web inform different modes of assertion and response: the wish to be alone at the top and the consequent fear that others will get too close; the wish to be at the center of connection and the consequent fear of being too far out on the edge. These disparate fears of being stranded and being caught give rise to different portrayals of achievement and affiliation, leading to different modes of action and different ways of assessing the consequences of choice.

The reinterpretation of women's experience in terms of their own imagery of relationships thus clarifies that experience and also provides a nonhierarchical vision of human connection. Since relationships, when cast in the image of hierarchy, appear inherently unstable and morally problematic, their transposition into the image of web changes an order of inequality into a structure of interconnection. But the power of the images of hierarchy and web, their evocation of feelings and their recurrence in thought, signifies the embeddedness of both of these images in the cycle of human life. The experiences of inequality and interconnection, inherent in the relation of parent and child, then give rise to the ethics of justice and care, the ideals of human relationship—the vision that self and other will be treated as of equal worth, that despite differences in power, things will be fair; the vision that everyone will be responded to and included, that no one will be left alone or hurt. These disparate visions in their tension reflect the paradoxical truths of human experience—that we know ourselves as separate only insofar as we live in connection with others, and that we experience relationship only insofar as we differentiate other from self.

REFERENCES

Freud, Sigmund. *The Standard Edition of the Complete Psychological Works of Sigmund Freud,* trans. and ed. James Strachey. London: The Hogarth Press, 1961.

———. "On Narcissism: An Introduction" (1914). Vol. XIV.

———. *The Question of Lay Analysis* (1926). Vol. XX.

———. *Civilization and Its Discontents* (1930/1929). Vol. XXI.

Horner, Matina S. "Sex Differences in Achievement Motivation and Performance in Competitive and Noncompetitive Situations." Ph.D. Diss., University of Michigan, 1968. University Microfilms #6912135.

Maccoby, Eleanor, and Jacklin, Carol. *The Psychology of Sex Differences.* Stanford: Stanford University Press, 1974.

May, Robert. *Sex and Fantasy.* New York: W. W. Norton, 1980.

Miller, Jean Baker. *Toward a New Psychology of Women.* Boston: Beacon Press, 1976.

Pollak, Susan, and Gilligan, Carol. "Images of Violence in Thematic Apperception Test Stories." *Journal of Personality and Social Psychology* 42, no. 1 (1982): 159–167.

Terman, L., and Tyler, L. "Psychological Sex Differences." In L. Carmichael, ed., *Manual of Child Psychology.* 2nd ed. New York: John Wiley and Sons, 1954.

Whiting, Beatrice, and Pope, Carolyn. "A Cross-cultural Analysis of Sex Difference in the Behavior of Children Age Three to Eleven." *Journal of Social Psychology* 91 (1973): 171–188.

4

REAL BOYS

THE TRUTHS BEHIND THE MYTHS

William Pollack

"Sometimes just because you're a guy, people treat you like you're a little hoodlum. I think if they opened up their eyes, they'd see that most of us are actually pretty good people."

—Dirk, age seventeen

THOUGH THE STEREOTYPES about what boys are and how boys should behave continue to be perpetuated, in our hearts many of us know that these outdated ideas are simply untrue. And we now have research confirming what most of us have always known.

There are three major myths about boys that persist in all kinds of situations and among all sorts of people, even among the most thoughtful and progressive families, schools, and communities. They are so deeply embedded in the culture, that without realizing it, they often short-circuit our ability to see and love the real boy before us—the true boy behind these old-fashioned ideas.

Myth #1: Boys Will Be Boys: Nature and Testosterone Win Out over Nurture

One myth, which recent studies, including my own, show to be untrue, is that nature controls much about a boy's behavior. More specifically, that where there are boys there is testosterone, and where there is testosterone there is aggression, and where there is aggression there is violence, or at least its potential. The phrase "Boys will be boys" is saying, in effect, that boys are prisoners of biology, that their behavior is predetermined, an inherent part of their nature. "Typical" boy behavior is assumed to involve insensitivity and risk-taking. The phrase is used when a little boy breaks a window with a baseball and runs away laughing. Or when a teenager skateboards into traffic, narrowly avoids a collision, and zooms away. Or when an older adolescent stays up until four in the morning playing Doom, and drags himself to school the next day.

"Boys will be boys" is not said, however, when a little boy brings a present to his teacher or gives his crying mother a hug. Or when a teenage boy obviously feels racked with guilt for breaking up with his girlfriend—unless he covers it up with a convincing show of apathy. Or when an older boy spends time with a dying parent in the hospital—unless he takes the opportunity to watch football on the hospital-room television.

The great danger in subscribing to the myth is that it tends to make people assume that they have less power to affect a boy's personality, behavior, or emotional development than in fact they do.

Truth #1: A Boy's Behavior Is Shaped More by Loved Ones Than by Nature

Underlying the "boys will be boys" myth is a misconception about the role of testosterone. Testosterone does contribute to a boy's natural patterns of behavior, but testosterone is not necessarily the major factor in determining a boy's behavior.

It's true that many boys enjoy being active. For most little boys, running hard across the playground, kicking a soccer ball, or zooming down the slide is action enough. I might add that plenty of little girls take delight in these very same activities. We don't apply the "boys will be boys" myth to that kind of "typical" boy behavior until it takes on a careless edge—when the running turns into a race, when the ball gets kicked *at* someone, or when the boy leans over the edge of the slide daring himself to fall off.

The unfortunate effect of the myth is that it allows us to shrug off a boy's behavior when it crosses the line from active to aggressive. We are more inclined to throw up our hands and say, "We can't do anything about it—that's the ways boys are!" But I strongly believe that a boy's behavior *can* be shaped, that any natural need for action can be encouraged and satisfied, and any impulses toward violence and aggression can be discouraged and channeled in creative, positive directions. The case of Kyle illustrates my point.

Kyle was six when his sister, Charlotte, was born. "We expected Kyle to show the usual sibling jealousy," says his mother, Roberta. "But he was much worse with her than we'd expected. Kyle showed no delight in having a new member of the family, and demonstrated no affection for her. He would poke her with his toys, and make faces at her as if he was completely disgusted with her existence.

"One day, we put Charlotte down for a nap. She slept longer than usual, and my husband, Don, went in to check on her. He found Kyle in the room with her, with his hands close to her neck. It looked for all the world like Kyle might strangle his baby sister. Don rushed to grab him, and realized that Kyle was just pretending. The baby was fine—she hadn't even woken up—but both Don and I completely lost our tempers.

"I rarely yell at my kids, but this time I just went over the edge. I felt as if there was something horribly wrong with my son, that he had a violent nature or something, and this incident had revealed his true self. I didn't try to understand what prompted his action. I viewed my baby daughter, a girl, as a helpless victim, and my boy as the aggressor."

Roberta told her friends about what had happened, and asked them for advice. "I was very worried about Charlotte's well-being. Don was an only child in his family, and I was the youngest child in mine, so neither one of us could really relate to what Kyle was going through. Finally, my friend Gloria helped me understand how Kyle might be feeling."

Gloria, the oldest of three children, explained how her life had changed when her two siblings came along. She had not been consulted in the decision to bring other children into the home—children rarely are. When her siblings first arrived, Gloria lost her status as the special, the only, child. She received far less attention than she'd had before. She had to share her parents and their limited resources of energy with two other children. "Gloria made me understand how much better things were for Kyle before Charlotte appeared, and I had to admit it was true. Kyle got our undivided attention before. Now it was hard to find the time or the energy to play with him."

Roberta and Don determined to work with Kyle to change his attitude toward Charlotte, to curb his "aggression," and to help him understand that his parents still loved him as much as ever. Together, the three of them read stories about big brother/little sister relationships, which sparked lots of conversation about the topic. "Once we convinced Kyle that we weren't going to blame him or punish him for his natural feelings," Roberta recalled, "he opened up. We had some really good talks with him, and we told him he would always be our special boy."

"Kyle's become a very caring brother," Roberta now says. "One day, he spent an hour drawing an elaborate picture of our family—including Charlotte—and he told me he wanted to give it to his baby sister as a present. Today, he's the kind of brother I'd hoped he would be. He knows that we're not going to abandon him for Charlotte, and he feels comfortable enough to share us with her. I can even laugh now at the memory of him pretending to strangle Charlotte, because I know he never would and never could do such a thing. He's not a violent person. He was just in a very difficult situation and couldn't express his feelings about it, and we certainly weren't helping him any."

My clinical experience and research—as well as work done by others—have shown that most boys, when lovingly nurtured themselves, will in turn nurture and show empathy for others. We have learned that the way parents care for their sons has an even more powerful effect on a boy's behavior than we had realized, an effect at least as strong as biology in determining a boy's nature. How you treat a boy has a powerful impact on who he becomes. He is as much a product of nurturing as he is of nature.

The Myth About Testosterone

The idea that high levels of testosterone equate with high levels of violence stems from a mistaken assumption that testosterone is the only force that inclines boys toward both active, rough-and-tumble play and violent behavior. This is not the case. Boys do play differently than girls, but their style of play is not solely a function of testosterone and it certainly does not prove a proclivity for violence. Boys, in general, like play that is competitive, physically rough, and forceful. They like games that involve interaction in large groups and take place in large spaces (such as playing fields, gymnasiums, stadiums) as well as those that follow rules and have a hierarchy of authority. Girls, on the other hand, generally enjoy play that is more interpersonal, often one-on-one, and less physically aggressive.

Although scientists have long recognized the differences between the play styles of girls and boys and continue to debate the evolutionary and hormonal influences, they have not been able to establish a clear link between boys' rough play and aggression or violence.

While testosterone does, in fact, contribute to boys' proclivity for action, scientists over the years have tried without success to establish an unequivocal link between testosterone and violent behavior. The fact is that testosterone is just one of many biological factors (including serotonin) that have an influence on aggression. In addition, testosterone can have a variety of different effects on boys' behavior. A high testosterone level in one boy may enable him to play a chess match with great intensity and alertness; in another, it may give him the energy and concentration to make complicated arrangements for a political rally. In a third case, it may contribute to his involvement in a brutal fistfight. But the amount of testosterone in a boy's system fluctuates depending on when it is measured and the activities he has been involved in—rather like the pulse rate. In older men the effects of testosterone vary from man to man. Research has also shown that when older men are given supplemental testosterone they become calmer and less aggressive than before. By contrast, when athletes take anabolic steroids, the cousins of testosterone, they become ornery and excitable. No simple scientific link has been made between testosterone levels and the tendency for aggression and violence.

The level of testosterone in any boy—and the way that testosterone affects him—has less impact on his behavior than how the boy is loved, nurtured, and shaped by his parents and by the context of the society within which he lives. The hormone may well predict a certain type of energy in boys. But the way in which that energy is funneled and expressed lies in our hands.

The Potency of Connection: The Power of Parenting to Affect Our Boys' Brains

Parents, and others who love and look after boys, are empowered in their efforts by their boys' own deep yearning for connection. This is what I call the *potency of connection*. The power of love can dispel the myth that, in boys, nature and nurture are at odds, or, indeed, have distinct separate influences on a boy and his life. The way we interact with boys, and the connections we make with them, can have a permanent effect on a boy's biology, his brain, and his social behavior. Scientists have found that early emotional interaction can actually alter a boy's brain-based biological processes.

When a boy (or girl) is born, the baby's brain—unlike the brain of any other primate—is not fully developed. In the first year of life a child's brain doubles in size, and then doubles again. By the time a child reaches the age of two, his or her brain has as many synapses (connections between brain cells) as an adult's. During this period of development, the human brain is very pliable and plastic, and—more than in any other species—is very open to learning from emotional and cognitive experiences. The human brain can, in fact, be permanently altered by its environment in these early years of its life. Scientists have demonstrated that at birth the human brain is wired to accommodate developmental interactions that further shape the nervous system after birth, with profound consequences for lifelong functioning.

How we respond to our baby boys and young sons—the manner in which we cuddle, kiss, and reassure, teach, comfort, and love—not only determines a young boy's capacity for a healthy emotional start in life but deeply affects a boy's characteristic style of behavior and the development of his brain. Our behavior fundamentally, and at times irrevocably, alters a boy's neural connections, brain chemistry, and biological functioning. The capacity to use language, to tolerate distress, to show and name feelings, and to be timid or eager to explore are all dramatically affected by the emotional environment created for a boy during early childhood. While nature creates boys whose behavior is influenced by biological proclivities—more than we used to believe—nature also creates boys who are more receptive to interaction with their caretakers than we had ever imagined.

Bruce Perry, a developmental neurobiologist at Baylor College of Medicine, summarizes it this way: "a child's capacity to think, to laugh, to love, to hate, to speak—all of it is a product of interaction with the environment. Sensory experiences such as touching . . . literally stimulate activity in the brain and the growth of neural structures."

The people in a boy's life—moms and dads, teachers and siblings, coaches and ministers, day-care providers and doctors—may have an effect equal to that of testosterone in shaping a young boy, not only by influencing his formative experience but by affecting his brain structures and neurotransmitters. The potency of connection is not just about the power adults have to create safe, nurturing, "holding environments." It is also about how these caring environments, in turn, affect the biological development of infant and toddler brains. Modern science has demonstrated how easily nurture becomes nature; there is no rigid dichotomy between the two.

So, let's rid ourselves of the myth that boys can never escape their biological fates. The truth is that we can do a great deal to shape how a boy behaves. We can search for ways to celebrate our boys' energy and channel it into positive and productive activities. If they feel the urge to hit, let's give them a punching bag and help them learn to box. If they want to scream and yell, let's play a game that gives them a chance to cheer. If they want to argue, let's engage them in a conversation that allows them to develop their debating skills. If they refuse to do what's on the family agenda, let's challenge them to come up with an alternative plan.

Myth #2: Boys Should Be Boys

The myth that "boys should be boys"—that they *must* fulfill the stereotype of the dominant and "macho" male—inhibits some parents and their sons from living in the way that comes most naturally to them. The Boy Code says that boys should be tough, should demand respect from others, and should never act "like a girl." As soon as a boy behaves in a way that is not considered manly, that falls outside the Boy Code, he is likely to meet resistance from society—he may merely be stared at or whispered about, he may be humiliated, he may get a punch in the gut, or he may just feel terribly ashamed.

When eight-year-old Ethan tells his physical education teacher that he would rather jump rope than play basketball with the boys, some of his second-grade classmates cannot contain their laughter. The teacher smiles indulgently but pushes Ethan firmly in the direction of the basketball courts.

Thirteen-year-old Steven arrives at school with flesh-toned acne lotion covering an embarrassingly large pimple on his nose. His peers tease him about how "pretty he looks." They humiliate him by asking whether he "forgot to put on his lipstick," or what color dress he plans to wear to the dance that night.

When seventeen-year-old Brad reads a poem in English class with dramatic intensity, there are a few sniggers from the back row. Later, someone mocks his recitation, adding an exaggerated lisp, and whispering loud enough for all to hear: "Faggot."

When boys act in less than conventionally "masculine" ways, their peers—both boys and girls—can be quick to tighten the laces on their gender straitjackets. Some parents, teachers, coaches, and other mentors also act in ways that reinforce society's myths about masculinity by letting boys know when they are violating the Boy Code.

Jennifer, a teacher at a Boston-area preschool, is thirty-six years old and holds degrees in childhood development from Wellesley and Harvard. She asked for my advice about one of her students, four-year-old Benjamin. "He still wants to play the mother and put on jewelry in the dress-up corner," she told me. "When I suggest something else for him to do, he cries in front of all the other kids. He seems perfectly healthy otherwise," she explained, "but I'm getting worried about whether he's really ready for kindergarten."

"Didn't I see Lisa wearing a cowboy hat and slapping her thigh like a horse the other day?" I asked.

"Sure," Jennifer said, "but *all* the girls do that."

Even this well-educated, highly competent, and sensitive teacher was influenced by the "boys should be boys" myth—playing mother and putting on jewelry did not constitute "healthy" boy behavior.

I witnessed similar attitudes at another private school that prided itself on being progressive. Recently they had instituted a coed program called Boxing Can Be Safe, designed to help kindergarten kids express their anger. I attended one of these kindergarten boxing matches and watched as five-year-old Michael, who stood no taller than three feet, made an awkward attempt at a punch. "Not like that, Michael," the coach admonished him. "You're swinging like a girl!"

It's hard to imagine how damaging these reproaches must be for boys. As a therapist—working with young people as well as adults—I have been through countless sessions with adult men who shared painful memories about being shamed as children for not being "manly" enough, for not being "like the other boys." Especially for very young boys, the humiliation leaves them feeling that there is no place to turn.

Without safe places where they can voice their pain or discuss their shame and deep embarrassment, many boys begin to toughen themselves up into little men. They become cut off from their own feelings, and their voices no longer fully connect with their emotional selves.

As difficult as the shame-hardening process is for boys, it is almost equally difficult for parents to watch. In many ways the myth that "boys should be boys" shields us, as adults, from dealing with our own pain and frustration as we observe our boys going through this extremely upsetting process. Perhaps by accepting the myth that boys must learn on their own how to act, must be like other "masculine" boys, and "tough it out," we somehow make ourselves feel more comfortable that this process is a necessary rite of passage, a natural part of growing up as a boy. Adult men in particular may rely on this myth to protect themselves from remembering how hurtful this "hardening" process was in their own childhood.

Truth #2: There Are Many Ways to Be a Boy— The Diversity of Masculinity

The truth is that the Boy Code is based on a stereotype unique to our culture and time. There is no *one* correct pathway to healthy masculinity.

Boys have been defined very differently in other countries, other cultures, and other eras. For example, in one country crying may be expected of boys and men, whereas in another it may be expressly forbidden. Many parents today feel terribly ill at ease and struggle with the myths of boyhood, knowing in their hearts that they do not truly reflect the true nature of their own boys. Others, who have taken the time to fully examine the validity of the myths, refuse to accept the Boy Code and actively seek to break free of it. Often these parents are able, in turn, to help their sons break free of the code.

When they feel comfortable that they will not be humiliated by girls or other boys for doing so, many boys derive tremendous joy from participating in a full range of playful, expressive, and creative activities—which was how a young man called Kip was able to create a wonderful life for himself. In high school Kip had spent every waking hour—when he wasn't doing schoolwork or helping out at his father's small business—practicing, living, and breathing basketball. He dreamed of being the next Larry Bird, Michael Jordan, or Shaquille O'Neal. He was good enough to make the all-state team and received a basketball scholarship to Duke University. During his first game of the season, Kip's career aspirations came to an abrupt end. An elbow to the ribs caused a hard fall to the parquet and a serious knee injury. That night the Duke doctors told him the bad news: his knee could not be repaired. He would have to forget about a career in the NBA. Kip spent months moping and feeling sorry for himself; he relived the moment when he took the hit, wondering if he could have turned away from that fateful elbow or fallen differently to avoid the injury. Finally, he faced up to the fact that he would not be the next Larry Bird. He decided that he would have to "reinvent" himself. But, because he was a mediocre student, Kip figured that he would not be accepted into business school and that a business career was not an option for him.

One day he had an inspiration. He had another skill besides basketball, although he had never taken it very seriously. He was an inventive cook. He had grown up in a close and loving Italian family and had often helped his mother in the kitchen. She had always said that he had culinary talent, and she loved to tell her friends about his skill with bruschetta and fresh pasta and osso bucco. Kip wondered if he could make a career as a chef. He also wondered if it would be an acceptable career for an ex-basketball player, a jock.

Kip mentioned the idea to his father and hinted at his reservations. "Hey, Kip, there's nothing wrong with wearing an apron," his father responded. "It's a uniform, just like wearing basketball shorts. Maybe even better. Anybody who thinks you can't be a man and be a chef has never tasted a really great fettuccine Alfredo."

The next month Kip enrolled at the Cordon Bleu cooking school in Paris. Five years later Kip was one of the most celebrated chefs in Denver and had employment offers from three restaurants in New York City. A well-known food-and-wine magazine hailed him as one of the stars of American cuisine. If you had told Kip when he was ten that he would become a chef, he probably would have scoffed at the idea. But he came to understand that his ability to be effective with the big round ball was not so different from his ability to be creative in the art of cooking.

"I'm not doing what I expected to do when I was a kid," Kip concluded. "But I think I had a very limited view of what a man should do with his life. Now I don't think there's anything less masculine about being a chef than being a forward."

There is no single path to a healthy and mature masculinity. A good school or home environment will send the message that activities like sports, acting in a school play, and volunteering at the local nursing home all provide equally good ways to succeed in the journey from boyhood into manhood.

When I am advising parents about boys, I encourage them to follow their own instincts about their sons' need for love and nurturing. Mothers and fathers need to feel secure that there is no such thing as giving their son too much love. Within appropriate limits you will never spoil a boy by showing him affection or by providing him with the freedom to follow his own path.

The Reverend Tony Jarvis, headmaster of one of Boston's most prestigious independent schools for boys, ends many a private interview with a troubled high school senior—perhaps a six-foot 250-pound fullback—with "You know I love you." We can all set up this kind of caring environment in which thoughts and feelings can be freely expressed and encourage boys to experience childhood in an entirely natural way. By doing so, we allow our sons to talk, mourn, and grieve openly about the shame they may feel when they fail to live up to the Boy Code. By doing so, we show boys that we love them for who they really are.

Myth #3: Boys Are Toxic—The Anti-Boy

A third myth of boyhood follows from the first two, but it can be even more devastating. Not only does society see boys as prisoners of their biological makeup ("boys will be boys"), and as properly confined by the gender straitjacket ("boys should be boys"), but we also tend to believe that there is something inherently dangerous or toxic about boys—that they are psychologically unaware, emotionally unsocialized creatures. This myth adds a potentially damaging element to the social environment.

Karen decided to send her daughter, Alison, to an all-girls school, but kept her son in a coeducational environment. The reason, she explained, was that her daughter needed to learn that "all roles in society are open to women." Her son, on the other hand, needed to learn in the company of girls because they would help to make him more "sensitive and polished." She was saying, in other words, that the presence of boys might have a toxic effect on her daughter, while girls could help mitigate the noxious disposition of her son. Barbara, another parent, put the same anti-boy sentiment a little more directly when she said, "Girls have a civilizing effect."

Such views must be seen as discriminatory to boys, but they are seldom challenged by other parents or by teachers because of the prevalent myth that boys *are* in fact toxic. This myth manifests itself in both subtle and dramatic ways. When a seven-year-old boy impulsively plants a kiss on a somewhat unwilling female playmate, he is branded a sexual delinquent and suspended from school. A fifth-grade boy coming directly from a "sex education" class jokes with a girl that her sagging belt looks like a penis and gets accused of "sexual harassment." It is as if we are in the midst of an irrational society-wide backlash against boys and young men.

Put aside for the moment the obvious double standard of how teenage girls who joke about the "bulge" in football players' pants are unlikely to be branded as sexual harassers, and ask why we have confused boys' childish exploratory play with adult predatory behavior. No doubt some components of boys' and girls' play go beyond the bounds of acceptability and are deserving of redirection or even reprimand. Yet, when it is a *boy* involved, we seem to forget his need to play, experiment, and fail in order to grow. Instead, we respond as though he is a full-fledged aggressor.

Truth #3: Boys Are Empathic

Although empathy is considered to be one of the strongest attributes of girls, there is ample evidence that boys are highly empathic as well. An interesting study was conducted of boys raised in a two-parent household in which the father was the primary emotionally nurturing parent. In addition to all the other typical traits of well-adjusted male children—self-confidence, exuberance, action-orientation—these boys also showed a greater flexibility of personality and a positive attitude toward girls and the ability to connect with them. In other words, men are capable of raising their boy children to have empathy in all their relationships. Even when raised without a predominant female presence, boys can learn to be sensitive and to care deeply about other people, including girls, and their feelings.

Seth's friends were just such boys.

Seth was a slight sixteen-year-old who excelled at soccer. In his junior year in high school he was elected cocaptain of the varsity soccer team. Not only was he respected by his teammates, but he was a model student and high achiever. But Seth had a sadness in his eyes, and an uncertainty in his bearing that seemed at odds with his popular and physically confident self. However, it was not difficult to see why he seemed to be bearing a burden. His mother, a warm and active woman named Cindy, had been diagnosed with a severe and rapidly growing form of breast cancer.

The entire family—Seth; his thirteen-year-old sister, Amy; his father; and Cindy herself—had met with Cindy's oncologist. Seth talked about that meeting with great emotion. His father, who owned an insurance business, had broken the ice by asking the doctor for some straight answers about Cindy's condition and her chances. "There's no good way to tell you this," said the doctor. "Your wife has a very serious form of breast cancer. We're going to do everything we can, but the average life expectancy from tumors like this is less than five years."

The family rallied around Cindy as best they could. Seth seemed particularly able to provide her with special comfort and support. He was aided in his efforts by an unexpected source—the members of his soccer team. The boys pitched in, helping with the formidable day-to-day tasks of caring for a seriously ill person. They hosted a bake sale to raise funds for the hospital, donating the proceeds in her name. Perhaps most important, Seth's buddies offered him their shoulders to cry on. And cry on them he did. When his mother's hair fell out from chemotherapy, when radiation treatments didn't work, Seth wept openly, at lunch hour, at study hall, or on his way to soccer practice in the afternoons. By his side were one or two, sometimes three or four, of his friends—tears streaming down their cheeks, as well.

His mother died four years later, when Seth was a sophomore at Yale. Although the news came as no surprise, it still hit him like a fist in the chest. He remembers doubling up with pain, worrying that he couldn't make it through the funeral. That night he called his best buddy from high school, Bill, a student at Stanford.

"Don't worry, Seth," Bill assured him. "We'll be there for you."

Seth assumed that Bill meant that his friends would be thinking of him, there for him in spirit. But on the day of the funeral almost all of the twenty-five young men who had composed Seth's soccer team showed up at the church to attend the funeral. Outside the church, they joined together in a circle of shared love and grief, poured out their sadness to one another, and gave Seth the strength he needed to get through the service.

The priest remarked to me that he had never seen anything like this. "I'm struck not only by their open affection and caring," he told me, "but by the fact that this is coming from *boys*."

"They're men now, Father," I replied, "real men."

This is just one example of the kind of caring, deeply supportive, empathic behavior that boys can show for their loved ones—their parents, their friends, their families—and that I have seen boys display in a wide variety of situations and circumstances.

REFERENCES

Blum, D. (1996). Boys May Be More Emotionally Fragile. *Sacramento Bee,* June 10.

———. (1997). *Sex on the Brain.* New York: Viking.

Fausto-Sterling, A. (1992). *Myths of Gender.* New York: Basic Books.

Halpern, D. F. (1997). Sex Differences in Intelligence: Implications for Education. *American Psychologist, 52(10),* 1091–1102.

Kimura, D. (1992). Sex Differences in the Brain. *Scientific American,* September, 119–25.

Pleck, J. (1981). *The Myth of Masculinity.* Cambridge, Mass.: MIT Press.

Pollack, W. S. (1995). "Reframing Masculinity: Men, Empathy, and Empathy for Men." Paper presented at the Cambridge Symposium, Cambridge, Mass., Winter.

———. (1995). "Men's Erotic Desires: Love, Lust, Trauma, Sex, Biology, and Psychoanalysis." Paper presented at the 103rd annual convention of the American Psychological Association, New York, August.

5

WHERE IT ALL BEGINS

THE BIOLOGY OF BOYHOOD

Michael Gurian

The past is prologue.

—Shakespeare, *The Tempest*

IN ISRAEL, AT A SOCIAL gathering, I met an emigré from India, a physician. I've never forgotten what he said.

Educated at Texas A & M, he had returned to India to work in Madras, then moved with part of his family to Haifa. Standing together at a party in Haifa, Dr. Jagdish Kulanapoor and I reminisced about India, where I had lived as a boy. We got onto a nature-versus-nurture conversation, which led him to the importance of ritual. Ritual, he said, is how children learn and adults flourish. When I got us onto the topic of boys' rituals, we agreed that American male rituals emphasize material acquisition and social education at the expense of spiritual growth.

He said: "Of course it would be this way in America. You have turned completely away from the primacy of biology. You pretend that human socialization, not natural inheritance, is the prime mover of the human animal. You pretend that human beings and human societies have so much power they can make boys and girls what they are. Believing this, what need have you for pervasive ritual whose job it is to honor nature's course?

"In my culture, we do not have this arrogance. We know that boys and girls are made very differently. We know and respect this even before birth. Not to do so, we believe, is to bring trouble upon us. We make separate spiritual rituals for each sex's natural and predetermined being."

This conversation took place in the early eighties. At that time in my life, I assumed, as did the vast majority of my colleagues, that nurture—"human beings and human society"—was most of why boys are boys and girls are girls. The "nature" view—that biology determined male and female behavior—had resulted, many of us could see, in women being oppressed for centuries.

So I smiled politely at Dr. Kulanapoor, and the conversation moved on.

But more than ten years later, I've realized how wise Jagdish was—not just wise in his commonsense knowledge that boys and girls are naturally different, but wise in his ability to connect biology to spirituality. For boys, no matter the tribe or culture, that link has been essential to healthy maturity. That link is missing in our families, schools, and culture.

Nature Versus Nurture

Camilla Benbow and Jullian Stanley, of Johns Hopkins University, studied 100,000 boys and girls, paying close attention to sex-different approaches to learning and living. In the late eighties, they let their results be known: "After fifteen years of looking for an environmental explanation and getting zero results," Benbow said, "I gave up." Benbow became popular on talk shows. But in many of the places she went to show her evidence that biologically inherited brain and hormone differences basically control the way males and females operate, she was treated with suspicion.

Now, in the mid-1990s, she and researchers like her have been more than vindicated. Researchers like Roger Gorski have discovered marked differences in physiological structures between the male and the female brain. Researchers at the University of Pennsylvania have measured, with brain-scan equipment, what parts of the brain males and females use during different kinds of stimulation. Amazing things have been discovered, which we'll look at in this chapter.

It requires pretty effective blinders these days to think as I did in the early 1980s—that boys are boys and girls are girls predominantly because of environmental forces. It's more accurate to say that much of who we are is determined by body chemicals, brain differences, hormones, and by society's efforts to honor this biology through its socializing influences.

Society has the choice of whether to fight our natural and inherited abilities or channel them effectively. With males especially, the "environment is the prime mover" view to which I adhered more than a decade ago has backfired. Boys as a group have not changed, despite decades of trying to make them. Not only have they not changed, they've gotten more randomly aggressive and more antisocially dangerous, the very things we thought, decades ago, we could nurture out of them by demeaning masculine culture and elevating feminine culture.

This chapter lays out information toward this view: that a boy is, in large part, hard-wired to be who he is. We can't, in large part, change who he is. We can teach him how to develop who he is with confidence, and toward a direction that contributes to our world. In this view, our best choices in nurturing him revolve around *knowing who and what he is,* then *channeling his energy in ways appropriate to him*—not to what or who we believe politically he ought to be.

Saying this does not deny the importance of environment and socialization on boys. They are important factors. Nor does it deny the importance of individual personality, both genetically driven, then individually developed, on a boy's life experience. However, as I will present in this chapter, I believe that helping boys to grow up well, and helping culture to progress, requires us to do some informed generalizing about a boy's nature, and requires us to put socialization and environmental influences in perspective. When we return to the common sense of nature in our upbringing of boys, we work with boys, give them the structure, discipline, and wisdom they, in particular, need. When we accomplish this, we don't create more random violence, we ensure less of it; we don't make boys into men who victimize women, we ensure less victimization of women. In our lives as parents, mentors, and educators, we stop feeling as if we're fighting against boys and masculinity; we start realizing how to work with boys and maleness. Consequently, our homes, schools, streets, and bedrooms start looking very different.

The Prime Mover: Testosterone

Marti, a mother of a now-grown son, recounted something many mothers in a workshop could identify with: "No matter what I did, Artie was just more aggressive than his sister. When Artie was four, five years old I'd try to get him to play with dolls. He'd play with them, sure, just not the way I meant. He'd take the biggest one, make it into a gun, and blast away at the others!"

Sheila Moore and Roon Frost, authors of *The Little Boy Book,* recalled this comment by a mother:

> The biggest things in my daughters' lives right now are Barbie dolls and nail polish . . . Jonathon—he walks like the Incredible Hulk, shovels down his food, and wrestles with every boy he sees—and he's only three and a half!

Don and Jeanne Elium recounted the words of Sam, father of a ten-year-old, in their book, *Raising a Son:*

> My son is quiet and sensitive. He doesn't go in for rough-and-tumble play with the other boys. But he is like a madman when he turns on his computer.

Because of their dominance by the hormone testosterone, aggression and physical risk-taking are programmed into boys. It's important to distinguish between "aggression" and "violence." As psychologist Aaron Kipnis has put it, "Violence is not hard-wired into boys. Violence is taught. Aggression is hard-wired."

Aggression will show itself quite overtly, as with Artie and Jonathon, or it will mask its predominance, as with Sam's son, until one of its channeling activities—like a debate or a computer videogame—begins. The quality and quantity of aggressive behavior in a boy always depends on the boy's age and how he has been taught to channel it. Boys who are mentally ill, have attention deficit disorder (hyperactivity), are genetically female, have a female brain, are homosexual, or are by personality describable by parents as "more sensitive" than most may prove to be more or less aggressive than "the average boy." Yet, still, one of the best ways to deal with a boy is to focus on his aggression and risk-taking—his domination by the hormone testosterone.

The effect of testosterone on a boy in the twentieth century has millions of years of history. Going back as far as four million years ago, males needed more testosterone than females in order to be able to reproduce. That testosterone created more body-muscle than body-fat, and that it made males more aggressive, were probably secondary functions four million years ago. Now higher levels of male sex drive than female (on average), higher levels of muscle mass, and higher levels of aggression all seem to be primary functions of testosterone.

Millions of years ago males produced trillions of potentially fertile sperm in a lifetime but were required to mate with human females who created a few hundred potentially fertile eggs—approximately one per month between the age of puberty and either death or menopause. Humans, in this male/female difference, are like most primates. In order for a male to fulfill his predominant biological imperative—to reproduce himself—he had to constantly mate with females. Back then, all a male knew was that a female was ovulating "estrous" (even now, in the 1990s, timing isn't sure). He had no way of knowing when the fleeting moment of egg-in-its-place would occur, or whether one particular ejaculation of his semen would connect with it. He was also in constant competition with other males and their sperm for the female's egg. The male's sperm competition and need for constant arousal and mating required high sex drive.

It required high testosterone.

Things have not changed much since the first humans started walking about the African savannah. Males are still in competition for females and will do nearly anything to get females to have sex with them, and love them. Females still decide (except in the case of rape) with whom they will mate based on how the males around them compete to win their affection. Males still need higher sex drives than women and still possess them, through their higher levels of testosterone. Testosterone is still the defining agent of whether a fetus will be male or female, even more lasting in its impact on the child than the chromosomal fusion that occurs in egg and sperm, for if a boy is created chromosomally but not enough testosterone exists to make him a boy, he will come out of the womb looking like a girl.

Here's how it works.

First, genetic fusion occurs between the sperm and egg to make a chromosomal boy (XY). Then the hormone testosterone surges through the chromosomally male fetus early in the pregnancy, making a boy's genitals drop. Then, in the middle months of the pregnancy, testosterone surges again, giving the boy a male brain. If, during the pregnancy, traumatic stress on the mother, for instance, inhibits testosterone release, an XY genetic boy may be born without male genitals and/or without a male brain. He may also be born homosexual without realizing it until later in life. Many external factors—traumatic stress on the mother, a mother's intake of drugs or alcohol—and many internal causes, the exact shape of which neurobiologists are still not certain, affect testosterone release in the womb.

Testosterone and Aggression

If you have a "normal" boy—meaning, he is an XY boy whose body and brain were created male by appropriate testosterone surges—he will himself be dominated by the hormone that made him what he is.

As an infant and little boy, he will show on average more aggressive tendencies than girls. Studies done with six-month-old infants have shown that when boys and girls both pull a string to get a happy result, like a smiling image on a screen, and then testers take the image away, the boys will keep pulling and pulling, more stubbornly and aggressively. Girls will, within a few pulls of not getting the image, put the string down and cry out for help.

It also shows in a boy's motor activity. From infancy, a boy's motor activity is more vigorous than girls', but the duration of each motor act is shorter and the peak of the motor act happens more quickly. So a boy will push his arm out in a jab and bring it to rest quickly, where a girl might bring her arm out more slowly and smoothly.

From infancy, boys tend to be more irritable. A factor that adds to this natural tendency might be the higher incidence of prenatal and birth complications in boys.

A little boy (on average) will turn toys into guns or swords with more frequency than girls will. He will hit more. He will try to one-up more. He will tend less toward empathic first-responses to others' pain and more toward provocative first-responses. He will be generally more competitive than his sister and especially in the few activities in which he perceives the potential to dominate over or be superior in. He will assess his potential to dominate based on his understanding of his personality, talent, and skill strengths. He will seek rough-and-tumble play or, if he perceives himself as physically weak, another outlet for aggression.

Testosterone and Independence

Boys, especially after the toddler years, often navigate independence differently than girls—some of this relates to testosterone and continues throughout a male's life. One mother, Mary Beth, said to me: "My husband and I were together until Casey was five. At about two, Casey was independent and just stayed that way, unlike his sister who was always more attached to me. Then when we divorced, Casey started clinging to me. Which one is more 'Casey'? The independence or the clinging?"

Mothers like Mary Beth often report having "independent boys," and just as often, seeing that independence change when a divorce occurs. Boys, dominated by testosterone, often feel compelled to gain independence earlier than girls, but only when they feel safe and confident that they are not losing a parent's love. If a parent misunderstands this equation—holds onto the boy longer than he wants to be emotionally controlled; or disrupts his sense of safety through a circumstance like divorce—his natural and very testosterone-controlled urge to separate and force himself into the world is disrupted.

Often single mothers will say things like, "I liked the clinging my son did with me after the divorce. It made me feel like I could have more influence on him. But at the same time, I knew there was more going on for him." They are wisely sensing the complexity of a boy's response to his sudden loss of confidence in becoming independent. They often find that loving him appropriately means getting him—with, hopefully, the divorced father's help—back on his independent feet again.

The more we study testosterone in a boy's life, the more explanation we have for boys' hitting, playing style, physical risk-taking, flirtations with danger, desires for independence, and general difficulty from many parents' points of view. Again, of course, we're talking averages. Some parents will say, "Are you kidding? My boys were easy. It was my girls who drove me nuts!"

Testosterone, Puberty, and Beyond

When a boy hits puberty, the influence of testosterone on his body and brain increase manifold. His testosterone level itself will increase in quantities ten to twenty times more than girls. His genitals will increase to eight times their previous size. His body will process anywhere between five to seven surges of testosterone per day. You can expect him to masturbate continually, bump into things a lot, be moody and aggressive, require a great deal of sleep, lose his temper, want sex as soon as he gets up the emotional guts to propose to a partner, have a massive sexual fantasy life, and so on. And this is just during adolescence.

When he becomes an adult, you can expect him to be more aggressive and competitive than the average woman—remember, we are again speaking of averages—more ambitious about workplace superiority; more prone to one-up in conversation; quicker to react physically to external stimulation. He will be more likely to hit when he feels accosted, and to seek rough-and-tumble play, competitive sports, or any physical or motor activities through which he can release tension, take risks, and show competitive prowess. Often he will show his prowess only to himself, and often that is enough. He will be more likely to force his way up the corporate ladder.

Testosterone so influences aggression and even assertiveness that studies done on women have shown an increase in both qualities when women have been injected with testosterone-like androgenic hormones. They take more risks, discover more ambition within themselves and in the work-place, and feel more assertive in everyday life.

Testosterone and Tension

Testosterone also affects the way boys, male youth, and men release ten-sion. This in turn affects vast portions of male life. Don and Jeanne Elium, in *Raising a Son,* put it well:

> The instant when the hunter makes the kill, the thrill of the long touchdown pass, and the closure of a big sale are all moments that live in the dreams of men from prehistoric times through today. Central to these moments is a powerful cycle of energy, fundamental in the makeup of a man: a short buildup of tension followed by a quick, grat-ifying, and decisive release. This short-term, immediate-gratification cycle prepares a male's body to act.

Understanding how a boy's (and man's) energy works is fundamental to loving him. That energy, propelled by testosterone, and guided by the specific structure and workings of the male brain structure, is the primary cause of three behavior patterns you've probably noticed in boys:

1. the search for instant or quick gratification, whether in eating quickly, jumping from activity to activity, or quick sexual conquest;
2. the tendency to move quickly to problem-solving, even in emotion-ally complex experiences;
3. the tendency to find activities through which his body will build physical tension—like sports or other concentrated, single-task experiences—then release the tension with an "Ahhh."

The male sex act is the best metaphorical and literal way of seeing this tension-release cycle with clarity. The male's reproductive job, unlike the female who will carry the child, is to plant the seed in a female, then find another female to plant it in, and so on: quick sexual tension and release, and as often as needed. We teach boys to do much more, of course, but their bodies are still built on the basis of their sexual biology. To try to teach boys to "rise above instant gratification," "become more like girls," "be more sensitive," "not like sports as much," and so on without first teaching them personally fruitful and socially acceptable ways to do all those things is to shoot ourselves in the foot. Boys don't believe adults who don't understand boys.

How a Boy Thinks: The Male Brain

"What we are and how we live," say Anne Moir and David Jessel in *Brain Sex,* "is largely dictated by the messages that mould and inform our brains."

Centuries ago—even just a few decades ago—when people talked about "the male brain" or "the female brain" they often did so in order to prove that one—usually the male—was superior to the other. When it was discovered, for instance, that the weight and volume of the male brain is ten to fifteen percent greater than the weight and volume of a female's brain, social thinkers were quick to say, "You see, the male brain is bigger and therefore men are better—smarter, more capable of doing the most important jobs." In this and so many other ways, brain "science" was used to put women down. As a result, talk about male and female brains has been avoided and even called "dangerous" in the last quarter century. In this absence of neuroscience in our political and social dialogue, we've avoided one danger but replaced it with another. We have constructed a late-twentieth-century society that specifically tries not to tailor child-raising techniques to boys and girls themselves. In the absence of this tailoring, boys whose brains work one way are told they're not okay; and girls whose brains work another way are also told they're not okay.

Nevertheless, brain research has been going on throughout our social changes so that now its evidence of male/female brain differences is so vast that responsible parents, mentors, educators, and social thinkers cannot avoid it if they are going to do right by children. Thankfully, research has advanced beyond the "my brain is smarter than her brain" stage. Now we are able to see differences between a boy's brain and a girl's without saying, "So this means girls can't do what boys can do and boys can't do what girls can do."

Brain research does not mean biology is destiny. It means biology is proclivity. The brain is so wonderful a mechanism that anyone can be most anything, given the drive, skill, and right nurturing. Opportunity need not be curtailed to anyone based on sex or gender. At the same time, because biology is proclivity, when our children are young, we must do everything we can to help boys and girls feel comfortable in the development of their own separate ways of doing things. Not to do so is to teach them that their core self is inadequate by nature and will not be nurtured by society. Our children, brought up this way, will take their revenge.

Structural Differences in the Brain

If we had X-ray glasses and could look into our children's heads, what are some differences we would see?

We would notice, as Laurie Allen, brain researcher at UCLA has pointed out, that in at least seven of the measured brain structures there are structural differences between female and male brains.

We would notice a difference in size—the boy's brain at least ten percent larger than the girl's.

We would also notice that within the smaller girl's brain is a larger corpus callosum than in the larger boy's brain. The corpus callosum is the bundle of nerves that connects the brain's right and left hemispheres. Moore and Frost have summarized how this happens:

> During fetal life when the brain and nervous system are being organized, the female cortex (brain) develops in advance of the male cortex. The left half of the cortex (the part of the brain that controls thinking) develops somewhat later than the right (the part that works with spatial relationships). In males, though, there is an even greater lag. "As a result," one neurologist says, "when the right side is ready to hook up with the left side (by sending over connecting nerve fibers), in the male the appropriate cells don't yet exist on the left. So (the fibers) go back and instead form connections within the right hemisphere. You end up with extremely enriched connections within the right."

One of the results of this structural difference is increased focus in the male brain on spatial relationships and activity. Little boys, much more so than little girls, manipulate objects like blocks to see how they use up space.

Because the female cortex develops faster than the male, it is able to create the larger corpus callosum, and because that bundle of nerves is larger, it is able to enjoy more cross-talk between the left and right hemispheres of the brain than does a boy's brain. Boys in general do less well in reading than girls—one reason is the smaller corpus callosum. The brain that will read better is the brain that can draw more heavily on both sides of the brain *at once,* which is what reading requires. The smaller corpus callosum in boys is also one of the reasons boys find it more difficult to identify with accuracy the emotions on another person's face. That, too, is an activity that is better done when more of the brain is being used.

If we could look with our X-ray vision even deeper into the brain, we would identify a neurotransmitter, serotonin, which inhibits aggressive behavior, and which exists in higher levels in girls than boys. Serotonin works with hormones secreted in the hypothalamus of the brain, hormones like testosterone. A boy's brain secretes more testosterone than a girl's *and* transmits less serotonin. Boys become all the more aggressive, girls less aggressive.

If we could continue our X-ray journey into the brain we would notice, as has Rubin Gur at the University of Pennsylvania, structural differences in the way girls and boys use their left and right hemispheres. Gur uses brain-scan equipment to generate computer photographs of brains in use. He hooks males and females (college age and older) to the equipment, then gives them tests. The scanning equipment photographs the brain in different colors, each color showing a different degree of intense cortical activity. So the photographs end up looking like those maps we studied as children, where different heights each got their own color—mountain ranges different from plateaus, plateaus from deserts, deserts from oceans.

When males and females are asked to do a spatial task—like figure out how two objects fit together in space—most of the male's right hemisphere lights up in various colors representing various degrees of right hemisphere intensity. Much less of his left hemisphere lights up with higher degree colors. The colors and their intensity are pretty much equal on both sides of the female brain. This very visual and state-of-the-art process for putting our X-ray glasses into the brain gives us clear visual evidence of why males of all ages (except the very old) do on average better than females in spatial tasks—from complex use of blocks as children to architectural design as adults. The male brain is set up to be intensely spatial, the female brain is not.

On the other hand, Gur has shown through his process how the male brain is not set up to be verbal but the female is. When verbal skills are tested, much less of the male brain is used than the female, and the intensity of activity in the left hemisphere is increased in the female over the male.

Overall, brain research has shown how the female brain is at work in more sections than the male *just about all the time*. It is on call in a way the male is not. To use an analogy: the male brain turns on, like a machine, to do its task, then turns off; the female brain is always on. This is an exaggeration, of course, for parts of the male brain are also always on, but when Gur compares the two brains in non-active states, the difference between the constantly "on" female brain and "on/off" male brain is startling.

This difference is a primary reason males are so "task-oriented," testing out as less able than females to do a number of different kinds of tasks at once; and why males react to interruptions in their thinking with more of a sense of invasion than females tend to, and combined with testosterone-based aggression, more forcefully.

Brain Differences and Your Children

Once I was speaking to a school group about brain differences. Sally, a mother of one boy and two girls, told me:

> My son is just like his father. He spreads things all over the floor, taking up more space than his sisters. It's like having a huge dinosaur living in the house. His sister can draw in a neat stack on the table, not Sandy. He's got to pretend the whole world belongs to him. Does this stuff about space relate to the way his brain works?

Sally hit the nail on the head. Boys tend to use up far more space than girls. When my daughter was in daycare, our friend and daycare provider once complained to me about three brothers, ages five through nine, she looked after. They were always active, always throwing things, "uncontrollable." I suggested she send them outside more. As I said it, she realized what common sense it was. It had crossed her mind too, but she hadn't acted on it. "I just wish they'd do what I say in here. Why should I have to give them special treatment?"

Yet her daycare space was very small. When she did make more space for the antsy boys, both inside her house by converting another basement room for "the boys," and by letting all the kids go outside more (supervised, of course), she discovered that her discipline problems decreased.

So often the boy's brain cries out to us like these boys did: "Give me more space!"

The boy's brain tries to recreate itself in the outside world by creating and playing games—like basketball, football, etc.—that fill large spaces and challenge the male brain to hone its skill at moving objects through space. The girl's brain tries to recreate itself in the outside world by creating situations and playing games—like house, doll life, imagined community life—that use lots of verbal skills, require lots of one-on-one communication between actors, and involve overtly complex emotional behavior.

Here are a few other behavioral differences you might notice between boys and girls—differences that begin in the brain.

From infancy, boys look at objects for shorter but more active periods than girls do. Girls pay attention longer than boys. This tendency continues throughout a boy's life. When parents complain that boys don't pay attention, part of the reason is innate. One thing parents find helpful in getting boys to pay attention is to wrap the activity or theme they want attended to around a concomitant activity involving objects moving in space—whether in a game, on the computer, or in a physical job.

Boys and men take in less sensory or "proximal" data than girls and women. They smell less, taste less, get less soothing and input from tactile information, hear less, and see less.

Let's take hearing as an example. Girls complain that boys don't listen, women complain that men don't hear, people don't feel heard by boys and men. This begins from the very beginning of life, in the brain. Males in general hear in one ear better than in the other. Females in general hear more data and hear equally well in both ears. All the way through life, males hear less than females say, which creates profound problems in relationships. Boys from very early on are reported to ignore voices, even parents' voices, more than girls do. In some of these cases, they are simply not hearing. Boys also do less well than girls at picking out background noises. Boys, quite simply, hear less background noise and differentiate less. This is one of the reasons parents and anyone around a boy often report having to speak more loudly to the boy than to a girl.

When parents or educators feel unheard by boys, some of the frustration needs to be replaced by an understanding of how the boy's brain is working. If he's not hearing, try another sense—especially the visual, which is the boy's best sense on average. Also try to get the message to him through stories, games, objects that move through space. Start by learning which is his better ear.

It probably comes as no surprise to anyone that girls and women want prolonged touch more than boys and men. The brain has set us up this way. Boys, especially as they get older, often feel demanded upon when they are forced to hug, etc. Simultaneously, girls often feel diminished and unloved when they don't get a higher amount of prolonged physical touch. Much of this is hard-wired by the brain.

Boys do better with visual problems and interpreting visual information when it is presented to their left eye—the one that feeds the right hemisphere, their strongest hemisphere, the hemisphere that specializes in spatial relationships. Girls do equally well with visual information no matter which eye it's presented to. Even in infancy, boys gaze at their mothers one half the amount of time girls do. Often mothers feel they are doing something wrong with their boys, or feel unloved because the boy doesn't seem to attend to their face for as prolonged a period of time. The real reason for his quick visual fix, then eye movement to whatever objects are in the room, lies in his brain's need to move quickly from object to object in space.

Television, videogames, and the whole computer culture is very much a creation of the male brain. It is predominantly a visual means of communication, providing lots of quick moving images and objects moving through virtual space. Televisions and computers can, of course, be used too much, at the expense of a boy's development of other senses. But still, it is important to realize that when a boy channel surfs and a girl wants him to stay on one program for a longer period of time, or when a boy seems preverbal unless he's at his computer, rather than say to ourselves, "Let's change that boy," we'd be better off saying, "Let's help that boy expand who he is through the skills he already enjoys."

Boys have three times more reading difficulties than girls. Preschool boys often come into their verbal skills up to a year later than girls. On the other hand, they test out on average better at math than girls. The brain holds the key. Math is an abstract, spatial construct of the right hemisphere. Boys will on average do better at it. Verbal skills originate in the left hemisphere. Girls on average do better at them.

These brain differences continue robustly throughout male and female life. Females tend to choose ways of relating, people to relate to, and jobs that utilize their verbal and empathy skills and thus will make them feel comfortable. When the hormonal and emotional drive to mate takes over, they will often choose mates who do not verbalize well, have lower empathy skills, and so on. But for the most part, girls pick girls to relate to. By the same token, boys pick boys to relate to.

This is not to say romance and other kinds of social life can't lead a man and woman or boy and girl to gain the skills of the other sex, or that parents and educators can't teach children and adults the skills of the other brain, or that boys relating to girls and girls to boys is somehow antineurological. Those sorts of interpretations are overreactions. A rich community life means relating to as many people as are helpful to community spirit. Brain information is a pathway to a child-raising system in which boys and girls discover who they are in large part by seeking out the people, both peers and elders, of the same sex with whom they feel comfortable, and innately at one.

How the Different Brains Were Created

When we talked about testosterone we talked about how our male and female ancestors adapted to life and brought their very different hormones along with them. They did the same with the brain.

Until about 10,000 years ago, when we shifted to agriculturally based societies, we spent millions of years hunting and gathering. Females carried and birthed the babies, took care of home and local governing, and "gathered" food and nesting material from the local agricultural environment. Males inseminated females, formed intra-local alliances, and hunted over millions of years. The female brain developed to do well at what survival required it to do; the male brain did the same.

It is no wonder, then, that the female brain should be better at sensory data. It needed to hear, smell, touch, taste, and see more minutely and effectively than the male because children's cues are more subtle than a lion's or a deer's, and because gathering roots and tubes, and figuring out which ones are poison, needs more sensory excellence as well.

It is no wonder, too, that the female brain developed better handling of emotive data. Kids and local community life required more emotive processing strength than did large or very isolated hunting parties, which were single-task focused rather than multi-task focused.

It is no wonder the male brain developed better spatial capacities. Hunting needs a very acute sense of dimensionality, depth perception, and distance.

It is no wonder the male brain developed better abstraction skills. Hunting, then large-population society building and edifice building, required an acute sense of abstract design.

Given, too, the daily necessity of the male to kill animals and, in war or other protection activity, humans, it is no wonder the male brain de-emphasized emotive and verbal skills, as well as empathy skills.

These different brains developed so our ancestors could survive. These brains are still in us. They will not change biologically or structurally for countless years. If we train these brains well, they can help us not only survive but spiritually flourish. Through our understanding and nurturing of these aspects of a boy's nature, we can take better care of life itself.

Often people who are aware of the evolution of brain differences will worry that if we nurture boys according to how their brains and hormones work, we'll be saying, "Boys will be boys." They fear that in saying this we'll be nurturing more violence, destructiveness, less intimacy with spouses and children, and more sexual stereotypes that will keep women out of architecture, engineering, and police work and keep men wary of social work, daycare, and primary parenting. This does not need to be the case. Knowledge of the evolution of brain differences teaches us that societies are capable of creating intimate and fruitful human relationships that nurture *both* the best of the female and best of the male brains. Our mistake is not in letting "boys be boys"; it's in letting boys be boys without the proper care, love, and discipline.

Essential also as we adapt our growing knowledge of brain differences to our own parenting and living is to look at how we have defined intimacy between people, especially women and men. Perhaps the single most important influence on our boys is how they see their parents be intimate. We live in a time and culture that defines how people should be intimate through the X-ray vision of the female brain—most self-help books are about how men are too absent, too incapable of intimacy, and how women know how to be close but men don't. *The standard most of these books use is the female brain's standard.* Our marriages, and thus the way we raise our kids, will change significantly for the better when we develop a standard that honors both the male and the female brain. Thoughts along this direction are the focus of books like John Grey's *Things Your Mother Couldn't Tell You and Your Father Didn't Know,* Harville Hendrix's *Getting the Love You Want,* my own *Love's Journey,* and videotapes for couples put out by Gary Smalley, Barbara DeAngelis, and The Learning Channel, on Brain Sex.

The Way Boys Feel: Feelings and the Brain

Once at a training I was doing for Big Brothers and Big Sisters, a case worker shared this story with me. She had been working with a single mom whose son had been a "crier," her word for a boy who cried on her chest when he was hurt, like any little boy would. But then sometime around seven or eight he stopped crying. "He changed," the mom reported. "He used to be honest with me about his feelings, but around eight he started keeping to himself more, he wanted more fighting, he kind of turned away from me. Once he told me I was no good to him. I just nagged him and wouldn't let him be."

Many mothers notice changes between five years old and ten years old in the way their sons process feelings and take care of their emotional needs. This mom's observations caused her pain, yet what was happening to her son was normal. Even given the other external factors in their lives—the father's departure from the home, the mom's return to work, an elder brother's exit from the home to live with dad—still, the eight-year-old boy's way of processing feeling was forming into a way he would use throughout his life.

The male brain and hormones give a boy a natural tendency toward processing feeling and emotion in a very "male" way. This way becomes quite clear by the age of ten, or if not by then, certainly by the time puberty hits.

There is a great deal of cultural misunderstanding of how boys process feelings, just as there are huge cultural expectations of the way some people want boys to process feelings. Boys are in their way "sensitive" and "compassionate." That is a given. Every person has this capability. And boys can always be trained to become more sensitive and empathic toward others than they are. These are givens. But still, their testosterone and brain wire them naturally to process their feelings and react emotionally in some boy-specific ways, and it is traumatic to try to make a boy change the very way he processes his own feelings. They are his, no one else's, and he needs to be able to do them his way.

How Boys Experience Their Feelings and Emotions

Here are eight internal processing methods favored by males. You'll notice as you read them that they grow logically out of things we've learned about testosterone and about the brain.

1. *The action-release method.* Boys process and release feeling in quick bursts of displayed energy. Often they angrily yell at us, or "fly off the handle," or slam a door, or hit their fist into a table, or "turn us off" and bury themselves in some activity, like a videogame. They are processing and releasing feeling through action. Sometimes this feels like rejection to us because they are processing the feeling through actions that seem to isolate us or even seem dangerous.

2. *The suppression-delayed reaction method.* Males are wired for a certain degree of delayed reaction. The male brain is very much a problem-solving brain, so it delays emotional reactions in order to solve a problem. It is very common to see boys who do not come to their parents with problems they've had in school until a week or more later. The boy is irritable or "a little off kilter" for a week, then finally allows us to help him get at what's bugging him, then in expressing it realizes it has been bugging him. Often the boy never even realized he had experienced emotional pain or trauma. Our best strategy when we see a boy in suppression-delayed reaction is to be patient, let him know we're there, and as always with boys, show him that a safe structure exists for him to continue living his life despite his twisted insides.

3. *The displacement-objectification method.* Let's say a boy I'm with is angry but won't talk about it. We happen to walk by a car that's dented. I say, "I'll bet that car is pissed off to have been smashed up that way. Look how pretty that chrome was, look how someone waxed that car up, and now some putz trashed the car. Sometimes I

feel like that. I feel like I've done my best and I just get trashed anyway. I know you feel like that sometimes . . ."

This is a strategy we use that acknowledges the boy's tendency to make objects even of emotions, to project emotions into outside space, and to displace emotional responses from original sources to safe, inanimate receptacles. If I can get the boy to put his emotional experiences into a story on a movie screen or a piece of mythology or a personal story involving objects around him, he is more likely to be able to talk. This often works much better than saying to him, "What's wrong, tell me, I'm sitting across the table from you, talk to me," and meaning "I've got only a few minutes, so just talk already." Boys often need us to give them more time than girls need, and they often need us to connect their feelings to objects in the outside world.

4. *Physical-expression method.* Boys will experience, express, and expel their feelings physically to a greater degree than girls (on average). This is, of course, common sense to everyone. In order to facilitate this method of expression, we must give boys enough physical space, enough disposable objects, and enough training in boundaries of physical space and disposability. The father who puts a punching bag in the basement and says, "This is your space. Come here when you need to, punch the bag when you need to" is wisely giving the son an object and a space. Simultaneously, he must teach the son that punching bags and having physical space is not to be confused with giving the boy carte blanche to punch anything or anyone. Just the opposite: by providing the boy with space and receptacle, the father is showing the son the proper boundaries for his feelings. "When they overwhelm you," he is teaching, "you bring them here. They will be contained here. When you return to the company of others, you'll know how to bring your feelings appropriately back to others because you've felt them cleanly here."

5. *The going-into-the-cave method.* Boys on average do not process feelings as quickly as girls. The social anthropologist Jennifer James told me of a study that showed males can take up to seven hours longer than females to process "hard emotive data"—in other words, stimulation that requires complex emotive responses. Boys often feel overwhelmed by a mother's swirl of feelings, sisters' myriad verbalizings of feelings. They often need time away, just time in the cave of their room, or a fort, to get away from the stimulation.

With boys who go into the cave a lot, it is essential that caregivers hold them accountable once they come out. That is, if we let the boy walk away while we're trying to get him to process emotional material, we must make sure we have his general agreement that once he's processed it, he'll bring the insights back to the family, the relationship. Boys often need us to show them that it's okay to go into the cave and it's essential that the boy feel good about coming out of the cave, (and we'll be waiting) to be reaccepted and refined by his insights.

6. *The talking-about-feelings method.* Most parents have noticed how hard it is, once the boy is seven, eight, or older to get a boy to process his feelings by talking about them. It's a lot easier to ask him later what he felt; at the time the experience is happening, he often just does not know what he feels and feels invaded when we force him to say what he does not know.

Because the two halves of the male brain are connected by a smaller group of fibers—the corpus callosum—than in the female brain, we can expect males in general to have greater difficulty than females expressing feelings. Information flows less easily from the right side of the brain to the verbal, left side. As the male and female brains mature in the first decade of life, then through the hormonal adjustments of puberty, we see boys getting less and less able to connect feeling and verbal information in comparison to girls. So, often, talking about feelings with boys does not work like it works for girls.

On the other hand, we have to keep trying. We have to pick and choose the right moment to ask him, "How do you feel?" Or "How was that (experience) for you?" Timing is everything here. We may need to wait until he's in a place where he feels emotionally safe. We may need to ask once, wait a few moments, then let it go—letting him come to us on *his* timing. Boys who are constantly asked how they feel will, for a while, feel good that their caregiver cares so much; but soon, if we just keep prodding the boy to talk about his feelings and he won't, what he's doing inside is building up resentment.

7. *The problem-solving method.* Often boys do not invest as much emotive energy in certain low-level problems as we think they do or think they should. For boys, the solving of a problem often releases the emotive energy of the experience. With men, of course, this is frequently true as well. This is one reason males in general move to problem-solving as quickly as they can. Yes, part of it is that they've been trained that way, but most of it begins in their hormones and

brains—they see a problem, it agitates them, once they solve it they feel much better.

8. *The crying method.* In his classic story of boyhood, *The Little Prince,* Antoine de Saint-Exupéry wrote: "It is such a secret place, the land of tears." For boys, especially as they get older, it is secret indeed.

Boys, by the time they are school age, will cry only under very stressful and very safe circumstances. As their brains form more completely and testosterone dominates them more fully, they feel unsafe in the activity of crying, especially toward puberty. It is about the most vulnerable a boy can be. That vulnerability, in his natural composition, is frightening not only because culture teaches him not to cry but because in order to cry he must be processing hard emotive data at such a fast and confusing rate—something his brain, unlike the female's, is not as well wired to do—he feels he is losing himself.

Part of why boys (starting at about four or five) don't tend to cry as much as girls, or men as much as women, is certainly that we have taught them not to. Much of that teaching, however, has been a result of centuries of human understanding and acceptance of the male brain. Boys process a lot more of their feelings through other methods than tears—through action, through problem-solving, through displacement. As much as possible, we need to help boys perfect these methods because these methods are natural to them.

At the same time, we must realize that the danger in male biology is its tendency to repress feeling. "I don't know what I feel," a boy (or man) will say. "I just don't know, help me." This is a terrible problem for males. Thus, many of our cultural efforts to help boys and men feel more, even cry more, are worthwhile. Yet emboldening the male-specific methods might be more fruitful than some of the methods for sensitivity training in which we try to get males to talk about their feelings and cry on call. This is often unnatural for them, whether they are a boy or a man.

From Biology to Culture

Wherever we turn we see the biology of boyhood at work. We drive by the park and see boys playing football: developing self-image by moving an object through space in a highly organized way, following highly complex rules of spatial conduct.

We walk past the street B-ball court and see boys, shirtless, sweating, and dissing each other: moving an object through space in a competitive way while verbally one-upping each other.

We walk past a building and watch men constructing the building from ground up, first having abstracted the spatial dimensions, then designed them onto paper, then organized a team of people to build the building into the local geography of the land.

We enter the information age—its e-mail, computers, televisions, video-phones—and find the visually and spatially oriented male brain manifesting its best functioning onto computer screens.

We also face increased antisocial violence every day, by males, as the male brain and its recently untrained, undisciplined testosterone do increasing damage in the world.

Everywhere we turn we see male biology at work. Usually, though, we say to ourselves, "There's those boys again, forming their boy society, their boy culture. Look how they've been socialized. If only we could change it." We say, "that masculine culture has got to go. It trains males to stare at TVs, keep women out of the workplace, play violent games, and make war." We say, "Male culture and female culture—they'll never get along. Let's change one or the other."

What about boy culture? What can we do about it? Or, more helpfully, what can we do for it? It will form whether we like it or not because the male brain will create it. The question we must answer as parents, mentors, and educators is: Will we guide it, or turn away from it in confusion and fear?

NOTES

The material about the effects of sex-different brain and hormonal systems is very controversial. One physiologist will come to one conclusion about pieces of it, one endocrinologist to another. Researchers argue vehemently over the quality of sources of research. The only thing all researchers agree on is that human beings are each individuals, with sex differences existing on a spectrum rather than at polar oppositions.

My own research into the biology of boyhood relies on three primary sources: biological material, anthropological material, and personal observations. I have been able to resolve the ambiguity and controversy to my own satisfaction by taking specific items of brain research and comparing them individually with historical and anthropological trends, then confirming those "hard science" and "soft science" facts with personal observations of 1990s' boys and families.

When, for instance, brain research tells me a boy will tend, because of his testosterone and brain structure, to process emotive information in a certain way, I will see if anthropological information indicates that tribes and societies have set up cultures and left cultural residues that support that biological trend, and I will observe boys in my life and work for that trend. If all three confirm each other, I feel comfortable that the brain research is robust.

NATURE VERSUS NURTURE Many researchers in the fields of evolutionary biology and brain science have discovered the same things simultaneously. The fact about how testosterone and the male brain work are gleaned from a number of sources the reader might want to pursue simultaneously.

The most valuable resource I've discovered—packed with information and delightfully readable—is *Brain Sex,* by Anne Moir, Ph.D., and David Jessel. *Brain Sex* culls information from endocrinology, neurology, and numerous other medical journals. I suggest it as a place to begin if you are looking for a book-length work. The material is primarily from the following sources:

Mary Batten. *Sexual Strategies.* Los Angeles: Tarcher/Putnam, 1992.
T. Berry Brazelton, and Bertrand G. Cramer. *The Earliest Relationship.* Reading, Massachusetts: Addison-Wesley, 1990.
Helen Fisher. *Anatomy of Love.* New York: Fawcett, 1992.
Lynn Margulis and Dorion Sagan. *Mystery Dance.* New York: Summit Books, 1991.
Anne Moir and David Jessel. *Brain Sex.* New York: Laurel, 1989.
Sheila Moore and Roon Frost. *The Little Boy Book.* New York: Ballantine, 1986.
Robert Pool. *Eve's Rib.* New York: Crown Publishers, 1994.
Carl Sagan and Ann Druyan. *Shadows of Forgotten Ancestors.* New York: Random House, 1992.
Robert Wright. *The Moral Animal.* New York: Vintage, 1994.

In presenting research of this kind, textbooks in the medical field become essential, as does the assistance of individuals trained in the medical sciences. Darl W. Vander Linden, Ph.D., and Jeff Hedge, D.O., were of invaluable assistance in helping me interpret medical information, and in providing me the use of their textbooks:

Eric R. Kandel, James H. Schwartz, and Thomas M. Jessel. *Essentials of Neural Science and Behavior.* Norwalk, Connecticut: Appleton & Lange, 1995.

Constance R. Martin. *Textbook of Endocrine Physiology.* New York: Oxford
    University Press, 1976.
Arthur C. Guyton. *Textbook of Medical Physiology.* Philadelphia: W. B. Saun-
    ders and Company, 1976.

Since *Time* magazine ran an article on brain differences as its cover
story on January 20, 1992, other magazines have followed suit. More
recently, *Newsweek* ran a cover story on brain differences (March 27,
1995). The November 28, 1994, issue of the *New Republic* featured an
article by Robert Wright, "The Moral Animal," comparing feminist views
with evolutionary theory. These articles are well worth looking at if you
don't have time to go through whole books on the subject.

THE PRIME MOVER: TESTOSTERONE
Don and Jeanne Elium. *Raising a Son.* Hillsboro, Oregon: Beyond Words, 1992.
Moore and Frost, *The Little Boy Book.*

TESTOSTERONE AND AGGRESSION
Margulis and Sagan, *Mystery Dance.*
Sagan and Druyan, *Shadows of Forgotten Ancestors.*
Batten, *Sexual Strategies.*
Brazelton and Cramer, *The Earliest Relationship.*

TESTOSTERONE, PUBERTY, AND BEYOND
Moir and Jessel, *Brain Sex.*
Wardell B. Pomeroy. *Boys and Sex.* New York: Delacorte, 1991.
Holly Nadler, "My Life as a Man," *LEARS,* December 1993.

TESTOSTERONE AND TENSION
Elium and Elium, *Raising a Son.*

HOW A BOY THINKS: THE MALE BRAIN
Moir and Jessel, *Brain Sex.*

STRUCTURAL DIFFERENCES IN THE BRAIN
Moir and Jessel, *Brain Sex.*
Moore and Frost, *The Little Boy Book.*
The Learning Channel, "Brain Sex" (a three-part video series based on the
    book).
Michael D'Antonio, "The Fragile Sex," *LA Times magazine,* December 4, 1994.

BRAIN DIFFERENCES AND *YOUR* CHILDREN
Brazelton and Cramer, *The Earliest Relationship*.
Moir and Jessel, *Brain Sex*.

HOW THE DIFFERENT BRAINS WERE CREATED
Margulis and Sagan, *Mystery Dance*.
Sagan and Druyan, *Shadows of Forgotten Ancestors*.
Wright, *The Moral Animal*.

THE WAY BOYS FEEL: FEELINGS AND THE BRAIN
Moir and Jessel, *Brain Sex*.

6

DO GIRLS AND BOYS HAVE DIFFERENT CULTURES?

Barrie Thorne

. . . a play of differences that is always on the move,
and can neither be reduced to gender differences
nor considered apart from them.

—Edward Snow, "The Play of Sexes in Bruegel's *Children's Games*"

A FAMILIAR STORY LINE runs through the literature on gender and the social relations of children. The story opens by emphasizing patterns of mutual avoidance between boys and girls and then asserts that this daily separation results in, and is perpetuated by, deep and dichotomous gender differences. Groups of girls and groups of boys have contrasting ways of bonding and expressing antagonism and conflict; they act upon different values and pursue divergent goals; in many ways they live in separate worlds. The story often concludes by drawing lessons for adults.[1] For example, in one popularized version, Deborah Tannen argues that because they grew up in the gender-separated worlds of childhood, adult men and women are locked into patterns of miscommunication, with women repeatedly seeking intimacy, while men are preoccupied with marking status.[2]

Reading the social science literature and sorting through my own observations, I have circled around and around this influential portrayal. The separate-and-different worlds story is seductive. It gives full weight to the fact that girls and boys often *do* separate in daily interactions, especially when they create more lasting groups and friendships. The marking of boundaries between groups of boys and groups of girls further drives the genders apart and creates spaces in which they can build and teach different cultures. And when I, like other observers, have compared the dynamics of groups of girls with those of groups of boys, I have been struck by apparent differences.

Furthermore, boys and girls—the "native informants"—sometimes use different rhetorics to describe their same-gender relationships: boys talk about "buddies," "teams," and "being tough," whereas girls more often use a language of "best friends" and "being nice." And when girls and boys come together, they occasionally comment on experiences of gender difference. When a troupe of Ashton sixth-grade girls grabbed a football from the ongoing play of a group of boys, the aide tried to reason with the warring parties by asking the boys, "Why can't the girls play football with you?" The boys hotly replied, "They don't do it our way. They can't tackle; when we tackle 'em, they cry." A similar episode emerged on the Oceanside playground when a group of girls vied with a group of boys for use of a foursquare court. The adult on yard duty tried to resolve the dispute by suggesting that the girls and boys join into one game. This time the girls protested, saying, "They don't play our way." One of the girls later explained, "The boys slam the ball, and we don't."

In short, much of what has been observed about girls and boys, especially in the relationships they create apart from the surveillance of adults, can be fitted into the model of "different worlds or cultures." But as I've tried to line up that model with my own empirical observations and with the research literature, I have found so many exceptions and qualifications, so many incidents that spill beyond and fuzzy up the edges, and so many conceptual ambiguities, that I have come to question the model's basic assumptions.

I have aired one major objection to the model of "different cultures": it implies that girls and boys are always apart and gives no theoretical attention to the moments of "with" and comfortable sharing. Girls and boys interact in many families, as well as in neighborhoods, churches, and schools, but the different-cultures model basically ignores these experiences. Here I add other criticisms of the different-cultures approach: it embeds the experiences of dominants and marginalizes many other groups and individuals; and it collapses "a play of differences that is always on the move" (in Edward Snow's compelling phrase) into static and exaggerated dualisms. The different-cultures framework gains much of its appeal from stereotypes and ideologies that should be queried rather than built on and perpetuated as social fact. It is, I have concluded, simply inadequate as an account of actual experience and is, in many ways, a conceptual dead end.

But before I unravel and then create a more complex account, I knit a fuller portrayal of the "different cultures of boys and girls," drawing on the extensive literature that is organized along those lines. I use my own data in the initial knitting *and* in the unraveling and reknitting in order to demonstrate that the same realities can be seen in varied ways and to argue that the complex reknitting is the more insightful version. I frame the initial portrayal in the tone of factual assertion found in the literature; my doubting voice comes later. The generalizations center on ages nine to twelve, although parts of the portrayal are echoed in studies ranging from preschool through high school.

Contrasting the Different Cultures of Boys and Girls

After emphasizing patterns of avoidance and separation between boys and girls, the different-cultures portrayal shifts to a series of contrasts. The structure and dynamics of boys' groups are usually described first, organized around a series of key characteristics—large, public, hierarchical, competitive—that are then contrasted with the features of all-girls' groups—smaller, more private and cooperative, and focused on relationships and intimacy. The strategy of contrast is often built into the design of research, for example, sociolinguists separately tape the interactions of groups of boys and groups of girls and then look for differences. Working from the contrastive model in the initial analysis of my fieldnotes, I also went searching for group gender difference. I highlighted the incidents that fit the prevailing generalizations about, and cultural images of, boy-boy versus girl-girl interactions. But, as I later discuss, I also found many incidents that contradicted the model, which, along with various theoretical concerns, gradually led me to question the dualistic approach.

The Boys' World

Contrasts between the world of boys and the world of girls usually begin with themes of location and size. Boys more often play outdoors, and their activities take up much more space than those of girls.[3] As Janet Lever has argued in much-cited articles comparing the play of fifth-grade boys and girls, boys' groups tend to be larger. They form "flocks," "gangs," "teams," or groups of "buddies," while girls organize themselves into smaller, more intimate groups and friendship pairs.[4]

Many researchers have reported that boys engage in more rough-and-tumble play and physical fighting than do girls.[5] In a description of the chasing melees on an Ashton playground, boys more often grabbed one another from behind, pinned down one another's arms, pushed and shoved, wrestled one another to the ground, and continually pressed the ambiguous line between "play" and "real" fighting. When girls chased other girls, they pushed and pinned from behind, but they rarely shoved one another down or ended up wrestling, and their physical encounters never resulted in physical injury.

In separate observational studies, Raphaella Best, Janet Schofield, and Andy Sluckin found that boys' talk, as well as their actions, frequently revolve around themes of physical strength and force.[6] On the first day of Mrs. Smith's kindergarten class when Karl loudly announced, "I'm tough," a chorus of boys (but no girls) joined in: "I'm tough too"; "Me too"; "Me too"; "My daddy says I'm tough." In the Ashton cafeteria I listened to a group of fourth-grade boys talk excitedly about a game they called "tackle": "You push 'em down, or you trip 'em." "When they're running real fast, that's when you trip 'em; I jump on 'em." "We play anything that's fun and rough, don't we, Tom?"

Standing near the "boys' side" of the fourth-fifth–grade classroom in Oceanside, I more often heard verbal threats than when I stood near the "girls' side." The threats—"Shut up Kevin, or I'll bust your head"; "I'm gonna punch you"—were sometimes issued in annoyance or anger, and sometimes in a spirit of play. Groups of boys in both schools talked at length about who had and could "beat up" whom. And when arguments erupted into serious physical fights, crowds gathered on the playground, and talk stretched out the events for hours.

It is often asserted that boys' social relations tend to be overtly hierarchical and competitive. They repeatedly negotiate and mark rank through insults, direct commands, challenges, and threats.[7] John, the highest-status boy in Miss Bailey's classroom, successfully directed the actions of the other boys (and one girl) in the bonded group of seven or eight that seemed to anchor "the boys' world." John, who was the tallest boy in the class and one of the best athletes in the school, deftly handled challenges to his authority. Dennis, who was not very good at sports or at academics, was at the other end of the pecking order. John and the rest of the group called Dennis "Dumbo" and insulted him in other ways; in a kind of ritual submission, Dennis more or less accepted the insults.

Not only do boys compete in sports; they also, as Best has observed, turn other activities into contests.[8] On the Oceanside playground I watched four boys from Miss Bailey's classroom start to climb up the "dirt pile" at the edge of the grassy playing field. As they climbed and compared the gripping power of their shoes, Matt suggested that they have "a falling contest; see who can fall the farthest," which they proceeded to do, negotiating and arguing about the rules as they climbed and slid. On the wintry Ashton playground I watched a similar episode: a group of boys competed to see who could slide the farthest on a patch of ice. Contests sometimes take the form of bragging, as in a classroom interaction on the "boys' side" of Miss Bailey's classroom. Bill began, "I got a science lab." Matt retorted, "I got a zoom 750 microscope." Bill replied, "So what, I got a telescope." Freddie chimed in, "I got an 880 microscope." Matt, "There isn't such a thing. My dad has a 750." This kind of technical talk was also more typical of boys' than of girls' conversations.

Lever has argued that the larger size of boys' groups, and their preoccupation with competition and with relative position, may be related to their involvement in organized sports, both as a favored activity, and as a metaphor for their social relations (boys sometimes talk about their cliques as "teams" with a "captain"). She contrasts the complex structure of team sports (many separate and independent positions; a large number of explicit rules) with the simpler, turn-taking structure of "girls' games" like hopscotch and jump rope.[9] I also noted that more Oceanside and Ashton boys than girls were caught up in team sports, both on the playground and in later conversations, when they retold their sports encounters, play by play.

Boys like to make and argue about rules, and they also collectively break them more often than girls do. Combining our data from Massachusetts, Michigan, and California, Zella Luria and I noted that boys more often publicly violated rules, for example, against saying "dirty words" on the playground. Their larger numbers give a degree of anonymity and support for transgression that is lacking in girls' friendship pairs. Boys bond through the risk of rule-breaking and through aggressing against other boys (called "girls," "fags," or "sissies") who are perceived to be weaker. Boys also bond by aggressing against girls.[10]

The Girls' World

The different-cultures literature contrasts the larger, hierarchical groups of boys with the smaller groups that girls typically form—pairs of "best friends" linked in shifting coalitions.[11] These pairs are not "marriages"; the pattern is more one of dyads moving into triads, since girls often participate in two or more pairs at one time, resulting in quite complex social networks. Girls often talk about who is "best friends with," "likes," or is "being mean to" whom. Relationships sometimes break off, and girls hedge bets by structuring networks of potential friends. Girls often carry out the activity of constructing and breaking dyads and maneuvering alliances through talk with third parties.[12] In her vivid memoirs, Toth recalls the intense but unstable friendships, the staking of rival claims, and the "triangles of tension" among her and her close friends.[13]

This pattern of shifting alliances, wrapped in skeins of talk, was especially evident among three of the girls in Miss Bailey's class. Jessie frequently said that Kathryn, the most popular girl, was her "best friend." Kathryn didn't proclaim the friendship as often; she also played and talked a lot with Judy. After watching Kathryn talk to Judy during a transition period in the classroom, Jessie went over, took Kathryn aside, and said in an accusing tone, "You talk to Judy more than me." Kathryn responded defensively, "I talk to you as much as I talk to Judy."

In gestures of intimacy that one rarely sees among boys, girls stroke or comb their friends' hair.[14] They notice and comment on one another's physical appearance such as haircuts or clothes, and they borrow and wear one another's sweatshirts or sweaters. (In contrast, touch among boys is rarely relaxed and affectionate; they express solidarity through the ritual handslap of "giving five," friendly teasing, and through the guise of mock violence—pushing, poking, grabbing from behind—whose context affirms good feelings.)

Among girls, best friends monitor one another's emotions.[15] They share secrets and become mutually vulnerable through self-disclosure, with an implicit demand that the expression of one's inadequacy will induce the friend to disclose a related inadequacy. In contrast, when a boy discloses a weakness to other boys, it is far more likely to be exposed to others through joking and a kind of collective shaming. Boys tend to be more self-protective than girls.

On school playgrounds, as Lever and others have documented, girls are less likely than boys to play team sports. They more often engage in small-scale, turn-taking, cooperative kinds of play, and by fifth and sixth grades many of them spend recess standing around and talking.[16] When they jump rope or play on the bars, girls take turns performing and watching others perform in stylized movements that may involve considerable skill. On both playgrounds I saw girls work out group choreographies, counting and jumping rope in unison, or swinging around the bars. In other synchronized body rituals, clusters of fifth- and sixth-grade girls practice cheerleading routines or dance steps.

Thus, the different-cultures literature concludes, boys stress position and hierarchy, whereas girls emphasize the construction of intimacy and connection. Girls affirm solidarity and commonality, expressing what has been called an "egalitarian ethos." In a study of conversations among children in an urban African-American neighborhood, Marjorie Harness Goodwin found that when they were engaged in shared tasks, groups of boys more often used direct commands ("go get the pliers") that marked hierarchy, while groups of girls more often used language like "let's" and "we gotta" that generated action in a collaborative way. The girls also criticized girls who acted conceited, or seemed to place themselves above the others.[17] Donna Eder has described the "cycle of popularity" among junior high girls, whom other girls seek to befriend, but also resent because they stand out from the others.[18]

Although they talk about being "nice," girls are far from goody two-shoes; beneath that rhetoric and overt concern with group harmony often lies considerable tension and conflict.[19] But the conflict is not expressed as directly as among boys. Goodwin found that girls more often talked about the offenses of other girls in their absence, as I noticed during an extended argument between Jessie and Kathryn. When their friendship was in a rocky period, they each told third parties that the other was "mean," and Jessie called Kathryn names like "flywoman" behind her back but rarely to her face. The protracted dispute, much of it carried out through reports to and by third parties, illustrates the indirect forms more characteristic of conflict among girls than among boys.[20]

Problems with the Different-Cultures Approach

The central themes of the different-cultures portrayal—large versus small, public versus private, hierarchy versus connection—operate like well-worn grooves on a dirt road; when a new study is geared up, the wheels of description and analysis slide into the contrastive themes and move right along. This path may be compelling because it evokes experience; adults have seen groups of boys insulting and challenging one another and girls negotiating who is "best friends" with whom. These patterns may also resonate with childhood memories. I, for one, remember a time in the fourth grade when Kitty, my best friend, and I had a falling out. Feeling like an outcast, I took a pencil and paper and mapped the alliances then in place among the girls. My diagram indicated that Marlene was also without a best friend and hence the logical girl with whom to pair up. My problem was that I didn't like Marlene very much and couldn't force my feelings to abide by the logic.

But does the evocative power of these themes come solely from the force of reality, or in part from deep-seated cultural beliefs about "the nature" of girls compared with boys? Because the portrayal skirts around stereotypes (e.g., boys are tough, girls are nice), and because the contrastive grooves by no means cover all the pathways of experience, we should view the different-cultures approach with a degree of skepticism.

I will now give voice to the questions, to the array of "but what about . . . ?"s that kept popping up as I tried to fit my own observations into the dualistic framework. When I searched through my fieldnotes to see how they related to patterns put forward in the literature, I found that much of the supportive evidence came from my observations of the most popular kids in Miss Bailey's classroom. This tips off one central problem with the separate-and-different-worlds literature: not everyone has had an equal hand in painting the picture of what boys and girls are "like." Furthermore, because it is based on dichotomies, the different-cultures approach exaggerates gender difference and neglects within-gender variation, including crosscutting sources of division and commonality like social class and ethnicity. These facts seriously undermine the tidy set of contrasts that build up the different-cultures view, and they raise the challenge of how to grasp complex patterns of difference, and commonality, without perpetuating stereotypes.

Whose Experiences Are Represented?

In an early phase of my project, when I largely accepted the different-cultures framework, I went through my fieldnotes on Miss Bailey's fourth-fifth–grade class and tried to compare the dynamics of boys' groups with those of girls. During this search I felt like an explorer shining a flashlight on selected parts of a dark cave. Guided by prior expectations (e.g., that boys would move in larger, more hierarchical, and girls in small, more intimate groups), I could indeed light up those patterns in my fieldnotes. But the light mostly hovered around the "popular kids"—the group of six or seven boys (and one girl) who deferred to John as their leader, and, to a lesser degree, the dyads and triads that maneuvered around Kathryn, the most popular girl in the class. I am not alone; *a skew toward the most visible and dominant—and a silencing and marginalization of the others— can be found in much of the research on gender relations among children and youth.*

John's group was visible in part because it was the largest and most stable clique in the classroom, including John, Nick, Kevin, Allen, Tony, Jessie, Freddy, and Dennis at the margins or on the bottom, depending on one's perspective. Members of the group shared food, maneuvered to sit together, and called one another "buddies"; they routinely played team sports (soccer, baseball, and basketball, depending on the season) and talked about their games in the interstices of the school day. (Here lies a striking "but what about?" The group that seemed to anchor the boys' world included a girl, Jessie. She acted out what has been called "boys' culture" more dramatically than did many other boys in the classroom, and she was also part of a shifting alliance among girls. Not irrelevantly, she was the only African-American student in the classroom.)

John's group not only was large but also included the most popular boys in the classroom. Kathryn shared this source of visibility since she was by far the most popular girl. The lives of the popular often become public drama, and Kathryn's break ups and renewed affiliations with Jessie and Judy drew attention and even participation, as gossips and messengers, from the rest of the class. Kathryn also got more than her share of attention in my fieldnotes; socially constructed contours of visibility skew ethnographic reports.

THE "BIG MAN BIAS" IN RESEARCH ON BOYS What about the other boys? Apart from John's group, they did not hang out in large, bonded "gangs," "flocks," or "teams," as the literature claims boys do. Matt, Roger, Eddie, and Don were sociable and regularly played team sports, so they could be seen in large groups heading to and from the soccer or baseball fields. But they were not part of a stable clique. Others were loners, including Joel, who was overweight, afraid of sports, and brought extra food and fancy toys from home to gain momentary attention; Neil, who was shy and physically uncoordinated; and Bert, who was slow on the uptake and at the bottom of the class in academic performance. Miguel and Alejandro, the recent immigrants from Mexico, hung out on the playground with a group of Spanish-speaking boys and girls who played zone dodgeball day after day. Their mixed-gender experiences are, of course, totally obscured by the different-cultures approach, which assumes virtually total separation between boys and girls.

The relationships of four of the boys—Jeremy, Scott, Bill, and Don—fit the "dyad into triad" description better than relationships among any girls in the classroom, except for Kathryn, Jessie, and Judy.[21] Jeremy, who had a creative imagination, spun fantasy worlds with one other boy at a time—acting as detectives tracking footprints on the playground, or as Starsky and Hutch, the television police buddies. Jeremy and his partner of the moment would also share treasured objects; for example, Jeremy brought in a compass and put it in his desk. He loudly told Scott (thereby announcing it was off-bounds to everyone else), "You can take my compass, but don't let nobody touch it."

The identity of Jeremy's adventuring partner shifted between Scott and Bill via a "break up" process often claimed to be typical of girls. The boy on the outs would sometimes sulk and talk about the other two behind their backs. When Scott was excluded, he would activate a long-standing affiliation with Don; when Bill was on the outs, he went solo. Over the course of the school year I saw each of the shifting pairs—Jeremy and Bill; Jeremy and Scott; Scott and Don—celebrate themselves as "best buddies." Once Jeremy and Scott toasted each other ("Here's to you and me!") with milk cartons at lunch. The overall pattern fit the shifting alliances claimed to typify girls' social relations, but *boys* were the protagonists.

In short, when I mold my data into shapes provided by the literature characterizing boys' social relations (in this case, the claim that boys are organized into large, hierarchical groups), I have to ignore or distort the experiences of more than half the boys in Miss Bailey's classroom. And I am not alone. The literature on "the boys' world" suffers from a "Big Man bias" akin to the skew found in anthropological research that equates male elites with men in general.[22] In many observational studies of children in preschools and early elementary school, large, bonded groups of boys who are physically assertive, engage in "tough talk," and actively devalue girls anchor descriptions of "the boys' world" and themes of masculinity. Other kinds of boys may be mentioned, but not as the core of the gender story.[23]

By fourth grade, as in Miss Bailey's classroom, the Big Men are defined not only by physical self-assertion and group bonds, but also by their athletic skill. In the United States, ethnographers typically detail the social relations of older boys from the vantage point of a clique of popular athletes: "Don's group" in Robert Everhart's study of a junior high; "the athletic group" in Philip Cusick's ethnography of a high school; in a participant-observation study of Little League baseball teams, Gary Alan Fine chose the "leaders" as his chief informants.[24] I detect a kind of yearning in these books; when they went back to scenes from their earlier lives, the authors couldn't resist hanging out at the top. Cusick writes about his efforts to shake off male "isolates": "I was there to do a study not to be a friend to those who had no friends."[25]

British sociologists and anthropologists have done pioneering ethnographic research in schools and on "youth culture" more generally. This literature also has a systematic bias, but because Marxist assumptions guide the British researchers, the "Big Men" who get attention are the ones—again bonded in larger groups—who are working-class, flamboyantly masculine, and resisting dominant class structures. *Learning to Labor,* an ethnography done in a vocational high school in England, is the classic of this genre. The author, Paul Willis, focuses on "the lads," a group who created an oppositional culture of aggression and joking tied to the working-class masculine subculture of factory workers. The lads' subculture, different from that of more conforming boys (whom the lads called the "ear 'oles"), ironically helped reproduce their eventual position in the working class. We have yet to see an ethnography written from the experiences of more "conformist" working-class boys like the "ear 'oles."[26]

Bonded groups of boys who uphold stereotyped masculine values may grab the attention of ethnographers for a variety of reasons. Acting in groups increases the power of individuals, and the boys' groups that are most often studied exert added influence through the charisma of being popular or because they disrupt classroom order. Ruth Goodenough observed that in kindergartens one group of this kind can "set the tone" for the other boys and draw them into contempt for girls.[27] Bonded and disruptive male groups cause trouble for teachers; Vivian Paley, a kindergarten teacher, has reflected on her ambivalence toward a male "superhero clique," and Ellen Jordan has discussed the problems that bonded aggressive groups of boys raise for teachers in preschools in Australia. The eyes of school researchers are often linked to the eyes of teachers.[28]

Finally, large bonded groups of boys may get more than their share of attention because their talk and actions fit prevailing images of masculinity. And here the literature moves in a circle, carting in cultural assumptions about the nature of masculinity (bonded, hierarchical, competitive, "tough"), then highlighting behavior that fits those parameters and obscuring the varied styles and range of interactions among boys as a whole. For example, in his study of Little Leaguers, Fine observed a lot of variation from team to team, but when he writes specifically about "preadolescent male behavior," he emphasizes the themes of aggression and sexuality found, by his own statement, more often among the Sharpstones (the focus of his discussion of masculinity) than other teams. Fine's data seem far more complex than his generalizing claims about masculinity.[29]

In *Making the Difference*, a pathbreaking ethnography of class and gender relations among secondary school students in Australia, R. W. Connell and his colleagues argue that there are multiple masculinities, some hegemonic and others submerged or marginalized; the patterns are contradictory and continually negotiated. The authors also point to varied forms of femininity, ranging from the "emphasized" (a term they have chosen because masculinity claims ultimate hegemony over femininity) to less visible forms.[30] Connell and his colleagues observe that although powerfully symbolic, "hegemonic masculinity" and "emphasized femininity" are not necessarily the most common patterns. This useful approach pries open unitary notions of masculinity and femininity and raises the question of why and how some forms come to be seen as masculinity and femininity in general.

Kids of various ages themselves recognize varied, albeit stereotyped, ways of being a boy or a girl. I overheard two first-grade boys arguing about whether it's better to be "mean" or "nice." They sorted themselves and other boys into the typology; the self-professed "nice" boy also used the term "machos" and "show-offs" for the ones who were "mean." A woman of college age described three types of girls she remembered from her year in fifth grade: "cootie kissers," "ugly girls," and "nerdy girls." Another woman distinguished "fast," "pretty," "smart," and "tough" girls. A man recalled that in his fifth-grade class the boys fell into three types: "intellectual," "athletes," or "troublemakers."

By junior high and high school, named cliques, or "groups," as kids call them, consolidate; some are same-gender and others include both girls and boys. Joyce Canaan, an anthropologist who did extensive participant-observation in the middle school and high school of a suburban U.S. community, found that from sixth to eighth grade, kids' social relations became increasingly hierarchical. Middle-school girls and boys enacted a three-tiered ranking system: "popular" (with two "cool" subgroups, "jocks" and "freaks"), "middle," and "low" ("scums," "wimps," and "fags"—the latter two terms used for boys; "brains," including both boys and girls, had an ambiguous status). Students more often labeled and talked about the "popular" than other groups. Canaan found that over the course of high school the group system became more open and ambiguous; it was both present and not present as kids manipulated contradictory values.[31] Research of this kind helps challenge overly coherent and monolithic portrayals of "boys' culture" versus "girls' culture." (As I discuss later in this chapter, metaphors like "culture" and "world" are themselves part of the problem.)

WHAT ABOUT GIRLS? The different-cultures portrayal is as problematic for girls as it is for boys, although in both cases the conventional picture does illuminate some recurring patterns. Among the girls in Miss Bailey's classroom there were no large, bonded groups of the sort that John led.[32] And there indeed were "tense triangles" and shifting alliances, notably the axis of Kathryn, Jessie, and Judy. Judy also had strong ties to Connie, and Jessie bridged to John's group. Another shifting threesome, rife with conflict, encompassed Nancy, Jessica, and Shelly. Shelly was also friends with Lenore from the other fourth-grade classroom; together they formed the core of a wandering playground troupe. Sheila and Tracy, another pair, often hung out together, especially during baseball season when they journeyed across the playground to seek entry into the boys' games. Neera, Beth, Rosie, and Rita didn't seem to have close friends, at least not at school. As with the more isolated boys, their experiences spill beyond the generalizations.

The conventional emphasis on friendship pairs and shifting alliances masks not only the experience of those without intense affiliations, but also the complex range of girls' interactions. In some activities girls interact in large groups. For example, playground troupes sometimes included as many as five or six girls, and shifting groups of six to eight girls often played on the bars, talking, doing tricks, and sometimes lining up in a row to twirl their bodies in unison. Although games of jump rope and foursquare involved only three or four active players at any one time, other girls lined up waiting for a turn and joined in the general and often contentious disputes about whether a given player was out.

Drawing on a detailed study of fourth- and fifth-grade girls on a school playground, Linda Hughes has challenged the depiction of foursquare as a simple, turn-taking type of play. She notes that within the formal rules of the game, the focus of Lever's generalizations about turn-taking, there may be varied ways of playing. (When the Oceanside girls said that boys "slammed the ball" and didn't play foursquare "our way," they recognized this point.) Hughes found—and, alerted by her insights, I could also see this in my observations—that in their playing of foursquare, girls created "complex, large-group activity," elaborating a complicated structure of rules.[33] These patterns cannot be grasped if one adheres to Lever's contrast between the play of boys (large-scale, competitive, with complex rules) and that of girls (small-scale, cooperative, with a simple structure).[34] Girls, and not just boys, sometimes play in larger groups and negotiate and argue about rules.[35] In short, *separate-worlds dichotomies gloss the fact that interaction varies by activity and context.*[36]

This point is also central to Goodwin's research in an urban neighborhood. The girls who used collaborative language like "let's" and "we gotta" when they were engaged in the shared task of making rings out of bottles shifted to hierarchical interaction, repeatedly giving and obeying direct commands, when they played house.[37] And while these girls used more mitigated and indirect (e.g., gossip) forms of conflict among themselves, they used aggravated verbal forms, including insults, when they argued with boys.[38] Other researchers have also found that African-American girls, as well as boys, tend to be skilled in direct verbal conflict, and several studies also report insult exchanges among white working-class girls who value "being tough."[39] *Generalizations about "girls' culture" come primarily from research done with girls who are class-privileged and white; the experience of girls of other class, race, and ethnic backgrounds tends to be marginalized.*

My own fieldnotes contain enough instances of girls using insults, threats, and physical fighting to make me uncomfortable with the assertion that these behaviors are somehow distinctively "male." Girls directly insulted boys, and occasionally they insulted one another. One day on the Oceanside playground, Nancy held her legs apart, jumped up and down, and yelled, "Jessica goes to the toilet." Jessica bent her head, fighting off tears. Nancy then ran around Jessica saying, "Bye, hot dog. Jessica is Mr. Hot Dog." Jessica walked away, and Nancy ran behind her, jumping up and down like an ape. Then the bell rang and cut off the barrage of insults.

On another occasion, as Miss Bailey's class was gathering by the classroom door at the end of recess, Matt yelled, "You faggot!" at Nancy. Nancy, who was taller and bigger, ran after and knocked Matt down, pulled at his hair while she kicked him hard, and then walked away with a triumphant look on her face. Matt crumpled over and sobbed, "She pulled my hair." A group gathered round, discussing how "a girl beat him up."

Nancy was white. Jessie, who was Black, also didn't shrink from physical fights with boys; in fact, it was widely acknowledged that she could beat up any boy in the school. Both Nancy and Jessie were skilled at insulting and threatening ("Shut up or I'll punch you out"). It's true that these two girls were relatively exceptional compared with others in Miss Bailey's class. But either by ignoring the occasions when girls hurled insults, made threats, and got into serious physical fights, or by rendering them as forms of gender deviance, the different-cultures framework diverts us from examining important sources of complexity.

What Does It Mean to Have Different Cultures?

As the difficulties multiply, I find myself wanting to return to fundamentals: What does it *mean* to claim, as Deborah Tannen does, that "boys and girls grow up in what are essentially different cultures?"[40] The literature is often ambiguous. Sometimes the claims—for example, that girls' groups tend to be smaller than those of boys or that boys use more direct insults—clearly refer to the relative frequency of various patterns of behavior or social action. At other points, the claims seem to refer to the symbolic (normative, ideological, or discursive) dimensions of gender. For example, boys talk about "being tough" and girls talk about "being nice," and these discourses bring somewhat different meanings to what is sometimes similar behavior. When boys got into physical fights, kids talked differently than when a girl was involved; "a girl beat him up" added extra significance to Nancy's triumph over Matt.

Assertions about gender differences in actual behavior refer, at best, to *average* differences between girls and boys, or between groups of girls and groups of boys. The issue of relative frequency appears in words like "on average," "more than," and "tend to" that sprinkle through the contrastive rhetoric of different-worlds stories. Since qualitative researchers generally avoid careful counting, our "tend to"s and "more often"s are, at best, general impressions or perhaps "quasi statistics" gleaned from counting up descriptions in fieldnotes. But some of the evidence cited in the different-cultures literature comes from quantitative studies. The patterns are instructive.

For example, in a widely cited study of sex differences in rough-and-tumble play, Janet DiPietro coded observations of preschool girls and boys at play. Comparing boys and girls as groups, she found an unusually large difference: 15 to 20 percent of boys scored higher than any of the girls on the measure of rough-and-tumble play.[41] Nonetheless, as Carol Jacklin has observed, in this study "80 to 85 percent of the boys remain indistinguishable from 80 to 85 percent of the girls."[42] Rough-and-tumble play may be a "sex-related difference," but it is *not* a dichotomous difference since the behavior of most of the boys and girls overlapped.

Other studies show not only commonalities between girls and boys, taken as a whole, but also complex variation within and across those groups. For example, Elliott Medrich and his colleagues interviewed 764 children from different racial-ethnic backgrounds about how they spent their time outside school.[43] Forty-five percent of the boys and 26 percent of the girls reported playing team sports (note the sizable overlaps between boys and girls who did, and boys and girls who did not, play team sports). There was no gender difference in the median number of reported close friends (three), but African-American girls and boys reported more friends than either whites or those of other ethnic backgrounds. For all racial-ethnic groups and for both genders, being involved in team sports correlated with reporting more friends. African-American boys had the highest rates of sports participation, and number of friends, and African-American girls had higher rates than white girls. It is a serious distortion to reduce this complex variation into dichotomous claims, like "boys play team sports and girls engage in turn-taking play" or "boys organize into large groups and girls into dyads and triads."[44]

In these studies, as in other statistically based research on sex/gender differences, *within-gender variation is greater than differences between boys and girls taken as groups.* Although the variation may be dutifully reported, the point gets lost when the conclusions and secondary reports fall into the binary language of "boys versus girls." Some methodological writings caution against translating statistical complexity into a discourse of "the pinks and the blues," the tellingly dichotomous title of a popular television documentary on sex differences among children.[45] And they note another distortion in the literature on sex differences: although this is not "good science," findings of difference are much more often reported and published than findings of no difference. These problems seriously qualify general assertions that boys have a different "culture" than girls, if "culture" is taken to mean clearly differentiated patterns of behavior.

Claims that boys and girls have different cultures sometimes seem to refer not to externally observable behavior, like the amount of rough-and-tumble play, but to the *symbolic dimension of experience*—patterns of meaning, stereotypes, beliefs, ideologies, metaphor, discourses. (Each of these concepts has a different twist, but they cluster at the symbolic level. Note also that in daily experience "behavior" and "meanings" are not easily separable; human conduct is always infused with meanings.) As feminist scholars have thoroughly demonstrated, gendered meanings are deeply embedded in many of the discourses we draw on to make sense of the world. As Valerie Walkerdine has written, femininity and masculinity are powerful fictions or ideas, "imbued with fantasy and lived as fact."[46] The discourses of "girls are nice" and "boys are tough" enter kids' experiences, but so do other, sometimes contradictory discourses, like the argument of a boy who insisted that boys could be "nice," or the talk of girls who value being "tough."

An ambiguous mixing of the symbolic with claims about differences in behavior can be found in Carol Gilligan's research on gender and moral reasoning. After close and respectful listening to girls and, to a lesser degree, boys as they discussed moral problems, Gilligan concluded that girls have a "different voice," emphasizing relationships and care, in contrast with boys' preoccupation with individual rights and abstract principles of justice.[47] There is some ambiguity about what Gilligan intends to claim. In some statements she seems to be arguing that there are actual empirical gender differences in modes of moral reasoning, but the evidence for this has been much contested.[48] In her more recent work, however, Gilligan acknowledges that the same individual (male or female) may use both voices, mixing them as "contrapuntal" themes.[49] The voices may be gendered nonetheless because themes of "connection and care" are historically and symbolically associated with girls and women, and "rights and justice," with boys and men.

Once they are identified, systems of meaning—for example, the belief that caring and connection are "feminine"—can be studied in the context of social action. In her research on girls playing foursquare, Hughes pressed beyond the imagery of girls as cooperative and seeking intimacy by situating girls' talk about "being nice" within their ongoing interaction. She found that the girls "competed in a cooperative mode," using a language of "being friends" and "being nice" while aggressively getting others out so their friends could enter the game. The girls did not seem to experience "nice" and "mean" as sharply dichotomous; they maneuvered their rhetoric (associated with symbolic notions of femininity) and expressed nuances through mixed phrases like "nice-mean" and "not really mean."[50]

In a related vein, Amy Sheldon, who analyzed conversations among preschoolers, describes the girls as using a "double-voice style" that enmeshed or masked self-assertion within an orientation to relationships and maintaining group harmony. In interacting with one another, girls tried to avoid the appearance of hierarchy and overt conflict, but much else—conflict, self-assertion, sometimes aggression—went on beneath the surface. Sheldon found that boys sometimes used this double-voice style, although she argues that it is more often a feature of girls' talk because they are constrained by gender prescriptions to display themselves as egalitarian and harmonious.[51]

Sensitivity to gender meanings within varied social contexts and practices may enrich our understanding of boys as well as girls. In an interpretive study of the sex talk of a group of boys in a London secondary school, Julian Wood observes that "masculinity has at its heart not unproblematic strength but often weakness, self-doubt, and confusion." The outward face may be brash and full of "presence," or the promise of power, but the inward face is often the reverse.[52]

In short, a given piece of social interaction may be simultaneously cooperative and competitive, self-assertive and oriented to others, and brash and vulnerable. And these qualities do not sharply divide by gender. This subtlety and complexity become lost when analysis proceeds through a series of gender-linked contrasts (e.g., competitive versus cooperative, agency versus communion), and when varied dimensions of gender are compressed into static dualisms.

Ethnographers of education who work within "social reproduction" or "resistance" theory have also provided insight into multiple gender ideologies (the former emphasize the reproduction of inequalities of social class and gender through schooling; the latter give more attention to how individuals and groups resist this process).[53] For example, Connell and his colleagues argue that although dominant ideals of masculinity and femininity may exert powerful influence, they do not simply determine individual behavior. Individuals and groups develop varied forms of accommodation, reinterpretation, and resistance to ideologically hegemonic patterns.[54]

Joan Anyon, who interviewed and observed fifth-grade girls in the United States, found that some girls acquiesced in one kind of prescribed femininity: they wore dresses and skirts, were quiet in class, and avoided aggressive physical activities. Others used exaggerated feminine behavior (giggling, whispering; being coy and flirting with a male teacher) to resist schoolwork. Some girls actively resisted stereotyped femininity by refusing to wear skirts and frilly clothing, and by playing sports and engaging in verbal aggression.[55]

Rather than casting children as "objects of socialization," this approach grants them agency, tracing varied responses to and interpretations of gender prescriptions. By positing a complex and plural approach to gender, these ethnographies also challenge simplistic dualisms like girls' culture versus boys' culture. On the other hand, the "reproduction and resistance" literature analyzes gender primarily by emphasizing separation between boys and girls and by comparing the dynamics of varied same-gender groups or styles. While the groups and subcultures are multiple, a sense of deep division between girls and boys persists; how far such divisions may vary by situation or context is not made clear. Dualistic assumptions poke through the multiplicity.

Beyond Dualisms

The separate-and-different-cultures model has clearly outlived its usefulness. But before I draw together alternative approaches, I want to briefly celebrate a breakthrough that was, I believe, facilitated by feminist work within the model of different cultures. Prior to the mid-1970s the experiences of girls were excluded from or devalued in most of the research on the social relations of children and youth. Within the United States, the child development literature on "peer relations" was based primarily on research on boys, as were historical studies of childhood and adolescence.[56] And, as Angela McRobbie observed in a trenchant critique, British youth culture studies either ignored or marginalized girls; for example, in Willis's study, girls are seen through the eyes of the "lads," as objects to be possessed.[57] Although Lever paid close attention to girls in her extensive research on sex differences in children's play, her work still suffered from a tendency to see them as deficient; for example, she described girls' play as "immature" and claimed that their groups had a "vacuum of leadership."[58]

The feminist movement has helped scholars focus more directly on girls, to be critical of the many ways in which they have been stereotyped and devalued, and to grant girls voice and agency in knowledge. The different-worlds framework, animated by feminist revaluing of "things female," cleared space to learn directly about girls and their interactions with one another.[59] One valuable result, exemplified by Gilligan's work, has been the articulation of dimensions of experience, such as relationality and caring, that were previously trivialized or ignored. Once these experiences have been conceptualized, they can then be studied in the context of the lives of boys and men, as well as girls and women, leaving open the issue of empirical gender difference.

But the contrastive framework has outlived its usefulness, as has the gender ideology that it builds on and perpetuates. The view of gender as difference and binary opposition has been used to buttress male domination and to perpetuate related ideologies like the division between public and private.[60] A sense of the whole, and of the texture and dynamism of interaction, become lost when collapsed into dualisms like large versus small, hierarchical versus intimate, agency versus communion, and competitive versus cooperative. (The portrayals often sound like a Victorian world of "separate spheres," writ small and contemporary.)

Furthermore, by relying on a series of contrasts to depict the whole, the approach of girls' culture versus boys' culture exaggerates the coherence of same-gender interaction. Terms like "culture" and "subculture" are too often used to reify contrastive images; as R. W. Connell argues, these terms suggest a place which people inhabit rather than an "aspect of what they do."[61] We need, instead, to develop concepts that will help us grasp the diversity, overlap, contradictions, and ambiguities in the larger cultural fields in which gender relations, and the dynamics of power, are constructed.[62]

If the separate-cultures story has lost its narrative force, how can we grasp the gendered nature of kids' social relations? To move our research wagons out of the dualistic rut, we can, first of all, try to *start with a sense of the whole rather than with an assumption of gender as separation and difference.* If we begin by assuming different cultures, separate spheres, or contrastive differences, we will also end with a sharp sense of dichotomy rather than attending to multiple differences and sources of commonality.

One way to grasp this complexity is by *examining gender in context* rather than fixing binary abstractions like "boys emphasize status, and girls emphasize intimacy." Instead we should ask "which boys or girls, where, when, under what circumstances?" As I have shown, the organization and meanings of gender vary from schools to neighborhoods to families, and from classroom to playground to lunchroom settings. Some situations, like cross-gender chasing and invasions, evoke a sense of gender as dualism, but other situations undermine and spread out that view. Furthermore, gender takes shape in complex interaction with other social divisions and grounds of inequality, such as age, class, race, ethnicity, and religion. As Joan Scott suggests, we should "treat the opposition between male and female as problematic rather than known, as something contextually defined, repeatedly constructed."[63] An emphasis on social context shifts analysis from fixing abstract and binary differences to examining the social relations in which multiple differences are constructed and given meaning.

NOTES

1. There have been several widely circulated versions of this argument: (1) Janet Lever emphasizes sex differences in the play of fifth-graders and argues that because they more often engage in team sports, males have a later advantage in the world of occupations and organizations. See Lever, "Sex Differences in the Complexity of Children's Play and Games" and "Sex Differences in the Games Children Play." Carol Gilligan uses Lever's work to support her claim that in the process of moral reasoning, girls use a voice of connection and care that is different from boys' emphasis on abstract rules. See Gilligan, *In a Different Voice: Psychological Theory and Women's Development.* (2) Daniel N. Maltz and Ruth A. Borker ("A Cultural Approach to Male-Female Miscommunication") claim that there are different patterns of talk in all-girl and in all-boy groups, leading to miscommunication between adult women and men; Deborah Tannen's popular book, *You Just Don't Understand: Women and Men in Conversation,* elaborates this basic thesis (for criticisms, see Henley and Kramarae, "Gender, Power, and Miscommunication"). (3) Eleanor E. Maccoby argues that gender-separated groups teach different forms of prosocial and antisocial behavior ("Social Groupings in Childhood: Their Relationship to Prosocial and Antisocial Behavior in Boys and Girls").

Collaborating with Zella Luria, I have also followed this story line, arguing that groups of girls and groups of boys teach different sexual scripts, leading to tangles in the more overtly heterosexual experiences of adolescents, with girls emphasizing intimacy and romance, while boys are oriented more to active sexuality. Some of our analysis is included, although with serious caveats. See Barrie Thorne and Zella Luria, "Sexuality and Gender in Children's Daily Worlds."

2. Tannen, *You Just Don't Understand.*

3. This generalization is supported by the studies finding that on average, boys roam twice as far as girls. In research on children in neighborhoods Ellis et al. ("Age Segregation in Children's Social Interaction") and Medrich et al. (*The Serious Business of Growing Up*) found boys more often played outdoors and girls, indoors.

4. Lever, "Sex Differences in the Games Children Play." Similar conclusions are drawn by Mary F. Waldrop and Charles F. Halverson, "Intensive and Extensive Peer Behavior: Longitudinal and Cross-sectional Analyses"; Donna Eder and Maureen T. Hallinan, "Sex Differences in Children's Friendships"; and Schofield, *Black and White in School.*

   In *Culture Against Man*, a 1960s study of adolescent culture in a high school, Jules Henry generalized: "Boys flock; girls seldom get together in groups above four. . . . Boys are dependent on masculine solidarity . . . the emphasis is on masculine unity; in girls' cliques the purpose is to shut out other girls" (p. 150). This frequently cited paragraph influenced many later researchers.

5. See reviews of research in Hartup, "Peer Relations," and in Eleanor E. Maccoby and Carol Nagy Jacklin, *The Psychology of Sex Differences.*

6. Best, *We've All Got Scars;* Schofield, *Black and White in School;* Sluckin, *Growing Up in the Playground.*

7. See Goodwin, *He-Said-She-Said,* for careful sociolinguistic documentation of this pattern among a group of boys in an African-American urban neighborhood.

8. Best, *We've All Got Scars;* also see ibid.

9. Lever, "Sex Differences in the Games Children Play" and "Sex Differences in the Complexity of Children's Play and Games."

10. See Thorne and Luria, "Sexuality and Gender in Children's Daily Worlds." For a related analysis of bonding among adult men, enacted through forms of joking, see Peter Lyman, "The Fraternal Bond as a Joking Relationship."

11. Best, *We've All Got Scars;* Eder and Hallinan, "Sex Differences in Children's Friendships"; Lever, "Sex Differences in the Games Children Play"; Schofield, *Black and White in School;* Thorne and Luria, "Sexuality and Gender in Children's Daily Worlds"; Waldrop and Halverson, "Intensive and Extensive Peer Behavior."

12. Goodwin, *He-Said-She-Said,* and Berentzen, *Children Constructing Their Social World.*

13. Toth, *Blooming.*

14. Schofield, *Black and White in School.*

15. Lever, "Sex Differences in the Games Children Play," and Eder and Hallinan, "Sex Differences in Children's Friendships."

16. Lever, "Sex Differences in the Games Children Play"; Evans, "Gender Differences in Children's Games"; Finnan, "The Ethnography of Children's Spontaneous Play"; Schofield, *Black and White in School.*

17. Goodwin, *He-Said-She-Said.*

18. Donna Eder, "The Cycle of Popularity: Interpersonal Relations Among Female Adolescents."

19. *Cat's Eye,* a novel by Margaret Atwood, vividly depicts subterranean conflict and hostility among a small group of girls.

20. Three different teachers, who may have been responding to these patterns and/or to cultural stereotypes, have told me that it's easier to discipline boys than girls; boys' arguments, they said, are more direct, and they "forgive and forget." But girls are "sneaky in their behavior"; "when girls are bad they're nasty."

21. In a study of primary school children in Australia, Davies (*Life in the Classroom and Playground*) also describes a group of boys as well as several groups of girls who maneuvered between "best friends" and "contingency friends." She notes that the availability of a contingency friend heightens one's bargaining power over a best friend. Davies does not locate the analysis within the rubric of gender difference.

22. The term and the observation about anthropology come from Sherry B. Ortner, "The Founding of the First Sherpa Nunnery and the Problem of 'Women' as an Analytic Category."

23. For example, see Carole Joffe ("As the Twig Is Bent") on the "masculine subculture" of four boys in a preschool; Vivian Gussin Paley (*Boys and Girls: Superheroes in the Doll Corner*) on "the superhero clique" in a kindergarten; and Best (*We've All Got Scars*) on "the Tent Club," a dominant male group that continued from first through second grade.

24. Everhart, *Reading, Writing, and Resistance,* and Cusick, *Inside High School;* Fine, *With the Boys.*

25. Cusick, *Inside High School,* p. 168.

26. AnnMarie Wolpe similarly observes that British ethnographies of schooling include little about "the ordinary boy who goes through school doing minimal work, but not necessarily domineering or sexually harassing" (*Within School Walls: The Role of Discipline, Sexuality, and the Curriculum,* p. 92).

27. Goodenough, "Small Group Culture," p. 217. In comparative observations she found that four of nine kindergarten classrooms had a bonded group of disruptive and aggressive boys; relations between boys and girls were more harmonious and mutual in classes without such a group.

28. Paley, *Boys and Girls,* and Ellen Jordan, "Gender Theory and the Construction of Masculinity in the Infants School."

    As another example of this process, both teachers and ethnographers have paid more attention to boys than to girls; girls have a "semi-ignored status" in traditional educational research *and* in teacher practices. However, the interests of ethnographers may also counter those of teachers; for example, whereas the teacher may want an orderly classroom, the observer may want juicy material about kids' underground cultures or, as in Paul Willis's *Learning to Labor,* about school resisters.

29. Fine, *With the Boys.*

30. Connell et al., *Making the Difference.* On the conceptual pluralizing of masculinities and femininities, also see Connell, *Gender and Power.*

31. Canaan, "A Comparative Analysis of American Suburban Middle Class, Middle School, and High School Teenage Cliques." Michael Messner ("Masculinities and Athletic Careers," p. 82) quotes an African-American man from a lower-class background who recalled that in junior high "you either got identified as an athlete, a thug, or a bookworm."

    In an insightful ethnography of a largely white high school in the Detroit area, Penelope Eckert traces the dynamic opposition between two categories that dominated the social life of the school. The jocks, with a middle-class orientation, controlled school athletics and other adult-sponsored activities. The more working-class burnouts were estranged from the school and rebelled against its authority. Girls and boys were in both categories, and, significantly, the majority of students fell in between. See Eckert, *Jocks and Burnouts: Social Categories and Identity in the High School.*

32. On the other hand, in an observational study in a British classroom of twelve- and thirteen-year-olds, Robert J. Meyenn ("School Girls' Peer Groups") found that groups and not pairs were the dominant form of social organization. He identified four distinct groups of varying sizes and with different patterns of behavior: the "PE" girls (nine members, physically mature and noisy, who "rough and tumbled" more than the boys); the "science lab girls" (four members; popular and liked by teachers); the "nice girls" (five members; unobtrusive and less physically mature); and the "quiet girls," four girls who were socially uncertain). Groups maneuvered to be together throughout the school day, and members gave one another help and support. Meyenn writes the girls found it "inconceivable to just

have one best friend," although there were patterns of "breaking friends" internal to each group (p. 115).

33. Linda Hughes, " 'But That's Not *Really* Mean': Competing in a Cooperative Mode," p. 684.

34. Lever, "Sex Differences in the Complexity of Children's Play and Games."

35. For a detailed analysis of arguments about rules during the playing of another turn-taking "girls' " game, see Marjorie Harness Goodwin, "The Serious Side of Jump Rope: Conversational Practices and Social Organization in the Frame of 'Play.' "

36. Luria and Herzog ("Sorting Gender Out in a Children's Museum") also found that context makes a difference in the organization of same-gender groups. On a class field trip to a children's museum, elementary school boys clustered in much smaller groups than one typically sees on school playgrounds.

37. Goodwin, *He-Said-She-Said.*

38. Ibid., and Marjorie Harness Goodwin and Charles Goodwin, "Children's Arguing."

39. For a review of literature and a description of insult exchanges among white working-class girls in a junior high cafeteria, see Donna Eder, "Serious and Playful Disputes: Variation in Conflict Talk Among Female Adolescents." This point relates to discussions of "hassling" and "meddlin" in multiracial schools, and white students being quicker than Black students to interpret the hassling as intimidation.

40. Tannen, *You Just Don't Understand,* p. 18.

41. J. A. DiPietro, "Rough and Tumble Play: A Function of Gender."

42. Jacklin, "Methodological Issues in the Study of Sex-related Differences."

43. Medrich et al., *The Serious Business of Growing Up.*

44. In a careful review of empirical research, Nancy Karweit and Stephen Hansell ("Sex Differences in Adolescent Relationships: Friendship and Status") conclude that the conventional view that boys have larger friendship groups than girls is overdrawn. Some studies find that up to age seven, boys are either situated in smaller groups than girls, or that there are no gender differences. The research literature does suggest that the *average* size of friendship groups fits the conventional depiction from age seven to adolescence, but patterns vary by setting, such as type of classroom, and by type of activity, for example, participation in team sports. Findings are mixed for junior high and high school.

45. In addition to Jacklin, "Methodological Issues in the Study of Sex-related Differences," see Maccoby and Jacklin, *The Psychology of Sex Differences,* and Fausto-Sterling, *Myths of Gender.*

46. Walkerdine, *Schoolgirl Fictions;* also see Davies, *Frogs and Snails and Feminist Tales.*

47. Gilligan, *In a Different Voice.*

48. For example, see Linda K. Kerber et al., "On *In a Different Voice: An Interdisciplinary Forum.*" For a critical discussion of Gilligan's recent research on girls entering adolescence and its neglect of race, ethnicity, and social class as they interact with gender, see Judith Stacey, "On Resistance, Ambivalence, and Feminist Theory."

49. Carol Gilligan et al., eds., *Making Connections: The Relational Worlds of Adolescent Girls at Emma Willard School.*

50. Hughes, " 'But That's Not *Really* Mean.' "

51. Amy Sheldon, "Conflict Talk: Sociolinguistic Challenges to Self-Assertion and How Young Girls Meet Them."

52. Julian Wood, "Groping Towards Sexism: Boys' 'Sex Talk,' " pp. 60–61.

53. For a helpful review of "reproduction" and "resistance" theories, see Dorothy C. Holland and Margaret A. Eisenhart, *Educated in Romance: Women, Achievement, and College Culture.*

54. Connell et al., *Making the Difference,* and Connell, *Gender and Power.*

55. Joan Anyon, "Intersections of Gender and Class: Accommodation and Resistance by Working-Class and Affluent Females to Contradictory Sex-Role Ideologies."

56. This point is made in Hugh C. Foot et al., eds., *Friendship and Social Relations in Children;* Hartup, "Peer Relations"; Gilligan et al., *Making Connections;* and Carol Dyhouse, *Girls Growing Up in Victorian and Edwardian England.*

57. Angela McRobbie, "Settling Accounts with Subcultures"; Willis, *Learning to Labor.*

58. Lever, "Sex Differences in the Games Children Play." A deficit approach to girls can also be found in Finnan, "The Ethnography of Children's Spontaneous Play."

59. Reviewing the evolution of the "separate spheres" metaphor in social history, Linda K. Kerber analogously observes that the notion of separate spheres "enabled historians to move the history of women out of the realm of the trivial and anecdotal and into the realm of analytic social history"

("Separate Spheres, Female Worlds, Woman's Place: The Rhetoric of Women's History," p. 37).

60. Judith Shapiro, "Gender Totemism."

61. R. W. Connell, *Which Way Is Up?: Essays on Class, Sex, and Culture,* p. 226.

62. Goodwin (*He-Said-She-Said*) resists the temptation to chalk up her findings as "children's culture," "gender cultures," and/or "African-American culture." Instead she asks how participants assemble and interpret activities through arguing, telling stories, and gossip. Starting with activities rather than an assumption of binary gender difference led her to discover both differences and commonalities between boys and girls.

63. Scott, *Gender and the Politics of History,* p. 49.

PART TWO

NEGOTIATING
THE CLASSROOM

FOR MANY YEARS experts in the field of gender in education
have argued that girls are shortchanged in the classroom,
receiving far less attention from teachers than their male
counterparts. Lately, a different perspective has been voiced:
it is boys, not girls, who are disadvantaged in school, an environment that rewards "female" traits and punishes boys for
being who they are. Who is really missing out?

Dan Kindlon and Michael Thompson tackle the challenges
of boys' first years in school in "Thorns Among Roses: The
Struggle of Young Boys in Early Education." With verbal
skills that develop more slowly than girls' and a great need
for physical activity, the boys that Kindlon and Thompson
depict are ill-prepared for the demands and expectations of
school. Myra and David Sadker echo this concern in "The
Miseducation of Boys," contending that while boys are more
likely to be the "stars" of the classroom, they are far more
likely to be the most troubled students as well.

Lyn Mikel Brown and the AAUW address the problems of
girls in class in "The Madgirl in the Classroom" and "How
Girls Negotiate School." Each examines the effect on female
students of being overlooked and ignored: the ways they react
to, resist, and cope with an environment that rewards the

"bad" behavior of boys with attention and the "good" behavior of girls with silence.

Although each of these pieces focuses on one gender in particular, taken together it becomes clear that both boys and girls are facing obstacles to their education that must be addressed.

7

THORNS AMONG ROSES

THE STRUGGLE OF YOUNG BOYS
IN EARLY EDUCATION

Dan Kindlon and Michael Thompson

I love all children, except for boys.

—Lewis Carroll

IT IS MIDMORNING circle time in Ms. Alvarez's kindergarten class, and fifteen children—six boys and nine girls—sit on a carpet in a cozy corner of the room waiting for her to begin reading.

On one side of the circle, the girls sit shoulder to shoulder, some with legs crossed, some with hands clasped in their laps, some waiting quietly, expectantly, others chatting happily as they wait for a sign that Ms. Alvarez is ready to begin. Beside them sits a boy, Daniel, equally self-possessed, relaxed, and waiting. Daniel is the best reader in the class; he spends hours at home and at school poring over books. For him story time is the happiest time of his day. As one kindergarten girl told a visitor, "All of the girls in my class can read, but none of the boys can, only Daniel."

A few feet away from Daniel sit four boys who are a study in contrast. Justin leans sideways onto Will's chest; Will collapses onto Bashir's shoulder while Bashir presses against Ryan, who is doing all he can not to tip over. Surprisingly, this falling tableau does not turn into a total collapse; it seems frozen in space. The boys are quiet; they will rest in this partially upright pile for a long time, waiting for Ms. Alvarez to begin reading. They are doing their best to follow the classroom rules, and she knows it. Yet she cannot start reading until Christopher comes to join the circle.

Christopher had been playing with Tangrams when Ms. Alvarez had rung the bell and called for circle time. On the way to returning his Tangrams to their appointed spot, he had run his finger through the chalk swirls on the blackboard, leaving a satisfying green line, bumped into Justin as Justin walked toward the circle, and stopped to pick up the plastic pears and tomatoes in the play kitchen. Now he is standing at the supply shelves, idly sifting through the colored markers in a plastic box, lost in thought.

"Christopher, are you going to join us?" asks Ms. Alvarez. Her question catches his attention. He looks over but doesn't move.

"Christopher, we're waiting," she says, firmly. Christopher hesitates, then drops the markers and starts to make his way across the room. In the meantime, the domino boys have begun to collapse. Justin has fallen into Will, and Will is trying to push him out of his lap and onto the floor. "Will, don't push Justin," says Ms. Alvarez. "Well, he's on top of me," complains Will. "Justin, please sit up and leave some space between you. Will, there's no need to push him. Let him do it by himself," she says. Then, "Christopher, everyone is waiting to read. Would you join us, please?"

Christopher negotiates the last few feet to the circle and sits down expectantly. Then Bashir decides to lie on his back, and only his knees and shoes are now part of the circle. He is staring at the ceiling. "Bashir, would you sit up like everyone else?" Bashir hauls himself up. "Good," Ms. Alvarez says. "Now we're ready to read."

Though the entire process of getting the boys to sit quietly in the reading circle has taken only two to three minutes, it is hard not to be annoyed at Justin and Christopher. They do waste a disproportionate amount of class time every day. The gender split is obvious; the girls bring energy and exuberance to the circle, too, but it is contained; they readily follow instructions. The boys have a much harder time sitting still. How does the activity of these boys impose upon these girls? What is the impact on Daniel, who waits patiently alongside the girls, aware that he is not one with these other boys? And what about the bumping, jostling boys? Or the distractible Christopher? What lessons do they learn from being reprimanded at circle time or anytime their behavior sets them apart? As mothers often recall about their son's grade school years: "I have a wonderful son, but he spent a lot of time on the bench outside the principal's office." What *is* it about boys? These are the questions that occupy teachers and parents and dominate discussions about boys in school.

In recent years the public discussion of fairness in schools has focused almost exclusively on girls and the ways they have been short-changed in a system that favors boys. As right as the concern for girls is, we are disturbed by the dialogue when it seems to pit boys against girls in the quest for fairness. The unchallenged assumptions that, if girls are suffering in school, then boys are not. Yet research, statistics, and our own experience as school psychologists and with boys and men in private therapy contradict this.

From kindergarten through sixth grade, a boy spends more than a thousand hours a year in school, and his experiences and the attitudes of the teachers and other adults he encounters there are profoundly shaping. The average boy faces a special struggle to meet the developmental and academic expectations of an elementary school curriculum that emphasizes reading, writing, and verbal ability—cognitive skills that normally develop more slowly in boys than in girls. Some boys are ahead of the others on that developmental curve, and some girls lag behind, but when we compare the average boy with the average girl, the average boy is developmentally disadvantaged in the early school environment.

Grade school is largely a feminine environment, populated predominantly by women teachers and authority figures, that seems rigged against boys, against the higher activity level and lower level of impulse control that is normal for boys. As one disappointed first-grade boy remarked unhappily at the end of his first day of school: "You can't *do* anything!" The trouble wasn't really that he couldn't do anything, of course, but that everything he loved to do—run, throw, wrestle, climb—was outlawed in the classroom. In this setting a boy's experience of school is as a thorn among roses; he is a different, lesser, and sometimes frowned-upon presence, and he knows it.

We went to talk with a third-grade teacher who we thought was particularly effective with boys. They seemed to enjoy her, and we wanted to know how she viewed boys in her class. When we mentioned that school might be a feminine place, she reacted somewhat defensively. "School isn't a feminine place. It is a human place, a civilized place," she said. "It's just easier for girls to adapt to it."

As much as she would like the school environment to be just a place where instruction and expectations present both boys and girls with the same opportunity for success, the fact that it's clearly easier for girls to adapt to it means that, in some unseen way, the expectations reflect girls' abilities and sensibilities.

This is the reason that David Trower, the headmaster of the all-boys Allen Stevenson School in New York City, says, "If boys need the protection of the single-sex environment at all, they need it most in elementary school because of the developmental disparity."

We are not suggesting that boys are good and schools are bad, or that teachers don't care about boys. Quite to the contrary, much of what we know about boys' difficulties in school is confirmed by the many caring, creative teachers we know who struggle with the challenge of working with boys in the school setting. We know, too, that there are boys whose talents or temperaments make them exceptions, but if we're going to talk about the ways in which boys' life experiences complicate their emotional development or compromise it, we have to talk about the hidden hurt that the early school years inflict on so many boys.

Studies that track children's development through the school years suggest that, by the third grade, a child has established a pattern of learning that shapes the course of his or her entire school career.[1] We see this clearly with boys: the first two years in school are a critical moment of entry into that world of learning, but boys' relative immaturity and the lack of fit they so often experience in school set them up to fail. Many boys who are turned off to school at a young age never refind the motivation to become successful learners. Even among those who press on to achieve success later in life, the emotional scars of those troubled years do not fade.

Karl was a frequent no-show at his two sons' grade school plays and other programs. A successful corporate consultant, he found it difficult to get away from the office in time for early evening programs and certainly couldn't break away for the midday plays and chorus concerts at the school. He steered clear of parent-child conferences, despite the teachers' efforts to accommodate his schedule.

Karl wanted to be a good father, a responsible parent, but he felt ill at ease and impatient at these school functions. As his wife began to pressure him to come more often, he went dutifully, but his hostility toward the teachers made the conferences uncomfortable for everyone. Finally, his wife told him not to bother. But her resentment grew.

After one particularly heated exchange of words, he recalled later, he was surprised by his wife's angry accusation that he didn't care about his children's education. His own response surprised him almost as much. His first thoughts weren't about his work or the office or deadlines—or even his children. They were about his feelings: shame, resentment, and anger that had smoldered for more than forty years.

"I walk into a school building, and I can feel my chest get tight," he explained later. "It's a place that's up to no good. I had a difficult time in school when I was a kid over stuff I had no control over. What I learned in school was that, in some essential ways that matter to other people, I didn't measure up. Now, as far as I'm concerned, all the kid art on the wall doesn't change the fact that school is a place where kids suffer, and it makes me angry to have to pretend otherwise, to have to sit there and make small talk with teachers who are part of the problem—smug, small-minded, inflexible people who think they're qualified to sit in judgment of children, and in judgment of me as a parent, when I know they're not. It's a sham."

Never mind that Karl's boys were successful students with talented, enthusiastic teachers. Neither time nor success had dimmed the hurt and anger of those years. When Karl walked into a school building, he was forty-eight going on eight years old.

Whether they have achieved enormous success in life or are struggling to make their way, we hear similar stories from countless men for whom school was a painful endurance test.

This is the struggle we witness in boys who, often by third grade, have already disengaged their energy from the task of learning, tuned out of school, and written it off as a place where they can't do anything right. Others achieve but feel the same alienation of spirit. They bide their time and make the grade, but experience no joy in learning and, like the others, lose the greater potential of these best learning years of their life.

More than two thousand years ago, the Hebrew sage Hillel advised that "a person too anxious about being shamed cannot learn." Today many boys face a steady diet of shame and anxiety throughout their elementary school years. From it they learn only to feel bad about themselves and to hate the place that makes them feel that way. Emotionally estranged from their life in school, these are boys already in deep trouble before they've even learned to spell the word.

Michael with Alan: A Boy's-Eye View of School and Teachers

Alan's mother called me to say that he was having a tough sixth-grade year. He'd been angry at several teachers, and despite his high IQ, his grades had dropped to an all-time low for him, from As and Bs to Bs and Cs. Furthermore, he had "hated" school periodically throughout the year—a stronger version of the unhappiness he had expressed occasionally since kindergarten. A school administrator had recommended Alan for psychological testing and possibly therapy because he seemed, at moments, to be so withdrawn and angry. The administrator told Alan's mother that he was worried that Alan might be depressed. She asked me to provide an independent opinion of her son's situation. Because Alan's family lived far outside Boston, I couldn't be his therapist, but I could review his records and talk with Alan to hear his own views.

I learned later that Alan had been reluctant to talk with me, but he gave no indication of that the day we met. This twelve-year-old with a marvelous smile, freckles, and a wiry athlete's body was an articulate spokesperson for the average boy in school. He was polite and responsive, but from the beginning he grappled with the questions I asked about school. Since teachers had been the focal point of his anger of late, we started there. Which teachers did he like, and which didn't he like?

He remembered his fourth-grade teacher: "She was just nice, and she had a sense of humor, and she wasn't always yelling and stuff."

He didn't like his social studies teacher from the year before, he said. She seemed perpetually angry, to hear him describe her, and "she was always getting mad at me over little things."

"Like what?"

"Lots of things. Like when I'd come to class without my pencil. Or . . . no . . . I know . . . we had these little assignment books that we had to keep track of on a field trip. We went to a museum, and we were at a fountain outside, and my little book fell in. Stuff like that."

"Was she that way with the other kids in the class?"

"Well, she was harder on boys because they do things, I guess. I don't think she ever really liked me. We didn't get along very well."

He recalls other teachers who he believes did not like him. His second-grade teacher stands out in his mind. That was the year Alan's slight learning disability in spelling became clear. This particular teacher discouraged him from writing poetry until he could spell better, he says.

"When you have had a teacher who has really liked you, how have you known?"

"Well, they don't get mad at me that easily. Just . . . they're easy to be around. They're like Mr. Clarkson . . . He pays attention, and he has more stuff you want to learn about."

We discuss the "stuff" Alan likes to learn about and some of his favorite teachers and the qualities he liked about them. There aren't many more.

To dig a little deeper, I turn the focus of the questions away from Alan's feelings about himself and ask instead about teachers and boys in general.

"Is it difficult for boys to have all women teachers?"

"They're pretty used to it," he says of boys.

"Is it easier for boys to have men teachers?"

"Yeah. They understand us more or something. They understand what we're trying to say."

"What do women have trouble understanding about boys?"

"They don't like to be gotten mad at."

Alan makes a simple point—that boys don't like being yelled at and yet that makes up a large part of their lives.

I'm reminded of a librarian—a woman—who lamented once: "Adults feel justified in yelling at boys because they are so 'bad' all the time."

The assumption is that yelling helps, especially in communicating dissatisfaction to boys, and that boys don't suffer from it as much as girls might. That is not my experience. Boys typically don't show that they suffer from yelling because being a boy requires that they not show it. But it hurts.

I ask Alan what aspects of school he finds most satisfying. Not surprisingly, it is sports.

"I know this may sound stupid, but why are sports so much more satisfying than anything else you do?"

"It's fun. It's something you can get better at by working hard . . . I don't know. You can excel in an area—like if you really like hockey, you can do that. If you really like soccer, you can do that. I look forward to sports every day. It is kind of like a big organized recess where you get to *do* stuff."

"But you're learning good things in school, aren't you?"

"Yeah, but running around is better than sitting. I have all these sitting classes all morning, and then I get to stand in art and in science when we go outside."

He talks some more about classes he likes—not many—and those he doesn't like, and it is clear that, whatever sophisticated planning has gone into curriculum design at Alan's school, the distinction between a good class and a bad class, from his point of view, has a lot to do with the freedom it offers to stand up and walk around.

In his weary review of life at school, Alan has described the nature of the problem so many boys have there. In essence, they sit all morning, and they have to keep track of those little books and not drop them in the water. And if they can't move around, they feel trapped and turned off to anything the teacher might have to offer.

In my previous experience working with children on the South Side of Chicago, I saw so many boys whose education had already, by second grade, been so scarred that they were truly done with schools—and as good as done for in life because the gangs were ready to snap them up. And yet, when school is not like this, not "charged" with tension the way their family lives and neighborhoods are, it becomes a "neutral" place where children can feel their own success. To the extent that a child is able to hook on to school as a place of achievement and support, school becomes a lifeline.

The interesting thing about Alan is that the same principle applies, even though he comes from an educated and affluent family. If school becomes a negatively "charged" environment, he will come to dislike it as a place where his personal achievement simply doesn't count for much. Much of the time a boy's experience of school is as a thorn among roses; he is a different, lesser, and sometimes frowned-upon presence, and he knows it. Alan is at that point now, and he is at risk for taking his soul out of school.

The "Differentness" of Boys: When Assets Become Liabilities

Jane, a fifth-grade teacher, mused on the differences she had observed in the way boys and girls worked on projects in her woodworking class. Every year, as the first project of the year, she offered the children their choice of working on a model bridge or a catapult. Typically, the girls chose to build the bridge and set about organizing the group effort very cooperatively, listening to one another's ideas, drawing rough sketches, and then working together to carefully construct the bridge. The boys, she said, typically chose the catapult, but their work didn't begin coopera-tively. Instead, each boy would hurry off to throw together his own best idea for a catapult that could hurl a rock; there was no sharing or listen-ing to one another's ideas. They sprawled across floor, chairs, and tables; lunged at materials; and yelped each time they stabbed themselves with pencils or got stung by a backfiring rubber band. In the rush, they usually built a catapult that didn't work, but they seemed unfazed by the setback. As they experimented with failure and the better catapults emerged in competition, the group began to coalesce as well, with each boy learning from the others' mistakes and the boys eventually cooperating to produce the best-of-all catapult.

It would be easy to criticize the boys for the predictable failure of their hurried and flawed first-round catapults, easy to shame them by comparing their rambunctious work style to the calmer, more efficient style of the girls. But this teacher saw something different. In addition to the well-executed planning and building by the groups of girls, she recognized in the boys a risk-taking energy and an enthusiasm that were of real value to the class.

Most educators—like Ms. Alvarez in her kindergarten class—strive to make school a place where boys and girls alike can grow to be responsible, caring individuals and enthusiastic learners. But we know that there are days when even caring teachers like Ms. Alvarez, who believes absolutely in the potential of each of her boys, wish that boys weren't so different or that the parents of boys raised them differently; days when parents raising just girls wish the same thing; and days when parents raising girls *and* boys are saying to one another, "You know, they *really are different!*"

The "differentness" of boys is not inherently bad, but it does present a challenge to teachers, to the school culture, and to boys themselves.

Boys generally are an active lot, and often impulsive. Their energy is contagious, especially among other boys, and that physical energy can translate into a kind of psychological boldness. They often are the risk takers, seemingly oblivious to the potential hurt of a fall or sting of a reprimand. Whether their choices might eventually prove to be brave or reckless, boys are often in the middle of an action before they consider the consequences.

Boys are direct; they act and speak in simple terms. Their more slowly developing language skills are apparent in their often blunt and unsophisticated humor or their preference for action over negotiation—grabbing the box of markers rather than negotiating a turn for using them. Boys' emotional immaturity allows them to celebrate themselves unabashedly, strutting, boasting, clamoring to be noticed. They're not terribly concerned about pleasing others. When the fabled little boy declared that the emperor wore no clothes, he spoke with the candor characteristic of boys.

Boys' need to feel competent and empowered leads them to express a keen power-based, action-oriented sense of justice, fairness, good and evil. Spiderman, Batman, Ninja Turtles—heroic action figures dominate the landscape of young boys because they want so much to be seen in heroic proportions—to be big instead of small, to have power in the world instead of the role of powerless child, and to be the arbiter of right and wrong rather than a negotiator or an observer.

Boys and girls alike bring energy, curiosity, and a desire for competence to their lives at school, but those gifts come wrapped in gender patterns that are recognizably different, as teachers and parents so frequently tell us. How many playful, imaginative girls will use their energies to fashion guns out of twigs or toast? How many playful, imaginative boys will use their energies to pretend they're beautiful, wild horses running across the plains?

The average boy's gifts are wrapped in high activity, impulsivity, and physicality—boy power—and the value of these gifts depends on the teacher, the boy, and the moment. These qualities serve boys beautifully on the playground, where there is room and respect for bold strokes of action and impulse. In the classroom, however, alongside girls—who are typically more organized, cooperative, and accomplished school learners—those "boy qualities" quickly turn from assets to liabilities. Even among those who aren't considered problem boys, many teachers identify the ordinary boy pattern of activity, attitudes, and behaviors as something that must be overcome for a boy to succeed in school.

Gender Differences: Worlds Apart in a Classroom Together

Two important developmental distinctions define boys' readiness for the tasks of elementary school and help explain their generally inferior performance compared with girls. First, boys mature more slowly than girls. Second, boys are more active and slower to develop impulse control than girls. This developmental pace appears largely biological, influenced by parents and teachers only to the extent that they provide support for that growth or fail to do so. Current scientific thinking about the nature-nurture debate highlights the inextricable link between biology and experience.[2] A boy's early ease with throwing a ball or climbing may begin with developmental readiness, but his skill and interest grow when he finds encouragement for his hobby at home. A girl's greater ease with reading and language also appears to begin with an early neurological advantage, enhanced when she is encouraged in her reading habit. These influences—some biological, some cultural—combine to nurture a child's developmental progress. Nurture and nature cannot be separated.

The fact that girls mature earlier than boys means that they frequently achieve cognitive milestones at younger ages.[3] They generally learn names for things sooner, such as the names of colors, and how to do simple counting. Because of this, girls are more ready when, in first grade, teachers commence with the first serious attempts to teach reading. The fact that many boys start out behind girls in these prereading skills means that boys are more likely to be miscategorized as learning disabled in the early grades.

In terms of activity level—and by this we mean motor activity, as in moving one's body around while running or walking—not many studies find sex differences until preschool. Or put slightly differently, gender differences in activity level between boys and girls become more pronounced as children approach school age. Recent research suggests that the main differences between boys and girls occur in social interaction. Boys in a group behave quite differently than boys alone, and boys are stimulated by the challenges presented by other boys. As with any gender difference, there is a lot of overlap between the populations of boys and girls: thus, there are girls who are more active than many boys. But by school age, the average boy in a classroom is more active than about three-fourths of the girls, and the most active children in the class are very likely to be boys.[4] And even the more active girls don't seem to express their energy in the unrestrained way more characteristic of boys.

When we examine extremes of activity—hyperactivity, for instance—the sex differences become even greater.[5] Most research finds that two to four times as many boys are diagnosed with attention deficit–hyperactivity disorder (ADHD) as are girls. For example, in a study of 8,258 kindergarten through fifth-grade children in Tennessee, all students in sixteen schools in one heterogeneous county, almost 4 percent of boys were diagnosed with the hyperactive-impulsive variety of ADD, whereas this was true for less than 1 percent of girls. So every class of at least twenty-five students is likely to find itself with one hyperactive boy.

The profile of boys as troubled learners stands out clearly to anyone who spends any time in elementary schools. As a second-grade girl commented ruefully one day: "Why are the bad kids always boys?" Our own experience is mirrored in research that indicates that a boy is four times more likely to be referred to a school psychologist than is a girl.

Some researchers have suggested that the preponderance of boys among the learning disabled (60 to 80 percent of learning disabilities occur in boys) would disappear if eight-year-old boys were taught in classes with six-year-old girls, because learning disabilities are diagnosed based on assessment of reading ability at a certain age compared with intellectual potential (IQ test results) at the same age. For decades, the Ethical Culture School in New York admitted five-year-old girls and six-year-old boys to kindergarten, because of the developmental disparity between boys and girls. The school eventually modified the practice because of the protests of that minority of parents who had very school-ready five-year-olds, but believes that the underlying wisdom of the earlier policy still holds. In the United States, at least some of the Waldorf Schools, with a creative arts–based curriculum, use a "pictorial introduction" to reading in the early grades in place of the more traditional reading skills and drills found in most schools. An administrator at one school where the curriculum takes a similar, less performance-based approach to early reading, once told us: "If you start teaching it any earlier, it looks as if all your boys have reading disabilities."

In short, the early age at which we teach reading favors girls, on average, and puts boys at a disadvantage. As a consequence, boys, on average, do not feel as able or as valued as the girls in the central learning tasks of elementary school. In therapy with boys, we frequently hear them describe themselves as losers or failures, even when they are developing skills at a pace that is normal for boys their age. Boys who struggle with genuine learning disabilities face even greater obstacles to school success, and their disheartening struggle as students easily comes to define their lives as boys.

Dan with Joe: A Paper Trail of Trouble to Come

In her phone call, Joe's mom tells me that she and her husband are worried about Joe. He has been having trouble in school and doesn't seem very happy. Lately, he has complained of stomachaches in the morning and begs to stay home. Joe is only six years old. It is April, and he is nearing the end of first grade. I am going to meet him in about an hour. I have his file open before me, and I read it while I eat my lunch. The folder contains some reports from his first-grade and kindergarten teachers as well as a few pages of preschool reports. It also has the completed questionnaires that his parents mailed back to me. These contain information about his medical history, which I will include in my report of the neuropsychological evaluation I am about to perform. I find myself mentally writing the report while I read over the information.

> Joe is the product of a full-term birth by cesarean section. He weighed seven pounds seven ounces. His five-minute APGAR was a 9. Medical history is remarkable for frequent ear infections requiring prophylactic antibiotics between the ages of six and eighteen months.

The questionnaires also tell me about Joe's early development and behavior at home and school. They contain quite a bit of information. Putting together a diagnostic report always reminds me of doing a puzzle. The pieces come from different sources—parents, teachers, physicians—and the precise significance of each piece isn't entirely clear. Sometimes a boy's problems are fairly straightforward; the big picture is clear before you start, and you can see easily how the pieces fit. But with Joe, as with many boys, we're not sure what that big picture is.

Joe's mother reports that there were some areas in which his development lagged behind peers. Although he walked early, Joe did not speak
until he was two, which he reportedly found very frustrating. He initially had quite a bit of difficulty separating from his mother at
preschool.

When I read the comments from his teachers, I sense that they like Joe.
I am familiar with the school he attends, and over the years I have been
uniformly impressed with the teaching staff. Because of this, I pay special
attention to what the teachers have to say. I have arranged to call Joe's
first-grade teacher at home tonight. For the purposes of diagnosis, the
observations of a good teacher are invaluable.

By teacher report, Joe has difficulty working independently, and his
attention to task is described as "variable." Math skills are developing
more rapidly than reading skills. Since February Joe has been in a language arts group, where he is beginning to acquire basic information
about how letters and sounds go together. This work is not easy for Joe,
but he has been making some progress, especially lately. Socially, he
tends to keep to himself or interact with a small group of friends.

Although I haven't even seen Joe yet, I find myself thinking about his
not-too-rosy prognosis. I know that my pessimism is due in part to my
interaction with Aiden, a fifteen-year-old boy who left my office a half
hour ago. This was a boy who had been ground down by his years in
school. He told me as much.

Aiden thought of himself as "stupid." "I can't do the work," he told
me. But his test scores told a different story. Aiden wasn't stupid at all.
He had just fallen further behind the pack each year, and now, like a tired
marathon runner, he had pulled off the road. I couldn't help thinking that
someday Joe would look like this—that in a few years a fifteen-year-old
Joe would be sitting in my office, his folder as fat as Aiden's.

Aiden had been evaluated every three years since he was six, and his
folder contained stacks of report cards, IQ scores, and reading comprehension test results. I dutifully added more paper to his file. It is part of
my job. Parents, teachers, and special education directors all want to
know the "scores"—as if they would provide some magical insight into
what is wrong with Joe, as if they were like the "scores" one would get
from a biopsy.

My mood is also fueled by a conversation I had with a colleague a few
weeks ago. We were talking about how busy we were and how many

reports we had to write. I had been asking him how much detail he put into the "Background and Medical History" section of his reports. For kids with thick folders, reading the information and summarizing it can be very time consuming. I found that his approach was very similar to mine; he had no shortcuts to offer. But then he said something tongue in cheek that contained too much brutal truth to laugh at: "We probably shouldn't waste the time because the reports really all say the same thing: 'Kid has trouble learning to read in first grade; starts to hate school; his self-esteem goes to hell; and when he's a teenager, he's pissed off or taking drugs.' " This is what we see.

Young Joe will walk through my door in a few minutes, and so I try to shake my pessimism. I want to be able to see him separate from this apocalyptic vision. Like my colleague, I have read hundreds of these thick folders, and too many of them read this way. It is what I try to communicate in my meetings with parents and teachers, what I try to emphasize amid the ten or more pages of test scores, interpretation, and recommendations:

> The most important thing to remember, the guiding principle, is to try to keep your son's self-esteem intact while he is in school. That is the real risk to his success and to his mental health. Once he's out of school, the world will be different. He'll find a niche where the fact that he can't spell well, or didn't read until he was eight, won't matter. But if he starts to hate himself because he isn't good at schoolwork, he'll fall into a hole that he'll be digging himself out of for the rest of his life.

Wild Animals and Entitled Princes: Destructive Boy Archetypes

"We expect too much of boys—and we don't expect enough," said a second-grade teacher reflecting on the way our culture's view of boys often scrambles messages they get from parents and teachers. "On the one hand, we expect them to do things they're developmentally not ready to do, and to be tough 'little men' when they're really just little boys who need goodbye hugs and affection. On the other hand, when they behave in cruel and thoughtless ways, we say, 'Oh, boys will be boys.' We let them off the hook over issues of respect and consideration for others."

Teachers and parents are in a position to help boys find success at school, to help them avoid the black hole of failure or help them out of it, but only if they see boys in need. Too often, instead, they react to boys from unconscious assumptions about the way all boys are. We call these unconscious images of boys *archetypes* to distinguish them from the more conscious and more easily recognized stereotypes in popular culture. Archetypal images of boys limit our understanding of them. Nevertheless, these views of boys are held by people of intelligence and goodwill, by parents and teachers who work with boys. Two of the most common of these images we see are those that cast a boy as a wild animal—out of control and incapable of responsible behavior or intelligent thought—or as an entitled prince who isn't held accountable to the same moral standards as the rest of us. Plato, in the fourth century B.C., called boys "of all wild beasts, the most difficult to manage," and his view of boys remains popular to this day. The trouble with this boy-view in classroom management philosophy is that if teachers are set up by our deepest assumptions to view a boy's energy and activity as "wild" and threatening, then we feel justified in responding with harsh action, correcting or reprimanding him more than necessary, or becoming ferociously controlling and determined to "whip him into shape." A boy's most common response to controlling behavior is not to be controlled—to become confrontational or defiant.

When we view boys as entitled princes, when we assume that a boy's gender or talents entitle him to a future of leadership, success, and power, we excuse him from the labor of learning to live and work wisely with others, protecting him from the consequences of acting badly, and hold him to a different, lesser standard of moral accountability in his actions and behavior toward others.

When our responses are distorted by these and other archetypal ideas, boys suffer for it. If the school culture or teachers react to a boy in ways that suggest that they are fearful of him, baffled by or uncomfortable with him, then he assumes he is fearsome and somehow not quite right, even unlovable. If they excuse him from reasonable childhood expectations because he is a man in the making and need not be bothered, then lessons of empathy and accountability are replaced by a creed of entitlement void of responsibility. Boys who feel feared, discounted, or unduly revered in school suffer a kind of emotional isolation that only intensifies their own fears, feelings of unworthiness, or arrogant expectations of entitlement.

It is easy to forget how powerful our expectations can be. Research conducted in the 1960s by Harvard psychologist Robert Rosenthal and his colleagues shows convincingly how this occurs in the classroom. In this study, teachers were told that, based on sophisticated psychological testing, certain of their pupils were "bloomers" who would show remarkable intellectual gains over the course of the school year. What the teachers were not told was that the tests were fake and that the students had been selected randomly. Despite this, the "bloomers" did end up showing greater intellectual gains than their "non-bloomer" classmates. When teachers were prepared to see students as learners, they communicated high expectations and their confidence in the students' abilities. Students who were "bloomers" fulfilled the expectations.

Unfortunately, our stereotypical or archetypal images of boys rarely cast them in a promising light. Instead, they typically obstruct the view of a boy, keeping teachers and other adults from recognizing a boy's inner life and responding to him in meaningful ways. This happens in every realm of a boy's life to some degree, but it is particularly destructive in the school environment, because so much of a boy's experience in school is shaped by the quality of his relationship with teachers.

When Boy Activity Is Misinterpreted, Mismanaged

The crisis call came about three weeks into the new school year at the small coed private elementary school in a suburb of Boston. "Help! This is one of our worst fourth grades ever," the desperate school director said. She rattled off a list of concerns. It was a small school, with one class per grade, and in our subsequent discussion with teachers, we learned that, due to a series of departures and arrivals of new students, the school had ended up with an extremely boy-heavy fourth-grade class: twelve boys and six girls. The tenor of the class seemed more confrontational than it ever had felt before, and it was sometimes hard to maintain control. Said one teacher: "It's just not nearly as *nice.*"

Clearly, this was the worst fourth grade these teachers had ever experienced at this school, but was it a *bad* fourth grade, or was it just not like the others? As we explored the complaints and concerns, it became clear that *worst* meant that it was very boy-flavored. Nothing extreme—no threats or intimidation, no fistfights or vandalism—just an ordinary level of ten-year-old boy energy that expresses itself in greater activity than does ten-year-old girl energy. And that was the crux of the problem. The preponderance of boys in the class had introduced a new standard that made the teachers uncomfortable. The students picked up on that discomfort and reflected it back in their own behavior toward one another, creating a climate of tension and tempers in the classroom.

Schools do need to maintain order, and boys can be difficult. This can be problematic, and every educator has to find a philosophical position with respect to the kind of disruption and disorder associated with the presence of boys. A teacher has to deal with boys' physical activity and disruption without always interpreting this behavior as malevolent or animalistic, because boys turn to activity as an outlet for a host of emotions—especially when their feelings outstrip their language skills or other options.

Music Room Melee Hits Sour Note of Aggression

At a small, private coed school in the Northeast, we worked with administrators and teachers during the first year after the formerly all-girls school was opened to boys.

Traditionally, during the lunch hour the girls had eaten their lunch and then sat in the spacious cafeteria to talk. With the first wave of boys into the school, it became apparent that boy style was to eat lunch in ten minutes and immediately go outside. This worked fine during the fall months, when the weather and lunchtime staffing allowed for the supervised outdoor recess. When winter came, the boys and supervising staff took over the gym instead, but when faculty members balked at the lunchtime recess assignment, the gym was closed.

A couple of days later, several boys took an unauthorized and unruly after-lunch run through the building, damaging some instruments in the music room.

Before talking with the boys and getting the facts straight about the extent of the damage, we heard two different tales of destruction. One was from the faculty members who, truth be told, weren't happy about the presence of boys at their school. The other report came from teachers who supported the coed environment.

The first version, told and retold by many of the unhappiest teachers, insisted that the boys had willfully set about to vandalize the music room and did so to the tune of $2,000 in broken instruments.

The second version held that, after a short but energizing lunch, the boys had engaged in a spontaneous game of tag, used poor judgment in racing through the music room, and accidentally bumped three instruments. Teachers who told this version prefaced it with the opinion that school officials had screwed up in the first place by closing the gym and eliminating an acceptable space for boys—or anyone—to work off the excess energy after a morning of sitting in classes.

After talking with the boys, we saw that the second version was more accurate. Clearly, the boys' behavior was unacceptable, and they were held accountable, but it was not an act of willful aggression. Nor was it abnormal, antisocial, or fraught with violent psychological undertones. But it's easy to understand how the image of boys as rampaging vandals (the wild-animal archetype) could spring to the minds of those who were predisposed to view the boy presence at their school as a negative. Any school day is full of similar, though less dramatic, misunderstandings regarding boys' motivations.

The emotional turmoil a boy feels—shame, anger, sadness—and his difficulty expressing those feelings may contribute to high activity and impulsiveness. A usually well behaved third-grade boy described being reprimanded by his teacher for climbing a fence in an outdoor play area in the minutes after his team lost the day's kickball game. Later, when the teacher sat the boy down to discuss consequences, the embarrassed boy confessed that he'd been on the verge of tears, but to avoid crying in front of his classmates, he had run to the fence and climbed it.

A friend, forty-three, recalled that, when he was young, he had an obsessional habit of counting the letters of words and sorting them into groups. His teachers, family, and friends considered this an odd piece of behavior but let him be. He never admitted to any of them that he immersed himself in this diversion to keep himself from crying in front of his classmates at school when he was upset. Here was a young boy with an impressive facility with words who chose to hide behind them, literally, rather than use them to express his emotional distress and his need for comfort. When boy activity is misinterpreted as aggression or willfulness, a boy is punished twice: once for the "willful" act and again in the loss of opportunity to reflect on the emotional dimension of the moment. In our work in schools, we often serve an "undercover" role in helping teachers and boys find a channel for communication that is free from the static of misunderstanding.

Michael with John, Norman: Negativity as a Cover

In my school consultation work, I often try *not* to see a boy who is struggling with the school environment. I prefer to work through his teachers and his parents, helping them to understand the issues without labeling the boy as a "patient" or a "problem." My meeting with a boy may alarm him or make him feel bad about himself, no matter how kind I am. This effect is called "labeling," and mental health professionals have always been aware of the simple and potentially negative impact of seeing a child for a diagnostic session. Perhaps the effect is diminished a bit these days, because so many children are seen and tested, but it is always a bit shocking for a child to be told he has to see a psychologist.

A second-grade teacher talked to me early in the new school year, already sensing trouble ahead for a boy in her class. John was relentlessly negative about school. In his first conversation with the teacher, he made his position clear. "I don't want to go to school. No one plays with me. No one likes me," he said. He had a whole set of adultlike mechanisms that were a bit baffling for the teacher because they were so confrontational and precocious: sarcasm, irony, trying to "dis" things or shrug them off. When John called a boy in his class an idiot, his teacher took him out into the hall to speak with him privately.

"He *is* an idiot," John snapped at her defiantly. "Do you think if he had any brains he'd keep coming here every day?" But even as John lashed out with his angry words, she could see he was terrified to be standing in the hall having this confrontation with her.

In reviewing John's history with his teacher, I saw that John's reading skills were very poor. He had been the only total nonreader at the beginning of first grade, and he was still the least capable reader in his second-grade class. Without question, his life at school had become a series of traumas for him, in which he experienced his self-esteem as being attacked daily.

John's situation required a change in strategy. He didn't appear to have a learning disability, but his slower developmental pace was going to keep him behind the pack. Indeed, because he was close enough to the group, the teacher had not wanted to single him out by praising his efforts too obviously or specifically. When John felt bad about reading, he felt bad about himself and exported that bad feeling in critical comments and defiant behavior. The teacher and I decided that she needed to let John know that she understood his feelings and that she needed to acknowledge his daily efforts and give him a lot of positive feedback. This she did and very soon reported back that, when she praised John on his reading effort, he smiled more and his negative banter faded out. And I faded out as a consultant as well. John didn't need to have a meeting with a psychologist. That would simply have complicated his already cloudy feelings.

John's reading skills developed slowly over time, but his behavior improved dramatically and quickly. He could cope with being a slow reader, but not with a vision of himself as a loser. With his teacher helping him feel competent and competitive—still in the game—John developed a more positive attitude. More confident of his potential for success, he no longer felt diminished or threatened by the successes of his classmates.

Norman was another boy I was consulted about but with whom I never met. Norman, a second grader, was consistently negative and loud. If someone said he or she had been to the beach for vacation, Norman would yell out, "The beach sucks." His teachers dreaded the new school year with him. They experienced him as a thin-skinned, self-centered, thoughtless little boy who expected to dominate his environment and everyone in it. Behavior like Norman's can be very hard to sympathize with, but I suggested to the teachers that, instead of responding to him as a negative person, they could help him "externalize" that negativity—define it as something separate from himself—and encourage him to rise up and defeat it.

This is a classic narrative therapy technique in which, instead of locating the problem inside the boy, you place the problem outside the boy and stand at his shoulder, allied with him in his struggle against it. When Norman acted in those negative ways, for instance, I encouraged his teacher to say to him, "I see that your bad mood has a grip on you today." Or to say, when he was having a great day, "How did you keep your bad mood from ruining your day at school today? You must have tricked it. How did you do that?"

This was a boy who wanted to feel good about himself and his life, but he had felt powerless in the face of his negative feelings. The approach helped him see himself as fighting an enemy. Every boy likes to fight an enemy; every boy likes to feel that he has allies. Norman's teacher was able to escape the trap of becoming Norman's enemy or viewing him as an entitled prince who was going to ruin her class for a year. It is particularly a boy thing to lead with this kind of negativity; many more boys do it in school than do girls. It is a challenge for every teacher to meet boy negativity with finesse and a deft response.

Despite the fact that boys are more active and impulsive than girls in the early grades and that there appears to be some biological basis for this, we should remember that activity and impulsivity are also produced by other forces. We can all remember a time when we've been very anxious—waiting for the results of a medical test, pacing the floor while a loved one was undergoing an operation, standing in front of a large audience, or meeting some very important person for the first time—and remember how this anxiety was translated into jitteriness and pacing or talking without thinking. Or think of a baby pumping his arms and legs while he cries; at young ages there is a direct connection between the centers of emotion and the brain's control center for movement, the motor cortex—and the infant's movements are a direct window on his emotional state.[6]

Similar principles are at work in all of us. We know that ease with verbal expression improves impulse control. So does emotional understanding, or being able to be conscious of your emotions and the reasons why you feel a certain way. When this literacy is absent, the emotions tend to be expressed through movement or action.

This developmental lack of ease with verbal expression, combined with the cultural edict against talking about feelings, channels boys' emotional energy into action. When boys are excited and happy, they often get loud and physical: they shout, they jump, they run, they push and shove one another around, they run it off. But when the emotions are painful, a good run isn't good enough. Physical activity can relieve some stress, but it doesn't eliminate the source of it, and for that reason, physical activity—whether it's running laps or punching a hole through the wall—isn't enough. It discharges the energy around the feeling but not the feeling itself. It lets off steam but doesn't turn off the burner under this emotional pressure cooker.

When school is not a good fit for a boy, when his normal expressions of energy and action routinely meet with negative responses from teachers and classmates, he stews in feelings of failure—feelings of sadness, shame, and anger, which can be very hard to detect beneath that brash exterior. Unable to "talk out" the emotional pressure, boys typically act out through verbal or physical aggression that walls them off emotionally from others, straining or severing emotional connections to the people and circumstances they find painful. And the worse a boy behaves, the more he invites negative reactions from teachers and other adults.

Medicating Boyhood: A Question of Culture, Philosophy

For many years, boys who were extremely distractible or extremely active were judged very harshly. Parents and teachers routinely labeled them as contrary, lazy, or morally deficient. With advances in the diagnosis of attention deficit disorder (ADD) and attention deficit–hyperactivity disorder (ADHD), there is now a somewhat more tolerant understanding of boys who struggle to pay attention or to sit calmly and who have trouble comprehending what everyone else gets with greater ease.

Over the years we have worked with many, many boys who suffer from ADD or ADHD and whose lives have been transformed through treatment with Ritalin or other drugs. However, as the number of boys taking Ritalin (the drug most often prescribed in the treatment of ADD) has topped 1 million in the United States—tripling from 1990 to 1995 alone— we have begun to see an even more frantic new version of the old view of a boy as someone who needs "fixing."[7] In this fix-frenzied spirit of the times, ADD/ADHD is the explanation of choice for any boys who have trouble paying attention, and with that explanation comes the willingness—even an eagerness, on the part of some adults—to medicate boys, not just to make them clinically "better," but to make them *better boys*.

They want a boy who makes As instead of Bs, a boy who can focus on the seriousness of building his future rather than the frivolous pursuits of the afternoon. They want a boy who always listens up when he's told to do something, a boy who reliably remembers instead of forgets.

Many thoughtful parents with genuine concerns about whether their son "has ADD" ask us, "How do you tell?" After all, the list of symptoms of ADD or ADHD is identical to the list of complaints most parents have about most boys at least some of the time: "fidgets or squirms in seat, loses things, doesn't seem to listen when spoken to directly, interrupts or intrudes on others, has difficulty playing quietly."[8] There is no simple answer to this question, and it is not even the best first question to ask. Attention problems don't generally show themselves in the same way as a typical medical condition. ADD isn't like the chicken pox; the question isn't "Does he have it, or does he not?" There are gradations of ADD severity, and many other factors about the boy's personality, intellectual abilities, and environment will affect how problematic ADD is for him. Two boys could have the same "degree" of ADD and be affected by it very differently.

All boys fit somewhere on a spectrum of distractibility, impulsivity, and hyperactivity. The fact that they are more physically restless and impulsive than girls makes many more boys than girls "look" ADHD.

That leaves you with the question, which boy is just "boy" and which boy is ADHD? We find in our work with schools and families that ADD/ADHD has added a new opportunity for turning away from the inner life of a boy, a new detour away from more complex issues of a boy's emotional life, of parenting issues and teaching styles, in favor of a drug that offers the promise of quick improvement.

Parents can fall into this trap as easily as can teachers and educators, like the parents of eight-year-old Evan, who they believed was "impulsive" because he sometimes didn't think carefully about a move when he was playing chess. Not a lot of eight-year-old boys could even sit through a whole game of chess. More typical was the case of the mother who said that her son had thrown a lamp at her and she thought he probably had ADD. When asked what she had done about the lamp incident, it became clear that she had done nothing and, what's more, that she rarely set any firm limits on her son's behavior. It would be hard to tell if he had ADD until more active parenting was in place.

The parents of a sixteen-year-old boy in therapy, Mark, asked for an ADD workup because his grades had slipped and they were wondering about his "organizational skills." This boy was a highly motivated achiever. Mark studied very hard, sometimes late into the evening. He also wanted to excel at sports and usually had practice every day after school and a game or meet on the weekend. He was also a good guitarist and had just started a rock band with some of his friends. As you can imagine, Mark didn't sleep much. When his parents made the request for the ADD evaluation, we felt that the only responsible reply was to suggest that we consider that option once they could demonstrate that he was getting close to eight hours of sleep every night.

Last, there are boys with other psychological conditions that get mislabeled as ADD. We have seen cases in which a parent or teacher wants us to check for ADD because a boy is having trouble concentrating and we find other factors that would clearly disrupt a boy's train of thought in math class: there was a boy whose best friend had recently tested HIV-positive, a boy whose father had died of a cancer with a strong genetic link, and a boy new to a school who was being unmercifully teased. These are fairly extreme cases, but they point out that, when thinking about ADD and normal boy behavior, the first question to ask is, "What are the reasonable expectations for a boy his age, and are there any plausible non-medical explanations for his behavior?" Plausible explanations may include family and parenting issues or a lack of fit for a boy in school, in the match of either teacher, school culture, or overall expectations.

Mitch Williams, a former major league baseball player who had the affectionate nickname of "Wild Thing," once told a sportswriter that, when he was a kid, his parents had been told that he was hyperactive, that he had ADD. The writer asked, "Did they put you on medication?" "No," Williams replied, "my dad bought a farm." Williams's father had a perspective that worked in his son's favor. He gave the boy an environment where his activity level did not present a problem.

We're not suggesting that all parents of active boys should move to the country, but only that it is important to think about the boy and his environment as a package. Even very active boys do quite well in a school with a high tolerance for a lot of movement. Alternatively, we have seen ADD-type distractible boys who fare very badly in an "open" classroom environment because of their organization and attention problems. Such children tend to need a great deal of structure and do better when they know exactly what is expected of them at all times. We have seen boys whose behavior suddenly improves when they move to a class with a teacher who likes them and doesn't think they are willfully bad. We've known boys who became "normal" overnight when they moved from a school with a very demanding environment in which they were expected to do homework for two or three hours a night to a school with more moderate requirements.

This is not to say that we don't believe that there is a medical condition that makes it very difficult for some people to sit still and pay attention in a minimally stimulating environment. The discovery of Ritalin and other drugs prescribed for ADD has been a lifesaver for them and their families. But in the less clear cases—and these are the majority—in our experience it is evident that most of what is being called ADD today would not have been called ADD fifteen or twenty years ago and that much of it falls within the normal range of boy behavior. We think it is very important to pause and think about the whole boy and the environment in which he finds himself before one jumps in with a diagnosis of ADD.

Then the challenge is to find the right combination of school program and environment, parental support, structure, and medication for boys with classic ADD and ADHD. And that's the challenge for all boys: to find the combination of support, empathy, appropriate structure, and expectations that works for boys, especially boys who are so significantly more distractible than their female classmates, boys whose level of spaciness or distractibility fits in least well in their school environment.

Boys Will Work for Schools That Work for Boys

When normal boy activity levels and developmental patterns are accommodated in the design of schools, curricula, classrooms, and instructional styles, an entire stratum of "boy problems" drops from sight. When a boy's experience of belonging at school is greater than his sense of differentness, then the burden of shame, inadequacy, and anger drops away, and he is free to learn.

Any school—coed or all-boys—can do this well or do it poorly.

If we look at all schools as laboratories for educational insights and strategies for engaging boys with developmentally appropriate challenges and learning opportunities, here is what we find:

Boys respond to a full range of academic, athletic, and extracurricular opportunities when the school culture supports their involvement. For instance, at an all-boys school, boys fill all the roles—artist, actor, athlete, editor, cook, cheerleader, and cellist—embracing experiences that often go to girls in a coed environment.

Boys can achieve a high standard of self-control and discipline in an environment that allows them significant freedom to be physically active. The headmaster of a boys' school known for its high standards of conduct noted that running, wrestling, and other benign physical expressions of boy energy are commonplace there during "downtime" between classes or other quieter activities. Not all boys wrestle whenever they have free time, but it helps every boy that this administrator welcomes a full range of boy behavior as normal and healthy and creates an environment in which boys feel that acceptance.

Boys benefit from the presence of male teachers and authority figures as role models of academic scholarship, professional commitment, moral as well as athletic leadership, and emotional literacy. The presence of men can have a tremendously calming effect on boys. When boys feel full acceptance—when they feel that their normal developmental skills and behavior *are* normal and that others perceive them that way—they engage more meaningfully in the learning experience.

These are the qualities that make some boys' schools—with their largely male faculty and boy-centered curriculum—particularly effective learning environments for boys. But a more boy-friendly school environment can be created at any school where educators want it to happen. Teachers and principals at all-boys and coed schools share with us success stories that underscore the power of even small details to transform the school setting for boys and, in so doing, transform boys' experience and behavior.

One boys' school serves students their midmorning snack of milk and chocolate-chip cookies outside well into the winter. The stated rationale is that the spot is centrally located on the campus. But the large open space also minimizes the effects of the inevitable bumping and shoving of groups of large boys.

The teacher of a coed kindergarten told us about her simple solution to "the unmanageable-boys problem" that routinely overwhelmed the first two hours of her class each day until the eleven A.M. recess. One day, following the start-up circle time, she turned the children out for an early recess before bringing them back in for class work. The release of physical energy made it much easier for the boys to settle in to work afterward, and both boys and girls were delighted with the early running-around time.

Other teachers have described rearranging the play areas in their classrooms to accommodate a greater range of boy activity with more open spaces or using the placement of desks as natural speed bumps to help reduce running with less nagging.

A third-grade teacher said she sends fidgety boys or girls on errands in the building for her. She places students who need her physical closeness in desks nearer to hers.

A kindergarten teacher told us how she uses hugs to welcome her students each day and has seen the transformative calming effect of that simple act on the most troubled and disruptive boys in the class. "It's about communicating what's important to that child," she explained. "Kids pick up on how you feel about them as human beings. If they feel respected, if they feel liked and cared for, those boys are a piece of cake. These cold, angry boys melt in your hand because their basic needs are to be loved, cared for, respected. Boys have the same human needs as the girls."

Meeting the Challenge of Boy Energy, Boy Potential

History is full of great men who were notable misfits in the school environment. In *The Life and Death of Mahatma Gandhi,* author Robert Payne wrote that Gandhi was "often boisterous" as a schoolboy and that he later described school as "the most miserable years of his life" and recalled that he "was never more than a mediocre student[;] . . . he had no aptitude for lessons and rarely appreciated his teachers[;] . . . he had no gift for learning and might have done better if he had never gone to school."

How can we "ask more" and "ask less" of boys in school in ways that respect who they are and each one's potential to grow up to be a decent, caring, successful man in his own way? This is the riddle that schools confront, the knot that schools have to untie every day. It can't be untied with a simple moral argument that concludes boys are "worse" than girls, nor can it be that boys are wild and must be forcibly civilized.

At our neighborhood ice-skating rink, skaters of all ages and expertise are welcome, and so it makes an interesting mix on an average Saturday night. Ice tag—one of boys' favorite activities on the ice—is prohibited. This is a very good rule, a great rule, because if skaters played tag openly, they'd be darting in and out and sometimes going against the orderly flow of skaters, many of them less able, gliding in a single direction around the rink. Or they might disturb those figure skaters who take to the middle of the rink to practice or perform their graceful maneuvers.

To enforce the ice tag ban, monitors—the equivalent of skating cops—patrol the crowded ice rink to guard against unruly behavior and roust rowdies from the rink. But boys love to play ice tag, and the ban on it only adds to the challenge of doing it so deftly that one avoids getting caught. Occasionally a girl joins in a tag game, but most often it's boys you see darting furtively through the gliding mass of leisurely skaters, clearly loving this marvelously intricate game of stops, starts, and smooth getaways. Inevitably, however, a few are collared by the monitors and escorted off the ice for a time-out. Just as inevitably, they return, refreshed and not at all discouraged from resuming their illicit game of speed and skill.

In a classroom setting, it can be hard to make this kind of allowance for "defiance within reason," but the bold energy it represents is life-affirming. If you never had that, you'd miss it. It would be a diminished world if everyone skated in precisely the same way around the circle or if the only deviation allowed were to skate graceful, skillful turns in the center of the ring. On the ice, in our schools, and in our lives, there is a need for some moments of anarchy, for a sprint of the spirit, not only for boys but for us all.

NOTES

1. See K. L. Alexander and D. R. Entwisle, "Achievement in the First 2 Years of School: Patterns and Processes," *Monographs of the Society for Research in Child Development* 53, 2 (1988), serial, 218.

2. Diane Halpern gives a cogent discussion of this in "Sex Differences in Intelligence: Implications for Education," *American Psychologist* 52 (1997): 1091–1102. She reviews the literature and although she finds a few differences between boys and girls on aspects of intelligence, rather than discuss these as part of the nature-nurture debate, she adopts a psychobiosocial model wherein the inextricable links between the biological bases of intelligence and environmental events are emphasized. From the article: "A predisposition to learn some behaviors and concepts more easily than others is determined by prior learning experiences, the neurochemical processes that allow learning to occur (release of neurotransmitters) and change in response to learning [such as] changes in areas of the brain that are active during performance of a task" (1092).

3. These findings are discussed in J. Huttenlocher, W. Haight, A. Bryk, M. Seltzer, et al., "Early Vocabulary Growth: Relation to Language Input and Gender," *Developmental Psychology* 27 (1991): 236–48; and S. E. Shaywitz, B. A. Shaywitz, J. M. Fletcher, and M. D. Escobar, "Prevalence of Reading Disability in Boys and Girls: Results of the Connecticut Longitudinal Study," *Journal of the American Medical Association* 264 (1990): 998–1002.

4. Gender differences in activity level are reviewed in G. A. Kohnstamm, "Temperament in Childhood: Cross-cultural and Sex Differences," in *Temperament in Children,* ed. G. A. Kohnstamm, J. E. Bates, and M. K. Rothbart (New York: Wiley, 1989), 483–508; and E. E. Maccoby, *The Two Sexes: Growing Up Apart, Coming Together* (Cambridge, MA: Belknap Press of Harvard University Press, 1998).

5. There has been a recent debate about whether boys really have a higher prevalence of ADHD than girls, especially for the primarily inattentive (i.e., non-hyperactive) type of ADHD. But when the prevalence statistics include

only the impulsive-hyperactive type of ADHD, boys are shown to have a higher prevalence. This is discussed in a recent review: E. A. Acia and K. C. Connors, "Gender Differences in ADHD?" *Developmental and Behavioral Pediatrics* 19 (1998): 77–83; and a recent epidemiological study in Tennessee: M. L. Wolraich, J. N. Hannah, T. Y. Pinnock, A. Baumgaertel, and J. Bown, "Comparison of Diagnostic Criteria for Attention-Deficit Hyperactivity Disorder in a County-Wide Sample," *Journal of the American Academy of Child and Adolescent Psychiatry* 35 (1996): 319–24.

6. This is discussed in J. Kagan and N. Snidman, "Infant Predictors of Inhibited and Uninhibited Profiles," *Psychological Science* 2 (1991): 40–44.

7. See J. W. Safer, W. Zito, and L. Fine, "Increased Methylphenidate Usage for Attention Deficit Disorder in the 1990s," *Pediatrics* 98 (1996): 1084–88.

8. The "official" diagnostic criteria for ADHD can be found in American Psychiatric Association, *Diagnostic and Statistical Manual of Mental Disorders,* 4th ed. (DSM-IV) (Washington, DC: American Psychiatric Association, 1994). See also N. Hallowell and J. Ratey, *Driven to Distraction* (New York: Pantheon, 1994).

REFERENCES

Acia, E. A., and K. C. Connors. "Gender Differences in ADHD?" *Developmental and Behavioral Pediatrics* 19 (1998): 77–83.

Alexander, K. L., and D. R. Entwisle. "Achievement in the First 2 Years of School: Patterns and Processes." *Monographs of the Society for Research in Child Development* 53 (1988): 2, serial 218.

American Psychiatric Association. *Diagnostic and Statistical Manual of Mental Disorders,* 4th ed. (DSM-IV). Washington, DC: American Psychiatric Association, 1994.

Cantwell, D. P. "Attention Deficit Disorder: A Review of the Past 10 Years." *Journal of the American Academy of Child and Adolescent Psychiatry* 35 (1996): 978–87.

Hallowell, N., and J. Ratey. *Driven to Distraction.* New York: Pantheon, 1994.

Halpern, D. F. "Sex Differences in Intelligence: Implications for Education." *American Psychologist* 52 (1997): 1091–1102.

Huttenlocher, J., W. Haight, A. Bryk, M. Seltzer, et al. "Early Vocabulary Growth: Relation to Language Input and Gender." *Developmental Psychology* 27 (1991): 236–48.

Jackson, A. W., and D. W. Hornbeck. "Educating Young Adolescents: Why We Must Restructure Middle Grade Schools." *American Psychologist* 44 (1989): 831–36.

Kagan, J., and N. Snidman. "Infant Predictors of Inhibited and Uninhibited Profiles." *Psychological Science* 2 (1991): 40–44.

Kohnstamm, G. A. "Temperament in Childhood: Cross-cultural and Sex Differences." In *Temperament in Children,* ed. G. A. Kohnstamm, J. E. Bates, and M. K. Rothbart. New York: Wiley, 1989, 483–508.

Luria, A. R. *The Role of Speech in the Regulation of Normal and Abnormal Behavior.* London: Pergamon Press, 1961.

Maccoby, E. E. *The Two Sexes: Growing Up Apart, Coming Together.* Cambridge, MA: Belknap Press of Harvard University Press, 1998.

Rothbart, M. K. "Temperament in Childhood: A Framework." In *Temperament in Children,* ed. G. A. Kohnstamm, J. E. Bates, and M. K. Rothbart. New York: Wiley, 1989, 59–73.

Safer, J. W., W. Zito, and L. Fine. "Increased Methylphenidate Usage for Attention Deficit Disorder in the 1990s." *Pediatrics* 98 (1996): 1084–88.

Shaywitz, S. E., B. A. Shaywitz, J. M. Fletcher, and M. D. Escobar. "Prevalence of Reading Disability in Boys and Girls: Results of the Connecticut Longitudinal Study." *Journal of the American Medical Association* 264 (1990): 998–1002.

Wolraich, M. L., J. N. Hannah, T. Y. Pinnock, A. Baumgaertel, and J. Bown. "Comparison of Diagnostic Criteria for Attention-Deficit Hyperactivity Disorder in a County-Wide Sample." *Journal of the American Academy of Child and Adolescent Psychiatry* 35 (1996): 319–24.

8

THE MISEDUCATION OF BOYS

Myra Sadker and David Sadker

TO ALL THE WORLD boys appear to be the favored gender, heirs apparent to society's rewards. They are the recipients of the lion's share of teacher time and attention and the featured figures in most textbooks. Sitting atop high standardized test scores, they haul in the majority of scholarship dollars, claim more than half of the openings in the most prestigious colleges, and are destined for high salaries and honored professions. Few would consider boys "miseducated," but gender bias is a two-edged sword. Girls are shortchanged, but males pay a price as well.

While boys rise to the top of the class, they also land at the bottom. Labeled as problems in need of special control or assistance, boys are more likely to fail a course, miss promotion, or drop out of school. Prone to take risks, they jeopardize not only their academic future but their lives as they dominate accident, suicide, and homicide statistics. In fact, because the educational failures of boys are so visible and public, schools invest extra resources on their behalf, and yet the catastrophic results continue. Girls suffer silent losses, but boys' problems are loud enough to be heard throughout the school.

> Sitting in the back of the social studies classroom to supervise one of our practice teachers, we have a student's-eye-view of events. A group of eighth-grade boys storms into the room, careening off desks and one another as they make their way to their places. By the time the noise subsides and the new teacher begins her lesson, the last row has been claimed entirely by males.

When the teacher tells the class to divide into geography groups, six are formed: three all-male and three all-female. The all-girl groups work quietly to complete their maps while the boys talk loudly, joke, and roam around the room. About five minutes before the class ends, they slam their books closed and stuff them into bookbags, any pretense of work over. Shouting above the racket, our student teacher tries to give the homework assignment, but only lip readers have a chance of hearing it. The boys in the back are already shoving one another on their way out the door.

When we ask the cooperating teacher, the veteran who is helping our novice, about the boys in his class, he pulls no punches: "They're sloppy, noisy, immature. I don't know the reason, but compared to boys, the girls are a pleasure to teach. Actually, these boys are not bad. When I was teaching in Baltimore, we were warned about being hit or shot. Here the boys are difficult but not dangerous. We just try to keep them calm and working."

Raised to be active, aggressive, and independent, boys enter schools that seem to want them to be quiet, passive, and conforming. In an uneasy compromise, many walk a tightrope between compliance and rebellion. To keep the balance, schools go the extra mile for males and give them more resources and attention. For some this isn't enough, however. They fail, are left behind, and never make it to graduation. Others become stars. They climb to the head of the class only to discover increasing pressure and the steep price of success.

Starring Boys

When teachers are asked to remember their most outstanding student, boys' names dominate the list. Teachers say males are brighter, better at science and math, and more likely to become the nation's future leaders. When students are asked to choose outstanding classmates, they also name boys. But boys are also on another roster. When teachers remember their worst students—the discipline problems, the ones most likely to create a classroom disturbance or to flunk out of school—they still list boys.[1] As one teacher at a workshop put it, "Boys at school are either in the process of becoming the Establishment or fighting it. Either way, they are the center of attention."

While boys stand out, girls blend in, do their work, wait their turn, and become the supporting cast. But the main parts, the starring roles of hero and villain, are usually reserved for the boys. Training for stardom begins at home. An elementary school principal in Connecticut described an interview she had with a mother and her young son, a new kindergarten prospect:

> There they were both in my office, the mother sitting across the desk with her son on her lap. As I was explaining the kindergarten program, I watched the boy squirm. He began tapping his mother on the arm to get her attention. She asked him to wait, but he only tapped harder. I began to hurry my explanation, but I wasn't fast enough. Finally the little boy grabbed his mother's chin, pulled it down to him, and said angrily, "I need you *now!*"
>
> That image sums it up for me. Many boys come to school the center of attention, the pride and joy of the family. Then the shock hits: They're not the center anymore. As one of many, they must wait, learn to take their turn, and follow the rules. They come to school the Prince of Everything, and here they lose their royal standing.

Arriving at school as the entitled gender, boys decide which is the best lunchroom table and take it. During recess they claim the schoolyard as their own. In the classroom, attention is the prize. Boys start by raising their hands, but if the teacher does not call on them, the more assertive literally call on themselves, shouting out the answers, sometimes even interrupting the teacher midsentence. But not every boy can be at the head of the class. Only a few rise to the very top. We watched two boys fight for star status in a suburban elementary school:

> Twenty-eight students file into the room, hang up their coats, and take their seats. The teacher, a nine-year veteran of the classroom, reviews the day's agenda. Math is first on the schedule.
>
> It is then we meet Jim and Matt, without being formally introduced. With the teacher's first question their hands shoot up. First Matt answers, then Jim, as each competes to be the center of attention. Hands waving, they edge out of their seats. Jim sits on his knees, gaining a full six inches and a visible advantage over Matt. The next question goes to the now-elevated Jim, stirring Matt to even greater heights—literally. He stands beside his chair and waves his arm, "Settle down, guys, and give someone else a chance," the teacher says. Several other students are called on, but within a few minutes the "Matt and Jim Show" returns. When the teacher writes difficult problems on the board, the questions no one else can answer, she turns to her two male stars for answers. "Matt and Jim will be great mathematicians

when they grow up," the teacher comments as math class ends and she erases the problems from the board.

Evidently, Matt will grow up to be a great historian as well, for he dominates social studies, too. With Jim less involved, Matt has the floor all to himself. During language arts, the class works in small groups on stories for a school newspaper, and the achievements of Jim and Matt are featured in several articles. The last class before lunch is science, and Matt is called up for a demonstration. As he stands in front of the room and reads the results of the science experiment, the other students dutifully copy his calculations into their notebooks.

During lunch we review our observation forms. Although almost evenly divided between boys and girls, males in this class have benefited from a more active learning environment; but Matt and Jim were in a class of their own. Matt received more of the teacher's time and talent than anyone else, with Jim coming in second. Calling these two boys future mathematicians, the teacher further distanced them from the rest of the class. At the end of three hours, Matt and Jim have answered almost half of the teachers' questions, leaving the other twenty-six students to divide up the remainder of the teachers' attention. Nine students, six girls and three boys, have not said a single word.

Warmed by the academic spotlight, students like Matt and Jim reap school rewards. In the elementary grades their future careers are the talk of the teachers' room. By high school, prestigious colleges and scholarships loom on the horizon. But school life can be marred by clouds even for stars. Since their performance is head and shoulders above the other students, boys like Matt and Jim no longer compete with their classmates; they are vying with each other. These superstar students, who are more likely to be male, face ever-increasing pressure and cutthroat competition in their fight to get to the top—to win state honors, the most lucrative scholarship, a place at an Ivy League college. From Jim's vantage point, although ahead of his classmates, he just can't seem to catch up with Matt. Frustration and despair often haunt and depress smart boys who find themselves "runners-up" in the competition for top prizes.

Star students are not the only ones who capture the teacher's attention. When schools are not able to meet their needs, some boys cross the line and go from calling out to acting out. On the classroom stage these males take the bad boy role, sometimes using it as a passport to popularity. Interviewing elementary school students, researchers have found that the most admired males are those ready to take on the teacher. Here's how two fourth graders described these popular boys:

MARK: They're always getting into trouble by talking back to the teacher.

TOM: Yeah, they always have to show off to each other that they aren't afraid to say anything they want to the teacher, that they aren't teachers' pets. Whatever they're doing, they make it look like it's better than what the teacher is doing, 'cause they think what she's doing is stupid.

MARK: And one day Josh and Allen got in trouble in music 'cause they told the teacher the Disney movie she wanted to show sucked. They got pink [disciplinary] slips.

TOM: Yeah, and that's the third pink slip Josh's got already this year, and it's only Thanksgiving.[2]

If teachers were asked to "round up the usual suspects"—the class clowns, troublemakers, and delinquents—they would fill the room with boys. Teachers remember these boys for all the wrong reasons. In fact, so pervasive is the concern over male misbehavior that even when a boy and a girl are involved in an identical infraction of the rules, the male is more likely to get the penalty. Scenes like this one are played out daily in schools across America:

> Two seniors, Kyle and Michelle, arrive at their high school English class fifteen minutes late. The teacher stares at them as they enter the room. "Kyle, do you need a special invitation? Is it too much to ask that you get here on time? Never mind. Sit down and see me after class. (Pause; voice softens.) And Michelle, I'm disappointed in you."

In most cases when boys get tougher discipline, however, it is because they deserve it. Their disorderly conduct sets into motion a chain reaction with steep costs and lasting impressions. When men at our workshops looked back on their school days, some of their most unpleasant memories were of the tough disciplinary incidents they experienced. A man who is now a high school teacher in New England said: "I was in fifth grade, and it was the first time I had a male teacher. This teacher would treat the girls almost like princesses, but when the boys were disciplined, it was very physical and very rough. He would grab us by the hair and slam our heads down on the desk."

> Ann, a student teacher in a Maryland middle school, is already learning the disaster potential of problem students, mainly male. Observ-

ing her class, we keep track of which students she calls on, what she says, and where she moves in the room. When we show her our notes, she sees that most of her questions went to six boys sitting at two tables near her desk.

"I know I usually call on those boys up front. I put them there so I can keep an eye on them."

"Did you realize that more than half of the questions you asked went to those six boys?"

"I didn't think I was talking with them that much, but I do use questions to keep them on task."

"Were they on task?"

"At the beginning, but toward the end they weren't paying attention."

"What about the other twenty-four students, the rest of the class? How were they doing?"

Ann looks confused. "I don't even know," she says. "I was so concerned about that group of boys, so worried they would act out, I didn't pay much attention to the rest of the class."

Ann was devoting her energy to boys at the bottom, the ones with potential to undermine her authority and throw the class into turmoil. So powerful was their influence, they determined where she walked, whom she questioned, and even how the room was arranged and where students sat.

Boys at the bottom and boys at the top are magnets that attract a teacher's attention either as a reward or as a mechanism for control. Teachers hope their male stars will become tomorrow's corporate presidents, senators, and civic leaders, but they do not hold high hopes for the boys at the bottom. Instead they fear those males could become involved in very serious trouble. Both groups are taught very different lessons and socialized into distinct aspects of the male role in America. Whether they are first or last, those boys pay a price.

Field of Broken Dreams

The principal of the Indiana high school obviously enjoyed showing off his school. He took us on a tour of the new computer center, the science labs, and a vocational training area. Then he began to smile broadly.

"This is our jewel," he said.

We turned a corner, he opened a door, and we entered the gym. It was enormous. Thousands of seats terraced up all sides, and the ceiling was at least four stories high. The gym was almost as big as the entire rest of the school.

"It's incredible, but why so large?" we asked.

"Intimidation," the principal responded.

"Intimidation?"

"When the other teams come here, to this small town, they expect a small gym. This place intimidates the hell out of them. The whole town comes out and screams for our boys. This is the town's entertainment center, our sports cathedral."

The Feminine School and the Emasculation of Boys

Through athletics boys are taught that competition, aggression, and endurance build real men, on the playing field and in the workplace. It was precisely because they intensified traditional notions of masculinity that educators found sports so attractive and incorporated them into the official school program. By the early part of the twentieth century, athletics had become an important line of defense, a counterweight against a frightening educational development: the arrival of women teachers.

From the 1870s into the twentieth century, schools experienced a gender revolution. During the Civil War men left their teaching positions to join the army. When schools posted vacancy signs, women lined up. By the early 1900s they had become more than 85 percent of the nation's teachers, more than half the school principals, and in the Midwest, 60 percent of school superintendents, numbers that far exceed today's statistics. Once a world managed by men, schools were being taken over by women.

Not everyone was pleased with these developments. Critics argued that schools had become a battleground between female teachers who were stressing decorum and conformity and free-spirited boys who were struggling to grow into real men. In this battle of the sexes, boys were the victims and losers. Critics had a name for these new instructors: the "woman peril."

By the early part of the twentieth century the public had come to believe that the arrival of female teachers represented a serious threat to the healthy development of boys. These concerns were fanned by critics such as military leader Admiral F. E. Chadwick, who declared that a boy taught by a woman "at his most character-forming age is to render violence to nature [causing] a feminized manhood, emotional, illogical, noncombative." According to the admiral, female teachers represented a threat to healthy male development and endangered the national security.[3]

Psychologist G. Stanley Hall agreed, explaining that a time of rough and uncouth development was necessary so boys could forge their masculine identity. Women as teachers or mothers harmed males by feminizing them, taming them, and transforming them into unnatural "little gentlemen." Denied a "wild period" of toughness and independence, these boys would never mature into "real men."

Hall's warnings resonated across the nation. A principal in Louisville, Kentucky, advised his colleagues that American boys were losing their competitive edge and becoming effeminate. The culprit was the female teacher. A University of Wisconsin professor termed the entry of women into teaching an unwanted "invasion."[4] And an educator from England observed that "the boy in America is not being brought up to punch another boy's head or to stand having his own punched in a healthy and proper manner; that there is a strange and indefinable air coming over the man; a tendency toward a common, if I may call it, sexless tone of thought."[5]

To develop tougher males while controlling wild ones, some school administrators experimented with an innovative plan. They co-opted the rough-and-tumble games boys played during recess and in their free time, and made these part of the official curriculum. By sponsoring athletic contests, schools not only developed "manly" boys but also subdued unruly ones, exhausting them into compliance. A New York principal observed in 1909 that when "the most troublesome and backward boys" played basketball for an hour each day, miracles were achieved: "An incorrigible class was brought to the gymnasium; a tired but tractable class left it." The administrator also found that sports created school spirit and helped solve discipline problems. "Many instances have come to my notice where big, strong, incorrigible, and stupid boys have been stimulated by the opportunity to represent their schools."[6]

As part of the educational curriculum, athletics was seen as a panacea, one that would reduce the dropout problem, create a masculine environment, and give unruly males an energy outlet—and schools a public relations bonanza. The community flocked to sporting events, especially football and basketball games; they even paid to attend. School sports were a regular newspaper feature, and high school athletes became local celebrities. But even sports did not stem the tide of the "woman peril." Male teachers continued to feel threatened.

Registering its opposition in 1904, the Male Teachers Association of New York City came forward with its position: Men are "necessary ideals for boys" and are "less mechanical in instruction."[7] Consequently, they are more effective teachers and deserve more money. Woman-bashing reached the highest levels of government when Theodore Roosevelt lamented the arrival of the female teacher and publicly spoke out against her negative impact on boys. But neither presidents nor professors could deter school boards from a good deal. By 1920 a school with forty teachers was typically staffed by thirty-four women and six men, saving thousands of tax dollars since women worked for less pay. As females took the helm of America's classrooms, citizens scrutinized school performance. What they saw only added to their concern.

Less than a century ago, girls' faltering performance on standardized tests, their loss of self-esteem, and their underenrollment in higher education and professional schools were not seen as problems. Back then, girls and schools seemed a match made in heaven. When it came to grades, girls excelled. Sitting on the graduation stage, they sparkled like perfect academic jewels while boys fidgeted. Many males didn't even stay in school long enough to make it to graduation. At the turn of the century, the term for male failure was not "grade repeater"; boys who were left back were called "retarded."

Throughout the first half of the twentieth century, critics continued to blame female teachers for boys' academic problems. As late as 1965, Patricia Sexton wrote in the *Saturday Review:*

> Boys and the schools seem locked in a deadly and ancient conflict that may eventually inflict mortal wounds on both. . . . The problem is not just that teachers are too often women. It is that school is too much a woman's world, governed by women's rules and standards. The school code is that of propriety, obedience, decorum, cleanliness, physical and, too often, mental passivity.[8]

Sexton continued her male distress call in *The Feminized Male,* an influential book published in 1969.[9] Echoing Hall's half-century-old criticism, Sexton argued that schools emasculated boys by imposing feminine norms that demanded docility, neatness, and silence—all the qualities males lacked. Forcing a boy to go to school was like putting a bull in a china shop. Males who submitted to the feminine school environment added new entries to the school vernacular: "mama's boy," "teacher's pet," and "apple polisher." Those who resisted were punished. Because of female teachers, boys were put in an impossible situation—forced to choose between feminization or failure.

In the 1960s and '70s, worry over the "woman peril" was replaced by concern for women in peril as the modern feminist movement took shape. By the time Sexton's *The Feminized Male* arrived in bookstores, Betty

Friedan's *The Feminine Mystique* was already there. As women's spheres continued to expand, men's territory shriveled. Like hunting game or fighting intruding tribes, the male role of family protector and breadwinner was becoming a thing of the past.

The early position of the fledgling men's movement was that masculinity had been too long measured by the size of a man's paycheck, by his ability to win, by repressing emotions, toughing it out, and beating other males. In the end this behavior proved self-defeating, and the costs were daunting: alienation from others and early death. Men were advised to allow their "feminine" side to emerge. Caring fathers and sensitive husbands were promoted in movies, books, and talk shows. But a second wave of authors marked a different path, calling upon men not to discover their feminine qualities but instead to reclaim their masculine roots.

In 1991, Robert Bly's *Iron John* sold more copies than any other nonfiction book in America, and a few months later Sam Keen's *Fire in the Belly* became a best-seller. Credited by some with reinventing the modern men's movement and criticized by others as a lunatic fringe leader, Bly asked males to join him on a mythological journey to relive their past through an ancient folktale: Iron John's initiation into manhood. To reach true masculinity Iron John needed to detach himself not only from woman as mother but from all females and return to a legendary past of ancient forests, physical challenge, and male mentors. Bly wrote, "The Industrial Revolution in its need for office and factory workers has pulled boys away from their father[s] and from other men, and placed them in compulsory schools, where the teachers are mostly women."[10] There boys suffocate under female influence that is "not balanced by positive male values."[11] In his resurrection of fears about the "woman peril," Bly's warning is a reminder: When it comes to gender, parents and teachers have spent most of the twentieth century worrying about boys at school—and the kind of men they will become.

Out of Control

The importance of initiation into manhood has been a perennial theme. Bly's *Iron John*, G. Stanley Hall's "wild period," and Teddy Roosevelt's call for "manly" contests with nature all describe the rite of passage from boy to manhood. And all claim that when women are in charge of this passage, males are at risk of feminization. But without the influence of women, the traditional characteristics of masculinity—aggression, toughness, and strength—may become intensified and distorted; sometimes they spin out of control. In all-male groups, females are more likely to be objectified and treated as less than human. Then, as in sports, sexuality is turned into an arena where boys must prove they are real men. Some males take extreme action to "score."

On the television screen he looked clean-cut and handsome, the all-American boy. The Lakewood senior explained to the television audience that school athletes like himself were "the popular men on campus," so popular that they had formed their own group called the Spur Posse. The posse's purpose was to have sex with as many girls as possible, counting each girl as 1 point. The rules were quite clear: Multiple sex encounters with the same girl still counted as only a single point, so different girls were needed for the score to climb high. The star Spur had a score of 67. Other members had much lower scores, having slept with only 40 or 50 girls. "I'm Reggie Jackson," said one, referring to the number 44 worn by the baseball player as the number of points he had accumulated. Expressing no remorse, regret, or second thoughts, posse members viewed themselves as male role models and claimed that "eight out of ten guys would like to have the life we lead." The posse's extreme exploits, covered by national media, gave the Lakewood Secondary School a new nickname: "Rapewood High."

Initially seven girls, ranging in age from eleven to seventeen, brought criminal charges against Spur Posse members, but all but one of the charges were dropped due to lack of evidence. One girl's mother said, "We're living in fear. They're hoodlums." Another girl transferred out of Lakewood to a new high school. But not everyone viewed the posse's behavior as a problem. Some parents saw it as a case of "boys will be boys" and described the girls as willing participants. A father of one of the boys said that the posse was just a group of athletes, an adolescent group like "band, choir, or the PTA." The boys were simply "sowing a few wild seeds" before college.[12]

College life is supposed to be a world apart from the transgressions of groups like the Spur Posse. But stereotypic masculine qualities can become magnified and distorted in higher education, too. Our students at The American University were discussing all-male rites of passage, from Eagle Scout initiation ceremonies to criminal acts required to join street gangs. A week later a young woman stopped by our office with a videotape.

"My friends shot this tape themselves. They go to college in Pennsylvania."

Not knowing what to expect, we loaded our VCR and watched what turned out to be a game called "physical challenge." The first boy on the tape was drinking directly from a hot chili bottle. With his face red and his voice hoarse, he yelled "Challenge!" and then passed the bottle to the next boy. Moaning and screaming, each took a mouthful. Next the boys challenged one another to eat live insects and then to walk down a public street naked. The final scene was called "riding a tree." Each boy crawled onto a second-story ledge and jumped, trying to reach a nearby tree to break the fall. Some caught branches, but others missed and hit the ground hard. The next day we told the student how upsetting we found the tape.

"I know. It's so dangerous," she said. "One boy broke an arm 'riding the tree,' and another didn't get anywhere near it. He plunged to the ground and received a concussion. But they still do it."

"Are they in a fraternity?"

"No. They're just college friends who share an apartment. This is their fun."

In a few colleges, this macho quality permeates campus life. Visitors to Wabash, Morehouse, and Hampden-Sydney, three of America's five remaining all-male colleges, say that a trip to campus is like experiencing a quantum leap back in time. At Wabash in Indiana, freshmen pledges still wear beanies, tip them when they pass a professor, and remind observers of the 1950s when Ivy League schools were all-male worlds.[13] To critics these colleges are historical oddities with little relevance to today's world. To advocates they represent unique and effective academic environments that are worth saving and nourishing. But two all-male colleges, The Citadel and Virginia Military Institute (VMI), both quasi-public and all military, have generated far more intense controversy. The Citadel and VMI argue that when females become students, military toughness and tradition are lost, so women are not welcome. While accepting taxpayer money, these colleges close their doors to half the taxpayers, a policy that has landed them in court.

Although The Citadel and VMI appear to be miniature versions of West Point, they are not. Unlike West Point, where the primary purpose is to prepare army officers, a minority of the students at these two colleges actually enter the military. But a military-style education is regarded as a way of teaching toughness.

At The Citadel, first-year students, called knobs, are closely supervised every waking minute. They must ask permission for each action—eating, leaving, passing, even sneezing or coughing. They salute everyone, talk to no one, serve upperclassmen at mess, and try to swallow a few quick mouthfuls before mealtime is over. This humiliating and grueling system is designed to develop discipline and the ability to function under intense stress and pressure. Many graduates praise their military-style education: "It gives you the feeling that you will confront nothing in life you can't handle. . . . You will not freeze, you will not choke up, you will do what has to be done." Not all students agree.

When Chad was recruited by The Citadel, he looked forward to the experience. "I thought a little responsibility and discipline might be good for me," he said. But when Chad missed crucial field goals and lost a football game, the young man learned firsthand about The Citadel's reputation for "building men." One night he was dragged from his bed, his head was wrapped in a blanket, and he was dunked repeatedly in a utility sink filled with water. Finally he passed out. Another night he was strung up by his fingers and left hanging in a closet with a saber perched between his legs. After three weeks of these lessons in self-discipline, Chad had had enough. He dropped out of school.[14]

Intensified masculinity is not just a situation of "boys will be boys." These rites of initiation and the sexual and physical proving grounds go beyond boyhood. Adult men also push the boundaries of masculinity to the danger point and beyond:

> Anthony Roberts was about to be initiated into a rafting and outdoor group called Mountain Men Anonymous. The Oregon carpenter's rite of passage seemed easy enough: hold a one-gallon fuel can above his head as a friend demonstrated his outdoor skills by shooting an arrow through the elevated vessel. Unfortunately, his friend's aim was low; Roberts lost his eye and almost his life. Recovering in the hospital, he told reporters, "I feel really stupid."[15]

Groups like Mountain Men Anonymous create a cultural time warp, idealizing a time in the past when males battled nature and each other. But today's culture calls for other skills—cooperation in the workplace and parenting at home. When risk-taking, violence, and sexual aggression are out of control and caring and nurturance are repressed, a distorted profile emerges, one that is detrimental to the good of society and to the healthy development of men.

Changing the Script

Boys confront frozen boundaries of the male role at every turn of school life. They grow up learning lines and practicing moves from a time-worn script: Be cool, don't show emotion, repress feelings, be aggressive, compete and win. As the script is internalized, boys learn to look down on girls and to distance themselves from any activity considered feminine.

Dutifully they follow the lines of the script, but now changes are being made in the plot. Today's schoolboys are learning lines for a play that is closing. Consider these statistics:

- From elementary school through high school, boys receive lower report card grades. By middle school they are far more likely to be grade repeaters and dropouts.[16]

- Boys experience more difficulty adjusting to school. They are nine times more likely to suffer from hyperactivity and higher levels of academic stress.[17]

- The majority of students identified for special education programs are boys. They represent 58 percent of those in classes for the mentally retarded, 71 percent of the learning disabled, and 80 percent of those in programs for the emotionally disturbed.[18]

- In school, boys' misbehavior results in more frequent penalties, including corporal punishment. Boys comprise 71 percent of all school suspensions.[19]

Beyond academic problems, conforming to a stereotypic role takes a psychological toll:

- Boys are three times more likely to become alcohol dependent and 50 percent more likely to use illicit drugs. Men account for more than 90 percent of alcohol- and drug-related arrests.[20]

- Risk-taking behavior goes beyond drug and alcohol abuse. The leading cause of death among fifteen- to twenty-four-year-old white males is accidents. Teenage boys are more likely to die from gunshot wounds than from all natural causes combined.[21]

- Many boys are encouraged to pursue unrealistically high career goals. When these are not attained, males often feel like failures, and a lifelong sense of frustration may follow.[22]

- Males commit suicide two to three times more frequently than females.[23]

The problems for minority males are more devastating:

- Approximately one in every three black male teenagers is unemployed, and those who are working take home paychecks with 30 percent less salary than white workers.[24] It is estimated that 25 percent of black youth's income results directly from crime and that one in every six African-American males is arrested by age nineteen.[25]

○ The odds of a young white woman being a murder victim are one in 369; for a young white man, one in 131; for an African-American woman, one in 104; and for an African-American man, a shocking one in 21. Homicide is the leading cause of death for young black men.[26]

City by city, the statistics are even more alarming. In New York City, about three out of four black males never make it to graduation, and in Milwaukee, 94 percent of all expelled students are African-American boys.[27] Milwaukee, Detroit, and Chicago consider black males an "endangered academic species" and have resorted to some radical solutions.

Milwaukee was one of the first cities to create black male academies, public schools that serve only African-American boys. The idea spread to other metropolitan areas, along with the notion that the best teachers for black boys are black men. At Matthew Henson Elementary School in a poor, drug-infested section of Baltimore, Richard Boynton teaches a class of young black students. Most of them grew up without fathers, so Boynton's responsibilities go beyond the classroom. "There are three things I enforce," he said, "three things I want them to know in that room: responsibility, respect, and self-control. I feel that these three things will not only carry you through school, they'll carry you through life."[28] So Boynton checks to make sure that all the boys have library cards. On weekends he takes them to the Smithsonian or to play ball in the park. "It's almost as if I have twenty-seven sons," he said. Boynton tries to create a school that will turn each of his "sons" on to education. But not everyone is convinced that teaching black males separately is the best approach.

"I read these things, and I can't believe that we're actually regressing like this," said African-American psychologist Kenneth Clark. "Why are we talking about segregating and stigmatizing black males?"[29] Clark's stinging observations are particularly potent since his research paved the way for the 1954 *Brown* decision that desegregated America's schools. Other critics charge that black male academies are little more than a return to the cries of "woman peril," scapegoating female teachers, criticizing black mothers, and ignoring the needs of African-American girls. NOW, the ACLU, and several courts have found separate black male education to be an example of sex discrimination and a violation of the law.

Morningside Elementary School in Prince Georges County, Maryland, is not a black male academy, but its students take special pride in their school team, the Master Knights. Tuesdays and Thursdays are team days, and the members, wearing blue pants and white shirts, devote recess and afternoons to practice. But the Knights, the majority of whom are young black boys, differ from other school teams. Their practices take place in the school library, and the arena in which they compete is chess.

The idea for the team originated in the office of Beulah McManus, the guidance counselor. When children, most often African-American boys, were referred to her as behavior problems, she pulled out a worn chess set. Somehow the game got boys talking, and eventually they found out they enjoyed chess, with its emphasis on tactics and skill, and the chance to compete on a field where size and strength mattered less than brains. As Gregory Bridges, the twelve-year-old president of the Master Knights, said, "When you see someone who is big and bad on the streets, you hardly see anyone who plays chess. . . . You have to have patience and a cool head, and that patience carries outside the chess club."[30] While Morningside emphasizes the importance of getting African-American boys excited about education, girls are not excluded, says principal Elsie Neely. In fact, the school is trying to recruit more female players for next year.

While Morningside stresses extracurricular activities in order to involve boys, some teachers are bringing lessons that challenge the male sex role stereotype directly into the classroom. Often they use the growing number of children's books that show boys expanding their roles. In a fourth-grade class we watched a teacher encouraging boys to push the borders of the male stereotype. As we observed her lesson, we were struck by how much effort it took to stretch outmoded attitudes. She began by writing a letter on the board.

Dear Adviser:

My seven-year-old son wants me to buy him a doll. I don't know what to do. Should I go ahead and get it for him? Is this normal, or is my son sick? Please help!
Waiting for your answer,

Concerned

"Suppose you were an advice columnist, like Ann Landers," the teacher said to the class, "and you received a letter like this. What would you tell this parent? Write a letter answering 'Concerned,' and then we'll talk about your recommendations."

For the next twenty minutes she walked around the room and gave suggestions about format and spelling. When she invited the students to read their letters, Andy volunteered.

Dear Concerned:

You are in big trouble. Your son is sick, sick, sick! Get him to a psy-chiatrist fast. And if he keeps asking for a doll, get him bats and balls and guns and other toys boys should play with.
Hope this helps,

Andy

Several other students also read their letters, and most, like Andy, rec-ommended that the son be denied a doll. Then the teacher read Charlotte Zolotow's *William's Doll,* the story of a boy who is ridiculed by other children when he says he wants a doll. Not until his grandmother visits does he get his wish so that, as the wise woman says, he can learn to be a father one day.

As the teacher was reading, several students began to fidget, laugh, and whisper to one another. When she asked the fourth graders how they liked the book, one group of boys, the most popular clique in the class, acted as if the story was a personal insult. Their reaction was so hostile, the teacher had trouble keeping order. We heard their comments:

"He's a fag."

"He'd better learn how boys are supposed to behave, or he'll never get to be a man."

"If I saw him playing with that baby doll, I'd take it away. Maybe a good kick in the pants would teach him."

"Dolls are dumb. It's a girly thing to do."

Next the teacher played the song "William Wants a Doll" from the *Free to Be You and Me* album. Several boys began to sing along in a mocking tone, dragging out the word *doll* until it became two syllables: "William wants a do-oll, William wants a do-oll." As they chanted, they pointed to Bill, the star athlete of the class. Both boys and girls whispered and laughed as Bill, slumped in his chair, looked ready to explode.

Belatedly the teacher realized the problem of the name coincidence; she assured the class that there was nothing wrong with playing with dolls, that it teaches both girls and boys how to become parents when they grow up. When the students began to settle down, she gave them her next instructions: "I'd like you to reread your letters and make any last-minute corrections. If you want to change your advice, you may, but you don't have to."

Later we read the students' letters. Most of them said a seven-year-old boy should not get a doll. But after listening to William's story, six modified their advice, having reached a similar conclusion: "Oh, all right.

Give him a doll if you have to. But no baby dolls or girl dolls. Make sure it's a Turtle or a G.I. Joe."

For some nontraditional programs, reading *William's Doll* is just a first step. At Germantown Friends School in Philadelphia, parenting classes begin in elementary school where children learn to observe, study, and interact with infants. By the sixth grade both boys and girls are in charge of caring for babies at school. Programs that make child-rearing a central and required part of school life find that boys become more nurturant and caring in their relationships with others.

Schools in New York City and other communities are downplaying aggression and encouraging cooperation through programs in conflict resolution. In these courses students learn how to negotiate and compromise while they avoid attitudes and actions that lead to violence. Students learn techniques in how to control anger, to listen carefully to others, and to seek common ground.

These innovative courses are rare. Most schools are locked in a more traditional model, one that promotes competition over cooperation, aggression over nurturing, and sports victories rather than athletic participation. Some boys thrive on this traditional male menu, and most students derive some benefit. But the school program is far from balanced, and the education served to boys is not always healthy despite the extra portions they receive.

From their earliest days at school, boys learn a destructive form of division—how to separate themselves from girls. Once the school world is divided, boys can strive to climb to the top of the male domain, thinking that even if they fall short, they still are ahead of the game because they are not girls. Boys learn in the classroom that they can demean girls at will. Schools that do not permit racist, ethnic, or religious slights still tolerate sexism as a harmless bigotry.

In *American Manhood*, Anthony Rotundo writes that men need to regain "access to stigmatized parts of themselves—tenderness, nurturance, the desire for connection, the skills of cooperation—that are helpful in personal situations and needed for the social good."[31] Studies support Rotundo's contention: Males who can call on a range of qualities, tenderness as well as toughness, are viewed by others as more intelligent, likable, and mentally healthy than rigidly stereotyped men.[32] But boys cannot develop these repressed parts of themselves without abandoning attitudes that degrade girls. Until gender equity becomes a value promoted in every aspect of school, boys, as victims of their own miseducation, will grow up to be troubled men; they will be saddened by unmet expectations, unable to communicate with women as equals, and unprepared for modern life.

NOTES

1. Safir, Marilyn, Rachel Hertz-Lazarowitz, Shoshana BenTsui-Mayer, Haggai Kupermintz. "Prominence of Girls and Boys in the Classroom: School-children's Perceptions," *Sex Roles* 27:9–10 (1992), pp. 439–53.

   Bentsvi-Mayer, Shoshana, Rachel Marilyn Hertz-Lazarowitz, and P. Safir. "Teachers' Selections of Boys and Girls as Prominent Pupils," *Sex Roles* 21:3–4 (1989), pp. 231–45.

2. Adler, Patricia, Steven Kless, and Peter Adler. "Socialization to Gender Roles: Popularity Among Elementary School Boys and Girls," *Sociology of Education* 65:3 (July 1992), pp. 169–87.

3. Tyack, David, and Elisabeth Hansot. *Learning Together: A History of Coeducation in American Schools.* New Haven, CT: Yale University Press, 1990, pp. 155, 157.

4. Keller, Arnold Jack. *A Historical Analysis of the Arguments for and Against Coeducational Public High Schools in the United States.* Unpublished doctoral dissertation, Columbia University, New York, 1971, pp. 323–24.

5. Tyack and Hansot, *Learning Together,* p. 157.

6. New York City Report for 1909, p. 475. Quoted in Tyack and Hansot, *Learning Together,* p. 193.

7. Male Teachers' Association of New York City. "Are There Too Many Women Teachers?" *Educational Review* 28 (1904), pp. 98–105. Quoted in Tyack and Hansot, *Learning Together,* p. 159.

8. Sexton, Patricia. "Are Schools Emasculating Our Boys?" *Saturday Review* (June 19, 1965), p. 57.

9. Sexton, Patricia. *The Feminized Male: Classrooms, White Collars and the Decline of Manliness.* New York: Random House, 1969.

10. Bly, Robert. *The Pillow and the Key: Commentary on the Fairy Tale of Iron John, Part One.* St. Paul, MN: Ally Press, 1987, p. 17.

11. Bly, Robert. *When a Hair Turns Gold: Commentary on the Fairy Tale of Iron John, Part Two.* St. Paul, MN: Ally Press, 1988, p. 15.

12. Interview quotes from NBC's "Dateline" and the "Sally Jesse Raphael Show."

13. DePalma, Anthony. "Picture a Men's College Circa '56; That's Wabash," *The New York Times* (April 22, 1992), p. B8.

14. The discussion of VMI and The Citadel is based on the following sources:

    "Cadet Claims Shooting Probe Was Inadequate," *Charleston Post-Courier* (January 1, 1993), pp. 1A, 13A.

Hackett, George, and Mark Miller. "Manning the Barricade," *Newsweek* (March 26, 1990), pp. 18–20.

Harris, John F., and Joan Biskupic. "High Court Rebuffs VM Appeal," *The Washington Post* (May 25, 1993), pp. A1, A7.

Reilly, Rick. "What Is The Citadel?" *Sports Illustrated* (September 14, 1992), pp. 70–74.

"Is VMI Getting Soft? School's Changes Displease Alumni," *The Washington Times* (September 13, 1992), p. A11.

15. "Arrow in Skull, Man Lives," *The Washington Post* (May 6, 1993), p. A18.

16. Brophy, Jere, and Thomas Good. "Feminization of American Elementary Schools," *Phi Delta Kappan* 54 (1973), pp. 564–66.

Sadker, Myra, and David Sadker. *Sex Equity Handbook for Schools*. New York: Longman, 1982.

17. Kessler, R., and J. McRae. "Trends in the Relationship Between Sex and Psychological Distress, 1957–76," *American Sociological Review* 46 (1981).

McLanahan, S. S., and J. L. Glass. "A Note on the Trend in Sex Differences in Psychological Distress," *Journal of Health and Human Stress* 2 (1976).

18. Sadker, David, and Myra Sadker, updated by Mary Jo Strauss. "The Report Card #1: The Cost of Sex Bias in Schools and Society." Distributed by the Mid-Atlantic Equity Center, Washington, D.C., and the New England Center for Equity Assistance, Andover, Massachusetts, 1989.

19. Duke, D. L. "Who Misbehaves? A High School Studies Its Discipline Problems," *Educational Administration Quarterly* 12 (1976), pp. 65–85.

Office for Civil Rights. *1986 Elementary and Secondary Civil Rights Survey, State and National Summary of Projected Data*. Washington, DC: U.S. Department of Education, 1988.

20. Kimbrell, Andrew. "A Time for Men to Pull Together," *Utne Reader* (May–June 1991), pp. 66–75.

Watts, W. David, and Loyd S. Wright. "The Relationship of Alcohol, Tobacco, Marijuana, and Other Illegal Drug Use to Delinquency Among Mexican-American, Black, and White Adolescent Males," *Adolescence* 25:97 (Spring 1990), pp. 171–81.

21. Unpublished data of the National Center for Health Statistics, Public Health Service, U.S. Department of Health and Human Services, 1986.

"Death Rates from Accidents and Violence: 1970 to 1985," *Statistical Abstract of the United States, 1988*. Washington, DC: Bureau of the Census, U.S. Department of Commerce, 1988.

Poinsett, Alvin. "Why Our Children Are Killing One Another," *Ebony* 43 (December 1987).

Children's Defense Fund. *The State of America's Children: 1992.* Washington, DC: Children's Defense Fund, 1992.

22. Pleck, Joseph, and Robert Brannon (eds.). "Male Roles and the Male Experience," *Journal of Social Issues* 34 (1978), pp. 1–4.

Komarovsky, M. *Dilemmas of Masculinity: A Study of College Youth.* New York: Norton, 1976.

Sadker and Sadker, *Sex Equity Handbook for Schools.*

23. Lester, David. *Why People Kill Themselves: A 1990s Summary of Research Findings on Suicide Behavior,* third edition. Springfield, IL: Charles C. Thomas, 1992.

Maris, R. W. *Pathways to Suicide: A Survey of Self-Destructive Behaviors.* Baltimore, MD: Johns Hopkins Press, 1981.

24. Dewart, J. (ed.). *The State of Black America, 1989.* Washington, DC: National Urban League, 1989.

Garibaldi, Antoine M. *Educating Black Male Youth: A Moral and Civic Imperative.* New Orleans: Orleans Parish School Board, 1988.

Collison, Michelle N.-K. "More Young Black Men Choosing Not to Go to College," *Chronicle of Higher Education* 34:15 (December 9, 1987), pp. A1, 26–27.

Gibbs, Jewelle Taylor (ed.). *Young, Black, and Male in America: An Endangered Species.* Dover, MA: Auburn House, 1988.

25. Whitaker, Charles. "Do Black Males Need Special Schools?" *Ebony* (March 1991), pp. 17–18, 20.

26. Simons, Janet M., Belva Finlay, and Alice Yang. *The Adolescent Young Adult Fact Book.* Washington, DC: Children's Defense Fund, 1991.

Children's Defense Fund, *The State of America's Children: 1992,* p. 52.

27. Lawton, Millicent. "Two Schools Aimed for Black Males Set in Milwaukee," *Education Week* X:6 (October 10, 1990), pp. 1, 8.

28. Dunkel, Tom. "Self-Segregated Schools Seek to Build Self-Esteem," *The Washington Times* (March 11, 1991), pp. E1–2.

29. Clark quoted in Whitaker, "Do Black Males Need Special Schools?" p. 18.

30. Leff, Lisa. "Maneuvering to Win Young Minds, P. G. School Chess Club Teaches Boys Self-Discipline, Self-Esteem," *The Washington Post* (May 17, 1993), pp. A1, A3.

31. Rotundo, E. Anthony. *American Manhood*. New York: Basic Books, 1993, p. 291.

32. Cramer, Robert Ervin, et al. "Motivating and Reinforcing Functions of the Male Sex Role: Social Analogues of Partial Reinforcement, Delay of Reinforcement, and Intermittent Shock," *Sex Roles* 20:9–10 (1989), pp. 551–73.

Osborne, R. W. "Men and Intimacy: An Empirical Review." Paper presented at the American Psychological Association, San Francisco, California, 1991.

9

THE MADGIRL
IN THE CLASSROOM

Lyn Mikel Brown

*The tension between theory and practice becomes a chasm of
alienation when private sorrows are suffered silently, unre-
deemed by collective reflection and response.*

—Peter Lyman

TYPICAL DESCRIPTIONS of girls in school classrooms, at least in recent
literature, are likely to conjure up images of cooperation, compliance,
polite silence, or, perhaps, invisibility, hands raised or waving patiently
but rarely called upon by teachers who, while well armored with good
intentions, may be unaware of their own biases.[1] The assumption seems
to be that what you see of girls is what you get.

In ways both obvious and subtle, the girls in this study counter such
assumptions. Irrespective of class, these girls express a good deal of anger,
annoyance, and frustration with school, often focusing on teachers who
they feel ignore them or attend to unruly students, usually boys, or who
abuse their authority in the classroom. Sometimes they complain of school
policies that leave them feeling unsafe or uninformed; other times they
speak to the sexism or stereotyping that seems to pervade school grounds.
The middle-class and working-class girls differ, however, in the intensity
of their anger, the issues that arouse the strongest feelings, and the manner

in which they express these feelings. Such differences have much to do with class-related definitions and views of appropriate feminine behavior.

Acadia: Behind Closed Doors

The Acadia girls are in touch with their angry feelings. They make considered choices about whether or not to speak or act on their own behalf, often choosing silence because they have little evidence that speaking would change the situation, but ample evidence that doing so would "cause a scene" and invite trouble or unwanted attention. The patience and politeness that might lead one to imagine these middle-class girls as the educational counterparts to Virginia Woolf's "angel in the house" belie their frustration and annoyance.

"My English teacher . . . there's like two boys in the class that she really favors," twelve-year-old Elizabeth tells us, speaking in measured tones. "They're the ones that misbehave and act out and don't get their work done very much." Irritated by her teacher's "unfairness," Elizabeth sees no benefit to pointing out her observations. Although she admits that she and her friends usually talk only among themselves about such favoritism, she is quick to justify their silence: "It's happened so often that we don't really think about it anymore." Instead, she writes her angry feelings down in her notebook.

Kirstin complains that it is sometimes difficult "being smart."

> I hate [it]. There's a lot of times when I know answers and I want to say them [and don't] because I get dirty looks and people laugh and call me . . . it's just embarrassing . . . it's sometimes humiliating to be the only person raising her hand and you know other people know the answer . . . I guess . . . it's just cool to be dumb . . . But they're not. They're smart . . . It's like, "Well, why don't you raise your hand if you know the answer?" I don't understand the logic. Are they too lazy to lift their arm? [And then] some teachers just won't call on me . . . I'll be the only one raising my hand and . . . they'll call on everyone and then not call on me at all. Go on to the next question. Even if I have an answer to a question, all period, all week, they just won't.

In spite of her frustration, Kirstin plays down her strong feelings: "It doesn't really make me mad . . . I'm used to it . . . I don't really think about it that much." When she's angry, she explains, "I just try to ignore things and it just builds up inside me until I can't stand it anymore."

Instead of expressing her anger, Kirstin reads fiction. Revealing the extent of her disconnection from others, she admits, "I don't really think about what—how I feel when I'm angry. I just know that I'm angry and usually I can blow it off by reading. Reading fiction helps a lot . . . [It helps] to know that other people have problems too and they get angry."

"Junior high," announces thirteen-year-old Robin in disgust, "is the virus that causes stupidity." "Teachers would be horrified by my opinions," she continues. "They are very descriptive and colorful—even purple . . . I get really mad at people because they don't want to learn or because they're just dumb . . . I can't imagine anybody wanting to be stupid and not learn." And yet Robin, who gets "really mad," sometimes "furious," does not say much in class. "I used to do a lot of talking. I don't talk as much anymore in class . . . When it comes to class discussion I speak when I'm spoken to or if I really have something to say that needs to be said." Instead, Robin finds other outlets for her strong feelings— directing them at herself or incorporating them into her art: "I usually do something destructive like shave part of my head . . . or rip stuff or punch things, you know? . . . I express my anger in my writing and my art and stuff."

These girls speak candidly about who lurks behind the quiet, well-behaved, middle-class "angel" in the classroom: a girl who is frequently irritated, frustrated, and angry, and almost always measured and polite about it, at least in public. Given the opportunity in the privacy of their interviews and focus groups to talk about themselves, however, the girls candidly express their strong feelings and—against perceptions of adolescent girls as a passive, amorphous group—boast about their unique qualities and individual abilities, saying such things as "I'm very good at math"; "I'm being myself . . . I'm different"; "I like stuff my own way and I'm bossy"; "I'm trying to go ahead in everything"; "I play hockey . . . I'm pretty good"; "I've never been a follower . . . it's not in my personality"; "I'm creative."

But even though the Acadia girls agree that it is important to express their feelings and to say what they think, they are also well aware that girls who do so are perceived as "loud and obnoxious" and are not well liked. Such awareness leads them to mitigate, question, and even at times disconnect from their feelings. Anger begins to seem like too strong a word. As Jane explains, "I don't think I get angry . . . I just get very, very, very annoyed . . . I'm never angry at anybody. I'm just annoyed and I dislike them."

The Acadia girls also know that there are consequences for expressing their strong feelings publicly, and they know that they are judged by different standards than their male counterparts. "In school it's definitely not as acceptable [for girls to get angry as it is for boys]," Kirstin complains:

> Like boys get away with so much. It's just that we're good all the time. If we do something moderately bad, like Theresa got in big trouble for calling a teacher by their first name. She just was so frustrated. She must have, you know, raised her hand saying so and so, so many times, saying, "Hey, listen to me," and it got [the teacher's] attention . . . [She] was like, "Excuse me. You have no right to call me by my first name." [Theresa] was just like—she didn't say it because she was—I could tell she was [saying to herself], "You have no right to ignore me every day. Do you remember I'm in your class?"

Theresa, usually a model student, "got in big trouble" for her inappropriate address, while the boys, Kirstin explains, "get away with so much, [like] swearing, being really rude to teachers, fighting." "You know," she contends, "teachers let a lot of things slide [with boys]. They're like that all the time. If we did anything half that bad, they'd be all over us." But in what begins to sound like the refrain from a Greek chorus, she adds, "It doesn't really make me mad though. I'm just used to it."

The Acadia girls also know that the boys are judged differently because they are perceived differently. "Like Devon," Jane explains,

> We had a student-teacher once, and [Devon's] in my class, and she was just a science class student-teacher, and he's pretty outgoing and he made her laugh and stuff like that and he also got detention. But she sent a card back to us and he was the one she mentioned and remembered . . . out of all the seventh-graders she teaches. So they remember the boys a lot better, because they're louder . . .

ELIZABETH: Of all the classes she teaches!

JANE: I know, all sixth period!

It becomes apparent to these girls that if you're a boy and "if you're outgoing and outspoken, and you have enough money," if you're "loud" and "have the right clothes," you've got it made.

Although boys are supposed to be "brighter," Jane explains, they "don't have to get good grades." Girls, by contrast, find themselves in a dilemma. "Girls are all expected to be smart, all of us," Jane says at one point, and then at another, "Well, girls shouldn't talk at all [in class] and shouldn't be smart." "Yeah," Kirstin agrees, "you have to be dumb." "Girls are too opinionated," Lydia adds sarcastically. What appears at first to be a contradiction is, rather, an accurate reading of the social scene that these middle-class girls confront daily. Girls are supposed to *be* smart and *appear* dumb. The point is not whether you are smart, but whether you are in tune with the social cues and willing to hide your capabilities in public, something these girls refuse to do.

JANE: If you're really really smart then . . . it's not that bad, but you have to be pretty smart . . . But not too much.

LYN: What happens if you show too much?

JANE: I, I don't know . . . Elizabeth gets picked on.

KIRSTIN: If you're smart and people know it, then, "See ya!" Because like Sandy is really smart, but she never raises her hand that much, because she knows people will know she's smart. And I can't do that. I can't *stand* to sit and not raise my hand and watch people get the wrong answer, and go . . . I explode, and so I raise my hand.

Because she is smart and cannot hold herself back, Kirstin explains, she has to deal both with getting picked on and, more difficult for her, with people who "just use you for the answers," who copy from her in class, something that makes her "really mad." "I really hate it! Because people have copied off my paper for a test forever. I'm so used to it. I mean, they always do. I mean," she adds, incredulous, "some people ask me to please not put my hand there because I'm blocking the answers!"

And yet despite their awareness of different standards, expectations, and treatment, these white middle-class girls generally espouse a strong belief in meritocracy and the American Dream. By and large they trust their teachers and other authorities to be fair, to judge them on their merits; they firmly believe that hard work and perseverance, in school and in society, will eventually yield a happy and prosperous life. And so perhaps it is not surprising that their most intense feelings of anger center on the frequent times when this ideology is disrupted or violated, when others receive credit or favoritism or special privileges for unearned work, either because they are popular or wealthy, or simply because they demand attention and credit.

Not surprisingly, the girls are most annoyed by the special favors and attention lavished on the "popular" kids in the school. In story after story, they illustrate the privileges these students receive simply for being who they are. Kirstin tells how a "really conceited, cocky" boy who "thinks he's everything in the world . . . was kicked off the [school] trip" for swearing and hitting a teacher, but ended up being able to go anyway:

> He had done something very wrong . . . And the night before the trip . . . he decided he really wanted to go. And the thing that really upset me was he got to go because his parents called and threatened to sue [the teacher] for not letting him go. Really. You know, and they're very rich and so he's so used to getting his way. I mean he even gets on the sports teams even though he's not very good . . . [And] he really didn't get any other punishment at all . . . And it's really unfair and a lot of times they get an advantage over us for something that we really deserve.

"It's ridiculous," Robin says. "My parents say if you earn your punishment, you better serve it."

Recalling another situation where a student nearly received a scholarship over a smarter and more needy classmate because he protested loudly and arrogantly that he deserved it most, Kirstin comments bitterly: "Yah, you're right, you [deserve it]. You never pay attention. You just think it's all a big game."

The irony, of course, is that it is, to a degree, a "big game," and though the girls are learning the social codes and rules well enough—the manners of speech and behavior and dress that will assure them a place in upper-middle-class society—they have yet to appreciate the socially constructed nature of the rules and who they are meant to benefit most. The girls constantly struggle with a tension between what they are told, and indeed practice religiously, and what they see and hear in the public world of their school.

The girls are especially angered by teachers who give special attention to boys simply because they "act civil and normal." If they "act like everyone else for the rest of the week and turn in their homework," Kirstin complains, "they get 'Student of the Week,' when, when other people have to like try and do extra credit and stuff." "Yeah, I know," Lydia interrupts. "We like work our butts off every single time and we don't get squat!" As Elizabeth observes, "They're getting special treatment because they're behaving badly or not doing what they're supposed to do . . . or doing half the work." "I mean," Kirstin continues, "a lot of times their definition of good is like not even normal. And just, you know, they still mouth off. And the teacher gives them second chances [*said in an overly nice voice*]: 'Shhh, Eric, you better raise your hand or you won't get Student of the Week!' "

Whether or not the stories the Acadia girls tell are fully accurate, they reveal their perceptions of school and justify their anger and frustration at their teachers' favoritism:

KIRSTIN: And now Mrs. Cronin is going to change David's chaperon. I know she, I know she's going to relent to that because she wants him to go [on the school trip] and she'll be like, "Oh, OK David. I guess you can be with me."

JANE: If *I* wanted a different chaperon—

KIRSTIN: Mrs. Cronin would be like, "That's nice. You don't get your initial $50.00 back."

JANE: She's like [*said primly*], "Yeah, well, we'll refund the money that you've already given me except the $50.00 in the beginning. And we do have a few people lined up that want to go."

VALERIE: So she wouldn't relent?

KIRSTIN: But she didn't say that to David. She's like, "Oh c'mon David. Please come. Please."

JANE: "We'll change your chaperon."

The girls are incredulous when teachers dole out unearned privileges to popular or favorite students, but they resist any suggestion that such transgressions undermine the school's ideology of meritocracy and just rewards. Jane, for example, complains about a teacher who "really favored this student . . . let [him] get away with a lot of things," and then tells a story of deceit and betrayal:

> [She] said that he won a scholarship [to go on a class trip], but [that it] had only been available after everyone had signed up and he had gotten it because he was like the only contestant. And there was a girl that had wanted it too, and she said, "Why couldn't girls enter it?" and [the teacher] said, "Because this grandfather had a little boy and the little boy died and before he gave the scholarship to someone it had to be a boy."

LYN: Was that true?

JANE: No, of course it wasn't true. And she paid it herself. She paid it herself because she really favored this student, and it was really unfair.

Although Jane chalks up this teacher's behavior to "her personality," this narrative suggests another, more troubling theme in the girls' stories of students "who are kind of getting a free ride." In every case the teachers in their stories of unfair treatment are women, and the favored students are boys. What makes such treatment most disturbing to the girls are the irreverent bantering and informal camaraderie that accompany it, compared with the more formal, unresponsive voices their teachers use with them. The boys "talk back," publicly challenge their women teachers, and engage in verbal play with them. Underlying such public performances are messages about power relations, particularly about women's desire for male approval, and also about women's relationships with other women. A sense of betrayal, more than infractions of school ideology, may explain the intensity of the girls' confusion and anger.

The fact that most of those who "act out" and get special favors are the more popular boys does not immediately occur to Elizabeth, though upon reflection she knows this to be true. Nonetheless, she concludes that she and her friends, not the teachers, are to blame for their being "overlooked":

> Sometimes it's because I think she doesn't hear us because we're not very loud . . . It's happened so often that we don't really think about it anymore . . . how it's kind of unfair and how the people who misbehave get all the attention . . . One of my friends is very quiet and I'm not as quiet as she is, so she sometimes gets overlooked. But the boys . . . they don't even raise their hands. They just call out if they think it's right or something. If they get it wrong she'll like kind of lead them to the right answer. She'll like, "Oh, no, maybe it's . . . No, I think that . . . Maybe, it's . . ."

There have been times, Elizabeth admits, when she has spoken out in this class, but she has been "told not to talk that loudly." She concedes that in those situations she probably was being a bit disruptive and deserved to be told to quiet down.

Whereas Jane, Elizabeth, and Kirstin are likely to attribute such favoritism to individual teachers' personalities and to share the blame for their invisibility, Lydia is more critical, more likely to delineate the structural outlines of privilege in her school and how it "typically" benefits those at the top. But though she comes close, she, too, falls short of condemning the classism and sexism she witnesses at school:

LYDIA: Like, one time like in class the teacher, we were trying to get this project, it was a yearbook, and you had to sign up for stuff really quick before it would be all full. Well, the teacher, she was of course wanted by kids, and I was right in front of her, and I was asking her, and she didn't seem to listen to me, but when one of the people from the popular group asked her to put down a subject, she immediately wrote down his name. And it's, I thought it was rather unfair . . . I was right in front of her . . . it was kind of hard to . . .

LYN: Do you think that's typical?

LYDIA: Yeah. I don't see why they get better treatment . . .

LYN: Why do you think it's like that?

LYDIA: Because not everybody saw it my way or they wouldn't be . . . They're always the best dressed, and they have the most money and they're always dressed up so people tend to label them the popular ones.

LYN: Do you think teachers do too?

LYDIA: Yeah, they really do. Like we went on this school trip, and all the really fun chaperons and everything, they all picked them . . . and a lot of people and myself think that [the sign-up sheets] were rigged because all of the like popular, awesome people got all the awesome chaperons. Because they think they're the crazy ones, but actually we're, we're actually a lot more crazier than them; they think they're crazy but the things that they do are like stupid crazy. We're more crazy in the sense of mature. Like we, we're crazy like high school students . . . but they're more like fifth-graders.

For Lydia the difference in treatment, while typical, ultimately comes down to a more general problem of perception grounded in a failure of relationship. If only the teachers *really* knew us, she implies, they would prefer to be with us. The teachers, Lydia believes, are simply taken in by the surface of things. Embedded in Lydia's explanation is her desire to expose the popular kids for who they really are and to redefine popularity so that it would be judged on more genuine terms. Thus while Lydia challenges her teachers' perceptions, she does not, perhaps cannot yet, see the connections between such perceptions and classism on a more systemic level. Rather, she reveals her very deep belief in the ideology of meritocracy. In fact, she believes that she and her friends ought to have the attention and the social standing that the popular kids now enjoy so undeservingly.

Thus there is no explanation in the Acadia girls' ideology of meritocracy for their observations that popular kids and, more often, boys, generally get more attention in class and more breaks, for their longing for the freedom boys enjoy to express strong feelings in public, or for their own personal experiences of invisibility in the classroom. Although the girls collectively know that these differences exist, the white middle-class culture of individualism into which they have been invited threatens to particularize and personalize their stories, so that they blame themselves for not being or doing enough, individual boys for talking and taking too much, and certain misguided teachers for encouraging them to do so.

And yet their strong feelings continually reemerge, indicating that something is wrong, that the issue is not yet resolved. Infuriated with the way things go in school, they also sound genuinely confused about the discrepancy between the ideal and the real. Theresa, for example, struggles openly with the invisibility she experiences when she is her usual good-girl self in class.

THERESA: In a lot of classes, the teacher just seems like to ignore me. I don't know why but they—maybe because I don't speak out loud enough, but usually, I'm like trying to tell them something and they just kind of ignore me, so I just say, "Fine!" and go on.

LYN: How do you know they ignore you?

THERESA: Because I'm like talking to them and they don't see me. I'll like ask a question and then they just like don't seem to hear me and they just like keep on talking to the person and like if they're talking—well, they just like don't answer my question. And they just talk to someone else.

This invisibility is something Theresa experiences "all the time": "I'm always ignored by everyone!" she insists. While she explains her teachers' behavior in individualistic terms—"They might just have their minds on something else," or "They don't really care"—and while she is adamant, when I ask her directly, that her invisibility has nothing to do with her gender, the construction of her response to my question suggests that she experiences the problem somewhat differently:

> No. I think it's because these teachers, they won't listen to everyone, they just kind of . . . See, these boys—sometimes they have their hands up and everything but they never . . . They always say raise your hand but then when you raise your hand they never call on you. So you end up—you have to yell out and then you get in trouble.

Theresa, like the other Acadia girls, knows on some level that being "always ignored by everyone" has something to do with being a girl. The girls repeatedly either resist knowing or explain away their knowledge that gender pervades classroom interactions, even as they define the problem in gendered terms. "No," Theresa assures me, it's not about being a girl, but in the next breath she begins, "See, these boys . . ." A subtle shift in pronoun from the first-person "I" to the second-person "you" then underscores her awareness that her experience is shared by other girls. The problem for Theresa and her friends is thus not that they are girls, but that they are not boys.

That the Acadia girls' expressions of strong feelings and self-promotion are discouraged in public dialogue seems also, to them, unconnected to their success or failure to be recognized. Jane takes pride in her ability not to show her feelings—"I hide my feelings a lot better than my sister does. I'm an actress"—even as she struggles to be seen and known for her abilities. Calling attention to herself sounds too selfish, and yet she admits, "I'm trying to get good grades too and be recognized." Frustrated that she works "twice as hard" as others who get more attention, and that even her girlfriends don't notice how capable and smart she is, Jane sees no way to be recognized without being judged or ostracized. "I get better grades than [they do] in science and math . . . I can act better and write better than [they] can . . . I don't get anywhere in anything . . . I never get anywhere in anything . . . It's frustrating," she admits. "I just can't get anywhere . . . they'd think I'm bragging and I don't." When her friends vote for another girl for an orchestra award, Jane feels immobilized. She can't speak up and say, "I deserve this," because "I don't know, it would probably . . . I'm more liked . . . more well liked," and to do so might risk her reputation as someone who is "flexible," who "can take teasing," and who can "just laugh" things off. "I could still say something, but I don't know if I want to. I mean I never gave them a reason to believe that I'm good . . . I just don't do anything either way . . . and then I think, well maybe they're right and I just try to see it from their point of view . . .

That might be what they want me to see . . . I have about twenty pages of writing [about this in my notebook]."

Even as they feel unrecognized in their classrooms these girls ventriloquate and embody white middle-class femininity in ways that ensure their acceptability and yet blend them into the amorphous backdrop of "nice girls," existing just out of their teachers' conscious awareness. They seem caught in the uneasy tension between their descriptions of themselves as "bossy" and "smart" and expectations that they should wait patiently for things to happen, holding in their feelings and thoughts. Frustrated, they judge other girls for acting in ways they themselves secretly covet—that is, for being "outspoken," saying what they feel and want directly and publicly.

Because they are pressed to stay out of the limelight, and tacitly agree among themselves to keep their "real" feelings secret and their accomplishments private, any girl who breaks out and commands the public stage or works her way to the few token spots reserved at the top for the best female students risks eliciting feelings of anger and betrayal. Jane, who admits, "I like trying to be the best," pays the consequences. After she won a school contest, she explains, "[My friend] . . . wouldn't talk to me for two days. She was so mad at me and it wasn't my fault." All good students, the Acadia girls wish to succeed, to do well academically, and to be acknowledged for their excellence; unfortunately, their desires are in constant tension, not only with pressures to appear appropriately nonassertive, but also with their need to be in relationship, to stay together as a group, which often demands that they carefully downplay their achievements to their friends. Such group reliance offers them protection against mistreatment by those with more social and material power, and yet goes against the competitive spirit at the heart of their ideological leanings.

It is abundantly clear that the Acadia girls are neither passive recipients of nor victims to the ideology of white middle-class femininity. In their case, simply put, what you see is *not* what you get. Amid pressures not to speak too loudly or passionately or demand too much space or appear too smart, these girls find creative ways to express their feelings. In the face of bullying and denigration by the popular kids, for example, they rally to exhibit a collective condescension, manifest in a quick and clever wit and the creative use of language designed to confuse their perpetrators, or simply to make them look stupid or silly. Talking about a time when she wanted to say something but did not, Lydia comments:

> That happens a lot. I mean, the eighth-graders . . . and a lot of times
> they come up to you and a lot of times I have the right thing to say but

then I don't say it and later, I'm like Oh . . . and I don't. But like now, it's like I'm so sick of it that I'm starting to revolt . . . and I'm starting to . . . A lot of times they just come and say something . . . and I speak in a different language.

LYN: You speak in a different language?

LYDIA: Yeah. They're like [*makes a confused face*], and then they'll leave me alone, because they know how to respond to certain things, but when I'm a seventh-grader and they're an eighth-grader and I'm speaking strangely they want to leave me alone because I guess they figure I could . . . they don't understand and I say something and they say, "What'd you say to me?" It's so funny.

"I have other concerns more important," Elizabeth claims, explaining why she cannot be bothered with a boy who has been "annoying" her. The others agree with her. The boys who harass them, they have decided, are "childish," "stupid," "dumb," "bored," and "have no life." In response the girls show little patience. "Do you have a problem with keeping things to yourself?" Lydia recalls asking a boy when he hit her in the back with some balled-up paper. To another boy "who bothered me in the hall," Lydia is condescending: "I was already in the hall looking at music, and he came up and he was staring right over my shoulder," and he said [*in a voice meant to sound dumb*], 'What's that?' I go, 'It's called music' . . . and then I walked off." "Once at lunch," she continues, "these boys were trying to take over our table, and Jane said, 'Go find your own table,' but they didn't."

JANE: I said more but that was the basic . . .

LYDIA: They said they didn't hear her, and so . . .

JANE: They heard me, but they chose to ignore me because they didn't think a puny little seventh-grade girl could actually talk like that to [*feigning awe*] an eighth-grade boy.

LYDIA: Then they said the same to us. And it's like [*in a baby voice*], "The same to you." And then they left, and they started scowling like little children.

JANE: They bothered us for about half the lunch period, and finally Mr. Robbins saw them, came over, and told them to go find their own table. And ever since then they've been bothering us.

The Acadia girls quickly decipher and ridicule the cryptic phrases thrown at them by the popular boys, though if they pick up a sexualized edge to the boys' teasing, they do not share it with us. In response to the derogatory phrase "sad skid," they retort, "Sorry, I'd like you to answer me in English." When Theresa reports the newest insult in school, the girls laugh and joke about it and the other "stupid" phrases the popular boys use.

THERESA: Well, they have another like thing they say now. They call you—they say, "Smell good?"

ELIZABETH: "Smell good?"

THERESA: Yeah. Jeff says it all the time. "Smell good?"

LYDIA: "Yes, thank you. Thank you. I know, I smell wonderful, don't I?" . . . Also, you have to be able to say, "The rooster crows at midnight."

KIRSTIN: And go, "Skid in the hammock!"

JANE [laughing]: Yeah, you have to say, "Skid in the hammock" and—

KIRSTIN: I don't even know what that means—

LYDIA: A board or log in the hammock . . .

KIRSTIN: It doesn't even make sense . . . They say the dumbest things. They call people guacamole stains [lots of laughter].

The girls poke fun at the boys' "childish" retorts and their appropriation of what they consider the baser forms of culture. If you said anything to them, Jane explains, "they'd just laugh, like go 'huh, huh,' doing that stupid laugh, like Beavis and Butthead. When the fire drill happened, they said, 'Cool, fire, huh, huh, huh.' "[2] Elizabeth agrees: "My whole French class was going, 'huh, huh.' So annoying. Stupid." But Lydia is outraged at what she considers the boys' disregard for more serious matters:

LYDIA: Every time a person goes, "Beavis and Butthead are cool," I'm like, "No, they aren't cool. Do you want Beavis and Butthead for culture?" I think that's stupid. Have you heard what happened? I mean people are killing other people because of Beavis and Butthead. Somebody burned down their house because of them, and their baby sister was inside, she was only two years old. She died, and you think that's funny?

. . . And also they laugh about the Holocaust. I don't think that was very funny . . . I don't think it's funny when some child was under their bed, and they see their parents murdered in front of them. I don't think that's very funny, and I really, I *hate* it when they do that.

VALERIE: Do you ever say anything?

LYDIA: No, I haven't and I should. I mean, sometimes I say, "I don't think that's funny."

Whereas the girls reject the popular boys for being insensitive and rude, they distance themselves from the popular girls by underscoring their intellectual inferiority and silliness. "Hold your head high and stick out your tongue!" Lydia exclaims, in defense of her group against these girls. "They're making themselves the higher point of life when you know they aren't . . . It's like dumb to be smart. Stupid!"

The girls know that the popular kids' command of public space—in terms of both movement and language—gives them an advantage in school, and they openly resent it. "They're popular because they have like power," Lydia explains. "And last year they went around making everybody feel horrible. They ruin stuff that they don't like, and that's other people's property and they make kids cry."

This psychological terrorism infuriates the girls, as they witness and experience its power to control people's behavior. "They use embarrassment," Kirstin explains, and the girls give a multitude of examples: making fun of an exchange student's clothes, accusing a shy boy of reading dirty magazines, teasing and blaming someone for things he didn't do until he is in tears; calling an overweight girl who is "really nice" mean names and saying "I love you" or writing on the board "someone likes Katie." The girls struggle in these situations because, as Lydia confesses, "It's so hard. I mean, it's hard to stick up for people because you don't want to turn into how that person is being treated, so you have to be careful what you say." "A lot of times it does turn on you," Kirstin agrees. "It happens to me all the time."

The Acadia girls feel constrained by the power they and others have invested in the popular kids. "They feel like they can order people around," Jane says angrily. "And they can't," Lydia adds. "I'm not gonna stand for that." Whereas publicly Lydia and the others "just walk away" when the popular kids take over, in their underground groups they develop resistance strategies. Armed with their wit, and also with sarcasm, humor, and condescension, the Acadia girls counter the popular boys and girls' intimidation tactics. Feeling pressure to cheat from kids who are either "really popular" or can "get to the popular people," who either "have a lot of power" or are "real bullies," the girls devise creative responses:

JANE: What I do when people want the answer from me is, I say, "Well, what do you think?" And they give me an answer and then look at me like, "Is that right?" And I say, "Yeah," even if it's wrong.

LYDIA: Chills them out.

JANE: Yeah. Chills them down a little.

KIRSTIN: Well, I tell people wrong answers all the time. I told Mitch and Dan that Caroline and the Captain [characters in a book the class was reading] were married.

ELIZABETH: And they believed you?

KIRSTIN: Yeah, they were like, "Cool." And so I flipped to this one section in the book and I like found one sentence that said something like, "I bet they did it," or something, and I go, "See, look here [*the others are laughing*]," and they didn't even read it, they were like, "Cool."

The girls also explain that consciously speaking and performing stereotypically feminine voices and behaviors make it more difficult for the boys to respond. In a scene she plays out dramatically before the group, Lydia reveals this as a strategy for countering an annoying boy's behavior in class:

LYDIA: Dylan, he sits behind me in Mr. Ballard's class. He had his feet underneath my chair, 'cause I was sitting right on the edge. And he was picking it up and it was bothering me. I didn't say anything, but what I did—he had his toes under there, and I stood up a little, and he was tipping it and everything. I came back down, and he wasn't quick enough, and I sat down really hard on his feet. He goes [*in pained, startled voice*], "Why did you sit down on my feet?" and I go [*in innocent, sweet voice*], "Why were they under there?" He was . . . quiet.

Lydia's theory about such boys is that "they want to get you mad. I think they enjoy making people mad." In response to their teasing and flirting, she performs a kind of controlled, naive femininity. But she is hardly sweet or innocent; she knows this is a psychological battle and she is determined to win. "If you don't get mad," she explains, if "you give back responses without getting angry or changing your facial expression, and they can see that . . . that means you've conquered them, and they haven't conquered you."

Outside of class, in the hallways, the Acadia girls are likely to respond more aggressively to boys who bother them. They get more mad and annoyed than uncomfortable, they say, and are therefore unlikely to remain passive or unresponsive. In fact, they quickly pick up on and use to their advantage words they know have power.

ELIZABETH: They usually bother me in the morning, because I have a band locker . . . They'll like, stand in front of you, or—

JANE: Put their bags in front of your locker—

ELIZABETH: Or take their hands and put them in front of your face, or . . . stupid stuff like that.

LYDIA: To bother you.

JANE [smiling]: Yeah. Sexual harassment.

LYDIA: Yeah. You should do that.

JANE: Yeah. Because they know I come to my locker every morning, and I always find at least five bags piled up there, and I like kick them away. And none of them have yet said, "Don't kick my bag away," but if they do, I'll know what to say.

While the girls joke about reporting the boys for sexual harassment, in fact they are not always sure how to interpret the boys' behavior. Even when they feel they should report an incident, they are uncertain whether the school's policy would be enforced.

ROBIN: A lot [of boys] make really slime-like remarks. Like, "Why do you wear those baggy clothes? If you've got it, flaunt it." And it's much more graphic than that usually. It's really—it annoys me because I don't think I should have to put up with that . . . and it's really annoying that they can sit there and do stuff like that or . . . The school just this year had a sexual harassment thing, so then you know, anything that's done that makes you feel uncomfortable, you should go to the office and the person can get suspended. But I mean, the teachers, even if they see it, they pretend that they don't. I hate that.

LYN: You haven't had anybody use that policy and have it go anywhere?

ROBIN: It doesn't go anywhere! I mean I made comments in the office once . . . I mean it's certainly annoying. You walk down the hall and all of a sudden part of your anatomy is in somebody else's hand. It's just like, "Do you mind!" It's very annoying.

Pushed too far, however, the Acadia girls will fight back. "I like to keep away from violence," Lydia explains, "but once in a while you have to do it. I mean, it's not necessary but you can't control it."

> Like in gym the other day, we had a substitute, and we were doing . . . it was mostly girls against boys, that's the way she set it up . . . and the boys were like keeping the ball out of our hands . . . and they were making sexist remarks and stuff like that . . . and so I got so angry at this one kid . . . so I started hitting on *him*. It was funny but . . . and finally he just dropped the ball . . . He just kind of stayed away from me . . . but he's so unfair . . . he'd throw the ball really hard from the back . . . and so we'd do that, we'd throw it right at him . . .

LYN: Did you say anything?

LYDIA: I like went to sit down because I love gym, I mean, it's the only activity I really love, because it's so active . . . and that's the first time I ever sat down because of somebody else and . . . so he goes, "What are you guys doing sitting down?" And I just said, "You should be taken out and stripped naked." And he just kind of walked away.

Such moments are rare. As angry as they are with the boys' behavior in school, the Acadia girls would rather distinguish themselves from these boys than behave in kind. In a conversation about the popular boys' sense of entitlement in the classroom, Valerie pushes the girls to imagine being as demanding and insistent as the boys are.

VALERIE: But why don't you get mad? Why don't you come right up and say, "I'm not sitting there today!" Because if Kirstin was bothering David . . . don't you think he would come right up to me and say [*in an angry voice*], "I'm not sitting in that group anymore because she's bugging me and she's talking and she's cheating"? Why don't you guys do that?

KIRSTIN: I've tattled enough. I mean, it doesn't get you anywhere.

JANE: Don't you have enough problems as it is?

VALERIE: But you feel like, why do you feel like you can't . . .

KIRSTIN: Because . . . people like that, they just have a name like, they just have a name like that and they get away with those things. I mean, teachers don't give them detention.

VALERIE: But what if, what if Jacob [a popular boy] jumped up and said, "I'm not sitting in this group because they're bugging me." Why don't you?

ELIZABETH: Well, because it doesn't seem as important as other things like, getting on with the lesson, and then you know—

KIRSTIN: Making sure you get a silent reading book so you—

ELIZABETH: Not stopping up, stopping the class . . . the whole class, and trying to learn instead of interrupting.

VALERIE: Mmhmm. But they'll do it.

JANE: We're not them.

This conversation underscores the entanglement of visible and invisible threads that bind the Acadia girls' expressions of anger and resistance. The weight of expectations—including their perceptions of what Valerie might want them to say—the pain of exclusion, the knowledge of class status and also of male power and privilege, and the awareness of how their actions affect others all point to the complicated nature of white middle-class femininity. The lines between civility—respect for their teacher and their classmates—and a feminine selflessness that would obliterate their anger are nearly indiscernible as the girls rationalize their refusal to speak out. In the context of their persistent struggles to be heard and taken seriously, such a refusal seems particularly problematic. There is, it seems to these adolescent girls, no way to be both good and visible, responsive and successful, caring and outspoken.

Listening to the Acadia girls' struggles with the contradictory voices they have taken in, as well as with the gendered polarities of the dominant culture, one can appreciate their creative strategies for expressing their anger and resistance. Their convoluted pathway to success and visibility is a reminder that, particularly with these girls, things are seldom what they appear to be. The concern, however, is that the performances these girls give will become, in time, persuasive even to the girls themselves; that the role of feminine perfection, silence, and selflessness will become their guiding ideology.

It is important that these seventh-grade girls remain in touch with their strong feelings. Researchers report that emotional expressiveness relates positively to some measures of well-being, whereas ambivalence about such expression relates to several indexes of psychological distress.[3] And while a number of studies connect suppressed anger to depression, others find that depression scores relate directly to the degree to which women endorse "care as self-sacrifice."[4] Anger, in the case of the Acadia girls, would appear to be not only a justified response to the sexism and classism they experience in school, but also a necessary protection against depression and other signs of psychological trouble.

Mansfield: Just Say It

As noted, the Mansfield girls do not share the Acadia girls' relationship with or trust in authorities, their belief in the American Dream, or their definitions of femininity.

"People don't listen because they don't like us," eleven-year-old Cheyenne says, her expression solemn as she addresses her group. "I don't like teachers so much . . . If I'm talking to a teacher, I'll tell them what I think." Some days, Cheyenne confesses, she finds ways to get out of class: if "I'm in a bad mood and I'm really frustrated . . . I bug the crap out of someone."

> Some days I'll just want to get in trouble so I don't have to be in classes . . . [I'll] take their papers and throw 'em on the floor or just tell the teacher that I don't, keep telling her that I don't understand this and I don't understand that. So she'll just say, "If you don't want to do it, then go down to the office," and I'll just leave . . . If I'm in a bad mood and I'm really frustrated and I just don't want to be near no one else, I'll get sent down to the office.

"You want to know something that really makes me mad?" asks thirteen-year-old Rachel. "When teachers think that they can do and say anything they want to us and they don't care how it makes us feel, but we have to be so careful what we say to them. It's really stupid." Rachel feels her anger intensely. Sometimes she talks back to teachers when she feels treated unfairly, but she holds in her anger and violent impulses toward her classmates: "I feel like [hitting people] a lot. I don't. I haven't yet."

Donna, fourteen, conveys her frustration with a teacher who hollers and points her finger at students:

> Well, she aggravates me and she like says stuff, when she talks to me she like, I don't know, hollers and stuff. And one day she was hollering at me and I hollered right back at her . . . I've done it before, but she said if I did it again I'd get suspended . . . I told her I didn't like how she treats kids and stuff, and how she treats me, and I don't think she should holler at you. I think she should just talk. I told her that I just don't like how she points her finger and hollers at you and stuff . . . She sent me down to the office.

Thirteen-year-old Susan is known for speaking her mind: "I don't like people annoying me that much . . . and I don't like people talking behind my back about me," she admits during her interview, looking me straight in the eye. "I don't think there was a time," she assures me, when she wanted to say something but didn't.

Unlike the middle-class girls, the Mansfield girls do not hide their strong feelings from public view. Anger is not only more visible but frequently more intense, sustained, and sometimes physical than it is with the Acadia girls. In large part, these differences in behavior and expression hinge on their resistance to teachers and other authority figures in the school. Rather than trust teachers to be fair, these girls are angered and confused by what they perceive to be unpredictable and inconsistent treatment on the part of those in positions of power, particularly their women teachers. "What really makes me mad," Corrine complains, "is when teachers tell you to do something and then you do it and they say, and they go and tell you, 'Oh, why'd you do that?' and I'll say, 'Well, you told me to,' and they'll say, 'No, I didn't tell you to do that.' " "Like one day," Dana continues,

> I was drawing on a poster thing and I was using [Miss Thomas's] little marker and she said I could use it. The next day she was in a bad mood and I go, "Can I use that marker again?" And she said [*in a mean voice*]: "What? You used that marker? I told you not to!" And

she said I could use it the day before . . . She changes . . . And with
Mrs. Evans you never know.

"Mrs. Nugent came in and started hollering at me," Donna complains.
"I don't know why." "All the teachers are different," Patti adds. "Each
day, I think they are different each day." "I don't like Miss Damon that
much because she can get really moody," Cheyenne agrees. "You'll tell
her something the week before and she'll forget and then you can say that
and all of a sudden . . ."

It is not so much the teachers' anger that the girls resent, as the fact that
they cannot always determine what they have done to cause such a
response; there seem to be patterns of interacting and rules of communication inaccessible to them. The minute the girls think they have figured
out what their teachers want, the rules change. Because, from the girls'
point of view, their teachers are so unpredictable, the girls' attempts at
reading their moods inevitably fail. The result is often explosive. "Um,
Mrs. MacDonald, I get in trouble with her a lot," Rachel explains:

> Because like you can—everybody takes advantage of her because she
> puts up with so much and then once you push her too far, and she just
> stops putting up with it and you're in big trouble. Everybody thinks
> that they can do whatever they want in there because she don't do any-
> thing about it usually.

LYN: Is it unpredictable or can you tell when she's going to start to clamp
down on things?

RACHEL: Well, sometimes you can, but then you don't think it's . . . I
mean it's just like . . . she usually lets you go for a really long time and
then sometimes you just start and she tells you to leave the room. She's
known for it. She sends you down to the office or something.

LYN: How can you tell?

RACHEL: She'll tell you. She'll say, "One more time and you're down in
the office." And you're like, "Already?" and like, "You usually put up
with it longer than that."

What sounds like a conventional feminine response to anger—"putting
up with it" until she is "pushed too far," then exploding in frustration—

amuses the girls even though they don't quite understand it and don't know ahead of time how long things will be allowed to continue without consequence. The fact that "everybody takes advantage" of Mrs. MacDonald's tolerance, and tries, often without success, to predict her breaking point, signifies the distance the girls feel from their teacher and what she is about in the classroom. The girls and their teachers struggle to communicate, with limited success, across cultural realities firmly grounded in social class.

It seems odd that the girls would feel so distant from their teachers, given the long-standing relationship between the school and the Mansfield community, and given the relaxed, open structure of the school. In fact, a few of the women teachers grew up in the surrounding area and are considered community members. But such a personal history of enculturation would not necessarily ensure their connection to the girls or, for that matter, protect them from deep ambivalence about their role in the girls' lives. Although they are long-time Mainers and some have working-class backgrounds, they are also college graduates, students of teacher-training programs that are unlikely to address issues of class or critically examine dominant cultural norms and values. Indeed, in contrast with urban students, who may feel that their teachers cannot relate to them in part because they do not live in their communities, the Mansfield girls seem to feel betrayed that their teachers, many of whom *do* live in their community, either do not listen or cannot understand them.

Indeed, the Mansfield girls generally feel that their teachers cannot be counted on to respond, to care, or to understand what is *really* going on in the classroom; from the girls' point of view their teachers' moods are unreadable. Even the teachers she likes are confusing to Rachel:

> Well, Mrs. Harvey, she's fun, she like does fun stuff. And I learn a lot with her, but then she's easily not in a good mood. Like if somebody in one class gets her mad then the next class, when we come in, she's all mad still and it's like her mood changes easily. And she gets really mad when she gets mad . . . We're always saying, "Mrs. Harvey is in a bad mood" when we hear her hollering.

With a few exceptions, the Mansfield girls feel that their teachers do not take the time to listen or understand them. "I don't talk to the teachers about [my opinions]," Susan explains, "because I don't think they would listen to somebody that disagrees, and some of the students do and [the teachers] just say that they disagree and they don't find out our feelings about it." "It's like they're too busy to listen when we need to know something," Rachel explains, and we have to follow 'em all around to get something, to know something. The teachers [are] always hollering at us, [about] everything. Like when they tell us to go do something, we'll think, why can't they do it theirselves? They're sending us everywhere. And I don't know—they're just hollering about everything. They can't like *tell* us, because they just always have to holler.

Unlike the Acadia girls, the Mansfield girls seem not to know what their teachers want from them. They feel ignored and dismissed, even when they think they are playing by the teachers' rules. Group sessions are repeatedly punctuated with their frustration and outrage.

SUSAN: I think that it's mean when teachers, like Miss Davis . . . yells at you because you want to ask her a question. And then she says, "In a minute, when I get done working." So when somebody else goes and asks her, she just goes and helps them and then . . . it just pisses me off.

DIANE: So she's not listening to you when you ask for help. Well, why? Why aren't these people listening?

AMBER: 'Cause they're bitches . . .

SUSAN: 'Cause they're ignorant . . .

BRIANNA: Like, um, Donna and I walked up to Miss Davis and she was like playing with a map or something. And she goes, "Go sit down! Go sit down!" And we sat down, and she said, "Go sit down and raise your hands." So we raised our hands, and we didn't get, I didn't get spoken to until the end of class, the end of the day about what I wanted to talk about . . . And she was just ignoring me.

DIANE: Why don't these people listen?

STACEY: Because they're ignorant.

The girls' complaints about their teachers hold a place for the power of their interpretations and the reality of their experiences. Collectively insisting on their teachers' ignorance and rudeness confirms the legitimacy of their requests and their manner of communicating in the classroom. And yet the intensity with which the girls express themselves speaks to the sense of both longing and loss they experience in relation to their women teachers. Their teachers, the girls say over and over, are "ignorant"—that is, they do not know anything about them—and yet many of the angry stories about their teachers are examples of possibility turned to disappointment, the possibility of being known and understood, the disappointment of lost relationships and shared knowledge. "When we're doing a subject like on friendship or feelings or something," twelve-year-old Brianna explains, "she'll like try to help you as much as she can. But then the next week, she'll just start [ignoring you] all over again." Others are stories of what the girls describe as their teachers' overreaction to ordinary behavior, resulting from their lack of awareness of who the girls are and indicating their lack of respect for their feelings.

RACHEL: Today I was talking with James in [Mrs. Nugent's] room and he had [some things of mine] and he was passing them back to me and [Mrs. Nugent] told me to get out because she don't want . . . any of us in her room. She was really rude about things. She says, "Get out. I don't want any of you guys in my room." I go, "Yeah, just a second. Look, he's just passing them." And I was just holding out my hand ready for him to give them to me but he was being stupid, just holding them there, and she hollered, "Get out!" I go, "Will you wait a minute. I'm getting out!" . . . I was surprised she didn't come out and start yelling at me—but I just walked out.

Just as the girls cannot read their teachers, it would seem that the teachers cannot read the girls. From the girls' perspective, their women teachers allow no space for their ways of communicating and interacting. As a result the girls feel cut off, literally and figuratively pushed out of the classroom. In response to such situations, the Mansfield girls feel compelled to defend angrily their versions of reality and their behavior. For Rachel, "just being able to say what you want to say to a teacher, telling them what you feel," is something worth fighting for. "I'd get sent down to the office for it if I ever told Mrs. Damon what I thought about what she was saying to me," she adds. To others, watching teachers treat students "unfairly" or act as though "they don't care" is cause for resistance and reaction.

One day eleven-year-old Cheyenne shares with the group what she feels is a teacher's unfair treatment of her best friend, Donna. Her version of the story underscores a number of complaints the girls have with their teachers that surface and resurface over the course of the year; they complain about moodiness, overreaction, unpredictable behavior, and abuse of power:

CHEYENNE: Yesterday, Miss Davis came in from recess and was really mad and nobody knew why. And she goes to [Donna], she goes, "Take off your coat." And she wouldn't take off her coat . . . Because she didn't feel comfortable taking it off; and she said, "Go out in the hall," and then half an hour later she went out in the hall with Donna and before she did that she was walking around and everybody would ask her for something and she'd start screaming at 'em.

DIANE: Did she say why?

PATTI: Maybe she had PMS!

CHEYENNE: Wait! No. Anyways, they were out in the hall and she asked Donna why she wouldn't take off her coat and she goes, "Because I don't feel comfortable taking it off."

DONNA: No, I said, "I didn't want to."

CHEYENNE: Oh, because she didn't want to. And she goes, "I want you to write me" . . . two pages on why she wouldn't take off her coat.

DONNA: No, two pages why she should let me wear my jacket.

RACHEL: Oh, because she always . . . wears *her* jacket. [*some of the girls start to talk*] Listen! She's like, at the end of last year, she goes, "OK, when it's wintertime I'm going to have my window open and you guys are going to have to live with it." So, okay, we're wearing our coats. *She* can wear her coat when she's cold, but we can't, we get in trouble for it.

CHEYENNE: And then after that she says, "Go down to the office. I don't want your kind here."

DIANE: To you?

CHEYENNE: No, to Donna because she wouldn't take off her coat. And it's not fair because she can keep her coat on whenever she wants—

RACHEL: She thinks she can say whatever she wants.

DONNA: I wrote a two-page letter and I told her . . . that if I didn't want to take off my coat that I didn't have to and that she shouldn't make me do anything that I didn't want to do . . . and that she said that I'm going through a stage where I don't like my body.

DIANE: That's what she said?

SUSAN [laughing, squeals in a high feminine voice]: "I don't like my body!"

CHEYENNE: I don't like it when teachers say something and they don't know what's going on though, and they say something mean to you. They butt in and say, "Well, I know what's wrong with you," and think they know what is going on.

Miss Davis's insistence on a rule that seems to the girls both arbitrary and unreasonable outrages them. This particular incident, revisited a number of times over the course of the year, is emblematic of what appears to be off or wrong between the girls and their women teachers. Whether or not Cheyenne is quoting Miss Davis accurately, the girls generally feel that their teachers "don't want [their] kind here." In fact, it would seem, at least from this and other incidents the girls recount, that their teachers do not fully understand who "their kind" are. Miss Davis's explanation for Donna's resistance—that she is going through a stage where she does not like her body—echoes the voluminous literature on white middle-class girls' struggles with body image. But these white working-class girls are stunned and incredulous when they hear about the remark. Susan pokes fun at the very idea that this would be Donna's primary reason for resisting Miss Davis's no-coats rule. Cheyenne calls the teacher's comment "mean" and is angered by her presumptuousness. Donna, who refuses to write the letter Miss Davis asks for—flatly choosing to defend her actions rather than to submit to what appears to be a supercilious demand for explanation—concludes that Miss Davis "just wants something to bitch about." The girls' frustration and animosity toward their teachers center on the fact that, as twelve-year-old Stacey says at a later point, "teachers think they know what you are talking about."

When the coat problem resurfaces a number of sessions later, Diane encourages the girls to take their complaints before the school council. As they consider this possibility, the girls identify more clearly what most angers them about their teacher—it is not simply Miss Davis's unreasonable demands, but the way she uses her power to intrude on their lives, to presume that she has the requisite knowledge and intimacy to name their most private experiences:

STACEY: Miss Davis and her coats. What's her problem about coats?

DONNA: I like to wear my coat . . .

RACHEL: So why's it her business?

DONNA: She wears *her* coat!

DIANE: So, is this something you can bring up in student council . . . that you should be allowed to wear your coats if you want to?

AMBER: Yeah!

DIANE: Which one of you is going to bring it up at student council?

DONNA: I will . . .

RACHEL: It's not gonna work. I promise it won't. Miss Davis will explain, and it will all work out the way she wants it to.

DIANE: What will Miss Davis say?

RACHEL: What she says goes. No, she'll say, "There is no need to. Maybe it's not a school rule, but there will be no need to wear your coat. You can dress warm."

DIANE: Well, could one of you say, "I have a personal need to wear my coat?"

RACHEL: And she'll say, "What [is it]?" She thinks she has a right to.

AMBER: Say it's personal.

STACEY: Then she'd take you aside and say, "You can talk to me," and just bitch you out . . . She has no right to do that.

DIANE: Bring it up at student council then.

STACEY: Then she'll make us write a two-page paper on why we shouldn't—

AMBER *[who has been trying to speak]:* "Shut the hell up!"

SARAH: Say, "No, we don't have to."

AMBER: I know why she thinks we want to wear our coats. Because she thinks it's because we're afraid of our bodies, cause we're developing.

DONNA: Yes, that's what she told me.

RACHEL: I don't see why she should even have to know . . . If it's not a school rule, she shouldn't be able to say anything.

SARAH: She thinks she's so powerful, God, I'm so sick of it!

AMBER: Before I leave this school I'm going to tell her off.

DONNA: She thinks she can solve all the problems by telling us what to do and doesn't even know half the things she thinks she does.

AMBER: I think she's going senile. She's losing her brain.

RACHEL: I think she thinks that she knows everything, and that whatever she says is the whole thing . . . We're sick of her hollering.

DONNA: It really ticks people off.

DIANE: There has to be some way that this can get talked about with her . . . The coats you guys can work out, I think, because there's no rule that says you can't wear your coats.

RACHEL: So next time she tells us to take our coats off, "just say no."

STACEY: I'm just going to say, "Is there a rule, is there a school rule that we cannot wear our coats?" And if there's a problem, I'll say, "Well . . ." and I'll let Donna take it from there *[laughs]*.

The girls feel the weight of their teacher's "right" to their personal lives and the impossibility of publicly laying claim to their own interpretation of the situation. While Donna's desire to wear her coat might have something to do with her changing body, more likely it has to do with the obvious—the fact that Miss Davis keeps the window open in cold weather. Regardless of the real reason, the incident becomes something of a leitmotif for the girls, an example of their general resistance to their teachers' intrusiveness, a resistance Donna shows again later when another teacher catches her slouching in her chair: "She told me to sit up, and I go, 'No,' and she told me again and I said, 'No, I don't want to,' and she said go to the office." Whatever moves fourteen-year-old Donna to fold her arms stubbornly over her zipped coat remains unspoken in the face of Miss Davis's misinterpretation—and the girls' insistent belief that, no matter what they do, "it will all work out the way [Miss Davis] wants it."

Repeatedly, the girls point to a stalemate with their teachers—a failure of relationship grounded in an inability to read and accurately respond to each other's thoughts, feelings, and actions—that results all too often in frustration and anger and perceived hostility on both sides. At times during their group sessions anger fills the room. In frustration, Susan says of a teacher: "I'd just like to take her head and rip it off!" Amber shouts of yet another teacher: "I hate her! . . . I hate teachers!" "Teachers always make me mad," Rachel comments:

> [They] yell too much, get so mad . . . I think that teachers should learn to control themselves and they ought to have more patience if they're going to be teachers . . . I hate it. They shouldn't be able to [yell at someone] in front of the whole class or anything. They shouldn't be able to yell at you and stuff . . . that totally embarrasses you . . . they should talk to you later or something.

Teachers, Cheyenne says, have a "massive attitude." It begins to seem to the girls, as Susan puts it, like "everything we do is wrong."

Indeed, as the girls talk about their teachers during these moments, there seems to be no common ground. The girls cannot understand why their teachers are so upset with them and so out of touch with their lives. And yet from what the girls say and do not say about their behavior in school—about pushing teachers to the limit, angry outbursts, acting out or getting in trouble so they don't have to be in classes—one can imagine how this communication gap feels from the other side. The girls' anger, however, points not only to their disappointment and loss, but also to their full engagement with this school drama and their desire for something to change.

The image of the cooperative, quiet female student was not constructed from the expressions and experiences of these girls, nor were the categories that so often define conventionally feminine behavior—selflessness, polite passivity, and discomfort with anger and conflict. The Mansfield girls frequently get in trouble not only for swearing "wicked loud" and for rough-housing, but also for being their plain-spoken, unsubtle selves—that is, for not personifying the white middle-class norms and ideals of femininity so valued in school and society.

Thus it is perhaps not surprising that though the girls have strong feelings and are likely to express themselves openly, they pretty much agree that their desires have little effect on the way things go. Should they say what they think, Sarah explains, "the teachers will jump down our throats . . . [they] don't listen to what we say." "What makes me angry?" Stacey asks. "If things aren't fair or if nobody will listen or if you can't, you don't feel as if you can say anything at school or if you don't think it would do any good." If she did persist, she continues, "I don't think [things] would really change," since what she tells her teachers "goes in one ear and right out the other."

In spite of their strong feelings, or perhaps, in part, because of them, the Mansfield girls find it difficult to participate in academic classroom discussions. Even though Amber expresses her frustration and anger with teachers and thinks "you should speak your mind and let everybody know how you feel," she doesn't actually talk much or participate in class: "I don't usually talk in the classroom . . . 'cause I just don't want . . . I just don't feel right . . . I don't like talking in front of a big group. I don't like being the center of attention." The other girls struggle in similar ways. "I don't like . . . I won't really say much [in class]," Cheyenne confesses, "because I think that I'll say something and the kids will like say, 'Oh, she's stupid to say that,' and all that stuff . . . I've seen them do that to other people . . . just whoever they don't like." Rachel, too, is sure she is not very smart and that she will always carry the burden of this fact. "I'm kind of stupid, basically," she laments in her group session one day. "I just don't think I'm good enough" to go to college or get a "good enough" job. As a result, school for Rachel seems futile, just a constant reminder of her deficiencies.

The anger, frustration, and hostility these girls express in school seem as much about their fear, alienation, and anxiety about their potential to succeed in and beyond school, as it is about an active or conscious resistance to authorities or to upper-middle-class ideals of femininity.[5] The way they are used to speaking at home does not serve them well in the middle-class culture of their school, where a different set of codes and rules applies. School, in a vague sense, just "doesn't feel right" to the girls, but they cannot always articulate exactly why. While their teachers are explicit about their power, their demands and punishments seem arbitrary and irrational. Without explicit explanation about what manner of behavior and speech they expect and why—that is, without an introduction into the "culture of power"—these girls experience themselves as stupid and their teachers as unreasonable, "unfair," and unresponsive.[6]

Against the backdrop of seemingly unpredictable and unreasonable authorities, relationships with their friends take precedence for these girls. Because they count on one another to listen, such relationships are the focus of a great deal of energy. In sessions the girls relentlessly tease and verbally spar with one another. As is the case with other white working-class girls, such ritual teasing, particularly about romantic and sexual behavior, is not only playful but collaborative—a way to support one another and to distance themselves from dominant cultural notions of feminine behavior.[7] The ritual teasing that takes place in the context of school, then, is understandable.

The Mansfield girls are comfortable turning their strong feelings outward. They express their disgust at the way the boys in their class behave and the differences in the way boys and girls are treated in the school. Sarah explains the nature of their conversations over the course of the year and the emerging group awareness of this as an issue:

> Well, we started talking about it, about how the guys are being so macho . . . like they have to do everything and do stuff first and have privileges more than girls. And the girls, you know, they just don't care. But they're starting to now. They're starting to get sick of the guys always wanting to be the best in everything and to them it means just everything, but we just kind of have fun and it feels good, and the guys have to win, but we just did it for fun.

For Rachel, the problem is "the way [boys] act . . . They're always loud and they're always talking so the teachers are always yelling at them and we'll have to listen to it." She finds it particularly disturbing that the boys get away with saying and doing "sickening" and "disgusting things."

RACHEL: Like in one of the speeches Kevin wrote at graduation, they talk about sticks, and all that stuff and you know, like it sounds good if you're not thinking of it the way they are, but then all of a sudden they're laughing, because they . . .

LYN: They're not talking about sticks. They're talking about something else.

RACHEL: Yeah. And they always do it the same in all the classes because the teachers just think—they know that the teachers don't know what they're talking about.

Like the Acadia girls, the Mansfield girls notice that the boys are judged according to different standards; but unlike the Acadia girls, they acknowledge that these differences are gender based. The boys, Stacey notes, are usually "a lot louder" than the girls,

> and they usually try to be not as involved and they're usually the ones that get in trouble . . . I think they're allowed more time to do things. Say something needed to be typed and on a certain day and they didn't have it done. So, they will argue with the teacher and the girls don't really argue with them so they get more time to do it . . . They're, they're really pushy. But I don't think that's the only reason. I guess the girls are expected to have it done mostly.

And that, twelve-year-old Corrine adds, "is just the way it is."

Although Corrine, echoing the Acadia girls, sees this difference in treatment as almost inevitable—"it doesn't bother me, I guess, that much . . . it always happens, I guess, so it's just like life"—the Mansfield girls in general are more likely to fight the image of female subordination and to compete with the boys for time and space. When their teachers assume that the boys are "tougher," the girls react:

SARAH: Like if it's something like moving or stacking chairs, they'll say . . . they'll pick a bunch of guys to go out and do it. They never ask us and I think . . . we can stack chairs too. Because the boys think they're so macho. They think the guys are tougher than us or something . . . I think there are some guys that are tough but then there are some that aren't and I get sick of it, about the guys thinking they're so tough and the teachers thinking they're so tough.

Rather than wait around to be asked to stack chairs, Sarah, twelve, explains, "we just go and do it . . . We try to compete with them harder, trying harder and doing better than we were before, to try to knock the guys down and win over them."

This resistance extends to the school playground as well. "Boys don't think girls can play basketball as good," Susan says, explaining why the boys feel entitled to the basketball court and constantly encroach on the girls' time. "I think that they should just change their attitude about it."

Susan and her friends became so fed up with the boys' behavior that, with Diane's encouragement, they took their complaints to the school governing board. As a result, "the teachers decided that the girls will have the court one day and the boys will have it the next day." Although, as Susan points out, "it didn't work out" in the long run "because like the boys kept on coming on our court while it was our time," and because, Amber thinks, "the girls didn't push hard enough . . . and then it like died out," the girls, in typical fashion, continue on occasion to demand their full playing time.

Although these girls feel anger and often openly express it, they say that they are told time and again by their women teachers that anger is not an appropriate emotion to express in school. Since the teachers and administrators did respond to the girls' anger about unfair treatment at school, that is, about the basketball court, it seems that the girls are talking about the teachers' response to feelings that are more private. As Donna, who, with the encouragement of her mother and a therapist, has struggled for some time to express her anger about her father's physical abuse, explains:

> I think [expressing anger] is a relief because when my dad and mom were married, I never expressed my feelings at all. I just, I don't know, because my dad used to beat up on me, so I like wouldn't say anything, you know, and I had to go to counseling and stuff, and then it just came. And my mom thinks I still have a lot of anger because of my dad and stuff.

Donna knows her anger is sometimes out of control at school—"I take it out on people and I know it's not right, but they say something and it just comes out"—but she doesn't know how to be in school with these feelings or how to be herself without them.

> I either try to talk to [the counselor] when she's here or when she's not here I, um, if I can't talk to her, I just sit there and do nothin', and I won't talk. I just sit there . . . A lot of people think, Miss Davis says [school's] not the proper place to express it, like your family problems at school because, you know . . . [she] says we should take it out in recess, but I don't know, then I might beat up somebody.

These working-class girls, who do not reify the separate spheres of public and private in the way the middle-class girls do, and who tend to see school in terms of "embattled relationships," find it difficult to understand such boundaries placed around the expression of feelings.[8] When Donna says school is not the proper place to express anger she means, in effect, the "family problems" that give rise to her feelings. Given the significant role she has played as mediator in her family and the value she places on caring for others—especially her mother—much of who she is and what she values is thus rendered inappropriate or invisible in school.

Rachel talks about how she deals with her anger in school in ways that suggest that the intensity of her feelings are, in part, a response to the regulation of her voice. She tells what happened when a teacher, in a bad mood, "sent me [down] to the office for going to the stupid bathroom."

> But I didn't go down. I didn't go down. She said I had to go see [the principal]. I didn't. And today I wasn't going to, but Mrs. Nugent went and told Mrs. Higgins that I wasn't cooperating and going down . . . When I came back up, it was even worse.

DIANE: So how did you handle your anger over this situation?

RACHEL: I just sat there and I wanted to punch something.

DIANE: And you didn't do anything, you just held it all in?

RACHEL: I couldn't! Well, what I wanted to do I'd get suspended for . . . Well, I always go in the kitchen and talk to people.

In this way the Mansfield girls struggle, with few structured or safe places to sort through their anger and express their rage; in a very fundamental way, they feel alienated from school and abandoned by their teachers. Donna feels caught between the messages she receives from home, that it's good to let her anger out, and those she receives from school, that expressing anger in public is inappropriate. Getting the message, she says she holds her feelings in, until a classmate or teacher pushes too far. Like one day, she explains, "I told Mrs. Evans that she was a fucking liar and I had to stay down to the office from 9:30 until 12:30 . . . I thought it was good for me to sit in the office because I knew if I went back upstairs that real trouble would have started and I would have gotten suspended." Rachel, knowing the consequences of expressing her strong feelings in school, holds her anger in and seeks out the familiar faces of the women who work in the cafeteria; they seem to understand her and care for her.

I am not suggesting that any and all forms of anger should be tolerated in school—certainly the girls' yelling and swearing make both teaching and learning difficult, if not impossible. Rather, I wish to highlight what appear to be radically different communicative styles and a clash of cultures, and suggest that the Mansfield girls' intense anger toward many of their teachers is, in part, about their emerging awareness of the difference between who they are and what their teachers want them to be. That their teachers "holler" at the girls so much, even as they demand their public compliance with middle-class conventions of speech and behavior, intensifies the girls' confusion and anger and contributes to their sense of betrayal. At best school becomes a place where these girls negotiate the intersection of cultural and class values; at worse, it represents a disingenuous imposition of "appropriate" femininity and middle-class views that serve to denigrate their experiences and contribute to their growing distrust of authorities.

In many ways, these adolescent girls, both working- and middle-class, interrupt our often unexamined notions of idealized femininity. Neither group of girls represents the conventional ideal, and each enters the culture struggling against the demands and costs of female impersonation. Although the Acadia girls appear to capitulate to or appropriate white middle-class ideals of feminine behavior, beneath the surface they are frustrated and angry with the lack of recognition and the invisibility such conventions demand. The angel in the classroom has her counterpoint in the "madgirl." Like the madwoman in the attic of Victorian literature, she is rebellious, subversive, sometimes outrageous; she knows that her thoughts and feelings, especially strong feelings like anger, place her in danger of being called pathological or monstrous.[9] As with the madwoman, the girls' strong feelings are pushed out of view, cut off, figuratively locked away in the cultural attic, or perhaps more accurately, buried in the basement. The Acadia girls do say what they know, what they feel and want, if only in the privacy of their interviews and focus groups. They are aware at times that they are performing or impersonating idealized femininity— that who they present themselves to be is not who they feel they really are.

The Acadia girls' adoption of the American Dream and its radical individualism, in conjunction with their discomfort with anger and the direct expression of what they want and need, contributes to intense underground competition, undermining what began as a collective, potentially powerful political resistance. Moving out of touch with one another, they have little corroboration for their feelings and express doubt about their perceptions. More important, they lose the power of their shared feelings and common circumstances, a loss that prevents them from seeing or reacting to the larger cultural picture and their place in it.

By contrast, the Mansfield girls, because of their angry distrust of authority, learn from one another and, in spite of often difficult interactions, stay in much closer relationship with one another. Their resistance, with their capacity to be outspoken and publicly angry, gives them a shared vision of a hostile world and, with this vision, the power to organize. A number of times during the year the girls supported one another through trying incidents, and in two cases—the coat incident and the basketball court battle—with Diane Starr's encouragement, were so vocal as a group that they were able to affect school policy.

Unlike the middle-class girls, then, the Mansfield girls live their "madness" in full view of their teachers, administrators, and classmates. And yet, their distrust of authorities, the confusing, often contradictory messages they receive about appropriate behavior, and their justified belief that they will not be heard or taken seriously also prevent them from developing genuine relationships with their women teachers. Notwithstanding the girls' hostility and frustration, there are numerous signs that their teachers do care and are trying to listen. It was the school, for example, that notified the authorities about Donna's abuse, and it was a responsive teacher who raised concerns for Corrine's physical and emotional well-being; school policies *were* changed in response to the girls' complaints, and even though Miss Davis may have misinterpreted Donna's refusal to take off her coat, she seemed to try to engage Donna in a dialogue she thought was important for her student. The problem, in fact, seems not to be that the teachers do not care, but that unexamined class and cultural divides prevent shared understanding between the girls and their women teachers.

For both the Acadia and the Mansfield girls, anger is a source of knowledge and motivation. It points to the heightened regulation of their thoughts, feelings, and actions, and it announces their resistance. Although the politics of their anger is at times only barely discernible to others, much less to themselves, the disruptiveness of their response contests a construction of reality that denigrates, marginalizes, or buries their experiences. These girls, in their passion and struggle, hold the potential for deepening our understanding of idealized femininity by clarifying the damage it causes and alluding to the social and psychological forces holding it in place. Should we pay close attention to their anger, as well as to the discomfort it arouses in us, we may well find ourselves participating in a different kind of conversation, open to other meanings and new pathways.

NOTES

1. See, for example, AAUW, 1992; Sadker and Sadker, 1986, 1994. Peggy Orenstein's *Schoolgirls* (1994) is a notable exception. And yet, though

Orenstein relays the complexity and range of girls' experiences in junior high, her reliance on the overall framework of psychological loss at the hands of gender bias causes her at times to downplay the resistance and critique of the girls to whom she listens.

2. Given that *Beavis and Butthead* is a parody of the immaturity of adolescent boys, it is, of course, ironic both that the boys identify with the cartoon, and that the girls take the boys' imitation seriously.

3. King and Emmons, 1990.

4. Jack, 1991; Jack and Dill, 1992.

5. Valerie Walkerdine (1990) makes this point in *Schoolgirl Fictions*.

6. See Delpit, 1988, 1995.

7. Here I refer specifically to Donna Eder's research on white working-class girls' friendships and peer relations (1985, 1993). See also Peggy Miller (1986).

8. See Luttrell, 1993, p. 539.

9. See Gilbert and Gubar, 1984.

REFERENCES

American Association of University Women. 1992. *How schools shortchange girls.* Washington, D.C.: AAUW Educational Foundation.

Delpit, Lisa. 1988. The silenced dialogue: Power and pedagogy in educating other people's children. *Harvard Educational Review* 58: 280–298.

———. 1995. *Other people's children: Cultural conflict in the classroom.* New York: The New Press.

Eder, Donna. 1985. The cycle of popularity: Interpersonal relations among female adolescents. *Sociology of Education* 58:154–165.

———. 1993. "Go get ya a french!" Romantic and sexual teasing among adolescent girls. In Deborah Tannen, ed., *Gender and conversational interaction.* Oxford: Oxford University Press.

Gilbert, Sandra, and Susan Gubar. 1984. *The madwoman in the attic: The woman writer and the nineteenth-century literary imagination.* New Haven: Yale University Press.

Jack, Dana. 1991. *Silencing the self: Depression and women.* Cambridge, Mass.: Harvard University Press.

Jack, Dana, and D. Dill. 1992. The silencing the self scale: Schemas of intimacy associated with depression in women. *Psychology of Women Quarterly* 16: 97–106.

King, L., and R. Emmons. 1990. Conflict over emotional expression: Psychological and physical correlates. *Journal of Personality and Social Psychology*
58: 864–877.

Luttrell, Wendy. 1993. "The teachers, they all had their pets": Concepts of gender, knowledge, and power. *Signs* 18(3): 505–546.

Miller, Peggy. 1986. Teasing as language socialization and verbal play in a white
working-class community. In Bambi Schieffelin and Elinor Ochs, eds.,
Language socialization across cultures. Cambridge: Cambridge University
Press.

Orenstein, Peggy. 1994. *Schoolgirls: Young women, self-esteem and the
confidence gap.* New York: Doubleday.

Sadker, Myra, and David Sadker. 1986. Sexism in the classroom: From grade
school to graduate school. *Phi Delta Kappan* 68: 512–515.

———. 1994. *Failing at fairness: How America's schools cheat girls.* New York:
Charles Scribner's Sons.

Walkerdine, Valerie. 1990. *Schoolgirl fictions.* London: Verso.

10

HOW GIRLS
NEGOTIATE SCHOOL

Research for Action (American Association of University Women)

IN HER STUDY OF GIRLS and boys in elementary school, Barrie Thorne argues that while adults influence how children take up being female and male, children themselves "act, resist, rework, and create . . . as social actors in a range of institutions."[1] Likewise, young adolescent girls learn the social patterns of the adult world at the same time that they are actively interpreting the world and shaping their own values. In the face of an onslaught of cultural and personal messages about what it means to be female, their task is monumental. They must both prune and blossom, cope and strategize; they must invent themselves. Girls at this developmental crossroad share a set of challenges as they come to grips with issues of autonomy and connection. They also differ from each other in ways that shape their choices and emerging identities.

Developmental psychologists theorize that while boys are most psychologically at risk in childhood, for girls the time of greatest risk is adolescence.[2] Carol Gilligan and her colleagues track preadolescent girls who are resilient, lively, willful, courageous, and honest through their early adolescence. Then these same girls begin peppering their speech with "I don't know," signaling what these researchers describe as "a giving up of voice, an abandonment of self, for the sake of becoming a good girl and having relationships."[3] While some girls respond to the developmental crisis of adolescence by "devaluing themselves and feeling themselves to be worthless . . . others disagree publicly and dissociate themselves from institutions which devalue them—in this case, the schools."[4]

Much of the early research conducted by Gilligan and her colleagues has been with middle- and upper-middle-class white girls. Researchers focusing on the challenges for young adolescent girls of color have noted that these girls "are making this passage embedded within a family and a community that is most often negatively impacted by a sociopolitical context framed by racial, gender, and economic oppression.[5] Writing about Native American preadolescents, Ardy Bowker notes that their development is shaped by their early initiation into "adult problems and adult responsibilities."[6] Tracy Robinson and Janie Ward argue that the young woman of color must be taught "resistance that will provide her with the necessary tools to think critically about herself, the world, and her place in it."[7]

Three Behavioral Strategies

As our researchers talked with young adolescent girls across the country, we heard girls' accounts of the pressures to be "nice" and quiet, to get along with everyone, to avoid conflict or even notice. But we also heard girls describe themselves with pride as having a "loud voice," being tall, being willing to stand up for their beliefs. These girls were active agents using an amalgamation of strategies to negotiate their school days. In this chapter we describe three strategic approaches that we saw used by girls identified as "successful" in school. We call these approaches "speaking out," "doing school," and "crossing borders," terms we coined to describe what we saw.

Speaking Out

Some girls tend to assert themselves, speaking out and insisting on being heard in both friendly and unfriendly circumstances. This is an approach often used by a girl with a strong sense of herself, her identity, her ideas, and her place in the hierarchies of school and peer cultures. A girl using this strategy may describe herself and be described by peers as "not afraid to say what she thinks."

Across our research sites, some girls habitually speak out. They make themselves highly visible in their schools and become "maverick leaders" who are publicly acknowledged. Others become earmarked as "negative leaders" or "troublemakers," youngsters with notable potential who risk being tagged for failure unless they can change others' perceptions of them. Whether a girl who speaks out becomes identified by herself and others as a leader or a troublemaker may well have to do with her relationships with key adults and how these adults are positioned in the school. It may also have to do with how well her home and community cultures match the dominant culture of the school.

Doing School

Some girls behave in ways that have been traditionally expected of them in school, doing what is asked and speaking in turn, if at all. This approach, too, can be seen as two sides of a coin, as girls call up traditional "good girl" ways of negotiating school either with apparent comfort or to cover dimensions of who they are.

The "schoolgirl" who employs such commonly agreed-upon strategies for success as doing her work on time, listening, and complying with adults' expectations may experience a comfortable fit between her home persona and school culture. Her worlds may well overlap, minimizing daily dissonance. Although she may have put on hold ideas that contradict expected norms, for the time being she has used this strategy to negotiate a viable deal.

A girl who is "playing schoolgirl" employs similar strategies but with greater ambivalence and perhaps even strife. She may be trying to achieve or at least to define her own goals, which may be less congruent with school goals. A girl negotiating school in this way is outwardly compliant and successful in school but leaves clues to her other identity and worlds, which may fit uneasily with school culture. While she is likely to receive adult support in her schoolgirl guise, adults and even peers in the school setting may not be privy to other challenges she is facing. Therefore, she may not be receiving support for the deep work of constructing her own identity.

Girls "doing school" tend to receive adult approval, though perhaps they receive less attention in class than more demanding students. Adults may name them as "good girls" rather than as leaders.

Crossing Borders

Finally, girls who cross borders between different cultures or sets of norms and expectations may achieve success in school and with peers as well as in their home communities, becoming proficient in two or more codes of speech and behavior and gaining stature as "schoolgirls/cool girls." These girls tend to be recognized by adults and peers alike as "successful" and "knowing everybody."

Some of these girls emerge as school leaders who can act as "translators" because of their ability to understand, communicate, and even facilitate others' interactions across disparate worlds, such as school and community, or adults and adolescents. In some settings, border crossers may be recognized in their schools as girls who carry important knowledge, and their schools may call on them to act as "stranger handlers," helping new people enter the cultural sphere of the school. Elsewhere, these girls and their talents may go unrecognized by school authorities, particularly in settings where differences go unacknowledged and strangers are rare.

Girls' approaches align somewhat with their class and/or race—with middle-class and white girls more likely to present as "quiet" and "nice," and working-class girls and girls of color likelier to risk confrontation. Our observations confirm research describing white and black working-class girls as sharing approaches such as a willingness to speak out.[8] However, class and race alone are not necessarily predictive of where a girl falls in this typology. More critical is the match between a girl's own race/ethnicity and class and the dominant culture of her school, which might make a particular strategy feel more available to some girls than to others. For example, a Latina in a school setting where both adults and peers were also predominantly Latino might employ a different strategic approach from a Latina in a predominantly white setting. Additionally, this racial/ethnic match might influence the school's view: For example, a girl regarded as a maverick leader in a school setting where she's of the dominant culture might be viewed as a troublemaker in another, where she's a minority.

In practice, girls' strategic approaches seem sometimes to overlap fully with their identities. As girls assess and select available strategies, at some moments more consciously than others, they may "become" their strategies for periods of time as they sort through options in the process of forming identities. However, their strategic approaches must be distinguished from the girls themselves.

Distinguishing strategies from girls helps us see the ways that some approaches may be precluded and others assisted by environmental factors. Separating approaches from girls' personae also highlights the fact that the same strategies may be interpreted differently at different schools or at different times. Thus, behaviors that evidence "leadership" in one setting, for example, might elsewhere be interpreted as "bullying." Finally, separating strategies from girls allows us to assess opportunities girls have to change their approaches. During their middle school years, girls may try on different strategies like so many coats as part of their self-discovery process. As a boy at one school saw it, girls were "actors," "impostors" who "change instead of staying the same." But rather than indicating falsity, this process of exploration is essential for girls' growth. Understanding girls' experimentation with strategies can help educators re-examine girls' choices in light of their options.

This chapter will use the typology of strategies as a framework to introduce six girls from the study who represent a range of approaches to negotiating school. Like the other girls in this study, these girls were selected because they were deemed "successful." Our criteria for success in school were necessarily complex, given different definitions of success held by disparate cultures within and outside of school. While we looked at such conventional indicators as academic achievement measured by grade and test scores, we also sought the perspectives of adults in school as well as peers and our own research team to identify girls achieving success in a range of ways including academically, athletically, creatively, as school and/or peer leaders, and as reflective observers of their worlds.

Typology of Girls' Strategies for Negotiating School

Speaking Out

Some girls tend to assert themselves, speaking out and insisting on being heard in both friendly and unfriendly circumstances. A girl who speaks out may be perceived as a maverick leader or a troublemaker, depending on her relationships with key adults, the adults' positions in the school, and the degree to which a girl's identity and approach match the dominant culture of the school.

MAVERICK LEADER. Some girls who habitually speak out make themselves highly visible in their schools and become publicly acknowledged as leaders.

TROUBLEMAKER. Other girls who also speak out become identified as "negative leaders" with unrealized potential. Girls viewed as troublemakers may increase their risk of failure until they change others' perceptions of them.

Doing School

Some girls conform to traditional expectations of girls in school, doing what is asked and speaking in turn or not at all. Like speaking out, this approach is two-sided, and depending on the girl and her context, can play to girls' advantage or disadvantage.

SCHOOLGIRL. Some girls employ traditional "good girl" ways of negotiating school with apparent comfort, such as doing work on time, listening, and complying with adults' expectations.

PLAY SCHOOLGIRL. Other girls call up "good girl" behaviors partly to cover up who they really are. This pretense can involve ambivalence and perhaps even strife. Girls using this approach are outwardly compliant and successful in school but leave clues to their other identities and worlds, which may fit uneasily with school culture.

Crossing Borders

Some girls move easily between different cultures or sets of norms and expectations, bridging the gulf, for instance, between peers and adults or between different racial or ethnic groups. These girls are able to move into and out of various settings, taking on characteristics sufficient to "fit" wherever they are. While some maintain separation between their spheres, other border crossers take on the responsibility of "translating" across these different cultures.

SCHOOLGIRL/COOL GIRL. Some girls may achieve success in school, with peers, and in their home community, becoming proficient in two or more codes of speech and behavior, thus gaining stature.

TRANSLATOR. Some girls emerge as school leaders, able to understand and communicate across cultural groups and even facilitate or mediate others' interactions across such divides as school and community, or adults and adolescents.

Our work was complicated by the different ways in which schools interpreted the same strategies, so that what worked in one environment might not work in another. While it is critical to view girls as authors of their identities and agents in their lives, their ongoing interaction with their environments also tempers and shapes who they are becoming. The work was further complicated by shifts in girls' approaches and degree of success even within the period of the research. Within each set of strategies for making sense and making choices, girls may take different paths. For example, a girl who is well liked by peers and also achieves academically may seek low visibility to balance the demands of being both a "schoolgirl" and a "cool girl," or she may choose greater visibility for herself by taking on the work of translating school values for peers while also helping adults to penetrate adolescents' perspectives.

While we began this research looking for successful girls who could help us understand what about their schools worked for them, what we discovered was a richer picture involving a dynamic relationship between girls and schools and greater insight into both the meanings and the fragility of success for adolescent females.

This study is predicated on the notion that both girls and schools change. Historically, girls entering adolescence have been pressured to alter their school personae to fit a relatively narrow definition of success.[9] Research indicates that as young adolescent girls begin to suppress aspects of themselves that seem at odds with models of adult femininity, they may experience a sense of "inner division" symptomatic of a separation between what they know to be true and what they can publicly acknowledge.[10] Our research suggests that we reframe the problem, beginning with the girls themselves as lenses on the institutions they inhabit. Rather than asking girls to cut off limbs to fit the procrustean bed of schools, we ask how girls' needs can become visible and how schools can change to address the learning needs of all girls.

Speaking Out

A Maverick Leader

An African American eighth grader at Grath, a large urban middle school, Keisha is a solidly built girl whose expression behind silver-rimmed glasses shifts quickly from meditative to amused or critical. Her attire—a study in contradictions—may provide clues to her complex persona. On the day she is to be "shadowed," Keisha wears a white sweater with a long black skirt and patent leather shoes with bows. Her hair is tucked up under a purple and yellow Mickey Mouse cap worn with the rim to the back.

In elementary school, Keisha managed to be aggressive while also achieving in school. She recounts, "I used to fight a lot with boys. 'Cause they always like hittin' on girls and they don't think you're supposed to hit them back. So I hit 'em back." Meanwhile, she earned the place of class valedictorian at elementary school graduation and recalls the standing ovation after her speech as a shining moment of success.

The transition to middle school, however, seemed fraught with difficult choices. She describes herself as a "bad girl" in sixth and seventh grades; adults, she says, regarded her as "a firecracker." Still, Keisha knew she was smart and assertive even as she rejected the demands of school. At home her older sister was "running the streets," leaving high school and finally home.

Upset about the strife at home and restless in a self-contained classroom with a substitute teacher unable to manage thirty-three sixth graders, Keisha "went wild," fighting and cursing in school and more often than not "cut[ting] out of school and go[ing] to Kentucky Fried Chicken." There were frequent suspensions from school. Nonetheless, Keisha's native intelligence, the same assertiveness that often led her astray of the system, and her connections with several key adults enabled her to pass sixth and seventh grades while friends with whom she cut school were kept back.

As an eighth grader, Keisha is bright, strong, and outspoken, an honor roll student with a math and technology focus. She expresses herself clearly and directly, using so-called Black English or African American Language[11] adeptly to explain her point of view. She explains how she has learned to handle her teacher, Barbara Shane, a white woman with an acerbic style with whom Keisha has had several run-ins. As Keisha describes it, she has had to let her teacher know her abilities and what she can and cannot tolerate. In a reading class where relatively few girls volunteer, Keisha stands out as sharp and alert, both about the subject matter and about how to put herself forward.

MS. SHANE: Where does the story take place?

KEISHA: Paris. (There is a mild disturbance and Ms. Shane does not hear her.)

MS. SHANE: Carl, the major city in France?

CARL: Paris.

KEISHA: I said it!

MS. SHANE: Oh, I'm sorry, I couldn't hear you.

Thereafter, Keisha is called on several times, each time proffering the correct answer, and is also the one to name the opera *Tommy* from yesterday's discussion. She explains to the researcher with scorn that others at her table "don't pay attention in class; that's why they don't know nothing." Later, she is among the first to finish the workbook exercises. For Keisha, this structured and competitive classroom provides a setting where she is developing an academic self and voice. In another setting the teacher might have admonished Keisha for her "attitude," perhaps forfeiting her involvement and her contribution.

Keisha hopes to attend a competitive engineering and science magnet high school in the area. She scored high enough on standardized tests to be placed in eighth-grade algebra. In science, also taught by Ms. Shane, Keisha appreciates the opportunity to take part in active learning that requires collaboration and risk taking, much like doing science in the world. "We do a lot of experiments and we're not just writing out of the book and having a test next week. . . . All [the teacher] do is pass out materials. She let us do [the work]. As we grow up, if everybody tell us, then we don't learn to do nothin'."

Keisha negotiates the classroom from the highly visible position of stature and leadership that she has gained at her school. "Everybody knows me. Even people I don't know, know me," she says. This was not always the case. Cutting class and maintaining a reputation as someone not to be "messed with" taught Keisha how and when to raise and lower her visibility. Her self-assured gait and new status as a person of influence seem to guarantee her immunity as she walks through hallways while others are jostled in the crowd or admonished by staff for being in the hall during class.

The new principal, an African American woman who calls Keisha "my miracle baby," met Keisha in the course of hallway confrontations and invited her to join the leadership team she was forming to guide school reform. "I wanted [Keisha] to represent the negative element," the principal explains. This invitation coincided with other factors in Keisha's life to catalyze a change. Keisha describes her role on the reform team as one of knowledge and authority: "It's like having kids there at the meeting to discuss, and we put in our opinion about what should be done about certain things. We know what's goin' on. The teachers [who are not there], we can inform them." While the principal expresses confidence in Keisha's ability "to go on from here, to do whatever it is she wants to do," Keisha in turn acknowledges the valuable currency she has gained by her relationship with the principal.

Keisha credits other adults, mostly African American women, with offering her critical support as well as opportunities to engage in real work. Joann Sellers, a classroom aide in elementary and now in middle school, runs the Performing Arts Club in the community, where Keisha measures her success in terms of her own satisfaction with scripting and performance. Ms. Sellers sees Keisha as making an important contribution to the venture.

"[At the club] Keisha initiated poem writing, 'cause we're doing a calendar as a fund-raiser. It focuses on kids in the [club]. She initiated, 'Everybody take your name and come up with things that describe your personality.' I thought it was a great idea [and] the other kids loved it!"

Keisha also describes close relationships with both parents, who offer consistent support and express confidence in her ability to set and achieve her goals.

Invited to participate in this study, Keisha was quick to employ strategies to make herself known to the researchers, to leave her own classes legitimately to conduct research in others' classes, and to help construct the picture of her offered in this report. During an interview she sits erect, smiling slightly and gazing at a filing cabinet as she explains that she wants to be a pediatrician. She likes kids but "never wants to get married because I see how it is with my mom doing all the work in the house." Information she has gleaned from observing the division of labor in her household influences Keisha's plans for the future.

Keisha has gained a sense of efficacy in school. Working from a solid sense of herself, she sees and takes up opportunities at school. Adults in her reform-minded school as well as adults at home have helped Keisha value and use her strengths. By creating inroads in the school culture and modeling initiative, Keisha in turn helps to foster a climate where students and especially girls take on leadership roles in school reform, sustain meaningful connections with adults, and engage actively in their own learning. On the other hand, Keisha remains willing to break a rule or confront an adult when, as she sees it, the situation warrants.

"Troublemaker"

At a middle school in the rural Southwest, a researcher has been shadowing Alicia, a high-achieving Hispanic student. In the scene below, she leaves Alicia and has an encounter with Mona, a Native American youngster whom school staff identified as successful several months earlier. By this second visit, Mona is in trouble and on in-house suspension, spending her days in her advisory teacher's classroom. At lunch she is allowed to join friends.

> In the cafeteria I leave Alicia to her friends and take my tray to one end of a long and otherwise empty table. Suddenly Mona with five of her friends descends on me—smiling gleefully—and settles at my table. As an aide who monitors the lunchroom approaches, I realize that aides are seating students now as a way of maintaining order in the remodeled cafeteria. Mona has astutely used my presence to create a bubble of dissension. The aide directs the girls back to their seats. The

others look at Mona, who asserts challengingly, "We're sitting with a teacher!" After several failed efforts to move the girls, the aide insists, "No, you need permission from Mr. Lomas [the principal]!" which I hear as an effort to put an end to it. But Mona has taken off across the crowded cafeteria toward the principal's table and soon returns triumphant, nodding and smiling. "[The principal] said it was okay, ask him." Other students are looking our way now, wavering with their trays. The principal is striding up behind her, apparently figuring out as he approaches that Mona has played us adults against each other. He frowns, shifting gears and telling the girls to return to their places, that I will come sit with them. They retreat amid groans.

(From a researcher's fieldnotes, 1/30/95)

Mona is a slender eighth grader with a coffee-colored complexion, a crooked smile, and straight dark hair that she wears up with tendrils hanging. At the provocation of a familiar lyric, she bursts into rap or laughter.

A Native American living on the Santa Pueblo, Mona embodies some of the tensions of a traditional culture embedded in an insistently modern world. Like many adults on the pueblo, her parents speak *keres,* a native language of the Pueblo Indians, at home. In a school system where English is the official language and Spanish the language of preference and study, the distinction Mona and her friends gain by sharing a secret tongue is offset by their identification as language minority students. The pueblo's economy is dominated by the neon-lit bingo casino, where Mona's older sister works long night hours, often leaving her two-year-old to Mona's care. Mona's mother travels to the city for work as a police dispatcher. From her sister, a single working mom, and her mother who works outside the home and off the reservation, Mona receives information about the economic and domestic pressures on Native American females, whose traditional role is in the home and community.

Apparently comfortable, self-confident, and voluble in a variety of settings, Mona is seen by adults at Avila Middle School as a Native American girl who is atypically unreserved. In a group of girls she quickly stands out, responding readily, singing, laughing, and cursing before the others, as they eye her for behavior cues. But in an interview she admits to feeling alone, distrusting adults at school who "don't understand" or "might phone my dad," being uncomfortable "talking to people [at home]—It is like a weird feeling that grows inside of you when you talk to someone at home," she explains—and, despite a strong peer identification with a girls' gang, feeling unable to open up to other members about deep personal issues because "I don't know how they'd react." Although she is peripherally aware of school personnel such as the counselor and Native American aides designated to support girls like her, Mona does not look to these adults for guidance.

Described by a Native American teaching aide as a girl who showed great promise in the sixth grade, Mona is currently on in-house suspension as a consequence of her behavior in school. Her adviser, a young white woman new to teaching, explains that when she called home to discuss Mona's transgressions, "her mom got angry and told me not to call again. So I sent a registered letter." A conference is necessary to end suspension. The adviser lists Mona's offenses: "She's in big-time trouble. She was brought in by a teacher for screaming obscenities. She chews gum and comes to class late. She also threatened a kid." Like Keisha, Mona possesses intelligence and energy that draw attention to her as "a real leader even when she acts 'bad' . . . a bright girl making some wrong choices." Unlike Keisha, Mona is described by a teacher as exerting a potent "negative influence on peers"; for key adults, this may take her beyond the possibility of redemption. With regret, her social studies teacher, another white female, notes, "Mona is very smart, very interesting. She's the one I'll remember twenty years from now."

The aide from Mona's pueblo worries that Mona may get expelled: Her grades are poor, her behavior wild, and she shows too much interest in boys. The aide describes the pressures on many pueblo girls to put the community ahead of school:

> If the family is traditional, education is not first on the list. . . . Women play an important role: They make activities go in the pueblo. They carry it all. Girls grow up knowing what their responsibilities are within the community. . . . School could take the kids away from the community.

While Mona resists the pressures of school, often not bothering with work that does not interest her, neither does she seem to be complying with expectations in the pueblo, where she "chills" next door, hanging out with an older brother and his friends.

In Mona's home, she is seen as carrying talent and a sense of promise and achievement for the family. She muses on different goals family members hold for her:

> My sister wants me to be a model. My dad wants me to be a singer, 'cause I'm always singing. My brother wants me to be an artist, 'cause

> I'm like always drawing and everything. But my dad doesn't want me
> to be a model because I'll be away from home a lot.

She feels that her mother shows her concern by "always trying to straighten me out, like trying to keep me off of drugs, stop smoking, stop drinking. She's just there a lot. She talks to me." Mona's family holds different expectations for her than those typical for the pueblo, and these expectations suggest a more liberal approach to female roles.

Widely acknowledged as a "leader" in the school and particularly among girls, Mona struggles to understand the hazards and potential gains of leadership:

> It's like if you were a young person that no one really paid attention
> to. And then when you get into a fight it is like you have become
> popular. Or you are like a queen or something. It is a real good feel-
> ing but you got to know when not to get out of hand no matter if
> anyone tries to pressure you into doing something. It is kind of stu-
> pid in a way because people will only be around you 'cause they
> think that you can protect them. But to me, being a leader is being
> yourself.

Who is "herself" and can she find and be this self in school? Mona admits, "I don't think of myself [as smart]. I feel like I'm always in trouble," while on the other hand reflecting, "I'm smart. I can do the [work] but I'm too lazy to do it." Though she seems hardly to attend to official classroom agendas, Mona grasps concepts and plugs in relevant information easily. While she sits and reads during suspension, another class begins basic computer programming—learning to create a program and then use it to solve a miles-per-gallon problem. Alicia and her partner are attentive and take notes before getting on the computer. They proceed through the steps but miss a beat. Alicia asks the teacher, "Do I use the dollar sign with miles?" Mona looks up from her book and answers, "No, it's a variable," before focusing again on her lap. A girl who integrates new ideas quickly and can give creative expression to what she sees, Mona would be an excited, exciting student once engaged.

But Mona can name nothing in her school day that engages her energy and creativity except interactions with her boyfriend and the gang. This peer context seems critical. "Once you're involved," she says, "it's very hard to pull out. You lose everything." She pauses, puts three fingers over her heart. "You will have an empty place inside you that you cannot fill."

Reflecting on Girls Who Speak Out

Both Keisha and Mona entered their middle schools as girls who spoke out and were noticed. However, over the three years of middle school, Keisha moved into a position of leadership and centrality at school, whereas Mona increasingly asserted her difference and distance from the adult-defined culture of the school.

Keisha entered middle school exercising "bad girl" strategies that ironically honed her strengths and gained her recognition in the context of a large middle school. She has been supported by critically positioned adults who have encouraged her to define and be herself and have welcomed her voice in shaping core values at her school. The principal as well as a classroom aide familiar with Keisha's home, school, and community worlds have played important roles. An African American young woman at a school that is predominantly African American, Keisha has found a new role for herself with the help of adult mentors attuned to girls' needs, school reform that addresses the needs of girls and boys, and her own strategies.

The principal's creation of a leadership team helps Keisha make inquiry work for her. On the leadership team, she says, students "discuss" issues, "know what's going on," and "inform" teachers. This intervention gives students voice and promotes their inquiry into issues of relevance to all members of the school community. Keisha also recognizes this research project as an intervention and positions herself to construct her own portrait for the report.

Keisha employs the strategies of a maverick leader who is savvy and articulate about working the system. She undermines a bureaucratic regime of standardization and control in schools and, by reframing resistance to include often-marginalized voices, she bolsters the idea of school as a site for girls' initiative and leadership. Keisha likes being "good at school." Even so, the fragility of her newfound position is evident considering both her occasional blowups at Garth and the unknowns of her upcoming transition into a large urban high school where she may or may not find opportunities and support.

Like Keisha, Mona is aggressive both verbally and physically, speaking up and flouting norms with apparent ease. Yet school staff as well as peers see her as playing the "troublemaker" or, as a teacher called her, the "negative leader." She entered middle school an extrovert, a youngster whom adults expected to achieve and perhaps even break out of a culture and gender mold that seemed to limit participation for Native American girls. Adults at school continue to name her as a strong, bright, and vocal leader despite the plunge in her grades and her increasing gang involvement. Her peer and home (pueblo) cultures create dissonance with the school culture—and perhaps with each other.

Also, her relationships with adults are not clearing the way for Mona: Her mother is not in regular communication with the school, and the aide from her pueblo has been reluctant to get involved with Mona's "case." Her adviser does not act as her mentor. Mona reminds us that not all school personnel are equally effective with girls and not all girls respond to adult intervention, no matter how skillful or well-intentioned the adult. In any event, it may be that none of these adults is positioned to intercede effectively on Mona's behalf. For Mona, resistance to home and school cultures as defined by adults seems to leave her in the precarious position of defining herself largely in terms of who she is not.

Looking at Keisha and Mona together raises questions about how schools can help girls perceived as troublemakers to reframe their resistance into more constructive channels, perhaps as maverick leaders. With guidance, these energetic and sometimes inspired voices can lend credence to resistance and help schools create avenues of growth for students exhibiting a wide range of talents and sensibilities.

Doing School

A Schoolgirl

Hillary shoots up her hand to put a homework problem on the board. She is a seventh grader, a perky and petite white girl with honey-colored hair. It is third period and this is math—her favorite class.

> I'm good at it. I knew in second grade [that I was good at it]. I could tell then. I got all my sheets right. I always understand when the teacher explains it and lots of times I can figure it out myself. Like multiplying and dividing fractions. I'm real good at that. Geometry is hard for me though and I don't like it.

Hillary's teachers agree with her assessment of herself. This past report card she earned all A's—even in science, her least favorite class because of the "yucky dead things and dirty animals in the classroom." Hillary's literature teacher is very pleased with her work and her contribution to the class. "Hillary is a deep thinker," she says. Hillary returns the compliment: "My literature teacher is my favorite. She's like a mom." The current unit on mythology has caught Hillary's attention: "Myths are like soap operas. I love the stories."

In class Hillary is focused and efficient. She is second to finish an English test and forgoes reading for pleasure or playing a word game with friends in order to get started on the essay assigned for homework. In literature she and her partner quickly translate a poem from dialect to standard English. Her literature teacher explains that this kind of competence and discipline are new for Hillary: "I talked to a teacher from her old school and she told me that Hillary was very silly last year. But she's almost like a little woman this year." This year's Hillary is quite different from last year's as she tries out new strategies and identities in school.

Hillary began the year new to Fairfield, a rural middle school in the South. Over the summer, her family moved here from a smaller and more isolated rural community so her dad could take a job at Fairfield Industries and to be closer to Hillary's grandmother. Hillary's mother now commutes thirty minutes to her part-time job as manager in a doctor's office. Hillary is glad to be in Fairfield where she is able to spend more time with her grandmother, who lives in a trailer five minutes from Hillary's house. Closely connected to an extended family of aunts, uncles, and cousins, Hillary recounts stories of overnights with her grandmother who cooks her favorite foods and inscribed the "names of all of her grandchildren— even the baby who died—in the sidewalk outside her trailer"; weekly dinners with cousins who accompany her to a church study group; a family vacation to Florida that was "special and great" despite "a trashy motel that had a leaky roof and still cost a fortune to stay in."

Here at her new school, adults and students alike took quickly to Hillary. When she was hospitalized in the fall with a virus that caused severe vertigo, Hillary received what a teacher called "an outpouring of concern and affection. I'll never forget one little boy—one of our sweeter but slower students—wrote Hillary: "You're my best friend. You are always nice to everybody." Hillary displays this "nice" quality by helping a girl with fewer resources than she has:

> Gym: A test on tennis is scheduled for this period. Hillary sits on the bleachers going over her notes and complaining with a friend that scoring is "so complicated." Dawn, a heavy girl who had been sitting alone, approaches Hillary and asks if she can look at her notes because she has been absent. Hillary suggests that Dawn talk to the teacher about not taking the test. When Hillary sees that Dawn is unsuccessful with the gym teacher, she gives her notes to her.

> (From a researcher's fieldnotes, 2/1/95)

Table 10.1. Middle School Girls: Supports and Challenges.

Girls	School	One Strategy Used	What Helped	Some Challenges
Keisha	Garth Urban East Coast	Speaking out: Maverick leader	Principal asked her to join leadership committee Classroom aide and community member as mentors Parents behind her Own determination	Tendency to confront adults can be problematic Transition to high school means leaving mentors Societal class/race prejudice
Mona	Avila Rural Southwest	Speaking out: Troublemaker	Programs that develop creativity Family belief in her talents Ability to express herself Involvement in this research	Multiple cultural spheres to negotiate Adult perceptions of her as "negative leader" Societal class/race prejudice Gang culture
Hillary	Fairfield Rural South	Doing school: Schoolgirl	Teachers' affirmation Congruence of home and school values Own diligence and kindness	Overcoming conventional expectations Developmental changes Peer pressures

Table 10.1. (continued)

Girls	School	One Strategy Used	What Helped	Some Challenges
Josephine	Valley Stream Suburban West Coast	Doing school: Play schoolgirl	School counselor as mentor Involvement in peer mediation program Leadership opportunities at school Own self-awareness	Recent move to neighborhood Pressures to conform
Angela	Parkside Urban East Coast	Crossing borders: Schoolgirl/cool girl	Mother's involvement with school Small learning community with invested core teacher Teaching approaches that offer a range of roles	Racial/ethnic prejudices Own ambivalence about leadership Mother's involvement with school
Nikki	Madison Suburban Midwest	Crossing borders: Translator	School policies that emphasize commitment to equity Mother as mentor Administrative recognition Leadership role in school	Perception by some that she's a "bully" Societal racial/ethnic prejudices Own ambivalence about translator role

Frequently dressed in corduroys and plaid shirts neatly tucked into belted pants, Hillary has the "prep" look that Fairfield students contrast to "redneck" or sometimes "good ole country." She likes country music but "doesn't mind listening to gospel with my mom in the car. But I wouldn't tell her that I like it." One teacher perceives Hillary as "natural and less sophisticated than some of our students." When asked about leaders in her class, Hillary—like many of her peers—quickly names Megan and Angie because "everybody knows them and likes them. They're cheerleaders." Then, more thoughtfully, she adds one of the first girls to befriend her, someone unnamed by anyone else: "Elizabeth is good in school. She does all her work. She tells her opinion. She speaks up for herself."

During the course of the research, Hillary exhibits changes familiar to observers of middle school youngsters. In November one of her friends explains that when she first moved to Fairfield, all the boys, especially Kurt, wanted to be Hillary's boyfriend but "she wouldn't have any of them." Hillary retorts, "I don't want a boyfriend. Boys are annoying." In January Hillary identifies Kurt as a class leader and even expresses some admiration for him: "Kurt is a live one. He picks on people and plays with them and does well in school. . . . Him and Chevez won the story award." By March a teacher-researcher writes that Hillary and Kurt are now "going together" and that the science teacher had to speak to them about "sneaking a kiss" during class. She reports that she has spoken to Hillary's mother: "Issues with peer pressure are coming up for Hillary now. She is maturing physically and her mother is nervous about it."

Hillary's behavior in science class is interpreted in light of her image as a "schoolgirl." She's not bad, her teacher concludes, just "maturing physically" and responding to "peer pressure." Her new behaviors over the year alert us to the developmental dimension of girls' strategies. For example, as they begin seventh grade, girls may be more likely to employ a seamless schoolgirl strategy as Hillary does; as they move toward eighth grade, they must learn to balance school demands with changing social expectations.

Asked about her future, Hillary echoes the hopes and concerns that many Fairfield residents hold for area girls and young women:

> I want to be a teacher or a radiologist. If I am a teacher I want first- or seventh-grade kids. When I was at my old school I helped out with the first graders. I loved it. I really got attached to those kids and was so sorry to leave them. Those kids still remember me when I see them at church. I would like seventh grade because it would be a challenge.

If I was a radiologist I would go to Clayton Hospital. They have a two-year program there. I don't know if I'll have the money to go to college.

A Play Schoolgirl

Hundreds of miles away in a different school setting, a girl exhibits another dimension of the "doing school" strategy. Like Hillary, Josephine "does school" well, meeting traditional school expectations. Unlike Hillary, though, Josephine recounts considerable struggle in her effort to fit in and negotiate her eighth-grade niche at her academic award-winning, suburban West Coast middle school. A high-achieving young-ster, she keeps her uncertainty, her pain, and perhaps much of her cre-ativity under wraps.

Josephine is a tall, slender, blond Caucasian with delicate features and high cheekbones. The jeans and plaid oversized workshirt with sturdy san-dals suit the angularity of her body and mark her as knowing what is "in" at her school. Her name is mentioned by several Valley Stream girls as their "ideal," and their comments carry a wishful chorus of "if I could be like Josephine. . . ." When we discuss whether girls here can be both "suc-cessful with teachers" and "popular," her name comes up. Josephine also takes her role as the lead eighth-grade peer mediator very seriously.

Only after a researcher has gained her trust and pressed her to speak does she volunteer, "I moved here a year ago, which was really hard for me. I think I've changed a lot since that move. I've become a really dif-ferent person." She reflects on how sports are "a real priority" in this school and town, and sees herself as "a terrible athlete," more of an artist. She contrasts this setting with the urban school three hours south that she attended previously: "Where I came from, it wasn't a very good part of town and they had a lot of outreach to the students. They had all these clubs, drama, psychology, and all these exciting things to do." When her mother remarried and relocated here, it was the beginning of a "hard, dark time" for Josephine. "It was pretty bad for a while, but all of a sud-den, when you go through pain that's that intense you start to come out on the other side."

An adult at school, a female counselor, stepped in and made the dif-ference, Josephine readily acknowledges:

> She is definitely a role model for me. It's easy to talk to people who are a lot like you. And I think we have a lot in common. She kind of understood what I was going through and how it was hard for me to

adjust and everything. She took extra time to help me out, listened to me, understood that I was in real pain. A lot of people they said, "Okay, you'll get over it." And of course I did get over it. But it was nice to have somebody there who said, "No, what you're feeling is definitely valid and real."

The counselor identified peer mediation as a program in which Josephine could find her voice. Josephine trained to become a mediator. She credits her success in this program to her struggle to adjust: "When you have experienced pain, you then understand others' pain better." When asked about her strengths, she replies, "I feel like I can understand people really well. I have a real kinship with almost everyone I know. I'm really close to people."

In addition to being lead peer mediator with major responsibilities for training the "interns" in the seventh grade, Josephine is treasurer of the Student Government Association, a hands-on position that requires her to respond to weekly requests for activity funds from both staff and students. She takes honors classes and is in the top algebra class. She laments,

> I get A's and B's but I really want straight A's. I feel that I could be doing better but it's really hard when you have all kinds of other things that people want you to do. People are always saying, "Okay, you have to do this and this and this, and you only have this much time to do it."

Josephine values her relationships with adults at school and accepts responsibilities they place on her even when their expectations are "unreasonable."

Josephine has a good male friend—not a boyfriend, she's careful to say; she doesn't want one yet, though boys ask her out—who helps her put in perspective her need to conform to others' expectations. "We talk about stuff and he thinks it's hilarious that I worry about all these people and then think that I am not a good person unless I make everyone happy." Friendship, respect, and admiration mean a great deal to Josephine because "when I was younger, I was real skinny. I had kind of short hair and didn't wear nice clothes. I used to go out on the field and sit by myself and just sing to myself."

Now an aspiring opera singer, Josephine takes weekly voice lessons. "When I was real young, I knew that I wanted to sing. I wanted my voice to be beautiful. My parents tell stories where I would go around the house saying, 'Turn on the lady' [Julie Andrews singing *The Sound of Music*]."

Her mother celebrates her daughter's talents but also recognizes her struggle not to be subsumed by others' expectations.

Reflecting on Girls Who Do School

While both Hillary and Josephine provide examples of girls "doing school" in conventionally approved ways, they also demonstrate subtly divergent strategies. Their approaches reflect differences in their schools' cultures as well as in the girls' identities and choices.

New arrivals to their respective schools, Hillary and Josephine were named by their teachers only months into the school year as successful girls. Both take their roles as students seriously, completing all that is required of them, appreciating adults who take time with them, and meeting peers' as well as adults' expectations. Both take pride in their work and their grades. Both are white in predominantly white settings, though Hillary's is a rural Southern school while Josephine's is suburban and on the West Coast. But the two girls employ somewhat divergent strategies for success. While Hillary seems to fit easily into her new life and school culture, "doing school" without apparent effort, Josephine struggles to manage conflicting expectations as she both conforms to a schoolgirl role and seeks to know and be herself. The greater degree of pressure at her school ups the ante for Josephine in her effort to find a balance between others' needs and her own.

Hillary employs negotiating strategies that match traditional expectations for girls in this setting. Women in the school who grew up in the area can recognize in Hillary the same values with which they were raised, the same roles they assumed, and the same achievements and limitations reached. While at several points Hillary betrays her awareness that her family's modest means may limit her goals, nevertheless she seems confident that her abilities and her persona will pave future options.

Josephine boasts a strong school record, too. But in conversation she articulates a more complex picture involving pain and struggle. Although she evidences considerable skill at "playing school"—both academically and socially—Josephine is aware that she is indeed playing multiple roles expected by adults as well as peers in her life. By talking with her male friend about her conflict over her multiple roles, Josephine demonstrates a successful if private way to pursue inquiry into gender issues. At the same time, Josephine's ability to call up her own struggle as a way of connecting with others' challenges is a strength that lets her be more empathetic. It remains to be seen if her sense of her own emerging identity will balance the pressures to conform to others' expectations and meet others' needs as she moves on to high school.

For Hillary and Josephine, school presents a site for success, and school adults acknowledge and support their achievements. But looking at the ways in which these two girls "do school" also suggests the need for reforms that would help schools expand girls' possibilities. Both girls would benefit from the opportunity to try out a range of roles and personae in school without risking safety and acceptance. For Hillary, a structured opportunity to step into a leadership role might broaden her repertoire of strategies. For Josephine, fewer adult demands on her time and more opportunities to explore her own creativity might help her balance her emerging identity with her position as a school leader.

Crossing Borders

A Schoolgirl/Cool Girl

Angela presents herself as the epitome of what many middle school girls might aspire to become—well groomed, stylishly attired, attractive, poised, confident, popular, and excelling academically. A thirteen-year-old Puerto Rican girl, she attends a community middle school in an ethnically and racially diverse, working-class neighborhood in one of the major cities in the Northeast corridor.

Being physically attractive is not always an attribute that lends itself to popularity with both girls and boys in middle school. Nevertheless, Angela has developed a facility with her peers—relating adeptly with girls as well as boys while also preserving her sense of self. As a result of this ability, she is viewed as a leader in her advisory section, in her classes, and in the larger school culture.

Voted president of her advisory, Angela has a leadership style that mixes quiet reserve and steadfast determination. She has learned how to survive and flourish in a school culture where the values of adults who hold structural power are often at odds with the adolescent value system in which students must negotiate. Angela has figured out the behaviors adults hold in high regard. And she has discovered that behaviors that boys find acceptable—such as being outspoken, even argumentative at times, and not following the rules—differ from behaviors teachers expect from girls. Savvy about this tension, Angela manages on occasion to exhibit male-approved behaviors without rebuke, perhaps because her teachers are perplexed at this atypical stance.

Angela steps in and out of both the adult value system and her peer culture, which includes pressure and intimidation from boys, thus maintaining her integrity as a bright, able young woman. In the following vignette, Angela interacts with a male classmate and their science teacher, Joel Levy, keeping her self-respect and independence by not allowing males to dominate her intellectually or socially:

> Since Soeun, Gloria, and Angela missed their science period with Mr. Levy this morning, he used Advisory to give the girls their topics for their reports on constellations. When Angela was given Sevis, the whale, one of the boys snidely called her a whale. Angela stated in a steady, deliberate tone, "I am not a whale." The teacher, unaware of the boy's comment, offered, "You are doing a report on the whale constellation." Assuredly and in a tone bordering on arrogance, Angela retorted, "Yes, I know!" Mr. Levy, looking perplexed by her tenor, made no counter response.

> (From a researcher's fieldnotes, 10/12/94)

In this scenario, Angela demonstrates her capability and willingness not to "let things go." She steps out of her schoolgirl role. She could have opted to remain silent—first with the boy and then with the teacher—but instead makes a concerted and deliberate effort to have her voice heard. This behavior is somewhat inconsistent with her general demeanor, which is to court some degree of invisibility: Not standing out gives her favorable stature in both the adult and peer cultures in the school. Although Angela is rarely observed participating openly in class discussions, her teachers applaud her as an excellent student.

Angela also is able to identify male privilege and turn it to her own advantage. In this vignette, Angela tries out the conventional strategy of hand-raising before arriving at the more successful strategy of enlisting the aid of a male peer:

> The two eighth-grade classes were facing each other across a playing field. Camaraderie was fostered by the game's design and scoring system. Students screamed and supported classmates passionately. Angela stood on the sidelines, very much in control. Her long chestnut hair was pulled back in a ponytail that exposed gold hoop earrings, and she was stylishly attired in ivory jeans and a maize sweater. When teams were being switched, she raised her hand but was not selected. Angela gestured to a classmate, a large boy who had scored a number of goals. The noise in the gym was deafening, but she gestured to explain that she had not had a chance to play. The boy interrupted the gym teacher, risking losing points, to intercede. As a result, a girl left the original line-up and Angela went in.

> (From a researcher's fieldnotes, 10/12/94)

Referred to often as a leader, Angela demonstrates her individualism by controlling the degree to which she will allow adults to coerce her. Urged on by teachers to run for president of the student body, she resists. When asked about student council, she expresses disdain for the way boys make rude remarks about the girls' physical appearance in assembly: "I don't want to be bothered with all of that." Her rejection of the formal leadership role reminds us of how important it is to look with girls' eyes: While adults tend to view student council as an ideal "voice" mechanism in school, Angela is more concerned with the negative trappings of the position than with its possible advantages.

Angela's decision not to participate formally in school leadership is also interesting in light of the fact that her stepmother is president of the Home and School Association, the local equivalent of the Parent Teacher Association. An articulate and outspoken woman, the stepmother is more than willing to raise difficult issues for discussion by the school's administrators and teachers. Informed of a policy recently initiated in the lunchroom, Angela's stepmother reflects, "I didn't know about it because my daughter didn't tell me. She tells me some things but not everything because she doesn't want me to go into the office and talk about it." Being the middle school daughter of a high-profile mother may contribute to Angela's desire to maintain a low school profile.

In Angela's interactions with adults, she is not overly friendly and does not attempt to ingratiate herself. Her manner is cool and somewhat detached. In this way, she protects her privacy, increases her capital with her teachers who have certain expectations of female students, and simultaneously fits comfortably into her peer culture.

A Translator

In the Midwest, a girl of similar talents but without Angela's studied aloofness seeks to maintain her independence even as she mediates for others across disparate cultures in her school community. A tall, fully developed African American girl with a loud voice, Nikki has been identified by administrators, teachers, and peers as a "natural leader" in her mostly white, suburban middle school. Apparently able to code-switch at will, Nikki communicates and holds sway with adults and teens across lines of race and class. She acts as an ally to an administration striving for a safe and orderly environment as well as to students—perhaps particularly female and African American students—who appreciate the authority she bears. In fact, her word carries so much authority that at times she is perceived by some adults and students as wielding too much power in the school. Both her assertiveness and her cooperation with school authorities flout the rules of a peer culture that typically rewards invisibility and moderate insubordination.

Nikki herself is less interested in securing others' approval than in pursuing her own sense of right thinking and action. She exhibits the ability to stand firmly for what she believes; peer pressure seems to have less impact on her conscious decisions than it does for many young people. Nikki describes herself this way: "See, I have a very strong mind that you would have to persuade if you wanted me to do something. Like if you wanted me to try drugs or whatever, I would think about all the perspectives and everything." This demonstrably stable sense of self seems also surprisingly receptive, an identity being shaped over time by a reflective sensibility.

Although she values her own company, Nikki is not a loner. An appreciation of mutual respect seems to drive her relationships with peers as well as adults. A friend describes Nikki as "a leader to me because she gives 100 percent. I give her my 100 percent respect because she gives it to me. And a lot of other people give her their respect. So I look up to Nikki. I'm not going to say she's a role model but. . . ."

For Nikki, respect is central, though it may look different in different spheres of her life. "I know with my mother, I show my mother a little more respect than I show my friends. I respect my friends but in a different manner. With the teacher, I'm not two-faced or whatever. I just show more respect. That's how I was raised."

Nikki's life has not been a simple linear tale of achievement. Sexually abused by a neighbor when she was a young girl, she knew how to support a friend who was sexually assaulted. The abuse provided a harsh lesson and strengthened her resolve "not to let people walk all over me." Incidents of racism have also pressed her to call her own assertiveness into service. How has she used these challenges to gain an understanding of others' perspectives and not instead to justify anger, hatred, and blame? She answers the question this way: "I have a conscience and I have a heart."

Nikki reflects habitually on her own behavior, subjecting past actions to new scrutiny as her ideas mature. For example, she recalls that last year she sometimes felt she was "being treated differently in a class because I was black." Later she considered the possibility that "that wasn't the case . . . I realized I have to think from both sides." This year she sifts through others' sometimes contradictory expectations of her: "Boys, mom, the adults, they want me to do this thing, and my friends want me to come over here and do this, but you have to compromise. I'll be like, 'I'll do half of this and then I'll go and do this.' . . . It's about learning this year."

Adults in school demonstrate their high expectations of Nikki by placing her in leadership roles that require her to cross borders such as age and race to translate for people on either side. A peer mediator, Nikki is expected to use her mediating skills not only in occasional formal sessions but also daily in hallways and other public spaces to help students and minimize school disruptions. Nikki both internalizes and resents these expectations: "I get treated more strict than anybody in this school. Because I'm a big talker, I'm supposed to show an example." She describes an instance where her role seems impossible: "I'm trying to stop some playing around [in the hallway] and all these teachers start yelling at me and I'm trying to stop trouble for them! . . . All my friends are like, they get to have fun."

A friend describes how Nikki took on the usually adult role of disciplinarian at the basketball game the previous day:

> Before [the adults] could say, "Stop stepping on the bleachers," you could hear Nikki saying, "Stop stepping on the bleachers." . . . She was cheering for all teams. She don't take that. That's the good thing about her. If you have a fight she won't take sides. She'll say, "Why'd you all do this? Why don't you talk it out?"

The school's harnessing of Nikki's mediating abilities can also spell trouble for a strong, reflective girl who takes that charge seriously, as in the following incident:

> Before Christmas, Nikki was suspended in coming to the rescue of a student involved in an altercation with a girl "from the city." Nikki intervened, telling the girl, "That's not how we do things here. We don't fight." The city girl informed her that she would "kick her ass too" and the fight ensued. For this infraction, Nikki served a one day in-house suspension with her mom present, shadowing her daughter all day. Note that this is an option—either three days out of school or one day in school with a parent.

> (From a researcher's fieldnotes, 1/27/95)

Nikki's mother is a reliable, competent, and caring advocate for her daughter. In fact, Nikki names her mother and poet Maya Angelou as the two women she admires most: "[My mother] talks to me and respects me. She talks to me like I'm not just her daughter [but] her friend, her sister, whatever. I just like the whole style about my mother." And about Maya Angelou: "As soon as I read her book [*I Know Why the Caged Bird Sings*,

1969], I knew I wanted to be just like her. How she went places and made a difference, how she overcame the odds. . . . Like I don't want to be the president of the United States, but it would be nice."

While Nikki has internalized adult expectations that promote success, almost parroting her math teacher's caution that in high school "they expect so much more," she also uses her skills as a translator of others' cultures to figure out what's needed to succeed without forfeiting more of herself than she's willing to lose. She acts with restraint in a class where she sees the male teacher as sexist and racist, so as not to hurt her grade. But she tempers that restraint when he confronts her in the halls: "I'm gonna participate in class but if we're outside school or outside class . . . I'm gonna give him respect, because that's what my mom taught me, but I'm not gonna give him 100 percent."

Nikki's grades and national test scores are generally high, and she has high hopes for the future:

> I want to be a lawyer. . . . I know I'm gonna try, and I know I'm gonna succeed, but if I can't do that, I'll resort to like a juvenile worker, helper, assistant. I want to give back to the community what they gave to me. I just want to make a difference, because they say you can make a difference.

Reflecting on Girls Who Cross Borders

Angela and Nikki are recognized by adults and peers for their ability to cross borders, decipher complex messages, and respond appropriately in the several different cultures of school and community. Nikki describes herself as "tolerant" of a range of people and situations. Angela also demonstrates forbearance in the many situations that she observes without entering the fray. This ability to understand diverse perspectives seems to indicate a strong sense of self—or at least confidence in the process of coming into self—rather than the chameleon lack of self for which this ability is often mistaken.

Both young women are also experiencing considerable pressure from school adults to employ their talents in the service of the school. In both cases the pressure comes from female administrators committed to school reforms that include an awareness of gender issues.

Angela resists the pressure to use her skills as a border crosser in an official and ongoing way. Thus she evades a formal role while retaining the ability to step in when she chooses in support of a teacher, a girl or boy friend, or herself. Nikki, on the other hand, protests her assigned role as school leader and the expectation that she translate across cultures for the good of the school, but in fact accedes to these expectations. While peer mediation gives her a chance to use her strengths publicly, she is also burdened by the expectation that she, as mediator, identify with the institution rather than with her peers. This tension peaks when Nikki confronts an African American young woman "from the city" who is not yet acculturated to the school. While Nikki's strengths have been channeled into leadership at Madison, in this instance she confronts a girl whose strengths have developed differently; for Nikki, this young woman may provide a troubling reflection.

Young women who carry tremendous expectations from adults as well as peers, Angela and Nikki use a shared set of strategies but make different choices. As these girls are pressed to employ their considerable strengths in many arenas simultaneously, their stories compel us to ask how schools might help them to keep this balancing act from overwhelming them. When adults in schools make a conscious effort to acknowledge differences, raising questions of gender, age, race, and culture, for example, in discussions of classroom dynamics and in the curriculum, they transfer the job of understanding others from the shoulders of a few "border crossers" to the community as a whole.

Implications

Adolescent girls typically undertake the process of identity-making with conscious effort, pain, uncertainty, and creativity. As active agents choosing and revising their approaches, girls are engaged in a continuous cycle of action and reaction with their environments. Since school takes up a disproportionately large part of their lives, it is not surprising that a great deal of this identity work goes on in school.

Because all young adolescent girls—even those achieving marked conventional successes—are engaged in this developmental process, their emergent selves are likely to be new, fragile, vulnerable to assault. What works for one girl at one school may not work for another girl at another school or even for the same girl from one year to the next. Girls who speak out may be treated as leaders or renegades. Girls who "do school" may be seen as "good" or may be invisible to adults. Girls who cross borders may be perceived as talented or power-hungry. Thus Josephine, acclaimed in her Valley Stream school setting, continues to struggle with insecurities prompted by her family's relocation. Between the researchers' visits to Avila in the rural Southwest, Mona changes, at least in her teachers' estimation, from a "leader" to a "troublemaker." Schoolgirl Hillary "sneaks a kiss" with her first boyfriend. Eighth graders describe their journey through middle school: Many begin as "schoolgirls" but find peer expectations increasingly pitted against those of the school culture. Clearly, no single negotiating approach will benefit all girls in all settings. Shifting strategies may help girls cope.

School adults need to notice the different ways that girls negotiate school. This requires observing girls in hallways and classrooms, asking girls questions, attending to girls' voices. It is also important that adults understand girls' needs to try out strategies in the process of forming identities and recognize that girls' strategies may shift. When adults become aware of how the culture of their schools and classrooms helps to shape girls' strategies, then they can help girls understand and increase their options and make conscious strategic decisions.

In this chapter we have looked at how six girls are negotiating their school lives. Each of these girls adopts strategies and tries on identities in ways characteristic of many of the girls we met in this study. These girls' successes testify to the support of adults in their lives and to their schools' efforts to incorporate what we're learning about adolescent development and gender as well as to their own hard work. While we began this study by looking for a relatively linear connection between what schools are doing and how their successful girls are faring, what we found instead was that successful girls and their schools are engaged in a complex, dynamic relationship that is neither linear nor necessarily cumulative. What works for girls involves a repertoire of possibilities.

These cases help illustrate the complexity of all factors working on girls. Gender and the way society interprets gender are not the only factors influencing a girl in middle school, but they are critical factors. The cases also highlight the opportunity for schools—if they're aware of these factors—to tailor curricula and programs to match girls' needs.

NOTES

1. Barrie Thorne, *Gender Play* (New Brunswick, N.J.: Rutgers University Press, 1993): 3.

2. Carol Gilligan, "Women's Psychological Development: Implications for Psychotherapy," in *Women, Girls & Psychotherapy: Reframing Resistance,* Carol Gilligan, Annie G. Rogers, and Deborah L. Tolman, eds. (New York: Harrington Park Press, 1991): 5–31.

   Annie Rogers, "Voice, Play, and a Practice of Ordinary Courage in Girls' and Women's Lives." *Harvard Educational Review* 63, no. 3 (1993): 265–295.

Emily Hancock, *The Girl Within* (New York: Fawcett Columbia, 1989).

Janie Ward, "High Self-Esteem/Low Achievement: The AAUW Findings on Black Girls Growing Up," paper presented at a symposium on the psychology of girls and the culture of schools (Temple University, Philadelphia, 1993).

3. Gilligan, "Women's Psychological Development."

Lyn Brown and Carol Gilligan, *Meeting at the Crossroads: Women's Psychology and Girls' Development* (New York: Ballantine Books, 1992): 1.

4. Gilligan, "Women's Psychological Development": 14.

5. T. Robinson and Janie Ward, " 'A Belief in Self Far Greater Than Anyone's Disbelief': Cultivating Resistance Among African American Female Adolescents," in *Women, Girls & Psychotherapy: Reframing Resistance,* Carol Gilligan, Annie G. Rogers, and Deborah L. Tolman, eds. (New York: Harrington Park Press, 1991): 88.

6. Ardy Bowker, *Sisters in the Blood: The Education of Women in Native America* (Newton, Mass.: WEEA Publishing Center, 1993): 260.

7. Robinson and Ward, "'A Belief in Self Far Greater Than Anyone's Disbelief'": 89.

8. Donna Eder with Katherine Colleen Evans and Stephen Parker, *School Talk: Gender and Adolescent Culture* (New Brunswick, N.J.: Rutgers University Press, 1995).

Roberta Tovey, "A Narrowly Gender-Based Model of Learning May End Up Cheating All Students," *Harvard Education Review Newsletter,* July–August, 1995: 3–5. Tovey describes work by Gilligan and her colleagues in which white and African American working-class girls share speaking styles.

9. Myra Sadker and David Sadker, *Failing at Fairness: How America's Schools Cheat Girls* (New York: Charles Scribner's Sons, 1994).

10. Brown and Gilligan, *Meeting at the Crossroads:* 4.

11. Selase Williams, "Classroom Use of African American Language: Educational Tool or Social Weapon?" in *Empowerment Through Multicultural Education,* Christine Sleeter, ed. (New York: State University of New York Press, 1991).

PART THREE

GENDER EQUITY IN THE CURRICULUM

ONE OF THE CORNERSTONES of the debate over gender equality in schools surrounds the crucial issue of curriculum: what is taught, which students take which classes, and how do they perform? This diverse selection of readings delves deeply into these difficult subjects, addressing both the traditional questions about girls in science and boys in the humanities, as well as some new and perhaps more subtle concerns about what boys and girls are, and are not, being taught.

The AAUW's "Course-Taking Patterns" provides a statistical overview of the courses that girls and boys select during their high school years and how this impacts the overall quality of their education. "Breaking the Barriers: The Critical Middle School Years" addresses in detail the sharp decline in girls' interest in math and the sciences throughout middle school, exploring why this drop-off occurs and what can be done to remedy it. In "Misreading Masculinity: Speculations on the Great Gender Gap in Writing," Thomas Newkirk looks at another disturbing disparity between genders: why girls tend to outperform boys in writing skills. In his piece, Newkirk suggests that a misinterpretation of the male perspective is often behind the devaluing of boys' writing and language skills.

The second half of the discussion on curriculum ventures into less-familiar territory. Both "Girls and Design: Exploring the Question of Technological Imagination" and "Educational Software and Games: Rethinking the 'Girls' Game' " take on the assumption that computers are the domain of boys alone. Each piece probes girls' relationships to technology, exploring their particular interests and how to encourage and foster them. "The Evaded Curriculum," from the groundbreaking report *How Schools Shortchange Girls,* looks closely at subjects that are rarely covered in schools, including sexuality, sexually transmitted diseases, eating disorders, and emotional well-being. Michelle Fine's "Sexuality, Schooling, and Adolescent Females: The Missing Discourse of Desire" also takes on schools' treatment of sexuality, where sex is associated with violence and victimization, denying an important discussion of sexuality as desire and pleasure.

Each of these widely varied pieces looks at a particular aspect of the curriculum, the building blocks of the educational experience. From course enrollment disparities, to performance differences, to topics that are shortchanged or simply ignored, problems within the curriculum are some of the most crucial in the gender equity issue in schools.

COURSE-TAKING PATTERNS

American Association of University Women

THE COURSES STUDENTS TAKE in high school and the degree to which they master these subjects affect the choices open to them for years to come. College acceptances, scholarship offers, and employment opportunities can hinge on student course-taking decisions and subsequent performance. Understandably, this area has drawn researchers' attention over the past several years.

Much of this attention has focused on math and science courses, where boys have historically outnumbered and outperformed girls. This gap is a portent of the gender gap in college math and science programs and, later, in well-paying math and science careers. The rapid growth of technology has also fueled concern about girls' computer skills, which generally lag behind boys'. Boys significantly outnumber girls in higher-skill computer courses, while girls tend to cluster in lower-end data entry and word processing classes.

This chapter reviews girls' and boys' uneven participation across the entire curriculum. We review not just girls' much-researched and discussed participation rates in science, mathematics, and computer science, but also boys' participation in English, foreign language, social sciences, and the arts. Examining gender differences among boys and girls, across the curriculum, reflects the goals of educational equity research, which attempts to document different educational outcomes according to factors such as sex, race, or class, regardless of which group these differences favor.

As Valerie Lee explains, "reading, writing, social studies, and foreign language are seldom discussed in the [gender equity] venue, although gender differences exist in these areas. . . . Why should we examine only curriculum areas where girls are disadvantaged?"[1]

○

Emphasizing Math and Science

1992 Goal: Girls must be educated and encouraged to understand that mathematics and the sciences are important and relevant to their lives. Girls must be actively supported in pursuing education and employment in these areas. (*How Schools Shortchange Girls,* page 86).

Analysis: In 1992 virtually every aspect of mathematics and science education was found to be lacking: Stereotypes of mathematics and science as inappropriate for girls and women were ubiquitous, classroom bias was apparent in these content areas, and women were underrepresented among mathematics and science college majors despite having sufficient background and abilities. The report also found apparent differences in the effectiveness of new science curricula favoring males.

1998 Reality: Of all the 1992 goals, this one has perhaps seen the most, or at least the most measurable, success. Innumerable programs have debunked myths and stereotypes surrounding girls' involvement in mathematics and science. Girls' test scores and course enrollments have risen perceptibly in these areas, with the exception of computer science. The National Science Foundation in particular has funded a number of promising initiatives. An evaluation of these is in progress.

○

Subject Enrollments

Girls' participation is improving in some academic areas where it previously lagged, particularly in math and science. The number of courses taken in a discipline, however, doesn't tell the whole story; class-by-class comparisons show that girls are still less well represented in some higher-level courses in math, science, and computer science. Boys' participation, meanwhile, is lower in some of the humanities, including English, language, sociology, psychology, and the fine arts.

Girls' enrollments are up in mathematics and science courses, and the difference between girls' and boys' course patterns here appears to be narrowing. Girls still enroll in language arts courses (including foreign languages) with greater frequency than boys. In fact, course-taking patterns, when viewed as a whole, suggest that girls may be getting a broader education than boys by deepening their exposure to math and science and by enrolling in more courses in other subject areas.

Mathematics

A much-discussed gap between girls and boys—average numbers of mathematics courses taken—appears to be diminishing. But gender differences remain in the kinds of courses taken. In an encouraging development, more girls are enrolling in algebra, geometry, precalculus, trigonometry, and calculus than in 1990. However, girls are more likely than boys to end their high school math careers with Algebra II.

Both the Council of Chief State School Officers and the 1994 High School Transcript Study found that males and females take comparable numbers of high school mathematics courses.[2] In 1994—the most recent year for which data is available—both groups averaged nearly 3.5 credits of math courses.

Yet an examination of course-by-course enrollment figures for girls and boys reveals remaining gender divisions. A significantly larger proportion of male than female high school graduates took the lowest-level high school mathematics courses (basic mathematics and general mathematics), according to 1994 data from the High School Transcript Study.[3] Girls outnumber boys in algebra and geometry. Roughly equal proportions of girls and boys take precalculus or calculus prior to leaving high school.

In another sign that the overall math gap is shrinking, more girls entered Algebra I, Algebra II, geometry, precalculus, trigonometry, and calculus in 1994 than in 1990. This finding is encouraging in light of research that cites taking Algebra I and geometry early in high school—generally in the ninth and tenth grades—as the major predictor of a student's continuing on to college.[4] Additionally, in 1994, roughly equal numbers of girls and boys took precalculus, trigonometry, and statistics/probability enrollments.[5] (See Table 11.1.)

Among college-bound girls, enrollment in math courses has increased more over the past decade than it has for college-bound boys, according to ACT, Inc., a nonprofit organization best known for its college admissions testing program. In this population, more females than males now take geometry and second-year algebra. In addition, the proportion of girls taking trigonometry and calculus has increased by 7 and 9 percent respectively since 1987, while the percentage of boys taking trigonometry has held steady and the percentage enrolling in calculus has increased by only 6 percent. Between 1987 and 1997 college-bound girls' enrollment in geometry also increased by 8 percent; in Algebra II it increased by 15 percent. In contrast, college-bound boys' enrollment in those courses rose by 5 and 10 percent.[6]

Table 11.1. Percentage of 1990 and 1994 High School Graduates Taking Specific Mathematics Courses by Gender.

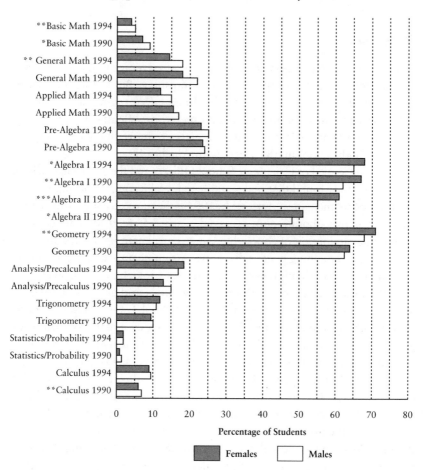

Source: *U.S. Department of Education, National Center for Education Statistics, 1994 High School Transcript Study, Tabulations, 1997.*
*Significant at p < .10
**Significant at p < .05
*** Significant at p < .01

State-level data collected by the Council of Chief State School Officers indicates that slightly greater percentages of girls enrolled in Algebra II/ Integrated Math in 1996 than in 1990. Seven of 18 states reporting data by gender indicated increases, ranging from 1 to 6 percent, from 1990 to 1996. Twelve of the 18 states reported an increase in girls' enrollments in trigonometry/precalculus (from 2 to 6 percent) over the same time period.[7]

However, girls are significantly more likely than boys to end their high school mathematics careers with Algebra II. Fifty-three percent of girls versus 47 percent of boys end their high school mathematics careers with the completion of this course. Stopping a math education at this level can close the door on future studies, scholarships, and careers.

○

Changes in Graduation Requirements

A high school's graduation requirements and the availability of honors and advanced placement courses provide the context in which students choose which courses to pursue.

Minimum high school graduation requirements in computers, mathematics, and science have risen since 1990. In 1990, 12 states required at least 2.5 credits of mathematics and four states required at least 2.5 credits of science. By 1996, 2.5 or more years of mathematics and science were required in 18 and 11 states respectively.

Students' selection of courses can be influenced by minimum high school graduation requirements. Since all students—girls and boys—must fulfill these minimum requirements, the type of course taken or timing of course enrollment may be a more accurate equity indicator.

○

Science

A greater percentage of female high school graduates took science courses in 1994 than in 1990. Girls are more likely than their male counterparts to take both biology and chemistry. Roughly equal proportions of girls and boys enroll in engineering and geology. Physics, however, remains a largely male domain. While more girls enroll today than in 1990, the gender gap here is sizeable.

Even though male and female high school students take a similar average number of science courses, males are more likely than females to have taken all three of the core science courses—biology, chemistry, and physics—by graduation. Girls' enrollment in physics has been increasing, but a significant gender gap persists. The science education community acknowledges the "physics problem" and has developed interventions to increase girls' participation.[8] Science reforms are more recent than those in mathematics, which may partly explain the lingering disparity between girls' and boys' participation in physics.[9] (See Table 11.2.)

Table 11.2. Percentage of 1990 and 1994 High School Graduates
Taking Specific Science Courses by Gender.

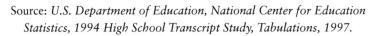

Source: *U.S. Department of Education, National Center for Education
Statistics, 1994 High School Transcript Study, Tabulations, 1997.*
*Significant at p < .10
**Significant at p < .05
*** Significant at p < .01

Computer-Related Studies

Enrollments in higher-skill computer courses show a puzzling drop for both
boys and girls, although boys clearly outnumber girls. In comparison, girls
tend to cluster in lower-end data entry and word processing classes that lead
to less stimulating jobs.

States' lavish investment in computers across K–12 education has vis-
ibly transformed the appearance and teaching philosophy of many public schools. Yet, for reasons that are unclear, fewer boys and girls are
enrolling in computer science classes that prepare students for careers in

Table 11.3. Percentage of 1990 and 1994 High School Graduates Taking Specific Computer Courses by Gender.

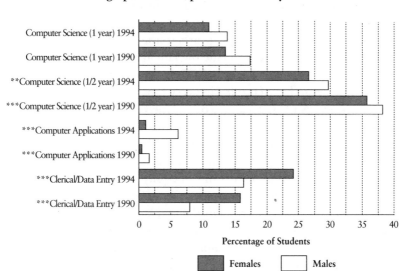

Percentage of Students

■ Females   □ Males

Source: *U.S. Department of Education, National Center for Education Statistics*, Vocational Course Taking and Achievement: An Analysis of High School Transcripts and 1990 NAEP Assessment Scores *(Washington, DC: 1995).*
*Significant at p < .05
** Significant at p < .01

computer programming and theory. The enrollment drop is puzzling in light of burgeoning industry needs for technically skilled workers.

Computer applications courses in graphic arts and computer-aided design, while not especially common, attract very few girls. Girls are significantly more likely than boys to enroll in clerical and data entry classes, the 1990s version of typing. (See Table 11.3.)

English

Girls outnumber boys in all English classes except remedial English, earning more credits here than boys.

No advocate of high educational standards and improved U.S. public education questions the need for literacy, reading, writing, and oral communications skills as prerequisites for success in all careers.[10] In the standards movement, literacy denotes not only reading comprehension and traditional courses in English literature, but also spoken language, technological communication, knowledge of written, spoken and visual texts, and knowledge of the processes involved in creating, interpreting, and critiquing such texts.[11]

Despite the centrality of language arts to the criteria of excellent education, boys and girls do not pursue the languages arts in equal proportion. In both 1990 and 1994, female high school graduates were more likely than males to have enrolled in every type of English course except for remedial English.[12] Girls as a group earned more than four credits of English in 1994, a slight rise from 1990. Boys as a population also score lower than girls on verbal skills on most standardized tests.[13]

Crucially, gender differences in language arts performance and course taking rarely are noted in discussions of equity or standards. According to Elizabeth Hayes, "one of the most striking findings" in a 1996 study of gender and literacy, in fact, "was the real lack of serious attention to gender issues in scholarship on reading education."[14] Yet equity means that an educational system does not produce uneven outcomes by any characteristic of social background—in this case, gender. The fact that boys do not perform to girls' level in certain subject areas therefore belongs in the gender equity discussion.

A few studies since 1992 have examined why girls excel in verbal, language, and writing skills, and how their strengths shape the school's overall approach to this important content area of the curriculum. (See Table 11.4.) A cross-national comparison in 1996 found that gender differences are more apparent for the language arts than for mathematics, and perhaps emerge out of a widespread cultural belief that language arts is a female domain. The perception of literacy, reading, writing, and verbal precocity as feminine characteristics shapes the way schools teach reading: They may cater to girls' interests and strengths, promoting "versions of literacy that appeal more to girls than boys."[15] Girls' acuity with language results in a deeper, more imaginative engagement with the writing process and with reading material. A 1992 study examined student journals of their reading experiences and reactions to a novel taught in school. Researchers discovered that "girls were much more apt to write their internal response as they read a novel than boys, and when the book had two strong main characters, girls made more entries about these characters [and identified them by name] than boys."[16]

Student acceptance of purportedly "natural" male and female strengths has undoubtedly fed the expectation that boys will lag behind in the language arts. When researchers in one study asked students why girls and boys differ in reading performance, the largest category of responses was, "It's the

Table 11.4. Percentage of 1990 and 1994 High School Graduates Taking Specific English Courses by Gender.

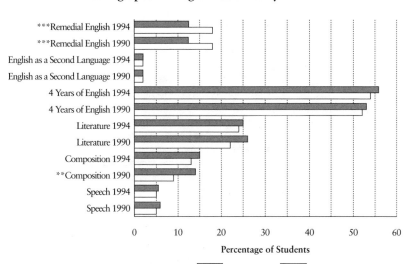

Source: *U.S. Department of Education, National Center for Education Statistics, 1994 High School Transcript Study, Tabulations, 1997.*
**Significant at p < .05
*** Significant at p < .01

way things are."[17] By the time they leave school, students exhibit deeply entrenched ideas of male and female domains of competency. Yet boys and girls do not begin their formal education with these notions. Perceptions of girls as uniquely suited for the language arts appear to intensify after the fourth grade and are most dramatic in the last years of high school.[18]

Social Studies

In the social studies field, encompassing such courses as history, geography, anthropology, economics, sociology, and psychology, more girls than boys tend to enroll in sociology and psychology.

Enrollment differences for males and females in social studies courses are not statistically significant. The one exception, in both 1990 and 1994, is sociology/psychology, where females are more likely to enroll than males. The pattern continues in higher education, where females are more likely to pursue college majors in certain social sciences.[19] (See Table 11.5.)

Table 11.5. Percentage of 1990 and 1994 High School Graduates
Taking Specific Social Studies Courses by Gender.

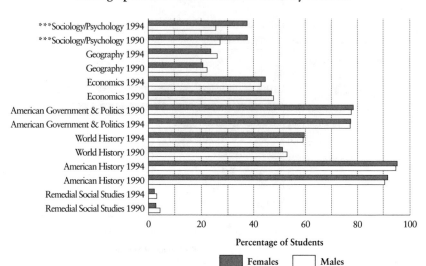

Percentage of Students

■ Females   □ Males

Source: *U.S. Department of Education, National Center for Education Statistics,* Vocational Course Taking and Achievement: An Analysis of High School Transcripts and 1990 NAEP Assessment Scores *(Washington, DC: 1995).*
*** Significant at p < .01

Foreign Languages

Female high school graduates were significantly more likely than male high school graduates to have taken French or Spanish in both 1990 and 1994.

The percentages of students, both male and female, who took Spanish increased across the four-year time period, while the percentages of both male and female students who took French declined slightly. (See Table 11.6.) More girls than boys took French or Spanish in 1990 and 1994.

Fine Arts

In both 1990 and 1994, female high school graduates were significantly more likely than males to have taken courses in music, drama, and dance.

Differences in both years were particularly large in music; in 1994, 44 percent of girls and 28 percent of boys had taken at least one semester of music, including participation in band or orchestra. Males and females enrolled in courses in art or music appreciation at fairly comparable rates

Table 11.6. Percentage of 1990 and 1994 High School Graduates Taking Specific Foreign Language Courses by Gender.

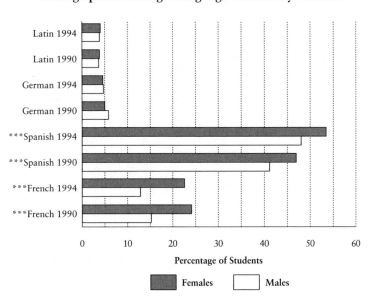

Source: *U.S. Department of Education, National Center for Education Statistics,* Vocational Course Taking and Achievement: An Analysis of High School Transcripts and 1990 NAEP Assessment Scores *(Washington, DC: 1995).*
*** *Significant at p < .01*

in 1990, although relatively few students of either sex had taken courses of this type while in high school. (See Table 11.7.)

There is some evidence that girls' higher enrollments in fine arts and music may enhance their performance in other subject areas. The National Education Association noted in 1997 that students who took four years of high school art or music classes scored an average 32 points higher on the verbal section of the SAT and an average 23 points higher in math.[20]

Health and Physical Education

Fewer students are taking physical education now than in 1990, and the drop-off is steeper for girls than boys.

Differences between males and females appear to have increased somewhat between 1990, when 67 percent of females and 70 percent of males had taken a year of physical education, and 1994, when the respective percentages declined to 61 and 67 percent.[21]

Table 11.7. Percentage of 1990 and 1994 High School Graduates
Taking Specific Fine Arts Courses by Gender.

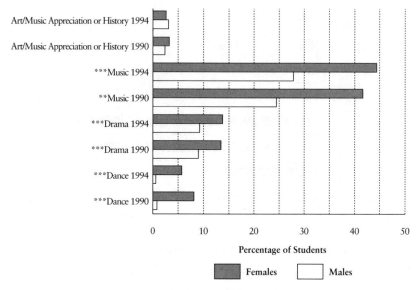

Source: *U.S. Department of Education, National Center for Education
Statistics,* Vocational Course Taking and Achievement: An Analysis of High
School Transcripts and 1990 NAEP Assessment Scores *(Washington, DC: 1995).*
** Significant at p < .05
*** Significant at p < .01

Research links physical activity for girls to higher self-esteem, positive
body image, and lifelong health. Young females are twice as likely to be
inactive as young males.[22] Male high school graduates were more likely
than females to have taken at least one year of physical education.
Although more girls now participate in a wider array of physical activities and sports than ever before, the decline in physical education is troubling, especially given the secondary academic benefits associated with
girls' athletic participation.[23] (See Table 11.8.)

Remedial and Special Education

Girls are likelier than boys to have their abilities overlooked, particularly
in math and science. Nonwhite and nonaffluent students—girls and
boys—are most likely to be steered to remedial classes.

Table 11.8. Percentage of 1990 and 1994 High School Graduates Taking Specific Health and Physical Education Courses by Gender.

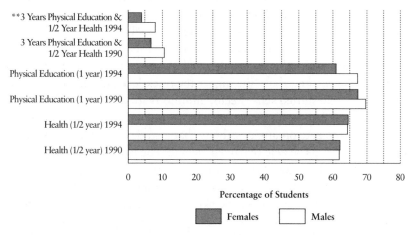

Source: *U.S. Department of Education, National Center for Education Statistics,* Vocational Course Taking and Achievement: An Analysis of High School Transcripts and 1990 NAEP Assessment Scores *(Washington, DC: 1995).*
** Significant at p < .05

○

Jennifer's Story

Despite the ubiquitous nature of informal tracking, teachers and schools often go to great lengths to prove to students that ability grouping does not exist. However, the argument does not fool the students.

"Hello. My name is Jennifer and I am in seventh grade, and I just turned 13 a little while ago. I have a teacher who puts us into groups, and the groups are smart group and dumb group.

"She doesn't say they're smart group and dumb group, but they are the smart group and dumb group. All the smart people are in the smart group, and all the other people are in the dumb group, and I'm always in the dumb group because I always have been in the dumb group."

Source: Kathleen deMarrais and Margaret LeCompte,
The Way Schools Work: A Sociological Analysis in Education
(White Plains, N.Y.: Longman Publishers, 1995): 214.

○

Schools play a pivotal role in allocating or withholding opportunities to students by identifying them as "regular," "college preparatory," "gifted and talented," or "learning disabled," or otherwise designating their ability level.[24] National data show that school policies of sorting or "tracking" students into lower-level classes result in less actual learning for both boys and girls overall. Maureen Hallinan asserts, "Empirical research provides considerable evidence that the quality and quantity of instruction increases with track level," and that "the higher the track level, the greater the students' academic status, self-esteem, and motivation to learn."[25] Jomills Braddock and Robert Slavin write that "being in the low track in eighth grade slams the gate on any possibility that a student can take the courses leading to college. The gate remained open for equally low-achieving eighth graders who had the good fortune to attend untracked schools."[26]

In theory, tracking might advance gender equity because it groups students according to their academic skills, rather than arbitrary variables such as race, socioeconomic status, or sex. However, some researchers have concluded that ratings of academic talents and skills are mediated by race, gender, and socioeconomic status, among other factors. Recognition of physical disabilities in schools are proportionate across the sexes, but recognition of more subjective disabilities such as learning disorders are not. This suggests that gender expectations bias tracking decisions.[27] Sally Reis and Carolyn Callahan found that male teachers, in particular, tend to stereotype girls and their talents.[28] Such critical judgments of their abilities deter many girls from persevering, particularly in mathematics and sciences.[29] Nonwhite and nonaffluent students—girls and boys—are especially likely to have their abilities overlooked.[30]

Significantly, placement into "remedial," special education, or lower academic tracks often occurs as students enter school in the fall—a difficult time for many students. Because tracking occurs so early in the school year, teachers and administrators may not have learned enough about individual students to challenge prior gender-stereotyped expectations. The earlier in the year a student is tracked, the more likely the decision is affected by stereotypes of performance and behavior rather than substantive knowledge—acquired only over time—of the student's abilities. Students who experience difficulties in the first few weeks of school often have trouble later with grades, behavior, grade retention, absenteeism, and dropping out of school.[31]

Advanced Placement, Gifted, and Honors Programs

In 1992 enrollments in gifted programs favored girls. No new data contradict this finding.[32] However, girls drop out of high school gifted tracks at a faster rate than boys.

Participation in top-level high school courses and in gifted and honors programs indicate, in large part, how teachers, parents, and students themselves perceive their academic abilities and interests. Participation in these courses also powerfully predicts enrollment in higher education.

Most schools identify children for gifted and talented programs at around third grade, on the basis of teacher recommendations and standardized tests.[33] Educators and administrators generally identify girls for gifted programs at equal or greater numbers than boys, yet students are identified for different kinds of programs, according to gender expectations. Schools do not identify girls for their mathematics and science talents in the same proportions as boys, who, likewise, are not identified for their English, language, or arts abilities in the same proportions as girls.[34]

Furthermore, girls are not retained in high-level gifted tracks to the same extent as boys. Despite the early identification of special talent in girls, Carolyn Read found that there is an abrupt reversal of this pattern around the tenth grade.[35] Something leads many girls not to enroll or to drop out of gifted and talented programs early in high school; others are not identified for these programs. What happens in middle school and early high school to discourage girls' identification with and participation in gifted programs? Read hypothesizes that, during elementary school, educators identify more girls for gifted and talented programs because girls are more likely to meet sex-role expectations.[36] However, as girls reach adolescence, their focus often shifts from being the "good girl" in school to fitting in with peer groups. For girls, fitting in often involves playing dumb, hiding their intelligence, and being quiet.

Sally Reis and M. Katherine Gavin also observed that although teachers in general did not engage in sex-role stereotyping, they did stereotype their best students in the area of mathematics, attributing characteristics such as volunteering answers, enjoying mathematics, and working independently to males.[37] Teachers rated females higher than males on the effort they put into schoolwork and on the quality of their work; however, teachers gave boys and girls the same grades, despite girls' higher ratings on effort and quality of work.[38] Perhaps this occurs because, as Pat Ross maintains, U.S. culture often equates higher expenditure of effort with lower ability.[39]

If educators and peers cast gifted white girls as quiet, good students, they sometimes cast gifted, academically successful black girls as troublemakers rather than as outspoken, independent leaders of tomorrow.[40] Signithia Fordham found "the most salient characteristic of the academically successful [black] females . . . is a deliberate silence, a controlled response to their evolving, ambiguous status as academically successful students."[41] Research on educational reform and gender has found that school response to girls' behavior plays a crucial role in recasting potentially "unfeminine" traits such as intellectual aggressiveness into positive and encouraged behavior. For example, one study notes, "girls who speak out may be treated as leaders or renegades," depending in some measure on the school's approach to the behaviors.[42]

AP and Honors Enrollment

Girls' AP and honors course enrollments are comparable to or greater than those of boys, except in physics. In AP and honors calculus and chemistry, girls' course enrollments improved relative to boys' from 1990 to 1994.

Advanced placement (AP) and honors courses are generally the highest-level courses high schools offer. Both kinds of courses are taught at an accelerated pace. Honors courses offer students a deeper understanding of the subject matter and challenge them to produce a higher quality of work. AP courses cover material at college level and can earn college credit for students who score 3 or higher on a 5-point voluntary course-end exam.

In 1997, 58 percent of all public high schools offered AP courses. Today, roughly the same percentage of males and females enroll in AP or honors courses in Western civilization, calculus, or chemistry—an improvement over 1990. Overall, girls' enrollments in AP or honors courses are comparable to those of males across all subjects except for AP physics. Girls are significantly more likely than males to enroll in AP or honors courses in English, foreign language, and biology. Except in foreign languages, girls' and boys' participation in AP or honors courses increased between 1990 and 1994.[43] From 1983 to 1993 there was a substantial increase (from 37 to 43 percent) in the proportion of female AP test takers in math and natural science subject areas.[44] (See Table 11.9.)

Summary

After lagging for years, girls' high school course enrollment patterns are beginning to look more like boys'—an encouraging sign because course selections can open or close future opportunities to students. But progress is not uniform.

In terms of *numbers* of courses taken, girls are closing the much-discussed gap in math and science. But important differences still rest in the specific courses taken. For example, more girls are taking Algebra I and geometry today than in 1990. The increase in girls' enrollments is

Table 11.9. AP Course Taking by Gender, Subject, Year.

Percentage of Students Taking the Course

Females   Males

Source: *U.S. Department of Education, National Center for Education Statistics, 1994 High School Transcript Study, Tabulations, 1997.*
** *Significant at p < .05*
*** *Significant at p < .01*

welcome news: Taking Algebra I and geometry by the ninth and tenth grade is viewed as a major predictor of a student's continuing to college. But more girls than boys end their high school math careers with Algebra II. Stopping a math education at this level is troubling because it can close the door on future studies, scholarships, and careers. Girls are also less likely than boys to take physics and high-level computer courses.

Girls' failure to take more top math and science courses remains an obstinate problem, with a long-term impact. Data on college majors and degrees earned indicate that girls may not make the transition from high school math and science courses to advanced postsecondary courses in these fields. This failure threatens to make women bystanders in the burgeoning technology industry of the 21st century and keep women underrepresented in high-salaried, intellectually challenging engineering, biochemistry, and biotechnology careers.

However, to review girls' enrollments in the sciences only is to subscribe to an arbitrary hierarchy of subject areas, and to relegate areas in which girls excel to a lesser status than they deserve. English, foreign languages, the social sciences, and fine arts are all educational prerequisites for higher education and career, particularly in the information-driven economy of the 21st century. Equally important, they are prerequisites for personal expression, informed citizenship, an understanding of global trends, and an ability to analyze and interpret contemporary culture. In these courses, girls outnumber boys. Boys' underenrollment in English, languages, and the arts warrants attention if public schools aspire to achieve high standards for all students.

Schools' practice of tracking students—formally or informally—affects girls' and boys' course-taking patterns differently. Girls are more likely than boys to have their abilities overlooked in math and science—a pattern that limits their future opportunities. On the other hand, girls are also more likely than boys to be identified at a young age for gifted programs. However, girls fall off this gifted track at a higher rate than boys, particularly once they reach high school. There, peer pressure tells many girls to hide their intelligence and be quiet.

The message is received differently by black and white girls, say some researchers. White girls are rewarded for fitting in, for meeting expectations of being the "good girl" in school. Those black girls who are outspoken and independent often find themselves cast as troublemakers rather than leaders. They may pay more of a social price for conforming to expectations of silence.

Roughly the same percentage of boys and girls enroll in the most challenging high school courses: AP and honors courses. Girls' and boys' enrollment in specific AP or honors courses reflects subject enrollment patterns elsewhere: Girls are more likely than boys to enroll in English, foreign language, and biology. Boys are more likely to enroll in physics.

Recommendations

In light of improving participation rates overall for girls in math and science, these recommendations focus on the types and timing of courses boys and girls take.

- In developing curriculum standards, states should make rigorous courses of Algebra I and geometry mandatory for all students, as the gatekeeper classes for college admissions and for advanced study in math, science, engineering, and computer science.

○ Schools and school districts should concentrate on increasing the percentage of girls who take the trio of core science courses: physics, biology, and chemistry. In this trio, physics shows the most obstinate gender gap.

○ Teachers and counselors should encourage talented girls to take math and science classes at the challenging AP or honors level.

○ Educators need to develop interventions at the classroom, school, district, or state level to equalize enrollments in computer science technology. Girls are dramatically underrepresented in regular and AP computer science courses, with the exception of word processing, the 1990s version of typing. This has ramifications beyond the classroom. There already is a shortage of talent to fill high-skill, well-paying jobs in the field.

○ Educators should develop curriculum and other incentives to encourage more boys to enroll in fine arts, foreign languages, advanced English electives, and AP languages and humanities courses. Areas such as these where boys underenroll or underperform girls are relevant to the equity agenda. Educators should ask: Why do these courses attract fewer boys? Are there curricular changes that might encourage their engagement in these crucial areas of the curriculum?

○ States and schools should reassess tracking policies not only in light of racial and class equity concerns, but also in light of gender equity. Currently, educators identify more girls than boys for gifted programs in the elementary years, yet girls are not retained in high-level tracks to the same extent as boys once they reach middle school.

○ State and federal data on participation in gifted and special education programs should be disaggregated by sex.

NOTES

1. Valerie Lee, "Is Single-Sex Secondary a Solution to the Problem of Gender Inequity?" in *Separated by Sex: A Critical Look at Single-Sex Education* (Washington, DC: American Association of Women Educational Foundation, March 1998): 42.

2. Rolf Blank and Doreen Gruebel, *State Indicators of Science and Mathematics Education: State by State Trends and New Indicators from the*

1993–1994 School Year (Washington, DC: Council of Chief State School Officers, 1995).

U.S. Department of Education, Office of Educational Research and Improvement, National Center for Education Statistics, *Vocational Course Taking and Achievement: An Analysis of High School Transcripts and 1990 NAEP Assessment Scores* (Washington, DC, 1995).

3. Throughout this report, statistical significance is reported either when such tests were noted in the material reviewed for this report or when the appropriate information was provided allowing calculation of such tests. Several test procedures were used depending upon the nature of the data. Significance levels of .10, .05, and .01 are noted on the tables. A finding that is statistically significant at the .05 level, for example, means that there is less than 5 percent chance that the differences can be attributed to random variation.

4. Michael Kane and Sol Pelavin, *Changing the Odds: Factors Increasing Access to College* (New York: The College Board, 1990).

5. Attention to and concern for the underrepresentation of women in mathematics and science fields has resulted in numerous gender equity initiatives focusing on these two curriculum areas (for example, the National Science Foundation's Program for Women and Girls, the Women's Educational Equity Clearinghouse within the U.S. Department of Education; the Collaboration for Equity Among the American Association for the Advancement of Science; Girls, Inc.; Educational Development Center, Inc.; and Campbell-Kibler Associates, Inc.).

6. "Females Taking More Math Courses Than Males," http://www.act.org, April 23, 1998.

7. Ruth K. Blank et al., *Mathematics and Science Content Standards and Curriculum Frameworks: State Progress on Development and Implementation* (Washington, DC: Council of Chief State School Officers, 1997).

8. Campbell and Steinbrueck, *Striving for Gender Equity.*

9. Sue V. Rosser, *Female-Friendly Science* (Elmsford, NY: Pergamon Press, 1990).

Sue V. Rosser, *Re-Engineering Female Friendly Science* (New York: Teachers College Press, 1997).

10. James Collins, "How Johnny Should Read," *Time* 150, no. 17 (October 27, 1997).

11. Arthur Halbrook and Katherine Woodward, *National and State Content Standards in English Language Arts* (Washington, DC: GED Testing Service, American Council on Education): 3.

12. With the exception of English composition in 1990, these differences are not statistically significant. We report these findings, however, because of the consistent direction of the differences and the importance of discussing and monitoring boys' participation in the English/language arts curriculum.

13. Nancy Cole and Warren W. Willingham, *Gender and Fair Assessment* (Princeton Educational Testing Service, Mahwah, NJ: Lawrence Erlbaum Associates, 1997): 122.

14. Elizabeth Hayes and Jennifer Hopkins, "Gender Literacy Learning: Implications for Research in Adult Literacy Education" (paper presented at the annual meeting of the American Educational Research Association, New York, April 1995): 15.

15. Elaine Millard, "Differently Literate: Gender Identity and the Construction of the Developing Reader," *Gender and Education* 9, no. 1 (March 1997): 31–48.

16. Kathleen Gormley et al., "Gender Differences in Classroom Writing: An Analysis of Sixth Grade Students' Reader Response Entries," *ERIC Digests ED353578* (Washington, DC: ERIC Clearinghouse, 1992).

17. Rebecca Cummings, "11th Graders View Gender Differences in Reading and Math," *Journal of Reading* 38, no. 3 (November 1994): 196–99.

18. Eileen McKenna, "Gender Differences in Reading Attitudes" (master's thesis, Kean College of New Jersey: May 1997).

19. *Women, Minorities, and Persons with Disabilities in Science and Engineering: 1996* (Washington, DC: National Science Foundation, 1996).

20. Elaine Woo, "Classroom Renaissance," *LA Times,* 4 February 1997.

21. Although not statistically significant, we note these findings because we believe the apparent widening gap between males and females deserves monitoring.

22. Linda K. Bunker et al., *The President's Council on Physical Fitness and Sports Report: Physical Activity and Sports in the Lives of Girls* (Washington, DC: President's Council on Physical Fitness and Sports, 1997).

23. U.S. Department of Education, Office of Educational Research and Improvement, National Center for Education Statistics, *Digest of Educational Statistics 1997* (Washington, DC, 1997).

24. Jeannie Oakes, "Can Tracking Inform Practice? Technical, Normative, and Political Considerations," *Educational Researcher* 21, no. 4 (1992a): 12–21.

    Jeannie Oakes, "Detracking Schools: Early Lessons from the Field," *Phi Delta Kappan* 73, no. 4 (1992b): 448–54.

Relsa N. Page, *Lower Track Classrooms: A Curricular Perspective* (New York: Teachers College Press, 1991).

25. Maureen T. Hallinan, "School Differences in Tracking Effects on Achievement," *Social Forces* 72, no. 3 (March 1994): 799–820.

26. Jomills Henry Braddock II and Robert E. Slavin, "Why Ability Grouping Must End: Achieving Excellence and Equity in American Education," in *Beyond Tracking: Finding Success in Inclusive Schools*, eds., H. Pool and J. A. Page (Bloomington: Phi Delta Kappa Educational Foundation, 1995): 7–20.

27. M. L. Wehmeyer and M. Schwartz, "Disproportionate Representation of Males in Special Education Services: Biology, Behavior or Bias" (Gender Equity in Special Education, unpublished).

M. Wagner, "Being Female—A Secondary Disability? Gender Differences in the Transition Experiences of Young People with Disabilities" (prepared for presentation to the Special Education Special Interest Group of the American Education Research Association annual meeting, San Francisco, 1992).

Wagner et al., "Youth with Disabilities: How Are They Doing? The First Comprehensive Report from the National Longitudinal Transition Study of Special Education Students" (prepared for the Office of Special Education Programs and the U.S. Department of Education, SRI International, 1991).

D. L. Caseau et al., "Special Education Services for Girls with Serious Emotional Disturbance: A Case of Gender Bias?" *Behavioral Disorders* 20, no. 1 (1994): 51–60.

28. Sally M. Reis and Carolyn M. Callahan, "My Boyfriend, My Girlfriend, or Me: The Dilemma of Talented Teenaged Girls," *The Journal of Secondary Gifted Education* 7, no. 4 (1996): 434–46.

29. Nancy Kreinberg and Ellen Wahl, eds. *Thoughts and Deeds: Equity in Mathematics and Science Education* (Washington, DC: American Association for the Advancement of Science, Collaboration for Equity, 1997).

Jane B. Kahle, "Opportunities and Obstacles: Science Education in the Schools," in Cinda-Sue Davis et al., *The Equity Equation: Fostering the Advancement of Women in the Sciences, Mathematics, and Engineering* (San Francisco: Jossey-Bass, 1996): 57–95.

30. Peter M. Hall, ed. *Race, Ethnicity, and Multiculturalism: Policy and Practice,* Missouri Symposium on Research in Educational Policy, vol. 1 (New York: Garland Publishing, 1997).

Barbara J. Bank and Peter M. Hall, eds., *Gender, Equity and Schooling: Policy and Practice*, Missouri Symposium on Research in Educational Policy, vol. 2 (New York: Garland Publishing, 1997).

31. Susan L. Dauber et al., "Tracking and Transition through the Middle Grades: Channeling Educational Trajectories," *Sociology of Education* 69, no. 4 (October 1996): 290–307.

32. Gail Crombie et al., "Gifted Programs: Gender Differences in Referral and Enrollment," *Gifted Child Quarterly* 36, no. 4 (1992): 212–13.

    Carolyn Reeves Read, "Achievement and Career Choices: Comparisons of Males and Females, Gender Distribution in Program for the Gifted," *Roeper Review* 13, no. 4 (1991).

    Digest of Educational Statistics 1997.

33. Pat O'Connell Ross, *National Excellence: A Case for Developing America's Talent* (Washington, DC: U.S. Department of Education, Office of Educational Research and Improvement, National Center for Education Statistics, October 1993).

    Thomas J. Ward et al., "Examination of a New Protocol for the Identification of At-Risk Gifted Learners" (paper presented at the annual meeting of the American Educational Research Association, San Francisco, April 1992).

34. Ross, *National Excellence*.

35. Carolyn Reeves Read, "Achievement and Career Choices: Comparisons of Males and Females, Gender Distribution in Program for the Gifted," *Roeper Review* 13, no. 4 (1991).

36. Ibid.

37. Sally M. Reis and M. Katherine Gavin, *Why Jane Doesn't Think She Can Do Math: How Teachers Can Encourage Talented Girls in Mathematics* (Reston, VA: National Council of Teachers of Mathematics, in press).

38. Donna Siegel and Sally M. Reis, "Gender Differences in Teacher and Student Perceptions of Student Ability and Effort," *The Journal of Secondary Gifted Education* (Winter 1994/1995): 86–92.

39. Ross, *National Excellence*.

40. Signithia Fordham, "Those Loud Black Girls: (Black) Women, Silence, and Gender Passing in the Academy," *Anthropology and Education Quarterly* 24, no. 1 (1993): 3–32.

    Signithia Fordham, *Blacked Out: Dilemmas of Race, Identity, and Success at Capital High* (Chicago: The University of Chicago Press, 1996).

41. Fordham, "Those Loud Black Girls."

42. Research for Action, Inc., Jody Cohen and Sukey Blanc et al., *Girls in the Middle: Working to Succeed in School* (Washington, DC: American Association of University Women Educational Foundation, 1996).

43. Virginia B. Edwards et al., "The Urban Challenge," *Education Week* 17, no. 17 (January 8, 1998): 6.

44. Cole and Willingham, *Gender and Fair Assessment.*

12

BREAKING THE BARRIERS

THE CRITICAL MIDDLE SCHOOL YEARS

Beatriz Chu Clewell

LOSSES OF ASPIRING or potential science and engineering students occur at each juncture in the educational process—elementary school, high school, and college (U.S. Congress, Office of Technology Assessment, 1988b). The greatest influence on the size and quality of the science and engineering work force is the precollege experience. Although the first intervention programs targeted students in high school or college, there has been a growing awareness that the factors impeding minority and female access to MSE careers are present long before high school. The research of Berryman (1983) and others suggests that intervention to increase the science talent pool is best undertaken before the ninth grade, while strategies to decrease attrition from the pool should be targeted at any point in the process.

What events occur at the middle school phase of the mathematics and science process that make it a crucial point for intervention? First of all, the middle school years (defined here as grades 4 through 8) determine whether a student will participate in the academic track, a prerequisite for access to advanced mathematics and science courses (which, in turn, predict higher performance levels in these subjects). Second, these years have been pinpointed as the period during which female and minority interest and achievement in mathematics and science decline. Third, the middle school years—the pre-adolescent period—are a time of great developmental change in the psychomotor, affective, social, and cognitive domains, dictating special educational needs (Dorman, 1981; Hill, 1980;

Lipsitz, 1977). Fourth, as students enter eighth grade, they must consider academic options and make decisions about course selections that will affect their future career choices.

The realization on the part of researchers, practitioners, and funding sources that intervention aimed at increasing the pool of potential MSE majors among minority and female students must begin before high school has resulted in an increase in the number of intervention programs targeting middle school students. A recent study funded by the Ford Foundation describes the nature and scope of these intervention programs, identifies gaps in service delivery, and makes policy recommendations based on its findings (Clewell, Thorpe, and Anderson, 1987). The Ford study identifies and describes 163 mathematics, science, and computer science intervention programs for middle school students in the United States, including Puerto Rico. Of these, 33 percent target minorities, 13 percent females, and 54 percent both minorities and females. Activities and services provided by the programs include exposure of participants to role models, direct instruction, counseling, field trips, guest speakers, hands-on experiences, special projects, contests and science fairs, study groups, tutoring, test preparation, and job shadowing. In terms of geographical distribution, the West has the highest number of programs—30 percent of the total. This region is followed by the Northeast, with 28 percent; the central states, with 24 percent; and the Southeast, with 18 percent.

In addition, the study found that there are many more intervention programs in mathematics and science serving middle school minority and female students than a review of the literature and anecdotal information led us to expect. In spite of this finding, there are gaps in service delivery. The number of programs focusing on middle school girls and minority students appears low in relation to the population of minority and female students within this age range (U.S. Department of Commerce, 1986). On a positive note, of the intervention programs that we identified that target minority students, many are incorporating strategies related to academic achievement. Some programs are also offering services that address motivational factors related to participation and achievement, including exposure to careers and opportunities to interact with role models or mentors.

For female students, a somewhat different picture emerges. Programs identified as female-focused are emphasizing attitudinal more than instructional activities. The preponderance of programs for both minorities and females focus at or above grade 6. Many of these programs also extend into the high school years. Only one-third serve students in the fourth or fifth grade. While many programs provide counseling or academic guidance critical to future academic and career planning, very few programs offer test preparation activities.

There is a dearth of intervention programs targeting middle school students in the Southeast. Since this area contains a large Black population, it is possible that Black middle school students in the Southeast are being underserved. The same situation exists for Native Americans. Several of the states with a high concentration of Native Americans seem to have no intervention programs for middle school students.

What implications do these findings have for policy? The following are specific recommendations generated by our look into the state of intervention in mathematics and science for females and minorities in middle school:

○ Increase the number of female-focused and minority-focused programs serving middle school students.

○ Increase the number of female-focused programs that offer activities to enhance the achievement and participation of girls in math and science.

○ Increase the number of minority-focused programs offering role models, career awareness, and counseling activities.

○ Add test preparation to programs offering awareness and motivational activities and substantive achievement activities. (Test preparation should not, however, be considered a substitute for substantive intervention.)

○ Serve greater numbers of Native Americans, especially in states where there is a high concentration of members of this group.

○ Establish more programs in the Southeast, especially in those states where there are none.

○ Expand the services of existing female- and minority-focused programs to fourth- and fifth-graders.

To be effective, intervention approaches must be grounded in an understanding of the growth and developmental needs of students in grades 4 through 8, as well as a sound knowledge of educational experiences and instructional strategies that promote learning and enjoyment of mathematics and science. The rest of this chapter addresses these issues and presents a framework that attempts to coordinate these components. A comprehensive approach to breaking the barriers will result in programs that have great potential for motivating, enriching, and possibly sustaining middle school students' interest and participation in math and science.

The Needs of Middle School Students

An understanding of the general developmental needs of middle school students, regardless of sex and race, can help establish guidelines for determining teaching strategies, including planning teacher-student activities, selecting materials, and organizing learning situations, and thus help make the teaching and learning processes profitable and rewarding experiences for both educators and students. Combining and synthesizing the work of social and behavioral scientists and clinicians, Hill (1980) offers a useful framework within which to consider what is known about adolescent development and how it affects adolescents' positions in the family, the peer group, and the school. Lipsitz (1977) reviewed the biological, socioemotional, and cognitive research on young adolescents as well as the social institutions that serve them, including the school. On the basis of the work of these two researchers, the Center for Early Adolescence (Dorman, 1981) compiled the following list of physical, social, emotional, and cognitive needs of young adolescents:

○ Diversity

○ Self-exploration and self-definition

○ Meaningful participation in their school communities

○ Social interaction with peers and adults

○ Physical activity

○ A sense of competence and achievement

○ Structure and clear limits

The following discussion briefly addresses these needs of students in grades 4 through 8 and notes implications for intervention efforts.

Diversity

The preadolescent years represent a period of rapid physical, sexual, psychological, cognitive, and social change to which the young person must adjust (Mussen, Conger, and Kagan, 1979). Students grow at varying rates and undergo changes at different ages. Students exhibit a wide variety of interests and social concerns, and individual differences are pronounced. In any one class of preadolescents, a range of maturity levels can be observed. To accommodate the wide range of abilities, interests, and skills of preadolescents, intervention programs should allow for variety in the curriculum and activities, varied instructional and resource materials, and flexibility in the schedule and use of available space.

Self-Exploration and Self-Definition

An important part of socioemotional development is the establishment of a sense of identity, which involves perceiving oneself as a distinct, consistent person in one's own right (Mussen, Conger, and Kagan, 1979). During this period, students must begin to develop their self-esteem through their own efforts and abilities. An intervention program should provide the kind of support that facilitates the development of independence, self-esteem, and self-reliance; be success-oriented; offer basic subjects, exploratory courses, activities on content and skills acquisition, and enrichment experiences to help students integrate their developing capabilities, interests, and relationships into a sense of who they are; encourage students to pursue answers to their own questions, in addition to their teachers' questions; offer guidance activities focused on self-exploration that are prevention-oriented, not problem- or crisis-oriented; and offer career guidance by exploring students' occupational and personal interests, not by making occupational decisions for them.

Meaningful Participation in School and Community

School and community are important forces in the socialization process. Schools need to provide a climate that makes learning a rewarding and relevant experience, one that makes the most of students' talents and interests. The socialization process is further strengthened when school activities are expanded to incorporate meaningful community experiences in and outside the classroom. Students' interests need to be considered and used as a basis for classroom and schoolwide activities (Bloom, 1971). Schools can provide the structure and the means for young adolescents to have a real voice in operating their schools and to make meaningful contributions beyond the classroom through student-initiated study and activities, student councils, and student committees. An intervention program should provide opportunities for young adolescents to identify and carry out projects that will both improve the school environment and allow them to contribute their knowledge, competencies, and skills to the communities.

Social Interaction with Peers and Adults

During the middle school years, the peer group becomes powerful and begins to replace parents as the major source of behavioral standards and recognition of achievement. It provides young people with an opportunity to learn to interact with age mates, to deal with hostility and dominance, to relate to a leader, to lead others, and to deal with social problems (Biehler, 1971). Positive adult relationships also provide an opportunity for young adolescents to learn social skills, control their behavior, and share their problems and feelings.

An intervention program must take into account young adolescents' need to be accepted by peers and respected by adults other than their parents. It should provide a supportive environment that protects young adolescents from the negative aspects of peer pressure and provide many opportunities (for example, small-group learning activities or cooperative learning) for positive peer interactions. Positive social interactions between adults and students are facilitated by adviser-student relationships, staff participation in student activities, and informal contact between students and staff outside the classroom.

Physical Activity

The challenging and sometimes difficult period of early adolescence is marked by spurts in the energy level. During this period, most students experience a period of very rapid physical growth, which often has an unsettling effect on the preadolescents' emotions and a spiraling effect on their physical and mental endurance. A responsive program will provide structured outlets for this physical energy. Breaks are needed to allow students to release tension. Since attention spans vary, activities should not be too long. Students should be allowed to move around in the classroom and to relax or work in unorthodox sitting positions, so long as such activity does not interfere with learning. To sustain interest during this period of much energy, a program should provide students with a variety of activities in a variety of educational settings.

Competence and Achievement

Improvement in cognitive processes is remarkable during this period of development. Attention spans continue to increase with all activities, with the most striking gains being in problem solving. According to Piaget (1956), students in this age range begin to shift from concrete to formal operations. Although concrete operations are logical and systematic, thinking at this stage is still tied to direct experiences. As students begin to shift to formal operations, they think more abstractly, formulate and test hypotheses, and consider what might be rather than merely what is.

In their efforts to facilitate the acquisition of these higher-level cognitive processes, intervention program developers must first realize that students differ widely in the attainment of higher-order thinking skills and that students initially need the opportunity to explore new concepts in concrete forms prior to dealing with more abstract, representational forms. Middle school students need hands-on experiences or activity-based instruction. In addition, a program to promote competence and achievement-oriented behavior among students should have positive academic expectations for all students, provide rewards and praise generously but honestly, and offer opportunities for students to increase their independence and responsibility to evaluate their own performance. If it does this, students will know what they are doing, why they are doing it, and whether they are doing it well.

Structure and Clear Limits

Young adolescents continue to need rules and schedules for the use of space and materials and standards for acceptable and unacceptable classroom and school behavior. Structure and clear limits can provide the security that young adolescents need to learn and grow during a time of rapid and pervasive change. Clearly stated limits should be accepted by students, teachers, and staff for the promotion of optimal learning in a setting of trust and responsibility.

Effective Strategies and Techniques at the Middle School Level

Most intervention programs at the middle school level employ multiple strategies for increasing female and minority students' interest and performance in mathematics and science. While no single method has emerged as most effective, a variety of instructional methods do work. Effective strategies include:

> Hands-on activities
>
> Sufficient time-on-task
>
> Adequate precollegiate training
>
> Contacts with role models in scientific and technical careers
>
> Laboratory work
>
> Cooperative learning
>
> Manipulative instructional materials
>
> Nonthreatening competition
>
> Independent projects
>
> Test preparation
>
> Support from parents, teachers, and peers
>
> Positive academic and personal counseling

Strategies should be related to both the developmental needs of students and intervention goals to enhance minority and female representation in math and science. A framework for linking intervention goals, strategies, and student needs is presented in Table 12.1.

Table 12.1. Intervention Approaches at the Middle School Level to Improve the Perception, Performance, and Participation of Minority and Female Students in Mathematics and Science.

Intervention Goals	Strategies and Techniques	Structure and Clear Limits	Competence and Achievement	Physical Activity	Positive Social Interaction with Peers and Adults	Hands-on Experience/ Meaningful Participation	Self-Exploration/ Self-Definition	Diversity
Math and science perceptions and career awareness								
Improve attitudes toward math and science	Increase the encouragement received from significant others				•		•	
	Socialize students to the demands and rewards of rigorous scientific work		•		•		•	
Increase career awareness	Acquaint students with varied math and science careers available and the preparation needed for them						•	•
	Arrange contacts with role models in scientific and technical careers (field trips, internships, demonstrations)	•	•	•	•	•		•
Increase confidence in doing math and science	Structure activities so that everyone can experience some success		•		•	•	•	•
	Recognize and provide awards for outstanding student achievement in math and science		•		•		•	

Performance in math and science and participation in advanced math and science courses

Goal	Action	Increase math and science knowledge	Increase use of math and science	Improve test performance in math and science	Increase enrollment in math and science classes	Increase out-of-school math and science activities
Increase math and science knowledge	Provide substantial time-on-task and homework at all levels	•		•		
	Be sensitive to individual differences in selecting cues, processing information, and analyzing data	•	•	•		
Increase use of math and science	Provide early hands-on experiences; "do" science in order to convey its utility	•	•	•		•
	Participate in math competitions, science fairs, and so on		•		•	•
	Enhance instruction through cooperative learning or small-group methods	•	•	•		
	Provide tutoring	•	•	•		
Improve test performance in math and science	Emphasize the mastery of scientific process and abstract thinking as well as the assimilation of facts	•		•		
	Provide test-taking workshops			•		
Increase enrollment in math and science classes	Counsel students to enroll in advanced-level math and science courses or help middle school students choose a direction for their high school studies and eventual math and science careers				•	
Increase out-of-school math and science activities	Establish high standards for minority and female participation in the sciences				•	•
	Encourage participation in math and science clubs, hobbies, and community programs		•			•

Intervention Approaches at the Middle School Level

There is general agreement that intervention programs are crucial to increasing the minority and female scientific pool. However, the focus of intervention at the middle school level remains an issue involving a balance between career awareness approaches and skill-building and enrichment approaches. Although there is a tendency to suggest working on interest first, then skills, it is important to remember that the two processes occur simultaneously and not in isolation from one another.

Career Awareness Approaches

Fostering positive attitudes toward mathematics and science and increasing students' interest in science and technology careers are critical to addressing the inequities in the participation of females and minorities in these areas. For interventions at the middle school level, the following recommendations are crucial for enhancing attitudes and increasing interest (Clewell, 1987):

- Intervention efforts to affect the attitudes of minority students should begin before the seventh grade. Career awareness programs for females should begin in the early elementary school years, followed by more intensive programs in the middle and high school years.

- Intervention efforts to affect the attitudes of minority students should ensure that the participants have access to skill enhancement.

- Intervention should emphasize that females and minorities can excel in mathematics and science.

- Minority and female students should be exposed to more mathematics and science experiences, activities, and hobbies at an early age, both in and out of school.

- Efforts should include combating the perception of math and science as a White male domain and stressing the usefulness of math, science, and technology in the present and the future.

- Intervention efforts for minority and female students should include role modeling and career information. Many opportunities to interact with people from industry, universities, and professional societies should be provided.

- Intervention approaches should focus on providing social support and acceptance of competitiveness of young females and reducing the degree to which characteristics of self are sex typed in order to combat females' negative attitudes about becoming scientists.

○ Parents should be made aware of their role in encouraging their minority and female children to participate in mathematics, science, and technology.

○ Teachers should be made aware of the importance of increasing minority and female students' self-concept and belief in their ability to succeed in quantitative and problem-solving activities.

○ Guidance counselors should be educated about the importance of encouraging minority and female students to participate in mathematics and science.

○ Intervention should provide means of utilizing the positive influence of peers on values, attitudes, and aspirations in helping minority and female students to maintain an interest in mathematics and science.

Skill-Building Approaches

It is critical during the elementary and junior high school years that minorities and females perform well in mathematics and science as well as plan to take high school science and mathematics courses. Minority and female students need a strong background in mathematics and science not only because college majors require it but also because there is a growing need for a more scientifically literate populace. Recommendations for improving performance of minorities and females in middle school mathematics and science and increasing the chances that they will opt to elect high school math and science courses are listed below (Clewell, 1987; Clewell and Anderson, 1987):

○ Math and science skills should be strengthened with the goal of preparing and motivating students to take advanced-level courses in high school.

○ Instruction should be activity-based, proceed from concrete to abstract, and encourage active involvement with a variety of manipulative materials at all ages.

○ Students should seek solutions to problems through hands-on experiences, and teachers should relate problems to the students' interest and experience.

○ Teachers should expect high achievement from every student and show confidence in each student's ability to learn. It is also important to give feedback and reinforcement as soon as possible, providing ongoing evaluation and routinely making growth apparent to the student. Teachers should help students to realize that they can succeed in mathematics and science.

○ Test preparation should be a part of intervention activities. Students should be tested in the language of instruction.

○ Teachers need to adapt their teaching methods to accommodate varying stages of cognitive development. Instructional approaches should also accommodate students' different cognitive styles and locus-of-control orientations.

○ Teachers should be aware of how their expectations, attitudes, behavior, and interactions with students affect students' achievement.

○ Minority and female students need early exposure to science and active participation in science projects.

○ Females should be exposed to male-oriented science activities that allow exploration of mechanical apparatus, computation, and the development of science-related skills.

○ Interaction among students enhances achievement. Grouping students according to ability is less effective than working with a mixed-ability group as long as differences are not too great. Peer tutoring can be a useful tool that benefits both tutors and the tutored.

○ Intervention concerning the selection of math and science courses in high school should begin in the fifth and sixth grades.

○ Parents should be provided with information and training to help them support their children academically and influence their career and high school study plans.

○ Intervention efforts should encourage minority and female students to enroll in hard-core science and mathematics courses.

REFERENCES

Berryman, S. F. Who Will Do Science? Trends and Their Causes in Minority and Female Representation Among Holders of Advanced Degrees in Science and Mathematics. New York: Rockefeller Foundation, 1983.

Biehler, R. Psychology Applied to Teaching. Boston: Houghton Mifflin, 1971.

Bloom, B. S. "Affective Consequences of School Achievement." In G. H. Block (ed.), Mastery of Learning. Troy, Mo.: Holt, Rinehart & Winston, 1971.

Clewell, B. C. "What Works and Why: Research and Theoretical Bases of Intervention Programs in Math and Science for Minority and Female Middle School Students." In A. B. Champagne and L. E. Hornig (eds.), Students and Science Learning. Washington, D.C.: American Association for the Advancement of Science, 1987.

Clewell, B. C., and Anderson, B. T. "Effective Math/Science Intervention Approaches for Middle School Minority Students: What the Literature Says." Paper presented at the annual meeting of the American Educational Research Association, Washington, D.C., Apr. 1987.

Clewell, B. C., Thorpe, M. E., and Anderson, B. T. Intervention Programs in Math, Science, and Computer Science for Minority and Female Students in Grades Four Through Eight. Princeton, N.J.: Educational Testing Service, 1987.

Dorman, G. Middle Grades Assessment Program. Chapel Hill: Center for Early Adolescence, University of North Carolina, 1981.

Hill, J. P. Understanding Early Adolescence: A Framework. Carrboro, N.C.: Center for Early Adolescence, Department of Maternal and Child Health, School of Public Health, 1980.

Lipsitz, J. Growing Up Forgotten: A Review of Research and Programs Concerning Early Adolescence. Lexington, Mass.: Heath, 1977.

Mussen, P. H., Conger, J. J., and Kagan, J. Child Development and Personality. New York: HarperCollins, 1979.

Piaget, J. The Origins of Intelligence in Children. New York: International Universities Press, 1956.

U.S. Congress, Office of Technology Assessment. Elementary and Secondary Education for Science and Engineering: A Technical Memorandum. Report no. OTA-TM-SET-41. Washington, D.C.: U.S. Government Printing Office, 1988b.

U.S. Department of Commerce. Statistical Abstract of the United States, 1986. Washington, D.C.: Bureau of the Census, U.S. Department of Commerce, 1986.

13

MISREADING MASCULINITY

SPECULATIONS ON THE GREAT
GENDER GAP IN WRITING

Thomas Newkirk

The push for men to express their feelings presumes that we have feelings, and we do have a few, but they remain submerged, and the airing of them often violates their authenticity.

—Roger Rosenblatt (1998, p. 244)

IN MIDDLE SCHOOL, during one of her periodic bouts of frustration, my older daughter met with one of her male friends to talk through her troubles. Midway through he stopped her, "I have an idea—do you have a bicycle?"

"Yeah," she said, puzzled.

"Well, ride it."

"What*ever!*"

When she told me the story, his logic made perfect sense: Simply recounting what makes you sad won't change anything. What you need to do is act, move, release this frustration. Talk, in other words, is an avoidance of action, of resolution, of decision-making. But when I told this story to a female friend of mine, her reaction was that his advice amounted to avoidance: rather than confronting the problems by talking through the frustration, he seemed to say you can run away—or at least ride away—from them. Furthermore, in a classic example of the mismatches that Tannen (1992) has made part of our gender folklore, my daughter's friend saw his role as offering advice, when my daughter wanted a listening partner who might *share* his own frustrations rather than *fix* hers.

If we view writing as drawing on strongly gendered attitudes, such as the ones on display in this conversation, it is small wonder that the writing of boys and girls differ from the first invented spellings they create. Vivian Paley once remarked that children "think they invented the differences between boys and girls, and, as with any new invention, must prove that it works (1984, p. ix). The difference was systematically explored first by Donald Graves in the early 70s, and subsequent researchers have confirmed the sharp and persistent differences in the writing of boys and girls. Perhaps more problematic is another set of studies which demonstrate, beyond any reasonable doubt, that the biggest gender gap that now exists is not in the areas that have received the most attention, girls falling behind boys in mathematics (a gap which *is* closing). It exists in writing (where the gap *is not* closing) (Cole, 1997). According to the most recent reports of the Educational Testing Service, the gap in writing between males and females at the eighth-grade level is over six times greater than the differences in mathematical reasoning (Cole, 1997, p. 15).

Another way to look at the magnitude of this gap is to compare it to the differences in writing performance of ethnic and racial groups. In the 1996 NAEP assessment for eighth graders, White students outperformed Black students by 29 points (on a 500-point scale) and Hispanic students by 21 points; females outperformed males by 25 points (Campbell, Voelkl, & Donohue, 1997, p. 167). In other words, the gap between females and males is comparable to that between Whites and racial/ethnic groups that have suffered systematic social and economic discrimination in this country.

I realize that this may seem a provocative comparison, particularly when one considers the historic economic advantage of males, particularly White males. It runs counter to the general thrust of most equity research (e.g. Sadker & Sadker, 1995) which has focused on the ways in which schools have "failed at fairness" in educating girls. My point is not to engage in a disadvantage competition, nor to deny the ways in which girls are often silenced in schools, nor to equate the gender gap (in language performance, particularly writing performance) to the ways Black and Hispanic students are more systematically discriminated against. I do, however, want to claim that male students often perceive school-defined literacy as excluding—or even dismissing—their own narrative preferences, and conclude early on that proficiency in school-based writing is more "natural" for girls. The subsequent, well-documented gap in performance may be a result of this perception.

I will begin by summarizing the research on gender differences in writing and then proceed to the more complex question of how these differences are read—or misread.

Aliens in the Hospital

Since Donald Graves' research on gender differences in the early 70s, researchers have documented consistent gender differences in writing:

○ When first graders were asked to imagine themselves as an animal in a story they might write, there were clear gender differences in the choices. Girls tend to choose domesticated animals (cat, horse), while boys choose animals that are dangerous and wild (cougar, monster) or comic (monkey) (Ollila, Bullen, & Collis, 1989).

○ Second-grade girls tend to choose "primary territory" (home, school, parents, friends) as topics for writing. Boys consistently choose secondary territory (professions) or extended territory (wars, presidents, space) (Graves, 1973; McAuliffe, 1994).

○ Second-grade boys write stories which focus on contests, physical and social, in which the protagonists act alone. Success is determined by winning or losing in these combative tests. By contrast, girls' writing tends to focus more on joint action and protagonists who struggle to remain connected to the community (McAuliffe, 1994; Trepanier-Street, Romatowski, & McNair, 1990).

○ When boys include females in their stories, they tend to be passive and, not coincidentally, professionless (Gray-Schlegel & Gray-Schlegel, 1995–96; Many, 1989). They tend to write about males in traditional roles of authority. When, for example, boys were asked to invert gender roles and write about a male nurse, one had the hospital invaded by aliens to change the terms of the task (Trepanier-Street, Romatowski, & McNair, 1990).

○ Because boys' writing deals so consistently with physical contests, it is far more violent than girls' writing (S. Peterson, 1998), a trend one pair of researchers called "disturbing" (Gray-Schlegel & Gray-Schlegel, 1995–6, p. 167).

○ In a study of first-year college students, women wrote autobiographical essays that were judged better than those of their male
counterparts (Peterson, 1991). In analyzing the differences, she
found that males tended to write about times when they acted individually, often in physical challenge that built confidence. Women
tended to write about a crisis in a relationship (boyfriend, family, or
an encounter with culturally different persons). In terms of writing
qualities, males showed no deficit at rendering detail; their lower
scores were due to a perceived difficulty in rendering "significance,"
in the capacity to reflect on the meaning of the experience.

○ Boys' preferences in reading and writing narratives are more
closely aligned with visually mediated storytelling—film, TV, video
games, computer graphics. They also rank humor higher than girls
do. Millard (1997) suggests that the traditional literature-based
curriculum may ignore the more visually-mediated narratives that
boys prefer.

It is one small step to turn these differences into deficits. The writing of
males can be read as endorsing a whole set of anti-social values: the use
of violence to resolve conflict; the lack of empathy for victims of violence;
the subordination of women; extreme individualism and competition; and
escapism. Even to allow such writing might be seen as complicity in a culture that condones male violence. Boys might also be viewed as drawing
inspiration not from good literature, but from the morally questionable
and exploitative visual media/toy culture. It is only one more small step
to take on a missionary role or at least a prohibitionary role—to ban the
violence, convert boys to more realistic and socially responsible fiction,
wean them from space and aliens, guns and blood. Yet I suspect that any
frontal assault on boyhood, as it has been culturally constructed, is a misreading of male students that is doomed to failure.

Reading "Violence"

A major difficulty with the debate about "violence," as it relates to the
media's effect on boys, is the almost unlimited scope of the term, often
covering everything from the first 30 minutes of *Saving Private Ryan*
(Bryce, 1998) to Roadrunner cartoons, from the Kennedy assassination
to the death of Kenny on *South Park,* from mass suicides to hockey
games. Of course, a waiver is granted to the violence in great literature—
Grimm's fairy tales, *Hamlet,* the Bible—which for some reason uplifts and
humanizes us. Can anyone doubt that the medieval audience listening to

Beowulf, which would become the first classic of British literature, didn't delight in Grendel's sheer awfulness? This waiver raises the question: is the criticism really about violence or is it about taste? Is it about all violence or just "low class" violence in the more popular media?

There is also a troubling—and in my view sexist—assumption of *extreme male susceptibility to any presentation of violence.* During one of the crackdowns on violent rap music, noted African American scholar Henry Louis Gates[1] often claimed that the critics of rap were holding a double standard. Black males, he argued, were being treated as "dry tinder" ready to ignite when they heard the rappers advocate violence. Yet no one worried that White women would start imitating Madonna (except in a campy way); everybody would assume that White women would maintain some ironic detachment, some bemusement at Madonna's antics, a presumption they would not extend to Black males. While I'm still troubled by some of the lyrics Gates defends, I think his caution is a good place to start in looking at boys' writing about violence. It is a mistake, I feel, to automatically equate boys' use of violence in writing with any desire to be vicious or sadistic. To do so ignores the possibility that "violence" can be mediated, viewed with humorous detachment, and appropriated for a variety of non-violent ends, including the maintenance of friendship.

We can see the way this appropriation works in a literacy narrative written by a White, first-year college student. Andrew Schneller[2] tried to identify the school practices that killed his love of writing. Andrew does not now enjoy writing, and he says he "want[s] to do . . . as little as possible." But it was not always this way:

> The first day of school that year I met Jon Cortis. Jon would later become my best friend through elementary school and in junior high we were inseparable. . . . I remember an assignment where we were supposed to draw a picture and write a sentence about it. I drew a shark (I used to spend my summers on the beach and developed a fascination with sharks). Jon drew a scuba diver covered with missiles and lasers. His sentence was "The underwater trooper kills all the sharks." Not to be upstaged I decided to add missiles and lasers to my shark and wrote: "Attack sharks kill underwater troopers." It was a very weak sentence, but I was (and still am) extremely competitive.
>
> Second grade Jon was in my class again. This year we focused on writing. We had to write a story each week. It seemed that all of Jon's stories were about underwater troopers killing my attack sharks. His stories always ended with a shark named Andrew dying in a different

gruesome manner each time. Again I retaliated by having my sharks destroying his troopers, always ending with a Trooper named Jon dying some humiliating death.

I suspect that if this writing were subject to the analysis traditionally used in studies of gender, Andrew's and Jon's stories would fit the familiar pattern—violent, competitive, individualistic, devoid of female characters, and, from a teacher's standpoint, numbingly repetitive. Yet in Andrew's account, the stories are intensely social; they help to form a continuing bond with his best friend. In fact, they remain the clearest—and most positive—memory that Andrew has of his literacy learning. Dyson (1993) has coined the term "social work" to describe the work writing can do to define and bond friendship groups in a classroom. This "work" may not be evident in the writing itself, appearing more in the talk and negotiation ("Can I be in your story?") that surrounds the writing. In Andrew's case, seemingly anti-social, violent writing paradoxically performed a positive collaborative function.

As Andrew moved through school, he lost the opportunity to make choices about reading and writing, and cites only one other positive experience, in seventh grade with his underwater opponent Jon.

That summer we read *Jurassic Park*. It was the first book I read on my own in a long time. I enjoyed it and recommended it to Jon, who also read and enjoyed it. There must be something about dinosaurs ripping people to shreds that appeals to twelve-year-old boys.

Here we see the pattern repeated; a book with sensationalist violence performs real social work, strengthening a social bond between friends. After they saw the movie they discussed the differences between the movie and the book, finding the book better. Andrew concludes, "I had regained my love of reading."

Another way to look at this affection for violence is to return to the opening conversation between my daughter and her friend. Recall his suggestion was to act, not to talk, to choose movement over reflection. When I asked one of my son's friends why he didn't do any voluntary reading, he responded, "Why should I choose to read, when I can *do* something?" Literacy gets in the way of the need to move, to talk, to play, to live in and with one's own body. In one sense, writing represents the choice of language over physical action; yet this choice can be mitigated by stressing action in the writing. Watch any first-grade boys composing and you will see the drama of hands simulating explosions, accompanied by sound effects, with intervals of consultation with friends about who is in which space ship. When I have asked boys how their writing differs from that of girls, they are dismissive of the *lack* of action in the girls' stories. As one said, making a face, "They write about walking home together."

Multiple Worlds

Dyson (1989) argues that writing, such as Andrew described, involves the intersection of multiple worlds. The texts are, in Bakhtin's terms, "heteroglossic" (1981, p. 293), containing echoes of various language systems. Note Andrew's comment on later elementary school writing:

> This was the year I read my first novel, *The Lion, the Witch and the Wardrobe* by C. S. Lewis. Jon also read the book and we used to discuss the parts we did and didn't like, incorporate some of the characters into our writing. By the end of the year I think I had read all of the books of Narnia and killed Jon off close to twenty times in my stories.

While I can imagine Andrew's teacher wondering aloud about Andrew and Jon, their sharks, laser guns, and mutual death, it is important to acknowledge the complexity, the multiple worlds integrated into these stories:

1. *Outside expertise*—Andrew's interest in sharks was tied to his fascination with the ocean and surfing.
2. *Visual representation*—the writing system was tied to a drawing system.
3. *A toy or video culture*—they drew on their knowledge of the laser weapons from video games, cartoons, and toys (modeled after this culture).
4. *A friendship culture or social world* (Dyson, 1993)—writing became a collaborative (*and competitive*) form of play that helps sustain his friendship with Jon.
5. *A curriculum culture*—where writing was expected at certain times, in certain amounts to fulfill an academic expectation. In transforming largely visual narratives to written narrative, students negotiate popular culture and academic work.
6. *A culture of established literature*—where characters from their reading of the Narnia Chronicles make their incongruous appearances among the sharks and lasers.

Paradoxically, this complex orchestration of cultures and symbol systems does not make writing harder—rather these systems serve as multiple supports, multiple inducements. They are the "complex and living" attractions of literacy. To strip the writing act of these systems—by prohibiting drawing, assigning uninteresting topics, isolating a child in a tutoring situation without peers, devaluing references to popular culture, or prohibiting "violence"—is to remove the possible appeal of writing itself.

Implicit in Dyson's (1989) argument for the "multiple worlds" of writing is what might be called a "piggyback" theory of literacy learning. The fundamental premise of this "theory" is that print literacy is made attractive and possible by being embedded in systems that are, at least initially, more attractive to the learner. Primary-school children regularly break into print by making elaborate drawings, with a label at the bottom—print literacy being pulled in the wake of the visual. Dyson (1997) shows how drama and performance can be a motivating culmination of the writing process, particularly for African American children whose writing is often rooted in voice, performance, and participation.

The greatest potential drawback for the young writer—perhaps the writer of any age—is the perception that writing entails solitude, isolation from peers, loneliness. Writing becomes much more appealing if it leads to peer solidarity, if it becomes a badge of membership. Israel (1999) has shown how the third grader boys in her class formed "clubs" based on their preference for either the Cowboys or the 49ers (two nationally popular American football teams). Some of the writing, early breakthroughs to print, took the form of ritual insult: "the Cowboys rule the 49ers drool." Membership in these clubs was the primary and indispensable inducement to write. Both Israel (1999) and Dyson (1989) reverse the logic usually used to explain collaboration. Normally collaboration is seen as the *means* to the end of producing a piece of writing. From the child's standpoint, though, writing may be viewed as a *means* to collaborate, a ticket to participate; the fundamental attraction is not producing a piece of writing but the social opportunities the writing opens up and maintains.

For boys, this language of affiliation will often be coded in the language of violence and assault, so it is essential to read the subtext of the message. While Andrew was repeatedly using his attack sharks to tear "Jon" apart, he was in fact maintaining a channel of friendship. And a decade later, he looks back to these stories as the high point of his literacy history.

Humor and the Burden of Sincerity

Devin Bencks, my son's best friend, has spent so much time at our house that for a while he would put items on the shopping list ("Heah Mr.

Newkirk, how about some Cool Ranch Doritos?"). Around sixth grade he developed an imaginary friend, Ed. If you asked Devin a question, like if the Red Sox would make the playoffs, he'd say, "I don't know, I'll have to talk to Ed." When the time came for the state sixth grade tests, Devin and the rest of New Hampshire's sixth graders were required to imagine they could be anyone for a day, and to write a story about their day as that person. Devin found this assignment "cheesy," calling for a predictable kind of hero worship which he was not about to give into. The very act of writing for a distant, examining body provoked his resistance, "They don't care who I admire; they just want to see if I can write, sentences, periods, that kind of stuff." So he wrote about Ed.

> If I could be anyone for a day, I would be Ed because he is so cool and he rules. If I was Ed I would wake up on a bed of nails surrounded by fire. I would then use my rat Binki's saliva to extinguish the flames.

He goes on to spend an afternoon dancing with Whitney Houston, later renting a herd of goats, and finally riding off with McNeill (of the McNeill/Lehrer NewsHour) "into the sunset with our goats." In fact, Devin memorized his essay and turned it into a performance, which, three years later, he can still do upon request.

While at first glance, this assignment might seem non-ideological (students can choose any person), I suspect that Devin found it unappealing for several reasons. The assignment suggests that the primary attitude of the writer should be open respectfulness, directed, most likely, to a member of his or her parent's (or grandparent's) generation. In other words, the assignment subtly calls upon the writer to "identify with the interests of those with power over him—parents, teachers, doctors, public authorities" (Pratt, 1996, p. 529). At the very least, it requires him to identify with authorities giving the test. Even to write about Martin Luther King Jr. in this context is to play the good student, dutifully respectful of a cultural icon, something Devin was unwilling to do. So he chose parody, a form of calculated resistance that went to the very edge of unacceptability.

This deep affection for parody and controlled resistance might be viewed as an example of what Erving Goffman (1961) calls "underlife." While Goffman studied "total" institutions, particularly mental hospitals, his theory fits the less-than-total institutions such as schools, and it offers an explanation of the psychological necessity of parody. According to Goffman (1961), institutions project an official view of what participants should be putting into and getting out of the organization, "what sort of self and world they are to accept for themselves" (p. 304). Yet for the inmates (and even employees) of the institution to completely accept "the embrace of the institution" is to lose a sense of personhood. Small acts of rebellion (silence, refusal to take pills, mockery of aides) constitute an "underlife," an attempt by the individual to "keep some distance, some elbow room, between himself and that with which others assume he should be identified" (Goffman, 1961, p. 319). While Goffman sees this "resistance" as necessary for institutional life in general, it may be especially attractive to some boys who find "good studenthood" to be acquiescent, unmasculine, a denial of who they are and want to be. Goffman clearly sees this form of resistance as a human need, not particularly a male need, and Finders (1997) provides an excellent account of the often parodic underlife of adolescent girls.

Boys are often in the difficult position of maintaining their standing as sons and students, while at the same time distancing themselves from "sincere" behaviors and language that they see as threatening and feminine. Parody is one way of meeting *both* these demands. Devin's Ed story is at once a rejection of the sincerity demand of the state assignment—yet it is also an identifiable genre that the evaluators recognized. So he was able to pull off the coup of mocking the assignment *and* getting a higher score than almost all of those who chose to take it seriously (such as my son, who wrote on Cal Ripken, Jr.).

We can see this balancing act in another piece co-written by Devin and my son in third grade. Devin and Andy wrote a progress report for their teacher, John (Jack) Callahan. The report contains some inside jokes that even the writers don't understand. But Nabu was an imaginary character Jack invented to teach a math unit—when the unit was over Jack told students that Nabu died. Here's the report:

JOHN RICHARD CALLAHAN   PROGRESS REPORT   DATE 2/6/93
Newkirk/Bencks

Jack is suffering since his good friend Nabu died. I think his donut cholesterol has gone up since. It has been affecting his work. I think he has donitides. I think he should be tutorhood and I think I found the person that would be perfect for jack madonna. I've talked to madonna and jack will meet her at 3:11 at wisconsin's bingo parlor she'll be wearing her Vogue uniform. I've heard they've made a new dunken donuts at _____. I think jack should take summer school because he needs to work on his cursive sevens. I think he should install a toilet in the room. We have not been able to see a successful ircele imitation if by the end of the week he doesn't do the imitation he will be exspeleed.

> This is the marking of how aubknockshis your sin has been this half
> year

The boys construct an elaborate rating system and then conclude:

> I hope you are plaesed with what we've written. So now you know
> how poor a student jack is. I hope you can get jack back on track.

> Sincerely Mr. Newkirk/Mr. Bencks

In this progress report, the two boys were both resisting and embracing
the institution of school—or rather, they were embracing *by* resisting.
They appropriate the language of authority and admonition, the presumption to rank, even the prerogative to threaten. They skate close to
potentially sensitive areas, Jack's affection for donuts and by implication
his concern for his weight; and they introduce the subjects of sexuality,
arranging the rendezvous with Madonna at the Wisconsin Bingo Parlor.
Yet their "progress report" is an unmistakable expression of affection,
and it's difficult to imagine a more effective vehicle.

If we view "sincerity" as a gendered attitude that boys may perceive as
threatening or at least best avoided, it calls upon us to reconsider literacy
practices that are usually advocated as universally good. Millard (1997)
raises questions about the "personal growth model," advocated by Dixon
(1967) and implicitly endorsed in much whole language practice. This
model which stresses personal relationships, "expressive" writing, direct-
ness of feeling, and sensory awareness may be perceived by boys as gendered female. Millard (1997) notes that a literature-based curriculum for
teenage readers usually stresses novels which explore character and making sense of individual experience. In her interviews with boys, these
books were often dismissed because "nothing of consequence ever happened" (p. 43). Yet realistic, introspective fiction often is considered "better literature" than comedy, science fiction, crime novels, and nonfiction,
in other words, genres that traditionally appeal to boys and could form
the models for their writing. Millard claims the school curricula have
"naturalized" a novel-reading practice that in the 19th century was
enjoyed almost exclusively by women.

Another invitation to sincerity that boys may resist is the introspective
self-analysis that has become part of the portfolio movement. Boys may
perceive the invitation to self-evaluate their development as something less
than an open request. In fact, they may see it as a double-bind; there are
two possible responses, neither very appealing. One option is to employ
the "sincere" language of self-improvement (e.g., "I think I am a much

better reader this quarter") which can feel like "sucking up," and is a much too close "identification with the interests of those who have power over them" (Pratt, 1996, p. 538). Yet if they suggest boredom, dislike for reading, lack of progress, they might find themselves in violation of the true intentions of the teacher, eager to see the student on the positive train to self-improvement. And if we accept Tannen's (1992) claim that males are sensitive to hierarchies of authority, boys may question the point of self-evaluation from a clearly subordinate position of power (i.e., when the grade ultimately comes from the teacher).

Converting the Natives

By arguing for a distinct culture of boys, I do not mean to suggest that these preferences should be considered inevitable, or in the long run entirely beneficial. As Peterson (1991) has argued, development in writing involves "cross dressing," a capacity to move out of stereotypical gender positions. This is clearly an important goal, for both boys and girls. But as Millard (1997) has shown, cross-dressing comes easier to females than males; "tomboy" has never been the pejorative term for girls that "sissy" is for boys. If masculinity is a more tightly constructed cultural category, with sharper penalties for deviance toward the feminine, it follows that to create equity in access to literacy, teachers will need to acknowledge the cultural materials (e.g., the affection for parody and action, interest in professional sports, cartoons, videos games) that boys (and *many girls*) bring into the classroom (for an example see Salvio, 1994). To fully engage this cultural material, it is necessary to understand the masculine distaste for sincerity, and the complex ways that the positive can be encoded in the negative, praise in criticism, friendship in violence, love in death.

One key to working with this cultural material is recognizing the openness of even the most "violent" writing to parody and humor. In fact, much of the violence boys like is "violence with a wink," violence that parodies itself or at least suggests its own unreality (the James Bond movies are full of such moments). The student who can engineer humor within the context of an action story almost invariably gains status. So, while it is tempting to bring boys into the "realistic fiction" camp, another strategy is to explore the ways in which they honor parody in their own stylized "violent" writing. Here are some other suggestions:

  o We need to recognize the ways writers do innovate within stereo-
     typical male genres. My sense is that this writing does evolve (as it

did when Andrew introduced the Narnia characters). Recall also how Jon killed off Andrew in "a *different* gruesome manner every time." I recently read a space adventure story which began with the usual group of boys in a plane, which came under attack, and as they got closer to the attacking plane they saw that it contained *their fathers*. Now, there's a twist.

○ We need to recognize cartooning as an important art form and narrative medium. It often seems there is an implicit hierarchy in school art programs where copying Monet's *Water Lilies* is seen as more valuable than creating a caricature; where the quilter comes in for an artist residency, and the cartoonist doesn't.

○ We need to be familiar with the narrative models that boys emulate. This may mean seeing some movies, watching some TV we might not otherwise choose to watch. Furthermore, we might ask how we can draw on these visual narratives to teach the conventions of story writing—plot, dialogue, detail, suspense, humor, character. How can we help students come closer to those models of narrative they find most appealing?

The most serious mistake, it seems to me, is viewing these preferences as pathologies, as anti-social ways of being that must be modified, or, if that is not possible, banned. I view this attitude as a form of cultural suppression that is sure to alienate male students from literacy and the school culture in general. Boys become the "natives" to be converted to more socially responsible preferences. It calls to mind W.E.B. Dubois' question—"How does it feel to be a problem?" (1989, p. 3)

NOTES

1. The comment noted here was made during a talk Gates did at the University of New Hampshire in the fall of 1989.

2. Andrew's quotes come from a literacy biography that he completed for my freshman English class.

REFERENCES

Bakhtin, M. (1981). *The dialogic imagination: Four essays*. (M. Holquist, Ed.; C. Emerson & M. Holquist, Trans.). Austin, TX: University of Texas Press.

Campbell, J., Voelkl, K., & Donohue, P. (1997). *NAEP 1996 trends in academic achievement*. National Center for Educational Statistics. Washington, DC: U.S. Government Printing Office.

Cole, N. (1997). *The ETS gender study: How females and males perform in educational settings.* Princeton, NJ: Educational Testing Service.

Dixon, J. (1967). *Growth through English.* Huddersfield, England: National Association for the Teaching of English.

Dubois, W.E.B. (1989). *The souls of black folks.* New York: Penguin. (Original published in 1903.)

Dyson, A. (1989). *The multiple worlds of child writers: Friends learning to write.* New York: Teachers College Press.

Dyson, A. (1993). *The social worlds of children learning to write in an urban primary school.* New York: Teachers College Press.

Dyson, A. (1997). *Writing superheroes: Contemporary childhood, popular culture, and classroom literacy.* New York: Teachers College Press.

Finders, M. (1997). *Just girls: Hidden literacies and life in junior high.* New York: Teachers College Press.

Goffman, E. (1961). *Asylums: Essays on social situations of mental patients and other inmates.* New York: Anchor.

Graves, D. (1973). Sex differences in children's writing. *Elementary English, 50* (7), 1101–1106.

Gray-Schlegel, M., & Gray-Schlegel, T. (1995–1996). An investigation of gender stereotypes as revealed through children's creative writing. *Reading Research and Instruction, 35* (2), 160–170.

Israel, A. (1999). *Peer collaboration in a dual language writer's workshop.* Unpublished Doctoral Dissertation, University of Arizona, Tucson.

Many, J. (1989). Sex roles from a child's point of view: An analysis of children's writing. *Reading Psychology, 10,* 357–370.

McAuliffe, S. (1994). Toward understanding one another: Second graders' use of gendered language and story styles. *The Reading Teacher, 47* (4), 302–310.

Millard, E. (1997). *Differently literate: Boys, girls and the schooling of literacy.* London: Falmer Press.

Ollila, L., Bullen, C., & Collis, B. (1989). Gender-related preferences for the choice of particular animals as writing topics in grade 1. *Journal of Research and Development in Education, 22* (2), 37–42.

Paley, V. (1984). *Boys and girls: Superheroes in the doll corner.* Chicago: University of Chicago Press.

Peterson, L. (1991). Gender and the autobiographical essay: Research perspectives. *College Composition and Communication, 42* (2), 170–183.

Peterson, S. (1998). Evaluation and teachers' perception of gender in sixth-grade student writing. *Research in the Teaching of Writing, 33* (2), 181–208.

Pratt, M. (1996). Arts of the contact zone. In D. Bartholomae & A. Petrosky (Eds.), *Ways of reading* (4th Ed.; pp. 528–542). New York: Bedford Books.

Rosenblatt, R. (1998). The silent friendships of men. *Time, 152* (23), 244.

Sadker, D., & Sadker, M. (1995). *Failing at fairness: How our schools cheat girls.* New York: Touchstone Books.

Salvio, P. (1994). Ninja warriors and vulcan logic: Using the cultural literacy portfolio as a curriculum script. *Language Arts, 71* (6), 419–424.

Tannen, D. (1992). *You just don't understand.* New York: Ballantine.

Trepanier-Street, M., Romatowski, J., & McNair, S. (1990). Children's responses to stereotypical and non-stereotypical story starters. *Journal of Research in Childhood Education, 5* (1), 60–72.

14

GIRLS AND DESIGN

EXPLORING THE QUESTION
OF TECHNOLOGICAL IMAGINATION

Margaret Honey, Babette Moeller, Cornelia Brunner,
Dorothy Bennett, Peggy Clements, and Jan Hawkins

Introduction

THE RESEARCH PRESENTED here began several years ago when a group
of us at Bank Street's Center for Children and Technology set out to investigate a range of issues around gender and technology. As part of that
research, we speculated that the activity of *design* was a promising way to
support alternative pathways for girls into the world of technology (Brunner, Hawkins, & Honey, 1988). The developmental and educational psychology literatures offer robust evidence that a richer understanding of a
task is developed when children actively construct their own knowledge
(Dewey, 1933; Piaget, 1972). In his book, *Knowledge as Design*, David
Perkins (1986) suggests that the act of designing facilitates the constructive

The research and development work for the Imagine project was originally
funded by the Spencer Foundation (Women and Technology: A New Basis for
Understanding). The research for this study was supported by the Center for
Technology in Education under Grant No. 1-135562167-A1 from the Office of
Educational Research and Improvement, U.S. Department of Education. This
paper appeared in Transformations, 2(2), Fall 1991.

and creative use of knowledge by the designer. The work that Seymour Papert and his colleagues at M.I.T. have undertaken on LEGO/Logo indicates that design is a powerful way to engage learners in making deep "cognitive connections with the mathematical and scientific concepts that underlie the domain in which they are designing" (Resnick & Ocko, 1990, p. 122). The LEGO/Logo researchers also found that, as an activity, design has the added benefit of helping students acquire a rich sense of achievement and purpose. At the start of our research, we hypothesized that through the activity of design, "it may be possible to develop situations in which technology comes alive for girls, where they are invited to engage in a new kind of conversation with materials and ideas in constructing artifacts" (Brunner, Hawkins, & Honey, 1988, p. 11).

Our gender research also began with certain suppositions about the nature of technology. In our view, there are specific discursive practices that have grown up around technology that need to be unpacked if we are to understand the social and psychological dimensions of engaging with technological objects. For example, there is a world of culturally produced meaning associated with technology. A recent article by Paul Edwards (1990) makes the point that "computer work is more than just a job. It is a major cultural practice, a large scale social form that has created and reinforced modes of thinking, systems of interaction, and ideologies of social control" (p. 102). There are also psychological meanings that we, as users, bring to the technology. For example, a common fantasy shared by women is that when something goes wrong with a technological device, it will blow up. These two meaning domains do not, however, exist independently of each other, and there are numerous ways in which personal fantasies or desires mesh with culturally produced meanings. Sherry Turkle's (1984, 1988, 1990) work has shown us that, in many respects, the cultural apparatus that surrounds technology is sustained by the ways in which gender operates as a social and psychological phenomenon. Her notion of "computational reticence" documents exactly this phenomenon—women are reluctant to engage with computers because, for a variety of complex social and psychological reasons, they experience this technology as threatening (1988, p. 42).

Background Research

With this perspective in mind, we collected baseline information that would help us to elaborate our hypothesis about design (Hawkins et al., 1990). We devised a paper-and-pencil projective task in which men and women and boys and girls were asked to imagine futuristic technological devices. Our purpose was to explore the symbolic aspects of technology by asking individuals to elaborate on their less-than-conscious associations to technology. Specifically, the adults were asked to write a reply to the following scenario: *If you were writing a science fiction story in which the perfect instrument (a future version of your own) is described, what would it be like?* The task was modified slightly for the adolescents, and read as follows: *If you were writing a science fiction story about the perfect school computer (a fabulous machine), what would it be like?*

The sample for these studies consisted of 24 adult technology experts (13 women and 11 men) and 80 early adolescents (41 girls and 39 boys) who were not particularly sophisticated about technology. While we found evidence suggesting an overlap between the genders, there was a definite and characteristic difference in the way adult men and women in our sample fantasized about the relationship between humans and machines (Brunner et al., 1990). Women commonly saw technological instruments as people connectors, communication, and collaboration devices. Their technological fantasies were often embedded in human relationships, and they served to integrate their public and private lives. For example, one woman, an industrial engineer, described a futuristic instrument in the following terms:

> The "keyboard" would be the size of a medallion, formed into a beautiful piece of platinum sculptured jewelry, worn around one's neck. The medallion could be purchased in many shapes and sizes. The keyed input would operate all day-to-day necessities to communicate and transport people (including replacements to today's automobile). The fiber optic network that linked operations would have no dangerous side effect or by-product that harmed people or the environment.

The men, in contrast, tended to envision technology as extensions of their power over the physical universe. Their fantasies were often about absolute control, tremendous speed, and unlimited knowledge. Consider this fantasy, written by a male computer scientist:

> A direct brain-to-machine link. Plug it into the socket in the back of your head and you can begin communications with it. All information from other users is available, and all of the history of mankind is also available. By selecting any time period, the computer can impress directly on the user's brain images and background information for that time. In essence, a time-machine. The user would not be able to discern

the difference between dreams and reality and information placed there
by the machine. (Perhaps this is all a nightmare.)

The results of our studies with adolescents were congruent with the
results of the adult subjects (Brunner et al., 1990). The difference in technological imagination points in the same direction as the adult fantasy
material. Girls' technological fantasies tended to be more about household helpers, contact bringers, machines that offer companionship, or
devices with which they could broaden their social and personal networks.
On the other hand, boys fantasized about extensions of instrumental
power, often thinking up tools that could make other technological objects
overpower natural constraints.

These differences between boys and girls were more concretely evident in
another task in which we had another group of early adolescents blueprint
designs of fantasy machines (Brunner et al., 1990). The boys often illustrated
fantastic cars or vehicles for flight that ventured through rocky terrain or
adventuresome landscapes propelled by powerful devices, such as rocket
boosters and turbo jets. Some went as far as describing the voltage of the
batteries or motors that their inventions included. The girls generally illustrated robots and devices with human-like qualities (e.g., smiles, eyes) that
could help with everyday chores, and they tended to embed their inventions
in social or real-life contexts, such as hospitals, bedrooms, or shopping malls.
They were less concerned with describing the internal mechanical parts of
their machines. Instead they often chose to include luxury features, such as
sensory devices (which one girl named "synergistic relaxation") or external
buttons and switches that would magically operate their inventions.

We gather from this that girls think about technology, when invited to
do so, as embedded in and facilitating human interaction. Clearly, such
an attitude toward technology should be encouraged and valued. However, if we consider the cultural and social discourse in which technology
is embedded, the obstacles girls may face in having their fantasies realized
become apparent. Margaret Lowe Benston (1988) suggests that

> Part of the technical world view is the belief in one's right to control
> the material world. Part of successful socialization as a man in our
> society involves gathering confidence in one's actual *ability* to exercise
> that control. (p. 20)

The male fantasy material in our studies reflects exactly this phenomenon. In addition, the kinds of design features that girls want to build into
their machines are not necessarily accorded the same privileged status as
the features of power, speed, and efficiency that boys emphasize. As the

writings of Cheris Kramarae (1988) and Cynthia Cockburn (1988) suggest, women's desire for communication, collaboration, and integration are not central to the masculine technological world view, which is increasingly accepted as the only legitimate model for discussing, developing, and evaluating technology.

Finally, there is a great deal of evidence that confirms the fact that gender-specific social expectations play a role in limiting girls' capacity to be creators, shapers, and producers of technology (Berner, 1984; Carter & Kirkup, 1990; Cockburn, 1988; Kramarae, 1988; Kramer & Lehman, 1990; Lewis, 1987; Weinberg, 1987). From a very early age, boys are expected and encouraged to learn about machines, tools, and how things work, and are given many opportunities to dismantle technological objects and toys. Girls, in contrast, are not expected to know about technical matters, and are often encouraged to be merely consumers and users of the technology.

The Design Tool

Our preliminary investigation into the question of girls and design led us to develop a computer-based design tool that enables girls to create machines by starting from their own imaginative vantage points. *Imagine* is intended to function as a legitimating environment in which girls are encouraged to think of themselves as designers and inventors of machines, without the traditional bottleneck imposed by math and science. *Imagine* is a graphics program that contains basic draw and paint tools as well as animation capabilities. After designing and drawing an object of their own, students can animate it by using a series of link procedures that are analogous to flip animation or the kind used in animated films. Sound and visual effects, such as a fade or black swipe across the screen, can be added to this type of animation. In addition, students can label the individual components of their machines and describe in as much detail as they wish what each component does and how it works.

The Research Context

To test the use and effectiveness of this program for encouraging girls' technological imaginations, an elective course in design based on *Imagine* was offered in an alternative junior high school in New York City.[1] The goal of the pilot research was to conduct a small-scale, qualitative investigation into the ways in which girls used *Imagine* in the context of a supportive but relatively unstructured classroom environment. In other words, we wanted to gather baseline information on how girls would make use of *Imagine* without the aid of a directive curriculum.

Six girls (five seventh graders and one eighth grader) met with the instructor once a week for an hour and twenty minutes. Because all of the girls were novice Macintosh users, the first two classes were devoted to an introduction to the computer. The girls learned such basics as using a mouse, the difference between the hard disk and a floppy disk, and file management. The skills needed to design and animate an object using *Imagine* were taught in the following order: draw tools, paint tools, animation, and labeling. Each session was organized so that the first 20 or 30 minutes were spent learning a new feature of the program, and the remaining time was spent working on projects. Once all of the important features of *Imagine* were introduced, students spent the entire period working on their projects, while the instructor traveled from student to student offering assistance where it was needed. The instructor spoke regularly with each student and encouraged her to articulate what she was working on and what she wanted to accomplish during the class.

Because we are ultimately interested in developing a more directive curriculum that will encourage girls to proceed from their own interpretive vantage points *and* think systematically about the mechanisms that make machines work, we analyzed students' inventions for the following information: (1) the kinds of machines they designed; (2) the range of functions they had their machines perform; and (3) the extent to which they posited a universal operating mechanism, and the extent to which they posited individual operating mechanisms for each discrete function through the use of *Imagine*'s labeling capabilities.

Findings

Of the six girls who took the elective, four became deeply involved in designing highly imaginative devices. The remaining two girls had less success using this environment for reasons that we will speculate about below. The nature of the imagining that girls did in this context was similar in many ways to the kind of imagining we found in our background research. The machines they designed often featured human-like qualities or emphasized solutions to real-life dilemmas. Three of the girls made extensive use of *Imagine*'s labeling capabilities. However, they tended to vary in terms of whether they specified a mechanism or set of mechanisms that made their devices work. The projects are briefly described below.

Beth, a seventh grader, designed a robot that was able to anticipate as well as fulfill a variety of human needs, including waking you up, serving breakfast in bed, and telling you the answers to homework problems. Beth's robot consisted of a drawing of a "creature who came from another planet." Figure 14.1 shows Beth's drawing and label descriptions for her robot.

Figure 14.1. Beth's robot and label descriptions.

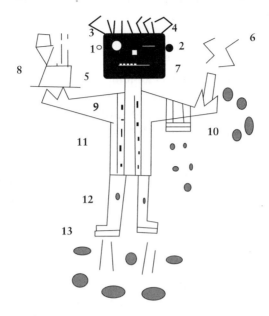

1: This is one half of the robot's brain. It sends messages to the robot and the robot will understand everything you say!

2: This is the other half of its brain. It knows when you want something to eat, drink, or just to rest or go to sleep, so it can tell you a bedtime story.

3: This helps the robot see where it's going, just like a human.

4: This also helps it see where it's going.

5: This helps the robot sense where.

6: This is a piece of soap they used in the robot's land before he landed on Earth. It's excellent for your face and wakes you up even more.

7: This is the mouth. It helps the robot to talk just like humans do. It also helps you if you want to watch a movie. You tell it which movie you want and it comes out of its mouth. The best part of all is that it tells you the answers to your homework if you need help.

8: This is a tray full of food for breakfast. It's brought to my bed every morning.

9: This is an arm that clips on to things. Every morning it picks me up by my shirt and carries me into the bathroom.

10: This is the towel that wakes me up every morning—but when it wakes me up, it's freezing cold!!!!

11: These are his suspenders from his old planet. They control all of his actions and sayings. Almost everything he does revolves around his suspenders.

12: These are his legs. They help him walk. The little buttons in the middle help all of his legs' actions.

13: These are pumps. They help him jump to all my needs.

Although she had a well-developed sense of the overall capabilities of her invention and had her robot performing a wide range of discrete tasks (she used a total of 13 labels to describe how the different parts of the robot functioned), she did not develop an explanation for an integrated mechanism that would enable the tasks to be carried out. For three of the robot's discrete functions, she alluded to biological mechanisms (e.g., brain, legs) and for another function, she made reference to a quasi-mechanical clip. Even though Beth had her robot performing complex tasks, there was no integrated mechanism that made the robot as a whole able to function. This device appeared to work magically—something like a fantasy caretaker who knows what you want even before the need has arisen.

Another student, Jessy, designed an improved subway car that made less noise, was more beautiful, had larger windows and a sunroof, more room to sit, and contained sensors for anything that could harm the subway or anybody in it. The project consisted of a relatively elaborate drawing and seven labels describing the improvements she envisioned. Figure 14.2 shows Jessy's drawing and label descriptions for her subway car.

1: These are the new wheels for the improved train. New and improved, it doesn't make a screeching sound when it puts on the brakes. It also doesn't send sparks flying when the train stops.

2: This is the door of the train. It has extra sensitive microchips that can sense graffiti cans, guns, knives, and any other weapon or object that can hurt the train or any person or thing on the train.

3: Are you tired of the old, boring, plain trains? Well, this piece of "art" makes the train nice to look at. Each and every train has an abstract painting on each side. These pieces of art have bright colors, and for once, you'll be riding in a train that looks good and NOT a train that looks like it had been through the city dump.

4: With the new and improved trains, you can finally have sunshine and fresh air. We have put in more windows than ever. Now, on the trains that run above ground, you can see out and love the scenery you never saw before. On the trains that run under ground, unfor-

Figure 14.2. Jessy's subway car and label descriptions.

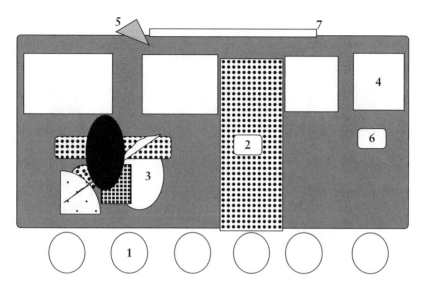

tunately, there is no such things as "beautiful scenery" but you can get fresh air and in the summers you won't have to suffocate. Windows are always needed.

5: With all these windows, how can a bird stop from doing its thing? This is the window washer that cleans not only bird markings, but also dirt and other things that keep the windows crystal clear. It cleans daily because it is programmed to at 12 o'clock midnight.

6: Finally, the body of the train. This is much bigger so everyone can have room to sit and not to stand. The special design has a secret spray on it that makes any dirt that comes near to go away. Its design urges people to come ride on the train. Each train has a different design. Isn't it beautiful?

7: Sun roof. See #4.

Jessy differed from Beth insofar as she began to speculate about the mechanisms that allowed for certain improvements to be realized. She borrowed from the world of computer technology and defined information-based mechanisms that made these parts work. For example, she described a window-washer that performed its function at midnight because it had been programmed to do so, and she described the door of the train as having extra sensitive microchips that could detect graffiti,

Figure 14.3. Pauline's intelligent television and label descriptions.

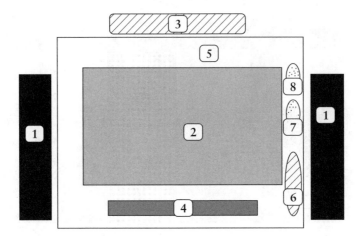

guns, knives, and other harmful weapons. Jessy, thus, appeared to be lean-
ing in the direction of thinking about the mechanism that allowed a device
to carry out its task.

A third student, Pauline, designed an intelligent television that performed
such tasks as serving food and answering mother when you really wanted
to avoid her. Like the others, she imagined a wide range of different functions (eight altogether) that her machine performed. Figure 14.3 shows
Pauline's drawing and label descriptions for her intelligent television.

1: These are the TV's speakers. If you want an ice cream float, just
   speak into the speakers and your words will be sent to the TV's central intelligence system. The TV's brain will make sense of your
   words and carry out your order.

2: This is the TV screen. You watch the screen, and your favorite
   shows are displayed on the screen and you just enjoy.

3: This is the TV's central intelligence. When you talk to the TV, your
   words are sent to the CI, and there they are made sense of.

4: This is the TV videotape player. You just pop your tape into the slot
   and tell the TV to rewind/forward wind or start wherever you want.

5: This is the TV's frame. It doesn't really have a purpose but without it,
   the TV would look kind of bare. It is supposed to be made of wood.

6: This is the TV push button which you push when you suspect that
   something is wrong with your TV's central intelligence system.

7: This is the TV's "Shut down button." If you are really sick and tired of your TV's cheerful and bright conversation, just press this button and you will be rid of all the annoyance your TV's CI brings to you.

8: This is the TV's duplicate button. If your mother is calling you and you don't want to answer, just activate the "DB" and (if you have your voice recorded in the CI) the TV will play your voice and it will seem like you are really talking.

Unlike Beth and Jessy, Pauline integrated the different components of her machine by making them responsive to a central processing unit known as the "central intelligence system." In her design, the CIS received and interpreted messages, provided feedback to the user, and was responsive to the different components of the machine. Of the three girls who concentrated on labeling, defining, and describing the functions of their devices, Pauline was the only student to conceptualize an operating mechanism.

Kathy, an eighth grader, was unique in that she was the only student to concentrate exclusively on using the animation component of the program to illustrate her design. She created a self-cleaning bathtub that featured a rotating brush and a button that released soapy water. Kathy's animation was composed of a series of twelve screens that illustrated the cleaning motion of the brush in the bathtub. Although she successfully showed how her machine functioned, she did not make reference to a mechanism that would underlie the operation of the brush. Figure 14.4 shows the drawing that Kathy used in her animation sequence.

The two girls who had difficulty using the program spent the majority of the course working together as partners. Although they came up with ideas for devices (e.g., a wristwatch that was also a VCR and Nintendo machine, a flying skateboard), they were never satisfied with the drawings they made. They spent class after class drawing and redrawing the object they wanted to design. Undoubtedly, both girls would have benefited from a version of *Imagine* that provided canned shapes and objects.

It was only toward the end of the course, when they began working independently of each other, that they started to make some progress. Hilda designed a flying bed. Her project consisted of a schematic drawing of a bed with pillows, a headboard, and controllers. However, the quality of Hilda's drawing suggested that she was struggling with the use of the tools. She identified five functions that the bed performed, but did not describe any mechanisms that made it work. Figure 14.5 shows Hilda's drawing and label descriptions for her flying bed.

Figure 14.4. Kathy's animation sequence.

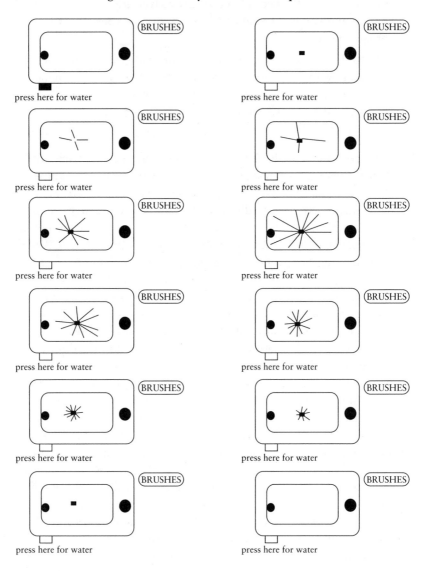

Figure 14.5. Hilda's flying bed and label descriptions.

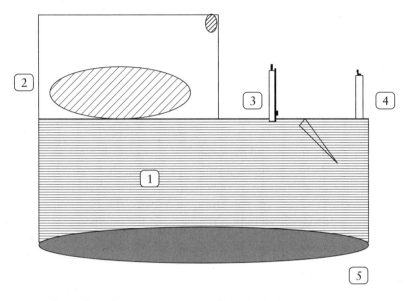

1: Headboard made to protect you while the bed is in motion!!!

2: Pillow for you to rest while you enjoy the moving bed!!!

3: Controllers used to steer the bed.

4: Nick! Nick! Controllers used to control the speed of it!!!

5: Bump. . . . Y! Bounces the bed up and down!!!!!!!! Fun?!!!!!?

The other student, Iris, with a great deal of support and guidance from the instructor, began to think through an animation sequence for a pinball machine. However, she was unable to put her plan into operation. Despite her difficulties in using the software, Iris was not discouraged and asked the instructor if she could take the class again the following semester.

Concluding Remarks

There is a growing body of psychological and sociological research which suggests that women and girls do indeed approach, interpret, and understand various facets of life differently from men. For example, Carol Gilligan's (1982) work on women's reasoning suggests that women tend to view the world in terms of interpersonal dynamics, and base their decisions, particularly in the moral realm, on an ethic of care and responsibility toward others. The work of Evelyn Keller (1985) suggests that the ways in which the mainstream scientific community represents its enterprise as an attempt to dominate nature, penetrate its secrets, and wrest knowledge from it runs counter to the ways in which women think about the scientific enterprise. In her work on the life of the molecular biologist Barbara McClintock, Keller found that the vocabulary McClintock used to describe her work was "consistently a vocabulary of affection, of kinship, of empathy" (p. 164). In the technological domain, sociologist Sherry Turkle (1988) has identified two different styles of computing: the *risk-taking style* (mostly male), which is preoccupied with testing the limits of both machine and self through mastery and manipulation of the computer environment, and the *relational style* (mostly female), which is "marked by an artistic, almost tactile style of identification with computational objects, a desire to 'play with them' as though they were physical objects in a collage" (p. 50). Our own research (Hawkins et al., 1990) suggests that gender is an important factor in the interpretation of engineered objects, understanding their symbolic significance, and exercising technological imagination. All of these findings have tremendous implications for creating alternative teaching and learning strategies that make room for differential patterns of understanding and interpretation employed by women and girls.

Based on the work that the girls in this study did during the course of a semester, it is clear that *Imagine* is effective in serving as a conceptual space where girls are encouraged to create and elaborate design ideas for technological devices. With minimal encouragement, the majority of these girls were able to develop imaginative devices that performed a range of creative functions. *Imagine* appeared to facilitate a process of mental and graphic tinkering. In the absence of a well-defined and rigorous design curriculum, what *Imagine* appears capable of doing is legitimating the *psychological* experience of thinking of oneself as an inventor. This, in and of itself, is an important first step in legitimating and affirming girls' technological imaginations.

NOTES

1. The students who attend this school are described as alternatively gifted. These are students who do not necessarily score exceptionally well on standardized tests, but are considered to be highly motivated and display a deep interest in one or more area of study. In addition, the school's curriculum is organized around project-based work and inquiry activities.

REFERENCES

Benston, M. L. (1988). Women's voices/men's voices: Technology as language. In C. Kramarae (Ed.), *Technology and women's voices*. New York: Routledge & Kegan Paul.

Berner, B. (1984). New technology and women's education in Sweden. In S. Acker (Ed.), *World yearbook of education 1984: Women and education*. New York: Kogan Page, London/Nichols.

Brunner, C., Bennet, D., Clements, M., Hawkins, J., Honey, M., & Moeller, B. (1990). *Gender and technological imagination*. Paper presented at the meeting of the American Educational Research Association, Boston, MA.

Brunner, C., Hawkins, J., & Honey, M. (1988). *Making meaning: Technological expertise and the use of metaphor*. Paper presented at the meeting of the American Educational Research Association, New Orleans, LA.

Carter, R., & Kirkup, G. (1990). *Women in engineering*. London: MacMillan Education Ltd.

Cockburn, C. (1988). *Machinery of dominance: Women, men, and technical know-how*. Boston: Northeastern University Press.

Dewey, J. (1933). *How we think*. Boston: Heath.

Edwards, P. (1990). The army and the microworld: Computers and the politics of gender identity. *Signs: Journal of Women and Culture in Society. 16*(1), 102–127.

Gilligan, C. (1982). *In a different voice: Psychological theory and women's development*. Cambridge, MA: Harvard University Press.

Hawkins, J., Brunner, C., Clements, P., Honey, M., & Moeller, B. (1990). *Women and technology: A new basis for understanding*. Final report to the Spencer Foundation. New York: Bank Street College of Education, Center for Children and Technology.

Keller, E. (1985). *Reflections on gender and science*. New Haven: Yale University Press.

Kramer, P., & Lehman, S. (1990). Mismeasuring women: A critique of research on computer ability and avoidance. *Signs: Journal of Women and Culture in Society. 16*(1), 158–172.

Lewis, L. (1987). Females and computers: Fostering involvement. In B. White (Ed.), *Women, work and technology*. Ann Arbor: The University of Michigan Press.

Piaget, J. (1972). *The psychology of intelligence*. Totowa, NJ: Littlefield, Adams.

Perkins, D. (1986). *Knowledge as design*. Hillsdale, NJ: Erlbaum.

Resnick, M., & Ocko, S. (1990). LEGO/Logo: Learning through and about design. In E. Harel (Ed.), *Constructionist learning*. Cambridge, MA: The Media Laboratory, MIT.

Turkle, S. (1984). *The second self: Computers and the human spirit.* New York: Simon & Schuster.

Turkle, S. (1988). Computational reticence: Why women fear the intimate machine. In C. Kramarae (Ed.), *Technology and women's voices.* New York: Routledge & Kegan Paul.

Turkle, S., & Papert, S. (1990). Epistemological pluralism: Styles and voices within the computer culture. *Signs: Journal of Women and Culture in Society. 16*(1), 128–157.

Weinberg, S. (1987). Expanding access to technology: Computer equity for women. In B. White (Ed.), *Women, work and technology.* Ann Arbor: The University of Michigan Press.

EDUCATIONAL SOFTWARE AND GAMES

RETHINKING THE "GIRLS' GAME"

American Association of University Women

THIS REPORT CONSIDERS educational software and computer games together because the line between them has become increasingly blurry. Parents buying games for their children often are hoping that they will have educational content, while educators choosing software for their classrooms are often comparing them to the engaging computer game as a gold standard.[1] Teachers reason that if designers can make computer games so entertaining as to be termed "addictive," why can't some of that talent be used to design educational materials? Furthermore, over the past two decades, generations of children have been socialized into the computer culture through computer games.

From the standpoint of gender equity, however, educators' interests in emulating games is very problematic. The commission noted that most computer games today are designed by men for men. They often have subject matter of interest to boys, or feature styles of interaction known to be comfortable for boys. They are also aggressively marketed to boys. Much educational software targeted for the classroom has similar short-comings. A review of popular mathematics computer programs intended for grades kindergarten through six showed that only 12 percent of the gender-identifiable characters were female, and that these characters played passive traditional roles, such as "princess." While male and

345

female elementary-age students could name software with male characters, only 6 percent could think of any software with female characters. Another study, reviewing 30 randomly selected software programs used in U.S. schools, found that of the 3,033 characters noted in the graphics and text, only 30 percent were female, and only 4 percent were identified as nonwhite or ethnic. Eighty-one percent of demonstrable "ethnic" characters were male. Women appeared more than men only in the categories of "domestic work" and "manual labor," and 80 percent of all characters featured in "adventure" or "leadership" roles were male. Male characters similarly had a broader range of roles, appearing in 90 separate activities, in comparison to the 55 activities in which female characters appeared. Global and multicultural perspectives in the software focused extensively on themes of war, colonization, aggression, and subjugation.[2]

A great many teachers surveyed for this report seem not to have noticed gender bias in software designed for the classroom. Twenty-one percent of the 900 tech-savvy teachers surveyed by the commission respond that they "don't know" how they would assess software for gender equity, a larger percentage of uncertain responses than for other questions. In response to an open-ended question that asked teachers to "describe the gender differences, if any, they have noted in educational software packages," more than half (58 percent) report that they have not observed any differences in the software, nor have they observed noteworthy gender patterns in use or content. A fair number say, "I haven't really noticed any, but haven't really looked for any, either."

When teachers do note gender bias—as did roughly 40 percent of the respondents to the Foundation's teacher survey—virtually all report that they feel the software caters to male students' interests or learning styles. "Most software 'feels' like it is targeted for boys: action packed, scoring points, winning situations," writes a teacher. "This is not how the teenage female mind works." Another observes, "If it calls for knocking things down or something, the girls perceive it as just for boys and they do not even bother with it. When it comes to communicating and creating writing and pictures, then the girls are way ahead of the boys. But one thing is for certain—when games are available during recess, nine times out of 10, the boys are [playing them]." Some teachers write of software that ascribes to girls what they characterize as "passive," "girly," "fluffy," or simply "traditional" roles. These teachers note that male characters "still get the juicy roles," the lion's share of "adventure" and "logic questions," and a "stronger and more competent" persona in the game. Others observe that girls' competencies and roles are linked to creative projects in software, with "action for boys and artsy stuff for girls."

Change: But in What Direction?

The commission believes that it is possible to have an impact on the game and software culture: The continuing growth of both industries depends on developing more of a relationship with girls. In recent years, the game industry has begun to target girls as a virtually untapped market niche. Analysts now predict that this segment of the computer entertainment market will experience the most dramatic growth of any in the coming years, expanding to more than $400 million in sales in the year 2000.

When the commission discussed possible directions for change in software, it began (as most people do) with Mattel's interactive CDs for girls, the computer games in the Barbie series. The first of these CDs was the Barbie Fashion Designer, in which users can design and fabricate dresses as well as select clothes for a virtual Barbie fashion show. The *New York Times* reported that "Barbie Fashion Designer sold half a million copies in its first two months—it is not only the biggest girl game on the market but the top-selling children's software title of all time."[3] Many consider Mattel's Barbie series as the signature "pink software"—software that is designed with girls' traditional interests in mind. Commissioners were divided in their opinions about pink software as an entry point for girls into computing. Some held very negative feelings, pointing out that the software is designed to include girls but it does so in a way that circumscribes their choices, often featuring them in passive, stereotypically "women's roles." Commissioner Yasmin Kafai's research shows that when the software industry uses market research paradigms to open up girls' markets, they create as much as they reflect gender-specific niches and, in the process, circumscribe the imaginations of both boys and girls.[4]

Other commissioners had less critical feelings about pink software. They argued that software has historically been "blue" for boys, "pandering" to male fantasies about violence and aggression. They noted that this software had made boys comfortable with computing: Boys grew into men who felt a sense of ownership of the computer culture. Why deny girls the same kind of access? Given the choice between killing and fashion designing, why criticize the latter? In the end, the commission was persuaded that some girls would develop a comfort with computing through games that are designed with conventionally feminine roles and tasks, but that the future of gender-equitable computing depends on rethinking the question of software. When girls from our focus groups describe the games and software that appeal to them, they speak about games that allow role playing, identity experiments, and simulations to work through real-life problems. If these were the attributes of pink software, few would object to them for either boys or girls. Indeed, one might well conclude that what would make girls more welcome in the software and game culture would enrich that culture for everyone—boys as well as girls.

○

Software targeted at a specific gender tends to deal with stereotypes too often. Software for girls tends to be frilly and cutesy, whereas material for boys tends to be tough and masculine. Software should be gender-neutral . . . as the real world is to a degree.

—teacher survey, on gender and software

○

To make play in the digital universe as appealing to girls as it now is to boys—and thereby to provide girls the same opportunities to encounter new technologies in a natural, playful way—digital play spaces have to become more sophisticated. They have to permit flexible decision-making, multiple stories, and perspectives, qualities that are not "girl-specific" so much as they are user-friendly, customizable, personalizable, and inviting to a range of players.

Token Gestures vs. Rethinking Games

It is not enough to make "token gestures" in software—as one teacher surveyed put it, "tossing a token female or black" into science software. As a solution to the problem, some teachers advocate the use of "neuter" characters: "Sometimes packages focus on male characters in their stories," one teacher writes. "But then again, sometimes software companies try to overcompensate because gender equity is such an issue that they make obvious and laughable attempts at creating female 'hero' characters. It's almost worse to try so darn hard. What's wrong with making the main character in these software packages be neuter?" A few other teachers find the effort to make "neuter" characters condescending and unreal. The world, after all, is not comprised of neutered bunnies. A few teachers suggest that since the characters presented in software are, in general, so far from students' experiences and life circumstances, the emphasis should be placed on making software that students are able to customize rather than trying to develop a set of characters that are appropriate for all.[5]

Differences of opinion over gender-neutral software are indicative of a larger state of confusion concerning software and equity. Parents, teachers, and school administrators shopping for "gender-equitable" software often lack criteria for selection. Even in the very few school districts that have gender equity criteria for the purchase of software, the criteria are fairly static, calling for "balanced representations" of cultural, ethnic, and racial groups. The criteria do not address design issues, play styles, or other less tangible content criteria.[6]

○

The problem with most gender issues within educational software is that they are gender-neutral. I teach eighth grade. [My students] are at an age when gender is something they are thinking about and confused about. The software should be addressing their needs instead of utilizing non-gendered beings such as animals and other animated creatures. Gender differences are not being given their just due. The students appreciate discussing the differences and negotiating roles. Even match programs can address differences.

—teacher survey, on gender and software

○

After their review of the literature on software, commissioners agreed that criteria for software selection and courseware evaluation needs to go beyond: "Is this software free of violent images?" or "Does this software involve clothes shopping?" Criteria must consider learning styles and students' attitudes toward computers to ensure that software does not appeal narrowly to only one (often male-identified) learning style or set of preferences. And criteria must consider models that empower students to be software "designers," to have greater control of their gaming environments. For example, Kafai's research finds that boys adopt more "female" design features in their game designs than vice versa, and demonstrate far more variability in their game preferences than is recognized in commercial models of "boys' " games. Hence, market research-driven paradigms of how to make games have gender appeal do not necessarily capture the range of interests and preferences that boys and girls would bring to games if they were put in the roles of empowered designers.[7]

○

Most programs are games and have no interaction between students or any other people.

—teacher survey, on gender and software

○

o

During my first year of teaching I taught a fourth-through-sixth-grade GATE class. After months of waiting, we finally received four computers for our classroom. My students strutted in and loudly exclaimed, "Show us the games! We've mastered them all." Since I've had a lot of training in multimedia and other aspects in technology education, I looked at them and said, "No, no, in this class we don't PLAY the games, we MAKE the games." Seeing all 31 pairs of eyes light up at that comment and become truly hooked in technology has been one of my favorite memories in seven years of teaching.

—teacher survey, on the "best moment" with technology

o

General Design Features

The girls who participated in focus groups for the Foundation's research were asked to design their ideal computer game for girls (software, online, or video) and to discuss their preferences among existing game options. For the most part, the girls describe characteristics that converge with some qualities that boys value in games, and challenge the notion that software should be designed and marketed to girls and boys as distinct market "niches." Appealing characteristics include:

- o Rich narrative and intricate, multi-level games. (Says a Richmond middle school teacher, "Make it a game where you have different options—each way you go there are different passages that lead you somewhere else.")
- o Engaging characters (preferably female or non-gendered, personalizable, and customizable).
- o Roles involving positive social action (such as guiding characters through a set of puzzles or challenges).
- o Challenge at the appropriate level of difficulty.
- o Social interaction both on-screen and between players—opportunities to build new relationships.
- o Opportunities to design or create. (One high school girl describes it this way: "Trivial Pursuit meets Tetris meets paintbrush.")
- o Strategy and skill requirements. (Says one respondent, "I like games that actually have like a strategy, not just shooting a gun at people.")[8]

Themes and Content

The girls in these focus groups say that they prefer games where they make things rather than destroy things. Many girls talk about computer games where they get to simulate real life, invent characters and personalities, or play with worldviews and identity on the screen. A Fairfax high school student imagines games where you "pick out a character, choose music, pick out a personality (job, hair, complexion), live [as the] person for a year, make their decisions, design a living space; [you] must give time to study for tests, must get an A at the end of the year to beat the game." She continues: "There would be a choice of being female or male. Then they would start in the morning and choose what they want to do that day. When they start the day, they would be faced with different situations, and, depending on how they choose to get out of the situation, it will become easier or harder." A middle school girl from Washington, D.C., would design "a video game for girls, telling the computer how your life has been and how you want it to be in the future, like a doll kind of thing." Other girls imagine more extensive identity games that entail the creation of personae and the building of worlds.[9]

○

The game would probably star a teenage girl. She would have to go through different challenges like choosing not to smoke, or real-life questions like that. It would help people not to ruin their lives and help people who might be having family problems, like parents who are getting divorced.

—Washington, D.C., middle school student

○

Many girls advocate games that simulate "realistic" adolescent experiences. Girls in the focus groups describe games in which characters must navigate the dangers and choices that are part of girls' lives—and of their lives. For example, one high school student from Baltimore says that her ideal games are closely related to everyday life: "My game would incorporate creativity, and it would be realistic, because I hate video games that are so fake." Girls elaborate these "real games" as ones where they can play out different life choices, especially those linked to gender roles and identity. Girls in these groups describe games that are the psychological and social extensions of popular girl software that involves cosmetic and wardrobe makeover and transformation. "The game would be based on real life, the action being in how you react in some situations," one middle school girl summarizes. Another high school girl imagines a game that shows different stages of growing up "so you learn from your mistakes and you can choose your own path. This way it can relate to everyone."

○

My game would be a game where you could describe your own image of a world that you would like it to be. Like you could design buildings, houses, whatever you would want the world to be.

—Baltimore high school student

○

A Richmond middle schooler writes a detailed account of a game with realistic scenarios and a moral message:

My game would be about a little girl in distress being saved and taken to freedom. The main figure would be a teenage girl between the ages of 16 and 18. The purpose would be to show girls how to overcome problems and fears. It would start with a girl facing boy problems with her parents at home, and lots of peer pressure. Different questions would come about and her answer to the questions would determine her outcome. During the game, different figures would appear, such as a teacher, a minister, and a friend. They would try to help her make a good choice or a bad choice, but the choice would be hers. At the end, if all the right choices were made, she would be greatly rewarded with her greatest desire.

○

Have a main character [a girl] who has missions to break stereotypes. For example, she would play baseball and win, and prove everyone wrong, or play a rock concert.

—Baltimore high school student

○

Other girls who describe games based on real adolescent experiences see the game as a "mentor," a proxy for parents or friends, perhaps, who could provide advice on topics that adults may not want to discuss. Realistic scenario games were particularly popular among two focus groups held with Hispanic and African American students. Some commissioners thought this may indicate a need for mentoring and positive images of problem solving. One student specifically describes a computer mentor— "someone or something that really does give you advice when you're going through a bad situation whether you're in school or anywhere. Also something that some parents don't want to discuss is sex, drugs, etc., and when your parents are divorced, a girl needs help on certain periods of her life to have your second parents."

[I want] something intellectual, fun, stimulating—[something that would] have tricky secrets that make you stop to think. The main figure, I don't really know, it wouldn't have to be a person—it could even consist of questions or pictures. The purpose would be to excel to higher levels nonstop. I would like it to take forever to win the game so it won't get boring.

—Washington, D.C., middle school student

By itself, becoming engaged in game-playing does not constitute technological fluency, but game and software cultures have been important factors in making boys and men feel comfortable with computing, and this path needs to be opened to girls and boys who have not found the style and themes of existing software appealing.

Nontraditional Software

Girls in many cases describe software characteristics that researchers have also found appealing to a wide variety of students, including those who are not "traditional" computer users. For example, in a study of third graders (ages eight to nine) in an urban elementary school, Anne L. Davidson and Janet W. Schofield observed the creation of a positive technology environment when one teacher offered children opportunities to use computers to develop relationships. The teacher used software that enabled children to build a virtual community. The particular software, known as MOO (short for multiple user, object-oriented) was used to engage children in reading and enhance their writing skills. The virtual environment contained storytellers, and the children could take on the roles of characters and have conversations with other users.[10]

○

The point would be to see what you would do in everyday situations, situations you may be faced with growing up.

—Richmond middle school student

○

Overall, Davidson and Schofield observed that girls who participated in this class showed decreased technical anxiety and increased technical confidence by the end of the course. Furthermore, girls developed new technical skills in the innovative MOO setting. Several features contributed to the teacher's success in creating an interesting and broadly appealing and equitable learning context: The teacher utilized an online environment that was not laden with traditionally masculine themes such as conquest. Instead, the online environment conveyed an inviting place for all students to communicate with others; the teacher played an active role in organizing students' work collaboratively. Students were assigned to work in pairs and the teacher rotated to different groups as they needed help. Collaboration eventually became the ethos of the whole class. Finally, the activities engaged girls' interests. They appreciated the ability to learn about online characters and to develop relationships online and off-line.

○

[I envision] students at computers, working on examples set up by teachers during lessons. The teacher could see who is understanding and who is not. Those who understand could move on, and those who need more instruction would receive it.

—teacher survey, on the future of the classroom

○

Another promising study explored games with gender-neutral themes and characters. Andee Rubin and her colleagues at TERC studied boys and girls using the CD-ROM "Logical Journey of the Zoombinis," a program designed to teach mathematics, logic, and set theory to eight-to-12-year-olds (third- to fifth-graders). The researchers found that while there were many individual differences in the ways students played the game, there was not a significant difference along gender lines. Software that engages both boys and girls, they conclude, tends to permit varied levels of collaboration, offer rich problems with multiple solutions, and provide a coherent, nonviolent narrative. Rubin writes that both boys and girls responded favorably to a "sense of conflict and potential resolution: The characters are in jeopardy and the player's actions can help them."[11]

○

Given the diverse ability levels of students and the emphasis on designing lessons appropriate for the individual student, I believe that computers and technology offer the best way to provide this. . . . Ironically, it seems that computers and technology will be the way to provide more personalized instruction tailored to individual interests and needs.

—teacher survey, on the future of the classroom

○

Sherry Hsi experimented with a tool to facilitate online discussions, investigating how students respond to anonymous and identified communication. Hsi found that students, especially female students, were more willing to participate when they could choose to remain anonymous than when all comments were attributed. She found that although the quality of contributions was similar for attributed and anonymous material, students had individual preferences for a particular format of discussion. In interviews, males and females both commented on the stereotyping that can occur in attributed electronic classroom discussions. Students believe that peer-anonymous discussions could open the discussion to more students. Students have the opportunity to get feedback on views that they fear might be ridiculed or misinterpreted by their peers in a face-to-face context. Adolescents are insecure and acutely worried about peer reception of their ideas. Women and minority students fear that their contributions, particularly about mathematics and science, might be received with prejudice. The opportunity to make anonymous comments in peer discussion allows these students to voice their own ideas without attracting potentially stereotyping responses.[12]

Finally, researcher Schofield analyzed the use of geometry computer "tutor" in several classrooms, and found that it allowed teachers to dispense more individualized attention and advice to their students. Further, it encouraged self-paced learning for slower and faster students, and introduced controls against students "skipping over" concepts in the curriculum that they did not truly understand. In partnership, rather than as substitutes for one another, the computer tutor and the teacher promoted more effective classroom techniques and individualized learning in unanticipated ways.[13]

Recommendations

Focus on Girls as Designers

Educators, parents, and others should help girls imagine themselves early in life as designers and producers of software and games, rather than as consumers or end users of games. Girls need opportunities at an early age to express their technological imaginations in a variety of media. Supporting activities that encourage girls to think further about the social history, purpose, function, and form of devices they see around them and envision for the future enable girls to become more attuned to observing, analyzing, and contributing to the built environment. This kind of activity paves the way for future hands-on technological design.

Rethink What Constitutes a "Girls' Game"
—and a "Boys' Game"

The computer game industry, educators, parents, software designers, and marketers do not need to label software specifically as "girls' games" or "boys' games"; instead, software for both classroom and home settings should focus on the many design elements that engage the interests of a broad range of learners, including both boys and girls, among them "nontraditional" computer users who do not identify with the "nerd" or "hacker" stereotypes.

The following 10 design characteristics are conducive to engaging a broader array of learners, boys and girls, with computer environments:

1. software that is personalizable and customizable. This type of software allows students to create their own characters, scenarios, and endings, and allows them to work independently or collaboratively

2. games with challenge

3. games involving more strategy and skill

4. games with many levels, intricacies, and complexities

5. flexibility to support multiple narratives

6. constructionist design—one that allows students to create their own objects through the software

7. designs that support collaborative or group work, and encourage social interaction

8. coherent, nonviolent narratives

9. "puzzle connections," such as rich mysteries with multiple resolutions

10. goal-focused rather than open-ended games

The following four content features have been found to be "girl friendly":

1. "identity games" that enable girls to experiment with characters and real-life scenarios. Some of these games enable girls to invent online personalities, identities, and worlds. Some of these games enable girls to experiment with choices about peer pressure, smoking, sexual relationships, etc., and "play out" the consequences of their action

2. software that has realistic as well as fantastical content; games that function as simulations of authentic contexts and situations

3. software structured around a conflict with potential resolution

4. games that have themes of mystery and adventure

Create a "Caldecott" Award for Software

Consumers—children, parents, educators, and school districts—need a "seal of approval" that denotes excellence in games just as the American Library Association's Caldecott medal recognizes excellence in picture books. The software "Caldecott" should reward games that are both "good" in that they engage the user's interest, and "equitable" in that they appeal to a variety of users. The American Association for the Advancement of Science is suggesting a similar strategy for books and films in science.

NOTES

1. School spending on software continues to increase, from $670 million in 1996 to $822 million in 1998. Software publishers, according to one report, are breaking up programs into "modules so that they can more easily be used to supplement than replace curricula." According to the most recent national survey of teachers, 53 percent use computer software. Charlene Blohm, *Software Publishers Association Education Market Report* (Washington, DC: Software Publishers Association, 1997); *Technology Counts '99*. On the interrelationship between educational software and games, see Dorothy Bennett, "Inviting Girls into Technology: Developing

Good Educational Practices," prepared for the AAUW Educational Foundation's Commission on Technology, Gender, and Teacher Education, 1999.

2. Carol Hodes, "Gender Representations in Mathematics Software," *Journal of Educational Technology Systems* 21, no. 1 (1995–96); Barbara Levin, "Children's Views of Technology: The Role of Age, Gender, and School Setting," *Journal of Computing in Childhood Education* 8, no. 4 (1997); Karen Birahimah, "The Non-Neutrality of Educational Computer Software," *Computer Education* 20, no. 4 (1993).

3. J. C. Herz, "Girls Just Want to Have Fun: When It Comes to Children's Software, Barbie Rules," *New York Times Book Review,* February 14, 1999; see Brunner, "Technology, Gender, and Education."

4. Yasmin Kafai, "Video Game Designs by Girls and Boys: Variability and Consistency of Gender Differences," in Justine Cassell and Henry Jenkins, eds., *From Barbie to Mortal Kombat: Gender and Computer Games* (Cambridge, MA: MIT Press, 1998).

5. For example, teachers note that when software depicts traditional family structures that don't reflect students' life experiences, students regard the software as coming from another world—an issue of social equity in computer that goes beyond the purview of this report.

6. Hsi, "Supporting Gender Equity through Design"; Software Publishers Association; EvaluTech "Criteria for Evaluation" CD ROMs, www.sret.sreb.org.

7. Maria Klawe found that boys, in fact, have a range of interests in games, and while violent games are popular, many boys prefer games that challenge them mentally. See Maria Klawe et al., "Exploring Common Conceptions About Boys and Electronic Games," *The Journal of Computers in Mathematics and Science Teaching* 14, no. 4 (1995). See Kafai, "Video Game Designs by Girls and Boys"; Kafai, *Minds in Play: Computer Game Design as a Context for Children's Learning* (Hillsdale, NJ: Lawrence Erlbaum Associates, 1995); Kafai, "Gender Differences in Children's Constructions of Video Games," in Patricia Greenfield and Rodney Cocking, eds., *Interacting with Video* (Greenwich, CT: Ablex Publishing Corporation, 1995); Kafai and Mitchel Resnick, eds., *Constructionism in Practice: Designing, Thinking, and Learning in a Digital World* (Mahwah, NJ: Lawrence Erlbaum Associates, 1996); Cornelia Brunner et al., "Girls' Games and Technological Desire," in *From Barbie to Mortal Kombat;* Andee Rubin et al., "What Kinds of Educational Computer Games Would Girls Like?" paper presented at the American Educational Research Association annual meeting, Boston, April 1997 [www.terc.edu/mathequity/gw/html/MITpaper.html].

8. On game characteristics, see Rubin, "What Kinds of Educational Computer Games Would Girls Like?"; K. R. Inkpen et al., " 'We Have Never-Forgetful Flowers in Our Garden': Girls' Responses to Electronic Games," *The Journal of Computers in Mathematics and Science Teaching* 13, no. 4 (1994); J. Mokros, Andee Rubin et al., "Where's the Math in Computer Games?" *Hands On!* 21, no. 2 (1998); M. J. Murray and M. Kliman, "Beyond Point and Click," *ENC Focus* (Washington, DC: Eisenhower National Clearinghouse, 2000); M. J. Murray, J. Mokros, and Andee Rubin, "Promoting Mathematically Rich, Equitable Game Software," in *Mathematics Teaching in the Middle School* (Washington, DC: National Council of Teachers of Mathematics, in press).

9. These findings are consistent with other research. While more boys than girls made positive comments about the sound and graphics in games, girls were often particularly invested in a game in which they could "design" some aspect of the characters—for example, their looks or personality. (Boys, in contrast, expressed interest in design primarily when it involved designing inanimate objects such as machines.) Rubin, "What Kind of Educational Computer Games Would Girls Like?" See Bennett, "Inviting Girls into Technology," for a summary of research on girls and games.

10. Anne L. Davidson and Janet W. Schofield, "Female Voices in Virtual Reality: Drawing Young Girls into an Online World," in K. A. Renninger and W. Schumer, eds., *Building Virtual Communities: Learning and Change in Cyberspace* (New York: Cambridge University Press, in press).

11. Chris Hancock and Scot Osterweil, "Zoombinis and the Art of Mathematical Play," Technology Education Research Center, 1996 [www.terc.edu /handson/s96/zoom.html]; Rubin, "What Kind of Educational Computer Games Would Girls Like?" See Hsi, "Supporting Gender Equity through Design" for a review of these programs.

12. Hsi, "Supporting Gender Equity through Design"; Hsi, "Facilitating Knowledge Integration in Science through Electronic Discussion: The Multimedia Forum Kiosk," Ph.D. diss., University of California, Berkeley (1997).

13. Janet Schofield, "Teachers, Computer Tutors, and Teaching: The Artificially Intelligent Tutor as an Agent for Classroom Change," *American Educational Research Journal* 31, no. 3 (1994). Among other qualities, the GP Tutor encouraged multiple learning styles and levels of expertise; helped to integrate computer technology into geometry, a subject that is not "about" computer technology, per se; helped to coordinate different mathematics ability levels in the classroom, as it allowed for self-paced learning; and

diminished the prohibitive consequences of students confessing to a lack of understanding. Further, the tutor allowed teachers to dispense assistance and help on a more individualized and private basis. These factors made computer technology in this example a valuable partner for better and more equitable learning.

16

THE EVADED CURRICULUM

American Association of University Women

THE EVADED CURRICULUM is the term coined in this report for matters central to the lives of students and teachers but touched upon only briefly, if at all, in most schools. These matters include the functioning of bodies, the expression and valuing of feelings, and the dynamics of power. In both formal course work and in the informal exchanges among teachers and students, serious consideration of these areas is avoided. When avoidance is not possible—as in the case of required health or sex-education courses—the material is often presented in a cursory fashion. Students are offered a set of facts devoid of references to the complex personal and moral dilemmas they face in understanding and making decisions about critical facets of their lives.

Youth is traditionally seen as a time of healthy bodies and carefree minds, but as numerous studies, reports, and television documentaries have outlined recently, young people in the United States are falling prey to what are being called the "new morbidities." These new morbidities are not necessarily caused by viruses or bacteria but rather by societal conditions that can lead young people into eating disorders, substance abuse, early sexual activity, unintended pregnancy, sexually transmitted diseases (including AIDS), and suicide.

Not only are many young people engaging in risky behaviors, frequently with lifetime consequences, but they are taking part in constellations of behaviors that are interrelated.[1] Young people who drink, for example, are far more likely than others to engage in unprotected sex or be involved in car accidents. Girls who are doing badly in school are five times as likely as others to become teen parents.[2] It is estimated that about one-quarter of all adolescents engage in multiple problem behaviors, often with devastating consequences.[3]

While the exact demographic makeup of the highest-risk groups is not known, data on separate risk behaviors indicate that there are more young males than females at high risk. When the different patterns of risk behavior are considered, however, it becomes clear that in some areas girls are at higher risk than their male classmates.

The health and well-being of young people are related to their ability to complete school.[4] It is obvious that girls who use drugs or liquor, suffer from depression, become pregnant, or give birth as teenagers cannot take full advantage of the educational programs presented them.

Substance Use

The initial use of harmful substances is occurring at younger ages than ever before. A recent survey showed that among the 1987 high school class, significant numbers of students first tried alcohol and drugs during elementary and middle school. Two out of three students using cigarettes began smoking before the ninth grade, and one out of four first used marijuana before the ninth grade. One out of twenty students who used cocaine used it before entering ninth grade.[5]

Differences between male and female patterns of reported drug use have declined over the past two decades to the point where researchers no longer consider the sex of an adolescent a good predictor of drug use.[6] One report states that "girls are more like boys in use of substances during adolescence than at any time later in life."[7] There are some sex differences in use patterns, however. Girls are more likely to use stimulants and over-the-counter weight-reduction pills, while boys are slightly more likely to report higher levels of illicit-drug use and episodes of binge drinking.[8] White high school students are more than twice as likely as black students to smoke cigarettes, and more white females are frequent smokers than students from any other sex/race group.[9]

Sexual Activity/Contraceptive Use

Initiation of sexual activity is also occurring at younger ages. Recent reports state that at least 28 percent of adolescents are sexually active by their fourteenth birthday; the average age at the initiation of sexual activity for this group is 12.[10] A recent survey from the Alan Guttmacher Institute indicates that 38 percent of girls between the ages of fifteen and seventeen are sexually active—a 15 percent increase since 1973.[11] There has been a dramatic increase in the numbers of sexually active teenage girls who are white or from higher-income families, reducing previous racial and income differences.[12]

Contraceptive use for adolescents remains erratic, and age is a significant factor, with younger adolescents using contraception far less frequently. Reasons adolescents give for not using contraception include (1) inadequate knowledge (both boys and girls state that they are not at risk of becoming involved in a pregnancy if they have unprotected sex), (2) lack of access to birth control, and (3) not liking to plan to have sex.[13]

DOES SEX EDUCATION TEACH WHAT GIRLS NEED TO KNOW?

Sex-education courses are particularly unenlightening about girls' physical and sexual development. Typically, the courses ignore female genital development and sexual response, often presenting the male body as the "norm."[1] For girls with physical disabilities, the absence of any mention of their particular circumstances, and indeed the too-often-made assumption that they are not sexual beings, further complicates the development of a positive sense of self. Even discussion of menstruation is inadequate and has been criticized as little more than a reinforcement of the menstrual taboo, to the extent that it treats menstruation as a hygienic crisis, emphasizes negative rather than positive aspects of the cycle, fails to address girls' psychosocial concerns about menstruation, and relies predominantly on a sex-segregated format.[2] All of these aspects combine to create an association of shame rather than pride with this aspect of female development.[3]

In early adolescence girls feel particularly vulnerable to boys teasing about menstruation.[4] When menstrual education is provided only for girls, the stage is set for suspicion rather than understanding between the sexes. With a limited forum in which to ask their questions and limited guidance about appropriate responses from either adults or female peers, boys express inappropriate responses that can be cruel and harassing to girls.

Even though girls may not want boys, fathers, or brothers to know about their particular menstruation, girls do wish boys knew more about menstruation in general.[5] The availability of more inclusive teaching about menstruation within the school setting might broaden boys' understanding, discourage their teasing, and make school more comfortable for girls.

1. E. Breit and M. Myerson, "Social Dimensions of the Menstrual Taboo and the Effects on Female Sexuality," in *Psychology of*

Women: Selected Readings, ed. J. Williams (New York: Norton, 1979); M. Fine, "Sexuality, Schooling, and Adolescent Females: The Missing Discourse of Desire," *Harvard Educational Review* 58 (1988): 29–53; J. Rury, "We Teach the Girl Repression, the Boy Expression: Sexuality, Sex Equity and Education in Historical Perspective," *Peabody Journal of Education* 64 (1989: 44–58); M. Whatley, "Goals for Sex Equitable Education," *Peabody Journal of Education* 64 (1989): 59–70.

2. Breit and Myerson, "Social Dimensions"; L. Whisnant, E. Brett, and L. Zegas, "Implicit Messages Concerning Menstruation in Commercial Educational Materials Prepared for Young Girls," *American Journal of Psychiatry* 132 (1975): 15–20; M. Stubbs, J. Rierdan, and E. Koff, "Becoming a Woman: Considerations in Educating Adolescents and Menstruation," Working Paper No. 160 (Wellesley, MA: Wellesley College Center for Research on Women, 1989); M. Stubbs, *Sex Education and Sex Stereotypes: Theory and Practice,* Working Paper No. 198 (Wellesley, MA: Wellesley College Center for Research on Women, 1989); J. Rierdan, E. Koff, and J. Flaherty, "Conception and Misconceptions of Menstruation," *Women and Health* 10 (1985): 33–45; M. Stubbs, *Bodytalk* (Wellesley, MA: Wellesley College Center for Research on Women, 1990).

3. Breit and Myerson, "Social Dimensions"; Stubbs, *Bodytalk.*

4. Stubbs, Sex Education and Sex Stereotypes.

5. B. Havens and I. Swenson, "Menstrual Perceptions and Preparation among Female Adolescents," *Journal of Obstetric, Gynecologic and Neonatal Nursing* 15 (1986): 406–11.

Before age fifteen, only 31 percent of sexually active girls report using contraceptives. By age fifteen, only 58 percent report contraceptive use; but by age nineteen, 91 percent report that they use contraceptives.[14] Meanwhile, there is some preliminary evidence that condom use is increasing; among seventeen- to nineteen-year-old males in metropolitan areas, reports of condom use at last intercourse more than doubled in the last decade—from 21 percent in 1979 to 58 percent in 1988.[15] Because of increased condom use, the proportion of teens using contraception at first intercourse rose from half to two-thirds between 1982 and 1988.[16] Unprotected sexual intercourse can result in too-early childbearing, discussed in detail earlier in this report. It can also result in sexually transmitted diseases (STDs).

○

○

"Rates of physical and emotional abuse for boys and girls are very similar, but rates of sexual abuse are four times higher for girls, and their abusers are overwhelmingly male."

—J. Gans and D. Blyth, *America's Adolescents: How Healthy Are They?* (Chicago: American Medical Association, 1990), p. 20.

○

Sexually Transmitted Diseases

Syphilis rates are equal for boys and girls, but more adolescent females than males contract gonorrhea.[17]

More than 1 million teens each year suffer from chlamydia infections, the most common STD among adolescents. Researchers speculate that teenage girls suffer high rates of STDs because the female reproductive system is particularly vulnerable during the early teen years.[18]

Nearly 715 teenagers age thirteen to nineteen have diagnosed cases of AIDS.[19] The number with HIV infection, which normally precedes AIDS, is much higher. The HIV infection rate for teenage girls is comparable to, and in some cases higher than, that for boys. While among adults, male AIDS cases are nine times more prevalent than female cases, the pattern of HIV infection among adolescents is very different. A 1989 study in the District of Columbia reports the HIV infection rate at 4.7 per 1,000 for girls, almost three times the 1.7 rate for boys.[20]

Other researchers who have been following the incidence of AIDS nationally state that teenage girls between thirteen and nineteen represent 24.9 percent of reported cases among females.[21] Women make up the fastest-growing group of persons with AIDS in the United States. The Centers for Disease Control (CDC) acknowledges that the number of reported cases is probably underestimated by 40 percent and the undercounting of women is probably more severe than for other groups because many of their symptoms are not listed in the CDC surveillance definition.[22]

Furthermore, there are differences in how AIDS is transmitted between men and women. Many more women (32.7 percent) than men (2.3 percent) become infected through a heterosexual contact; more women than men also contract AIDS through intravenous drug use.[23]

Body Image/Eating Disorders

Girls are much less satisfied with their bodies than are boys and report eating disorders at far higher rates. For example, more girls than boys report food bingeing and chronic dieting. They are also more likely to report vomiting to control their weight.[24] Severe cases of bulimia (binge eating followed by forced vomiting) and anorexia nervosa (the refusal to maintain an adequate body weight) can cause death.

Depression

An important longitudinal research study recently noted evidence of increasingly early onset and high prevalence of depression in late adolescence, with slightly more girls than boys scoring in the high range of depressive symptomology. One of the most striking findings of the study is that severely depressed girls had higher rates of substance abuse than did similarly depressed boys. Significant gender differences were found in school performance measures among the most depressed students. Grade point averages were lower for girls, and 40 percent more girls failed a grade than boys.[25]

Suicide

Adolescent girls are four to five times more likely than boys to attempt suicide (although boys are more likely to die because they choose more lethal methods, for example guns rather than sleeping pills).

A recent survey of eighth- and tenth-graders found girls are twice as likely as boys to report feeling sad and hopeless. This is consistent with clinical literature, which shows that females have higher rates of depression than males, during both adolescence and adulthood.[26]

Cohesive families, neighborhoods with adequate resources, caring adults, and quality schools all help protect teens.[27] But because the dangers they face result from a complex web of interactive social conditions and behaviors, there can be no single solution. For any program to succeed in reducing risks to teens, policymakers at every level must recognize that the needs and circumstances of girls and young women often differ from those of boys and young men.

The Functioning of Healthy Bodies

In spite of reports indicating strong public support for sex education in the schools and an increase in the number of sex-education programs offered, sex education is neither widespread nor comprehensive.[28] Few schools include sex education in the early grades, and most middle and junior high schools offer short programs of ten hours or less. It has been estimated that fewer than 10 percent of all students take comprehensive sex-education courses, i.e., courses of more than 40 hours or courses designed as components within a K–12 developmental-health or sex-education program.[29]

For most teachers, knowledge of human sexuality is largely a matter of personal history rather than informed study.[30] Such knowledge is often based on traditional male-defined views of human sexuality, including unexamined gender-role-stereotyped beliefs about sexual behavior. Knowledge about sexual development is usually limited, regardless of whether the teacher is male or female.

The content of sex-education classes varies from locale to locale, in part because program planners must address local sensitivities.[31] One of the few carefully controlled field studies on sexuality- and contraceptive-education programs recently compared the impact of a special sex-education class on thirteen- to nineteen-year-old males and females.[32] The findings indicate that publicly funded sexuality- and contraceptive-education programs as brief as eight to twelve hours appear to help participants increase their knowledge, initiate effective contraceptive use, and improve the consistent use of effective contraceptive methods by both girls and boys.

> The assumption of heterosexuality is a form of discrimination that is rarely discussed but that has an indelible impact on the roughly 10 percent of our youth who are homosexual or bisexual. By never raising the issue of sexual orientation as a legitimate developmental issue, by not placing informative and nonpejorative books in the school library, and by not seriously confronting homophobia in the classrooms schools abdicate their responsibility not only to adolescents who are questioning their individual sexual orientation but to all students. Homosexual girls and boys face many of the same difficulties, but lesbian students—like girls in general—are more often invisible. The few discussions of homosexuality that do occur tend to focus on gay men.

The experimental intervention appears to have been most helpful for males with prior sexual experience, improving the consistency of their use of effective methods of contraception. Females without prior sexual experience seemed to respond better to traditional sex-education programs; researchers hypothesize that the girls may have been uncomfortable with the structured, interactive, and confrontational aspects of the experimental program. The study also found that prior experience with sex education was an important predictor of contraceptive efficiency, suggesting that formal sexuality education may be an incremental learning process whose efforts may not be evident on short-term follow-up.

The absence of adequate instruction and discussion about menstruation and contraception is only a piece of the problem. The alarming increases in STDs and HIV infection among adolescents, the increase in childbearing among young teens, and the increase in eating disorders make the lack of comprehensive courses on sexuality, health, and the human body unacceptable. An understanding of one's body is center to an understanding of self. The association of sexuality and health instruction exclusively with danger and disease belies the human experience of the body as a source of pleasure, joy, and comfort. Schools must take a broader, more comprehensive approach to education about growth and sexuality. An awareness that relationships with others and the development of intimacy involve both the body and the mind should be critical components of these courses.

The Expression and Valuing of Feelings

By insisting on a dichotomy between feelings and emotions on the one hand, and logic and rationality on the other, schools shortchange all students. Classrooms must become places where girls and boys can express feelings and discuss personal experiences. The lessons we learn best are those that answer our own questions. Students must have an opportunity to explore the world as they see it and pose problems that they consider important. From Sylvia Ashton Warner to AAUW teacher awardee Judy Logan, good teachers have always known this and have reflected it in their teaching.[33] The schools must find ways to facilitate these processes.

When this is done, issues that may not always be considered "appropriate" will undoubtedly arise. They should. Child abuse is a brutal fact of too many young lives. Children must have a "safe place" to acknowledge their pain and vulnerability and receive help and support. While girls and boys are more or less equally subjected to most forms of physical and emotional abuse, girls confront sexual abuse at four times the rate of boys.

We need to help all children, particularly girls, to know and believe that their bodies are their own to control and use as they feel appropriate— and not objects to be appropriated by others.[34] This, of course, is particularly difficult in a culture that uses the female body to advertise everything from toilet cleanser to truck tires and where the approved female roles remain service-oriented. The so-called "womanly" values of caring for and connecting with others are not ones that women wish to lose, but they are values that must be buttressed by a sense of self and a faith in one's own competence.

> "Public schools posit separate spheres, that is, they presume that what goes on in school—the public—should be separated from what goes on out of school—the private. Issues that young women experience as private and personal—even if they affect large numbers of adolescents across social classes and racial and ethnic groups—are reserved for discussion inside counselors' offices rather than in classrooms. That domestic violence was a secret not to be discussed in social studies, English, or science, but only in the protected offices of a school psychologist or guidance counselor marks a betrayal of these young women's lives."
>
> —M. Fine and N. Zane, "Bein' Wrapped Too Tight:
> When Low-Income Women Drop Out of High School,"
> *Women's Studies Quarterly* 19 (Spring/Summer 1991):85.

In July 1991, *Newsweek* ran a story titled "Girls Who Go Too Far," about the newly aggressive pursuit of boyfriends by some young teens.[35] The comments of the girls themselves illustrate their dilemma in having grown up to believe that a man is an essential part of every woman's life, that only male attention can give them a sense of themselves, and that the culturally accepted way to achieve a goal is to resort to aggressive, even violent, behavior.

Rather than highlighting aggressive behavior among girls, we must address the degree to which violence against women is an increasingly accepted aspect of our culture. School curricula must help girls to understand the extent to which their lives are constrained by fear of rape, the possibility of battering, and the availability of pornography. Boys must be helped to understand that violence damages both the victim and the perpetrator, and that violence against women is not in a somehow-more-acceptable category than other violent acts. The energies and passions so routinely expressed in violence toward others in our culture must be rechanneled and redirected if our society is to fulfill its promise.

A strong line of feminist research and thinking, including the work of Jane Roland Martin, Jean Baker Miller, Carol Gilligan, Nel Noddings, and Mary Belenky and her colleagues, addresses the strengths girls and women can bring to communities through the sense of connection with and concern for others that is more often encouraged and "permitted" in their lives than it is in boys'.[36] Others, such as Alfie Kohn, have written extensively about the need for schools that can help students learn and grow as part of a "prosocial" community.[37] A democracy cannot survive without citizens capable of seeing beyond immediate self-interest to the needs of the larger group.

When asked to describe their ideal school, one group of young women responded:

> "School would be fun. Our teachers would be excited and lively, not bored. They would act caring and take time to understand how students feel . . . . Boys would treat us with respect . . . . If they run by and grab your tits, they would get into trouble."[38]

Care, concern, and respect—simple things, but obviously not the norm in many of our nation's classrooms. These young women are not naïve. Their full statement recognizes the need to pay teachers well and includes a commitment to "learn by listening and consuming everything" as well as a discussion of parental roles.[39] What they envision is needed by their male classmates and their teachers as well; it is what we as a nation must provide.

---

o

"It's important to have a guy so I can feel loved. It doesn't matter if he's ugly or disgusting as long as he pays attention to me."

—Junior high student, age fourteen,
"Girls Who Go Too Far," *Newsweek,* July 22, 1991.

o

Gender and Power

Data presented earlier in this report reveal the extent to which girls and boys are treated differently in school classrooms and corridors. These data themselves should be a topic of discussion. They indicate power differentials that are perhaps the most evaded of all topics in our schools. Students are all too aware of "gender politics." In a recent survey, students in Michigan were asked, "Are there any policies, practices, including the behavior of teachers in classrooms, that have the effect of treating students differently based on their sex?" One hundred percent of the middle school and 82 percent of the high school students responding said "yes."[40]

Gender politics is a subject that many in our schools may prefer to ignore, but if we do not begin to discuss more openly the ways in which ascribed power, whether on the basis of race, sex, class, sexual orientation, or religion, affects individual lives, we will not be truly preparing our students for citizenship in a democracy.

NOTES

1. R. Jessor, "Risk Behavior in Adolescence: A Psychosocial Framework for understanding and Action," paper prepared for Cornell University Medical College Conference "Adolescents at Risk: Medical and Social Perspectives," Cornell University, February 1991; J. Dryfoos, *Youth at Risk: Prevalence and Prevention* (Oxford: Oxford University Press, 1990).

2. *Preventing Adolescent Pregnancy: What Schools Can Do* (Washington, DC: Children's Defense Fund, 1986).

3. Dryfoos, *Youth at Risk,* p. 107.

4. J. Earle and V. Roach, "Female Dropouts: A New Perspective," in *Women's Educational Equity Act Publishing Center Digest* (Newton, MA: Education Development Center, 1988); M. Fine, *Framing Dropouts* (Albany, NY: State University of New York Press, 1991).

5. J. Gans and D. Blyth, *America's Adolescents: How Healthy Are They?* (Chicago, IL: American Medical Association, 1990), p. 28.

6. H. Adger, "Problems of Alcohol and Other Drug Use and Abuse in Adolescence," paper prepared for Cornell University Medical College Conference "Adolescents at Risk: Medical and Social Perspectives," Cornell University, February 1991.

7. *Facts and Reflections on Girls and Substance Use* (New York: Girls Clubs of America, Inc., 1988), p. 9.

8. Adger, "Problems of Alcohol."

9. U.S. Centers for Disease Control, Youth Risk Behavior Survey, quoted in Ellen Flax, "White Students Twice as Likely as Blacks to Smoke, Study Finds," *Education Week* 11 (September 1991):10.

10. D. Scott-Jones and A. White, "Correlates of Sexual Activity in Early Adolescence," *Journal of Early Adolescence* 10 (May 1990):221–38; Dryfoos, *Youth at Risk,* chart p. 67.

11. D. Forrest and S. Singh, "The Sexual and Reproductive Behavior of American Women," *Family Planning Perspectives* 22 (1990):208, Table 4.

12. C. Irwin and M. Shafer, "Adolescent Sexuality: The Problem of a Negative Outcome of a Normative Behavior," paper prepared for the Cornell University

Medical College Conference "Adolescents at Risk: Medical and Social Perspectives," Cornell University, February 1991.

13. M. Sullivan, *The Male Role in Teenage Pregnancy and Parenting: New Directions for Public Policy* (New York: Vera Institute of Justice, 1990), p. 21.

14. Irwin and Shafer, "Adolescent Sexuality."

15. Children's Defense Fund, unpublished paper, Washington, DC, 1991.

16. K. Moore, *Facts at a Glance* (Washington, DC: Child Trends, 1988). See also K. Moore, "Trends in Teenage Childbearing in the U.S.: 1970–1988" (Los Alamitos, CA: TEC Networks, March 1991).

17. Irwin and Shafer, "Adolescent Sexuality."

18. Ibid.

19. Quoted over the phone by the National AIDS Clearing House from U.S. Centers for Disease Control, *U.S. AIDS Cases Reported in July 1991*, 1991.

20. L. D'Angelo et al., "HIV Infection in Adolescents: Can We Predict Who Is at Risk?" poster presentation at the Fifth International Conference on AIDS, June 1989.

21. M. Wolfe, "Women and HIV/AIDS Education," paper prepared for the NEA Health Information Network, Atlanta, 1991.

22. Ibid.

23. Ibid.

24. *The State of Adolescent Health in Minnesota*, Minnesota Youth Health Survey (Minneapolis: Adolescent Health Database Project, February 1989).

25. H. Reinherz, A. Frost, and B. Pakiz, *Changing Faces: Correlates of Depressive Symptoms in Late Adolescence* (Boston: Simmons College School of Social Work, 1990).

26. Gans and Blyth, *America's Adolescents*, p. 11.

27. D. Hawkins, "Risk Focussed Prevention," speech to the Coordinating Council on Juvenile Justice and Delinquency Prevention, 1990; Jessor, "Risk Behavior"; J. Gibbs, *Not Schools Alone* (Sacramento, CA: California Department of Education, 1990); E. Werner, "Vulnerability and Resiliency: The Children of Kauai," paper presented at a conference on Vulnerability and Resiliency in Children and Families, Baltimore, March 1991.

28. U.S. National Research Council, Panel on Adolescent Pregnancy and Childbearing, C. Hayes, ed., *Risking the Future: Adolescent Sexuality, Pregnancy, and Childbearing* (Washington, DC: National Academy, 1987).

29. Hayes, *Risking the Future;* D. Kirby, *Sexuality Education: An Evaluation of Programs and Their Effects* (Santa Cruz: Network Publications, 1984); J. Leo, "Sex and Schools," *Time* (November 1986):54–60.

30. M. Stubbs, *Sex Education and Sex Stereotypes: Theory and Practice,* Working Paper No. 198 (Wellesley, MA: Wellesley College Center for Research on Women, ERIC Document Service No. 306–655, 1989), p. 7.

31. Ibid., p. 8; M. Rotheram-Borus et al., "Reducing HIV Sexual Risk Behaviors among Runaway Adolescents," *Journal of the American Medical Association* 266 (4 September 1991):1237–41.

32. M. Eisen, G. Zellman, and A. McAlister, "Evaluating the Impact of a Theory-Based Sexuality and Contraceptive Education Program," *Family Planning Perspectives* 22 (November/December 1990):261–71; M. Rotheram-Borus et al., "Reducing HIV Sexual Risk Behaviors."

33. S. Ashton-Warner, *Teacher* (New York: Simon and Schuster, 1963); J. Logan, *Teaching Stories,* paper presented at the American Association of University Women Fellowship, Washington, DC, 1991.

34. For some disabled girls and women, issues surrounding control and ownership of their own bodies are particularly problematic. For a full discussion of many of these issues see M. Fine and A. Asch, eds., *Women with Disabilities: Essays in Psychology, Culture, and Politics* (Philadelphia, PA: Temple University Press, 1988).

35. Emily Yoffe, "Girls Who Go Too Far," *Newsweek,* 22 July 1991, pp. 58–59.

36. J. Martin, *Reclaiming a Conversation: The Ideal of the Educated Woman* (New Haven, CT: Yale University Press, 1985); J. Miller, *Toward a New Psychology of Women* (Boston, MA: Beacon Press, 1976); C. Gilligan, N. Lyons, and T. Hammer, eds., *Making Connections: The Relational Worlds of Adolescent Girls at the Emma Willard School* (Troy, NY: Emma Willard School, 1989); C. Gilligan et al., eds., *Mapping the Moral Domain: A Contribution of Women's Thinking to Psychological Theory and Education* (Cambridge, MA: Harvard University Press, 1988); N. Noddings and P. Shore, *Awakening the Inner Eye: Intuition in Education* (New York: Teachers College Press, 1984); N. Noddings, *Caring: A Feminine Approach to Ethics and Moral Education* (Berkeley, CA: University of California Press, 1984); C. Witherell and N. Noddings, *Stories Lives Tell: Narrative and Dialogue in Education* (New York: Teachers College Press, 1991); M. Belenky et al., *Women's Ways of Knowing: The Development of Self, Voice, and Mind* (New York: Basic Books, 1986); see also P. Elbow, *Writing without Teachers* (London: Oxford University Press, 1973).

37. A. Kohn, "Caring Kids: The Role of the School," *Phi Delta Kappan* 72 (March 1991):496–506; A. Kohn, "Responding to Others: The Child Development Project," *The Brighter Side of Human Nature* (New York: Basic Books, 1990).

38. As quoted in *In Their Own Voices: Young Women Talk about Dropping Out,* Project on Equal Education Rights (New York: National Organization for Women Legal Defense and Education Fund, 1988), p. 12.

39. Ibid.

40. State of Michigan, Department of Education, Office of Sex Equity in Education, "The Influence of Gender Role Socialization on Student Perceptions," June 1990.

17

SEXUALITY, SCHOOLING, AND ADOLESCENT FEMALES

THE MISSING DISCOURSE

OF DESIRE

Michelle Fine

SINCE LATE 1986, popular magazines and newspapers have printed steamy stories about education and sexuality. Whether the controversy surrounds sex education or school-based health clinics (SBHCs), public discourses of adolescent sexuality are represented forcefully by government officials, New Right spokespersons, educators, "the public," feminists, and health-care professionals. These stories offer the authority of "facts," insights into the political controversies, and access to unacknowledged fears about sexuality.[1] Although the facts usually involve the adolescent female body, little has been heard from young women themselves.

This article examines these diverse perspectives on adolescent sexuality and, in addition, presents the views of a group of adolescent females. The article is informed by a study of numerous current sex education curricula, a year of negotiating for inclusion of lesbian and gay sexuality in a citywide sex education curriculum, and interviews and observations gathered in New York City sex education classrooms.[2] The analysis examines the desires, fears, and fantasies which give structure and shape to silences and voices concerning sex education and school-based health clinics in the 1980s.

Despite the attention devoted to teen sexuality, pregnancy, and parenting in this country, and despite the evidence of effective interventions and the widespread public support expressed for these interventions,[3] the systematic implementation of sex education and SBHCs continues to be obstructed by the controversies surrounding them.[4] Those who resist sex education or SBHCs often present their views as based on rationality and a concern for protecting the young. For such opponents, sex education raises questions of promoting promiscuity and immorality, and of undermining family values. Yet the language of the challenges suggests an affect substantially more profound and primitive. Gary Bauer, Undersecretary of Education in the U.S. Department of Education, for example, constructs an image of immorality littered by adolescent sexuality and drug abuse:

> There is ample impressionistic evidence to indicate that drug abuse and promiscuity are not independent behaviors. When inhibitions fall, they collapse across the board. When people of any age lose a sense of right and wrong, the loss is not selective. . . . [T]hey are all expressions of the same ethical vacuum among many teens.[5]

Even Surgeon General C. Everett Koop, a strong supporter of sex education, recently explained: "[W]e have to be as explicit as necessary. . . . You can't talk of the dangers of snake poisoning and not mention snakes."[6] Such commonly used and often repeated metaphors associate adolescent sexuality with victimization and danger.

Yet public schools have rejected the task of sexual dialogue and critique, or what has been called "sexuality education." Within today's standard sex education curricula and many public school classrooms, we find: (1) the authorized suppression of a discourse of female sexual desire; (2) the promotion of a discourse of female sexual victimization; and (3) the explicit privileging of married heterosexuality over other practices of sexuality. One finds an unacknowledged social ambivalence about female sexuality which ideologically separates the female sexual agent, or subject, from her counterpart, the female sexual victim. The adolescent woman of the 1980s is constructed as the latter. Educated primarily as the potential victim of male sexuality, she represents no subject in her own right. Young women continue to be taught to fear and defend in isolation from exploring desire, and in this context there is little possibility of their developing a critique of gender or sexual arrangements.

Prevailing Discourses of Female Sexuality Inside Public Schools

> If the boy is seen as endangered by uncontrollable forces, then presumably this is a society or social group which fears change—change which it perceived simultaneously as powerful and beyond its control.[7]

Public schools have historically been the site for identifying, civilizing, and containing that which is considered uncontrollable. While evidence of sexuality is everywhere within public high schools—in the halls, classrooms, bathrooms, lunchrooms, and the library—official sexuality education occurs sparsely: in social studies, biology, sex education, or inside the nurse's office. To understand how sexuality is managed inside schools, I examined the major discourses of sexuality which characterize the national debates over sex education and SBHCs. These discourses are then tracked as they weave through the curricula, classrooms, and halls of public high schools.

The first discourse, *sexuality as violence,* is clearly the most conservative, and equates adolescent heterosexuality with violence. At the 1986 American Dreams Symposium on education, Phyllis Schlafly commented: "Those courses on sex, abuse, incest, AIDS, they are all designed to terrorize our children. We should fight their existence, and stop putting terror in the hearts and minds of our youngsters." One aspect of this position, shared by women as politically distinct as Schlafly and the radical feminist lawyer Catherine MacKinnon, views heterosexuality as essentially violent and coercive.[8] In its full conservative form, proponents call for the elimination of sex education and clinics and urge complete reliance on the family to dictate appropriate values, mores, and behaviors.

Sexuality as violence presumes that there is a causal relationship between official silence about sexuality and a decrease in sexual activity—therefore, by not teaching about sexuality, adolescent sexual behavior will not occur. The irony, of course, lies in the empirical evidence. Fisher, Byrne, and White have documented sex-negative attitudes and contraceptive use to be negatively correlated. In their study, sex-negative attitudes do not discourage sexual activity, but they do discourage responsible use of contraception. Teens who believe sexual involvement is wrong deny responsibility for contraception. To accept responsibility would legitimate "bad" behavior.[9] By contrast, Fisher et al. found that adolescents with sex-positive attitudes tend to be both more consistent and more positive about contraceptive use. By not teaching about sexuality, or by teaching sex-negative attitudes, schools apparently will not forestall sexual activity, but may well discourage responsible contraception.[10]

The second discourse, *sexuality as victimization*, gathers a much greater following. Female adolescent sexuality is represented as a moment of victimization in which the dangers of heterosexuality for adolescent women (and, more recently, of homosexuality for adolescent men) are prominent. While sex may not be depicted as inherently violent, young women (and today, men) learn of their vulnerability to potential male predators.

To avoid being victimized, females learn to defend themselves against disease, pregnancy, and "being used." The discourse of victimization supports sex education, including AIDS education, with parental consent. Suggested classroom activities emphasize "saying no," practicing abstinence, enumerating the social and emotional risks of sexual intimacy, and listing the possible diseases associated with sexual intimacy. The language, as well as the questions asked and not asked, represents females as the actual and potential victims of male desire. In exercises, role plays, and class discussions, girls practice resistance to trite lines, unwanted hands, opened buttons, and the surrender of other "bases" they are not prepared to yield. The discourses of violence and victimization both portray males as potential predators and females as victims. Three problematic assumptions underlie these two views:

○ First, female subjectivity, including the desire to engage in sexual activity, is placed outside the prevailing conversation.[11]

○ Second, both arguments present female victimization as contingent upon unmarried heterosexual involvement—rather than inherent in existing gender, class, and racial arrangements.[12] While feminists have long fought for the legal and social acknowledgment of sexual violence against women, most have resisted the claim that female victimization hinges primarily upon sexual involvement with men. The full range of victimization of women—at work, at home, on the streets—has instead been uncovered. The language and emotion invested in these two discourses divert attention away from structures, arrangements, and relationships which oppress women in general, and low-income women and women of color in particular.[13]

○ Third, the messages, while narrowly anti-sexual, nevertheless buttress traditional heterosexual arrangements. These views assume that as long as females avoid premarital sexual relations with men, victimization can be avoided. Ironically, however, protection from male victimization is available primarily through marriage—by coupling with a man. The paradoxical message teaches females to fear the very men who will ultimately protect them.

The third discourse, *sexuality as individual morality,* introduces explicit notions of sexual subjectivity for women. Although quite judgmental and moralistic, this discourse values women's sexual decisionmaking as long as the decisions made are for premarital abstinence. For example, Secretary of Education William Bennett urges schools to teach "morality literacy" and to educate towards "modesty," "chastity," and "abstinence" until marriage. The language of self-control and self-respect reminds students that sexual immorality breeds not only personal problems but also community tax burdens.

The debate over morality in sex education curricula marks a clear contradiction among educational conservatives over whether and how the state may intervene in the "privacy of families." Non-interventionists, including Schlafly and Onalee McGraw, argue that educators should not teach about sexuality at all. To do so is to take a particular moral position which subverts the family. Interventionists, including Koop, Bennett, and Bauer, argue that schools should teach about sexuality by focusing on "good values," but disagree about how. Koop proposes open discussion of sexuality and the use of condoms, while Bennett advocates "sexual restraint."[14] Sexuality in this discourse is posed as a test of self-control; individual restraint triumphs over social temptation. Pleasure and desire for women as sexual subjects remain largely in the shadows, obscured from adolescent eyes.

The fourth discourse, a *discourse of desire,* remains a whisper inside the official work of U.S. public schools. If introduced at all, it is as an interruption of the ongoing conversation.[15] The naming of desire, pleasure, or sexual entitlement, particularly for females, barely exists in the formal agenda of public schooling on sexuality. When spoken, it is tagged with reminders of "consequences"—emotional, physical, moral, reproductive, and/or financial.[16] A genuine discourse of desire would invite adolescents to explore what feels good and bad, desirable and undesirable, grounded in experiences, needs, and limits. Such a discourse would release females from a position of receptivity, enable an analysis of the dialectics of victimization and pleasure, and would pose female adolescents as subjects of sexuality, initiators as well as negotiators.[17]

In Sweden, where sex education has been offered in schools since the turn of the century, the State Commission on Sex Education recommends teaching students to "acquire a knowledge . . . [which] will equip them to experience sexual life as a source of happiness and joy in fellowship with other [people]."[18] The teachers' handbook goes on, "The many young people who wish to wait [before initiating sexual activity] and those who have had early sexual relations should experience, in class, [the feeling] that they are understood and accepted."[19] Compare this to an exercise suggested in a major U.S. metropolitan sex education curriculum: "Discuss and evaluate: things which may cause teenagers to engage in sexual relations before they are ready to assume the responsibility of marriage."[20]

A discourse of desire, though seldom explored in U.S. classrooms, does occur in less structured school situations. The following excerpts, taken from group and individual student interviews, demonstrate female adolescents' subjective experiences of body and desire as they begin to articulate notions of sexuality.

In some cases young women pose a critique of marriage:

> I'm still in love with Simon, but I'm seeing Jose. He's OK but he said, "Will you be my girl?" I hate that. It feels like they own you. Like I say to a girlfriend, "What's wrong? You look terrible!" and she says, "I'm married!" (Millie, a 16-year-old student from the Dominican Republic)

In other cases they offer stories of their own victimization:

> It's not like last year. Then I came to school regular. Now my old boyfriend, he waits for me in front of my building every morning and he fight with me. Threatens me, gettin' all bad. . . . I want to move out of my house and live 'cause he ain't gonna stop no way. (Sylvia, age 17, about to drop out of twelfth grade)

Some even speak of desire:

> I'm sorry I couldn't call you last night about the interview, but my boyfriend came back from [the] Navy and I wanted to spend the night with him, we don't get to see each other much. (Shandra, age 17, after a no-show for an interview)

In a context in which desire is not silenced, but acknowledged and discussed, conversations with adolescent women can, as seen here, educate through a dialectic of victimization and pleasure. Despite formal silencing, it would be misleading to suggest that talk of desire never emerges within public schools. Notwithstanding a political climate organized around the suppression of this conversation, some teachers and community advocates continue to struggle for an empowering sex education curriculum both in and out of the high school classroom.

Family life curricula and/or plans for a school-based health clinic have been carefully generated in many communities. Yet they continue to face loud and sometimes violent resistance by religious and community groups, often from outside the district lines.[21] In other communities, when curricula or clinics have been approved with little overt confrontation, monies for training are withheld. For example, in New York City in 1987, $1.7 million was initially requested to implement training on the Family Life education curriculum. As sex educators confronted community and religious groups, the inclusion of some topics as well as the language of others were continually negotiated. Ultimately, the Chancellor requested only $600,000 for training, a sum substantially inadequate to the task.[22]

In this political context many public school educators nevertheless continue to take personal and professional risks to create materials and foster classroom environments which speak fully to the sexual subjectivities of young women and men. Some operate within the privacy of their classrooms, subverting the official curriculum and engaging students in critical discussion. Others advocate publicly for enriched curricula and training. A few have even requested that community-based advocates *not* agitate for official curricular change, so "we [teachers] can continue to do what we do in the classroom, with nobody looking over our shoulders. You make a big public deal of this, and it will blow open."[23] Within public school classrooms, it seems that female desire may indeed be addressed when educators act subversively. But in the typical sex education classroom, silence, and therefore distortion, surrounds female desire.

The blanketing of female sexual subjectivity in public school classrooms, in public discourse, and in bed will sound familiar to those who have read Luce Irigaray and Helene Cíxous.[24] These French feminists have argued that expressions of female voice, body, and sexuality are essentially inaudible when the dominant language and ways of viewing are male. Inside the hegemony of what they call The Law of the Father, female desire and pleasure can gain expression only in the terrain already charted by men.[25] In the public school arena, this constriction of what is called sexuality allows girls one primary decision—to say yes or no—to a question not necessarily their own. A discourse of desire in which young women have a voice would be informed and generated out of their own socially constructed sexual meanings. It is to these expressions that we now turn.

The Bodies of Female Adolescents: Voices and Structured Silences

If four discourses can be distinguished among the many positions articulated by various "authorities," the sexual meanings voiced by female adolescents defy such classification. A discourse of desire, though absent in the "official" curriculum, is by no means missing from the lived experiences or commentaries of young women. This section introduces their sexual thoughts, concerns, and meanings, as represented by a group of Black and Latina female adolescents—students and dropouts from a public high school in New York City serving predominantly low-income youths. In my year at this comprehensive high school I had frequent opportunity to speak with adolescents and listen to them talk about sex. The comments reported derive from conversations between the young women and their teachers, among themselves, and with me, as researcher. During conversations, the young women talked freely about fears and, in the same breath, asked about passions. Their struggle to untangle issues of gender, power, and sexuality underscores the fact that, for them, notions of sexual negotiation cannot be separated from sacrifice and nurturance.

The adolescent female rarely reflects simply on sexuality. Her sense of sexuality is informed by peers, culture, religion, violence, history, passion, authority, rebellion, body, past and future, and gender and racial relations of power.[26] The adolescent woman herself assumes a dual consciousness— at once taken with the excitement of actual/anticipated sexuality and consumed with anxiety and worry. While too few safe spaces exist for adolescent women's exploration of sexual subjectivities, there are all too many dangerous spots for their exploitation.

Whether in a classroom, on the street, at work, or at home, the adolescent female's sexuality is negotiated by, for, and despite the young woman herself. Patricia, a young Puerto Rican woman who worried about her younger sister, relates: "You see, I'm the love child and she's the one born because my mother was raped in Puerto Rico. Her father's in jail now, and she feels so bad about the whole thing so she acts bad." For Patricia, as for the many young women who have experienced and/or witnessed sexual violence, discussions of sexuality merge representations of passion with violence. Often the initiator of conversation among peers about virginity, orgasm, "getting off," and pleasure, Patricia mixed sexual talk freely with references to force and violence. She is a poignant narrator who illustrates, from the female adolescent's perspective, that sexual victimization and desire coexist.[27]

Sharlene and Betty echo this braiding of danger and desire. Sharlene explained: "Boys always be trying to get into my panties," and Betty added: "I don't be needin' a man who won't give me no pleasure but take my money and expect me to take care of him." This powerful commentary on gender relations, voiced by Black adolescent females, was inseparable from their views of sexuality. To be a woman was to be strong, independent, and reliable—but not too independent for fear of scaring off a man.

Deidre continued this conversation, explicitly pitting male fragility against female strength: "Boys in my neighborhood ain't wrapped so tight. Got to be careful how you treat them. . . ." She reluctantly admitted that perhaps it is more important for Black males than females to attend college, "Girls and women, we're stronger, we take care of ourselves. But boys and men, if they don't get away from the neighborhood, they end up in jail, on drugs or dead . . . or wack [crazy]."

These young women spoke often of anger at males, while concurrently expressing a strong desire for male attention: "I dropped out 'cause I fell in love, and couldn't stop thinking of him." An equally compelling desire was to protect young males—particularly Black males—from a system which "makes them wack." Ever aware of the ways that institutional racism and the economy have affected Black males, these young women seek pleasure but also offer comfort. They often view self-protection as taking something away from young men. Lavanda offered a telling example: "If I ask him to use a condom, he won't feel like a man."

In order to understand the sexual subjectivities of young women more completely, educators need to reconstruct schooling as an empowering context in which we listen to and work with the meanings and experiences of gender and sexuality revealed by the adolescents themselves. When we refuse that responsibility, we prohibit an education which adolescents wholly need and deserve. My classroom observations suggest that such education is rare.

Ms. Rosen, a teacher of a sex education class, opened one session with a request: "You should talk to your mother or father about sex before you get involved." Nilda initiated what became an informal protest by a number of Latino students: "Not our parents! We tell them one little thing and they get crazy. My cousin got sent to Puerto Rico to live with her religious aunt, and my sister got beat 'cause my father thought she was with a boy." For these adolescents, a safe space for discussion, critique, and construction of sexualities was not something they found in their homes. Instead, they relied on school, the spot they chose for the safe exploration of sexualities.

The absence of safe spaces for exploring sexuality affects all adolescents. It was paradoxical to realize that perhaps the only students who had an in-school opportunity for critical sexual discussion in the comfort of peers were the few students who had organized the Gay and Lesbian Association (GALA) at the high school. While most lesbian, gay, or bisexual students were undoubtedly closeted, those few who were "out" claimed this public space for their display and for their sanctuary. Exchanging support when families and peers would offer little, GALA members worried that so few students were willing to come out, and that so many suffered the assaults of homophobia individually. The gay and lesbian rights movement had powerfully affected these youngsters, who were comfortable enough to support each other in a place not considered very safe—a public high school in which echoes of "faggot!" fill the halls.

In the absence of an education which explores and unearths danger and desire, sexuality education classes typically provide little opportunity for discussions beyond those constructed around superficial notions of male heterosexuality.[28] Male pleasure is taught, albeit as biology. Teens learn about "wet dreams" (as the onset of puberty for males), "erection" (as the preface to intercourse), and "ejaculation" (as the act of inseminating). Female pleasures and questions are far less often the topic of discussion. Few voices of female sexual agency can be heard. The language of victimization and its underlying concerns—"Say No," put a brake on his sexuality, don't encourage—ultimately deny young women the right to control their own sexuality by providing no access to a legitimate position of sexual subjectivity. Often conflicted about self-representation, adolescent females spend enormous amounts of time trying to "save it," "lose it," convince others that they have lost or saved it, or trying to be "discreet" instead of focusing their energies in ways that are sexually autonomous, responsible, and pleasurable. In classroom observations, girls who were heterosexually active rarely spoke, for fear of being ostracized.[29] Those who were heterosexual virgins had the same worry. And most students who were gay, bisexual, or lesbian remained closeted, aware of the very real dangers of homophobia.

Occasionally, the difficult and pleasurable aspects of sexuality were discussed together, coming either as an interruption, or because an educational context was constructed. During a social studies class, for example, Catherine, the proud mother of two-year-old Tiffany, challenged an assumption underlying the class discussion—that teen motherhood devastates mother and child: "If I didn't get pregnant I would have continued on a downward path, going nowhere. They say teenage pregnancy is bad for you, but it was good for me. I know I can't mess around now, I got to worry about what's good for Tiffany and for me."

Another interruption came from Opal, a young Black student. Excerpts from her hygiene class follow.

TEACHER: Let's talk about teenage pregnancy.

OPAL: How come girls in the locker room say, "You a virgin?" and if you say "Yeah" they laugh and say "Ohh, you're a virgin. . . ." And some Black teenagers, I don't mean to be racial, when they get ready to tell their mothers they had sex, some break on them and some look funny. My friend told her mother and she broke all the dishes. She told her mother so she could get protection so she don't get pregnant.

TEACHER: When my 13-year-old (relative) asked for birth control I was shocked and angry.

PORTIA: Mothers should help so she can get protection and not get pregnant or diseases. So you was wrong.

TEACHER: Why not say "I'm thinking about having sex"?

PORTIA: You tell them after, not before, having sex but before pregnancy.

TEACHER (now angry): Then it's a fait accompli and you expect my compassion? You have to take more responsibility.

PORTIA: I am! If you get pregnant after you told your mother and you got all the stuff and still get pregnant, you the fool. Take up hygiene and learn. Then it's my responsibility if I end up pregnant. . . .

—Field Note, October 23, Hygiene Class

Two days later, the discussion continued.

TEACHER: What topics should we talk about in sex education?

PORTIA: Organs, how they work.

OPAL: What's an orgasm?

[laughter]

TEACHER: Sexual response, sensation all over the body. What's analogous to the male penis on the female?

THEO: Clitoris.

TEACHER: Right, go home and look in the mirror.

PORTIA: She is too much!

TEACHER: Why look in the mirror?

ELAINE: It's yours.

TEACHER: Why is it important to know what your body looks like?

OPAL: You should like your body.

TEACHER: You should know what it looks like when it's healthy, so you can recognize problems like vaginal warts.

—Field Note, October 25, Hygiene Class

The discourse of desire, initiated by Opal but evident only as an interruption, faded rapidly into the discourse of disease—warning about the dangers of sexuality.

It was in the spring of that year that Opal showed up pregnant. Her hygiene teacher, who was extremely concerned and involved with her students, was also quite angry with Opal: "Who is going to take care of that baby, you or your mother? You know what it costs to buy diapers and milk and afford child care?"

Opal, in conversation with me, related, "I got to leave [school] 'cause even if they don't say it, them teachers got hate in their eyes when they look at my belly." In the absence of a way to talk about passion, pleasure, danger, and responsibility, this teacher fetishized the later two, holding the former two hostage. Because adolescent females combine these experiences in their daily lives, the separation is false, judgmental, and ultimately not very educational.

Over the year in this high school, and in other public schools since, I have observed a systematic refusal to name issues, particularly issues that caused adults discomfort. Educators often projected their discomfort onto students in the guise of "protecting" them.[30] An example of such silencing can be seen in a (now altered) policy of the school district of Philadelphia. In 1985 a student informed me, "We're not allowed to talk about abortion in our school." Assuming this was an overstatement, I asked an administrator at the District about this practice. She explained, "That's not quite right. If a student asks a question about abortion, the teacher can define abortion, she just can't discuss it." How can definition occur without discussion, exchange, conversation, or critique unless a subtext of silencing prevails?[31]

Explicit silencing of abortion has since been lifted in Philadelphia. The revised curriculum now reads:

Options for unintended pregnancy:
(a) adoption
(b) foster care
(c) single parenthood
(d) teen marriage
(e) abortion

A footnote is supposed to be added, however, to elaborate the negative consequences of abortion. In the social politics which surround public schools, such compromises are apparent across cities.

The New York City Family Life Education curriculum reads similarly:

List: The possible options for an unintended pregnancy. What considerations should be given in the decision on the alternatives?

○ adoption

○ foster care

○ mother keeps baby

○ elective abortion

Discuss:

○ religious viewpoints on abortion

○ present laws concerning abortion

○ current developments in prenatal diagnosis and their implication for abortion issues

○ why abortion should not be considered a contraceptive device

List: The people or community services that could provide assistance in the event of an unintended pregnancy

Invite: A speaker to discuss alternatives to abortion; for example, a social worker from the Department of Social Services to discuss foster care.[32]

One must be suspicious when diverse views are sought only for abortion, and not for adoption, teen motherhood, or foster care. The call to silence is easily identified in current political and educational contexts.[33] The silence surrounding contraception and abortion options and diversity in sexual orientations denies adolescents information and sends the message that such conversations are taboo—at home, at church, and even at school.

In contrast to these "official curricula," which allow discussion and admission of desire only as an interruption, let us examine other situations in which young women were invited to analyze sexuality across categories of the body, the mind, the heart, and of course, gender politics.

Teen Choice, a voluntary counseling program held on-site by non-Board of Education social workers, offered an instance in which the complexities of pleasure and danger were invited, analyzed, and braided into discussions of sexuality. In a small group discussion, the counselor asked of the seven ninth graders, "What are the two functions of a penis?" One student responded, "To pee!" Another student offered the second function: "To eat!" which was followed by laughter and serious discussion. The conversation proceeded as the teacher asked, "Do all penises look alike?" The students explained, "No, they are all different colors!"

The freedom to express, beyond simple right and wrong answers, enabled these young women to offer what they knew with humor and delight. This discussion ended as one student insisted that if you "jump up and down a lot, the stuff will fall out of you and you won't get pregnant," to which the social worker answered with slight exasperation that millions of sperm would have to be released for such "expulsion" to work, and that of course, it wouldn't work. In this conversation one could hear what seemed like too much experience, too little information, and too few questions asked by the students. But the discussion, which was sex-segregated and guided by the experiences and questions of the students themselves (and the skills of the social worker), enabled easy movement between pleasure and danger, safety and desire, naiveté and knowledge, and victimization and entitlement.

What is evident, then, is that even in the absence of a discourse of desire, young women express their notions of sexuality and relate their experiences. Yet, "official" discourses of sexuality leave little room for such exploration. The authorized sexual discourses define what is safe, what is taboo, and what will be silenced. This discourse of sexuality miseducates adolescent women. What results is a discourse of sexuality based on the male in search of desire and the female in search of protection. The open, coed sexuality discussions so many fought for in the 1970s have been appropriated as a forum for the primacy of male heterosexuality and the preservation of female victimization.

The Politics of Female Sexual Subjectivities

In 1912, an education committee explicitly argued that "scientific" sex education "should . . . keep sex consciousness and sex emotions at the minimum."[34] In the same era G. Stanley Hall proposed diversionary pursuits for adolescents, including hunting, music, and sports, "to reduce sex stress and tension . . . to short-circuit, transmute it and turn it on to develop the higher powers of the men [sic]."[35] In 1915 Orison Marden, author of *The Crime of Silence*, chastised educators, reformers, and public health specialists for their unwillingness to speak publicly about sexuality and for relying inappropriately on parents and peers, who were deemed too ignorant to provide sex instruction.[36] And in 1921 radical sex educator Maurice Bigelow wrote:

> Now, most scientifically-trained women seem to agree that there are no corresponding phenomena in the early pubertal life of the normal young woman who has good health (corresponding to male masturbation). A limited number of mature women, some of them physicians, report having experienced in the pubertal years localized tumescence and other disturbances which made them definitely conscious of sexual instincts. However, it should be noted that most of these are known to have had a personal history including one or more such abnormalities such as dysmenorrhea, uterine displacement, pathological ovaries, leucorrhea, tuberculosis, masturbation, neurasthenia, nymphomania, or other disturbances which are sufficient to account for local sexual stimulation. In short such women are not normal.[37]

In the 1950s public school health classes separated girls from boys. Girls "learned about sex" by watching films of the accelerated development of breasts and hips, the flow of menstrual blood, and then the progression of venereal disease as a result of participation in out-of-wedlock heterosexual activity.

Thirty years and a much-debated sexual revolution later,[38] much has changed. Feminism, the Civil Rights Movement, the disability and gay rights movements, birth control, legal abortion with federal funding (won and then lost), and reproductive technologies are part of these changes.[39] Due both to the consequences of, and the backlashes against, these movements, students today do learn about sexuality—if typically through the representations of female sexuality as inadequacy or victimization, male homosexuality as a story of predator and prey, and male heterosexuality as desire.

Young women today know that female sexual subjectivity is at least not an inherent contradiction. Perhaps they even feel it is an entitlement. Yet when public schools resist acknowledging the fullness of female sexual subjectivities, they reproduce a profound social ambivalence which dichotomizes female heterosexuality.[40] This ambivalence surrounds a fragile cultural distinction between two forms of female sexuality: *consensual* sexuality, representing consent or choice in sexuality, and *coercive* sexuality, which represents force, victimization, and/or crime.[41]

During the 1980s, however, this distinction began to be challenged. It was acknowledged that gender-based power inequities shape, define, and construct experiences of sexuality. Notions of sexual consent and force, except in extreme circumstances, became complicated, no longer in simple opposition. The first problem concerned how to conceptualize power asymmetries and consensual sexuality. Could *consensual* female heterosexuality be said to exist within a context replete with structures, relationships, acts, and threats of female victimization (sexual, social, and economic)?[42] How could we speak of "sexual preference" when sexual involvement outside of heterosexuality may seriously jeopardize one's social and/or economic well-being?[43] Diverse female sexual subjectivities emerge through, despite, and because of gender-based power asymmetries. To imagine a female sexual self, free of and uncontaminated by power, was rendered naive.[44]

The second problem involved the internal incoherence of the categories. Once assumed fully independent, the two began to blur as the varied practices of sexuality went public. At the intersection of these presumably parallel forms—coercive and consensual sexualities—lay "sexual" acts of violence and "violent" acts of sex. "Sexual" acts of violence, including marital rape, acquaintance rape, and sexual harassment, were historically considered consensual. A woman involved in a marriage, on a date, or working outside her home "naturally" risked receiving sexual attention; her consent was inferred from her presence. But today, in many states, this woman can sue her husband for such sexual acts of violence; in all states, she can prosecute a boss. What was once part of "domestic life" or "work" may, today, be criminal. On the other hand, "violent" acts of sex, including consensual sadomasochism and the use of violence-portraying pornography, were once considered inherently coercive for women.[45] Female involvement in such sexual practices historically had been dismissed as nonconsensual. Today such romanticizing of a naive and moral "feminine sexuality" has been challenged as essentialist, and the assumption that such a feminine sexuality is "natural" to women has been shown to be false.[46]

Over the past decade, understandings of female sexual choice, consent, and coercion have grown richer and more complex. While questions about female subjectivities have become more interesting, the answers (for some) remain deceptively simple. Inside public schools, for example, female adolescents continue to be educated as though they were the potential *victims* of sexual (male) desire. By contrast, the ideological opposition represents only adult married women as fully consensual partners. The distinction of coercion and consent has been organized simply and respectively around age and marital status—which effectively resolves any complexity and/or ambivalence.

The ambivalence surrounding female heterosexuality places the victim and subject in opposition and derogates all women who represent female sexual subjectivities outside of marriage—prostitutes, lesbians, single mothers, women involved with multiple partners, and particularly, Black single mothers.[47] "Protected" from this derogation, the typical adolescent woman, as represented in sex education curricula, is without any sexual subjectivity. The discourse of victimization not only obscures the derogation, it also transforms socially distributed anxieties about female sexuality into acceptable, and even protective, talk.

The fact that schools implicitly organize sex education around a concern for female victimization is suspect, however, for two reasons. First, if female victims of male violence were truly a social concern, wouldn't the victims of rape, incest, and sexual harassment encounter social compassion, and not suspicion and blame? And second, if sex education were designed primarily to prevent victimization but not to prevent exploration of desire, wouldn't there be more discussions of both the pleasures and relatively fewer risks of disease or pregnancy associated with lesbian relationships and protected sexual intercourse, or of the risk-free pleasures of masturbation and fantasy? Public education's concern for the female victim is revealed as deceptively thin when real victims are discredited, and when nonvictimizing pleasures are silenced.

This unacknowledged social ambivalence about heterosexuality polarizes the debates over sex education and school-based health clinics. The anxiety effectively treats the female sexual victim as though she were a completely separate species from the female sexual subject. Yet the adolescent women quoted earlier in this text remind us that the female victim and subject coexist in every woman's body.

Toward a Discourse of Sexual Desire and Social Entitlement: In the Student Bodies of Public Schools

I have argued that silencing a discourse of desire buttresses the icon of woman-as-victim. In so doing, public schooling may actually disable young women in their negotiations as sexual subjects. Trained through and into positions of passivity and victimization, young women are currently educated away from positions of sexual self-interest.

If we re-situate the adolescent woman in a rich and empowering educational context, she develops a sense of self which is sexual as well as intellectual, social, and economic. In this section I invite readers to imagine such a context. The dialectic of desire and victimization—across spheres of labor, social relations, and sexuality—would then frame schooling. While many of the curricula and interventions discussed in this paper are imperfect, data on the effectiveness of what *is* available are nevertheless compelling. Studies of sex education curricula, SBHCs, classroom discussions, and ethnographies of life inside public high schools demonstrate that a sense of sexual and social entitlement for young women *can* be fostered within public schools.

Sex Education as Intellectual Empowerment

Harris and Yankelovich polls confirm that over 80 percent of American adults believe that students should be educated about sexuality within their public schools. Seventy-five percent believe that homosexuality and abortion should be included in the curriculum, with 40 percent of those surveyed by Yankelovich et al. (N = 1015) agreeing that 12-year-olds should be taught about oral and anal sex.[48]

While the public continues to debate the precise content of sex education, most parents approve and support sex education for their children. An Illinois program monitored parental requests to "opt out" and found that only 6 or 7 of 850 children were actually excused from sex education courses.[49] In a California assessment, fewer than 2 percent of parents disallowed their children's participation. And in a longitudinal five-year program in Connecticut, 7 of 2,500 students requested exemption from these classes.[50] Resistance to sex education, while loud at the level of public rhetoric and conservative organizing, is both less vocal and less active within schools and parents' groups.[51]

Sex education courses are offered broadly, if not comprehensively, across the United States. In 1981, only 7 of 50 states actually had laws against such instruction, and only one state enforced a prohibition.[52] Surveying 179 urban school districts, Sonnenstein and Pittman found that 75 percent offered some sex education within senior and junior high schools, while 66 percent of the elementary schools offered sex education units. Most instruction was, however, limited to 10 hours or less, with content focused on anatomy.[53] In his extensive review of sex education programs, Kirby concludes that less than 10 percent of all public school students are exposed to what might be considered comprehensive sex education courses.[54]

The progress on AIDS education is more encouraging, and more complex,[55] but cannot be adequately reviewed in this article. It is important to note, however, that a December 1986 report released by the U.S. Conference of Mayors documents that 54 percent of the 73 largest school districts and 25 state school agencies offer some form of AIDS education.[56] Today, debates among federal officials—including Secretary of Education Bennett and Surgeon General Koop—and among educators question *when* and *what* to offer in AIDS education. The question is no longer *whether* such education should be promoted.

Not only has sex education been accepted as a function of public schooling, but it has survived empirical tests of effectiveness. Evaluation data demonstrate that sex education can increase contraceptive knowledge and use.[57] In terms of sexual activity (measured narrowly in terms of the onset or frequency of heterosexual intercourse), the evidence suggests that sex education does not instigate an earlier onset or increase of such sexual activity[58] and may, in fact, postpone the onset of heterosexual intercourse.[59] The data for pregnancy rates appear to demonstrate no effect for exposure to sex education alone.[60]

Sex education as constituted in these studies is not sufficient to diminish teen pregnancy rates. In all likelihood it would be naive to expect that sex education (especially if only 10 hours in duration) would carry such a "long arm" of effectiveness. While the widespread problem of teen pregnancy must be attributed broadly to economic and social inequities,[61] sex education remains necessary and sufficient to educate, demystify, and improve contraceptive knowledge and use. In conjunction with material opportunities for enhanced life options, it is believed that sex education and access to contraceptives and abortion can help to reduce the rate of unintended pregnancy among teens.[62]

School-Based Health Clinics: Sexual Empowerment

The public opinion and effectiveness data for school-based health clinics are even more compelling than those for sex education. Thirty SBHCs provide on-site health care services to senior, and sometimes junior, high school students in more than 18 U.S. communities, with an additional 25 communities developing similar programs.[63] These clinics offer, at a minimum, health counseling, referrals, and follow-up examinations. Over 70 percent conduct pelvic examinations,[64] approximately 52 percent prescribe contraceptives, and 28 percent dispense contraceptives.[65] None perform abortions, and few refer for abortions.

All SBHCs require some form of general parental notification and/or consent, and some charge a nominal fee for generic health services. Relative to private physicians, school-based health clinics and other family planning agencies are substantially more willing to provide contraceptive services to unmarried minors without specific parental consent (consent in this case referring explicitly to contraception). Only 1 percent of national Planned Parenthood affiliates require consent or notification, compared to 10 percent of public health department programs and 19 percent of hospitals.[66]

The consequences of consent provisions for abortion are substantial. Data from two states, Massachusetts and Minnesota, demonstrate that parental consent laws result in increased teenage pregnancies or increased numbers of out-of-state abortions. The Reproductive Freedom Project of the American Civil Liberties Union, in a report which examines the consequences of such consent provisions, details the impact of these statutes on teens, on their familial relationships, and ultimately, on their unwanted children.[67] In an analysis of the impact of Minnesota's mandatory parental notification law from 1981 to 1985, this report documents over 7,000 pregnancies in teens aged 13–17, 3,500 of whom "went to state court to seek the right to confidential abortions, all at considerable personal cost." The report also notes that many of the pregnant teens did not petition the court, "although their entitlement and need for confidential abortions was as strong or more so than the teenagers who made it to court. . . . Only those minors who are old enough and wealthy enough or resourceful enough are actually able to use the court bypass option."[68]

These consent provisions, with allowance for court bypass, not only increase the number of unwanted teenage pregnancies carried to term, but also extend the length of time required to secure an abortion, potentially endangering the life of the teenage woman, and increasing the costs of the abortion. The provisions may also jeopardize the physical and emotional well-being of some young women and their mothers, particularly when paternal consent is required and the pregnant teenager resides with a single mother. Finally, the consent provisions create a class-based health care system. Adolescents able to afford travel to a nearby state, or able to pay a private physician for a confidential abortion, have access to an abortion. Those unable to afford the travel, or those who are unable to contact a private physician, are likely to become teenage mothers.[69]

In Minneapolis, during the time from 1980 to 1984 when the law was implemented, the birth rate for 15- to 17-year-olds increased 38.4 percent, while the birth rate for 18- and 19-year-olds—not affected by the law— rose only .3 percent.[70] The state of Massachusetts passed a parental consent law which took effect in 1981. An analysis of the impact of that law concludes that " . . . the major impact of the Massachusetts parental consent law has been to send a monthly average of between 90 and 95 of the state's minors across state lines in search of an abortion. This number represents about one in every three minor abortion patients living in Massachusetts."[71] These researchers, among others, write that parental consent laws could have more devastating effects in larger states, from which access to neighboring states would be more difficult.

The inequalities inherent in consent provisions and the dramatic consequences which result for young women are well recognized. For example, 29 states and the District of Columbia now explicitly authorize minors to grant their own consent for receipt of contraceptive information and/or services, independent of parental knowledge or consent.[72] More recently, consent laws for abortion in Pennsylvania and California have been challenged as unconstitutional.

Public approval of SBHCs has been slow but consistent. In the 1986 Yankelovich survey, 84 percent of surveyed adults agree that these clinics should provide birth control information; 36 percent endorse dispensing of contraceptives to students.[73] In 1985, Harris found that 67 percent of all respondents, including 76 percent of Blacks and 76 percent of Hispanics, agree that public schools should establish formal ties with family planning clinics for teens to learn about and obtain contraception.[74] Mirroring the views of the general public, a national sample of school administrators polled by the Education Research Group indicated that more than 50 percent believe birth control should be offered in school-based clinics; 30 percent agree that parental permission should be sought, and 27 percent agree that contraceptives should be dispensed, even if parental consent is not forthcoming. The discouraging news is that 96 percent of these respondents indicate that their districts do not presently offer such services.[75]

Research on the effectiveness of SBHCs is consistently persuasive. The three-year Johns Hopkins study of school-based health clinics found that schools in which SBHCs made referrals and dispensed contraceptives noted an increase in the percentage of "virgin" females visiting the program as well as an increase in contraceptive use. They also found a significant reduction in pregnancy rates: There was a 13 percent increase at experimental schools after 10 months, versus a 50 percent increase at control schools; after 28 months, pregnancy rates decreased 30 percent at experimental schools versus a 53 percent increase at control schools. Furthermore, by the second year, a substantial percentage of males visited the clinic (48 percent of males in experimental schools indicated that they "have ever been to a birth control clinic or to a physician about birth control," compared to 12 percent of males in control schools). Contrary to common belief, the schools in which clinics dispensed contraceptives showed a substantial postponement of first experience of heterosexual intercourse among high school students and an increase in the proportion of young women visiting the clinic prior to "first coitus."[76]

Paralleling the Hopkins findings, the St. Paul Maternity and Infant Care Project found that pregnancy rates dropped substantially in schools with clinics, from 79 births/1,000 (1973) to 26 births/1,000 (1984). Teens who delivered and kept their infants had an 80 percent graduation rate, relative to approximately 50 percent of young mothers nationally. Those who stayed in school reported a 1.3 percent repeat birth rate, compared to 17 percent nationally. Over three years, pregnancy rates dropped by 40 percent. Twenty-five percent of young women in the school received some form of family planning and 87 percent of clients were continuing to use contraception at a three-year follow-up. There were fewer obstetric complications; fewer babies were born at low birth weights; and prenatal visits to physicians increased relative to students in the control schools.[77]

Predictions that school-based health clinics would advance the onset of sexual intimacy, heighten the degree of "promiscuity" and incidence of pregnancy, and hold females primarily responsible for sexuality were countered by the evidence. The onset of sexual intimacy was postponed, while contraception was used more reliably. Pregnancy rates substantially diminished and, over time, a large group of males began to view contraception as a shared responsibility.

It is worth restating here that females who received family planning counseling and/or contraception actually postponed the onset of heterosexual intercourse. I would argue that the availability of such services may enable females to feel they are sexual agents, entitled and therefore responsible, rather than at the constant and terrifying mercy of a young man's pressure to "give in" or of a parent's demands to "save yourself." With a sense of sexual agency and not necessarily urgency, teen girls may be less likely to use or be used by pregnancy.[78]

Nontraditional Vocational Training: Social and Economic Entitlement

The literature reviewed suggests that sex education, access to contraception, and opportunities for enhanced life options, in combination,[79] can significantly diminish the likelihood that a teenager will become pregnant, carry to term, and/or have a repeat pregnancy, and can increase the likelihood that she will stay in high school through graduation.[80] Education toward entitlement—including a sense of sexual, economic, and social entitlement—may be sufficient to affect adolescent girls' views on sexuality, contraception, and abortion. By framing female subjectivity within the context of social entitlement, sex education would be organized around dialogue and critique, SBHCs would offer health services, options counseling, contraception, and abortion referrals, and the provision of real "life options" would include nontraditional vocational training programs and employment opportunities for adolescent females.[81]

In a nontraditional vocational training program in New York City designed for young women, many of whom are mothers, participants' attitudes toward contraception and abortion shifted once they acquired a set of vocational skills, a sense of social entitlement, and a sense of personal competence.[82] The young women often began the program without strong academic skills or a sense of competence. At the start, they were more likely to express more negative sentiments about contraception and abortion than when they completed the program. One young woman, who initially held strong anti-abortion attitudes, learned that she was pregnant midway through her carpentry apprenticeship. She decided to abort, reasoning that now that she has a future, she can't risk losing it for another baby.[83] A developing sense of social entitlement may have transformed this young woman's view of reproduction, sexuality, and self.

The Manpower Development Research Corporation (MDRC), in its evaluation of Project Redirection,[84] offers similar conclusions about a comprehensive vocational training and community-based mentor project for teen mothers and mothers-to-be. Low-income teens were enrolled in Project Redirection, a network of services designed to instill self-sufficiency, in which community women served as mentors. The program included training for what is called "employability," Individual Participation Plans, and peer group sessions. Data on education, employment, and pregnancy outcomes were collected at 12 and 24 months after enrollment. Two years after the program began, many newspapers headlined the program as a failure. The data actually indicated that at 12 months, the end of program involvement, Project Redirection women were significantly *less likely* to experience a repeat pregnancy than comparison women; *more likely* to be using contraception; *more likely* to be in school, to have completed school, or to be in the labor force; and twice as likely (20 percent versus 11 percent, respectively) to have earned a Graduate Equivalency Diploma. At 24 months, however, approximately one year out of the program, Project and comparison women were virtually indistinguishable. MDRC reported equivalent rates of repeat pregnancies, dropout, and unemployment.

The Project Redirection data demonstrate that sustained outcomes cannot be expected once programs have been withdrawn and participants confront the realities of a dismal economy and inadequate child care and social services. The data confirm, however, the effectiveness of comprehensive programs to reduce teen pregnancy rates and encourage study or work as long as the young women are actively engaged. Supply-side interventions—changing people but not structures or opportunities—which leave unchallenged an inhospitable and discriminating economy and a thoroughly impoverished child care/social welfare system are inherently doomed to long-term failure. When such programs fail, the social reading is that "these young women can't be helped." Blaming the victim obscures the fact that the current economy and social welfare arrangements need overhauling if the sustained educational, social, and psychological gains accrued by the Project Redirection participants are to be maintained.

In the absence of enhanced life options, low-income young women are likely to default to early and repeat motherhood as a source of perceived competence, significance, and pleasure. When life options are available, however, a sense of competence and "entitlement to better" may help to prevent second pregnancies, may help to encourage education, and, when available, the pursuit of meaningful work.[85]

Femininity May Be Hazardous to Her Health: The Absence of Entitlement

Growing evidence suggests that women who lack a sense of social or sexual entitlement, who hold traditional notions of what it means to be female—self-sacrificing and relatively passive—and who undervalue themselves, are disproportionately likely to find themselves with an unwanted pregnancy and to maintain it through to motherhood. While many young women who drop out, pregnant or not, are not at all traditional in these ways, but are quite feisty and are fueled with a sense of entitlement, it may also be the case that young women who do internalize such notions of "femininity" are disproportionately at risk for pregnancy and dropping out.[86]

The Hispanic Policy Development Project reports that low-income female sophomores who, in 1980, expected to be married and/or have a child by age 19 were disproportionately represented among nongraduates in 1984. Expectations of early marriage and childbearing correspond to dramatic increases (200 to 400 percent) in nongraduation rates for low-income adolescent women across racial and ethnic groups.[87] These indicators of traditional notions of womanhood bode poorly for female academic achievement.

The Children's Defense Fund recently published additional data which demonstrate that young women with poor basic skills are three times more likely to become teen parents than women with average or above-average basic skills. Those with poor or fair basic skills are four times more likely to have more than one child while a teen; 29 percent of women in the bottom skills quintile became mothers by age 18 versus 5 percent of young women in the top quintile. While academic skill problems must be placed in the context of alienating and problematic schools, and not viewed as inherent in these young women, those who fall in the bottom quintile may nevertheless be the least likely to feel entitled or in control of their lives. They may feel more vulnerable to male pressure or more willing to have a child as a means of feeling competent.[88]

My own observations, derived from a year-long ethnographic study of a comprehensive public high school in New York City, further confirm some of these conclusions. Six months into the ethnography, new pregnancies began showing. I noticed that many of the girls who got pregnant and carried to term were not those whose bodies, dress, and manner evoked sensuality and experience. Rather, a number of the pregnant women were those who were quite passive and relatively quiet in their classes. One young woman, who granted me an interview anytime, washed the blackboard for her teacher, rarely spoke in class, and never disobeyed her mother, was pregnant by the spring of the school year.[89]

Simple stereotypes, of course, betray the complexity of circumstances under which young women become pregnant and maintain their pregnancies. While U.S. rates of teenage sexual activity and age of "sexual initiation" approximate those of comparable developed countries, the teenage pregnancy, abortion, and childbearing rates in the United States are substantially higher. In the United States, teenagers under age 15 are at least five times more likely to give birth than similarly aged teens in other industrialized nations.[90] The national factors which correlate with low teenage birthrates include adolescent access to sex education and contraception, and relative equality in the distribution of wealth. Economic and structural conditions which support a class-stratified society, and which limit adolescent access to sexual information and contraception, contribute to inflated teenage pregnancy rates and birthrates.

This broad national context acknowledged, it might still be argued that within our country, traditional notions of what it means to be a woman—to remain subordinate, dependent, self-sacrificing, compliant, and ready to marry and/or bear children early—do little to empower women or enhance a sense of entitlement. This is not to say that teenage dropouts or mothers tend to be of any one type. Yet it may well be that the traditions and practices of "femininity" as commonly understood may be hazardous to the economic, social, educational, and sexual development of young women.

In summary, the historic silencing within public schools of conversations about sexuality, contraception, and abortion, as well as the absence of a discourse of desire—in the form of comprehensive sex education, school-based health clinics, and viable life options via vocational training and placement—all combine to exacerbate the vulnerability of young women whom schools, and the critics of sex education and SBHCs, claim to protect.

Conclusion

Adolescents are entitled to a discussion of desire instead of the anti-sex rhetoric which controls the controversies around sex education, SBHCs, and AIDS education. The absence of a discourse of desire, combined with the lack of analysis of the language of victimization, may actually retard the development of sexual subjectivity and responsibility in students. Those most "at risk" of victimization through pregnancy, disease, violence, or harassment—all female students, low-income females in particular, and nonheterosexual males—are those most likely to be victimized by the absence of critical conversation in public schools. Public schools can no longer afford to maintain silence around a discourse of desire. This is not to say that the silencing of a discourse of desire is the primary root of sexual victimization, teen motherhood, and the concomitant poverty experienced by young and low-income females. Nor could it be responsibly argued that interventions initiated by public schools could ever be successful if separate from economic and social development. But it is important to understand that by providing education, counseling, contraception, and abortion referrals, as well as meaningful educational and vocational opportunities, public schools could play an essential role in the construction of the female subject—social and sexual.

And by not providing such an educational context, public schools contribute to the rendering of substantially different outcomes for male and female students, and for male and female dropouts.[91] The absence of a thorough sex education curriculum, of school-based health clinics, of access to free and confidential contraceptive and abortion services, of exposure to information about the varieties of sexual pleasures and partners, and of involvement in sustained employment training programs may so jeopardize the educational and economic outcomes for female adolescents as to constitute sex discrimination. How can we ethically continue to withhold educational treatments we know to be effective for adolescent women?

Public schools constitute a sphere in which young women could be offered access to a language and experience of empowerment. In such contexts, "well-educated" young women could breathe life into positions of social critique and experience entitlement rather than victimization, autonomy rather than terror.

NOTES

1. M. Foucault, *The History of Sexuality*, vol. 1 (New York: Vintage Books, 1980).

2. The research reported in this article represents one component of a year-long ethnographic investigation of students and dropouts at a comprehensive public high school in New York City. Funded by the W. T. Grant Foundation, the research was designed to investigate how public urban high schools produce dropout rates in excess of 50 percent. The methods employed over the year included: in-school observations four days/week during the fall, and one to two days/week during the spring; regular (daily) attendance in a hygiene course for twelfth graders; an archival analysis of more than twelve hundred students who compose the 1978–79 cohort of incoming ninth graders; interviews with approximately fifty-five recent and long-term dropouts; analysis of fictional and autobiographical writings by students; a survey distributed to a subsample of the cohort population; and visits to proprietary schools, programs for Graduate Equivalency Diplomas, naval recruitment sites, and a public high school for pregnant and parenting teens. The methods and preliminary results of the ethnography are detailed in M. Fine, "Why Urban Adolescents Drop Into and Out of High School," *Teachers' College Record* 87(1986): 393–409.

3. L. Harris, *Public Attitudes about Sex Education, Family Planning, and Abortion in the United States* (New York: Louis Harris & Associates, 1985).

4. B. Kantrowitz, M. Hager, S. Winger, G. Carroll, G. Raine, D. Witherspoon, J. Huck, and S. Doherty, "Kids and Contraceptives," *Newsweek*, 16 February 1987, 54–65; J. Leo, "Sex and Schools," *Time*, 24 November 1986, 54–63.

5. G. Bauer, *The Family: Preserving America's Future* (Washington, D.C.: U.S. Department of Education, 1986).

6. Leo, "Sex and Schools," 54.

7. C. Smith-Rosenberg, "Sex as Symbol in Victorian Purity: An Ethnohistorical Analysis of Jacksonian America," *American Journal of Sociology* 84(1978): 212–47.

8. C. MacKinnon, "Complicity: An Introduction to Andrea Dworkin's 'Abortion,' Chapter 3, 'Right-Wing Women,' " *Law and Inequality* 1(1983): 89–94.

9. W. Fisher, D. Byrne, and L. White, "Emotional Barriers to Contraception," in D. Byrne and W. Fisher, eds., *Adolescents, Sex, and Contraception* (Hillsdale, N.J.: Erlbaum, 1983), 207–39.

10. Fisher, Byrne, and White, "Emotional Barriers to Contraception."

11. C. Vance, *Pleasure and Danger* (Boston: Routledge & Kegan Paul, 1984).

12. G. Rubin, "Thinking Sex: Notes for a Radical Theory of the Politics of Sex," in C. Vance, ed., *Pleasure and Danger* (Boston: Routledge & Kegan Paul, 1984).

13. A. Lorde, "Uses of the Erotic: The Erotic as Power," paper presented at the Fourth Berkshire Conference on the History of Women, Mt. Holyoke College, August 1980.

14. "Koop's AIDS Stand Assailed," *New York Times,* March 1987, A25.

15. A. Snitow, C. Stansell, and S. Thompson, eds., *Powers of Desire* (New York: Monthly Review Press, 1983).

16. N. Freudenberg, "The Politics of Sex Education," *Health PAC Bulletin* (New York: Health PAC, 1987).

17. C. Golden, "Diversity and Variability in Lesbian Identities," paper presented at Lesbian Psychologies Conference of the Association of Women in Psychology, March 1984; R. Petcheskey, *Abortion and Woman's Choice* (New York: Longman, 1984); S. Thompson, "Search for Tomorrow: On Feminism and the Reconstruction of Teen Romance," in Snitow, Stansell, and Thompson, *Powers of Desire.*

18. P. Brown, "The Swedish Approach to Sex Education and Adolescent Pregnancy: Some Impressions," *Family Planning Perspectives* 15, 2(1983): 88.

19. Brown, "The Swedish Approach to Sex Education and Adolescent Pregnancy," 93.

20. Philadelphia School District, "Sex Education Curriculum," draft (1986); New York City Board of Education, *Family Living Curriculum Including Sex Education Grades K through 12* (New York City: Board of Education, Division of Curriculum and Instruction, 1984).

21. P. Boffrey, "Reagan to Back AIDS Plan Urging Youths to Avoid Sex," *New York Times,* 27 February 1987, A14; "Chicago School Clinic Is Sued Over

Birth Control Materials," *New York Times,* 16 October 1986, A24; M. Dowd, "Bid to Update Sex Education Confronts Resistance in City," *New York Times,* 16 April 1986, A1; J. Perlez, "On Teaching About Sex," *New York Times,* 24 June 1986, C1; J. Perlez, "School Chief to Ask Mandatory Sex Education," *New York Times,* 24 September 1986, A36; L. Rohter, "School Workers Shown AIDS Film," *New York Times,* 29 October 1985, B3.

22. This information is derived from personal communications with former and present employees of major urban school districts who have chosen to remain anonymous.

23. Personal communication.

24. L. Irigaray, "When Our Lips Speak Together," *Signs* 6, 69(1980); H. Cíxous, "Castration of Decapitation," *Signs* 7, 41(1981): 55.

25. C. Burke, "Introduction to Luce Irigaray's 'When Our Lips Speak Together,' " *Signs* 6, 69(1980): 66–68.

26. O. Espin, "Cultural and Historical Influences on Sexuality in Hispanic/Latina Women: Implications for Psychotherapy," in C. Vance, ed., *Pleasure and Danger,* 149–64; B. Omolade, "Hearts of Darkness," in Snitow, Stansell, and Thompson, *Powers of Desire,* 350–67.

27. J. Benjamin, "Master and Slave: The Fantasy of Erotic Domination," in Snitow, Stansell, and Thompson, *Powers of Desire,* 280–99.

28. For a counterexample, see G. Kelly, *Learning about Sex* (Woodbury, N.Y.: Barron's Educational Series, 1986).

29. Fine, "Why Urban Adolescents Drop Into and Out of High School."

30. Fine, "Silencing in Public School," *Language Arts* 64(1987): 157–74.

31. M. Green, "In Search of a Critical Pedagogy," *Harvard Educational Review* 56(1986): 427–41; N. Noddings, "Fidelity in Teaching, Teacher Education, and Research for Teaching," *Harvard Educational Review* 56(1986): 496–510.

32. New York City Board of Education, *Family Living Curriculum Including Sex Education Grades K through 12.*

33. Fine, "Silencing in Public School"; Foucault, *The History of Sexuality.*

34. Leo, "Sex and Schools."

35. G. S. Hall, "Education and the Social Hygiene Movement," *Social Hygiene* 1(December 1914): 29–35.

36. M. Imber, "Towards a Theory of Educational Origins: The Genesis of Sex Education," *Educational Theory* 34(1984): 275–86; B. Strong, "Ideas of the Early Sex Education Movement in America, 1890–1920," *History of Education Quarterly* 12(1972): 129–61.

37. M. Bigelow, *Sex Education* (New York: Macmillan, 1921).

38. B. Ehrenreich, E. Hess, and G. Jacobs, *Remaking of Love* (Garden City, N.Y.: Anchor Press, 1986).

39. J. Weeks, *Sexuality and Its Discontents* (London: Routledge & Kegan Paul, 1984).

40. Espin, "Cultural and Historical Influences on Sexuality"; Golden, "Diversity and Variability in Lesbian Identities"; Omolade, "Hearts of Darkness."

41. Weeks, *Sexuality and Its Discontents.*

42. MacKinnon, "Complicity."

43. Petcheskey, *Abortion and Woman's Choice.*

44. Foucault, *The History of Sexuality;* Irigaray, "When Our Lips Speak Together"; Rubin, "Thinking Sex."

45. Benjamin, "Master and Slave"; Rubin, "Thinking Sex"; Weeks, *Sexuality and Its Discontents.*

46. Rubin, "Thinking Sex."

47. R. Weitz, "What Price Independence? Social Reactions to Lesbians, Spinsters, Widows, and Nuns," in J. Freeman, ed., *Women: A Feminist Perspective,* 3d ed. (Palo Alto, Calif.: Mayfield, 1984).

48. Leo, "Sex and Schools"; Harris, *Public Attitudes.*

49. Leo, "Sex and Schools."

50. P. Scales, "Sex Education and the Prevention of Teenage Pregnancy: An Overview of Policies and Programs in the United States," in T. Ooms, ed., *Teenage Pregnancy in a Family Context: Implications for Policy* (Philadelphia: Temple University Press, 1981).

51. J. Hottois and N. Milner, *The Sex Education Controversy* (Lexington, Mass.: Lexington Books, 1975); Scales, "Sex Education."

52. D. Kirby and P. Scales, "An Analysis of State Guidelines for Sex Education Instruction in Public Schools," *Family Relations* (April 1981): 229–37.

53. F. Sonnenstein and K. Pittman, "The Availability of Sex Education in Large City School Districts," *Family Planning Perspectives* 16, 1(1984): 19–25.

54. D. Kirby, *School-Based Health Clinics: An Emerging Approach to Improving Adolescent Health and Addressing Teenage Pregnancy* (Washington, D.C.: Center for Population Options, 1985).

55. Freudenberg, "The Politics of Sex Education."

56. Benedetto, "AIDS Studies Become Part of the Curricula," *USA Today,* 23 January, 1987, D1.

57. Kirby, *School-Based Health Clinics;* Public/Private Ventures, *Summer Training and Education Program* (Philadelphia: Public/Private Ventures, 1987).

58. M. Zelnick and Y. Kim, "Sex Education and Its Association with Teenage Sexual Activity, Pregnancy, and Contraceptive Use," *Family Planning Perspectives* 14, 3(1982): 117–26.

59. L. Zabin, M. Hirsch, E. Smith, R. Streett, and J. Hardy, "Evaluation of a Pregnancy Prevention Program for Urban Teenagers," *Family Planning Perspectives* 18, 3(1986): 119–26.

60. D. Dawson, "The Effects of Sex Education on Adolescent Behavior," *Family Planning Perspectives* 18(1986): 162–70; W. Marsiglio and F. Mott, "The Impact of Sex Education on Sexual Activity, Contraceptive Use, and Premarital Pregnancy among American Teenagers," *Family Perspectives* 18, 4(1986): 151–62; Kirby, *School-Based Health Clinics.*

61. E. Jones, J. Forrest, N. Goldman, S. Henshaw, R. Lincoln, J. Rosoff, C. Westoff, and D. Wulf, "Teenage Pregnancy in Developed Countries," *Family Planning Perspectives* 17, 1(1985): 55–63.

62. J. Dryfoos, "A Time for New Thinking about Teenage Pregnancy," *American Journal of Public Health* 75(1985): 13–14; J. Dryfoos, "School-Based Health Clinics: A New Approach to Preventing Adolescent Pregnancy?" *Family Planning Perspectives* 17, 2(1985):70–85; National Research Council, *Risking the Future: Adolescent Sexuality, Pregnancy and Childbearing,* vol. 1 (Washington, D.C.: National Academy Press, 1987).

63. Kirby, *School-Based Health Clinics.*

64. Kirby, *School-Based Health Clinics.*

65. Leo, "Sex and Schools."

66. A. Torres and J. Forrest, "Family Planning Clinic Services in the United States, 1983," *Family Planning Perspectives* 17, 1(1985): 30–35.

67. Reproductive Freedom Project, *Parental Consent Laws on Abortion: Their Catastrophic Impact on Teenagers* (New York: American Civil Liberties Union, 1986).

68. Reproductive Freedom Project, *Parental Consent Laws on Abortion.*

69. Reproductive Freedom Project, *Parental Consent Laws on Abortion.*

70. Reproductive Freedom Project, *Parental Consent Laws on Abortion.*

71. V. Cartoof and L. Klerman, "Parental Consent for Abortion: Impact on Massachusetts Law," *American Journal of Public Health* 76(1986): 397–400.

72. S. Melton and N. Russon, "Adolescent Abortion," *American Psychologist* 42(1987): 69–83; Reproductive Freedom Project, *Parental Consent Laws on Abortion.*

73. Leo, "Sex and Schools."

74. Harris, *Public Attitudes.*

75. Benedetto, "AIDS Studies Become Part of the Curricula."

76. Zabin et al., "Evaluation of a Pregnancy Prevention Program."

77. St. Paul Maternity and Infant Care Project, *Health Services Project Description* (St. Paul, Minn.: St. Paul Maternity and Infant Care Project, 1985).

78. Petcheskey, *Abortion and Woman's Choice.*

79. Dryfoos, "A Time for New Thinking"; Dryfoos, "School-Based Health Clinics"; Kirby, *School-Based Health Clinics;* Select Committee on Children, Youth, and Families, *Teen Pregnancy: What Is Being Done? A State-By-State Look* (Washington, D.C.: U.S. Government Printing Office, 1986).

80. National Research Council, *Risking the Future.*

81. Dryfoos, "A Time for New Thinking"; Dryfoos, "School-Based Health Clinics."

82. Weinbaum, personal communication, 1986.

83. Weinbaum, paraphrased personal communication, 1986.

84. D. Polit, J. Kahn, and D. Stevens, *Final Impacts from Project Redirection* (New York: Manpower Development Research Center, 1985).

85. M. Burt, M. Kimmich, J. Goldmuntz, and F. Sonnenstein, *Helping Pregnant Adolescents: Outcomes and Costs of Service Delivery, Final Report on the Evaluation of Adolescent Pregnancy Programs* (Washington, D.C.: Urban Institute, 1984).

86. Fine, "Why Urban Adolescents Drop Into and Out of High School"; Weinbaum, personal communication, 1987.

87. Hispanic Policy Development Project, *1980 High School Sophomores from Poverty Backgrounds: Whites, Blacks, Hispanics Look at School and Adult Responsibilities,* vol. 1, no. 2 (New York: Hispanic Policy Development Project, 1987).

88. Children's Defense Fund, *Preventing Adolescent Pregnancy: What Schools Can Do* (Washington, D.C.: Children's Defense Fund, 1986).

89. Fine, "Why Urban Adolescents Drop Into and Out of High School."

90. Jones et al., "Teenage Pregnancy in Developed Countries."

91. Fine, "Why Urban Adolescents Drop Into and Out of High School."

PART FOUR

VIOLENCE IN SCHOOLS

OVER THE PAST SEVERAL YEARS, the issue of school violence has received enormous media attention, mostly in relation to the myriad of suburban school shootings that have
become all too familiar. Violence in schools, however, takes
many more forms than just guns and mass murders, as these
pieces vividly demonstrate.

In "Bullying as Sexual Harassment in Elementary
Schools," Nan Stein takes a critical look at young children
and how bullying and teasing, both within and between genders, is played out in their lives. James Garbarino focuses
more specifically on boys in his piece, "How Early Vulnerability Becomes Bad Behavior: Hurt Little Boys Become
Aggressive Big Boys," investigating what factors in the lives
of young boys may lead them down a path of aggression and
violence. Peggy Orenstein takes on the issue of sexual harassment in her piece, "Striking Back: Sexual Harassment at
Weston." This ethnographic look at the experiences of middle-
school girls reveals how sexual harassment is enacted
between children and how the response, or lack thereof, of
school administrators can perpetuate or even worsen the
problem. Finally, in "Boys to Men: Questions of Violence,"
Carol Gilligan leads a discussion between renowned
researchers on boys'-related issues, exploring the many facets

and elements of male violence, particularly why it happens and how to prevent it.

While shootings may be the only kind of school violence that makes the evening news, violence is happening in schools every day, sometimes in small and subtle ways. As these pieces reveal, whether it is teasing and bullying, sexual harassment, or outright physical aggression, violence between children is a key issue for schools to address.

18

BULLYING AS SEXUAL HARASSMENT IN ELEMENTARY SCHOOLS

Nan Stein

NO DOUBT MANY OF US can still conjure up the image of Jonathan Pre-vette, that cute little blond 6-year-old boy with thick glasses from Lexing-ton, North Carolina, who said he kissed, at her request, a little 6-year-old girl classmate and was then accused of sexual harassment by his school dis-trict in late September 1996. While he, his parents, and the spokesperson for the school district could be found for several weeks on the evening news and talk shows, nothing was ever heard from the little girl and her parents. How-ever, through a secondary source (Craig Koontz, chair of the school board), two journalists (Goodman, 1996; D. Nathan, personal communication, 1996) reported that the kiss was not mutual, that the little girl had not asked for it, that it was she who revealed the kiss to the school's administrators, and that she had subsequently blamed herself for all the fuss. However, as long as the parents of the little girl maintain their silence, the public will never know, and the little boy's version of the events will dominate.

According to the sociologist Laura O'Toole (1997), who did an analy-sis of 25 articles appearing in the national and regional press during a 2-week period at that time, one of the major motifs of the events as con-structed by Jonathan's parents was that of Alfalfa, of *Little Rascals* fame. That metaphor may well indeed linger in the public's consciousness about this event, subsuming all rational discussion and analysis of the events, the context, and the actors.

A critical question that lies at the heart of this and any discussion of sexual harassment is that of mutuality. Had the kiss been mutually desired, requested, or performed, whether the children were 6 or 16, kissing might have been against school rules but it would not be sexual harassment— that is, behavior that is unwanted and unwelcomed. Yet, the fact that the school chose to cast this event as sexual harassment is revealing. On the one hand, it demonstrates their vigilance in regard to the existence of inappropriate, unwanted, and unwelcome behaviors of a sexual nature in schools. By leaping to call it sexual harassment, maybe they hoped to ward off litigation by the girl's family; fear of lawsuits with their negative publicity and monetary damage awards are a major concern for many school administrators and school board attorneys. On the other hand, the administrators' panic attack followed by their retraction that "we never called it sexual harassment," and the feeding frenzy of the press did nothing to illuminate the larger problem of bullying in schools or to acknowledge that sexual harassment could and does exist in elementary schools.

The interviews with the boy's family and with school officials reinforced for me the absurdity of attempting to have conversations with young children about sexual harassment. Common sense should lead us to use language and concepts that are already in young children's vocabulary to talk about interactions with their peers that are unwanted and wanted, whether those interactions are verbal, touching, or playing. I have found that the word and concept of *bullying* is one that young children understand and use, and may capture the coercive, invasive, unwanted, and intrusive nature of both bullying and sexual harassment. Unfortunately, never once did the national press during the Jonathan Prevette episode touch on this larger problem of bullying that is indeed omnipresent in children's lives.

In this chapter I will explore some of the research that has been conducted on bullying schools, particularly bullying research that has a bearing on gender. However, in no way will this chapter be an exhaustive review of bullying research. I will discuss my preference, for educational and developmental reasons, for framing the problem of sexual harassment as bullying when we talk about it with children under the age of 10- or 11-years-old. Yet, by using the word bullying, I do not deny the existence of sexual harassment in elementary schools nor mean to imply that elementary schools are exempt from legal scrutiny; sexual harassment is against the law whereas bullying is not. Rather, I am voicing my opinion, confirmed somewhat by research, that with elementary-aged children, discussions framed as bullying rather than sexual harassment might be more developmentally appropriate.

Bullying: Definitions and Research

The antecedents of peer-to-peer sexual harassment in schools may be found in "bullying," behaviors children learn, practice, or experience beginning at a very young age. All boys know what a bully is, and many boys as well as girls have been victims of bullying. Much of the bullying that takes place at this age is between members of the same sex. Teachers and parents know about bullying, and many accept it as an unfortunate stage that some children go through on their way to adolescence and adulthood. Left unchecked and unchallenged, bullying may in fact serve as fertile practice ground for sexual harassment (Stein, 1993; 1995a).

Like its older cousin, sexual harassment, bullying deprives children of their rightful entitlement to be educated and secure in the knowledge that they will be safe and free from harm. Although laws in 38 states prohibit the practice of "hazing" in educational institutions (with hazing defined as the organized practice of induction, usually into a fraternity or sports team, through degrading behaviors, physical assault, or both), bullying floats free from legal restraint and adult intervention and is often not discussed as a deliberate part of the school curriculum (Stein, 1995a).

Scandinavia

The preeminent researcher in the world in the field of childhood-bullying research is Dan Olweus (1993, 1994), professor of psychology at the University of Bergen, Norway, who has conducted more than 20 years of research on bullying. His research has largely focused on Scandinavia: a study of 17,000 schoolchildren in Grades 3–9 in three cities in Sweden conducted in 1991; a study of 130,000 children in Norway, ages 8–16, representing almost a fourth of the whole student population in his country (1993); and a more detailed study, known as the Bergen (Norway) study of 2,500 boys and girls in Grades 4–7, along with data from 300 to 400 teachers and principals and 1,000 parents, on effects of an intervention program that he designed.

Before we try to import the findings from Olweus's research to children and schools in the United States, there are two major differences that need to be articulated. First of all, Sweden and Norway are largely homogeneous countries, without much diversity in race, ethnicity, language, or religion—factors that often serve as triggers for bullying. Second, those countries, similar to most countries in Europe and the Western world, have a standardized, nationalized curriculum, allowing for more comparisons to be made across the country and classroom. Olweus's research and suggestions for interventions are predicated upon national regulation of the whole school environment, including classroom content, pedagogy, informal and formal activities, guidance and counseling, and activities to stimulate parental involvement.

Olweus defines bullying as activity occurring when someone is "exposed, repeatedly and over time, to negative actions on the part of one or more other students" (Olweus, 1993, p. 9; 1994). "Negative actions" for Olweus are intentional infliction or attempts at such, including threatening, taunting, teasing, name-calling, hitting, pushing, kicking, pinching, and restraining. He also acknowledges that it is possible to carry out negative actions "without the use of words or physical contact, such as by making faces or dirty gestures, intentionally excluding someone from a group, or refusing to comply with another person's wishes" (1993, p. 9). Bullying implies an imbalance of strength and can include a single incident of a serious nature, yet not all acts of meanness, pestering, or picking on someone constitute bullying. Olweus emphasizes that the salient feature of his definition of bullying is that the negative actions are repeated and carried out over time. Almost to a word, Olweus's definitions of bullying seem interchangeable with definitions of sexual harassment in the United States.

Olweus's major findings on bullying have indicated:

○ Fifteen percent of all children are involved in bully/victim problems at some point in elementary and junior high. He estimates that approximately 7% of children have been bullies and 9% have been victimized, 3% have been bullied "about once a week or more frequently," and somewhat less than 2% bullied others at that rate (1993, p. 14).

○ Boys tend to engage in more direct physical bullying than girls, but the most common forms of bullying among boys were with words and gestures.

○ Boys were more often victims and, in particular, perpetrators of direct bullying.

○ Girls engaged in more indirect bullying such as slandering, spreading rumors, and manipulation of friendships.

○ Boys carried out much of the bullying that girls were subjected to: 60% of the bullied girls in Grades 5 through 7 reported being bullied mainly by boys; an additional 15–20% said they were bullied by both sexes, whereas 80% of boys said that they were bullied chiefly by boys.

○ In secondary/junior high school, more than four times as many boys as girls reported having bullied other students.

○ Bullying peaks in elementary school, and then decreases; there is a steady decline as children get older, meaning there is less of it at high school; however, a considerable part of the bullying that exists is carried out by older students, particularly in the earlier elementary grades.

○ Most bullying happens in school rather than on the way to or from school, especially in those places where students tend to be less closely supervised by adults (playground, lunchroom, hallways); those students who were bullied on their way to and from school tended to be bullied at school, too.

○ Parents and teachers are relatively unaware of the extent and intensity of bullying that exists. Children tend to underreport it to their parents and teachers due to embarrassment and fear of retaliation if the adult were to become involved.

In addition, Olweus's research has disclosed important information about the victims and bullies. He pointed out that there is not one universal type of bully or victim, so therefore a variety of interventions need to be designed for different kinds of bullies and different kinds of victims. Moreover, he refined the types of bullying into direct and indirect bullying (Ross, 1996). Moreover, the victims have no aberrant trait for the most part, though bullies may focus on or look for such a characteristic. It is important to note that according to Olweus (1993), having an aberrant trait is not the root cause of the bullying. Bullies are popular and have friends, whereas a victim is often a loner; popularity is likely to decrease a boy's risk of being bullied, and popularity is very tied to physical strength. Interestingly, Olweus points out that for girls, it is not clear whether any factor serves a similar protection function against bullying.

Olweus's research also laid to rest some myths that bullying is a big-city problem or that the size of the school or class is a salient feature. His research as well as that of another researcher in Finland (Lagerspetz, 1982, p. 24, in Olweus, 1993) gave no support at all to these hypotheses. He states conclusively that size of the class or school appears to be of negligible importance for the relative frequency or level of bully/victim problems in the class or the school. What does matter and have major significance in terms of the extent of bullying is the responses and attitudes of the adults in the school community.

Other countries have conducted research into bullying, including Canada (Pepler, Craig, Zeigler, & Charach, 1993); Japan (K. Hirano, personal communication as cited in Whitney & Smith, 1993, p. 5, and Olweus, 1993, p. 14); the Netherlands (Junger, 1990); Finland (Lagerspetz, Bjorqkvist, Berts, & King, 1982); Spain (Garcia & Perez, 1989); Australia (Rigby, Slee, & Connolly, 1991); and the United Kingdom.

United Kingdom

In the United Kingdom, initially the research was focused on single-sex boarding schools (Keise, 1992; Tattum & Lane, 1988; Tattum, 1993), but since the late 1980s, the research has expanded to include coed schools and racial bullying (Ahmad & Smith, 1994; Whitney & Smith, 1993; Tattum & Lane, 1988; Tattum, 1993; Tattum & Tattum, 1997). A valuable contribution from the British researchers has been their acknowledging and documenting the more indirect bullying and exclusion that is more typical of the repertoire of girls when they bully. Ahmad and Smith (1994) found in their research studies that whereas boys engaged in both verbal and physical abuse, girls were mainly involved in verbal abuse. Moreover, girls seemed to be more involved in perpetrating indirect bullying, which includes name-calling, gossip, rumors, secret-telling, refusing to be friends, refusing to allow someone to play, shunning, and playing tricks on someone.

In particular, two British studies illuminate the gendered nature of bullying. Whitney and Smith (1993) in their 1990 study of 6,700 students, ranging in age from 8 to 16 years old, in 24 schools in Sheffield found that the sex difference for being bullied is slight, but that girls tended to be bullied less than boys. In addition, boys admitted to bullying other boys considerably more than girls. They found that most bullying was carried out mainly by one boy; next came bullying by several boys, then mixed-sex bullying, followed by bullying by several girls, and least of all bullying by one girl. They found this pattern to be consistent in both junior/middle schools and secondary schools. Moreover, their research confirmed previous findings on gender differences: girls are equally likely to be bullied (slightly less so in secondary schools), but are only about half as likely to be involved in bullying others; and boys are bullied almost entirely by other boys, whereas girls are bullied by both sexes. Furthermore, boys are more involved in physical forms of bullying whereas girls specialize in more verbal and indirect forms. In other words, boys bully both sexes, often in physical ways, but girls bully only other girls, often in indirect ways. It remains, however, that the most common form of bullying is "being called nasty names" (p. 22), and that the playground is the most common location for bullying.

Smith, along with researcher Yvette Ahmad, reviewed sex differences in bullying. They state unequivocally that "sex differences in all forms of aggression have been repeatedly found, and bullying is no exception" (Ahmad & Smith, 1994, p. 70). In their own study they modified Olweus's (1993) definitions and accordingly the questionnaires to include forms of indirect bullying, which were not explicit in Olweus's original definitions, in order to be able to capture those forms of bullying in which girls typically engage. They surveyed over 1,400 students in five schools (two middle and three secondary) with a mixture of racial groups. Their results confirmed that boys are more involved than girls in bullying others, whether one is looking at indirect or direct bullying. Boys in both middle school and secondary school are usually bullied by other boys and rarely by girls. For girls, however, the picture is different: At the middle school level, they are most likely bullied by boys, but at the secondary level, they are most likely to be bullied by other girls (Ahmad & Smith, 1994). Moreover, for girls and boys in middle school, the playground is the most common site for bullying, but by secondary school, the most common site for girls becomes the classroom, then the corridors, whereas for boys, the playground remains the most common location.

Their results were similar to Whitney and Smith's 1993 study. They found that bullying decreased with age; boys were more likely than girls to report being bullied by one or several boys whereas girls were more likely than boys to report being bullied by one or several girls, or by both boys and girls; it was unusual for boys to report being bullied by one or several girls. Furthermore, boys were more likely to be physically hit and threatened than were girls, whereas girls were more likely to experience verbal forms of bullying (being called nasty names and indirect bullying, such as no one talking to them). These sex differences were found in both middle and secondary schools. By secondary school, physical bullying has largely decreased for girls, but there is an escalation of their involvement in indirect bullying, especially spreading rumors about someone else (Ahmad & Smith, 1994, p. 81). Ahmad and Smith conclude that there are both qualitative and quantitative research findings that confirm the existence of male and female forms of bullying, but they assert that this finding does not mean that these forms are exclusive to each sex.

Canada

Recent studies in Canada (1991–1995), summarized in a paper by O'Connell and colleagues (1997), include for the first time a study of 588 children in Grades 1–3, the first study of bullying and victimization problems among such young children.

Results from this younger sample included the following developmental differences: Peers intervened (at 24% of the incidents) in bullying episodes for Grades 1–3 as opposed to interventions in Grades 4–6 (at 11% of the time) or Grades 7–8 (at 7% of the time). Other developmental differences emerged when the students were asked, "Could you join in bullying?" In Grades 1–3, 12% of the children answered yes, whereas 31% in Grades 4–6 said yes, compared to 49% in Grades 7–8. The final striking developmental difference was in the realm of willingness to help the victim. In short, it declined with age: 57% of the students in Grades 1–3 were willing, but only 39% in Grades 4–6, and 27% in Grades 7–8. Indeed, the cumulative results of this study provide a sad portrait of aging, compassion, and empathy.

Moreover, these Canadian studies showed a decline in adult involvement in bullying episodes. Children in the younger grades (1–3) reported higher (37%) adult interventions as opposed to 26% in Grades 4–6, and only 30% in Grades 7 and 8. In summary, the Canadian researchers found that with age children were more willing to join in the bullying and less willing to help a victim, and that there was a decrease in reports of peers helping victims. This final finding is consistent with the finding of decreased concern for victims in Rigby et al.'s (1991) Australian study.

United States

In the United States, on the other hand, most of the initial research on bullying was designed from a psychological/psychopathological point of view. There seems to have been a tendency to pathologize the problem, with a focus on bullies or on treatment programs to rid them of their bullying tendencies or to develop guideposts by which to judge potential bullies. Largely this research has consisted of interviews with criminals, including jailed molesters or pedophiles who traced back their conduct and behavior. Although this methodology may illuminate their trajectories, it is not a particularly good measure for making generalizations about normative behavior for the majority of boys and men.

Several recent studies have focused on school-aged children in the United States. A study conducted by Oliver, Hazler, and Hoover (1994) looked at children in Grades 7–12, and found that girls, significantly more than boys, felt that bullies had higher social status than did their victims. This study also found that even in small-town, allegedly safe environments, 81% of the males and 72% of the females reported being bullied by their peers, with ridicule and verbal and social harassment as the most common forms.

A second study from the Center for Adolescent Studies at Indiana University of 558 middle school boys and girls found that bullies, compared with other children, faced more forceful parental discipline at home, spent less time with adults, and had fewer positive adult role models or positive peer influences (Seppa, 1996). Gender was not teased out in this study.

The work of two U.S. researchers has a bearing on the issue of gender-based teasing and bullying. Barrie Thorne's book *Gender Play: Girls and Boys in School* (1993), although not explicitly about bullying, certainly raises questions about the nature of gendered play and interactions, and offers many insights into the development of gender relations in elementary school. She found that boys use sexual insults against girls, and that they regard girls as a group as a source of contamination. Boys and girls who don't conform to this prototype, and especially those who desire to be friends with one another, are at risk of teasing or ostracization. One girl, speaking of her friendship with a boy, at church and in their neighborhood, poignantly offers the reason why they don't speak to each other at school: "We pretend not to know each other so we won't get teased" (p. 50). The threat of heterosexual teasing may act as a deterrent to cross-gender friendships or may drive those friendships underground.

In addition, Donna Eder and colleagues at Indiana University in their book *School Talk: Gender and Adolescent Culture* (1995), and in a more recent book chapter (Eder, 1997), studies sexual aggression within the culture of middle school students. She and her colleagues have studied language and informal talk in middle school, including gossip, teasing, insulting, and story-telling. As with the European studies, Eder found that boys and girls alike used sexual put-downs toward girls, and that girls' use of words such as *sluts* or *whores* helped to maintain a hierarchy with male-oriented, tough, and sexually aggressive boys at the top. Girls also tormented boys who were friendly toward them by casting doubt on their heterosexuality. Eder points out these and other ways in which girls contribute indirectly towards sexual aggression.

Finally, my own research into sexual harassment through the survey in the September 1992 issue of *Seventeen* magazine garnered responses from girls as young as 9 and 10 years old. Out of 4,300 surveys returned by the time of the deadline, we randomly selected 2,000 of them to be analyzed (Stein, Marshall, & Tropp, 1993); of those 2,000 surveys, one came from a 9-year-old; seven from 10-year-olds; 38 from 11-year-olds, and 226 from 12-year-olds. There was no doubt from these responses that girls even at this young age knew about gender-based harassment—

either from their own experiences or from observing it happening in their schools.

Pilot Studies on Bullying

In the winter of 1993, I began a small pilot project that involved seven classrooms in three elementary schools in Boston and Brookline, Massachusetts. For a period of 8–10 weeks, I developed and taught fourth- and fifth-grade students a variety of lessons on teasing and bullying. Over the course of the following 2 years, these classroom lessons were further refined by some of the teachers and me, and were finally published as a teaching guide on teasing and bullying (Sjostrom & Stein, 1996).

Beginning in October 1995, further research was funded by the U.S. Department of Education (Women's Educational Equity Act Project, and Safe and Drug-Free Schools and Communities Act) to look at gender-based teasing and bullying in Grades K–3. With research partners in New York City (Educational Equity Concepts), our research was conducted at one elementary school on the Upper West Side of New York City that had a student population of mixed ethnic and socioeconomic status as well as in three schools in Framingham, Massachusetts. The three Framingham schools have a student population that is predominately White but with a sizable number of ethnic minority students, including Hispanic, African American, and Asian, and recent immigrants from the Azores and Eastern Europe. In addition, at two out of the three Massachusetts schools, there were students who lived in homeless shelters or shelters for battered women. The faculty in all the schools, in both cities, were almost exclusively White women, a major limitation of our research that will restrict the generalizations that can be drawn from this project.

In both cities, the schools that participated were self-selected; the principals were more or less recruited, as well the classroom teachers. In Massachusetts, we observed more than 450 children in a total of 17 classrooms in Grades K–3, as well as conducted interviews with 27 individual children. The children whom we interviewed were selected by the teachers to provide a sampling of those identified by teachers as initiators, recipients, or bystanders of bullying. Within each grade level, there were equal numbers of girls and boys interviewed. The sample of 27 students included numbers of children who were of different racial and socioeconomic backgrounds: one half of them were White, and the other half were Asian, African American, Hispanic, or biracial; four were children with an identifiable special need.

Moreover, we conducted focus groups with teachers and a separate set for parents at each of the schools. A total of 24 teachers participated in our focus groups, including teachers from Grades K–5, plus bilingual, special education, art, physical education, and music teachers. About 50 parents attended the information meetings that were held at two schools, but only 10 of the parents were able to actually participate in the organized focus group.

Within the parameters of our research, our results mirrored those of Olweus's as outlined above. We found that the responses and attitudes of the adults had major significance on the extent of bullying that occurred. In fact, we could identify distinct trends in the three different schools, with the principal's leadership style and responses playing a central role that also had a bearing upon the teachers' responses to children's teasing and bullying. In addition, the tone and climate that the teachers set in the classroom had an impact on the incidence of teasing and bullying that we observed. Our observations at two of the schools with the greatest difficulties, and later confirmed by comments from the teacher focus groups, pointed toward a lack of respect by the teachers toward their students and their families. Teachers tended to use authoritarian measures, such as yelling at students, or making comments that embarrassed them or demeaned them.

Findings from the Children

The interviews with the children confirmed and corroborated both our observations and the information provided by the teachers in the focus groups. This notwithstanding, the parents and teachers doubted the veracity of what the children would reveal to us; the adults assumed that the children would invent events or distort reality. However, the students we interviewed told it like we saw it.

In the Massachusetts sites, we observed little overt gender-based teasing and bullying except for teasing about body parts, and incidents of exclusion by gender. However, teachers and parents reported gender-based incidents largely occurring on the buses or in bathrooms. According to the parents and teachers, these incidents involved same-sex initiators and recipients. On the other hand, we observed numerous incidents of class and racially based bullying; for example, students were singled out because they were Hispanic or poor, new immigrants were targeted, students were excluded from informal-time playing on the basis of their appearance or ethnicity or both. Interestingly, we observed several students with obvious disabilities, but they were not targeted for their disabilities (one wonders if teasing about disabilities was "off limits").

There were some incidents of gender-based exclusion or teasing that we couldn't adequately document because those events were not overt or we were unable to hear comments or talk among the children. These gender-based incidents included two salient interactions. The first revealing incident that was typical and repeatedly occurred at both indoor and outdoor play times, when groups of girls or boys were able to effectively exclude (or systematically eliminate) opposite-sex peers by setting rules or tasks that the opposite-sex peers either couldn't or wouldn't follow. Examples from such strategies were giving opposite-sex peers undesirable roles in a game (roles that were eliminated once the offending peer, usually a boy, left), or creating new rules such as hitting hard slams during ball games, which stopped once the peer (usually girls) left. At no point did we overhear gendered exclusion spoken about; in other words, we never heard "no boys allowed" or "girls can't play with us." Whatever code was operating was unspoken and subtle, yet it was fully operative.

The second salient event occurred during recess at one school, where the boys typically played with balls and the girls typically played with jump ropes. Often these items were brought from home because the school didn't have any to offer to the children (particularly jump ropes); without these items, there was virtually nothing for the children to do other than run around the playground. In previous weeks, the boys had been teasing the girls by making a game of stealing their ropes. The teachers had become so annoyed at the fussing that resulted (girls complaining to the teachers about the boys' behavior) that the teachers responded by prohibiting jump ropes from the playground, thereby effectively taking away the girls' play. The boys seemed to recognize this development as a gendered triumph.

Our interviews with children about their experiences in schools produced findings similar to those reported in other research studies (Ahmad & Smith, 1994; Olweus, 1993, 1994). Those results include:

- Transition time, lunch, and recess were times when teasing and bullying were most likely to occur.
- Teasing and bullying were most prevalent when adults were not present, not paying attention, or not physically available. In the Massachusetts schools where we observed, transition times, recess, lunch, arrival, and departure times were supervised by untrained parent volunteers or other low-paid employees, individuals whom

the children viewed as people without much authority. Moreover, at these times, adult-to-child ratios were very high.

○ When students go to adults, or when adults witness incidents of teasing and bullying, the students feel they are not listened to or taken seriously; they are often admonished to work it out on their own. Ironically, the students felt that they were doing just what the adults told them to do, which was to try to work out their problems with other students, and if that didn't work, then they should tell an adult. But when they did approach an adult, students got a conflicting message because the adults were typically annoyed and impatient and seemed to brush them off by telling the child to go back and deal with it on his or her own. The adults typically didn't give students helpful guidance about how to do this, nor did they give support to them for attempting to do it.

○ Students felt that perpetrators were not punished; many children felt that the consequences (such as going to the principal's office) were fun, and did not carry a negative connotation or consequence. The victims were then often subjected to more teasing either because they told (other words for this behavior include *ratted, dimed, squealed*) or because the teasers felt that they could get away with it, because the adult hadn't intervened. So the cycle continued and often escalated.

○ Students surmised that children resort to bullying for fun or because they're bored.

As one might expect, when the adults were asked about this cycle, they put an entirely different spin on the events. Both parents and teachers felt that students came to them with very trivial concerns, and couldn't understand why the children couldn't work out these problems on their own. Nonetheless, teachers also frequently complained that principals trivialized their concerns with teasing and bullying, claiming that they had more important or difficult issues to manage, usually problems that involved the older students in the school. Teachers complained and hypothesized that if the little problems in Grades K–3 were appropriately handled with discipline, then there wouldn't be as many big issues in the upper grades.

From our observations and interviews with the children, it seemed that first the students were asking for better and more effective skills (what to say; models of conduct) to manage their problems on their own, and second for support, authority, and a belief in their attempts to deal with the offending peer. What we found particularly disturbing about this cycle was that it echoed exactly what my research has found with older students about their experiences of sexual harassment—that it happens in public, that adults were often watching, and that when students reported the sexual harassment to the adults, the adults either did not believe the students, trivialized the problem, or dismissed the events entirely.

Results from Focus Groups with Parents and Teachers

Two sets of separate focus groups were held, one set with parents and a separate set with teachers. The results revealed that both parents and teachers felt that teasing and bullying were problems that existed both at school and at home with siblings, and that the problem seemed to be getting worse, in both the amount and degree of teasing and bullying. The following is a long list of the behaviors that the adults noticed about teasing and bullying in children:

- "Teases du jour": cooties; being fat (directed at girls more than boys)
- Talk about "dating" or "love" (even among second and third graders); threatening to kiss or hug another child, a threat particularly used by girls toward boys
- "Meanness" which usually meant exclusion, won't be friends, name-calling; focusing on a feature of a child's appearance, typically their clothing, which seemed to be a stand-in for a socioeconomic-class commentary
- Put-downs that involved one's mother ("your mother . . . ")
- Physical behaviors that usually involved boys on boys; giving another child a wedgie (that is, picking up a child by their underwear), pantsing (which means pulling down a child's pants, or underwear)
- Body-part talk (especially boys teasing other boys about the size or shape of their penis)
- Using the F-word ("f— you") toward other adults as well as other kids
- Taking the possessions of other children
- Telling a child that he or she is a member of the opposite sex: "you kick/throw/[etc.] like a girl" and "you look like a boy/girl"
- Using derogatory words about sexual preference (*gay, fag, lezzie*) or race or ethnic background (*nigger, spic*)

○ Proclaiming "I don't like so-and-so because s/he's a — [racial epithet]"; calling girls "bitches"

Both parents and teachers indicated that they thought the children really did not understand the meaning of the words that they used, but knew that the words were bad. They also noted that verbal teasing quickly escalated to physical acts between students. In particular, teachers focused on:

○ Absence of students' qualms about swearing at or threatening teachers (e.g., "You can't touch me!")

○ Lack of support from principals (e.g., being sent to the principal's office was considered fun for students, and principals were afraid to take a stand against teasing and bullying)

○ Lack of support from administrators (ineffectiveness of guidance counselors designated to deal with serious or longstanding behavioral difficulties)

○ Principals not taking a stand with teachers who exhibited disrespectful or bullying behaviors

○ Principals being more concerned with older students and trivializing difficulties with the younger students

○ Too much leeway being given to children from so-called troubled backgrounds (e.g., "Don't do it again, OK?")

○ Lack of consistent, effective policies that held consequences for teasing and bullying (something beyond detentions, or telling the offending students, even those in kindergarten, to "write until their hands fall off" as a punishment for most infractions)

○ Frequency of stealing, fighting, and problems on the bus

Is Bullying Sexual Harassment?

The simple answer is yes, but if it is a boy-to-girl interaction, then it is more likely to be labeled as sexual harassment than if the interactions occurred between same-sex members or if it involved behaviors that came from girls directed toward boys; rarely are same-sex behaviors deemed to be sexual harassment. However, if all the protagonists are in elementary school, then sexual harassment will rarely be acknowledged. Words such as *pestering, annoying, bothering, hassling,* or *bugging* will more than likely creep into descriptions of the events; the law will rarely be seen as operative or having application. Yet, since sexual harassment is against the law, and bullying is not, more students, their families, and lawyers will try to frame the events as sexual harassment, rather than as bullying, regardless of the ways that school administrators try to characterize the incidents. Irrespective of the ways in which school officials frame or dismiss the incidents, parents may file self-standing criminal complaints against the individuals involved, as opposed to being limited to filing civil court actions against the school district and personnel. There have been lawsuits and complaints that involved children in elementary schools (fifth grader Aurelia Davis in federal court in Georgia; third grader Jonathan Harms and first grader Cheltzie Hentz in Minnesota under Minnesota state law; and the U.S. Department of Education's Office for Civil Rights complaints in Modesto and Newark, California, that both involved elementary school students).[1]

Although much of Olweus's research findings about children's behaviors might qualify as sexual harassment under U.S. law (Title IX), with liability falling on the school system, he never discusses sexual harassment. Nonetheless, his definition of bullying has many parallels to sexual harassment, particularly in the repeated and long-term nature of the behaviors targeted against an individual. Severity is not the salient feature in his definition of bullying; similarly with sexual harassment, severity is not the ruling feature: *repeated* and *pervasive* are defining terms that carry as much weight.

Our research in Grades K–3 points toward the existence of conduct that could be labeled and possibly litigated as sexual harassment. Our research also indicates the usefulness of conducting classroom discussions and a whole-school approach toward bullying; it is developmentally appropriate and seems to engage the students, appearing both relevant and helpful.

If educators and advocates pose and present the problem as "bullying" to young children, rather than labeling it immediately as "sexual harassment," we can engage children and universalize the phenomenon as one that boys as well as girls will understand and accept as problematic. Hopefully, such an approach will go a long way toward engendering compassion and empathy in the students. Moreover, we can simultaneously avoid demonizing all little boys as potential "harassers" by initially presenting these hurtful and offensive behaviors as bullying, a behavior found in the repertoire of both boys and girls. Activities that ask the children to distinguish between "teasing" and "bullying" can help them focus on the boundaries between appropriate and inappropriate, hurtful behaviors.

Returning to the voices of children, the reflections of fifth graders at the end of the 8–10 week unit on teasing and bullying display new conceptual connections as well as insights about themselves and their classmates.

> Well, since we started this, people in my class and I learned a lot. Now they stopped doing mean things to each other. Like now that people know how I felt when they called me "shrimp" and "shorty" and other mean things they stopped doing that. Now we don't hurt other people's feelings and respect one another even if the person is short, tall or opposite sex. (male)

> I see a big difference in myself since we started discussing bullying, teasing and sexual harassment. Example: when it was my turn to be captain of the kickball game I picked x as a player. As soon as I picked x, he started to pick all the players and suddenly x was the captain. Not only that but x also picked who was pitcher and the batting order (all stuff captain does). So, I stood up to x reminded him that I was captain (I would have never done that before). It made me feel good inside. (female)

> I do see a difference in the way that all of the boys in the class are treating the girls now. 1) They have mostly stopped teasing us and chasing us down the hallways while we are coming back from recess. 2) The boys have also mostly stopped insulting all of the girls and trying to dis us. I think that the girls have also mostly stopped teasing and bullying all of the shrimp or short boys. (female)

> I really think sexual harassment can hurt because sometimes people may tease you about your body parts and it really hurts our feelings because you can't change them in any way. It can also interfere with your school work because all your thoughts are on your anger and then you can't concentrate. If I am harassed in the future, I will stand up for my rights and if a teacher doesn't care, I will pressure him or her to punish my harasser. (male) (Stein, 1995a, p. 150)

Gaining a conceptual framework and common vocabulary that elementary-school-age children can understand, apply, and reapply will help them find their own links between teasing and bullying and sexual harassment. The connection between bullying and sexual harassment in schools is of critical importance—it is one that educators need to make explicit and public by deliberately discussing these subjects in age-appropriate ways with children.

NOTE

1. Davis v. Monroe County (GA) Board of Education, 1994; Harms v. Independent School District #47 (Sauk Rapids-Rice), 1993; Eden Prairie School District #272, MN, 1993; Modesto City Schools, CA, 1993; Newark Unified School District, CA, 1993 (also see Stein, 1995a).

REFERENCES

Ahmad, Y., & Smith, P. K. (1994). Bullying in schools and the issue of sex differences. In J. Archer (Ed.), *Male violence* (pp. 70–83). New York: Routledge.

Davis v. Monroe County (GA) Board of Education, 862 F. Supp. 863 (M.D. Ga. 1994), *rev'd*, 120 F.3d 1390 (11th Cir. 1997) (en banc), *rev'd and remanded to district court*, 119 S.Ct. 1661 (1999).

Eden Prairie School District #272, MN, No. 05–92–1174 (Office for Civil Rights, U.S. Department of Education, Chicago, Ill. April 27, 1993).

Eder, D. (1997). Sexual aggression within the school culture. In B. Bank and P. Hall (Eds.), *Gender, equity, and schooling: Policy and practice* (pp. 93–112). New York: Garland.

Eder, D., with Evans, C. C., & Parker, S. (1995). *School talk: Gender and adolescent culture.* New Brunswick, NJ: Rutgers University Press.

Garcia, I. F., & Perez, G. Q. (1989). Violence, bullying, and counseling in the Iberian Peninsula: Spain. In E. Roland & E. Munthe (Eds.), *Bullying: An international perspective* (pp. 41–52). London: David Fulton.

Goodman, E. (1996, October 13). The truth behind "the kiss." *Boston Globe,* pp. F1, 8.

Harms v. Independent School District #47 (Sauk Rapids–Rice). No. ED1990019 (Minnesota Department of Human Rights, May 14, 1993).

Junger, M. (1990). Intergroup bullying and racial harassment in the Netherlands. *Sociology and Social Research, 74,* 65–72.

Keise, C. (1992). *Sugar and spice? Bullying in single-sex schools.* Staffordshire, UK: Trentham Books.

Lagerspetz, K. M., Bjorqkvist, K., Berts, M., & King, E. (1982). Group aggression among school children in three schools. *Scandinavian Journal of Psychology, 23,* 45–52.

Modesto City Schools, CA, No. 09–93–1319 (Office for Civil Rights, U.S. Department of Education, San Francisco, Calif., Dec. 10, 1993).

Newark Unified School District, CA, No. 09–93–1113 (Office for Civil Rights, U.S. Department of Education, San Francisco, Calif., July 7, 1993).

O'Connell, P., Sedighdeilami, F., Pepler, D. J., Craig, W., Connolly, J., Atlas, R., Smith, C., & Charach, A. (1997, April). *Prevalence of bullying and victimization among Canadian elementary and middle school children.* Poster session presented at the Society for Research on Child Development, Washington, DC.

Oliver, R., Hazler, R., & Hoover, J. (1994). The perceived role of bullying in small-town midwestern schools. *Journal of Counseling and Development, 72*(4), 416–420.

Olweus, D. (1993). *Bullying at school: What we know and what we can do.* Oxford: Blackwell.

Olweus, D. (1994). Annotation: Bullying at school: Basic facts and effects of a school based intervention program. *Journal of Child Psychology and Psychiatry, 35,* 1171–1190.

O'Toole, L. (1997, August). *It was only an innocent kiss: On the use, mis-use and non-use of context in public discussion of sexual harassment.* Paper presented at Sixth Annual Sociologists Against Sexual Harassment Conference, Toronto, CA.

Pepler, D., Craig, W., Zeigler, S., & Charach, A. (1993). A school-based anti-bullying intervention: Preliminary evaluation. In D. Tattum (Ed.), *Understanding and managing bullying* (pp. 76–91). Oxford: Heinemann Educational.

Rigby, K., Slee, P., & Connolly, C. (1991). Victims and bullies in school communities. *Journal of the Australian Society of Victimology, 1,* 25–31.

Ross, D. M. (1996). *Childhood bullying and teasing: What school personnel, other professionals, and parents can do.* Alexandria, VA: American Counseling Association.

Seppa, N. (1996, October). Bullies spend less time with adults. *APA Monitor, 24*(10), 41.

Sjostrom, L., & Stein, N. (1996). *Bullyproof: A teacher's guide on teaching and bullying for use with fourth and fifth grade students.* Wellesley, MA: Wellesley College Center for Research on Women.

Stein, N. (1993a). No laughing matter: Sexual harassment in K–12 schools. In E. Buchwald, P. R. Fletcher, & M. Roth, *Transforming a rape culture* (pp. 311–331). Minneapolis, MN: Milkweed Editions.

Stein, N. (1993b). It happens here, too: Sexual harassment and child sexual abuse in elementary and secondary schools. In S. K. Biklen & D. Pollard, *Gender and Education: 92nd yearbook of the National Society for the Study of Education* (pp. 191–203). Chicago: University of Chicago Press.

Stein, N. (1993c, January). Sexual harassment in the schools. *School Administrator, 1*(50), 14–21.

Stein, N. (1993d, October 18). It breaks your soul and brings you down. *New York Teacher, 35*(4), 23. New York: New York State United Teachers.

Stein, N. (1995a, Summer). Sexual harassment in K–12 schools: The public performance of gendered violence. *Harvard Educational Review, 65*(2), 145–162.

Stein, N., Marshall, N., & Tropp, L. (1993). *Secrets in public: Sexual harassment in our schools. A report on the results of a* Seventeen *magazine survey.* Wellesley, MA: Wellesley College Center for Research on Women.

Tattum, D. P. (Ed.). (1993). *Understanding and managing bullying.* Oxford: Heinemann.

Tattum, D. P., & Lane, D. A. (Eds.). (1988). *Bullying in schools.* Stoke-on-Trent: Trentham Books.

Tattum, D. P., & Tattum, E. (1997). *Bullying in the early years.* London: Gulbenkian Foundation.

Thorne, B. (1993). *Gender play: Girls and boys in school.* New Brunswick, NJ: Rutgers University Press.

Whitney, I., & Smith, P. E. (1993). A survey of the nature and extent of bullying in junior/middle and secondary schools. *Educational Research, 31*(1), 3–25.

19

HOW EARLY VULNERABILITY BECOMES BAD BEHAVIOR

HURT LITTLE BOYS BECOME
AGGRESSIVE BIG BOYS

James Garbarino

WHAT COMES NEXT in the chain of events that leads from disconnection and hurt in the early years to the act of committing lethal aggression in adolescence? What stands between early psychological vulnerability and later youth violence? That is the question I am seeking to answer when I talk with Dennis.

Dennis was sixteen when I first met him, the youngest of two children. Tall with short hair and very intense dark eyes, he grew up in a small city in the care of his mother and father. Both parents worked—he at the post office, she in a hospital. While his parents worked, he was cared for by his grandmother a few days a week and at a day-care center the rest of the time. When he was six years old Dennis started first grade at the school three blocks from his home.

It is my first interview with Dennis. I have been going through the chronology of events in his life—where he lived and with whom, where he went to school and how he liked it, and so on. He lists four different elementary schools he attended as a child. "Why did you change schools so often when you were a child?" I ask. "I was bad," is his simple answer. "How bad?" I ask. "I'd get in trouble and get suspended," he replies with a smile. "After getting suspended a few times, I'd get expelled and then move on to another school. That's the way it went until I got to high school, and then I stopped going most of the time." He says his parents told him he was always more difficult than his older sister. "I did have one good year, though," he reports. "At the Alternative School." There, he tells me, he didn't get into much trouble. The classes were small, and there were only a hundred kids in the whole school. "The teachers made an effort to understand my problems," he says. Whatever good they did for Dennis, it was either too late or simply not enough to set him on the right track.

The following year, when he was transferred back to the regular high school program, all Dennis's old problems resurfaced, and by May of that year he had stopped going to school altogether. A year later he was arrested on a charge of being part of a drug-dealing network in his neighborhood. Convicted of this crime, he served four months in a juvenile detention center. After he was released, he didn't even bother to go back to school. He simply picked up where he had left off. Six months later Dennis was arrested again, this time in connection with the shooting of two boys in the park across the street from the school he no longer attended.

Fourteen-year-old Thomas tells much the same story. I talk with him while he awaits trial for murdering a seventeen-year-old in a street confrontation two blocks from his home in a small town in rural upstate New York. "I was a terror," he says, recounting a litany of troubles. Like Dennis's, Thomas's problems started in early childhood, beginning with an escalating pattern of disobedience and graduating to fights at school. He lived with his grandmother and her husband, the only child in a household with two middle-aged adults.

When Thomas talks about his childhood, he is quick to point out that he wanted to do better than he did—in school, with his grandparents, and with the neighbors. His grandmother says, shaking her head, "Thomas is a nice boy, but he was always a handful. My husband and I tried our best with him, but . . ." Her voice trails off. I've seen the records in Thomas's case, and they document an ongoing saga of misdeeds: stealing money from his grandmother's purse, calling in a false fire alarm to his elementary school, skipping school with some older boys when he was nine years old, smoking in the bathroom in sixth grade, not coming home when he was supposed to after school, and getting into fights on the playground.

Malcolm, too, was a difficult child whose problems started early. His mother was absent for the first four years of his life. She was in the army, and Malcolm lived those years with his grandmother. Once his mother did return, she tried to impose her will on a little boy who knew her only from pictures, cards, and phone calls, and he rebelled. Malcolm was a troublesome child in kindergarten, always into mischief. If there was a wad of gum in the goldfish bowl, Malcolm was the most likely suspect. If there was a tussle in the back of the line on the way to the gym, Malcolm was probably involved. In second grade he was suspended for a day for punching another boy so hard he knocked the wind out of him. By the time he was in third grade he had started fighting for real, not just the tussles common to many a boy's childhood but full-fledged fighting. At ten years of age he was suspended from school for a fight that landed another boy in the hospital with a seriously injured eye and a broken nose.

Such stories are not unusual in the accounts of childhood told by violent youths, who by and large started misbehaving early in life. These boys say that the adults who took care of them often remind them of their early misbehavior, even today. Such stories are in the social worker's notes in Michael's case file; Michael's mother had told the caseworker, "The boy has always been a problem—willful and disobedient. No matter how hard I punished him, he wouldn't behave." Michael has the scars on his back to validate her claim about using harsh punishment. But he also has taken her words to heart and has folded them into his own self-portrait. Now nineteen years old, Michael says that he was "a rogue" but that his brother Robert was "submissive." The pattern was set by the time the brothers reached elementary school: Michael fought with other children, disobeyed teachers, and destroyed property, whereas Robert submitted to adult authority in every situation in every way. Today's violent high school boys are, for the most part, the bad boys in elementary school from five or six years ago.

I saw such bad boys during my own brief stint as an elementary school teacher in the 1960s. I recall one such child as if it were yesterday. As I watched him on the playground, six-year-old Damon dropped a banana peel on the ground and ran off. The principal saw him commit this minor act of delinquency and tracked him down. "Pick it up," he said to the boy. Damon did, and then promptly dropped it again. "Pick it up and put it in the trash," the principal commanded. Damon did so, paused, and then pulled the banana peel out of the trash and dropped it on the ground again. "Pick it up, put it in the trash, and leave it there!" the exasperated principal yelled. These are the children who leave their teachers weary every day.

Coupled with aggression, this sort of chronic misbehavior lays down the foundation for bigger problems in later life unless teachers and parents intervene early to get these boys back on track. The good news is that this redirection is possible. According to the results of a study conducted by Johns Hopkins University psychologist Sheppard Kellam and his colleagues, violence prevention programs and effective classroom management techniques in first grade can have a dramatic effect on the likelihood that an aggressive six-year-old will become a violent thirteen-year-old. Kellam's group found that highly aggressive six-year-old boys placed within well-managed first grade classrooms run by effective teachers were three times less likely to be highly aggressive by the time they reached eighth grade than similarly aggressive boys who were placed in a chaotic classroom with ineffective teachers.

When Bad Behavior Starts Early

Research by psychologist Leonard Eron and colleagues documents that by age eight boys' patterns of aggressive behavior and attitude are already crystallizing, so much so that without intervention such patterns tend to continue into adulthood. When they began their studies in the 1960s, Eron and his colleagues asked eight-year-olds to identify the aggressive children in their classrooms. "Who are the children in your class who hit people, who start fights, who kick people?" they asked. When they followed up on these children three decades later, they found that, by and large, the children who had been identified as aggressive at age eight became adults who at age thirty-eight hit family members, get into fights in the community, and drive their cars aggressively. (By the way, this gives a developmental spin to the problem of road rage: it may start as "tricycle rage.")

There is a formal name for the pattern of behavior that Dennis calls being "bad" and Thomas calls being "a terror." Psychologists and psychiatrists call it Conduct Disorder. For children to be labeled as having conduct disorder, they must meet a set of criteria developed by the American Psychiatric Association and published in its official *Diagnostic and Statistical Manual of Mental Disorders* (DSM). The current edition, DSM-IV, defines Conduct Disorder as "a repetitive and persistent pattern of behavior in which the basic rights of others or major age-appropriate societal norms or rules are violated." The manual's criteria include aggression to people and animals, destruction of property, deceitfulness or theft, and serious violations of rules. This is a familiar pattern to me; I see it often with incarcerated boys. That is not surprising, for at least 80 percent of boys in juvenile prisons and rehabilitation programs, boys like Dennis, Malcolm, Thomas, and Kip, carry with them this rather cold diagnostic label.

Particularly important for understanding lethal youth violence is the question of when a boy's pattern of chronic bad behavior starts, that is, whether it begins early (childhood onset) or later (adolescence onset).

British criminologists Farrington and Hawkins report that when Conduct Disorder begins in childhood rather than adolescence, it is more likely to continue into adulthood. Other investigators, such as psychologist Alan Kazdin, agree that youths with childhood-onset Conduct Disorder are more likely than those with adolescence-onset Conduct Disorder to engage in aggressive and criminal behavior and are more likely to remain chronically dysfunctional into and throughout adulthood.

Why is childhood-onset Conduct Disorder more severe? There are no simple answers, but there are some compelling ideas from child development research. First, if bad behavior starts in childhood rather than adolescence, it has a longer period to build up and interfere with normal development. When it begins in adolescence, a boy is more likely to have positive experiences and relationships from the past to fall back on, and the troubling behavior is more likely to be a temporary phase reflecting difficulty in meeting the special challenges of being a teenager, such as dealing with complicated issues of peer relations. Indeed, surveys show that *most* boys and many girls exhibit some delinquent behavior during their teenage years, with more than 60 percent engaging in some combination of aggressive acts, drug abuse, arson, and vandalism. I know I did, as did most of the teenagers I have known.

The second reason childhood onset is a bad omen is that when young children exhibit a pattern of bad behavior, it more than likely is linked to some underlying problem in them rather than to simple negative peer influence. According to Kazdin's research, underlying problems include a difficult temperament, neurological deficits and difficulties (often associated with pregnancy- and birth-related complications), separation from parents, violence in the family, and harsh parenting practices.

Of the boys I've interviewed, nearly all would qualify as childhood-onset cases. Dennis reports that he regularly beat up other kids in school. Devon took money his mother gave him to buy sneakers and used it to purchase drugs instead. Adam stole a purse. All these things happened before any of these boys turned ten. Their own self-reports fit within the American Psychiatric Association's set of criteria for Conduct Disorder.

I sit listening to fifteen-year-old Aaron remember the places he lived in and the schools he attended over the years. He's a cherubic-looking kid with an engaging smile and a very dignified way of talking. (I can picture him with a herringbone tweed jacket, an ascot, and a pipe.) I am taking it all in, perhaps lulled by his apparently sweet disposition. After he has finished, I turn to the task of verifying the sequence of events he has just reported. "Why did you move from the house on Ferry Street?" I ask pleasantly.

His answer takes me aback. "I burned down the house playing in the kitchen," he replies, smiling sheepishly.

I pride myself on being unflappable with the boys, so I pause a moment and then say, "Tell me about that."

And he does: "I burned the house down 'cause I was playing with spaghetti sticks. I was putting them in straws, and the melting plastic was dripping on the floor. I think I was like seven."

I ask, "So when the fire started in the house, were you by yourself?"

"No, my mother, she was braiding my sister's hair in the living room. And I was running back and forth playing in the kitchen. My mother was telling me like, 'Don't be back there playing with nothing.' But I didn't listen, and I climbed up on the wood thing, I got some spaghetti strings and the straws, I took some straws out the drawer, and I stuck them in there. And I lit the stove and stuck it in the fire. And the straws was burning, the plastic was dripping. And when that happened, when the plastic on the floor started burning up, I went in the living room and sat down next to my mother. And she was like, she knew I did something 'cause usually I just was running around the house, but I came and sat next to my mother. I was sitting there watching her braid my sister's hair. She was like, she looked at me like, 'What did you do?' I was like, 'Nothing.' So she went in the kitchen and saw it, and that's when it was already burning up. So we had to leave, and we moved down the street by my grandmother."

I ask him, "Were you scared when the fire started?"

"Yeah," he says. "But my mother, she wasn't surprised I did it, 'cause I was always hyper."

Understanding, Not Labeling

Although violent boys obviously don't use the term Conduct Disorder to describe themselves, their self-descriptions certainly match the criteria for this disorder. But the term is only a label. It simply describes a pattern of chronic bad behavior: a boy steals, hits people, hurts animals, destroys property, disobeys parents and teachers, fights with other boys, and victimizes girls. When this behavior occurs over and over again, it is called a chronic pattern of behavior, or Conduct Disorder.

But using this label for a boy can easily become the end of the story rather than the beginning. To go beyond diagnosis, we need to know *why* a boy is behaving badly and what we—parents and professionals—can do to improve his behavior. We want to understand why a boy would engage in a pattern of chronic bad behavior, but it seems that the process of diagnosis often simply leaves us with the fact that he does habitually engage in such behavior, without shedding light on its origins. For example, during Thomas's trial, the prosecution's psychologist diagnosed him with "Conduct Disorder, childhood onset" and left it at that, as though simply pronouncing the diagnosis explained anything and everything the court needed to know. In fact, it explained nothing other than the fact that Thomas's act of homicide as a teenager was the culminating point of many years of aggressive behavior.

It took hours listening to Thomas's life story for me to understand how and why he reached the point of killing someone. It took hearing about his being emotionally abandoned by his mother and father, about his early problems controlling his temper and his grandparents' ineffective responses, about his frustrated attempts to find friends, about his being sent to visit his drug-addicted mother in the war zone of the city. In short, understanding him required hearing his life story, not just learning which diagnostic label he had been assigned.

What is more, labeling a child pushes us away from remembering the human being behind the diagnostic label or category, a consequence of most clinical diagnoses. No one likes to be reduced to a diagnosis. I don't like being known only as a "white adult male college professor" any more than Malcolm likes being seen only as a "black teenage felon with a history of Conduct Disorder." So while I rely on research that uses the term, I avoid the term Conduct Disorder as much as possible, and instead will simply focus on the questions of how and why boys get to be who and what they are.

Avoiding dehumanizing labels is particularly important when dealing with adolescents and issues involving adolescents. Many adults have a prejudice against teenagers. We make jokes about it as parents. I SURVIVED BEING THE PARENT OF A TEENAGER, says one bumper sticker. We tend to shy away from teenagers in groups, for example, at the mall or on the street. Thirty years ago, when I told people I had volunteered to teach junior high school, and thus to spend my day with classes full of kids just entering adolescence, many thought this was clear evidence of insanity on my part. One reason for this bias is that while most adults find children familiar and comprehensible, they find teenagers alien and inscrutable. Part of this is the myth that adolescence is a time of unpredictable changes and that it represents a disconnection from childhood. Child analyst Anna Freud promoted this view. In fact, as she saw it, there is something unhealthy about a child who *doesn't* go crazy and become rebellious, defiant, and troublesome as a teenager. Our culture has a tendency to see adolescence as a time of dramatic changes that come out of nowhere, unpredictably. In her book *Children Without Childhood,* social critic Marie Winn refers to the "myth of the teenage werewolf": the idea that well-behaved and nice children become monsters when the hormonal surges of adolescence take over.

But research conducted by psychologist Daniel Offer in the United States and psychiatrist Michael Rutter in the United Kingdom generally tells a different story. Only about 20 percent of kids demonstrate a tumultuous adolescence, one full of crisis and turmoil. Most kids do *not* evidence the dramatic changes for the worse that the myth of the teenage werewolf would lead us to expect. Rather, they show a pattern of continuity from childhood into adolescence, particularly if the circumstances of their lives remain relatively constant and supportive. Psychologist Aaron Ebata finds that children with depressive tendencies generally become depressed teenagers. A report compiled for the American Psychological Association documents that aggressive children generally become aggressive teenagers.

Yes, adolescence brings about changes and intensification, but generally these are along the lines laid out in childhood. Kids who experience a tumultuous adolescence generally had a difficult childhood. Violent boys are not so different from other boys in this regard. It is a question of their intensifying the negative while other boys are accentuating the positive. The process is the same, but the negative outcomes can be as disastrous as the positive outcomes can be wonderful. And in some boys it is a time when problems that were swept under the rug in childhood come bursting out into the world, as the suddenly powerful teenager replaces the previously powerless young child. For example, University of Pennsylvania sociologist Richard Gelles reports that most teenagers who assault their parents were once children assaulted *by* their parents. This is the domain of the lost boys, the boys who go beyond the bounds of normal male aggression to become violent teenagers. The recognition of adolescence as the culmination of what begins in childhood directs us toward an understanding of the core question, Why would a boy be so bad at an early age in the first place?

Are Boys Born Bad?

Some people are tempted to say that some kids really are just born bad. That is where the popular expression *bad seed* comes from. Some of the troubled boys' parents and grandparents seem to accept this explanation, as do some professionals who work with them. Yes, some boys are born with difficult temperaments; they are irritable, hyperactive, and resistant.

And, yes, being born difficult increases the challenges faced by parents and other caregivers and thus increases the likelihood that such boys will be rejected, abandoned, abused, neglected, and mishandled. But this is not synonymous with being "hardwired" in the womb to behave badly and become a violent teenager.

The question of whether bad behavior is preprogrammed genetically is one of the central controversies in child development. An informed starting point is to remember that child development requires the interplay of biology *and* society, the characteristics children bring with them into the world *and* the way the world treats them, nature *and* nurture. Sociobiology emphasizes a genetic origin for social behavior: some characteristics promote survival, and thus reproduction, more than other characteristics. In contrast, what researcher Benjamin Pasamanick calls social biology concentrates on the social origins of biological phenomena (e.g., the impact of poverty on infant health). Sociobiologists look for the origins of biological phenomena (i.e., genetically transmitted characteristics in a population) in its social history (i.e., the differential life success of individuals and groups in reproducing and thus passing on those characteristics). The key is that there are *social* implications of *genetically based* individual behaviors; the social impact of biologically rooted traits can affect the survival of individual people and groups of related people, and thus the likelihood that a particular genetic pattern will be passed along to surviving offspring.

From a social biological perspective, one can say that children face different opportunities and risks for development because of their mental and physical makeup *and* because of the social environment they inhabit *and* because of how well their inborn traits match up with what their social environment offers, demands, rewards, and punishes. Social environment also affects the very physical makeup of the child. These effects may be negative (e.g., the impact of poverty on birth weight or the influence of industrial carcinogens in one's neighborhood in producing birth defects) or positive (e.g., intrauterine surgery or nutritional therapy for a fetus with a genetic disorder). A social biological perspective on the question of lethal youth violence accepts the premise that biologically based predispositions to violence only translate into behavior when they occur in social situations that permit or encourage their expression.

So when all is said and done, I think the best theory of child development comes down on the side of a focus on the social context, what psychologist Urie Bronfenbrenner has called an "ecological" perspective on the question of nature and nurture. How genetic influences, such as temperament, and environmental influences, such as early trauma, will affect a child's development depends upon the context in which those influences are played out. One of the challenges we face in understanding human development is the central importance of these contexts. Few processes work universally and independently of specific situations. Rarely does any specific X cause a specific Y in every time and place and with every human being. Indeed, in matters of human development, when the question is "Does X cause Y?" the best answer is almost always "It depends." *It depends.*

The critical importance of social context is as true of the consequences of child temperament as it is of any other characteristic relevant to understanding youth violence. Does it matter if a child is born with a minor physical anomaly, such as low-seated ears and a slightly misshapen head, which are indicative of minor neurological problems arising from disorders of pregnancy, particularly in the first trimester? Does being born with these anomalies predict that a child will end up as an aggressive adolescent? *It depends* upon the family the child is born into and in which the child grows up.

Sarnoff Mednick and Elizabeth Kandel studied the impact of being born with such a minor physical anomaly on the development of violent behavior, speculating that the neurological damage signaled by the physical anomaly might be biologically linked to such behavior. They found that such children who grow up in well-functioning, stable families have no greater risk of being arrested for violent crimes by age twenty-one than do physically normal children (the arrest rate was about 15 percent for both groups). However, when such damaged children grow up in unstable, troubled families, they are three and a half times more likely to end up being arrested for violent crimes by age twenty-one than are physically normal children in similar families (70 percent vs. 20 percent).

A study conducted by German psychologists Friedrich Losel, Doris Bender, and Thomas Bliesener tells a similar story about the role of social context. These psychologists looked at the role of child temperament in high-school-age bullies and victims. They started from the general finding that a low resting heart rate in children is associated with antisocial behavior. Why? The hypothesis is that such children have a low resting heart rate because the emotional reaction system in their body is set low. This means, among other things, that they don't show as much fear in response to the threat of punishment and are more impulsive. Apparently, they are less likely to be frightened off by scary situations and are more willing to take the risks associated with antisocial behavior. By the same token, timid children typically have high resting heart rates, suggesting that their emotional response systems are highly reactive and that they thus are easily frightened.

Losel and his colleagues went beyond this simple dichotomy to look at the role of temperament (as measured by heart rate) in two situations: low-risk families (i.e., those with low levels of stressful events and trauma and a high level of effective family functioning) and high-risk families (high levels of stressful events and trauma coupled with a low level of effective family functioning). The heart rates of bullies and victims were quite different in the two groups of family situations. In low-risk families there were significant differences between the heart rate of bullies and that of victims: in contrast to other children (who had rates of 70 beats per minute), bullies had low heart rates (62 beats per minute) and victims had high heart rates (75 beats per minute). But in high-risk families there was no difference in the heart rates of bullies, victims, and other youth (at about 70 beats per minute). Context matters in the impact and expression of temperamental characteristics. We must never forget that.

The Story of One Difficult Child

Being born difficult does not mean that a child will end up displaying a chronic pattern of aggression and bad behavior in adolescence. I know this from firsthand experience. I myself was a difficult infant and toddler—cranky, troublesome, willful, and aggressive. At two I was found standing on the wall of the balcony outside our sixth-floor apartment and talking to the cats in the courtyard. When my mother ordered me in, I refused. That same year, I ran away from home one night and was found wandering the streets in my pajamas. When I was three, the neighbors routinely came to my mother to complain that I was beating up their six- and seven-year-old children. When I was six I would stand at the top of the monkey bars on the playground, let go with my hands and challenge other children to try to shake me off.

But by the time I reached adolescence, my aggressive days were over and I became something of a model citizen. I was vice president of the student council and editor of the yearbook in my high school; I was even sent to Washington in 1964 as an exemplary youth by the Lions Club in my town. Few who saw the difficult child I was at three would have predicted the model citizen I became at sixteen.

Why did I turn out as I did while other difficult children do not? My success had a lot to do with the social context in which I grew up—my family, my neighborhood, my community, my school. I was the first child in my family and for more than four years the only child, so I had my parents all to myself. My mother devoted her every minute to me, literally "taming" me as one would a wolf pup. My father was there for me, a positive force in my life. When I started elementary school, I was assigned to strong and effective teachers in the early grades who took charge of me and the rest of their students and made sure we behaved in a civilized manner. Although I lived some of my early years in a public housing project in New York City, it was when "the projects" were still a safe and sane place, before they began the descent that transformed them into a war zone twenty years later. I was taken to church every Sunday morning, and the president of our country was a trusted and reassuring father figure. When I turned on the television or went to the movies, the violence I saw was very tame by today's standards and the sexiest thing on either screen was a slow kiss. When I reached adolescence, I went to a small high school where I felt safe and was taught by teachers who cared for me. There were no gangs, guns, or drugs in my neighborhood.

Each of these elements of my life supported, protected, guided, and nurtured me. A boy like Malcolm experiences a negative mirror image of my early life: for each protective factor I experienced he is dealt a risk factor. Context matters, and one of the most important features of context is the balance between protective influences and threatening risk factors.

Risk Accumulates

Threats accumulate; support ameliorates. The presence of only one or two risk factors does not disable a child. Rather, it is the accumulation of threats that does the damage. And trouble really sets in when these threats accumulate without a parallel accumulation of compensatory "opportunity" factors. Once overwhelmed, defenses are weakened the next time the child faces threat. Children and adolescents become highly sensitive to any negative social influences around them. I look at it this way: Give me one tennis ball, and I can toss it up and down with ease. Give me two, and I can still manage easily. Add a third, and it takes special skill to juggle them. Make it four, and I will drop them all. So it is with threats to development.

This accumulation approach to developmental threats offers hope to those responsible for policy and programming on behalf of youth. It tells us that life need not be risk free for development to proceed successfully. And one way to succeed with kids is to inject compensatory opportunity factors into the equation of their life. Then we can expect to see positive results—as long as we can prevent the coping capacity of youth from being overwhelmed. If there are one to two threats to our children's development beyond our immediate control, they need not be destructive. At the same time, they should be an urgent warning, telling us to protect the children in our care from any further risks and to marshal our resources to build opportunities to enhance their development.

As threats accumulate, children's intellectual development suffers and they cannot bring to bear cognitive strength in mastering the challenges they face. In a study by University of Michigan psychologist Arnold Sameroff and his colleagues, eleven-year-olds with less than three risk factors had above-average IQ scores; those with four such risk factors had below-average IQ scores.

The threat to intellectual competence compounds the effects of negative social influences in the environment by undermining a child's resilience and coping processes. With the accumulation of threats—an absent father, a low resting heart rate, ineffectual teachers, whatever—children not only achieve less but, as a result, value themselves less. Thus begins a downward spiral: those who enter adolescence lacking the reservoir of skills and attitudes they need to deal with negative peer influences in their communities are drawn into or seek out aggressive peer groups, including gangs.

We always need to look at the whole picture, not just one element of the situation. Psychologist Alan Kazdin speaks of "packages" of risk factors that interact to produce chronic patterns of bad behavior in boys. Psychologists Carl Dunst and Carol Trivette speak of the "accumulation of opportunity factors" in improving the prospects of children with disabilities. When I look back on my own childhood, I see a healthy social environment rather than a toxic one; when I listen to Malcolm's story, I hear the opposite.

The Seeds of Bad Behavior

In her book *The Nurture Assumption,* Judith Harris pinpoints a series of temperamental traits that put a child at risk for becoming troubled and aggressive. These include high activity level, insensitivity to the feelings of others, lack of physical fear, being easily bored with routine, tendency to seek excitement, and less than average intelligence. Put these characteristics together in one child, and you have a parent who faces a very difficult challenge.

But why do some difficult children become well-socialized youth while others end up troubled or in trouble? One important reason lies in early experience. As I pointed out earlier, chronic bad behavior and aggression are more than a simple matter of male biology or hardwiring in the brain. They result from experience, experience that may start with an infant's non-responsiveness in the early months of life, which is mostly an adaptation to early mistreatment, rejection, and inept parenting. In a study by child psychologists Stuart Erickson, Byron Egeland, and Robert Pianta at the University of Minnesota, children who were maltreated at an early age were noticeably less cooperative than children who had not suffered harsh punishment at the hands of their parents or guardians. Indeed, the early badness of violent boys—that is, being noncooperative and resistant to parental directions and commands—often starts as a reaction to maltreatment. Many incarcerated boys echo sixteen-year-old Scottie when he recalls, "I wouldn't listen. I just was not going to be told what to do by anybody." This makes the task of anyone who would reform these boys very challenging indeed. By the time these boys reach prison, they often have a decade and a half of noncompliance under their belts. It's a tough habit to change, and much easier to prevent in the first place.

Some parents believe that the way to encourage cooperativeness and obedience in a child is to be harsh and punishing from the very start. But in her classic study of the relation between maternal responsiveness in the first three months of life and the child's compliance at twelve months, psychologist Eleanor Maccoby and her colleagues found just the opposite. Rather than producing "spoiled brats," responsive mothers were rewarded with obedient children. In fact, Maccoby found that the more responsive mothers were in the first three months of life—for example, going immediately to pick up the baby when he or she cried—the more obedient the child was at one year. Maccoby measured obedience by how long the child would stay away from a desirable toy if the mother said, "No. Don't touch." Babies who had more responsive mothers were more obedient than babies who had less responsive mothers. Of course, Maccoby's study did not directly measure how easy or difficult the children were, temperamentally, from the start. But psychiatrist Stanley Greenspan has taken this part of the equation into consideration, and he finds that although it takes a special kind of responsiveness from the mother (including a lot of physical soothing), even temperamentally difficult children can learn to behave well.

It is ironic. Mothers who seek to prevent the disobedience they believe comes from spoiling a baby can end up producing exactly the opposite of what they desire. University of Oregon researcher Gerald Patterson and his colleagues found that chronic bad behavior is most likely to arise in the early years of life when parents use harsh, inconsistent punishment practices instead of clear, firm, but warm responses when the child exhibits unacceptable behavior. The former approach reflects inept parenting, the latter competent parenting. As it turns out, parents who use harsh punishment and mainly pay attention to their child's negative behaviors and ignore the positive ones are unintentionally encouraging aggression.

This is a good starting point for understanding the seeds of a troubled boy's behavior. Mothers and fathers who parent according to the rules I have just described, or whose own psychological condition or history makes them emotionally unavailable to the child, are setting the stage for their child's disobedience and defiant behavior. Not surprisingly, early disobedience and defiance are building blocks for trouble later on, particularly if the child's peers are themselves disobedient and defiant.

One of Patterson's contributions to our understanding is to highlight the fact that parental behavior affects child behavior and vice versa. Alternative behavior patterns are possible for the same parents and children. Behavior is not fixed as a matter of personality. How a child eventually turns out is not decided solely by what goes on inside the family, between parent and child, of course. The world outside the family, particularly the school environment and peer group, plays a powerful role in translating the child's personality traits and predispositions into behavior.

Children may start off on a negative path in part because parents mistakenly withdraw from them in the first months of life (perhaps because they have been taught that leaving a young infant to cry in the crib is the best medicine or because they find the baby too much to handle). The truth is, in the early months of life the big danger is not too much attention but, rather, *in*attention. It is only later that effective parents begin to shape their child's behavior by responding to desirable and undesirable behavior in different ways. Infants require unconditional attention, regardless of how undesirable their behavior may be. "Discipline" only comes later.

It is hard to know what goes on inside the head and heart of an infant, but I believe babies are angry and confused when no one comes to them when they cry and that they are pleased and reassured when someone does come. Is this the beginning of a pattern of estrangement and isolation that builds up through childhood? It certainly seems so when I listen to violent teenagers talk about the way they see the world, that is, with distrust, suspicion, and rage. Malcolm says, "I don't trust nobody. You can't count on anyone except yourself. That's a fact." Scottie tells me, "I just say, forget them. They don't want me, I don't want nothing to do with them," and Bobby has arrived at this conclusion: "I've learned one lesson about life: it sucks." Where did they learn these bitter lessons about life? I believe they learned them first as infants and found reinforcement for those beliefs as they passed through childhood into adolescence.

Psychologist Byron Egeland and his colleagues report that children whose mothers are psychologically unavailable have more behavioral problems than other children. These problems include most forms of emotional and intellectual dysfunction and disability, as well as aggression. Why do some mothers ignore their children? There are many reasons, of course, some having to do with temperament and others with circumstances. Some mothers may be self-centered or self-absorbed or may be the product of an abusive childhood themselves; others may suffer from drug or alcohol abuse, depression, or domestic violence. Whatever its origins, a parent's psychological unavailability is a form of child maltreatment, and maltreatment plays a central role in the development of bad behavior and aggression in children.

Problems with early attachment are one of the sources of vulnerability among children. Byron Egeland, Alan Stroufe, and their colleagues at the University of Minnesota explored the relationship between attachment problems and aggression by studying preschool-age children in social situations. They identified two groups of children for the study: those who often took the role of victimizer and those who were frequently the victimized. They found that the "victimizer" children had displayed avoidant attachment as infants. (Recall that avoidant attachment describes children who fear their caregivers. It is often a sign of some significant disruption of the parent–child interaction early in life, perhaps including maltreatment.) Egeland's research suggests that early maltreatment plays a role in diverting the development of young children toward aggression.

The Psychological Cost of Adapting to Child Abuse: Negative Social Maps

Nothing tells us more about the link between child maltreatment and aggressive bad behavior than the research of psychologist Kenneth Dodge and his colleagues at Vanderbilt University. Child maltreatment teaches children to adapt their behavior and thinking to the harsh fact that those who are in charge of caring for them are the same people who hurt, terrify, ignore, and attack them. This very adaptation ultimately becomes the source of their problems in later years. According to the studies by Dodge and his colleagues, *children who are maltreated are much more likely than non-maltreated children to develop a chronic pattern of bad behavior and aggression.* The key lies in the fact that the child comes to understand how the world works through the lens of his own abuse. Put another way, a child's worldview is a matter of how he draws his social map.

Of course, all children develop social maps and codes of behavior, which are initially the products of their experiences as filtered by their temperament. For most children, the social map portrays the world in positive terms: *I can trust people. If I behave well, I will be treated well. I am lovable. I have allies in the world.* And as a result, these children naturally develop benign codes of behavior: *Listen to adults. Cooperation pays off. Be patient. Share. I will keep my hands to myself.* Such social maps and codes of behavior give direction to life.

Abused children develop their social maps by adapting to an abusive environment. The more they learn these lessons, the more likely it is that they will learn a code that is compatible with a pattern of bad behavior and aggression by the time they are eight years old. There are four specific elements of this code that are especially important for subsequent behavior and development.

1. *Children become hypersensitive to negative social cues.* Thomas sits with me watching staff and other kids pass by the window of the interview room. As each one goes by, he has something to say that marks them as dangerous. "This one looked at me funny yesterday," he says. "That one is bothering me," he tells me. "See that guy there? I think he's got a blade hidden." No one escapes his watchful eye. He continues: "Just the other day one of the teachers insulted me. She made me feel stupid for asking a question in a class."

2. *Children become oblivious to positive social cues.* Michael cannot think of one nice thing that anyone has done for him in the past year of his incarceration, yet I know of at least three staff members who have gone out of their way to offer him a kind word or some special bit of help. And I know that the teacher who Thomas says insulted him makes a point of praising him whenever she can.

3. *Children develop a repertory of aggressive behaviors that are readily accessible and can be easily invoked.* Malcolm tells me, "I know how to fight. Someone touches me, I'm going to finish it. Somebody hits me, I hit him back twice as hard. I hit him until he bleeds 'cause that way he's not going to hit me again. You know what I mean." I do.

4. *Children draw the conclusion that aggression is a successful way of getting what they want.* Dennis says, "I learned early in life that there's winners and there's losers. The winners end up on top. The losers bleed. I can take care of myself if I need to. I know the rules." He learned that lesson first at home, at the hands of his parents, and it was later reinforced on the playground and on the street.

The code of violent boys and the social maps it reflects partially explain the nature of their bad behavior. They are not dumb. They observe and they experience, and they draw conclusions based on what they see and feel. Specific experiences become general patterns that together become the lenses through which they see the world. In early childhood they begin to draw negative psychological conclusions about the world and about their place in that world. With these negative social maps in place, they act accordingly.

According to psychologist Alan Kazdin, about 4 to 7 percent of kids exhibit chronic patterns of bad behavior and aggression that are serious enough to constitute a diagnosable mental health problem, such as Conduct Disorder. Boys are anywhere from three to four times as likely to display this pattern as are girls. How specifically are the social maps that abused kids develop linked to their later bad behavior and aggression? Dodge and colleagues found that if a child is maltreated and develops none of the four critical code elements associated with a negative social map (described earlier), the odds that he will exhibit chronic bad behavior and aggression are 5 percent, about what's normal for the population as a whole. But if the child manifests at least three of the four code elements, we can expect a sevenfold increase in the risk that the child will exhibit the pattern of chronic bad behavior and aggression that defines Conduct Disorder.

Why Don't Most Abused Kids Develop Bad Behavior and Aggression?

While most kids don't become violent criminals, of course, it is true that the majority of boys incarcerated for violent crimes were subject to abuse or neglect as children. But what about the abused kids who don't develop the negative social maps and don't develop chronic bad behavior and aggression? What about them?

Only 35 percent of abused kids with negative and aggressive social maps become violent, according to Dodge. Why is it that 65 percent of the kids who have been abused and have negative social maps do not develop a pattern of bad behavior and aggression? Why do some boys who are abused develop some or all of the self-defeating behaviors and activities that characterize bad boys while others do not? Some children probably respond by developing other kinds of problems, perhaps confining their response to the internalizing problems of depression, low self-esteem, self-destructive behavior, and bodily troubles like headaches and stomachaches.

Some children do seem resilient. Why? With some boys, the answer seems clearly linked to a compensatory relationship—that is, a relationship with a devoted grandmother, a father who balances out an abusing mother, a loving mother who compensates for an abusive father, perhaps someone outside the family who is positively crazy about the child and who does not let the child's emotional life wither on the vine but lovingly helps redraw the child's social maps. The resilience of some children is due to the fact that the abuse they experience is limited to physical assault and they are able to feel a measure of love and acceptance from their parents at the times when they are not abused.

Some at-risk children are saved by an intervention program, perhaps a highly effective early childhood education program or the work of a child guidance clinic. Therapists can help children improve their attitudes and their behaviors. Some of the same psychologists who study the origins of bad behavior and aggression in children also remedy those problems. For example, the same Gerald Patterson who studies the emergence of aggressive and oppositional behavior among children develops and implements therapeutic programs to help parents and children escape from being entrapped in coercive relationships. All around the country there are professionals doing this good work with young children.

The mystery remains, however, as to why some children have the fortitude and strength to resist adapting to abuse and other experiences in ways that put them at risk for becoming violent. Some boys achieve a state of grace in which, though victimized, they find a positive path. This is resilience at its highest level.

There is, of course, another question implied by Dodge's research: Why do some *nonabused* children develop bad behavior and aggression? Perhaps the answer in this case comes from research on parents who withdraw from but do not actively abuse their kids. These are neglectful, passive parents, about whom much less is known. But some things are clear: neglect often results from parents who are incapacitated by drugs or depression, by what social worker Norman Polansky called the apathy-futility syndrome. Also, some parents find themselves unable to cope with temperamentally difficult children and gradually withdraw from them. Their goal each day is only to avoid the aversive experience of confronting the child and dealing with the resulting shouting, screaming, crying, hitting, punching, slamming of doors, stamping of feet, destruction of property, and general mayhem. These parents find an escape from their children, but the result is often emotional and physical neglect.

In fact, neglect is more common than abuse: more kids are emotionally abandoned than are directly attacked, physically or emotionally. According to the federal government's National Incidence Study of Child Abuse and Neglect, there are almost 900,000 cases of neglect and about 750,000 cases of abuse. Neglect leaves a social vacuum that may send a young child looking for connection somewhere else, or with someone or something else. That somewhere else may include television, where the child can learn countless negative lessons about violence and antisocial behavior.

Someone else may include peers who actually have been abused and who thus can model and teach neglected children the ins and outs of bad behavior and aggression. A significant proportion of the acts of violence committed by boys occurs in groups, and in groups there is often a psychological chemistry that makes the violence potential of the group greater than the potential for violence of the individual members. Acting under the influence of peers, any boy may be led to do things he might not do alone, and boys who have a desperate need to fit in may be particularly likely to join in hurtful, aggressive, and dangerous activities.

Beyond Social Maps: Dissociation and Emotional Numbing

There is more to the link between child maltreatment and the development of violence and antisocial behavior than its effects on the child's social map, however. Actual brain damage may be involved, perhaps accounting for some of the unexplained differences between children who become violent youth and those who don't. Baylor University psychiatrist Bruce Perry and his colleagues documented damaging effects to children's brains as a result of the trauma of child abuse. Particularly vulnerable to such damage is the cortex of the brain, where higher thinking that controls moral reasoning takes place.

There is a third explanation for the link as well, lying in the emotional disconnection that psychologists and psychiatrists call *dissociation*. Much has been made of the famous fight-or-flight response to threat. But as Bruce Perry points out, rarely do children have the option of either fighting or fleeing a situation physically, particularly when, as often is the case, the situation is their membership in an abusive family. Perry notes that the fight-or-flight response is mainly observed mostly in male adults, who, when confronted with a stressful threat, can actually choose between fighting or fleeing. Trapped in their home, in a schoolyard, or in a neighborhood, how do children respond?

The most likely option for children is to flee psychologically, that is, to shut down emotionally and disconnect themselves from their feelings *so that they don't have to feel them anymore*. It's a survival strategy that seems to work—in the short run. By cutting off or disowning the feelings that threaten to overwhelm them, children can survive traumatic threats. But at what cost?

John was six years old when his mother was murdered. He knows that because he was there. The day of the killing his stepfather showed up at the door at three o'clock in the morning, hoping to sneak back into the house after having been thrown out the day before by John's mother. The little boy awoke when he heard the kitchen door open, and he got out of bed to see what was happening. He found his stepfather opening the refrigerator to get a can of beer. "Shush," the man said as John appeared in the doorway to the kitchen. "I don't want your mother to hear me." "Welcome back, Daddy Bill," little John said. "Are you supposed to be here?" "It's okay, boy," John's stepfather replied, patting the boy on the head and moving down the hallway to the master bedroom. John stood in the middle of the kitchen, sleepy but hoping for a glass of milk. In a minute Daddy Bill was back in the kitchen, but he looked very angry. At first, John drew back in fear, because he had experienced his stepfather's anger before.

But Daddy Bill was not angry with little John this time. "Don't be scared, boy," the man said. "You okay. Now just reach in that drawer there," he continued, "and get me that big knife your mother uses to cut meat." John did as he was told. He reached into the drawer next to him and pulled out the big knife, then handed it over to Daddy Bill, who took it in his hand and disappeared down the hallway toward the master bedroom again. The next thing John heard was shouting and screaming coming from the bedroom. He stood there, frozen to the spot, for five or ten minutes, until he felt the pee running down his leg onto his foot. Then he walked down the hallway to the bedroom and looked in. Years later, he says that what he remembers is the red walls. His stepfather killed John's mother, stabbing her fifteen times.

"How did you feel?" I ask him, now two decades later. "I don't remember," he says. "I suppose scared, but I would be lying to you if I said I really remember anything but giving Daddy Bill the knife, hearing the screaming and the shouting, and seeing the red walls." He remembers the events, but he has no memory of the feelings. Poor little boy. As I talk with him, he sits on death row, awaiting execution for stabbing to death a fifty-year-old woman in her bedroom. "How did you feel when you killed that woman?" I ask. "I don't remember," he replies.

Emotional dissociation becomes a hard habit to break. It becomes generalized, giving others the impression that a boy has *no* feelings. In fact, the reverse is true: his feelings are so powerful that they must be put in a box and pushed aside to ensure his survival. When incarcerated boys talk about their lives—and sometimes their crimes—they often seem emotionless. But

I know it's not that they don't have feelings; their feelings are locked up inside the young child they have banished for his own protection.

This is emotional territory that is familiar to most males. Boys are routinely taught to ignore or deny their feelings by parents and others who are training them to be men in a culture that demands male stoicism. It is no secret that boys and men in many societies, including our own, are encouraged to put their emotions in boxes, to keep them out of consciousness, and to regard the expression of powerful feelings of pain and sorrow as a highly dangerous activity. We call this *compartmentalization,* and it is dissociation's first cousin. One of the emotions specially targeted for compartmentalization and dissociation is fear.

Fear

For teenage boys, particularly those who have to be tough on the streets or in their families, fear is a dangerous commodity. Boys often talk about the testing that goes on among their peers, whether it be in school, on the streets, or in prison. They are virtually unanimous in their belief that to *show* fear is to invite victimization. But do they *feel* fear? While the boys I see generally won't admit to feeling fear when they talk to their peers or even to adults who have power over them, they sometimes do so in the privacy of our interviews.

Sharnell is a tough kid. He's battle scarred from his life on the streets and in the juvenile detention facilities where he has spent four years of his life since he turned twelve (he is now sixteen). We sit and talk about his life. Forty-eight armed robberies. He tells me how he and three of his friends would take the subway out to middle-class neighborhoods and rob other teenagers there at gun point. Drug dealing. He explains how the most dangerous point in a drug deal comes when the money is in sight. Once he had to punish a buyer who tried to cheat him; he hit the man on the head with a lead pipe. "Did he die?" I ask. "No," he replies. "My mistake, 'cause a week later the guy surprised me in the hallway of my building and stabbed me in the chest." He shows me the scar. When I ask him about fear, Sharnell tells me, "Nah. I ain't afraid of nothing. Nothing." At which point he rocks back and forth in his chair and sucks his thumb, an act of self-soothing carried over from early childhood. What is going on inside this boy?

As I watch Sharnell rock back and forth, I think of Bruce Perry's study of the children who survived living in the Branch Davidian complex in Waco, Texas, and who had lived through the confrontation that took the life of its leader, David Koresh, and most of his followers. After the shooting and fire, when the surviving children were safely evacuated, Perry interviewed them. Even though they seemed calm on the surface, their hearts were beating at 148 beats per minute (far above the normal 70 beats per minute for young children at rest).

Violent boys often erect this facade of fearlessness early in their lives. I suspect for some it reflects a biological predisposition, an element of temperament. Recall the study in Germany conducted by Friedrich Losel and his colleagues showing that in low-risk families, high school bullies had unusually low heart rates (62 beats per minute, compared to 70 beats per minute for other boys) and victimized children had high heart rates (75 beats per minute). This may reflect a temperamental predisposition to fearlessness.

Some boys are temperamentally primed to take on aggressive roles, while other, more timid, boys are likely to be targeted as victims—and thus develop the elevated heart rate indicative of traumatic response. This pathway is evident in families where environmental conditions permit temperament to shine through. But in high-risk families the trauma affects all the boys, and neither bullies nor victims differ from the normal heart rate patterns found among other children of the same age (70 beats per minute). Perhaps this means the bullies among them have had their heart rates accelerated from dealing with traumatic experiences while the timid victims have used dissociation to train themselves to deaden their emotions so they can get through their stressful days without exploding.

Some boys are too fearful from the start to react delinquently to parental mistreatment or to the threatening environment they find on the streets. They simply try to conform to parental dictates and seek out some small measure of safety in conforming to adult conventions. Michael's brother Robert was one such boy, and Michael referred to him as "submissive," a highly undesirable trait for most boys because it flies in the face of dominant images of masculinity, images that are reinforced nightly on television and in the movies. Thomas reflects the culture around him when he derisively labels as "sissies" the boys who cave in to parental pressure or who stay at home to avoid dealing with the challenges of the streets.

This is always an issue for boys in a situation of social conflict and danger. I sat in a home in the Gaza Strip in 1988 with a fifteen-year-old Palestinian boy named Hamad and his parents at the height of the uprising against Israeli occupation. Hamad's older brother was serving time in an Israeli prison for his acts of political violence. While I sat in his living room with Hamad, other boys his age were on the street in front of the house throwing stones at the Israeli soldiers, and getting teargassed in repayment. His parents had made a deal with the authorities. If they kept him inside and out of the conflict for another three months, the police would release his older brother from jail and the whole family would be allowed to emigrate to Canada. If the younger son joined the conflict, he too would be arrested and both brothers would spend years in jail. I watched Hamad as the battle raged outside. His shame at being safe at home was terrible for him. He was a sissy in Thomas's terms, a "kit kat" in the local youth slang of the Palestinians.

Some boys do cave in, but other boys fight back against the world when they experience trauma at home. Compare Michael, who is facing the death penalty for first-degree murder, with his brother, who is working in a record store. But some boys are given no choice. They live in environments in which failure to participate in violent peer group activity is not an option. Billy was such a boy.

When I interview him on death row, Billy recounts his struggle as a timid child to find a way to avoid joining in with the violence that was all around him. He is now a slight man with fine features and a soft voice. I can imagine him as a small, skinny child, a frightened child, easily bullied. He tells me how the more aggressive boys in his neighborhood were bound and determined to get him to join them. They threatened him. They beat him up day after day, on his way to and from school. Finally, they threatened to kill his mother if he didn't join them. At that point he succumbed and joined the program. It was all downhill from there as he went further and further down the path of aggression and bad behavior, learning to hide and bury his feelings as he went. He was nineteen when he killed on the orders of his gang.

Unlike violent boys such as Billy, who start out as victims and later make the switch to bully as a matter of survival (who are, in effect, drafted), other boys seem to volunteer to join the ranks of violent youth. These boys often remember a physical fearlessness from an early age. Robert speaks of eight-year-old playmates with whom he jumped from second-floor window ledges onto mattresses below. Rasheen recounts walking a plank between two buildings four stories off the ground. "Was I afraid?" he said, extending my question when I asked him how he felt four stories off the ground on a single plank. "Nah. No problem, man. It was cool." "How about when you heard shooting outside your building?" I asked. "Nope. I ain't afraid of nothing," he replied. Where is the fear? More important, where are the feelings at all?

Dissociation as a Way of Life

The dissociation of violent boys is more than simple temperamental fearlessness. It goes beyond that, so far beyond that it makes me wonder about their overall emotional life. Where is the hurt? Where is the anger? I asked Michael what he did with the anger he felt toward his mother for the beatings she inflicted on him and for the favoritism she displayed toward his older brother Robert. He thought and thought with an intense look of concentration. Then he shook his head and said, "I guess I just held it inside." I asked him how he felt about his mother's preference for his brother. "It's just a fact of life," he replied. But it's an overwhelming *emotional* fact of his life. Most people would find the feelings intolerable. How did Michael deal with these feelings? One small clue appeared when he told me that the only thing he was ever afraid of was that he would lash out at his abusive mother and do to her what she had done to him, take an electric cord or a fist and even the score. Here was the fear that grew out of the hurt. And here was the anger. How are they related? Anger is repressed sadness, and sadness can mean depression.

In *I Don't Want to Talk About It*, Terrence Real provides a road map to the hidden emotional life of boys and men. He traces the links between masculine culture and covert depression, and the detour sadness takes to become violence. By burying their feelings in silence and externalizing them through aggression and addiction, sad and hurt men find a way to get through the day. Speaking of one of his patients, Real reports, "A lifetime of inattention to his emotions and his relationships was perched precariously over a childhood of profound psychological neglect."

That's what the future holds for aggressive boys if they are not helped to reconnect with their emotions and see clearly the role these feelings play in producing their acts of violence and thus wrecking their lives. This redirection can happen for boys, but it takes a lot of work and a lot of skilled psychological and spiritual leadership. Cuts to mental health services in schools and juvenile detention facilities and the secular nature of most programs put this desperately needed leadership in short supply. It is a major public policy issue for citizens and governments to address.

For a young child, this is not a grand issue of public policy or institutional practice. It is a matter of inner life or death. Without loving guidance, spiritual counsel, and psychological nurturance, children see little alternative but to cope as best they can, and that generally means dissociation—no matter its cost to a child's inner life and his external behavior. For a child, the intolerable can be made tolerable by being stripped of its emotional content and consigned to the world of simple fact, with the emotional content being locked away in a psychological vault. That's the point of dissociation as a survival strategy.

But while they are locked away in that psychological vault, the emotions that arise in response to rejection, abuse, and abandonment don't just sit there, inactive. They earn emotional interest. Rage compounds.

And the negative emotional bank accounts of the lost boys are often bloated with rage and shame and fear and humiliation. For some boys the psychological vault cannot hold all the hurt and anger that is stored there. Events—sometimes what appear to be trivial events—trigger a break that results in violence.

These boys need someone to help convert their negative emotional stockpiles, to therapeutically take the anger and make it over into insight and eventually into something constructive for the soul. Terrence Real and Robin Casarjian find in their therapeutic work with the men these boys become that without this psychological and spiritual help violence sometimes becomes a chronic addiction for the men, something to divert attention from their pain and sadness and a way to punish the world and themselves.

Hope

When I think of helping violent boys find their way, I often think of one particular troubled youth who grew up in Jamestown, New York, in the early years of this century. The boy had to deal with the emotional predicament of living in a household dominated by an alcoholic and abusive father. To escape his horrible family life, the boy wandered the hills and found solace in nature, particularly in birds. This fascination with birds sustained him, but by the time he reached high school he was a lonely, troubled boy. A teacher in his school formed a Junior Audubon Club so that the boy would have at least one positive setting at school in which his interest in birds could be nourished. This act of acceptance was decisive. It provided a positive link for the boy to peers and adults. As a result of this experience, the boy did not get lost. He went on to become an internationally acclaimed expert on birds and wrote a best-selling guide. His name was Roger Torrey Peterson. When I met him near the end of his long life, we talked about his personal history, and he told me this story as a testament to the potential power of a caring teacher, to the power of hope.

I believe that one of the most important elements in the developmental equation for violent boys is the larger social environment *outside* the family, for it is there that one of three things happens: (1) an early pattern of bad behavior and aggression is identified and treated; (2) an early pattern of bad behavior and aggression plays itself out in a socially benign setting (in which no matter how bad the boy's behavior gets, there is little danger); or (3) an early pattern of bad behavior and aggression falls on fertile ground and grows into chronic violence and delinquency as the child partakes of the dark side. All three courses are possible options.

Option one is the most likely outcome in families and communities that are rich in social and educational resources, where parents, teachers, and mental health professionals have the time and energy to focus on redirecting troubled little boys. I saw it in my own life when I was in elementary school. In my school and in our community, most boys were doing pretty well, but there was enough time and energy to go around for the boys who were in deep trouble.

Option two still exists in some places and certainly was more common in our society in decades past. When a troubled boy lives in a safe and peaceful social environment, there is a cushion for him. In the past, a boy living in a small town found a slow pace of life, without drugs and gangs and guns. In such an environment, a boy with bad behavior tests the limits, but his being bad is very unlikely to result in lethal violence. After all, other societies tell a different story from our own. For example, Canadian kids get in fights, too, but their youth homicide rate is less than a quarter of ours. Even American girls have a higher homicide rate than boys in many countries, such as Japan and Sweden.

Context is critical. Enter option three. It is because of the dangerous larger social environment many boys find themselves in today that we are so concerned that early "childish" bad behavior and aggression will turn into lethal behavior in adolescence and young adulthood.

REFERENCES

According to the results: Kellam, S. G., Ling, X., Merisca, R., Brown, C. H., & Ialongo, N. (1998). The Effect of Level of Aggression in the First Grade Classroom on the Course and Malleability of Aggressive Behavior into Middle School. *Development and Psychopathology, 10,* 165–185.

Research by psychologist Leonard Eron: Eron, L. D., Gentry, J. H., & Schlegel, P. (Eds.). (1994). *Reason to Hope: A Psychosocial Perspective on Violence and Youth.* Washington, DC: American Psychological Association.

There is a formal name: American Psychiatric Association (1994). *Diagnostic and Statistical Manual of Mental Disorders* (4th ed.). Washington, DC: Author.

That is not surprising: Edens, J. F., & Otto, R. K. (1997, Spring). Prevalence of Mental Disorders Among Youth in the Juvenile System. In *Focal Point: A National Bulletin on Family Support and Children's Mental Health.* pp. 1, 6–7. Portland, OR: Portland State University.

British criminologists Farrington and Hawkins: Farrington, D. P., & Hawkins, J. D. (1991). Predicting Participation, Early Onset, and Later Persistence in Officially Recorded Offending. *Criminal Behavior and Mental Health, 1,* 1–33.

Other investigators: Kazdin, A. E. (1997). Conduct Disorder Across the Life-Span. In S. S. Luthar & E. Zigler (Eds.), *Developmental Psychopathology: Perspectives on Adjustment, Risk, and Disorder.* Cambridge, MA: Cambridge University Press.

Indeed, surveys show: Loeber, R., & Farrington, D. P. (1998). Serious and Violent Juvenile Offenders. In R. Loeber & D. Farrington (Eds.), *Serious and Violent Juvenile Offenders: Risk Factors and Successful Interventions.* Thousand Oaks, CA: Sage.

According to Kazdin's research: Kazdin, A. E. (1994). Interventions for Aggressive and Antisocial Children. In L. D. Eron, J. H. Gentry, & P. Schlegel (Eds.), *Reason to Hope: A Psychosocial Perspective on Violence and Youth* (pp. 341–381). Washington, DC: American Psychological Association.

Child analyst Anna Freud: Freud, A. (1958). Psychoanalytical Study of the Child. *Adolescence, 13,* 255–278.

In her book: Winn, M. (1983). *Children Without Childhood.* New York: Pantheon.

But research conducted: Offer, D., & Offer, J. D. (1975). *From Teenager to Young Manhood: A Psychological Study.* New York: Basic Books.

Psychologist Aaron Ebata: Ebata, A. T. (1987, October). A Longitudinal Study of Psychological Distress During Early Adolescence. Dissertation Abstracts International 48(4-A): 1027.

A report compiled: Eron, L. D., Gentry, J. H., & Schlegel, P. (Eds.). (1994). *Reason to Hope: A Psychosocial Perspective on Violence and Youth.* Washington, DC: American Psychological Association.

most teenagers who assault their parents: Gelles, R. (1978). Violence Toward Children in the United States. *American Journal of Orthopsychiatry, 48,* 580–592.

Some people are tempted: Sleek, S. (1998, August). The Basis for Aggression May Start in the Womb: Is There Really Such a Thing As a Natural Born Killer? *American Psychological Association Monitor, 29*(8), 37.

In contrast: Pasamanick, B. (1987, Winter). Social Biology and AIDS. *Division 37 Newsletter.* Washington, DC: American Psychological Association.

So when all is said and done: Bronfenbrenner, U. (1979). *The Ecology of Human Development: Experiments by Nature and Design.* Cambridge, MA: Harvard University Press.

Sarnoff Mednick and Elizabeth Kandel: Mednick, S. A., & Kandel, E. (1998). Genetic and Perinatal Factors in Violence. In S. A. Mednick & T. Moffit

(Eds.), *Biological Contributions to Crime Causation* (pp. 121–134). Dordrecht, the Netherlands: Martinus Nijhoff.

As threats accumulate: Sameroff, A., Seifer, F., Barocas, R., Zax, M., & Greenspan, S. (1987). Intelligence Quotient Scores of 4-Year-Old Children. Social Environmental Risk Factors. *Pediatrics, 79,* 343–350.

Psychologist Alan Kazdin: Kazdin, A. E. (1994). Interventions for Aggressive and Antisocial Children. In L. D. Eron, J. H. Gentry, & P. Schlegel (Eds.), *Reason to Hope: A Psychosocial Perspective on Violence and Youth* (pp. 341–381). Washington, DC: American Psychological Association.

Psychologists Carl Dunst and Carol Trivette: Dunst, C., & Trivette, C. M. (1992). *Risk and Opportunity Factors Influencing Parent and Child Functioning.* Paper based upon presentations made at the Ninth Annual Smoky Mountain Winter Institute, Asheville, NC.

In her book: Harris, J. (1998). *The Nurture Assumption: Why Children Turn Out the Way They Do.* New York: Free Press.

In a study by child psychologists: Erickson, S. F., Egeland, B., & Pianta, R. (1989). The Effects of Maltreatment on the Development of Young Children. In V. Carlson & D. Cicchetti (Eds.), *Child Maltreatment: Theory and Research on the Causes and Consequences of Child Abuse and Neglect* (pp. 647–684). Cambridge, MA: Cambridge University Press.

But in her classic study: Maccoby, E. E., & Martin, J. A. (1983). Socialization in the Context of the Family: Parent-Child Interaction. In P. H. Mussen (Series Ed.) & E. M. Hetherington (Vol. Ed.), *Handbook of Child Psychology: Vol. 4, Socialization, Personality, and Social Development* (4th ed., pp. 1–101). New York: Wiley.

But psychiatrist Stanley Greenspan: Greenspan, S. I. (1992). *Infancy and Early Childhood: The Practice of Clinical Assessments and Intervention with Emotional and Developmental Challenges.* Madison, CT: International Universities Press.

University of Oregon researcher: Patterson, G. R., & Stouthamer-Loeber, M. (1984). The Correlation of Family Management Practices and Delinquency. *Child Development, 55,* 1299–1307.

Psychologist Byron Egeland and his colleagues: Egeland, B., & Vaughn, B. (1981). Failure of "Bond Formation" as a Cause of Abuse, Neglect, and Maltreatment. *American Journal of Orthopsychiatry, 51,* 78–84.

problems with early attachment: Egeland, B., & Stroufe, A. (1981). Developmental Sequelae of Maltreatment in Infancy. In R. Rizley & D. Cicchetti (Eds.), *Developmental Perspectives on Child Maltreatment* (pp. 77–93). San Francisco: Jossey-Bass.

Nothing tells us more about: Dodge, K. A., Pettit, G. S., & Bates, J. E. (1997). How the Experience of Early Physical Abuse Leads Children to Become

Chronically Aggressive. In C. Cicchetti & S. L. Toth (Eds.), *Developmental Psychopathology: Developmental Perspectives on Trauma: Vol. 9. Theory, Research, and Intervention* (pp. 263–288). Rochester, NY: University of Rochester Press.

4 to 7 percent of kids: Kazdin, A. E. (1994). Interventions for Aggressive and Antisocial Children. In L. D. Eron, J. H. Gentry, & P. Schlegel (Eds.), *Reason to Hope: A Psychosocial Perspective on Violence and Youth* (pp. 341–381). Washington, DC: American Psychological Association.

Some at-risk children are saved: Patterson, G. R. (1982). *A Social Learning Approach to Family Intervention: III. Coercive Family Process.* Eugene, OR: Castalia.

There is, of course, another question: Polansky, N. A., Borgman, R. D., & De Saix, C. (1972). *Roots of Futility.* San Francisco: Jossey-Bass.

In fact, neglect is more common than abuse: Sedlak, A. J., & Broadhurst, D. D. (1996, September). *Third National Incidence Study of Child Abuse and Neglect: Final Report.* Washington, DC: U.S. Department of Health and Human Services.

There is more to the link: Perry, B., Pollard, R., Blakley, T., Baker, W., & Vigilante, D. (1995). Childhood Trauma, the Neurobiology of Adaptation, and "Use-Dependent" Development of the Brain: How "States" Become "Traits." *Infant Mental Health Journal, 16,* 271–289.

There is a third explanation: Ibid.

As I watch Sharnell rock: Perry, B. (1994, March). *Children of Waco.* Presentation to the Chicago Association for Child and Adolescent Psychiatry.

for some it reflects a biological predisposition: Losel, F., Bender, D., & Bliesener, T. (1998, July). Biosocial Risk and Protective Factors for Antisocial Behavior in Juveniles. Paper presented to the 15th Bi-ennial Conference of The International Society for the Study of Behavioral Development, Bern, Switzerland.

Terrence Real provides a road map: Real, T. (1997). *I Don't Want to Talk About It: Overcoming the Secret Legacy of Male Depression.* New York: Scribners.

These boys need someone: Ibid.

These boys need someone: Casarjian, R. (1995). *Houses of Healing: A Prisoner's Guide to Inner Power and Freedom.* Boston: The Lionheart Foundation.

20

STRIKING BACK

SEXUAL HARASSMENT

AT WESTON

Peggy Orenstein

PRINCIPAL ANDREA MURRAY is on the phone when I enter her office. She motions me into a battered oversized chair and swivels away from me to continue her conversation, tapping the long, red-painted nails of one hand impatiently against her cluttered desk. Ms. Murray's office is small and, on this January day, overheated; there's barely room in it for her file cabinets, her computer terminal, and the two empty chairs that lay in wait for errant children. The walls are an unforgiving shade of institutional green, but on the corner of her desk nearest me, Ms. Murray has placed an enormous jar of hard candy, a gesture of warmth and approachability from the person whose position usually fills students with dread.

Ms. Murray completes her call and turns toward me. A small, amiable woman with carefully styled brown hair wearing a flower-sprigged dress and sensible shoes, she folds her hands in her lap and looks at me expectantly.

An eighth-grade girl, she informs me, is being sexually harassed.

Laying Down the New Law

Jeanie Mayes, a quiet, somewhat mousy girl, has lodged a formal complaint against a group of boys in her gym class who have been taunting her about the size of her breasts. The gym teacher, who is male, has largely

459

ignored the remarks, although he has occasionally punished the most insolent boys by making them run a lap around the school track. For the most
part, though, Jeanie silently endured the heckling until last week, when a
new, more physically developed girl moved to Weston and the harassment
escalated. The boys began to walk by Jeanie, their hands cupped a few
inches away from their chests, smirking, saying, "You've got competition,
Jeanie. Connie is bigger than you are, but we'll always remember that
you're second!" A few days later, one of the boys reached out and grabbed
Jeanie's breasts.

"The thing is," says Ms. Murray, "this girl is actually not large-chested,
this isn't happening because she's Dolly Parton. I suspect it's because they
know they're getting to her. She doesn't have a lot of friends, and she's
very nonassertive. She wouldn't even come in here on her own. Her
mother told me what was going on and asked me to call her out of class."

Ms. Murray tells me she has been concerned about the level of sexual
harassment on campus since she arrived at Weston last year. She describes
incidences of boys insulting girls; boys restraining girls; boys grabbing
girls' breasts, buttocks, and crotches. She's been mystified and frankly
exasperated over why, in the face of such ill-treatment, the girls remain
silent. They even remain deferential to some of the harassers who are
"popular" boys.

"They won't see this as something boys do to girls as one group to
another, like racism," Ms. Murray says. "If they could just see themselves
as a group, as powerful, if they just agreed to look at those boys as if they
had leprosy, the boys would correct their behavior immediately."

But January 1, 1993, brought an opportunity for change at Weston,
and that's why Ms. Murray has called me in here, that's why she looks
oddly energized by this unhappy situation. On that day a new, innovative
law took effect in California. Every school in the state is now required to
develop a written sexual harassment policy for staff and students, to display it prominently on campus, and to distribute a copy to each teacher
and parent. More to the point, a principal may suspend or even expel students as young as fourth graders who engage in sexual harassment.

Ms. Murray informed the students of the new law at a school-wide
assembly just after winter break, in which she also discussed a number of
other issues, such as the dates for upcoming standardized tests and the rising incidents of spitting on campus. The message was reinforced several
days later in the school bulletin, which is read aloud in each class during
first period.

Jeanie Mayes's complaint, Ms. Murray says, will be Weston's first test
of the new law.

Ms. Murray has already transferred Jeanie to another gym class, and her science class has been switched as well, since most of the boys who harass her go directly there with her after gym, where they continue their behavior. The next challenge is to confirm her allegations, so it won't be just her word against the boys'. At Ms. Murray's request, Jeanie has compiled a list of girls who have witnessed the harassment; one of the school counselors has been assigned to convene that group after lunch today. The hope is that the girls will not only identify the perpetrators but begin to build a sense of cohesion and power among themselves.

"I'd like Jeanie to see that she's not the sole victim of abusive talk," Ms. Murray says. "That's part of why she's been so distressed. I even want her to see, maybe, why other kids don't take it as hard." Ms. Murray also suggested to the counselor that the girls might want to write an anonymous open letter to the Weston boys about harassment that would be placed in the school bulletin.

Once she's built her case, Ms. Murray plans to suspend the instigators of the harassment, using the new law—there will be no expulsions unless the boys persist—then she'll call their *fathers* with the news. "No man wants to hear from a woman that his parenting hasn't been too good," Ms. Murray explains. "Let alone hear it in graphic terms. I'll just say, 'It's not my job to train your child to be civil in public. You need to take him home and tell him not to make references to girls' bouncing boobs at school.' " She smiles impishly. "If I were a man I'd be so mad at my son for getting me in this humiliating situation!"

If she meets with any resistance, Ms. Murray says, she'll take her crusade into the community. "It's one thing for *me* to say I find it despicable when boys call girls 'ho's' and 'sluts,' " she says, "but it's not as meaningful as if our PTA supports the idea that certain behavior—including certain comments and language used consistently on campus—has adverse effects on the psyche of the girls and affects their academic performance.

"I see this as an evolution of standards," she continues. "We used to tolerate people saying nigger, we used to tolerate physical abuse of children, we used to tolerate slaves at one point if you go back far enough. We've evolved. We don't tolerate those things anymore, and now we won't tolerate sexual harassment."

Sexual Harassment: Who Decides?

Ms. Murray's fervor on this issue is unusual among school principals, to say the least. Technically speaking, students have been protected from sexual harassment since 1972, when Title IX of the Education Amendments

banned discrimination based on sex and required school districts to des-
ignate an employee to handle complaints.[1] Up until recently, few administrators have enforced those regulations and students have remained
ignorant of their rights.[2] But just about the time that the Anita Hill–
Clarence Thomas hearings riveted national attention on sexual harassment among adults, a series of lawsuits brought it roiling to the surface
in public schools. In 1991, in what may be the most celebrated of those
cases, nineteen-year-old Katy Lyle won a $15,000 settlement from the
Duluth, Minnesota, school district, which, while she was a high school
student there, had failed to remove explicit graffiti about her from the
walls of a boys' bathroom even after her parents' numerous complaints.
The following year, in Petaluma, California, Tawnya Brawdy won a
$20,000 out-of-court settlement from Kenilworth Junior High School,
which did not stop boys who mooed at her and jeered about the size of
her breasts. In a third significant case, Christine Franklin took her $6 mil-
lion claim against the Gwinnett County, Georgia, school district all the
way to the Supreme Court after a lower court held that Title IX violations
were not subject to suit for punitive damages. In February 1992, the Jus-
tices unanimously sided with Franklin—even Clarence Thomas agreed.[3]
By the spring of 1993, nearly half of the forty sexual harassment cases
that were being investigated by the U.S. Department of Education's Office
of Civil Rights involved elementary and secondary schools.[4]

In spite of the Supreme Court verdict, it has remained contentious to
suggest that sexual harassment is possible—even has its behavioral roots—
among young children. Media outlets from the daily papers to the afternoon television gab shows to such *éminences grises* as *60 Minutes* have
served up reports on sexual harassment among schoolchildren. Yet, oddly,
no matter how many times the issue is raised, and regardless of the growing hostility toward girls exhibited in such disparate incidents as Lakewood, California's "Spur Posse" sex-for-points scandal and the recent
mob assaults on girls in New York City swimming pools, the media
remain piously skeptical, hinting that this "teasing," this normal adolescent rite of passage, is being taken too seriously.

Perhaps if sexual harassment—which includes unwelcome sexual
remarks that create a hostile learning environment[5]—happened in equal
measure between boys and girls (or men and women) that argument
might have merit. But it doesn't: overwhelmingly boys harass and girls (or
other boys) are harassed, indicating that the behavior is less a statement
about sexuality than an assertion of dominance. The prevalence of sexual
harassment reminds us that boys learn at a very young age to see girls as
less capable and less worthy of respect. One need only consider that the

most shameful insult that one boy can hurl at another is still *"girl!"* (or "pussy" or "faggot," which have similar connotations) to understand how aware children are of female powerlessness, how important it is for boys to distance themselves from that weakness in order to feel like men.

Ms. Murray is right about the girls, too: middle-class and affluent girls in particular tend to accept sexual harassment as inevitable. And why not? The sexual teasing, stalking, and grabbing merely reinforces other, more subtle lessons: it reminds them that they are defined by their bodies; it underscores their lack of entitlement in the classroom (in fact, the harassment frequently *happens* in the classroom);[6] it confirms their belief that boys' sexuality is uncontrollable while their own must remain in check. Without encouragement and proper information, these girls, who already feel diminished, have little reason to believe that they could have recourse against boys' ridicule.

Certainly, middle school children are exploring their sexual identity; but, as we've seen, from the outset those explorations are mired in inequity, and that, too, serves to silence girls when they are harassed. If boys wield the power to ruin girls' reputations, speaking out against boys who offend becomes too risky. Meanwhile, since girls look to boys for confirmation of their desirability (which they've learned is central to their self-esteem), they are left in a muddle: like adult women, they are expected to draw the line between flattery and harassment. Like adult women, they judge one another by where and how they draw that line.

Ideally, the new California law would help redress the power inequities between boys and girls. And the legislation does take a step in that direction: by requiring a sexual harassment policy it admits to the existence of a problem. By stipulating a punishment, it offers girls a measure of the institutional support that they've been sorely lacking, and puts the burden of change squarely on boys. Those shifts in perception alone could have a profound impact on girls' self-esteem. Yet in spite of its good intentions, the law, which may well become a model nationwide, is essentially toothless. Gender equity specialist Nan Stein has pointed out that the state offers no guidance for the development of these new sexual harassment policies and, more importantly, its approach is solely punitive: there are no provisions either for staff training or for a curriculum that would help students define the boundaries of appropriate behavior and dissect power relations.[7] In fact, since the state has no means of enforcing the law, principals are free to soft-pedal it. Those administrators who are concerned about sexual harassment, such as Ms. Murray, are forced to improvise their own plans. They are also left with the fallout if those plans fail.

Strength in Numbers: The Girl Group

Just after lunch, Edie Deloria, a half-time counselor at Weston, convenes the group of girls whose names Jeanie Mayes submitted on her list. Mrs. Deloria is a heavyset woman in her late forties, with heavily moussed hair and bright pink nails; she wears olive stretch pants with a matching sequined shirt and suede ankle boots. As we wait in her office for the girls to assemble, she confides, "I've never done anything like this before, so I don't really know what I'm supposed to do. Andrea kind of booted this onto me."

Seven girls file in and perch uncomfortably on the chairs that Mrs. Deloria has arranged in a circle. Some of them look familiar: I recognize Emily and Samantha from Evie's math class. Amanda is in Becca's English class. Jeanie is among the last to arrive, trailing on the heels of her best friend, a compact girl with flowing red hair named Angie. Jeanie has ruddy skin with a patch of acne on one cheek. She's wearing a baggy sweatshirt that makes her upper body appear formless, and she lets her blond hair, which is limp and a little dirty, hang across her eyes. She looks around nervously and takes a seat under a poster that reads: "Make It Happen!"

The group gets off to a crashingly slow start.

"There've been some things happening in gym class," Mrs. Deloria begins. "Some boys saying some sexual things to girls, and some of you know about it and some of you don't."

A few of the girls stare straight ahead; others look baffled. Jeanie blushes deeply.

"How many of you are aware of this problem?"

There is no response for several seconds, then, one by one, five of the girls raise their hands. Mrs. Deloria looks heartened.

"You may have some feelings about this," she says, "Would anyone like to comment?"

Several of the girls shrug. Some study the ground.

Mrs. Deloria glances at me, then tries another tack. "We want to make the school safe," she says. "We want you to be free from remarks and other things that keep you from feeling comfortable learning here. Do you agree that this needs to be stopped?"

The girls shift in their seats. Jeanie darts her eyes back and forth. Seeing only disinterest, she sinks back into her chair. The meeting appears to be a flop. Then Emily, who is tiny and brooding, winces and says, "Sometimes guys say to other people that they're sluts."

At that, Samantha, who has been staring resolutely at the linoleum while wrapping her hair into a bun, begins to speak. "Something happened today in another class," she says reluctantly. "This guy called this girl a slut and . . . things like that . . ." She trails off and the other girls appear even more uneasy.

"That was my brother," Emily says. Emily, it turns out, skipped a year in elementary school; she is now in the same grade as her older brother Sid, who is a ringleader among the boys.

"And sometimes guys say to girls that they're half guy if they like sports," Samantha continues, then adds, squirming, "but they don't use those words . . . exactly."

"Jeanie's too scared to talk," says Angie, who wears a floppy T-shirt and oversized jeans. Jeanie drops her eyes. "But boys talk about her breasts. And today when we were playing hockey, they'd take the stick and make this motion." She holds her hand near her crotch and pumps it up and down.

"Like masturbating?" Mrs. Deloria asks.

Several of the girls nod.

"Who does that?"

Angie names several names, then adds, "But a lot of the guys do it."

"Guys are just immature," says Samantha.

"It doesn't bother me," says Angie. "But it bothers Jeanie. They come up to her and say, 'Can I have some skim milk?' and stare at her breasts."

Amanda, who has been chewing her fingernails assiduously since the meeting began, snaps her head up. "Are you talking about all our classes?" she asks. "Because Robbie Jordan says he had sex with my mom and that . . . and other stuff."

"Can you say it?" Mrs. Deloria asks.

"Well, that my mom gave him a blow job."

The girls are loosening up now, and a tone of exasperation is replacing their initial reluctance. They begin recounting boys' remarks in detail: they talk about boys who say, "Suck my fat Peter, you slut," who call them "skank" and "ho'" (a variation on "whore" popularized by male rap artists). They talk about boys who pinch their bottoms in the hallways, or grab their breasts and shout, "Let me tune in Tokyo!" They insist that it isn't just "bad" boys who badger them: it's boys with good grades, boys who are athletes, boys who are paragons of the school. And, they all agree, their fear of reprisal is much too acute to allow them to confront their harassers.

Nonetheless, here in the safety of the counselor's office, the girls do name names, many of which are familiar to me: they are the same boys who interrupt and belittle girls in the classroom. They are often the very same boys whom I've seen demand—and get—the most teacher attention in the least productive ways.

During a brief pause in the girls' litany, Mrs. Deloria breaks in. "Girls think that guys 'just say these things,' " she says. "And after a while you think that this is the way that guys are supposed to talk to girls. But it doesn't have to be that way. Your feelings are important and you have to remember that. If you girls want them to stop, you have to tell them what's going to happen if they do it; and then you have to follow through. We take this very seriously at Weston."

"After assembly, the boys acted like it was a big joke," says Katie, a cherub-faced Asian girl. "Now they walk down the hall and touch you on the arm and say, 'Ooooh! Sexual harassment!' Like that's funny."

"I'm not saying it's easy," the counselor says. "But you have to be role models. I know it's just words, but you have to make it happen."

"Jeff Bellamy grabbed my breasts," Jeanie says softly, her eyes misting.

"How did you feel, Jeanie?" asks Mrs. Deloria.

"Jeanie was upset," Angie says. "I know, because I was sitting beside her and . . ."

"Let *Jeanie* finish," Mrs. Deloria interrupts.

"I'm finished," says Jeanie, who appears unaccustomed to speaking for herself.

Amanda, who has gone back to her fingernails, looks up thoughtfully. "I like guys who are your friends," she says. "Guys who talk to you for your personality, not just to get things from you."

The girls ponder this comment in silence; Jeanie looks morose.

"Would you girls like to meet again next week?" Mrs. Deloria asks. All seven girls raise their hands, as if they're in class; they decide, at that time, to work on a letter for the school bulletin.

As the girls get up to leave, Mrs. Deloria cautions, "This conversation is confidential, girls, it's between us. If anyone finds out about it, it was one of you who said something."

The girls nod solemnly; they won't tell a soul.

"Okay," the counselor continues, reaching for a jar of candy, "everyone have a piece of chocolate before you go. Like we need to add to our rear ends—that's where it goes on us!"

Mrs. Deloria shuts the door after the girls leave, leans back in her chair, and offers me the candy jar, apparently seeing no irony in her final remark. "I think that went pretty well," she says, relieved. "You know, a lot of these girls think they have to take this. They're taking it now, and by sixteen years old it will be so ingrained in them that they'll just accept it. Some of them, the girls who don't think they can fight back, they'll grow up and become depressed or battered, you can see it."

Mrs. Deloria's speech is cut short by Andrea Murray, who rushes into the room. "The group went very well," Mrs. Deloria begins to say, but Ms. Murray brushes her aside.

"You won't believe this," she says, turning to me. "Two eighth-grade girls just came into my office and they are livid about something that happened in *their* gym class—a different class. Sid Connelly called one of them a hooker, and another boy said, 'She can't be a hooker because she gives it away for free.' "

Ms. Murray shakes her head. "This girl was raped two years ago by a family member," she says, "so she's taking the remark pretty hard. Her friend brought her in to see me. I promised them I'd suspend Sid first thing tomorrow."

I Did It; So What?

At nine o'clock the next morning, Ms. Murray, wearing a "Distinguished California School" T-shirt, sits in her office with Gary Sanchez, the police officer who is assigned to work with her at the school.

"Are we going for tears here?" Officer Sanchez asks Ms. Murray. The principal nods.

Sid Connelly saunters in the door and, barely glancing at Officer Sanchez, sprawls in the chair next to Ms. Murray's desk. He's a tall, skeletal boy with dewy skin and crooked teeth. Like many boys at Weston, he's shaved the sides of his head and wears a baseball cap over the remaining thatch, giving the impression of total baldness. Since he's also wearing his jeans a fashionable three sizes too big and a huge T-shirt, the baldness makes him look vulnerable rather than tough, as fragile as an egg. He truly looks like a little boy dressed up in a bigger man's clothes, and the words he's been hurling at girls show just how important it is for him to convey that virile impression. Sid's eyes snap with defiance. He's been in here twice already this year for racial slurs and a number of times for other infractions, so he knows the drill.

Ms. Murray looks at him sharply. "We hear you've been talking about girls, Sid," she says.

"You mean Lisanne?"

"Yes, I mean Lisanne."

"So what, she calls me names and I called her one. I called her a hooker, so what?"

"What's a hooker, Sid?" Officer Sanchez asks. He's a big man, too big for the chairs in the office, which are the largest in the school. His graying hair is ridged around his head where his cap usually sits.

"A prostitute." Sid leans back in his chair and folds his arms.

"So you've been calling girls prostitutes," says Andrea.

"Sure," Sid says, shrugging. "She called *me* an asshole."

"Other girls say that's not all you call them."

Sid looks away. "I just did it once."

That's when Ms. Murray slips up, unwittingly identifying one of the girls. "Your sister and other girls say that's not true. They say you call them slut, ho', a lot of names. Are you calling them liars?"

"No," Sid says, kicking his feet against his chair.

Officer Sanchez turns to Sid, shaking his head. "Sid, Sid, Sid. Society doesn't accept boys calling girls sexual names anymore. It's illegal. You can be expelled for it. You can go to jail for it."

"Well, if they want people to know that, why don't they tell them," Sid says sullenly.

"We did, Sid," Ms. Murray says. "Weren't you at the assembly Friday?"

"I was absent."

"Well, didn't your first-period teacher read the note in the bulletin and discuss it this week?"

"I don't listen to him," Sid says.

The cop and Ms. Murray exchange a look.

"Expulsion means you're out of school for the rest of the year," Officer Sanchez continues. "You don't go on to high school next year either. And the parents of those girls? They can sue you, Sid. But since you're a minor . . . you live in . . ."

"Redwood Estates."

"Redwood Estates. There's a lot of nice homes up there," Officer Sanchez says, nodding appreciatively. He leans in toward the boy. "Since you're a minor," he says, "your mom could be sued by those girls' parents for what you did. And then you couldn't live in Redwood Estates anymore. Instead of your nice, comfortable house, you'd be down here in town living in a little apartment. Your mom wouldn't be too happy with you then, would she, Sid?"

Sid's eyes are getting a little glassy.

Ms. Murray interjects. "Do you see your dad on weekends?" she asks.

Sid nods.

"Do you live with him during the week at all?"

Sid shakes his head.

"Well, I'm going to call him right now and tell him to talk to you about how a man acts." She spins her chair around and places the call. "Will? This is Andrea Murray at the middle school. I have your son here. I'm calling you rather than his mother because we have a serious problem. I have girls complaining that he's making sexually harassing remarks to them." She recounts the incident. "I need your support in talking to him to say it's inappropriate to call girls sluts and hookers."

Sid's jaw tightens. He fights back tears as Ms. Murray goes on to explain the new law to his father.

"If you'd talk to him and explain how girls feel . . ."

She is interrupted as the father speaks. She tries to reiterate her point but is interrupted again. Sid looks, in addition to unhappy, uncomfortable. Something else is being exposed here.

"Well, the information really needs to come from you, Will," Ms. Murray says. "He needs to hear it from a father figure, he needs to identify with your values, to learn his behavior from you. You can help him if you can have that conversation with him. If you tell him . . ."

There is another long pause.

"Yes, I'll notify her, but if you could talk to him from a male perspective maybe you can have a greater influence . . ."

By now, Ms. Murray is fairly begging Will Connelly to talk to his son, and the father is clearly refusing. Sid runs a finger under his eyes. His face is pink.

Ms. Murray hangs up the phone. "You know what your dad tells me, Sid?"

Sid shakes his head.

"He says this might not do any good. He says suspension might not get the message to you. He says he's surprised this hasn't happened before."

Sid looks rigidly ahead, his eyes brimming, his lips full and moist. Ms. Murray ceremoniously fills out a suspension form and hands it to him. He snatches it from her hand and runs out the door, just as the bell signals the end of second period.

After he leaves, Ms. Murray rolls her eyes. "Well, that's where he gets it. You can tell that vulgarity is that man's main way of communicating. He says that it's all his ex-wife's fault, that she doesn't know how to raise them. He probably usually uses those words that Sid used to describe his ex-wife." She lets out a long breath. "Well," she says grimly, "I can't fix his family, but I'm going to stop his behavior."

She begins to brief Officer Sanchez on the next boy who is coming in today, the one who said Lisanne "gives it away for free." This boy is a good student, from a solid family with a mother whom Ms. Murray describes as a feminist; the principal believes he was motivated less by malice than peer pressure, so she plans to go easy on him, just giving him a Saturday detention. But just as she locates his third-period class on the computer, the secretary slips in with a note from Sid's sister. Emily is panicked; she was promised anonymity in the counseling group, but suddenly Sid is blaming her for his suspension. He's told some of his friends, too, and they're starting to come up to her calling her "a big fat ho'." According to Emily, the other girls from the group are terrified; what if their names were used, too? What will the boys do to them?

"They are so scared," Ms. Murray says, shaking her head, "it's unreal."

Ms. Murray calls both Sid and Emily into her office. Emily sits in a chair and folds her hands in her lap. Sid stands next to her.

"Did you see your sister after we talked?" she asks. "Did you say anything to her?"

"Yeah," Sid says. "You said it was my sister who came in here and said I call girls hookers."

"I said what?" Ms. Murray sputters. "Sid, you don't listen too well. I said, 'Even your sister knows what you do.' "

Sid shifts from foot to foot, his lips tight and his eyes wet with anger.

"Your suspension is now *two* days," Ms. Murray says. "And if any girl comes in here and says you're harassing her, I'll just keep adding the days. And I'm calling your mother right now." Sid sniffles. Emily casts her eyes downward. Ms. Murray dials the phone.

When Ms. Murray reaches Sid's mother, Mrs. Connelly tries to dismiss her son's behavior, making excuses for it. Then Ms. Murray hands the phone to Emily, who tells her mother exactly what Sid has been doing. When she hears her own daughter's frightened voice, the excuses stop.

"She just said, 'I'll take care of it, and it *won't* happen again,' " Ms. Murray says after the children leave. "She became completely supportive. I wish every boy had a sister in the same grade."

The More Things Change . . .

Over the next several weeks, Ms. Murray suspends five boys for sexual harassment, including two of the boys who were hounding Jeanie Mayes. She gives several other boys, whom she views as "followers," detention or Saturday school. Her thoroughness buoys the Weston girls' spirits; they believe that Ms. Murray is on their side and will protect them from harm. But this seismic shift toward equality leaves the boys confused and hostile. For the first time, they cannot do or say anything they want. Some of the boys are philosophical about the change, but most are unsure of—or unwilling to consider—what, exactly, constitutes inappropriate behavior. A few of the boys suggest that sexual harassment is too subtle to define, but if girls let them know that they're being offensive, they'll stop. Others are like Carl Ross, who was suspended for making masturbatory motions at Jeanie Mayes and asserting that several other girls "suck dick," and now complains, "The principal says it's degrading gossip, but you can't even say a girl's fine anymore, and how's that degrading?" Rather than try to work through the dilemma, Carl has simply decided to avoid girls for the rest of the year. "I'll just wait until high school," he says, "and talk to the girls then."

Even Jeff Bellamy, the boy who grabbed Jeanie's breasts, seems to have difficulty understanding the charges against him. I stop to chat with him the day after his suspension, while he is running an errand for his math teacher. "I was puzzled by the punishment," he tells me, stroking the few downy hairs on his chin. "I don't remember doing it, but maybe I did. All the guys do that stuff, it's no big deal. The girls don't mind. I mean, they don't do anything about it. I'd beat the crap out of someone if they touched me like that. But girls are different, they don't really do anything, so I guess it's okay to do."

On February 4, less than a month since her campaign to eradicate sexual harassment at Weston began, Ms. Murray calls me back into her office. Her sexual harassment policy, she announces glumly, has "all turned to shit . . . It's come back to bite me."

First, she says the father of one of the girls in the counseling group called her. At home. He wanted to know why the word "masturbating" had been used in front of his daughter without his consent. Apparently, she had yet to learn what the word meant and he wasn't anxious to fill her in.

"I tried to explain that boys in this school are talking about girls' mothers giving them blow jobs," she says. "I told him there's no underestimating the depth of these kids' knowledge or their misinformation. But he wouldn't listen."

Worse still, Jeanie Mayes's case has collapsed. Ms. Murray had told Jeanie's mother in confidence that according to one of the other girls in the class (who happened to be Lisa Duffy), Jeanie was not forceful enough toward her harassers; Lisa said Jeanie sent "mixed signals," and that the boys as well as some of the girls thought she invited the problem. Mrs. Mayes did not find this well-intentioned critique illuminating. She informed her daughter that a girl was spreading rumors about her, and the next day Jeanie retaliated, persuading the other girls in her former gym class to ostracize Lisa (something she never tried against the boys). At that point, Jeanie stopped being the "victim" and Ms. Murray called home again, to request that the mother have a talk with the daughter about her aggressive behavior. Mrs. Mayes exploded.

"She was happy as long as I met the agenda, as long as I suspended boys who misbehaved," Ms. Murray says. "But when her own daughter was held accountable she didn't like it. Now she's pulled Jeanie out of the school."

Before she did, though, Mrs. Mayes called the district superintendent to complain about the principal's mismanagement of her daughter's case. The superintendent agreed that Ms. Murray had botched the proceedings, but not because she hadn't attended to Jeanie. Her complaint was that the principal had failed to protect the boys. "The superintendent was upset that Mrs. Mayes had the names of the boys who had perpetrated this," Ms. Murray says. "But if one kid was hitting another, the parent would know that so-and-so hit his kid, so why is this different? She was also concerned that I'd allowed a group of girls to discuss what had happened. She said the girls could spread it around and stigmatize the boys. But individually, girls are afraid to speak out, and I thought that the group empowered them. And part of the point was supposed to be that these girls would identify boys who were doing this and make them stop by not accepting the behavior.

"I guess I misread the situation," she says. "I thought I should be applauded for this, I thought I was doing something for girls, and that I was developing a culture where girls stood up for their rights. But I guess it's more important to keep a lid on it."

Ms. Murray says the superintendent's reprimand has made her feel "burned" and "gun-shy," so she's not going to confront the remaining boys on her list of chronic harassers. And since she's met with outrage from the parents of both boys and girls, she is dropping her initial plan to rally community support at a PTA meeting. She has already told Edie Deloria to discontinue the girls' group, which, in spite of the counselor's promises, had yet to meet again anyway. That means the open letter for the school bulletin will be abandoned as well.

Maybe she folded without much of a fight, but, Ms. Murray claims, she can't effect broad-based change in her school without the backing of the superintendent. And, practically speaking, Ms. Murray says she has her own reputation to protect; if she crosses too many people, she could endanger her job. So instead of spearheading Weston's sexual harassment policy herself, Ms. Murray has decided to follow her boss's lead.

"There's still no procedure in place for dealing with this in the district," she says, "and no one seems to have any plans to develop one. There's been no discussion among the administrators, no talk about staff training, nothing. There's just the law, no way to carry it out . . . and I guess, looking back, I wouldn't try something like this again."

After leaving Ms. Murray's office that morning, I stop by the school gym. It is a rainy day, and the students are inside playing basketball. The boys dash back and forth, chiding one another for mistakes and slapping high fives over their triumphs. The girls, for the most part, hover on the periphery of the game, halfheartedly guarding one another. This is Lindsay's class, and at one point, when she is the only person on her team who is both near the basket and open, a boy passes her the ball. She purses her lips and shoots.

As the ball leaves her hands, I turn away. I don't want to know whether Lindsay makes the basket or not. I like to imagine that she does, that the ball arcs through the air and swishes perfectly through the hoop, that she embraces her friends, jumping up and down with glee. But perhaps that's not what happens. Perhaps the ball goes wild, and the boys in the class roll their eyes in disgust before continuing the game. Either way, I hope she tries again.

I leave the gym and walk through the rain to the parking lot. As I have on many days this year, I am splitting my time between Weston and another school. I slip into my car and turn it toward the freeway, toward Audubon Middle School, fifty miles and a whole world away.

NOTES

1. Nan D. Stein, "Sexual Harassment in Schools," *The School Administrator,* January 1993, p. 15. According to Stein, formerly the sex equity/civil rights specialist with the Massachusetts Department of Education, students are also protected from sexual harassment by Title VII of the Civil Rights Act, the Fourteenth Amendment to the Constitution, and numerous state criminal and civil statutes.

2. A 1989 study found that three-quarters of all high schools violate Title IX. Susan Faludi, *Backlash: The Undeclared War Against American Women,* New York: Crown Publishers, 1991, p. xiv.

3. *Franklin v. Gwinnett County Public Schools.* Christine Franklin claimed she had been subjected to continual sexual harassment since tenth grade by her economics teacher, Andrew Hill. She said that, initially, Hill had made a number of sexually oriented comments to her, phoned her at home, and

forcibly kissed her in the school parking lot; during her junior year he allegedly forced her to have sex with him in his office. Franklin informed the principal of the sexual assault, but the school dropped its investigation when Hill agreed to resign. Franklin subsequently filed her suit against the district, claiming her school had violated Title IX.

4. Millicent Lawton, "Sexual Harassment of Students Target of District Policies," *Education Week*, February 10, 1993, p. 1.

5. The following is the definition of sexual harassment according to the Equal Employment Opportunity Commission, modified by the Minnesota Human Rights Act to apply to educational institutions:

Sexual harassment consists of sexual advances, requests for sexual favors, and other inappropriate verbal or physical conduct of a sexual nature (student to student; employee to student or vice versa) when: 1) submission to such conduct is made either explicitly or implicitly a term or condition of an individual's employment or education, or when 2) submission to or rejection of such conduct by an individual is used as the basis for academic or employment decisions affecting that individual, or when 3) such conduct has the purpose or effect of substantially interfering with an individual's academic or professional performance or 4) creating an intimidating, hostile, or offensive employment or educational environment.

6. The American Association of University Women Educational Foundation, *Hostile Hallways: The AAUW Survey on Sexual Harassment in America's Schools,* researched by Harris/Scholastic Research, a division of Louis Harris and Associates, Inc., in partnership with Scholastic, Inc., Washington, DC: American Association of University Women, 1993, p. 12. The report found that classrooms were second only to hallways as a venue for harassment. More than half the students surveyed had been harassed during class. In *Secrets in Public: Sexual Harassment in Our Schools,* Wellesley, MA: NOW Legal Defense and Education Fund and Wellesley College Center for Research on Women, 1993. Nan Stein, Nancy L. Marshall, and Linda R. Tropp found the classroom to be the most likely single place for harassment to occur (p. 7).

7. Nan Stein, personal interview, June 16, 1993. Minnesota, the first state to enact legislation against sexual harassment in schools in 1989, requires every school to develop a process for discussing the policy with students and employees. The state has also generated a model curriculum, [Susan Strauss] *Sexual Harassment to Teenagers: It's Not Fun/It's Illegal, A Curriculum for Identification and Prevention of Sexual Harassment for Use with Junior and Senior High School Students,* St. Paul, MN: Minnesota

Department of Education Equal Educational Opportunities Section, 1988. Individual schools, such as Minuteman Tech and Amherst Regional High School—both in Massachusetts—have also developed sexual harassment policies that are educational rather than merely disciplinary. Both schools place a premium on mediation between students, allowing the harassee to maintain a sense of control over the proceedings.

BOYS TO MEN

QUESTIONS OF VIOLENCE

Harvard Education Letter

EVERY MONTH, the Harvard Graduate School of Education invites a number of educators, researchers, community activists, and policymakers from across the country to talk about such topics as school violence, multiple intelligences, teaching science, and the politics of school reform. We are pleased to be able to provide you with an edited transcript of some of these talks.

Below is an edited transcript of a talk that took place at the Harvard Graduate School of Education on April 15, 1999.

Introduction

CAROL GILLIGAN: I'm delighted to welcome you to this most important discussion, "Boys to Men: Questions of Violence."

Our panel members include Jim Garbarino, and Jim Gilligan, and Michael Thompson. Jim Garbarino is co-director of the Family Life Development Center and a professor of Human Development at Cornell University. He has authored or edited 13 books, most recently *Lost Boys: Why Our Sons Turn Violent and How We Can Save Them.* Dr. Garbarino has been a consultant on children and families and has received a number of awards for his work. It's a great honor to have him with us tonight. My husband, Jim Gilligan, wrote a book called *Violence*. The book is based on his 25 years as the medical director at Bridgewater (MA) State Hospital for the criminally insane, where he worked in the 1970s to take people out of chains. He's been associated with Harvard and Harvard Medical School for about 25 years and a supervisor at Cambridge Hospital. He's the father of three boys, so he knows what he's talking about and it's great to have him join this forum. Michael Thompson is a consultant, author, and child and family psychologist practicing in Cambridge, MA. He's the co-author, with Edward Howell, of *Finding the Heart of the Child*. Dr. Thompson has lectured widely on topics pertaining to the development of boys and has conducted problem-solving workshops with parents, teachers, and students around the country. He just wrote a book with Daniel Kindlon called *Raising Cain: Protecting the Emotional Life of Boys*, which is on the extended *New York Times* bestseller list which indicates the enormous interest in this subject. I'm going to start with a question and then we'll have a discussion. I hope you'll get involved in this important conversation.

Panel Discussion

CAROL GILLIGAN: There's been a fair amount of discussion recently about the emotional lives of boys and men. The emotional life of boys and men, or the inhibitions in their emotional life. What is your thinking on the specific needs and issues of boys that need to be addressed in order for them to grow into functional, productive, loving men? How are these needs different from those of girls and women?

THOMPSON: I want to explain that my co-author Dan Kindlon is the research half of our partnership; I'm much more the clinician. I haven't worked with many violent populations, but I'm concerned about the level of anger among the privileged boys I work with and about the narrowness of their decisionmaking with respect to emotional problems.

Boys are born with the same emotional potential as girls. Boys have faces as expressive as girls do. Boy babies cry more. There is every reason to believe that boys have as much neurological potential for an emotional life as do girls. But something gets lost in boys, and as somebody who has worked in elementary and secondary schools all of my professional career, I can tell you you can watch the loss of facial expression in boys as they turn into men. And we know that by kindergarten a girl is six times more likely to use the word love than is a boy.

○

It is as if they say, "Thank you for saving us from what we were about to do to each other" and that is a real resistance to what the culture requires of them.

○

By the time their boys are 8 or 9 years old, mothers routinely report to me that they can no longer read their boys' faces the way they used to, that they've gone–somehow—"stony." A teacher asked me the other day, "What is it that happens to boys in third grade? They're so open and innocent up until then and then we lose them."

By the age of 8 or 9 a boy is measuring everything he does on one dimension, from strong to weak. If you want to understand boy psychology, it's that they put everything through the strong/weak filter. Now girls care about strong and weak, they care a lot about strong and weak, but they also care about nice/not nice and close/far away. Working in co-ed schools, I see that girls are able to operate on more dimensions. Boys feel required to express only a narrow band of what they truly feel.

I was talking with some 15-year-olds last week and one of them said, "You can only show your strong side, not your soft side." And I said, "What happens to your soft side if you don't show it?" And this boy was stumped and another boy said, "You lose it because you become what you show." I might say they *think* they become what they show, and the problem that Dan and I see is that boys go into the adolescent years with a restricted range of emotional expression and a restricted language that we call "emotional illiteracy." This keeps a boy locked up because he may not be able to articulate his experience and he may be ashamed that he can't, and if he knows he cannot articulate it and he's ashamed that he can't, then the best course, the strongest-looking course, is to be silent.

JIM GILLIGAN: Let me pick up on some of those themes. My own work has involved a great deal of work with violent men and male adolescents. I want to mention that one of the most salient things that I noticed about boys and men was the degree to which there was a preoccupation with weak versus strong. It's not too difficult to see how quickly that evolves into a predisposition to prove one's strength by means of violence, particularly if a child doesn't have nonviolent means available to show that he is strong.

Working primarily with violent men, I've been struck by the degree to which the concern about proving that one is not a coward, not a weakling, will drive men, if they don't have nonviolent means available to uphold their sense of identity and their sense of self-worth, to engage in levels of violence that are not only destructive to other people but ultimately can even cost their own lives. There's something about proving that one is a man by means of showing how brave and courageous he is, which often means engaging in risk-taking behaviors, so that boys and men, for example, die and are injured from accidental injuries at several times the rate of women. And this is true in every culture on earth. And needless to say, boys engage in violence more than girls, and men more than women.

When I started asking myself why men are so much more violent than women, it struck me that from the time they are little kids, boys are taught that the worst thing to be is a sissy or a coward or a mama's boy. If we are ever going to raise a generation of males who grow into less violent men, then it seems to me we have to start challenging some of these stereotypes about masculinity.

There are some ancient traditions in our culture and in most patriarchal cultures that condition boys to feel that they are not really male unless they are willing to fight.

I think this is a theme that needs to be emphasized. We're all familiar with the many ways the polarization of sex roles is disadvantageous to women; I think it's important now to recognize how those gender roles are also disadvantageous to men.

GARBARINO: I've worked in the field of child abuse and neglect for about 25 years. Most recently I've been focusing on boys incarcerated for committing murder or other severe acts of violence. If you come at things from a psychological point of view, you know the term developmental psychopathology, which is a field based on the idea that by studying extreme and abnormal psychological developments, we can shed some light on normal development. The work that I am currently doing might be called *developmental social pathology*, in that it is looking at boys in really terrible social environments and seeing what light that sheds on normal social environments of boys. So that is part of the context for what I would have to say.

It is important to approach these issues from what we usually term an *ecological perspective*, meaning that individual development doesn't really become clear unless you understand the context in which it occurs. I was struck by Carol's question of what needs to be addressed in order for boys to grow into functional, productive, loving men. My first thought was, the context may make those mutually exclusive. The implicit thing is that the right context will allow boys to be functional and productive and loving men at the same time. I think that part of the problem is that those three goals are often in opposition from a boy's point of view, and in fact it may mean giving up one in order to achieve another.

○

I think teenagers, particularly boys, have a sense that there is nobody to provide order and stability in their world, and so they are left to this kind of dog-eat-dog world that takes its ultimate form in the prison.

○

On the other hand, there is some research that points to a kind of uniformity across many cultures, at least on the psychological level that is, when you look at the foundations for resilience, the ability to deal with stress and threats. Aimee Vernard, in her review on resilience, points out that androgyny, the combining in one person of traditionally masculine and traditionally feminine attributes and characteristics, emerges as one of the correlates or underpinnings of resilience across a wide range of cultures, which certainly would argue that what is needed then is literally to tame boys and to enhance their "softer" side to make them more resilient. That certainly flies in the face of what most boys and men think—namely, that they have to suppress their feminine side in order to be strong enough to survive. But, as you heard from Jim Gilligan, while it seems counterintuitive to boys, the fact is that the more narrowly masculine they become, the more likely they are to end up in early death and early incarceration and other damage. So there is certainly something to be said about using resilience as a criterion to promote this more well-rounded development.

Getting to Resilience

One of the big issues that pulls us all together is juvenile vigilantism, which is boys' adaptation to a situation in which their need to be strong seems to be threatened by the lack of adult strength in their environment. A boy in Michigan said to me, "If I join a gang I am 50% safe; if I don't join a gang, I am 0% safe." The bottom line is he doesn't see that aligning himself, allowing his aggression and his needs for power to be channeled into prosocial adult agendas, is likely to meet his basic need of safety. When I asked a nine-year-old boy from a dangerous neighborhood in California what it would take to make him feel safer here, the only answer he could come up with was, "If I had a gun of my own."

One 16-year-old boy we interviewed in our prison project pointed very specifically to one day, at age eight, that he understands now to be the turning point in his life. He says he was in third grade, on the schoolyard, when one of his friends was jumped by a bunch of older boys—fourth graders. He said the teacher turned her back and went inside. In that moment he realized that he was on his own out there. Given the essential priority of being safe and being strong, given that adults are not going to help that, obviously you are on your own and a lot of very dangerous things happen because of that.

CAROL GILLIGAN: Girls don't passively become what society wants them to become. We found evidence of resistance in our research on adolescent girls. Where are the sources of boys' resistance?

GARBARINO: The larger cultural contexts in which male and female resistance occur are pretty different. That is, a girl who is being called a tomboy is considered uppity, trying to be something better than she should. The boy who is called a sissy is considered to be lowering himself. And so the resistance is of a different nature. For that reason, it may well be easier to empower the girl because she is moving into a domain that is understood to be valuable by both sides. For boys to complete their humanity has a lot of overtones of giving up a privileged position to take on the attributes of something in a patriarchal culture that is viewed as being less.

The way I experienced resistance from boys is that boys who, in the collective of the youth prison, are fully functional in that they are almost completely affectless except for expressions of bravado. In public settings they are very guarded, in their tones of voice and posture, but in the intimate private setting that we create in the interview, they often find a space where they can participate in the other part of their humanity because my partner and I very clearly give them models of that and permission to do that and it is pretty clear that this is all confidential so nobody else is going to know that they have these feelings when they leave the room.

I think that speaks to a resistance movement which, if you also think about the masculine culture, does offer some stylized and ritualized opportunities to be expressive, which the boys gobble up. For example, in athletics, boys can hug and do things that are not permitted outside of the ritual context.

The other element of these boys in prison that complicates the task is that very often they have been cast into a kind of developmentally inappropriate relationship with their mothers. Because their fathers are often absent from their lives and often the men who are intimate with their mothers are aggressive towards their mothers, they early on become some combination of protector and confidante for their mothers. When they reach adolescence and they need a lot of structure and discipline, they don't respect their mothers. They may love their mothers but they see them as being weak and unable to protect them. The boys have had to protect their mothers. This complicates their ability to respect their feminine side because they associate it with victimization.

JIM GILLIGAN: What I am struck by is how little effort there is toward changing the traditional male role. What I am trying to say is, despite all the work on gender and the tremendous amount of discussion that we have had about expanding the opportunities and the expectations and so on, how very little we have said or done about changing male sex roles or gender roles. Our male leaders are so terrified of looking like wimps, are so terrified that somebody will say you are soft on crime, or you are not tough enough to stand up against this enemy or that. I think the silence about how problematic the male gender role is is just deafening. I think it would be healthy and rational and realistic to start recognizing how bizarre it is to say that one sex should be the only one that can be functional and active and so forth and that the other sex is supposed to be more restricted and passive. Regardless of where these ideas may have come from historically, they are so manifestly maladaptive now that one would think that ordinary rationality would lead to a much more powerful critique of them.

THOMPSON: I am the psychologist for the Belmont Hill School, an all boys' school. When I accepted the job there, a lot of people, men and women, said, oh, don't go there. Nobody will talk to you, you will be like the Maytag repairman, they have no use for you. It is not a psychological place and men won't open up. And though I work at the whole other end of the socioeconomic spectrum from where you two have worked, what you say resonates with me. So many boys come in and give me an indication that they are crushed by the culture, saying "I am not a real athletic boy" or "I am not a real Belmont Hill boy." What they are saying is, "I find myself lacking in those attributes which I know I am supposed to have." But if you can persist and stay with them and find a way to speak to their sense of humor or capture them somehow, boys will signal that they are suffering. In my work I see that they are grateful when I find a way to get behind the mask that they have put up.

The other thing I see, in the schools where I consult, is that boys claim they are tough and they claim they need to fight. I interviewed two boys from Concord, MA—a tenth grader and twelfth grader. I asked, what does it mean to be a man? And this tenth grader said, "You have to be ready to fight at any time." I looked at these two well-fed boys from Concord and I asked, has either of you ever actually had a fight? And the twelfth grader got my drift and he said, "No, but you have to be ready to fight at any time."

What I find is, in the schools where I have worked where the level of adult supervision is very high and the protections are great, how grateful boys are after there has been a possible threatening incident and adults have stepped in. It is as if they say, "Thank you for saving us from what we were about to do to each other" and that is a real resistance to what the culture requires of them.

GARBARINO: I think the boys that I speak with also are very grateful. The key to their being grateful is that when we begin to talk with them, we make it clear that the last thing we are going to talk about is their crime, because they are so used to the only entry point into their lives being their crime. And they have a sense of relief and gratitude that we want to hear about the rest of their life, and eventually, maybe weeks from now, maybe we will talk about their crime. I said at the opening, developmental psychopathology tries to shed light on normal development by looking at the abnormal. I think these boys in many ways are the most "American" boys, because in being ready to fight at any minute, if you are in a prison is not a hypothetical construct; that is the reality. I have interviewed boys in several different prisons. One that was remarkable was the New York State Youth Prison system, in that the adults really were in charge of the facility, unlike at the other four I visited. I spoke with boys who had been in the other four and they had the sense that they were now in an environment in which the adults really are in charge, perhaps for the first time in their adolescent lives, and they relax, they talk about not needing to be as hypervigilant as they were before. That was really summed up by one boy I interviewed. The director of the facility walked by, and the boy said to me, "That is the owner." Not the director, but the owner. And this is a boy who had been in a lot of other places and had been involved in a lot of violent activity in other places, but here he felt the owner was in charge and so all these implicit issues about aggression could stay implicit, and I think that is an important lesson in the microcosm of the prison, and also in the society at large.

○

Boys need a sense of order and a strong adult presence and I want to know how can we move to a sense of clear structure without moving back into a patriarchal structure.

○

With the decline of the sense of their being a benevolent adult authority, I think teenagers, particularly boys, have a sense that there is nobody to provide order and stability in their world, and so they are left to this kind of dog-eat-dog world that takes its ultimate form in the prison.

CAROL GILLIGAN: Jim, I was just thinking about what you said in the seminar about the conditions under which a boy with a history of trauma and abuse takes a violent pathway. I thought it would be useful if you would talk about that, and then I want to pick up on the point that you just made.

GARBARINO: One really illuminating study on this transition from early victimization to aggression is by Kenneth Dodge, who is now at Duke University. What Dodge asked is what do abused kids do that leads them into chronic violence and aggression? He found that only about 35% of the abused children moved into this pathway and it was almost entirely accounted for by whether or not they drew four conclusions or four adaptations to being an abused child. One, they become hypersensitive to negative social cues. That is, when exposed to a social environment, they perceive threatening looks, hostile gestures, negative tones of voice. Two, they become oblivious to positive social cues, so they don't see in the same social environment, the smiles, the warm tones of voice, the beckoning gestures. Three, they develop a readily accessible repertoire of aggressive behavior, so their first and almost exclusive answer is aggression. And fourth, they develop a conclusion about the way the world works; namely, that aggression is successful.

So thinking of children as anthropologists, we see that they look at their world and they conclude, yes, when my mother bugs my father, he punches her in the mouth and then she doesn't bug him. When my brother demands an ice cream cone and my mother kicks him down the stairs, he doesn't ask again. So they form these conclusions. What Dodge found was that if an abused child didn't develop those four conclusions he was no more likely to develop chronic aggressive behavior than non-abused children. But an abused child who did develop these four conclusions was seven times more likely to develop this pattern of chronic aggression. Those kids, who by age nine had this pattern of chronic aggression, acting out and violation of rules, are the group from which the most damaged and damaging teenagers come. About a third of those boys become serious violent chronic delinquents, and more than 90% of them will ultimately have such big problems that they will probably be institutionalized, maybe not in a prison, but somewhere. So this is a very important dynamic and the big question is why some kids draw those conclusions from being abused and others don't.

I think future research will focus on temperamental differences that lead to intellectual differences, that lead some kids to draw more diffuse conclusions. It is really helpful to pinpoint where the critical juncture is, and that leads us to think about what we could do about it. Another study that I think is very important is by Shepard Kellum at Johns Hopkins University. Kellum has found that first grade is a critical moment in boys' evolution. He finds that aggressive boys who come into a first-grade classroom and find a chaotic class and a weak teacher form aggressive peer groups that are evident in seventh grade. But when those same aggressive boys come in and find a strong, organized teacher they react differently. I think of my first-grade teacher, Mrs. Annunziata, a giant woman with an enormous bosom and a big wart on her face. You walked into her classroom and she said, "Children, this is my classroom, you are here to be civilized." Kellum finds that teachers who are loving but strong tame those boys and don't allow aggressive peer groups to form.

THOMPSON: I have been astonished by the capacity of very little boys to scare adults. That is, adults are fearful of boys in groups even in second and third grade and though they may not say it overtly, they manifest a kind of fear that is terrifying for the boys because they don't want to scare adults. But, having scared adults, they get hooked on it.

CAROL GILLIGAN: Now I heard Jim say that these boys need a sense of order and a strong adult presence and I want to know how can we move to a sense of clear structure without moving back into a patriarchal structure.

GARBARINO: I think the political answer is pluralism, which is diversity within a common purpose and a common structure. Mrs. Annunziata in my first-grade classroom was not a dictator, but she clearly said that adults set the context in which you can flourish and grow up. It may be that that reflects some primal need for hierarchy and structure and order, which may be particularly boys' primary characteristic wherever it comes from. In chaos you see the more barbaric elements emerging, whereas if you have at least a benign structure, I think boys will live within that but they will demand some kind of organization.

I am less concerned about boys being over controlled. I think if anything, the issue is to think about counter socialization—that is, to tame the boys and embolden the girls. Mrs. Annunziata did both in her classroom because she prevented the boys from dominating the girls and thus gave the girls a safe context in which they could be more active and assertive. Had she been weak, the aggressive boys would have set a chaotic tone, the chaos in the classroom would have been filled, that vacuum would have been felt by the aggressive boys and they'd react by seizing control, and I would rather have the teacher in charge than those boys.

JAMES GILLIGAN: One distinction I would like to make is between restraint and punishment or between control and punishment, when people's behavior is out of control. By punishment I mean the deliberate infliction of pain on somebody for the sake of making them hurt and for getting revenge, versus simply restraining people if they behave in ways that are dangerous to themselves or others. We all know what that means if we are talking about little children. Any of us who have raised children know that if a young child is running out in front of traffic and they don't respond to words, you hold the child so he or she won't run out and get run over. Or if a child is beating up his little brother or sister, and doesn't respond to words, you restrain the child. You pull him off, hold him back, but that does not mean you have to be violent toward the child. You hold the child, you try to teach, you talk. In fact you are trying to prevent violence and pain.

Now I wish we could make that same distinction on a more global scale. As parents, for example, you know you don't have to hurt your child to make him behave. But when we get to a larger context, I think of how punitive our society has become with respect to the boys who get into trouble. I was appalled when we went through this epidemic of schoolyard shootings over the last couple of years. What appalled me was not only the events themselves, which of course were horrendous and tragic, but the response of many adults. Instead of realizing what a tragedy this was for everybody involved, many said, "Gee, can't we try these kids as adults and can't we put them in adult prisons and can't we lock them up for the rest of their lives? And in fact, can't we even kill them?" A legislator in Texas introduced a law to bring the age of the death penalty down, so that we could start executing 12-year-olds. The United States is only one of a tiny handful of countries that still can execute children as young as 16. That puts us in the same company as Iraq and Iran and the Sudan and some other countries we don't ordinarily like to be in the same company with. We speak of the epidemic of violence among our youngsters or adolescents, and yes, there is an epidemic in relative terms. From 1984 to 1994, the rate at which teenage boys committed homicides tripled. Over the last 30 years, the homicide rate has increased about sixfold. But what people often forget is that the suicide rate has also increased fivefold for that age and, in fact, if you put these rates on a chart, the increase in the homicide rate and the increase in the suicide rate overlap each other. Both increased explosively. The people who are so eager to be more punitive toward our teenagers, as though we have raised a generation of evil children or something, seem to me to be asking the wrong question. The question is how have we raised a generation of young kids who reach their teenage years in such a state of despair that they don't care whether *they* live or die, let alone anyone else. That is a question we need to ask ourselves, as much as them.

I certainly don't pretend to have all the answers to that question. But I do know at least a few clues that might be worth considering. One is that far more children in America are killed by poverty than are killed by murder. The United States happens to have the highest poverty rate among its children of any developed nations on earth. The age group that has the highest rate of poverty is children, meaning people under the age of 18; the highest rate is among those under the age of 6. We have increased governmental support to keep older people out of poverty, which is a wonderful development, so that the lowest poverty rate is among those over the age 65. But the fact is the amount spent to do that has increased enormously over the last 30 years, while spending for children has just been flat.

I think we have taken an attitude toward our children that makes it understandable that the degree of trust they have in us has gone down. I think that we adults have to take the responsibility for that development.

THOMPSON: I couldn't agree with you more. I think we have deep underlying attitudes toward boys. We are far more violent toward boys than girls: 90% of American families still hit their children and boys are hit more and hit harder and are more likely to be physically abused. Yet when you said tame the boys, I felt provoked, because I actually think that we have an attitude that boys are more animalistic than girls. We react to the physicality and the impulsiveness of boys. By school age, three-quarters of boys in the class are more physically active than any girl. I believe that the psychological overlap between girls and boys is very great on most dimensions, but we know that on the physicality and impulsivity dimensions, there is a difference. And how you feel about boys' physicality, how you react to it, tells a boy a lot about what kind of a man you expect him to be. I was on a talk show in Minneapolis yesterday. I followed the governor, Jessie Ventura, by about ten minutes. He had endorsed corporal punishment in the schools. Shortly before I got on, he said that he had been paddled, it had gotten his attention, and hadn't had any damaging effect on him. He went on to say that the pain hadn't been all that bad, it was the humiliation that left an impression. There was a flood of calls. I took a position absolutely contrary to this and was baited by the talk show hostess, coming from Cambridge and being a psychologist. Then a

Minnesota state policeman called. He was a good man, but he said that this idea that corporal punishment for boys is violence, is entirely wrong. He argued that if boys need to be corrected and we need to get their attention and we need sometimes to spank them, that is not violence. He was trying to make a distinction between violence against boys, what would be REAL violence, and spanking. And I heard this state police officer really struggling with an idea, I thought struggling unsuccessfully. So I said to him, "If you are a small boy and the person you love most in the world is out of control and angry and hitting you, that you may be rationalizing it as you are doing this for his own good, but that boy experiences only violence. He is overwhelmed and frightened, and the moral content of the lesson is completely lost for him in the fear and the overwhelming effect of the moment. And what he remembers is not what he did wrong, but that he had this scary experience. And here an old concept of Freud's comes in, identification with the aggressor. If you are that frightened, there are only two things you can do: you can think, "I can be subjected to that again," or "I could hope to grow up and be like that and be on that side of it sometime," and then you start to act like that.

○

There are some ancient traditions in our culture and in most patriarchal cultures that condition boys to feel that they are not really male unless they are willing to fight.

○

When we discipline girls in school, we say to two girls who have had a rough go at each other, "Now, why did you do that to her? Don't you think you hurt her feelings? Put yourself in her shoes. How would you have felt?" I use it as an opportunity for empathy training, right? But with a boy, I am likely to stand over him and use my body and say, "Cut it out, I don't want to see it in this classroom." We have to look at the way we discipline boys and how much we frighten them, because what I see is that many boys are giving back exactly what they have seen. Sometimes, in a very raw and confrontational way, we are looking into a mirror of our view of boys.

CAROL GILLIGAN: I have one more question for this panel, then I am going to invite questions from the audience. You are three white men talking about boys and violence in a society in which we have a disproportionate percentage of black boys in prison and I wonder how as white men you feel about these issues of race and how you address the racism of the society and of the criminal justice system?

JIM GILLIGAN: The poverty rate is three times as high in the African-American community as it is in the white community. That is not unrelated to the fact that black babies die at three times the rate of white babies and African-American mothers die in giving childbirth at five times the rate of European-American mothers, and so on. The death toll that poverty inflicts on the African-American community is far greater than all of the death and violence caused by crime that we pay so much attention to. Let me give you one example.

We all know how much concern we have had in this country about the rate of murder and other violent crimes over the last 30 years. We really have been going through an epidemic, which has just begun to wane. Presidential elections have been won and lost over the issue of who can prove to the voters that they will be toughest on crime and murderers. The highest the murder rate in America has ever been is roughly ten murders per 100,000 people per year. If you look at the difference in the death rates of whites and blacks in this country, roughly 300 more black people per 100,000 population die than do whites. In other words, if the death rate is 1,000 among whites per 100,000 in a given year, it will be 1,300 for blacks. And we know that this death rate is not due simply to behavior. It has been studied very carefully. You can control for all the health risks like diabetes and hypertension and alcohol and drugs and murder, but a large percentage of those deaths can only be attributed to poverty and all the concomitants of poverty, which of course include poorer medical care, poorer nutrition, poorer housing, less access to knowledge, and so on. But that death rate of 300 per 100,000 never gets talked about. The death rate of 10 per 100,000, we absolutely get hysterical about. They both happen to be important, but we have our priorities totally contrary to where the real deaths are occurring and where the real violence is occurring. The real violence is in the social and economic system, much more than it is in the behavior of the relatively few individuals who respond to that inequitable social and economic system by exploding in violence.

GARBARINO: When I go into a youth prison, it is always going to be 90% African-American teenagers. Fox Butterfield has analyzed the role of Southern culture in the culture of violence. The Southern states have had the highest homicide rates going back over 200 years, and he has done a pretty nice job of illuminating why that might be. It actually has a lot to do with the settlement patterns in the old South, particularly the Scots. The Scots are about the most aggressive group going. They were sent to Ireland to beat the crap out of the Irish and they sent them over to the colonies to beat the crap out of the Indians and the slaves and everyone else. I was in Scotland a month ago, and if you look at the homicide rates among youth, Scotland is number two, after the U.S. Walking the streets in Scotland one night with a colleague, as a bunch of rowdy, aggressive, boisterous, Scots boys came by, he said that if they had guns the way your boys do, we would beat you out for the homicide rate. So that is something to think about, that the disproportionately high homicide rate among African-American young men is much more a function of their Southern heritage than their African heritage, and there are a lot of ways to explain that. A fascinating study done by a psychologist at the University of Michigan had Northern young men and Southern young men walk down a hall, and the experimenter's ally bumps into them and says, "Jerk." What they measure is the physiological level of arousal in the youth bumped into, and they are able to demonstrate that Southern young men are more aroused than Northern young men. Certainly when I talk with boys, you encounter this Southern heritage very clearly. Although they may live in New York State, their family origins are in the South. They are sent back to the South and there is a constant infusion of that Southern culture of a particular kind of violence. That is one particular issue in Fox Butterfield's case study. The other thing is the psychological significance of racism as a day to day reality.

Some of you probably saw the study conducted in Washington State, in which they asked whites and African-Americans "How often does race come into your mind as something that is going to affect what happens to you today?" Among whites, some 2% said "often," and among African-Americans I think it was at least 65% who said, "virtually every day." So the added element of dealing with racism always has to be factored into the equation and when it is complicit with poverty, when it is complicit with the Southern tradition of vengeful violence, and when all that is mixed together in an accumulation of risk model, it is not surprising that it pushes over the edge, without even getting into institutionalized racism and the dealing with kids and who gets suspended and all of those kinds of issues.

Let's remember that the life course of these boys often begins with early suspensions in elementary school and the failure to deal with that issue and with truancy, and allowing this momentum to build up figures very prominently. There is clearly a racist overlay there in what is tolerated and expected. I think it is necessary that we confront those effects to really make progress on this. Of course we are loathe to talk about race as an active force in the social environment of kids, but I think it is very powerful. In many of the boys I know, the opening for their transformation is to begin a kind of academic study of racism as students in their prison. And it is when they begin to read Malcolm X and Eldridge Cleaver and all the rest of the visionaries that they begin to develop a level of self-awareness and consciousness which I think is often an opening to transformation that they never got through their education before.

THOMPSON: As a clinical matter, in working in schools that are largely white and where African-Americans are in a very small minority, I know that they suffer from the need to look strong because to open up, particularly to white people who want to be helpful, to open up and articulate feelings of sadness or vulnerability feels to them that they are going to confirm in some way the racist notions of the white people around them. I think it is almost impossible to do clinical work with African-American teenagers without addressing racism as the first agenda, because they can't talk honestly and openly until you have talked to them about it, and there has been some acknowledgement about what the racist environment is and what the impact on them is. It is the only way that you can develop whatever trust you can develop, so that they can articulate their feelings and find other strategies for dealing with the humiliations in the environment and begin to feel comfortable enough to do something other than to seem strong and closed and potentially explosive.

GARBARINO: If given a little more time, we could explore the significance of the word taming, but I think of "The Horse Whisperer" as opposed to those who break horses. We tend to stand the boys up and say, what did you do? We ought to take them on our laps and cuddle them, and that is what is meant by taming, the horse whisperer, rather than the breaking model.

Questions from the Audience

THOMPSON: I do not believe that hormones are responsible for anger in teenagers. I have worked with teenagers all of my professional career and when boys get testosterone, they get erections. They don't get aggressive. Most of the men in this room didn't suddenly become aggressive when they got hormones. The mood changes I think are less hormonal and more connected to the American teenager's idea of autonomy and their wish to put their childhood behind them and their reaction against their parents, which is not a reaction against their parents who are still loved, but a reaction against their own childhood, which they are trying to put behind them, and become the rugged individualist that they all think they have to be. I think the research is that most teenagers don't get angry, that in fact they have highs and joys and pleasures and their highs are higher than ours and their lows are lower than ours, but they move up and down. And if you have a chronically angry, irritable, challenging teenager, you probably have a depressed teenager or a teenager whom has been traumatized or a teenager for who something is going terribly wrong in their home.

JIM GILLIGAN: One aspect of this I want to emphasize is the degree to which males in our culture are socialized to be violent and to think of themselves as not masculine if they are not violent. I think there is also a lot of pressure on males, particularly adolescent males, to be sexually active, more than many of them are ready for, and it seems to me that these are related. I think they both represent a macho image of masculinity rather than a realistic one. I think that we could reduce the pressure on adolescence, or at least we could not increase the pressure, if we could relax a bit this notion that somehow to be a real man, you have to be hopping into bed with whoever is available, starting as soon as puberty arrives. As far as the violence of the United States, yes, I referred earlier to the degree to which people, our male leaders, got us into some pretty violent incidents or kept them going out of the fear that they will look like wimps. I think that is what Margaret Thatcher said to George Bush, which inspired him to start the first war against Saddam Hussein. We also know that our leaders kept us in Vietnam for years beyond the point at which they thought it made any sense to be there because they didn't want to lose face by being the first president to have a "defeat," which means, in other words, they wanted to live up to the traditional male gender role. It is irrational and it led to the deaths of tens of thousands or more human beings. I think there are times that one has to resort to violence, but I think that when we do, we need to realize that it is a tragic choice and it means that we failed. And when we have to resort to violence, it means that we failed and we need to really examine what it is we did wrong that we couldn't have prevented the need for that. So I think your observation about the U.S. is on target.

GARBARINO: There are a number of studies that document at least a significant correlation between involvement at the political level in warfare and a follow-up increase in internal violence somewhere down the line. So certainly the correlation in general is there, but it is also worth pointing out that it isn't automatic. I think there is at least some kind of case study historical information that societies can go through a process of increased self-awareness and come out of a period of high political violence into a new kind of national culture. Sweden is an example of a society that has a really violent, aggressive past, which eventually went through a period of self-awareness training, if you will, and came out of it with a very different orientation. Are adults who have been sexually abused, better or worse as therapists with kids who were sexually abused? My answer is yes. Better or worse—it depends on what comes out of that experience and I think that war is like that.

AUDIENCE: How can we not look at boys' development decontextualized from their relationships with caring adults, and how do we explain what we see happening in boys, intergenerationally?

THOMPSON: I don't agree with some folks who think that middle-aged men are such emotional waste cases that we can't raise a new generation of boys. What I see is a tremendous readiness in men to actually speak about their experience, have some empathy for what happened to them as boys, and resolve to do better for boys, but we have to first make men safe, and men don't feel safe. They haven't felt safe since the age of 8 or 10 or so and it is hard on them. We have to work with caretakers who are going to work with boys, to work with boy anger and physicality and the things that can be provocative and bring our inner demons out. I knew a man who came from a fundamentalist family in which all the children had been beaten quite systematically, and he swore he would never do it. And then when his son got to a certain age and was big enough, almost an adolescent, and sassed him, he hit his son right across the face. He was mortified that this had come out of him and desperate to talk to somebody about it, so that whatever that was wouldn't come out of him again. And that seems to me the great hope here in this discussion about boys.

PART FIVE

THE INTERACTION OF GENDER, RACE, AND CLASS

MUCH OF THE RESEARCH currently performed on gender issues in education centers around white, middle-class girls and boys. While these findings are significant, it is also important to look at the role of gender in connection to issues of race and class: how is the importance or meaning of gender affected across a variety of ethnicities and social strata?

"Diversity in Girls' Experiences: Feeling Good About Who You Are" uses a quantitative approach to examine the values and self-esteem of girls across five different ethnic groups. Janie Ward uses a different tactic in examining questions of gender and race in "School Rules," exploring how black girls and boys and their families each react and respond to a system that is simultaneously the gateway to their future and, all too often, an instrument of their oppression.

"Characteristics of Communities Affecting Participation/ Success" takes a close look at Latina girls, examining the effects of Latino culture, including family structure, cultural values, and views on gender roles, on girls' success in an academic environment. Ann Ferguson, in contrast, investigates how stereotypes about black masculinity influence the treatment of African-American boys in school in her piece,

"Naughty by Nature." Switching gears once again, Beatriz Chu Clewell and Angela B. Ginorio explore how girls in a variety of ethnic groups participate in the sciences throughout their school years.

Each of these pieces reveals important information about the connection between gender, race, and class in an educational environment. By moving away from the traditional emphasis on white, middle-class children, these authors demonstrate both the significance of looking at gender in conjunction with a variety of other elements as well as the research that is still lacking in many areas. While key investigations into African-American and Latino communities are growing, there is still far too little information on Asian-Americans, Native Americans, and many other ethnic groups. It is clear that the progress on these topics must continue in order to create a comprehensive understanding of how gender, race, and class interact in our schools.

22

DIVERSITY IN GIRLS' EXPERIENCES

FEELING GOOD ABOUT WHO YOU ARE

Sumru Erkut, Jacqueline P. Fields, Rachel Sing, and Fern Marx

THE EVOLVING DEMOGRAPHIC PROFILE of the young female population in the United States today poses a critical challenge to a growing body of research on adolescent girls, a challenge that is not solely theoretical. It also has profound practical implications for policies and programs to promote gender equity for girls and young women.

Research on women and girls until relatively recently focused primarily on white middle-class females. There is growing recognition, long overdue, in mainstream gender research circles that the absence or underrepresentation of girls from certain communities and contexts calls into question the generalizability of findings. Participation in mainstream academic knowledge building by different kinds of women, not only as study subjects but also as researchers, will require a reevaluation of the assumptions, approaches, and purposes that have shaped research on women and girls to date.

Inclusion of diverse experiences and perspectives undoubtedly will also challenge mainstream views in unforeseeable ways. We contend that race or ethnicity, social class, and urbanization of residence do not merely account for variations on a universal or essential experience of being female. Instead, these factors mediate gender in ways that produce qualitatively different "female" experiences for girls and young women.

In this chapter we briefly summarize some central concerns that have framed our own research on girls' sense of themselves and their world in different communities. We then report the results of a study of girls from five racial and ethnic backgrounds and their answers to the question "What activities make you feel good about yourself?" Self-regard is a construct that provides a lens for exploring girls' development in a social context in which race, ethnicity, class, and gender are inseparable defining features. We use the term *self-regard* to include a range of terms and concepts that refer to the feelings one has about oneself, such as self-esteem, self-perceived competence, self-concept, efficacy, and so forth.

Are Adolescent Girls at Peril for Not Having Positive Views of Themselves?

In popular forums in the United States in recent years, from television talk shows to best-selling books, conventional wisdom about the connection between a person's psychological outlook and her or his success (e.g., academic attainment, career and income level, and social status) has proliferated. The notion that feeling good about yourself is a prerequisite for success has been prevalent. Similarly, in academic research, a prominent view is that positive self-perceptions of ability are more important in determining an individual's level of achievement than actual ability or competence (Bandura 1990; Seligman 1991). A positive personal outlook yields positive results. Conversely, low self-esteem and low self-appraisals of competence have been linked with low motivation and achievement. At the same time, some proponents of self-esteem have observed that success does not ensure high self-regard (Steinem 1992). It has been noted that particularly among females, who tend to attribute their achievement to external factors or good fortune rather than to innate ability, success does not guarantee high self-esteem (Clance 1985).

Concern about young women's self-regard converged with concerns about gender equity in such landmark reports as *Reflections of Risk: Growing Up Female in Minnesota, A Report on the Health and Well-being of Adolescent Girls in Minnesota* (Minnesota Women's Fund 1990) and the AAUW poll conducted by Greenberg-Lake, *Shortchanging Girls, Shortchanging America* (American Association of University Women 1991). Girls' high self-regard has been associated with motivation to achieve (academically and in a career) and confidence in their ability to achieve (AAUW 1991; Baruch 1975; Phillips and Zimmerman 1990). While some research indicates that an adolescent's self-concept generally remains positive (Marsh and Gouvernet 1989), other research notes a low point in many girls' self-regard beginning in early adolescence (AAUW 1991).

Longitudinal studies have found that a decline in positive self-regard among adolescent girls contrasts not only with males' experiences, but with younger girls' self-confidence, self-concepts, and optimism about their lives (Brown and Gilligan 1992; Phillips and Zimmerman 1990). Low self-regard has been associated with low personal aspirations (both academic and in career goals) and, in some cases, with low academic achievement (AAUW 1991). Other studies have reported that dissatisfaction with one's body, eating disorders, depression, and suicide attempts all occur at much higher rates for adolescent girls than for adolescent boys (Gans and Blyth 1990; Reinherz, Frost, and Pakiz 1990).

Increasingly, being female is being defined as a factor that puts a young person "at risk" (Earle, Roach, and Fraser 1987), and early adolescence is regarded as a critical time in girls' lives (AAUW 1991; Brown and Gilligan 1992). Indeed, in their recent work, Gilligan and her colleagues view adolescence as a "crossroads" for girls. They describe it as a time of crisis when girls become uncertain of what they know and can speak, a time when girls confront new prescriptions about their responsibility to themselves and to others and rules about knowledge and understanding that may be publicly expressed but may not be knowledge based on their own experience and intuition (Brown and Gilligan 1992; Debold, Wilson, and Malave 1993; Gilligan, Rogers, and Noel 1992). However, because this construction of girls' adolescence is based largely on research with white, privileged girls, it leaves open the possibility that these findings may be a product of that particular context.

Limitations of Existing Notions of Risk and Resilience

An assumed correlation between self-regard, motivation, and success has informed most theories and interventions around "at risk" youth (see Luthar and Zigler 1991). However, risk, to a large extent, is a matter of perspective. The risks that Michelle Fine (1991), Signithia Fordham (1988), or Maxine Baca Zinn and Bonnie Thornton Dill (1994) associate with systemic and institutionalized racism, cultural corrosion, and disconnection from the supportive ties of family and community contrast with the antisocial outcomes that Gary Wehlage (Wehlage, Rutter, and Turnbaugh 1987) associates with risk (e.g., repeating a grade, school tardiness, pregnancy).

Notions of "resilience" and "protective factors" (e.g., Bernard 1991) often reflect white, middle-class cultural models of child rearing, interpersonal relationships, and lifestyles (e.g., Baumrind 1989; Luthar and Zigler 1991) that are not necessarily practiced or valued in every community. The sociocultural specificity of such concepts as "at risk" and "resilience" speak to the degree to which self-regard itself is a cultural construct. For example, the notion that the more an individual believes in her own capability, the more persistent she will be in the face of obstacles or adversity (Bandura 1990) is a cultural model that is not necessarily meaningful in all social contexts. One can argue that a girl's ability to rely on others, to access knowledge and resources in her community, and to cultivate a support network are just as important in enabling her to be persistent in the face of obstacles and adversity. In our exploration of "feeling good about who you are" among different girls in different communities, we have asked what "feeling good" means, what it entails, and how it manifests itself for different girls.

Intersections of Gender, Race or Ethnicity, and Social Class

Critiques of feminist research on girls, such as the work of Carol Gilligan and her colleagues, have been directed at the tendency to universalize or essentialize characteristics and experiences observed among certain girls as the characteristics and experiences of all girls (for a summary, see J. M. Taylor 1994). Developmental models that may be appropriate in certain white, middle- and upper-middle-class settings cannot be generalized to all girls in all contexts (Robinson and Ward 1991; Stack 1994). One study has found that girls in different racial or ethnic groups exhibit different patterns of self-esteem (AAUW 1991). Indeed, self-regard among African Americans has been found to match or exceed that of their white peers (Powell 1985; Rosenberg and Simmons 1971; R. L. Taylor 1976).

A recent study on racial and ethnic differences in academic achievement (Steinberg, Dornbusch, and Brown 1992) demonstrated that, in addition to important differences between white adolescents and adolescents of color, there were notable differences among students of color that defy simple categorization. The researchers found that parenting styles, peer values and support, and historic social status in the United States interacted in such different ways for young people in different racial and ethnic groups that there was no simple formula—no single key factor—for students' academic success or failure. Their study points to the need for research on young people that explores not only between-group differences but also differences within groups, including gender differences. For example, Diaz-Guerrero (1987, cited in Rotheram-Borus 1989) notes a shift in cultural expectations of Latino males' behavior and attitudes during adolescence (i.e., to be assertive and to question authority) that is not paralleled in cultural expectations of Latinas, which, instead, continue to emphasize cooperation and respect for authority.

Research indicates that for adolescents of color, developmental processes may differ from those of white youth (Tatum 1992). Race and ethnicity generally are salient for adolescents of color, particularly in their identity formation, in ways that they are not salient for white adolescents (Phinney 1989; Rotheram-Borus 1989). "Racism," Tatum notes, "defined as a system of advantage based on race, is a pervasive aspect of U.S. socialization" (1992, 3). For white girls, gender may indeed be the principal site for struggle and negotiation in terms of personal identity and social place. For girls of color, culturally and linguistically different girls, working-class girls, and girls living in poverty, gender is not the only site for struggle and negotiation, nor is it necessarily the most salient site. There is also a need for exploring the implications of white identity in development, rather than viewing whiteness as neutral or as a norm.

There is significant social and cultural diversity within major racial and ethnic groups based on language, nationality, religion, socioeconomic status, immigration or migration history, and even skin color. This diversity suggests the need for exploring the "diversity within diversity." The research described below is based on responses of a racially, ethnically, and socioeconomically diverse group of girls. We present findings on their descriptions of what activities make them feel good about themselves.

Diversity in Girls' Views of What Activities Make Them Feel Good

The data for this study were collected as part of a larger project on racial and ethnic diversity in Girl Scouting, which was carried out in twelve states.[1]

Sample

The sample was recruited from the five broad ethnic classifications: Native American, African American, Anglo-European American, Asian Pacific Islander, and Latino. The field sites were three states in the East, three in the South, three in the Midwest, and three in the West. The field sites included a mix of urban areas, suburbs, small cities and towns, rural areas, and Native American reservations. We collected information from 77 Native American, 94 African American, 41 Anglo-European, 76 Asian Pacific, and 74 Latina girls. In total, we obtained data from 362 girls, 175 of whom were current Girl Scouts, 65 of whom were ex-Girl Scouts, and

122 of whom had never been associated with Girl Scouts in any way. The ages of the girls ranged from 6 to 18 with a mean of 12.4 (SD = 2.6).

Procedures

The data collection occurred in small groups of three to five girls who met with an interviewer of the same race or ethnicity as that of the girls. The focus group interview included a question on activities that made the girls feel good about who they were and a follow-up question asking what about the activity made them feel good.

Results

Because there were no statistically significant differences among current Girl Scouts, former Girl Scouts, and girls who had never joined Girl Scouting, we combined the data on all girls for further analyses. Close to half of all girls (46%) gave answers that mentioned an *athletic* activity, such as playing basketball or baseball, swimming, or gymnastics. The next most frequently mentioned activity dealt with the *arts*, such as music, painting, ballet, drama, and arts and crafts activities, mentioned by 19%. Responses indicative of *service to others* were given by 14% of the girls, and *playing* was mentioned by 13%.

When asked what about the activity makes them feel good about themselves, 28% of the girls gave responses that were coded as indicative of *mastery or competence*—for example, "I can do it," "I'm good at it." Twenty-five percent indicated that they *enjoyed the activity,* 14% said it *helped people,* 10% said it was an opportunity to *be with friends,* and 6% said it was a way of "*expressing who I am.*"

There were a number of patterns related to race or ethnicity, socioeconomic status (SES),[2] and urbanization of residence and interactions among these variables. Native American and Asian Pacific American girls were most likely to mention athletics as an activity that made them feel good about themselves (52 and 50%, respectively). In general, high SES girls were less likely to mention athletics (chi square = 23.3, df = 8, p = .003) but much more likely to mention an arts-related activity (chi square = 15.7, df = 8, p = .05). The tendency to find athletics self-enhancing was most pronounced for low SES Native American girls.

The arts appear to be an option most frequently available to middle and high SES girls who live in urban areas. Of all the girls who said an arts-related activity made them feel good about who they were, fully one-third were high SES girls who lived in big cities. The pattern of SES and urbanization interaction was even stronger for community service, whereby girls who lived in big cities and high SES girls were more likely to mention that being of service to others made them feel good (chi square = 17.0, $df = 6$, $p = .009$). This pattern of high SES and urban residence interaction was most pronounced for Asian Pacific American and European American girls (chi square = 31.4, $df = 8$, $p = .001$). Over 90% of the girls who reported service to others made them feel good said the reason was that they liked helping people.

The finding that mastery of the activity ("I can do it") was one of the main reasons it made one feel good is particularly relevant to a discussion of positive self-regard. Here again, we found race, ethnicity, and SES differences (chi square = 28.9, $df = 8$, $p = .0003$). Overall, Asian Pacific American and Latina girls were more likely to say that mastering an activity made them feel good about who they were than were Native American, African American, or European American girls. However, SES interacted with racial and ethnic group. Among Asian Pacific Americans and European American girls, SES was positively related to mastery: high SES girls were most likely to report mastery, followed by middle SES girls, and then low SES girls. Among Latinas and Native Americans, however, it was negatively related to mastery: low SES girls from these groups were more likely to report mastery than high SES girls. Among African Americans, SES had no effect on reporting mastery.

African American and Asian Pacific American girls were more likely than the other groups of girls to say their enjoyment of the activity was the reason it made them feel good (30 and 28%, respectively) (chi square = 26.4, $df = 6$, $p = .059$). Indeed, low SES Native American girls were the group most likely to give this response, accounting for 21% of girls who said being with friends was the reason the activity made them feel good. Opportunity for self-expression (through art, music, or drama) was given as a reason by a small number of girls (6%). The majority of them were middle SES, African American girls who lived in big cities. They accounted for nearly a third of all who gave this reason.

Discussion

An unexpected finding was the frequent mention of athletics as an activity that made girls feel good about themselves. This finding was unexpected for two reasons. First, for a large number of girls, involvement in sports is a relatively new phenomenon in the United States, dating to the passage of Title IX in 1972. One of the provisions of the Title IX Education amendments of 1972 is that schools must provide equal athletic opportunity for both sexes. Although it is true that some girls have participated and excelled in school sports for a long time, before Title IX the range was limited, and cheerleading was the only "athletic" outlet available to girls in many public schools, and often even that was not an option for nonwhite girls in integrated schools. Since then public schools have attempted to provide more opportunities and support to girls' athletic activities. Title IX has by no means eliminated unequal access to sports for girls, but it has made sports programs more widely available to girls in institutions that receive federal financial assistance (see National Advisory Council on Women's Educational Programs 1986). In twenty years sports have become sufficiently available to girls to be a source of self-enhancement. This finding underscores the importance of historical time as a social context.

In addition, deriving self-enhancement from participating in a physical activity, and reporting mastery as the primary reason for such enhancement, has not been generally recognized in traditional or even modern female roles in the United States. Women (and girls) have been described as deriving their worth from relationships (see Brown and Gilligan 1992; Miller 1976). Yet only 10% of the girls in our study stated that a certain activity made them feel good about themselves because it gave them an opportunity to be with friends. The findings about sports and mastery suggest that the availability of opportunities, which may be context specific, plays a major part in defining gender roles.

It appears that sports are a relatively inexpensive, widely available source of self-enhancement, whereas the pursuit of arts-related activities requires a financial outlay for lessons or supplies and is more readily available to high SES girls. However, socioeconomic level appears to have the opposite impact on Asian Pacific American girls. In this group, high SES girls most frequently reported athletics as an activity that made them feel good, followed by middle SES girls, and then low SES girls. The finding that low SES Native American girls and high SES Asian Pacific American girls were most likely to find self-enhancement in athletics again underscores the importance of social context—in this case, the intersection of race or ethnicity, SES, and urbanization. Among low SES Native American girls, many of whom lived on reservations and in rural areas, more than three-quarters reported that sports made them feel good because it was a way to be with their friends. On the other hand, for high SES Asian Pacific American girls, sports is an activity that gives them a sense of mastery and enjoyment. Moreover, the finding that these girls discovered self-enhancement in sports, which has not been part of the traditional definition of Asian Pacific female identity, suggests the possibility of the high SES Asian Pacific American girls' greater resistance to the stereotype of the demure Asian female.

Overall, our results show a relationship between high SES and the desire to be of service to others; an association between living in rural areas, feeling good about oneself, and being with friends; and a correlation between high SES, urban residence, and finding arts-related activities to be a source of feeling good. These findings suggest that the presence or lack of opportunities and resources plays a major role in determining what makes girls feel good about who they are.

Conclusion

Our research on activities that make a girl feel good about who she is and the reason why that activity makes her feel good is but one approach to the larger question of girls' self-regard. These data illustrate the diversity of girls' experiences and the importance of social context for understanding their development. Our data point to SES and rural/urban residence differences among girls from diverse racial and ethnic groups. These three broad categories (race or ethnicity, SES, and urbanization or residence) merely scratch the surface of relevant contexts of girls' lives. An important factor left out of our analysis because of sample size constraints is the diversity within racial and ethnic groups. Racial and ethnic groups can encompass diversity with respect to language, national origin, recency of immigration, religion, and skin color. Our data did not take into consideration the implications of differing abilities or of sexual orientation. Both are major determinants of one's identity and self-regard. Nor did it take into consideration perceived discrimination, which is another important social context for how one feels about oneself.

There is a need for exploration of girls' life experiences in multiple and diverse contexts in order to (a) illuminate gender as one kind of socially constructed difference among other kinds of difference that are equally significant (e.g., race or ethnicity and class), (b) detail how gender is configured and plays out differently in diverse communities and contexts, and (c) examine how gender as a configuration of power relations interacts with other asymmetries of power, including asymmetry based on race or ethnicity and class.

A girl's self-regard does not develop in a social or cultural vacuum. The gender roles, expectations, and relations that prevail in one community do not necessarily map well onto roles, expectations, and relations in another community. Qualities associated with "female" in one community may not translate to "female" in another community. The meaning of puberty and values around female sexuality can vary considerably. Attitudes, values, and behaviors that lead to survival and success for females in one context do not necessarily serve a girl's interests in another. The challenges that many girls face in constructing meaning, negotiating different environments, and finding affirmation of "who they are" are considerable. Orenstein (1994) depicts detailed examples of how similar and how different risks and opportunities can be for girls, depending on race or ethnicity, class, and urbanization of residence.

Similarly, as Fine and Zane (1989) note, the social context of girls' lives fundamentally shapes the choices girls have. Schooling for many girls of color, as well as immigrant and working-class or economically poor girls, may be experienced not as an enhancing process but instead, as Fordham and Ogbu (1986) state, as a "subtractive" process that involves denying, abandoning, or repressing important pieces of oneself. Fine (1991) echoes this perspective in her study on young African Americans who left high school before graduating. Fine observed that many students who left school departed as "feisty social critics." Their short-term strategy for self-preservation, however, did not serve them well in the long run. Four years later, Fine found many of them no longer feisty and critical, but depressed and struggling economically.

Robinson and Ward (1991) similarly find that girls' strategies to survive do not always serve them well. In their study of young African American girls' resistance to oppression, Robinson and Ward distinguish between "resistance for survival" and "resistance for liberation." Resistance for survival, which is short-term and often short-sighted, can include food addictions, substance abuse, school failure, and early pregnancy. Robinson and Ward associate it with internalized negative images, excessive individualism, and disconnection from community. Resistance for liberation, by contrast, involves girls' naming and addressing the oppressions in their lives.

In conclusion, the major point we raise is that the questions that have guided most research on adolescent girls have not been informed by the wisdom of women and girls who are different from the white, middle-class mainstream. Nor have there been sufficient investigations of the diverse experiences of *all* girls. Just as studying women's and girls' experiences in the world opened many minds to seeing female development in a new, nonpathologizing, nondeviant perspective, so studying girls' experiences in the full social context of their lives will bring forth more valid and accurate understandings of female development.

NOTES

1. For greater detail on the methods employed in the Girl Scouts study see S. Erkut, J. P. Fields, D. Almeida, B. De León, and R. Sing, *Strength in diversity* (New York: Girl Scouts of the U.S.A., 1994).

2. Socioeconomic status is estimated using a composite index based on parent reports of parent(s)' education and total family income. The sample was divided into thirds—low, middle, and high SES groups—on the basis of their scores on the SES index.

REFERENCES

The research reported here was funded by a contract from Girl Scouts of the U.S.A. for a study on racial and ethnic diversity. The literature review is based in part on Rachel Sing's qualifying paper submitted to Harvard Graduate School of Education. The collaboration of Deirdre Almeida, Brunilda De León, and Stephanie Geller in the research is gratefully acknowledged, along with the support provided by Sylvia Barsion, national director for research and evaluation for Girl Scouts of the U.S.A. We also thank the forty-five interviewers who participated in the collection of the data.

American Association of University Women. 1991. *Shortchanging girls, shortchanging America.* Washington, D.C.: AAUW, Analysis Group, Greenberg-Lake.

Baca Zinn, M., and B. T. Dill. 1994. Difference and domination. In *Women of color in U.S. society,* edited by M. Baca Zinn and B. T. Dill. Philadelphia: Temple University Press.

Bandura, A. 1990. Conclusions: Reflections on nonability determinants of competence. In *Competence considered,* edited by R. J. Sternberg and J. Kolligan, Jr. New Haven: Yale University Press.

Baruch, G. K. 1975. Girls who perceive themselves as competent: Some antecedents and correlates. Unpublished paper, Worcester Foundation for Experimental Biology, Shrewsbury, Mass.

Baumrind, D. 1989. Rearing competent children. In *Child development today and tomorrow,* edited by W. Damon. San Francisco: Jossey Bass.

Bernard, B. 1991. *Fostering resiliency in kids: Protective factors in the family, school, and community.* Portland, Oreg.: Western Regional Center for Drug-Free Schools and Communities, Far West Laboratory.

Brown, L. M., and C. Gilligan. 1992. *Meeting at the crossroads: Women's psychology and girls' development.* New York: Random House.

Center for Research on Women, Wellesley College. 1992. *How schools shortchange girls: A study of major findings on girls and education.* Washington, D.C.: American Association of University Women.

Clance, P. R. 1985. *The imposter phenomenon.* Atlanta, Ga.: Peachtree.

Debold, E., M. Wilson, and I. Malave, 1993. *Mother daughter revolution: From betrayal to power.* Reading, Mass.: Addison Wesley.

Diaz-Guerrero, R. 1987. Historical sociocultural premises and ethnic socialization. Cited in *Children's ethnic socialization: Pluralism and development,*
edited by J. Phinney and M. Rotheram. Beverly Hills, Calif.: Sage Publications, 1989.

Earle, J., V. Roach, and K. Fraser. 1987. *Female dropouts: A new perspective.*
Alexandria, Va.: National Association of State Boards of Education.

Fine, M. 1991. *Framing dropouts: Notes on the politics of an urban public high
school.* Albany: State University of New York Press.

Fine, M., and N. Zane. 1989. Bein' wrapped too tight: When low-income
women drop out of high school. In *Dropouts from school: Issues, dilemmas, and solutions,* edited by L. Weis, E. Farrar, and H. G. Petrie. Albany:
State University of New York Press.

Fordham, S. 1988. Racelessness as a factor in black students' school success:
Pragmatic strategy or Pyrrhic victory? In *Facing racism in education,*
edited by N. M. Hidalgo, C. L. McDowell, and E. V. Siddle. Reprint Series
no. 21. Cambridge: Harvard Education Review.

Fordham, S., and J. U. Ogbu. 1986. Black students' school success: Coping with
the "burden of acting white." *Urban Review* 18 (3):176–206.

Gans, J., and D. Blyth. 1990. *America's adolescents: How healthy are they?*
Chicago: American Medical Association.

Gilligan, C., A. G. Rogers, and N. Noel. 1992. Cartography of a lost time:
Women, girls, and relationships. Paper presented at the Lilly Endowment
Conference on Youth and Caring, February, Miami, Florida.

Luthar, S. S., and E. Zigler. 1991. Vulnerability and competence: A review of
research on resilience in childhood. *American Journal of Orthopsychiatry*
61 (1):6–22.

Marsh, H., and P. Gouvernet. 1989. Multidimensional self-concepts and perceptions of control: Construct validation of responses by children. *Journal of
Educational Psychology* 81 (1):57–69.

Miller, J. B. 1976. *Toward a new psychology of women.* Boston: Beacon Press.

Minnesota Women's Fund. 1990. *Reflections of risk: Growing up female in
Minnesota, a report on the health and well-being of adolescent girls in
Minnesota.* Minneapolis: Minnesota Women's Fund.

National Advisory Council on Women's Educational Programs. 1986. *Title IX:
The half full, half empty glass.* Washington, D.C.: U.S. Government Printing Office.

Orenstein, P. 1994. *Schoolgirls: Young women, self-esteem, and the confidence
gap.* New York: Doubleday, in association with the American Association
of University Women.

Phillips, D. A., and M. Zimmerman. 1990. The developmental course of perceived competence and incompetence among competent children. In *Com-*

petence considered, edited by R. J. Sternberg and J. Kolligan, Jr. New Haven: Yale University Press.

Phinney, J. 1989. Stages of ethnic identity development in minority group adolescents. *Journal of Early Adolescence* 9 (1–2):34–49.

Powell, G. J. 1985. Self-concepts among Afro-American students in racially isolated minority schools: Some regional differences. *Journal of the American Academy of Child Psychiatry* 24:142–49.

Reinherz, R., A. Frost, and B. Pakiz. 1990. *Changing faces: Correlates of depressive symptoms in late adolescence.* Boston: Simmons College School of Social Work.

Robinson, T., and J. V. Ward. 1991. "A belief in self far greater than anyone's disbelief": Cultivating resistance among African American female adolescents. In *Women, girls, and psychotherapy: Reframing resistance,* edited by C. Gilligan, A. G. Rogers, and D. L. Tolman. Binghamton, N.Y.: Harrington Park Press.

Rosenberg, M., and R. Simmons. 1971. *Black and white self-esteem: The urban school child.* Rose Monograph Series. Washington, D.C.: American Sociological Association.

Rotheram-Borus, M. J. 1989. Ethnic differences in adolescents' identity status and associated behavior problems. *Journal of Adolescence* 12:361–74.

Seligman, M. 1991. *Learned optimism.* New York: Random House.

Stack, C. B. 1994. Different voices, different visions: Gender, culture, and moral reasoning. In *Women of color in U.S. society,* edited by M. Baca Zinn and B. T. Dill. Philadelphia: Temple University Press.

Steinberg, L., S. Dornbusch, and B. Brown. 1992. Ethnic differences in adolescent achievement: An ecological perspective. *American Psychologist* 47 (6):723–29.

Steinem, G. 1992. *Revolution from within: A book of self-esteem.* Boston: Little, Brown.

Tatum, B. D. 1992. Talking about race, learning about racism: The application of racial identity development theory in the classroom. *Harvard Educational Review* 62 (1):1–24.

Taylor, J. M. 1994. Adolescent development: Whose perspective? In *Sexual cultures and the construction of adolescent identities,* edited by J. M. Irvine. Philadelphia: Temple University Press.

Taylor, R. L. 1976. Psychosocial development among black children and youth: A reexamination. *American Journal of Orthopsychiatry* 46:4–19.

Wehlage, G., R. Rutter, and A. Turnbaugh. 1987. A program model for at-risk high school students. *Educational Leadership* (March):70–73.

23

SCHOOL RULES

Janie Ward

A PHILADELPHIA FATHER described his daughter's struggle with, and his response to, an issue far too many black teenagers face at school: the low expectations that many teachers and administrators have of black students.

My daughter Tiffany is 14 now, and at this age you never know who you're going to meet at any given moment. Sometimes she's Miss Independence, other times she acts like she's scared to death to try anything new on her own.

We've always been really involved parents. We go to all the PTA meetings, all the parent conferences—my wife bakes cookies for the bake sales, you know. Tiffany has watched us deal with these schools over the years. If we had a question or a concern, boom—we're there in a flash. If we don't like the way a teacher does something, ring, ring, ring. Me or my wife, one of us is on the phone.

Recently we had this situation. Tiffany came home and she said, "Daddy, I'm in a new reading group and I don't think it's the right one for me." So I said, "Really? What's the problem?" She said, "Well, I used to be in a higher reading group, but two weeks ago the teacher moved a few of us around and now I'm in a lower group and I shouldn't be because I'm not being challenged." "Challenged"— that's the word she used. So I said, "So what do you want me to do about it?" "Talk to the teacher and tell her I should be in another group." So you know what I said to her? I told her, "No." She looked at me with this shocked look on her face and I repeated myself. "No. I'm not doing nothing. This is your problem and I expect you to take care of it." She started to protest and whine. "But Daddy, you're a teacher. You know how to talk to these teachers . . ." I said, "You do, too. And if you don't know exactly what to say, we'll talk about it and find the right words. But this one is on you. You are old enough and smart enough to handle this situation."

Now I don't know why that teacher switched the groups around. I do know that Tiffany feels she can work harder. And I want her to always remember that she has the power to get her needs met. Tiffany is smart; she's got her evidence, put the pieces together, and since she presented her argument to me, I know she has the ability to argue her case in front of a teacher. Right now she's nervous, and that's okay. I'll work with her, help her find the right words, make the best case. That I'll do. But I think that a large part of my responsibility as a parent is to help my child to be able to appreciate the value of working hard in school and to feel she has the power to make the school respond appropriately to her educational needs.

Schooling is an intensely charged issue for black Americans. Teenagers and parents alike recognize its critical importance—as a gateway to better jobs, better housing, and a strong, healthy, powerful black community. Teenagers and parents alike also recognize the obstacles that impede blacks' access to full and forceful education, like inferior resources, stereotyping, the low expectations that teachers and administrators often have for black students, and the quagmire of complacency into which too many blacks surrender. Parents know how important it is to teach their children to counter low expectations, resist complacency, and help their children reap the intellectual, financial, and social rewards of a strong and positive educational identity.

Tiffany's father is teaching his daughter how to resist responsibly. By placing the power to oppose her teacher's presumption of low performance into his daughter's hands, he has taught her how to appreciate and exercise her own power. In doing so, he helps her to replace a situation that had the potential to disempower her with an opportunity to be empowered.

Not long after I talked with Tiffany's dad, I heard a similar story from a teenage boy's perspective. Sixteen-year-old Antoine riveted me with the clarity of his understanding of his teachers' power. He was describing the day-to-day problems of attending his black urban school—loud noise, weapons checks, broken elevators, teacher and student frustration—when he blurted out, "My teachers that have a problem with me, they take it out on my brain." His summation was right on the money. The truth is, teachers possess astounding power: they can decide to teach black children or not to teach them. Possessing this power means possessing a weapon that can inflict permanent damage.

At 16, Antoine had a grip on the power dynamic, at his school and at schools across the country. He may even have been aware of the ever-widening gender gap that also marks the black educational experience, a gap that starts early on in school, and a gap that my female African American college students often observe and comment on. Black women significantly outnumber black men enrolled in colleges. And the ratio of black men to black women attending college is widening steadily. This not only takes a toll on black college women's social lives; it also perilously affects the economic future of black men, and ultimately black families. We know that the gap begins early, when teachers react adversely to boys' behavior (which is often rambunctious and loud, or marked by distractibility), responding with more negative attention, negative evaluations, suspensions, and referrals to special education programs than they dole out to girls. To compound this problem for boys, some of us black parents, perhaps because we are so worried about our sons' mere physical survival in a world that is intensely and increasingly perilous for black males, focus primarily on protecting them, neglecting to push them to raise their own standards and expectations.

The fact that over the past two decades something in our educational system has gone terribly wrong (for both black boys and girls, but particularly for boys) is well known in the black community, and the parents and teenagers with whom I spoke were eager to talk about it. Stories about school spilled out in every context—identity formation, what it means to be black, what parents wanted for their children, what they believed their children weren't receiving—even before I asked any formal questions about education. Education is a hot-button issue for African Americans. We know at the deepest, most visceral level that a strong educational foundation is critically important for blacks. It means better career and economic opportunities, the chance to make large-scale change in the black community, the opportunity to genuinely influence the power dynamic between blacks and whites. But at the same time we are profoundly suspicious of our country's educational system, which continues to be controlled by whites—a system that formally disenfranchised us for decades, and informally continues to do so.

This tension informed many of my talks with families. Parents and teenagers alike speak of the value of education, most often in terms like these: Even if they're poor, they can become whatever they want to be—if they get that background, that resource, that education. Black parents should urge their children to stay in school and learn as much as they can about anything and everything. If you're given the tools, then you can work with it.

Others see the need for each generation of blacks to exceed the last, and education is the means to that end. "If that doesn't happen," one father said, "we will perish as a race."

At the same time, parents and teenagers alike are acutely aware of the shortcomings of the system. Although some teenagers that I talk to describe themselves as academically strong, most teens I know describe their educational programs as marginally "okay," and some use even less positive terms. Their parents are even more disenchanted with their children's education. Most had been educated in the legally segregated schools of the South or in racially segregated neighborhoods in Boston and Philadelphia. By contrast, either due to desegregation bussing programs, or because they lived in integrated neighborhoods, their children were members of integrated school communities.

These mothers and fathers voice a profound distrust of a system that has actively participated in subordinating blacks. Many complain about the low expectations set for blacks by teachers and administrators. Others speak of the profound apathy and sense of complacency many black teenagers feel because of poor schooling. Still others talk about issues of identity that their children face at school, especially when they feel pressure to choose between performing well academically and fitting in with their black peers.

Parents find that designing resistance strategies in the context of school is particularly demanding, since it requires treading a delicate path between encouraging education and compliance to teachers' demands while at the same time inculcating the right degree of suspicion about the system.

Certainly the distrust is well founded. After all, generations of black slave children in America were not allowed to learn how to read or write for fear that they would use these tools to gain freedom, and even after emancipation, blacks were confined to separate and definitely not equal schools. And although the mandate of the U.S. Supreme Court in *Brown v. Board of Education* technically changed that in 1954, the parents with whom I spoke retained painful memories of the violence against, and denigration of, black students that became commonplace as desegregation took hold. Soon after the decision in *Brown* came down, W.E.B. Du Bois spoke of the tension that continues to haunt black parents today.

The decision, he said, confronted "[n]egroes with a cruel dilemma." On the one hand, "they wanted their children educated. That is a must, else they continue in semi-slavery." On the other hand, he continued, "with successfully mixed schools they know what their children must suffer for years from southern white teachers, from white hoodlums who sit beside them and under school authorities from janitors to superintendents who hate and despise them."

To fuel the distrust we parents already possess, for the past two decades the nation has crept again toward resegregation, especially with the conservative movement's relentless attacks on court-ordered bussing and affirmative action. Gone is the black history and literature movement that flowered in the 1960s and 1970s; and many of the black teachers are gone as well. Teaching, once the top vocational choice of African American college graduates, has dwindled in popularity, and the number of black teachers decreases each year. Moreover, black schools in low-income rural areas and the inner city have had their attention distracted from race-specific learning to more immediate concerns: children from broken homes; the effects of drugs, violence, and poverty; and the difficulties of maintaining discipline under circumstances like these.

Although some schools—public and private, predominantly white and predominantly black—are doing an excellent job of creating an environment where all students feel they belong and where expectations are high for all students regardless of race, many are not. And although some teachers are committed to changing the existing educational system to make sure the best is brought out in all children, too many are stymied by school administrations bent on maintaining barriers to change, focusing on the bottom line, and stalling, fearful of political backlash.

Statistics describe gross underachievement by black students, not just in low-income urban and rural schools, but now in more affluent middle-class schools as well. Reports show gaps in black achievement that seem to increase the longer children stay in school: gaps in standardized test scores, disproportionate dropout rates, and questionable mastery of basic skills upon graduation. We black parents have to question why it's always our children who fail in school, and many of us reject the notion that we are entirely to blame for the situation. Instead, we point to the color-blind ideology of racial innocence—the belief that if we don't talk about race, race won't matter—as part of the problem. Many others believe that white educational institutions consciously and deliberately hold blacks back, denying us access to tools that develop the critical skills that might put us at a true economic advantage, as well as to accurate information about our cultural history and the achievements of our forebears. Or, as one man in Raleigh put it, the schools have deliberately "trained us to be stupid."

Many of us resent the high cultural price we have paid for the privilege of attending integrated schools: the surrender of racial solidarity and culture in exchange for an opportunity that includes sharing space and taking instruction from those who often don't see blacks as worthy of full and fair inclusion. We feel the loss is profound: Gone is the richest mission of the segregated black schools: the creation of a set of educational practices and beliefs that were culturally relevant and specific to the needs of blacks. In its place stands unrelenting low academic achievement by black children across the country, and persistent patterns of underfunding and mismanagement of black schools, with high teacher-turnover rates, diluted curricula, and significant discipline problems.

Many black baby-boomer parents describe having attended what they believe were good, caring, educationally solid schools, where the teachers held the futures of their black students close to their hearts, and where they felt a sense of racial solidarity and common purpose. Teachers felt free to teach racialized messages about school success and failure, messages that started, "We as blacks are up against . . ." and "We as blacks must succeed because of . . ." and "A lack of education leads to our failure as individuals and as a people because . . ."

In private conversations out of the earshot of white colleagues and school officials, I've often heard African American educators privately complain about bussing and racial desegregation. Much like the parents with whom I spoke, they maintain that to successfully educate black students, to genuinely promote academic achievement, personal growth, and development in black children—particularly black males—we must redirect our efforts to achieve racial integration in schools and once again build our own educational institutions, separate from whites.

There is, of course, an inherent paradox in an argument that says we must return to the past to create fair, caring, successful schools for black children today. I've never heard an argument in favor of the underfunded, resource-poor, segregated black schools of the past. With the loss of those old segregated schools, however, we have lost a battery of caring teachers who had the requisite knowledge to teach black children well, to foster their self-esteem, and to expand their understanding of black cultural history. These were teachers who could recognize that cultural differences present both opportunities and challenges, who had the skill and the will to build upon cultural resources, and who recognized and understood the relationship between academic and personal development as well as social and moral development. They knew that black children need to possess a sense of efficacy—a belief that they possess the power to make things happen—and teachers like these worked hard to develop that power within.

The parents' descriptions of this loss reminded me of the story a relative once told me about her father, a black teacher in a black school in Kansas, who found himself fired from his teaching position immediately after the *Brown* decision. Maybe the law could require the school administrators to admit blacks to the same schools as whites, but they certainly weren't going to let any black teachers teach white kids. Just like that, he and many other black teachers were dismissed from their responsibilities of teaching black children. And gone with the black teachers were the essential lessons for black students about who they were in the world and how to take their place in it—stories of black achievement and history.

Even against this bleak background, we black parents know that to be psychologically strong and socially smart, our children must be well educated in order to get ahead. We continue to stress the importance of holding the bar high, and we expect our children to succeed, often invoking the same sorts of encouragement our own parents had provided to us. Most important, we maintain that our most critical task as parents is to instill in our children an unwavering belief in their own intellectual competence.

One father told me about an incident that occurred when his daughter, Marian, was in the sixth grade. Each year at her school, the teachers selected students to receive achievement awards. Marian had earned all A's throughout the middle grades, and she had the highest grades in the most academic subjects, a fact that was known to all because of the school's policy of making grades public. Nevertheless, when it came time to present the awards in a schoolwide assembly, Marian received only two of them. Both she and her parents were surprised and upset. After the awards ceremony, at a party organized by the teachers to recognize Marian as the top student of the sixth-grade class, her father took her aside to talk. "Dad," she told him, "I had the highest grades in all those areas. I should have gotten all the awards." "Yeah," he told her, "but you didn't get all the awards. And this is exactly what I been telling you about. Sometimes even when you achieve, you may not get what you are due, but if you don't achieve, you have no hope of ever getting it. So you're always handicapped, but that's your lot in life because you are black."

Marian's father used this difficult and painful event in his daughter's life to teach two essential lessons. First, that life is not always fair for black folks, but that's no reason to give up trying. And second, that you mustn't assess yourself by the criteria designed by others; you must always strive to do your best, know you've done your best, and hold on to that truth in the face of those who might suggest otherwise. While it might sound bleak, this harsh negative critique of the world set in motion the design of resistance strategies for coping with the unfairness of race and gender bias that empowered Marian. Rather than having a demoralizing effect, her father's truth-telling was ultimately liberating because it replaced negative critique with positive recognition.

The fact that the people who had changed the rules in the middle of the game were teachers—adults whom his daughter had trusted and her parents had told her to listen to and obey—was disturbing, but it is a fact of life for which black teenagers like Marian must remain ever vigilant. They must also resist becoming discouraged by such behavior, and instead should take a stand for educational excellence, personal achievement, and tenacity.

Another father, Bob Fraser, described with pride the way his daughter pushes herself. If she gets an 85 percent on a test, he says, she wants to take it again because she won't be happy unless the score is in the upper 90s. "I'm trying to be a fair, good parent," he says, "and not push her. At the same time, I'm saying, 'You're as good as the top student in that class. Don't be dragging in any inferior grades in this house. Your daddy is a teacher. We're top people and you're part of us. So you've gotta do it— you've gotta get those A's and B's.' And she hears that."

He explained that he was passing on the same messages about education that he had heard growing up in much harsher times:

> I could remember my mother saying, "I'm not scrubbing these floors on my knees for you to come in here speakin' bad and talkin' in a way that does not say I'm sending you to school to get an education." My mother didn't have one herself, but she pushed and she's still pushing on me to excel and to do well. If I heard anything about race, it was "you're as good as the next person." And that's what I came up believing.

Parents and adolescents who talk about responsible resistance emphasize the need for teenagers to resist pressures by other teenagers—black or white—to treat academic achievement with disdain. In particular, they worry about the tendency of some blacks to equate academic achievement with "acting white" and something to be avoided. They worry as well about sliding into complacency: of black teens not bothering to resist the messages of their own inferiority. When we envision responsible resisters in our educational systems, black parents stress the importance of holding standards for black achievement high, even in the face of institutionalized low expectations. But underachievement by black students is not just the fault of careless teachers and institutional racism. Most disturbing of all is the disservice some black parents do their children when they emphasize athletic achievement, hipness, or entertainment at the cost of academic success.

I heard these strongly held ideas expressed by parents who were college graduates and by those who weren't, by teenagers in school and by dropouts who had recently returned, by pregnant girls and teenage mothers who were struggling to stay in school, and by achieving college students. But the theme raised most often had to do with the disastrous effects of low expectations—most often held by teachers and administrators, but also at times by peers and parents—and the urgent need we have as black parents to help our children resist and exceed them.

Low Expectations

Felicia, a 15-year-old from North Carolina, told me that her parents had attended all-black schools in the South. From the stories they told her, she felt sure that it was easier to be a black student in a pre-*Brown* segregated school than it was to be a black student in an integrated school today. "[I]t was easier," she said, "because they wouldn't be judged because they were black." The hardest part about being in school today, she told me, was dealing with the teachers' low expectations of blacks. "The teachers," she said, "they don't expect blacks to be smart. You have to prove them wrong. So you have to work hard and show them that you really are a different person than some of the rest."

Mrs. Freeport told me the story of her teenage daughter, who had been thoroughly engaged in academics when the elementary school she attended was all-black, but faced increasing difficulties as she grew older and the school became integrated.

> My daughter was brought up basically with black kids. She had a tremendously good experience. By the time she was in the sixth grade, the schools were integrated. But with her personality, she didn't have any problems in terms of her teachers and her schoolwork, because she had black teachers and, even through junior high, we didn't face any problems with her. When she got into high school and went to an integrated school, she found that there was prejudice there. The teachers expected less of her and the few other black students in her class. [But] she would conceal things that happened to her. She wouldn't share them, because she didn't know what the outcome would be. We had to find out later.

Over time, the mother came to understand that her daughter was under attack in the predominantly white high school.

There was nothing that was done to her physically, but it was just that she was a part of the group of kids that were mistreated by the students. The white kids were ganging up on the black kids, because there were so few of those kids. Til she finally says, "Mama, I cannot stay at that school." And we started to question her at that point. "What is happening?" [The daughter described an incident with a dance teacher who forbade the black students from performing with the dance group.] She felt the tension with the teachers because she felt that the teachers were not giving [the blacks] adequate attention, and she was very withdrawn from them. We knew she was capable of doing her work, but it was like she just got so disinterested in it because the teachers didn't care anything about her. And they made a distinction in the homework with the black kids and the white kids. Especially in biology and science. Several times they had separate sets of homework, until we were made aware of it. They're always saying that black females are dumb in math and science and stuff.

After she had confirmed her daughter's claims, Mrs. Freeport decided to take action.

By that time, my pressure had started to rise, and so I went to the school. I'm not the kind of person who can sit back or go to the bottom. I go to the top when there's a problem with my kid.

Although the daughter's reaction to the problem (to be silent in the face of prejudice and mistreatment) was in keeping with where she was developmentally at that stage in her life, it's an example of a maladaptive resistance strategy—one that works in the short run only, to allow avoidance of immediate conflict, but it changes nothing and, if allowed to continue, can lead to depression and despair.

It's tough to take on the world at such a young age, and no one should expect her to. Mrs. Freeport's strategy—to first ask questions, gather evidence and make connections, and then, when it appeared necessary, to challenge the school directly and make herself visible and heard—is an example of a healthy resistance strategy that leads to empowerment and long-term change. She told me that with her younger sons she is even more intent on being a constant visible presence at their schools.

I'm more visible to them [the teachers], so they know that they're not going to get by with so much. I don't think it's overprotection. It's just that I'm more aware of the prejudice and what they can and what they

can't get away with. And my concern is on education now—that they
get the best they can get.

This mother understood that it is only by showing teachers that you
care and are watching that you can require them to rethink their assumptions about black students, give them the attention and respect they
deserve, and understand that mistreatment won't be tolerated.

Mrs. Freeport also told me about the tremendous value she places on
open communication, and how it pained her that her daughter hadn't
brought her concerns to her earlier. If she had, the mother told me, "I
think I would have been able to go in and get a group of parents to say,
'Let's see what's going on.' " She encouraged her children to talk about
racial matters and work together to solve problems, and planned to continue to do so, despite the difficult lapse with her daughter. She understood the value of preparing her children for incidents like the ones her
daughter had endured.

Many of us parents know of the destructive assumptions teachers often
hold about black students, the stereotypes of black children—all black
children—as dumb and deficient. As a result, black children and teenagers
often become withdrawn and fearful, falling victim to the "rumors of inferiority" that become self-fulfilling prophesies. Black parents sense as well
that some teachers have low expectations for black children based on
assumptions about the parents' sometimes low level of education. This is
so even though research shows that parental education doesn't always correlate with academic performance in black adolescents (the same way that
it does for whites).

As an educator and a mother of a black child, I have an insider's sensitivity to this issue. I know that not all teachers hold to the false and insulting stereotype of black intellectual inferiority. I also know that not all of
the teachers who have low expectations of black students are white women
and men. But it would be irresponsible and inaccurate not to identify and
speak out about the fact that far too many education professionals insist
on expecting less of our children and youth. It happens, and all too often.
Why do the stereotypes persist and why do some teachers take to them so
readily? One possibility is that teachers in large school settings have only
a short time to connect with each child, to try to understand him as an
individual and learn about his intellectual and social needs. When schools
are overcrowded, teachers are overworked, and children have multiple and
often extreme needs, making these meaningful connections can be terribly
difficult. For some, holding on to the stereotypes can be a form of admin-

istrative efficiency. On the other hand, as recent research shows, even in well-funded schools with smaller class sizes, blacks don't always fare as well as their white counterparts. What we need are more educators, parents, and programs that target the "stereotype threat" of genetically based intellectual inferiority and low expectations by building black students' sense of competence and self-efficacy in the domain of academics.

Although these wrong-minded assumptions about the black intellect can serve to light a fire under some black students—"I'll show them I can succeed"—they can just as easily backfire, creating the negative, self-destructive attitude of "Why even try?"

Yet black parents are aware of characteristics that incite and reinforce the stereotype in teachers ready to receive it: black English dialect, a child's social class, the neighborhood he lives in, and who he hangs out with. At the same time, we know that "acting white" isn't the answer; staying involved and visible, and preparing our children for the inevitable, is.

Teenagers, because of their lack of experience, frequently need help from adults in discerning teachers' often-subtle expressions of prejudice.

A father, Mr. Ephat, and his teenage daughter told me about a time when the two of them together detected and countered the unfairly low expectations inflicted on the girl by her teachers, which nearly cost her the opportunity to achieve in an honors course, and which created in her a crisis of confidence, making her doubtful of her already-proven abilities. Although she had consistently received high grades in social studies for a number of years, her teachers did not place her in the honors curriculum for social studies in high school. Her parents, sensing that something was wrong, went immediately to the school to discuss the matter. Their daughter, for the first time in her life, lost confidence in her academic abilities. As she told me, she kept thinking to herself, "I can't do honors, I can't do honors."

The father was horrified by his daughter's response, because it brought home how easily a teacher's assumptions about black intellect can undermine even a previously confident student:

> You have to be so careful as a black parent. Here we had a child who was confident that she was fairly bright and could do the work. And because of the teacher's recommendations, she had a little crisis in confidence. This "I can't" stuff—this is something that I'd never heard before. Now, I have no illusions that she was an across-the-board honor student in every subject. I knew that it would be tough for her, because I see how hard she works to make the grades that she makes.

> But I'd never heard this "I can't" before. And it was all brought up by
> the recommendations and how her teachers saw her.

At her parents' insistence, the girl's school counselor pulled her records and noted both her good grades and the fact that every year since third grade she had performed better than the year before. "Oh my God," the teachers admitted, "we *have* made a mistake." The girl was placed in the honors curriculum. This family's strategy, to take the school head on, helped their daughter resist internalizing an attitude of defeat, and saved her from languishing in a curriculum that would do little to challenge her.

The girl's reaction to the school's initial decision (anguished self-doubt) could as easily have been to give up, to mentally check out, or to put her energy, as so many students choose to do, into other activities—athletics, being a class clown, driving the teacher nuts—instead of academics. Black teens, who are so often victims of low expectations, can come to believe it and stop trying at all, or stop trying so hard, or apply themselves inconsistently, out of a fear of failure.

In *Souls Looking Back: Life Stories of Growing Up Black,* a book for which I was an editor and to which I contributed, there is a young African American college student whom I call Chantal. In her autobiographical essay she wrote that when she was a top student in elementary school, her teachers frequently told her that she was "different." Her mother advised her daughter not to accept this backhanded compliment as flattery and warned her to be careful of those who wish to see her as a "token nigger." The psychiatrist James Comer writes that in the perception of too many white Americans, "when Blacks achieve in significant numbers or in areas held to be beyond the group's capacity, it is threatening; and most problematically, it does not change the negative perception of the group or of blackness." Chantal's mother, like many other African American parents, recognized what Comer speaks of, and she was determined to teach her daughter how to identify and resist negative appraisals from the wider society, how to debunk its myths and filter out racist messages.

Sometimes parents feel compelled to take steps beyond challenging the teachers, staying visible, and socializing their children to recognize racism in school settings. One father told me that after years of conflict with his sons' school over the importance of holding high expectations and other related issues (proper teaching, good instructional materials, timely communication when his sons were having problems), he turned to home schooling. He was especially disturbed by the tremendous influence teachers have over students and the power imbalance that leads youngsters to believe that teachers always know what they're doing even when they don't. "In this instance," the father said,

> I had to exert a tremendous amount of parenting authority. I had to have my kids recognize that they're not going to submit to the authority of teachers who knew less than their father and mother, and that they should not trust their teachers as much as they normally would have, because we know different and we know better at home. The authority of home has to be much more important than the authority of schools.

Because he travels internationally as part of his job, he took pains to take his sons with him as much as possible.

> I was trying to open their minds to the diversity and richness of experience that was not American. And in that sense I found that this was a parenting duty and that I was kind of shaping the world for them, that I wanted them to see, as opposed to the world that the schools were giving them.

This father's resistance strategy was twofold: first, to teach his sons to think critically about the quality of the education they were receiving rather than to blindly accept it (which is similar to resistance strategies for helping children and teenagers critique and understand the role the media plays in fostering racial stereotypes), and second, to clarify the importance of the home as the foundation for learning. Like many of the other parents, he had little confidence in the school's ability or commitment to delivering the kind of education black students need and deserve: an education that holds them to high expectations and respects their individuality as well as their collective strengths. Like the other parents, he was well aware of the power of schools to destroy confidence and interest and produce silence, self-doubt, disconnection, and suffering among black students. And he knew that only by resisting—in his case, taking the highly visible act of withdrawing his children from school and the less visible act of teaching his sons to critically examine the education they were receiving—could he empower them. Although his financial resources provided him with options that other black families may not have (including international travel with his children), it's important to remind ourselves that there are many other resources that can help enrich our children's lives that are close at hand and less expensive, including libraries, films, museums, and cultural events.

Resistance Strategies

Unhealthy (Short-Term, Survival-Oriented) Strategies

○ Using silence and withdrawal as a way to avoid conflict

○ Disconnecting and disengaging from school

○ Succumbing to self-doubt

○ Promoting achievement in areas like sports and entertainment at the expense of academic achievement

Healthy (Long-Term, Liberating) Strategies

○ Instilling in our children an unwavering belief in their intellectual competence

○ Setting goals high for ourselves and our children

○ Having continued, open discussion as a family of all race-related issues, including those that have to do with school (especially stereotyping and low expectations of blacks)

○ Staying visible, vocal, and vigilant at school, and teaching the importance of these traits to our children

○ Teaching youngsters to critically evaluate the education they are receiving, rather than blindly submitting to the demands of a system that devalues them

○ Remembering and emphasizing the importance of home as the base of learning and authority

Psychologically Strong, Socially Smart

A psychologically strong teenager resists self-doubt and self-silencing. She refuses to suffer alone and shares her worries or concerns with trusted adults, like her parents, who can intervene on her behalf. She knows that a teacher's low expectations can affect her self-esteem and that this is wrong. She has self-confidence, knows her strengths and weaknesses, and believes in herself and her ability to resist and to make change.

A teenager who is socially smart knows that not all teachers assume that blacks are intellectually competent. But he knows that most schools do have some teachers who will serve as allies and advocates for individual blacks, and who are also committed to helping advance blacks as a group. He knows to seek out teachers like these and to be willing to work with them. He also understands that sometimes—especially when school issues are involved—it is better to enlist adults as advocates rather than challenge the system alone.

Countering Complacency

Not all the negative stories I heard about schools revolved around bad teaching. As several parents were quick to point out, not all underachievement by black students can be tied to low expectations for blacks held by teachers. We blame ourselves as well.

Many parents tell me that, to their regret, we blacks sometimes participate in our own oppression by failing to set our goals high enough. Parents and teenagers alike point out that students all too often become complacent about their schooling. That is, they are either satisfied with their educational progress (lackluster though it may be), or they have become apathetic and unconcerned about the consequences of school failure. Some parents and teenagers acknowledge that black teens appear clueless about the obstacles that confront them now and will continue to confront them in a society dominated by a white power base. We fear that too many black adolescents simply don't appreciate how important education is for our group, and we worry that the "stay-in-school" messages conveyed by the schools themselves in this post-civil-rights era have become homogenized and fail to stress, or even note, the special significance of the message for blacks. And they are afraid that the complacency is fed by other messages that do filter through, messages that say to our youth that education isn't really important, or that it's less important than other things. As one teenage girl, Francine, who was ashamed of the conduct and appearance of some black boys at her school, put it,

> They don't really show respect for themselves. I wish they would realize that they are going to need education, and they're going to need the people that they're hurting now—they're going to need them later. And they're going to need the education in order to succeed in life.

Francine is concerned that the "so what" attitude that these boys at her school had lapsed into prevents them from envisioning themselves in the future—from seeing themselves in the role of responsible men, caring for and financially supporting families, and contributing meaningfully to the black community and larger society. As one father, Mr. Murphy, put it:

> As black people, we can't afford to be as complacent as we are today. We can't afford to be complacent about how we are viewed by the world, what we do and our effect on the world. I think we have to be very intentional about preparing our children for this society.

Another father, Fred Prentice, was deeply disturbed at what he saw as black teenagers failing to take advantage of the educational opportunities they are offered, and again, failing to understand how vitally important education is, especially for blacks.

> I get upset when I am in the school system and I see "poor" kids behaving like middle-class white kids. By that I mean the way they respond to activities that are presented to them, like being in the band or whatever. I feel that they neglect the same things I see a lot of middle-class white kids neglect. They don't take it serious enough. They don't see it as a ticket out. They don't see it as being an important part of their lives.

According to him, the white students who are slacking off now will be able to fall back on connections or other resources, but the black students won't. He, too, attributes this complacency to a lack of understanding of the realities of the future. He is deeply worried about the high numbers of underachieving black students in our high schools, young men and women who are headed toward dead-end jobs with low-end pay, unable to support their families or build their communities. His proposed strategy to help teenagers resist this complacency is to help them develop a racialized lens, a way of seeing themselves as part of a larger political and social struggle.

Fred Prentice feels fortunate to have had an upbringing that he feels many black teenagers today don't have, to have had teachers and parents who made him understand how important education is for blacks. Despite their own limited education (his mother was a high-school graduate; his father had only a third-grade education), his parents always emphasized the importance of school and of accomplishing something with your life. "The schools don't emphasize it today," he said.

> When I was coming along, I was fortunate because I got it twice. I grew up with kids who were as poor, or poorer than I was. When we were coming along, we got it first from the teachers. And some of us were fortunate, we got it again from our parents. The teachers would say things to us like, "If you're going to compete in this world . . ."

And they were saying, "In this white man's world, you've got to be more than good, you've got to be this, that, and the other." It was a priority for the teachers.

Today, he says, things have changed:

> It's no longer a priority for the teachers, because teachers are very satisfied now to let our kids do what they will. [They say to black kids] "If you can do that, fine. If you can't do it, fine." There's not the same sense that your future depends on it. If your future depended on it, and you had that future at stake in your own heart, you wouldn't let them fail—not in the ways they are failing. [If they failed], it wouldn't be because of neglect. It would be because they tried their best and they still failed. But that's not what's happening now.

This dad, like many other parents, feels that too many teachers are disconnected from the schools and communities they teach in, and from their students as well. The problem isn't just in the suburbs, where white or many black middle-class teachers may not know the black students they teach—because the students are bussed in, or because the students aren't part of the community. The problem also exists in city schools because so many teachers live outside the community or in parts of the city far away from where they teach. Although they have daily interactions with the same students, they don't get to know them the way teachers did when Fred Prentice was growing up, at a time when teachers tended to live in the communities in which they taught, or at least visited the families of their students at home. (A parent in a low-income neighborhood laughed when I asked her if a public-school teacher had ever visited her home. "Of course not," she said. "They're too afraid to visit, or don't care to.")

Compounding this lack of connection by teachers is a lack of accountability for the futures of black students that appears to be built into the system. When Fred Prentice was in school, black teachers couldn't disengage so readily from their students' failure. They knew that if their students failed to learn, they would cripple the black community as adults. As members of the same community as their students, they felt a more immediate stake in their futures—in helping to prevent the difficulties (increased violence, drug traffic, and delinquency) that would have an immediate effect on the teachers and their families as well.

Many of us, along with our children who are enrolled in some schools, are made to feel like interlopers. This happens most often in the suburban school, where our children say they feel out of place, uncomfortable, or disadvantaged. Because they feel they can never fit in, some resort to complacency and stop competing academically. Celia Pinkney, a mother in a Boston suburb, told me that it was disturbing to see black students at her daughter's school "acting out" when the white students seemed so serious about their schoolwork:

> You'd see a bunch of white kids in a little huddle, studying for a test or something, or talking about an exam that's coming up or a science project. And then you'd see ours chasing some boy, jumping on his head, fighting and talking loud. Believe me, I'm not making this up. I don't even want to have to repeat it, but this is what I see.

The black kids' behavior makes Mrs. Pinkney angry. And although she understands it as a reaction to being unable to fit the norm at the school they attend, she wants them to overcome their complacency and make the norm of achievement their norm, too:

> I think it's kind of an acting out because they need to feel comfortable. The parents don't live in the area. They know there's a big gap in the area, so they're not going to fit the norm which here is, "We're going to achieve. And we're going to have the best grades." That's the norm. And that's what I want to see our people feel in the same way. And I don't like group standards and ethical behavior and morality and excellence in grades associated with "this is a white phenomenon." It's a people phenomenon and we are people too.

When I asked her where she thought the black students had learned their behavior, she told me that she thought they had picked it up from older black teenagers and young adults who had similarly discounted and devalued their education. She was sure that these bad attitudes were not grounded in the larger black community. Her husband, on the other hand, had a different take on the issue. The black kids' behavior, he said, "[i]s taught by a white racist system that would like to eliminate the economic competition and [in order to do so] they have created this awful thing called 'black' and they try to make you act like that, and then we're dumb enough to get out there and start doing it."

He's not alone in his judgment. Research shows that black students today are buying into the destructive notion that the concepts of ethics, morality, and excellence are white ones. Opposition to acting white is a kind of socialization perspective that many of today's black teenagers hold toward authority and toward economic and political oppression. Many feel forced to decide between racial identity and Eurocentric definitions of academic success. The conflicts they face are both ideological and developmental as they struggle to "balance conflicting needs to define themselves within their cultural frame versus fitting in or doing well in school."

This attitude can take root in any school (integrated, predominantly black, suburban, urban, or rural) where the school culture allows, or even condones, such ways of thinking. White curriculum materials, ability-tracking programs that in effect segregate students by race and class, a school climate where only the academically successful students receive positive attention and praise and academic underachievers (often minority students) are ignored and derided, all breed cultures in which minority students reject school success. Such cultures lead to a disconnect—the students' refusal to identify with school—which results in poor academic performance.

A mother of a teenage girl told me how important it is to make sure our children know that although we as parents are there to provide support, we can't—and shouldn't—do the real work for them. She told me about the time she attended a student seminar at her daughter's school in recognition of Black History Month. The students in the mother's group were black. One of them told her, "You know, these white teachers, they're flunking me and they're doing this and they're doing that."

> "Well," I said, "do you do your homework every night?" and he looked at me and said, "No." So I said, "well, that's your responsibility. [And] if after you've done your homework, and you've studied, you come back and tell me this white teacher still flunked you, I'll come back. I'll come to battle them down to the wire. I will fight with you all the way down the line. But first you've got to deliver."

This mother could have agreed with the student that he was a victim, but she chose not to. Instead she challenged the victim characterization, a challenge all the more powerful because she, the challenger, was black. Rather than endorsing the teenager's feelings of victimization and complacency, she took them head-on, educating the group in the importance of reading a situation, and naming it as racism only if it truly is. Racism exists, she told them, and must be countered, but laziness is not racism.

These feelings of alienation and complacency are probably compounded by the developmental fact of life that junior high and high school are times when cliques kick in and social comparisons become important. They are also times when the social and psychological implications of ability-tracking systems are fully entrenched, making intellectual differences (or perceived intellectual differences) even more pronounced. And when the numbers are great enough, black students do band together. This can be for emotional or social support, which is to the good, because it allows black students to gain a better sense of who they are. But it can also contribute to an "us versus them" mentality, especially if the blacks already feel alienated and angry, and a spilling of collective venom on white students through teasing, sarcasm, and interference with other students' learning. For some students at this age, however, fitting in—especially if they're attending a school where they don't feel comfortable—is far more important than doing well.

But complacency—equating school success with acting white, slacking off, pressuring other blacks to reject school, refusing to participate in "white" activities like going to museums or the library—is a thoroughly ineffective, maladaptive way to deal with devaluation and alienation. In the short run it may make students feel better; it's easy and it offers a ready identity tied to the images of black success that dominate the culture—that is, blacks as cool and hip, blacks as athletes and entertainers. But what the teenagers who lapse into complacency don't realize is that this attitude is perilously close to the identity that too many school personnel expect of blacks: that we are simply not as smart as the white kids. And the strategy fails dramatically in the long run; it marginalizes black students, turns teachers off (even those teachers who do truly wish to improve the educational status of our youth), and does nothing to change the wrong and deeply embedded assumptions that many teachers hold about blacks. Worst of all, it reinforces them.

It can be hard to understand why our teenagers might buy into the stereotypes so readily, and harder still to acknowledge that sometimes they really do believe the stereotype and internalize the inferiority. Some, we hope, are simply unaware of what they're doing. Once we wake them up, we hope, they will come to their senses and refuse to buy in. The long and the short of it is that our black teenagers are lost and searching for role models of African American achievement that they can relate to. They need models of blacks with integrity who achieve intellectually and possess a black identity that is proud and comfortable, but who still can have fun. Our job as parents is to supply these models for our youth.

Parents who want their children to resist internalizing low expectations and intellectual laziness need to emphasize three simple ideas: first, that if black people under much worse circumstances have painfully and successfully struggled to get an education, you can, too; second, that if black people under much worse circumstances have struggled to make certain you can get the best education possible, then you must participate and achieve that goal as a moral imperative; and third, to turn your back on education is to participate in your own oppression.

By teaching the history of black folks' struggle for education, often by sharing our personal stories of what family members have had to endure to gain admission to our nation's schools and colleges, parents teach their children that they are connected to a long line of people who have refused to allow others to shape their destiny. We can also teach our children that they have a personal and collective responsibility to honor that connection and to do their best. Finally, we must communicate to our youth, clearly, precisely, and repeatedly, the paramount importance of education. I believe that this message is most powerful when delivered as a racialized one: that because they are *black*, it is critical that they devote to their education every ounce of their determination, strength, and energy. As part of this ongoing teaching, parents also need to be brutally honest with their teenagers about the grave consequences of an inadequate education for black people: poverty, social and political disenfranchisement, and further marginalization. They must make their children aware of the dominant culture's insidious message that a black teenager's future work won't require advanced education or training; that the larger society expects blacks to work in service professions as orderlies, security guards, clerk-typists, and at menial and manual labor. They need to know that society doesn't expect black people to use their brains.

Parents who are determined to raise their children to resist becoming complacent about their schooling must also be prepared themselves to resist the attitudes of other African Americans who devalue education. It is frightening to contemplate the teenagers and their families who have lost their motivation to improve their educational status, or who aren't hurting enough to push themselves harder or to figure out how to navigate a system that isn't pushing them hard enough. But the situations that are particularly difficult to comprehend are those where black parents actually enable their teenagers to be academically unsuccessful. I fear for the children of these parents and for the black community as well.

One mother, Bridget Reed, told me about her exasperation with black parents who don't take education seriously themselves and make it easy for their children to buy into racist notions of intellectual inferiority. A single mother, she had worked her way through college and saw the urgency of staying on top of her own daughter's education. If she could choose a single thing for blacks to work toward together, she told me, it would be education.

Education is just a low, low point for black people. I don't think it's as important as it should be. I mean, it's just that a lot of black parents do not particularly push their kids to do well. Like my sister-in-law; she got D's in math. And my brother [her husband]; he got D's in math. So now their daughter has D's in math. And that's okay, you know—it's not even a question for them. They would never think, "What can we do to make her get a C?" It's just too much of that "it's in the genes being a dummy" stuff.

She offered this practical advice:

If you know you didn't go to school and you didn't learn enough to be able to help your kids with some new math, I suggest you find somebody out there who can. Find out who's the smartest kid in the class and make friends with his mother. That way, when they come over, their kid can help your kid, or whatever. But a lot of black parents I know, they don't even try to get tutors.

She went on to describe things she had done with her young daughter as she grew up: trips to museums and libraries, and reading aloud at home. Friends and relatives, she said, had told her these activities were "too white."

What's wrong with taking your kids to the museum? There's nothing wrong with it. Why does it always have to be barbecue pits in the park? The best party, the best dance. Why can't it be like something more positive? All that body rhythm is great, but we can't all be dancers and make a living out of it.

Ms. Reed saw her sister-in-law's complacency as affecting her daughter in areas other than school, as well. She says that when the girl announced that her mom "showed me how to get all the men, so I ain't got to worry," she was horrified. What if the man she caught with her hip ways turned out to be poorly educated, unemployed, and unemployable?

When she returned to the subject of her niece's D's in math, she was outraged:

If you can stand up there and dance with your kids and play games with your kids and show them how to be hip, and show them how to be cool, why the hell can't you show them how to learn?

The problem is that some black parents settle for too little. We may say all the right things about our children's education, but we behave as though we ourselves don't really believe them. D's and C's are passing grades so why worry? For some, the attitude arises out of feelings that "if it was good enough for me, it's good enough for them," or we project our own perceived deficiencies on our children: "I wasn't good in school so why should I expect my kids to be?" In some cases, it may mean that a parent, driven by shame and guilt over her own school experiences, unconsciously doesn't want her child to succeed too much—at least not more than she has. In others, it may be too hard to have to think of their children as smarter than their parents—at least not in the basics. Knowing that your child can do algebra or write a research report and you can't, can be tough to take. To avoid the feeling of shame, the parent devalues the source of the feeling. "School doesn't matter." "Don't even try to do well."

Some parents unwittingly support school failure by adopting the "bad genes" theory. A father might say, "I wasn't good in math, so I don't expect my son to be either" (and that's okay with me). This attitude is dangerously close to notions of racial genetic inferiority—that intelligence is immutable and unaffected by effort. Parents who think like this are, I believe, unaware of the implications of this line of reasoning.

In addition, some parents may refuse to take part in activities that might enrich their children's educational achievement (visiting museums and libraries, and attending lectures and plays) because they feel those activities are "too white." This could well be the reason why there are often so few blacks at cultural events and activities. If you are a black adult for whom crossing over feels dangerous, you may choose to stay put, even at a cost to your children. It's not that blacks don't see the value of these activities, or that they are nonintellectual or anti-intellectual. It's just that for many, it feels too treacherous, too hard to be the first to or the only one.

It's tough to be the only black eighth grader enrolled in an art class at the museum, or in a swimming class at the YMCA, especially if your black peers are not supportive; and it can be hard as well for the parent who stands by waiting in a crowd of all-white parents. Parents need to take a deep breath and dive in, summoning their courage and maintaining an unwavering focus on the good that can result for their children.

Complacency is an insidious issue for blacks. An attitude of doing just enough to get by, adopted because it's easy to adopt, can just as easily become a habit that influences other areas of life as well. The complacent attitude, with its deemphasis of education and its overemphasis of dance, popular culture, and being slick, is short-sighted and makes no positive change for blacks. Although historically we blacks have valued and adopted being cunning and slick as survival strategies, we did this because there were precious few other options available in the past. Today, especially with regard to education, the strategy is dysfunctional. Systems have changed, yet for far too many of us the old approach—getting over and getting by—hasn't.

Teenagers who do just enough to get by (to pass the test or the class or receive a diploma) haven't internalized the message that they will inevitably be in competition with white people, as well as many other potentially well-trained and better-educated nonblack people, and that getting by won't necessarily get you ahead, or even get your foot in the door. They will vie for employment and advancement with people who have certain unearned privileges and the advantages that go with those privileges—like being assumed competent and trustworthy until proven otherwise.

When it comes to our children's schooling, we must be explicit about race, creating and delivering messages about intellectual development and academic achievement in racially specific ways. Chances are that by adolescence our children have already heard the rumors of inferiority; most have been threatened head-on by the stereotypes of black intellectual incompetence. Having heard the rumors, they must know what to do with the information. It isn't healthy to ignore information like this, or to deny that the stereotype exists. That kind of response leads to psychological vulnerability, anger, fear, and escapism. And the more a child fears the stereotype, the more powerful it becomes.

The parents and teens with whom I talked agreed: the healthy response is to resist the stereotype. To do this, we must teach our teenagers the facts. They must know in their hearts that rumors of black intellectual incompetence are not true, despite what they hear from school officials reporting black students' low SAT scores, or, in many schools, their low achievement grades. We must teach them that achievement is directly tied to effort. You work hard, you achieve more. It's that simple. It's not about genetics; African Americans are not intrinsically less able.

We also need to teach them to understand the origins of the stereotypes—that they are the creation of those who wish to maintain existing systems of oppression and domination. Once again, this is a black folks' truth: the idea that for some people the only goal is to maintain whatever power they possess. And one way to maintain that power is by discrediting "the other." These attitudes are part of the ideology of many American institutions; they are even woven into the fabric of many of our schools.

Finally, they must understand how to effectively navigate around and across the racial barriers built into the system, keeping in mind that the system is so well entrenched that some of us African Americans end up believing the stereotypes about intellectual inferiority ourselves. And they must beware: some of those who are settling for low achievement may indeed be their friends. They must know that only by resisting the stereotypes, aiming high, and applying themselves—diligently, every day—will they reap the educational rewards to which they are entitled.

Resistance Strategies

Unhealthy (Short-Term, Survival-Oriented) Strategies

- Emphasizing achievement in sports, entertainment, and popular culture over academic achievement
- Avoiding academic involvement and success as "acting white"
- Adopting a complacent attitude—that is, doing only enough to get by (pass the test, pass the class, get the diploma)
- Believing you are limited by "bad genes"
- Settling for low achievement in school

Healthy (Long-Term, Liberating) Strategies

- Presenting constant messages to children of the critical importance of education for blacks; helping them understand the disadvantages for black teenagers and young adults associated with low achievement, now and in the future (low-level jobs mean low income, difficulty raising families, inability to buy what you want and need, and few prospects for financial stability in retirement); knowing this means internalizing the message on an individual level as well as taking to heart what it means at a group or community level
- Teaching children to recognize and repel stereotyping of blacks as intellectual inferiors and believing, instead, in their intellectual competence; understanding that the notion that we are intellectually inferior is socially constructed to prevent us from competing economically
- Teaching children to develop a racialized lens: to see themselves as part of a larger political and social struggle

○ Providing children with models of intellectual black achievement, from the public arena and from close by (family, coworkers, community members)

○ Taking steps to ensure academic success at school: holding standards high, finding tutors, risking the discomfort of being the "only one" at museums, libraries, plays, and other events in order to enrich your child's education; making clear that they must apply themselves and persevere, with a full understanding that for a black teenager, getting the very best education possible is the most important task in life; emphasizing that part-time jobs, athletics, parties, dating, and learning to drive are secondary to schooling, which must be paramount

○ Staying vigilant, visible, and involved at school; intervening when a child is mistreated; and letting teachers and administrators know directly that you will not tolerate unfairness or disrespect

Psychologically Strong, Socially Smart

A psychologically strong teenager knows that education is essential. He works hard, stays focused, and knows that he's in school to learn and gain skills. He resists family patterns of failure and underachievement, and he knows to get help when he needs it.

A socially smart teenager knows that as a black person she can't afford to be complacent. She knows that the risks of complacency are severe: low-level education, low-level jobs, permanent low-income status for oneself, family, and community. She knows her enemy (a system that's designed to keep blacks subservient) and resists participating in her own oppression.

Shaped by School: Education and Identity

Black parents and teenagers have much to say about the interplay of schooling and issues of identity, about the effect that an educational setting can have on a student's sense of self, as an individual and as a member of a racial group. Some of the stories were positive; others were negative. All of them demonstrated the critical effect that feeling part of a group, or not part of a group, can have on knowing who you are. Clearly, wherever teenagers are thrust daily in close quarters with other people—students and teachers, blacks and whites—is a crucible in which a sense of self is formed, for better or for worse.

Diane, a ninth grader, told me how happy she was after she transferred to a public exam school in the heart of the city. An exam school is one that requires that students pass an entrance exam for admission. These schools tend to enroll and graduate high-level students. This school was filled with students who, like her, took education seriously, and in so doing taught her a tremendous amount about being black and smart. She told me what the change meant to her:

> Well, I met a lot of other black girls, you know, who had really good images and stuff and who never gave up. And they knew where they wanted to go, they knew where they came from, and things like that. That was really helpful. As opposed to some of the people who I went to school with before. They were like, "I'm here because they made me come, and I'm not going to do nothing while I'm here."

For Diane, studying among other blacks who were equally intent on achieving served as nourishment to her soul, providing her with a sense of support and community that the complacency at her previous school had not.

Other stories I've heard are not as positive. One mother told me a different story about her son. Although he had what she called "brains" and "book sense," and didn't smoke or drink, she was worried that he didn't have enough of a sense of himself to say, "Get off my back," or "Stay away from me; I don't need your cigarettes," if he were pressed hard enough. "He takes a lot from his peers," she said. "The other kids call him 'nerd.'" She said that when she pointed out to him that he had no friends, he responded with, "Well, I don't need a lot of friends, Mom. They get you into trouble."

This mother was understandably concerned. A peer group of other achieving black teenagers could have provided her son with a foundation of power, the comfort of numbers, a stronger base from which to resist. Alone, he would be easy prey for complacent or disconnected teenagers; it might well be easier to join them than to resist.

A mother in Boston, Susan Lyons, told me about her 11-year-old daughter who attended a predominantly white suburban school and who, from earliest childhood, had taken her schoolwork and grades seriously. Then, when she was in fifth grade, her grades plummeted. "All of a sudden," the mother said, "we didn't know what had happened. And all the little white girls who used to call or come around, or who she would visit—all that was out." All this happened at the same time a group of black children from another part of the city enrolled in the school.

Luckily, a sensitive black teacher saved the day. She called the Lyonses to a meeting at school, and, as Susan remembers it, told them,

> Your daughter is a very lovely girl and she's having an identity crisis. And I think you should know that she's chosen to be with the black kids, you know, as an identification thing, and not be with those who were affirming [her] doing their homework and taking school seriously.

Mrs. Lyons was outraged at the situation:

> I said, "I'm not living in this town, paying this much money for this kind of school, to have my kid want to play around just because the other kids are black." I don't care about the color. I really don't. I said, "I want her to be prepared to go to college. And she's not going to be prepared if she doesn't get good grades."

She and the teacher came up with a plan: to make her daughter's seating in the class conditional on her grades. They would move her away from the seating block where this group of black students sat. If her grades went up again, she could move back to the area with her black friends. But she could stay there only if she kept her grades up.

I asked the daughter to talk about what happened with her black friends after she was forced to separate from them.

> Well, they, I mean, they just went back to their norms—where you know [they said], "You're white." I was white because I was hanging around with whites. So they ignored me, and I ignored them.

Mrs. Lyons acknowledged that the girl had been in an extremely difficult situation, because consciously she did have to choose. And what we said was, "There are blacks who are just as serious about school as you are. Unfortunately, these are just not the ones."

So we tried to still affirm the race, and let her know that people just had different choices, and that at this point in their lives they chose to play and get C's. And that she couldn't afford to do that. [We told her] "You are a person and that has to take precedence over any color identification."

The parents recognized the important part the black teacher had played in the experience. When I asked the mother if she thought a white teacher would have been as responsive to the problem, she said no, she didn't think so. Mr. Lyons added,

> There are a few white teachers that I see who may have been as sensitive to what was going on as the black teacher was, but for the most part, the white teachers probably would have just thought that [our daughter] was just one of those [academically lazy] black kids and put her in that category. There's unconscious prejudice, and there's stereotyping, even with the white teachers that I like. It comes up and you say, "My God, we have to do something." It's still there.

This story shows a clear, fascinating interplay of bad resistance and good resistance strategies. The new black students' adoption of a complacent, underachieving attitude in response to their new white environment, and the girl's decision to sacrifice her academic status in order to take on the racial identity that the black group dictated (and be part of the group) are both short-term survival strategies. Fortunately, in response, both the teacher and the mother reacted with healthy resistance strategies: The teacher recognized the daughter's developmental need for racial identity and affiliation and took immediate steps to communicate this need to her parents. The mother took fast action as well, working with the teacher to stop the conduct that threatened her daughter's future. The point she made of affirming to her daughter her racial connection—reminding her that there are other academically successful black kids out there, and that she was not alone—was a brilliant final strategy.

Another mother described her daughter's brush with academic failure and how she had helped her surmount it. She was in her first year of boarding school in New England, and she was having a hard time academically. The mother was afraid her daughter, who had always received good grades in the past, was attributing her difficulties to the fact that she was from a single-parent, working-class black family and had attended a city school. As the semester progressed and her struggles with the subject matter intensified, her daughter started to doubt her own abilities, having convinced herself that she had entered boarding school with an inferior educational background. The mother knew better:

> But, what I tried to do is tell her, "The problem is you didn't study. You just did your homework, and beyond that you made absolutely no effort." And now she can see, you know, because now she calls me and tells me, "Mom, I did my work and now I'm studying more in the library."

The daughter continued to work hard and, at her mother's urging, stayed to repeat the year. The strategy was a success: the daughter raised her grades and her self-confidence and was nearly an honors student when I talked with her mother. The most critical part of this mother's very effective resistance message was about gaining power and control through effort and hard work, refusing to allow her daughter to buy into the notion that she was inferior, or a victim of her previous schooling.

As active, involved parents, we can (and should) encourage our schools to create learning environments where black students can feel comfortable being both black and smart. A teacher I know told me the story of an all-black school where the superachievers have turned both the "acting white" stereotype and the stereotype of the academic nerd on its head. These academically successful students have developed their own style of dressing and acting. They are not copying the white nerd look, nor the sitcom character "Urkle the dweeb" look—the goofy over-sized glasses, the plastic pocket protectors, the high-water pants pulled up over the waistline. Instead, their clothes are fitted, neutral, slightly retro, and urban—an image that's both consistent with the broader aesthetic of the school culture and uniquely black. By doing this, the achievers made sure they weren't singled out as freaks, or as white wanna-be's. They are perceived as the smart kids, which is fine with them. In fact, they feel proud of the image of being black and smart. They can integrate those two identities because they are in a school culture that supports black students' success. Most important, the image of the successful black student in this institution is an indigenous creation; it evolved from, and found a secure home within, the culture of the black students themselves.

Resistance Strategies

Unhealthy (Short-Term, Survival-Oriented) Strategies

- Identifying with peers who deemphasize academics and cut classes
- Feeling victimized by inferior schooling, and internalizing notions of incompetence
- Succumbing to the erroneous belief that a person can't be both black and smart

Healthy (Long-Term, Liberating) Strategies

- Teaching children that they have the power within themselves to achieve academically, if they expend the effort

○ Teaching teenagers that identity is not to be externally imposed (by whites or other blacks) but internally defined

○ Finding and involving your children in groups of achieving black youth who value education

Psychologically Strong, Socially Smart

A psychologically strong, socially smart teenager has a positive attitude toward education, and at the same time maintains her racial connection. She stays focused on what she must do in order to succeed: stay in school and resist the pull of friends who avoid schoolwork. She has developed the ability to negotiate the school world, be it predominately black or predominately white, while developing a strong racial identity and sense of self. She looks for friends who will support her in this effort and is mindful that not all black social groups will have her best interests in mind. She knows that black students have special needs and face special challenges in school. She musters her energy and talents in order to be ready, willing, and able to develop intellectually, despite the obstacles.

REFERENCES

Black women significantly outnumber black men: (1999, Spring). Special Report. "College Degree Awards: The Ominous Gender Gap in African American Higher Education." *Journal of Blacks in Higher Education,* 6–9.

The fact that over the past two decades: Kunjufu, J. (1989). *Developing Self-Images and Discipline in Black Children.* Chicago: African American Images.

The decision, he said, confronted "[n]egroes with a cruel dilemma": W.E.B. Du Bois, quoted in Weinberg, M. (1977). *A Chance to Learn: The History of Race and Education in the United States.* New York: Cambridge University Press, p. 87.

and many of the black teachers are gone as well: Teaching, once the top vocational choice of African American college graduates, has dwindled in popularity, and the number of black teachers decreases each year.

Statistics describe gross underachievement: Belluck, P. (1999, July 4). "Reason Is Sought for Lag by Blacks in School Effort." *New York Times,* p. 1.

the schools have deliberately "trained us to be stupid": Note: Carter G. Woodson wrote that American schools intentionally "mis-educate the Negro," stating that the identity of the black students is intentionally distorted and misrepresented in the curriculum's Eurocentric approach to education and history.

understood the relationship between academic and personal development: See research on caring, committed segregated black schools in Siddle Walker, Vanessa (1996). *Their Highest Potential: An African American School Community on the Segregated South.* Chapel Hill: U of NC Press, and research on black teachers in Michele Foster (1997). *Black Teachers on Teaching.* New York: New Press.

The destructive assumptions teachers often hold: See Steele, Claude M. (1997). "A Threat in the Air: How Stereotypes Shape Intellectual Identity and Performance." *American Psychologist, 52,* 613–629; and Steele, Claude M. (1999, August). Thin Ice. "Stereotype Threat and Black College Students." *The Atlantic Monthly,* pp. 44–54. In these works on stigmatization he argues that there can be a devastating effect to black student performance caused by the negative-ability stereotype threat, which states that blacks do not belong in the domain of academic and intellectual excellence.

"rumors of inferiority": Howard, J., and Hammond, R. (1985, September 9). "Rumors of Inferiority." *New Republic,* pp. 18–23.

On the other hand, as recent research shows: Belluck, "Reason Is Sought."

target the "stereotype threat": Steele, C. (1999, July). *Atlantic Monthly.*

building black students' sense of competence and self-efficacy: Howard, J. (1995, Fall). "You Can't Get These from Here: The Need for a New Logic in Education Reform." *Daedalus, 124*(4), 85–92.

it does not change the negative perception: Comer, J. (1995). "Racism and African American Adolescent Development." In C. Willie, P. P. Rieker, B. Kramer, and B. Brown (Eds.), *Mental Health, Racism and Sexism.* Pittsburgh: University of Pittsburgh Press, p. 160.

Souls Looking Back. Garrod, Ward, Robinson, and Kilkenn. (1999). *Souls Looking Back: Life Stories of Growing Up Black.* New York: Routledge.

Research shows that black students today: Fordham, S., and Ogbu, J. (1986). "Black Students' School Success: Coping with the Burden of 'Acting White.' " *Urban Review, 18,* 176–206.

"Balance conflicting needs to define themselves": Murrell, P. (1993). "Afrocentric Immersion: Academic and Personal Development of African American Males in Public Schools." In T. Perry and J. Frasier (Eds.), *Freedom's Plow.* Boston: Beacon Press, p. 251.

24

CHARACTERISTICS OF COMMUNITIES AFFECTING PARTICIPATION/SUCCESS

Angela Ginorio and Michelle Huston

THIS PAPER WILL EXPLORE AND DISCUSS some of the factors that contribute to the educational trends just presented and to Latinas' formation of possible selves. In this section we approach families, peer groups, and schools—both K–12 and postsecondary—as forms of community, each of which contributes to an individual's perception of future outcomes and opportunities. We cannot stress strongly enough the interaction among the factors discussed in all of the sections to follow. Any one characteristic is nearly meaningless without simultaneously considering all the elements of Latinas' lives. "Socialization can be fully understood only by examining the role of parents in light of the influence of other settings in which children and families function" (Collins, Maccoby, Steinberg, Hetherington, & Bornstein: 2000, p. 228).

For many Americans, particularly middle-class Anglos, the communities of family, peer groups, and school reinforce shared social values and agendas. The behaviors and expectations rewarded in the home are largely congruent with those rewarded in school and articulated among peers. In this sense, these communities echo and reinforce one another. For many other young people, especially people of color, messages sent by these various communities can conflict with one another. In school, this can result in a "subtractive education" (Valenzuela: 1999) that leads to increasingly bifurcated worlds: academic versus family, culture of origin versus culture of choice/identification, individualist versus community-focused values, and so on. In the ideal community, families find support for their belief systems and lifestyles from their neighbors and other social institutions. In cases where conflicts and differences exist among the values of the school, families and communities, children may face multiple, conflicting views of who they can and should be. Schools and other institutions can approach these differences in a way that is affirming of a Latina's culture and that encourages individual academic identification and personal creativity or in a way that exacerbates a student's sense of alienation or fragmentation by dismissing the student's values.

Family

A Latina will form the first images of who she can be and what should be considered realistic and rewarding options for her future self within her family of origin. A young girl's sense of possible selves benefits from a family environment that supports an array of educational and career options. Latino families are also shaped by their connections to other cultures in the United States and often characterized by marginal economic survival, segregation in poor urban neighborhoods, and an uneasy distrust of a dominant culture that is often typified by racism and intolerance. In many cases, the local school system may embody or represent these characteristics, which in turn shape the family's relationship to the school.

Family Structure

As is true of every group in the United States, there is no single "typical" Latino family. Family structure is diverse and covers the spectrum: two-parent families with no children or many living at home; single-parent families; and extended families with grandparents, adult siblings and their children, or family friends living in one home. In some homes, only Spanish is spoken; in others, only English. In still others, both are used.

Yet family structure is most often conceived in the research literature as simply the presence or absence of a father in the home. According to the U.S. Census Bureau, Hispanic families are more likely than non-Hispanic White families to have a female householder with no spouse present. Twenty-three percent of all Hispanic families, compared with 13 percent of non-Hispanic White families, were maintained by a female householder with no spouse present. Not only are Hispanic female-headed households more numerous, they also tend to be poorer than White female-headed households, with a median income of $12,406 compared to $17,414. Puerto Rican female householders have the lowest income of all Hispanic families in the country (U.S. Census Bureau: 1993b).

It is generally assumed that children in single-parent homes fare worse than children from two-parent homes due to reduced economic circumstances, limited supervision, and so on. However, not all research supports this assumption. Reyes and Jason (1993) found that 9th graders classified as being at high risk and low risk for dropping out of high school did not differ in their family structures; that is, students from high-risk groups were no more or less likely to come from single-parent homes.

Much less is known about additional elements of family structure, such as the impact of siblings, grandparents, or other adults in the home. We know very little about how different household configurations—aside from the one- or two-parent family—may affect achievement and education for Latinas. This omission in the research base has particular significance for understanding Latina/o education, since Latina mothers may draw on other adults—not spouses—in the home to cope with low wages and earning potential and to alleviate economic distress (Ortiz: 1997).

Even less is known about the influence of siblings on a child's academic achievement. While many theorists suggest that decision-making about education in Latino families takes into account whole family needs so that an older child may curtail his or her own education to support the family economically or to allow younger children to succeed, this proposition is not well studied. Some evidence suggests that the effect of older siblings may be particularly powerful if they curtailed their own aspirations because of the need to leave school and work (Gándara: 1995). Anecdotal data suggest that siblings can play a crucial role by supporting one another through sharing chores and responsibilities, among other things (Ginorio & Grignon: 2000; Ginorio & Huston: 2000). Larger-scale data suggest that students who drop out are more likely to have siblings who dropped out, and students who graduated are more likely to have siblings who graduated (Valverde: 1987).

Themes and Questions for Further Research:

○ What influence do different household configurations have, aside from the absence or presence of a father, on educational outcomes?

○ What influence do siblings have on Latinas' educational outcomes and choices?

Centrality of Family

Two values that cut across many distinct "Hispanic" cultures are the centrality of the family and the importance of religious affiliation, most commonly, Catholicism (Ginorio, Gutiérrez et al.: 1995). Thus, many Latinas' possible selves are more intrinsically tied to the family than are those of other ethnic and racial groups in the United States (see Sidebar Two).

Unsurprisingly, then, qualitative research also suggests that parental involvement, especially for low-income Latina/os, boosts educational outcomes (Delgado-Gaitan: 1991; Durán: 2000; Perna: 2000). Federal initiatives for Hispanic education have prescribed a positive focus on the family, noting that we "need to recognize that Hispanic families have social capital on which to build" (Lockwood & Secada: 2000). Yet there has been little discussion in research or policy of how the centrality of family life may affect Latinas and Latinos differently, despite the gendered nature of roles and responsibilities in most families in the United States. A 1998 report on college-bound students, for example, finds that the greatest discrepancy between Hispanic and White seniors has to do with the compatibility of students' home life with schooling. "One-third of Hispanic seniors, at a level at least 10 percent higher than Whites, worry about money problems, family obligations, a lack of a good place to study at home, and parental disinterest in their education" (College-Bound Hispanics: 1998). Family care-giving obligations, especially, fall more on Latinas than on their male counterparts (Chacón, Cohen, Camerena, Gonzáles, & Strover: 1983).

---

o

A principal of a Denver high school that aggressively works to keep Hispanic students in school notes that "The Latino Culture values education, but it values family above all. And when it comes to choosing between going to school and helping the family, the family will win." This principal combated the dropout rate by establishing flexible schedules so that students could accommodate work demands and family roles as well as school, including a program for pregnant and parenting Latinas to continue their education.

—(Vail: 1998)

---

o

By the same token, however, family ties and supports are a resource for Latina/os' educational achievement when schools are equipped to build on this strength in the community. They may provide powerful incentives and resources for Latinas to pursue education and to excel (Valenzuela: 1999), a theme that invites further research. Qualitative studies of high-achieving Latina women in academia confirm Gándara's 1995 findings

Table 24.1. Home/School Cultural and Value Conflicts for Latina/os.

Home	School
Nurtures dependency	Values independence
Children loved and enjoyed	Teacher seen as distant or cold
Nurtures cooperation	Values competition
Authoritarian style	Democratic style
Low-income children usually do not have preschool experiences	Expects preschool experiences
Low-income families are forced to value daily survival more than the educational needs of their children	Expects parents to value education above other values
Girls do not need to be educated as much as boys	Both sexes should be educated equally
Admonishes immodesty in girls	Physical education requires changing in front of others
Promotes ignorance of sexual matters	Advocates sex education
Achievement is for family satisfaction	Achievement is for self-satisfaction
Nonsegregated age groups	Segregated age groups
Segregated sex groups	Nonsegregated sex groups
Machismo for boys	Less sexually typed male ideal
Marianismo for girls	Less sexually typed female ideal
Some low-income families do not see the connection between school-related behaviors, such as daily school attendance, and doing well in school	School assumes that families know the types of child and family behaviors that lead to good school performance

Source: *Vásquez-Nuttall & Romero-García (1989, p. 67)*

that: "family support was mentioned over and over" in their narratives of success. "Their families believed in education despite wide differences in educational backgrounds." Support from mothers was especially important, as it seems to be in families in which parents have little in the way of social capital. However, "being in school was never an excuse to shortcut family duties as daughter, wife, partner, mother, or caregiver. The family held very high expectations for her fulfilling family responsibilities at whatever age" (García & Associates: 1998). Similarly, the concept of family, rather than individual, success through education can lead parents to place a high value on Latina education as a means to elevate children, siblings, and other family members.

○

Neither my father nor my mother ever gave up trying to socialize me—
"civilize" me, my mother would often say.

Throughout those years, they inculcated in me that intellectually
and artistically I was as capable as my brothers. So they provided me
with the best education they could afford. They made clear to me,
nonetheless, that all this was being done not just to satisfy my own
needs as an individual, above all I was being educated to serve the
needs of the family I would one day have.

"When you educate a man," my father would often tell my younger
sister and me, "you educate an individual, but when you educate a
woman, you educate the whole family." . . .

It wasn't unusual for Mexican fathers—almost regardless of class—
to deny their daughters the advantages of formal schooling on the false
premise that as women they would always be supported and protected
by their husbands. The important thing was, then, my uncles perfunc-
torily stated, to get as successful a husband as could be found for the
girls in the family. Problem solved.

My father was not quite the typical Mexican father in this respect.
But even this atypical man, who has been and will continue to be one
of the most influential people in my life, was subject to the social
norms and pressures that made the education of woman a separate (if
equal) experience.

—Lucha Corpi, "Epiphany: The Third Gift" (Castillo-Speed: 1995)

○

Social Class and Cultural Capital

Contrary to popular beliefs about Hispanic communities, most parents
hope that their children will excel in school, yet Latino families' economic
and social contexts often preclude the realization of those dreams. One
of the most pervasive difficulties with interpreting data about ethnic/racial
minorities in the United States is untangling the effects of poverty from
the effects of culture. By most measures, Latina/os are among the most
impoverished members of the U.S. society (U.S. Census Bureau: 1993b).
In areas where the Latino population is new to the country and in which
English is a second (or not even spoken) language, poverty is rampant.
But language is just part of the problem: even in areas where the Latino
community is largely born in the U.S. and fluent in English, the poverty
rate is twice as high as it is for Anglos (Aponte & Siles: 1994).

Both poverty and cultural differences—in terms of language and other values—create barriers to parents' effective mobilization of resources on their children's behalf. Conversely, cultural values can create assets—such as bilingualism and family support networks—for students in education-affirming schools. Social scientists use the term "cultural capital" to refer to resources such as familiarity with educational terms and jargon, the provision of reading materials in the home, and exposure to (European-based) cultural enrichment such as museums, literature, art, and music. Parents with little disposable income and a lack of familiarity with English (not to mention academic terminology) and American schooling procedures do not have the same levels or types of cultural capital as middle-class Anglo families. This is particularly problematic when schools assume that children come to their classrooms with these resources at their command and that parents can and will aggressively advocate on their child's behalf.

In 1995 12 percent of Hispanic children had parents whose highest education level was college or above, compared with 38 percent of White children and 14 percent of African American children. More than one in four—27 percent—Hispanic children have parents whose highest level of education was "less than high school," a notably higher percentage than for African American children (16 percent) or for White children (4 percent) (U.S. Department of Education: 1997).

The Family Economy and Latinas' Contributions

Parents who have high educational goals for their children nonetheless may require labor contributions or economic support from their children for the family to survive. For children from poor families, economic need often results in poor attendance at all levels of the schooling process. Many Latinas contribute to their families with unpaid labor before the laws governing legal employment age allow them to contribute with a paycheck. For young women, this often means providing child care before and after school. For many, family labor often means they must miss their first classes of the day to look after children whose schools start later in the day. Paid and unpaid labor curtails a student's participation in extracurricular activities as well as time to spend studying and forming relationships with classmates.

Anecdotal evidence suggests that even young children may spend substantial time acting as translators to their non-English-speaking parents, a topic that deserves further exploration. A recent article on Latina/os in Washington, D.C., describes children who "connect [their families] to the English-speaking world." A director of community education interviewed for the article finds that "more often students lost time from school and lose time from learning. They simply do not come in, because they have to translate for their parents at the doctor's [office] or social services or some-where else." It is possible, although it requires further research, that girls and women, charged with the maintenance of family ties, shoulder more of the "translation" responsibilities than male siblings and view their role as integral to the family's well-being, rather than an individual sacrifice. A Nicaraguan daughter-translator explains, "My mom came [to the U.S.] because she wanted a better life for us. She wants me to get a good educa-tion, and this is what I can do to repay her" (Stockwell: 2000).

○

The reason we came here, my mother had a lot of problems, money situations. But again, my family was always there for us, too. But she felt kind of embarrassed to ask for help . . . I'd try to help her as much as possible, you know, like taking care of my little sister while she was working. She had two jobs. She was working during mornings and nights to support us. And even though it was very hard, she wanted us to go to a private school. She always tried to give us the best, the excellent education for us.

—"Refusing the Betrayal: Latinas Redefining Gender, Sexuality, Family, and Home" (Fine & Weis: 1998).

○

Family and School

○

For Latino students—particularly girls—child care is a common bur-den that can compete with school. One of six children, Magdaly Mar-roquin, 16, shares regular responsibility for babysitting her 3-year-old brother John until their mother, Bibiana, returns from work. Two days a week, the Guatemala native leaves her class early at her Wheaton, Maryland, high school to collect John from daycare. Sometimes she misses basketball practice. On other days, the babysitting task falls to her 13-year-old sister.

"It's hard sometimes," says Marroquin, "because you want to do your homework and . . . he wants to play. Sometimes you can't go out at all."

For a long time she used her childcare duties as an excuse for blow-ing off her homework. Her stock refrain to her mother's questions about homework was "I did it during lunch." No more. Marroquin, who wants to teach math, says she knows her future hinges on her school performance. Says the 10th-grader, "I wanted to do something better with my life. Everything before was socializing."

—Magdaly Marroquin (Morse: 2000)

○

Contrary to popular assumption, family responsibilities and unpaid labor may not negatively affect achievement. A study of high- and low-achieving Latinas in the San Diego City Schools find that high achievers tend to have *more* responsibility at home than low achievers. Half of the high achievers take care of younger siblings in comparison with 20 percent of the low achievers. The majority of all Latinas—70 percent of the high achievers and 80 percent of the low achievers—also report paid work experience in addition to family responsibilities (San Diego City Schools: 1989).

On a more abstract level, children are aware of the limitations their families face and may curtail their educational goals to remain in line with their perceptions of their parents' ability to support them in their choices (Ginorio & Huston: 2000; Ginorio & Grignon: 2000).

Migration Patterns and Farm Work

While immigration status is a relatively common variable in studies, few studies explore the impact of migration. Children of migrant workers are more likely to transfer frequently and miss school—primarily to act as translators for their parents (Martínez, Scott, Cranston-Gingras, & Platt: 1994). According to the Migrant Attrition Project, the dropout rate for migrant students is close to half (Pérez: 2000). Yet migrant students are notoriously underidentified and underreported in states with large Hispanic populations. A recent preliminary study found that 70 percent of migrant students in districts with large Latino populations were not identified as they moved to a new campus (Pérez: 2000). A qualitative study of Latina migrant mothers who traveled with their families to pick tomatoes in northeastern Pennsylvania reveals contradictory values that they and their children experience, particularly around differences in sex roles between their own and the dominant culture and the choice between continuing education to seek careers outside farm work or taking advantage of the *immediate* availability of work and the opportunity to make money. Although Latina mothers would like to help their children out of the migrant life, they face daunting exigencies (Bressler: 1996).

Children raised by parents who settle in one community will have at least that community on which to rely for consistency and adult supervision. Children raised by parents who follow the growing season of various crops all over the country may be less likely to find themselves integrated into larger social structures that facilitate educational attainment in school.

Themes and Questions for Further Research:

○ Work, family responsibilities, and education: how are family responsibilities allocated? How do they influence schooling and achievement?

Family Acculturation

When individuals or groups with different cultures come into contact, social and psychological processes take place that lead to changes in the culture of one or both groups. In cultures of equal status, the changes are assumed to be of equal magnitude for both groups. In the case of the United States, it is assumed that immigrants will change their culture to resemble that of the Anglo majority. Acculturation refers to changes wherein one group acquires some of the characteristic values or behaviors of the other without giving up its own values or behaviors. Assimilation refers to the acquisition of new values or behaviors that replace original values or behaviors with the intent of becoming like the group being copied.

Researchers try to measure the acculturation of immigrant groups in a variety of ways, such as years or generations of residence in the United States, use of the English language, educational attainment, and number of non-Latina/o friends. Conversely, they may measure attachment to Latino culture by use of the Spanish language, participation in Latino cultural festivals, and constructed scales of Spanish pride, among other indicators. The result of all this variable creation is that acculturation may refer to very different things from one study to another. Unlike assimilation, which requires the abandonment of the culture or origin, acculturation does not necessarily involve the rejection of one culture for another. Families attached to Latino culture are not necessarily less attached to Anglo culture. It is entirely possible—and even beneficial— for Latinas to maintain strong ties to their Latino heritage while simultaneously participating in Anglo culture (Gómez & Fassinger: 1994; Valenzuela: 1999).

The ongoing heated debate over who is to "blame" for the low academic achievement of many ethno-racial minorities has often centered on the culture of the ethnic group in question. Researcher Guadalupe Valdés explains: "In its strongest form, proponents of [the culture argument] argue that poor children are trapped in a culture of poverty and locked into a cycle of failure. Those who subscribe to this position maintain that children succeed in school only if their many deficiencies are corrected and if they are taught to behave in more traditionally mainstream ways" (Valdés: 1997, p. 398). Others have suggested that renouncing one's culture of origin actually deters achievement through a subtraction of cultural and linguistic resources critical to success (Valenzuela: 1999) and that the best path to economic well-being lies through celebrating one's culture while simultaneously participating in the institutions of the dominant culture.

For Latino families, much of the discussion around acculturation and academic achievement centers on language. In general, Latina/o parents seem to support their children's participation in Anglo culture through the use of the English language (LaVelle: 1996).

Lack of familiarity with the English language or lack of understanding of how schools work may have a negative effect on parents' ability to either help their children with schoolwork or effectively interact with school personnel on their children's behalf. Despite a nearly universal desire to help with homework, only 77 percent of Latina mothers surveyed felt they could help with reading and 66 percent with math (compared with 97 percent and 86 percent of Anglo mothers) (Stevenson, Chen, & Uttal: 1990). Hispanic parents with similar characteristics to other parents in all other aspects (evaluation of the child, definition of giftedness, etc.) are significantly less likely to request that a school test their child for placement in a gifted classroom (Scott, Perou, & Urbano: 1992). This tendency to be less likely to pursue enrollment in gifted programs could be due to language differences between parents and school personnel, or cultural views that hold excellence as something to be achieved and recognized in the group—not the individual.

In a qualitative study of tracking practices across several communities in Baltimore, first-generation Americans whose parents emigrated from countries "linguistically and culturally distinct from the U.S." described how the families' "social positions as immigrants also limited the families' understanding of the American educational system. As a result, these families heeded the advice of teachers and counselors who sometimes recommended that students move up the tracking hierarchy, but more often suggested that students move down" (Yonezawa: 1998, p. 9).

Children are sometimes caught between their families' efforts at cultural retention and their own exposure to the larger culture through media, peers, and schools. Some children end up feeling alienated from Anglo school culture, as well as from the culture of their parents. In these cases, children may adopt an urban street culture that has more in common with other urban youth than with other Spanish-speaking children or with Anglo classmates at school (Katz: 1996). Children who present themselves as part of the urban street culture are easy for teachers to stereotype and discount or dismiss, regardless of their actual participation in it, or their true academic abilities or aspirations (Valenzuela: 1999). This is one route through which a student's sense of self becomes bifurcated, leaving some students to disengage from education.

Values, Expectations, and Norms

Most Latina/o parents value education and encourage their children to do well in school (Huston, Ginorio, Frevert, & Bierman: 1996; Romo & Falbo: 1996). More than 90 percent of Latina/o children report that their parents want them to go to college—the same rate that Anglos report (Smith: 1995). Latina/o students in high school are as likely as Anglo students to report that their parents check their homework, talk about their classes and studies, limit their social and TV activities, and visit their classrooms (U.S. Department of Education: 1995).

Academic success is seen as the ticket to a better life for both the child and the entire family, especially in a context where the American Dream is a powerful incentive for immigration and heavily promoted in the school and popular culture. However, this desire for academic achievement must be embedded within other cultural values. For example, Latino families commonly value respect for authority over individual assertiveness (Vásquez-Nuttall & Romero-García: 1989) and reward achievement most highly when it benefits the collective. The Latino emphasis on respect as part of education (Valenzuela: 1999) may lead to students being labeled apathetic or insolent and receiving less attention in the classroom than their Anglo peers. This value system runs contrary to the Anglo school culture, where individual achievement is prized over group achievement, where outspoken—even aggressive—students receive more attention in the competitive classroom, and where submissive behavior is seen as a negative trait, often associated with a lack of engagement (Vásquez-Nuttall & Romero-García: 1989).

○

Women are strong in spirit and I think they are stronger than men emotionally. It is better for them to make their minds strong. They are

just going to be a strong person. They are the—how do you say it—
the prop for the family. They are the head of the household—the kids
and everything. The kids look up to them. They go to them for advice.
The don't go to the father—well sometimes. The woman has to be
strong.

—AAUW Educational Foundation, focus group with
high school Latinas on education, Los Angeles, 1998

○

Parents may also hold expectations about children's commitments to
the family (as exhibited through work, participation in religious activities,
choices in residential location, etc.) that run contrary to the expectations
of the school system. Furthermore, these expectations may be affected by
gender norms within the culture, a possibility we discuss at more length
in the next section.

Although education in the abstract is valued, many families are
ambivalent about the American school system, having encountered and
resisted the assimilationist approach prevalent in many schools (Brown &
Stent: 1977). Families unfamiliar with and often alienated by school
may have a generalized fear and distrust of the educational system
(Rendón & Amaury: 1987), which leads to decreased involvement in
educational programs. For example, Latino families are less likely than
others to take advantage of preschool programs for their children, even
after controlling for income, employment status, and education (Fuller,
Eggers-Piérola, Holloway, Liang, & Rambaud: 1996). From 1973 to
1993, Hispanic three-and four-year-old preschool enrollments remained
flat (at 15 percent), while White preschool enrollments steadily grew
from 18 to 35 percent. White and African American preschool enrollments were roughly equal in 1995 yet Hispanic enrollment continued to
lag, despite considerable learning advantages associated with *quality*
preschool programs (President's Advisory Commission: 1996; U.S.
Department of Education: 1995). Parents with preschool children perceive a mismatch between the school's expectations for children and
those endorsed by the family. The President's Advisory Commission on
Educational Excellence for Hispanic Americans confirms this, noting that
"low-income Hispanic families often believe their home environments
are better for their children than programs like Head Start, because many
early childhood services are not prepared to deal with the linguistic and
cultural diversity of their children" (President's Advisory Commission:
1996, p. 2).

Schoolwork Comes First

○

Luisa Camacho, mother of 4-year-old Chantelle, 10-year-old Cheri, and 9-year-old Sharon, says she doesn't worry that her daughters may drop out of school one day. The girls—born here after Camacho emigrated from the Dominican Republic 10 years ago—know education is "muy importante," says their mother, that homework has precedence over "televisión." "They love to study," she says. "They can get whatever they need as long as they study. Education is a top priority."

After Sharon began attending weekend sessions of a support program called Educación 2000, the sprinkling of C's on her report card turned into A's and B's. The fourth-grader who attends school in Prince George's County, Maryland, credits hard work and positive thinking. "Always listen to your teacher and do your work, and think good stuff," she says, "and don't think you're gonna get bad grades because if you think that, you will."

—Luisa Camacho (Morse: 2000)

○

At the other end of the educational process, postsecondary education is often perceived as coming at the cost of maintaining close family ties and personal interdependencies that are highly valued in Latino culture (Ginorio & Martínez: 1998; Seymour & Hewitt: 1997). Schools that dismiss or simply overlook the importance of family support fail to capitalize on an important factor in the success of Latinas. Research by Helen García and another study by Norma Martínez-Rogers found that family support was mentioned repeatedly by Latino doctoral recipients, most of whom were first-generation women college students. The great majority names family and community involvement as measures of their personal worth and academic success (Why Hispanic-American: 1998). As in other cultures, women are charged with the maintenance of family ties. Thus, for many Latinas, possible selves imagined for the postsecondary years must include some integration of those conflicting expectations, or they will be forced to choose between education or loyalty to the family.

Gender Role Socialization

Given the centrality of the family in many Latino cultures, it is unsurprising that many families emphasize or highly esteem traditional roles for women as wives and mothers. Although there is variance within families and Latino cultures on this issue, residual, traditional expectations for women persist. For example, among Puerto Ricans with lower socioeconomic status (SES), gender roles for women are extremely restrictive; many traditional adults question the value of any education for women (Vásquez-Nuttall & Romero-García: 1989). For many Latinas, however, this traditionalism interacts with educational expectations and family ambitions to produce conflict for young women trying to follow contradictory prescriptions (González: 1988; Flores-Niemann, Romero, & Arbona: 2000).

ɔ

The point is nobody really went to college and my parents—I'm the last girl at home—my parents are looking at me saying okay, you have to do this and you have to do that. They set my goals for me but it is my choice if I want to follow what they want me to do. To prove to them, to make them happy—I have to go by their rules.

—AAUW Educational Foundation, focus group with high school Latinas on education, Los Angeles, 1998

ɔ

Conflicts about gender-appropriate behavior are another element that may bifurcate Latinas' sense of their possible selves. Parents see peer influence as affecting their daughters more than their sons and therefore closely monitor or restrict their daughters' activities as a guidance strategy (Azmitia & Brown: 1999). This strategy remains active even at the college level where parents prefer that unmarried daughters live at home (Guerra: 1996). Alternately, parents may see Latino-affirming schools as places where girls can explore and harmonize various gender roles and expectations.

Pregnancy and Sexuality

Teen pregnancy has often been treated as a health crisis in the United States—one that limits educational opportunities for both mother and child. Both families and schools play an important role in this phenomenon. Because the subject demands more attention, we have moved this discussion to its own section.

Family and Sociocultural Factors

The roles of mother and/or wife are highly valued for women in virtually all cultures. However, every culture has expectations about what constitutes acceptable timing of these events in the course of life. Teenage motherhood is considered a natural, normal process in many cultures. Many Latinas in the country come from areas where teenagers often marry and bear children as their primary (or only) rite of passage to adulthood, and the status associated with these events is highly rewarding. Researcher Pamela Erickson notes, "Pregnant women are afforded a prestigious position. . . . for many young women from disadvantaged homes . . . pregnancy may be the first time in a long time that they have received attention and respect." Ideally, the communities where this idea is prevalent are also organized so as to better support young couples with minimum education and life experience (Erickson: 1998).

○

Having a baby is a lottery ticket for many teenagers. It brings with it at least the dream of something better, and if the dream fails, not much is lost. If America cares about its young people, it must make them feel they have a rich array of choices, so that having a baby is not the only or the most attractive option on the horizon.

—Kristen Luker, 1997

○

In the United States, marriage and motherhood are more likely to be rewarded by middle-class Anglo society if they occur after high school and preferably after college. Pregnancy has particular relevance for Latinas. The National Center for Health Statistics reported in 1998 that for the first time, Hispanic teenagers are having babies at higher rates than White or African American girls. Almost 11 percent of Latinas aged 5–19 gave birth in 1995 (this figure described births rather than pregnancy rates).

The effect of pregnancy on Latinas' educational achievement, however, is ambiguous. One comparative study found that teen birth was the most predictive factor of the chances of a Latina's dropping out of school. The only other significant predictor found in that study was whether or not the family received federal aid (Forste & Tienda: 1992). Latinas tend to cite concerns about sex and pregnancy at earlier ages than their Anglo and Asian age peers (Haag: 1999), although Latinas drop out due to pregnancy at about the same rate as Anglo girls. Three out of 10 Latinas report leaving school due to pregnancy, despite their higher rates of childbearing during the high school years (Forste & Tienda: 1992; Portner: 1998; U.S. Department of Education: 1995; Smith: 1995; Kaplan, 1990 cited by Erickson: 1998). Another study argues that the effect of teen marriage and pregnancy on high school completion was significant only for Whites, in both the short term (Forste & Tienda: 1992) and for eventual pursuit of postsecondary degrees (Rich & Kim: 1999).

It is not clear, then, that teen pregnancy precipitates a disruption of a low-SES Latina's life plan or trajectory (although it clashes with middle-class, Anglo culture and life plans), or that it would precipitate dropping out of school. In fact, a study of poor Latinas in East Los Angeles finds that the opposite may be true: although conventional wisdom holds that teen girls drop out of school because they are pregnant, a majority in this study (63 percent) were not attending school when they became pregnant. Dropping out of school may encourage Latina teen pregnancy, rather than the converse. We discuss this possibility below in the section on schools.

Once Latinas give birth, it is less likely that they will return to high school to complete a degree: only 27 percent of Latinas who gave birth during their teen years completed a degree by their mid-20s, compared to 66 percent among Whites and 67 percent of African Americans (Yawn, Yawn, & Brindis: 1997). Some research suggests that this may be so because teen Latinas, unlike African Americans, may not be encouraged to pursue further education once they are mothers, as they are "viewed as having entered the realm of motherhood with primary responsibilities for the home rather than finishing their education" (Yawn et al.: 1997). Indeed, although Latinas are more likely to be sexually active than Whites, they are also more likely to be married than other groups of girls (Yawn et al.: 1997).

---

o

As soon as I got out of high school I was pregnant but as soon as I had my baby I got right back in and this is like what I'm going to do for the rest of my life and I'm not going to wait and not go to school because this is the money I'm going to be supporting my family with. So I've got to rush it.

—AAUW Educational Foundation, focus group with high school Latinas on education, Los Angeles, 1998

---

o

Family Support

Some studies suggest that strong family support is one major reason that higher birth rates among Latina teenagers do not lead to higher dropout rates (Romo & Falbo: 1996; Erickson: 1998). However, this support varies across Hispanic communities and according to immigration status. A 1995 study based on U.S. Census data shows that "foreign-born" young mothers, in a "distinctive immigrant strategy, especially for Mexicans," are more likely than their U.S.-born counterparts to rely on family resources and help to raise their children. Among young Latina mothers, economic support from families further differs, with Puerto Ricans appearing worse off financially than others, and Cuban mothers better off than other groups (Kahn & Berkowitz: 1995).

Schools

One of the most difficult subjects schools teach is sex education. Pressure from parents and community members often results in sexual education ending up on the "evaded" curriculum—never discussed, and its side effects ignored and relegated to the area of "personal problems." Even if sex education is taught as part of the formal curriculum in health class, *meaningful* school-based support systems for teen mothers are still relatively rare. Teen mothers rarely have good options for child care and alternative scheduling that will allow them to work toward, and complete, their high school degree. "Sex education school initiatives tend to place primary responsibility for adolescent pregnancy on girls" (AAUW Educational Foundation: 1998).

Furthermore, schools are implicated in this process when they are inattentive to students who are struggling: "Girls with previous academic difficulties (e.g., poor grades, grade retentions) were more likely to become pregnant, use drugs and alcohol, and engage in delinquent behavior" (AAUW Educational Foundation: 1998, p. 116).

Similarly, a 1998 sociological study argues that "girls who are discouraged at school will often escape through getting pregnant," which reverses the common argument that pregnancy precipitates dropping out. Manlove explains that among dropouts, female Hispanics have the highest rate of pregnancy at almost half (48 percent), and African Americans, the lowest at one-third (Manlove: 1998).

A study of the effects of pregnancy and childbearing on dropping out in the Southwest concludes that although pregnancy was one of the reasons (accounting for one-third of school dropouts), it was not the primary cause of dropping out among Latina females. Being behind a grade and traditional family sex roles emerged as important causes of dropping out (Kaplan: 1990).

> School then enters the equation on education in three distinct ways: conducting sex education classes to discourage pregnancy, offering support services to pregnant teens and young mothers, and ensuring that girls are engaged in school.

○

It's like I have to go to college because neither of my parents did. They know I do have high expectations for myself . . . if I didn't go to college my mom would kick me out. That is what I have to do. So it's like I have to prove to them that yes, I will do whatever I say I can.

—AAUW Educational Foundation, focus group with
high school Latinas on education, Los Angeles, 1998

○

Among a sample of academically successful Latinas (mostly Puerto Rican), Thorne (1995) found low levels of sex role traditionalism. Adherence to traditional sex role stereotypes is a barrier to college retention (Castellanos & Fujitsubo: 1997; Flores-Niemann et al.: 2000). Research by Cardoza in 1991 found a strong relationship between sex-role status and college attendance and persistence among Hispanic women. Women who adhered to "traditional" sex roles (i.e., married with children or placing a high value on these qualities) were not attending or persisting in college to the same extent as "nontraditional" Latinas (Cardoza: 1991).

Themes and Questions for Further Research:

○ How, if at all, do Latinas and Latinos differ in their views of education, and why?

○ How does acculturation of women affect educational outcomes?

Peers and Peer Groups

While parental wishes and expectations clearly influence every student's life, peers can also play a pivotal role in either limiting or expanding a person's pool of possible selves. For girls still shaping their sense of self, peers play an important role in deterring or encouraging academic achievement and forming a self that aspires to academic excellence. The influence of peers can be either encouraging or dismissive of academically successful selves (Ginorio & Grignon: 2000; Ginorio & Huston: 2000). In a sample of rural girls, 40 percent report that their friends are supportive of their plans to go to college and 9 percent report that their friends are barriers to their college plans. Among a matched sample of dropouts and students who graduated, those who graduated were far more likely to have friends who did *not* drop out and who encouraged their success in high school. The author concludes, "The impact of peer group was a stronger determining factor in the student's decision to drop out or remain in school than any other factor with the exception of grades" (Valverde: 1987, p. 324). One area of discord between parents and children is the choice of friends whom parents often see as deterring their children, particularly boys, from "el buen carnino" (the path of life) (Azmitia & Brown: 1999).

Adults often dictate different roles from those dictated by peers (Cohen, Blanc, Christman, Brown, & Sims: 1996, p. 60). Young people may be faced with pressure from their friends to choose among the stereotypical roles found within those communities. "Will they be 'schoolgirls' approved by adults, 'cool girls' popular with peers and doing well in school, or 'cholos' (sic) involved with gang culture?" (Cohen et al.: 1996). The strategy chosen by a particular girl will reflect not only her personal preferences but also the school setting. The choices for a Latina in a majority Latina/o school may be different from those she would make in a school where she is a distinct minority.

Peers', schools', and families' rewards and penalties for these roles and behaviors are not always in agreement. For example, both schools and families may be opposed to premature sexual activity even while boyfriends (and the larger peer network) encourage a young woman to engage in sex. Furthermore, while schools and parents are opposed to this activity, the sanctions each would impose on sexually active women may be quite different. Of particular importance is the 33 percent of 10th grade girls who report that boyfriends or fiancés make it more difficult for them to go to college (Ginorio & Grignon: 2000; Ginorio & Huston: 2000). This finding at the high school level is consistent with college-level findings that more traditional Latinas worry about being labeled too educated by prospective Latino husbands. Therefore, a young woman's choices of possible selves may be conditioned not only by the pressures she perceives from these various sources, but also by her understanding of the consequences her choices may carry for those people who are most important to her.

Some peers resent Latinas' engagement and success in school, and Latinas who do well in their classes may find themselves the target of harassment.

○

In DeAnza Montoya's Santa Fe Latina neighborhood, it was considered "Anglo" or "nerdy" to do well in school. So DeAnza cruised in wildly painted cars with her "low rider" rides and didn't worry about the future. She claims she was simply doing what was expected of her: "In school they make you feel like dumb Mexican," she says, adding that the slights only bring Hispanics closer together.

—(Headden: 1997)

○

Many girls of color (regardless of ethnicity/culture) report that they are accused of "acting White" when they try to engage in academic studies (Fordham: 1996; Dietrich: 1998; Haag: 1999). This perception of achievement as "White" is probably more pronounced in schools whose environment is perceived as assimilationist or dismissive of minority cultures. Often, this leads to a bifurcation of academic and Latina identity, making it difficult for a young woman to craft an identity that is both Latina and academically successful.

At the group level, participation in extracurricular activities (such as leadership, student government, and sports) has been reported as facilitating academic success. Among the factors that nurture academic ambivalence or rejection, gangs are the most discussed factor in the literature.

"Gangs" appear in the educational literature in two ways—as discouraging education by making schools less safe for particular individuals and as dismissing education by their oppositional relation to the adult authorities in school and society. Although popular media associates Latino gangs with males, around 3 percent of Latinas also participate in gangs (Rodríguez, personal communication, 2000). While few Latinas participate in gangs, their presence in the school environment and neighborhood may cause conflict or fear for personal safety among nongang members.

If gangs are present in the community, some Latinas will face pressure to participate in gang activities in their neighborhoods. Latina/os are almost three times as likely as Anglos to report having many gangs in their schools (Smith: 1995). The Department of Justice reports that in 1995, among students ages 12 to 19, half of Hispanic students reported that street gangs were present in their schools, an increase of 18 percent from 1989. Hispanics were two times more likely than all other groups of students to report gangs in their schools (Educational Testing Service: 1998). There is little research on how these experiences affect Latinas specifically.

Researchers believe that gang formation for boys or girls from any ethnic/racial group results from feelings of alienation from other institutions such as the family or school. Gangs thereby function as a support system and community (Katz: 1996).

○

They gave me power that I never had. At home, I was always the mother, always taking care of the kids. Getting no respect, never going anywhere because I was too young, this and that.

—Latina gang member quoted in
"Women, Men, and Gangs" (Portillos: 1999)

○

Portillos notes that Latina gangs are hardly a sign of "liberation," but rather one strategy whereby Latinas deal with a bleak present and a harsh future that seems to offer little hope. A study of Hispanic girl gangs in New York describes that members "exist in an environment that has little to offer young women of color. The possibility of a decent career outside of 'domestic servant' is practically nonexistent. Most have dropped out of school and have no marketable skills. Future aspirations are both gendered and unrealistic" (Chesney-Lind & Hagedorn: 1999, p. 215). Gang membership usually involves ditching classes and a general disdain for the formal educational process. In Harris's 1988 study of gang members, none of the respondents had finished high school.

Risk Factors Related to Peer Culture and School

Recent research by the Urban Institute and the Commonwealth Fund explores teen risk-taking and risky behaviors such as using alcohol, tobacco, marijuana, or other illegal drugs; binge drinking; fighting; carrying weapons; thinking about attempting suicide; and engaging in sexual activity. These reports found that Hispanic and White girls were more likely to engage in risky behaviors and take multiple risks than African American or Asian American girls (Commonwealth Fund: 1997). While teen involvement with these "risk behaviors" has declined overall over the past decade, this has not been the case for Hispanic males and females. The share of Hispanic students engaging in five or more risk behaviors increased from 13 percent in 1991 to 19 percent in 1997, an increase of nearly 50 percent. Among Hispanic 9th and 10th graders, participation in five or more risk behaviors nearly doubled in the same time frame, while the number remained relatively stable for White and African American students (Lindberg, Boggess, Porter, & Williams: 2000).

Data from the U.S. Centers for Disease Control and Prevention on illegal drug use similarly find that Latinas are more likely to use marijuana, inhalants, and cocaine than their African American or White peers. Lifetime use of powder cocaine by Latinas (12.5 percent) is nearly twice that of White girls (7.5 percent), and more that 12 times that of African American girls (1 percent) (CDC: 1998). These figures, based on a sample of high school students, do not reflect risk behaviors among Latinas who have dropped out of school and are thus conservative estimates from actual drug use among adolescent Latinas.

Themes and Questions for Further Research:

- ○ What is the role of boyfriends' educational aspirations in shaping young Latinas' education plans?
- ○ What school practices foster school disengagement among Latinos or Latinas?
- ○ Is gang participation a result of school disengagement, or does school disengagement result from gang membership?
- ○ Are there differences in Latinas' and Latinos' involvement with risky behaviors? If so, why?

Schools

A school with adequate resources, including teachers, technology, and support staff, may succeed well with students whose values and experiences harmonize with those of the school. However, these same well-equipped schools may be far less successful if the school is dismissive of education that is consonant with students' cultural background. These incongruities are likely to occur when the school adheres to a monocultural view of education—a view that defines the school experience, environment, and norms narrowly, with one kind of student in mind. Education-dismissive schools may lack adequate economic resources to provide education to *any* student, have detrimental tracking practices, and fail to address life circumstances and needs of any students. Since only 6 percent of the national budget is allocated to K–12 education and additional resources are based on property taxes, poor students and students of color are far more likely to attend underfunded schools (Fairchild: 1989; U.S. Department of Education: 1996a; Oakes: 1990). These schools have low test scores and graduation rates, and students within them are faced with increasing detachment to school because of the extreme dissonance between their school, family, and social worlds. But well-supported schools may still be dismissive of the education of Latina/os if they see these students in stereotypically negative ways.

Education-encouraging schools successful with students of color also fit a profile: they provide a good education—not just good instruction. They acknowledge and respect possible selves that arise from cultural backgrounds, and work with families to support and guide a rich and congruent pool of possible selves.

Schools also have different degrees of human resources in the communities around them. In areas characterized by high congruence between the goals of the school and the goals of families, a large number of parents participate in school planning, fundraising, and the curriculum. However, where schools fail to reach out to parents and provide a welcoming, supportive environment for their values and ideas, children are more likely to experience the bifurcation of their school and community possible selves.

Gándara (1995) cites many studies suggesting that racially concentrated schools produce lower achievement than racially integrated schools, possibly related to funding and the quality of teachers. Among her sample of professional first-generation Latinas, most attended integrated schools and considered this important for their educational success in college. In addition, residential and school segregation have been argued to promote linguistic and class isolation that deter academic attainment (Arias: 1986).

Preparation of Teachers to Work with Latina/o Students

Substantial evidence suggests that an individual teacher can have a profoundly positive effect on a child's eventual adult achievements. However, *as a group*, many teachers are underprepared or unprepared to deal effectively with gender issues in the classroom. Furthermore, Anglo school teachers have been criticized for their lack of preparation and interest in learning about their students who come from ethno-racial backgrounds different from their own (Rendón & Amaury: 1987). Even Latina/o teachers may not feel adequately prepared or equipped to deal with "limited English proficiency" students or predominantly Hispanic classrooms. A 1990 survey of 438 Latina/o teachers, 77 percent of whom were women, found that only 41 percent felt that they were "well prepared to teach Latina/o students" and only 34 percent felt well prepared to teach limited-English-proficient students (Monsivais: 1990).

Teachers may have little in the way of college or in-service preparation for working with these populations, and Latina/o teachers are few and far between. In 1994, 12 percent of students were Hispanic, but only 4 percent of teachers were Hispanic (Meek: 1998).

○

We continue to prepare teachers for nonexistent students: middle-class students who speak English and have plenty of resources at home.

—María Robledo Montecel, Intercultural Development
Research Association (Archer: 1996)

○

Teachers may have trouble moving beyond their own stereotypes of Latinas' educational possibilities (or probabilities, in their minds) and thus promote an education-dismissive environment. Many Latina/o students report that their teachers did not encourage them to consider college (Rodríguez: 1993). Evidence suggests that Anglo teachers have lower expectations for the academic performance of Hispanic students than do Hispanic teachers and that these expectations may be a crucial—and rectifiable—element of teacher education. However, teachers' expectations about academic performance are related to a student's chances of attending college. When evaluating students who are expected to attend college, Anglo and Hispanic teachers had similar academic expectations for their students. In this way, teachers may be education-encouraging for individual students while simultaneously endorsing an education-dismissive environment. However, Hispanic teachers' evaluations remained high for non-college-bound students, while Anglo teachers' expectations were lower (So: 1987b).

Well-intentioned and committed teachers may also be hampered by state-dictated curricula, the effects of standardized testing (Patthey-Chávez: 1993), and the questionable application of the "standards" movement. Teachers in urban Hispanic schools also suffer great stress—much of it caused by a lack of administrative support, a lack of resources, and disengaged students (Bruno: 1983).

By the same token, effective, skilled teachers with an understanding of their students can make a substantial difference, particularly for Latinas who value personal connections with teachers. Some of the characteristics associated with Latinas' high achievement in school, by conventional measures, often diverge from the way education is delivered in public schools. Several studies find, for example, that high-achieving Latinas in K–12 and postsecondary education emphasize the role of "personalism" in accounting for their success. As a report from the San Diego City school district on high- and low-achieving Latinas explains, "the traditional Mexican culture values personalism; that is, warmth, expressions of personal interest, and connectedness with others." This report finds that "the things both groups like and dislike about attending their school focused on relational/human interaction aspects" (San Diego City Schools: 1989, p. 59). The study found that "worst" school experiences focused on negative human interaction and that, conversely, Mexican American girls "respond more positively to positive reinforcement than do Anglo females" or males in general. High achievers focused on the personal qualities of teachers and counselors, such as helpfulness, caring, and personal regard (San Diego City Schools: 1989, pp. 5–6). Valenzuela's work in Houston re-affirms this finding, leading her to assert that care from teachers is a prerequisite for Mexican American students' engagement with education (Valenzuela: 1999).

Among a sample of 9th grade Latinas who excelled in science, virtually all of them reported encouragement by one or more teachers to continue their studies (O'Halloran: 1995). A national study suggests that Latina/os are as likely as Anglos to say their teachers are interested in their students, teaching in their school is good, and discipline is fair (Smith: 1995). Other high-achieving Latinas cite cultural traditions, such as story telling, caring for others, interacting, and communicating with style, as particular strengths that encouraged academic success (García & Associates: 1998). Students characterized as likely to finish high school are significantly more satisfied with their schools than students who are at high risk of not graduating from high school. These students' satisfaction does not make them insensitive to their teachers' treatment of others; in fact, they are likely to say that teachers' treatment of their at-risk peers is unfair and distracting (Reyes & Jason: 1993).

Themes and Questions for Further Research:

- Are there teaching techniques and styles that are especially effective with Latina/o students? If so, what are they?
- How can teachers and counselors build on the strengths of the family to foster high educational expectations among Latinas?

Counseling

Guidance counselors play a potentially powerful role—whether positive or negative—in students' lives and for Latinas, who may especially value personalized interaction with a school administrator. Although counselors may come into contact with children only once or twice a year, they greatly influence which courses a student will take and which tracks the child might pursue. They also formally supervise students' course-taking during secondary education and the preparation of students for academic opportunities beyond high school. In this regard, counselors are critical to young people envisioning their possible selves. However, their cursory contact with each student may necessarily limit their positive impact.

○

My counselor, I don't know. . . . She tells you—you go in and tell her what you want to do and she'll tell you you can't do it. She picked out all your stuff and goes, no you can't do that. I told her I wanted to do something in medicine . . . and she's like "nope, you can't. I'm sorry."

—AAUW Educational Foundation, focus group with Latina high school students on education, Los Angeles, 1998

○

The literature on counseling is quite mixed. Counselors have been accused of the same lack of preparation and interest as teachers, and some reports indicate that Latina/os are not so likely to use counselors as Anglo students, nor are counselors likely to reach out to Latina/os (Hispanic Children: 1985). Other reports indicate that Latina/os may have more contact with counselors than White students but related to nonacademic concerns such as discipline (Huston et al.: 1996). Counselors' low expectations of Latina/os' achievement lead them to place Latina/os in college preparation classes at much lower rates than their Anglo peers (Hispanic Children: 1985). In one study, half of the sampled Latinas who were excelling in their science classes in high school reported that their counselors were not at all helpful in their studies or career and college planning (O'Halloran: 1995). However, other reports indicate that Anglo and Hispanic sophomores in 1990 were equally likely to report that guidance counselors had encouraged them to go to college (U.S. Department of Education: 1995).

To the extent that counselors' interaction styles reflect or perpetuate Anglo cultural values, they contribute to the creation of an environment that may be overtly or covertly hostile to young people from cultures not versed in tracking school bureaucracies, SAT tests, financial aid options, or the college admissions process. In one study of students' perceptions of counselors, Anglo-acculturated students were significantly more likely to rate a counselor as trustworthy than were bicultural or Latino-acculturated students. Furthermore, Latino-acculturated students seemed to prefer a different counseling style and were significantly more likely to rate a counselor using a nondirective style as being more understanding of their problems and needs (Pomales & Williams: 1989).

○

My college counselor at my high school . . . wasn't supportive of me at all, because I did have low grades at the time, but I still thought I could do whatever I really wanted to and she just didn't recommend me to apply to any of my colleges. Even though I did, I got accepted to every single one. I made her feel real stupid.

—AAUW Educational Foundation, focus group with Latina
high school students on education, Los Angeles, 1998

○

Case studies suggest that guidance counselors can help a young woman better manage demands placed on her time by providing flexible scheduling options, suggesting tutoring programs as appropriate, and recommending other academically supportive programs. In these cases, counselors can serve as significant ambassadors between the Latina student and the worlds of college, work, and after-school programs, even if that support is short-lived or limited in scope (Romo & Falbo: 1996).

English as a Second Language Classes

English as a Second Language (ESL) classes are too complex and contentious an issue to cover fully in this review, yet they must be mentioned as a critical component of Latinas' school experience. The U.S. Department of Education's Office for Civil Rights shows that nationally, a substantial percentage of Hispanic students—40 percent of males and 37 percent of females—are identified as "in need of LEP (Limited English Proficiency)" classes or programs, and the same percentages are in fact "enrolled in LEP" (Office for Civil Rights: 1999).

ESL classes provide education in basic academic subjects in Spanish, while offering intensive English language classes concurrently. A great deal of research and theory suggests that doing away with ESL classes would be a disservice to students: for many, these classes are essential for building strong basic skills. Some evidence indicates that students—at least those in integrated schools—find language-based tracking useful because it separates them from an otherwise hostile environment and cocoons them with teachers and peers who support their success and ambition (Gándara: 1995). Furthermore, to deny students a learning environment that supports their native language, some researchers conclude, "guarantees(s) . . . intellectual passivity" (Fuentes: 1994) and may limit their cognitive proficiency, which is best developed through a language in which students are fluent.

However, in many districts, there are serious ramifications to being placed in the ESL track. Once in an ESL track (where classes are usually remedial and rarely college-preparatory), students have a very difficult time moving into mainstream classes even if they excel in school and have their parents' and teachers' support (Romo & Falbo: 1996). Students themselves say that language classes contribute to the stereotyping and maintenance of a social hierarchy in which they are forever on the bottom rung (Burke: 1995; Genesee & Gándara: 1999; Genesee: 1999). Some argue that this segregation deters academic attainment by narrowing a student's options—especially of entering college, but even for receiving a high school diploma (Arias: 1986).

Themes and Questions for Further Research:

  ○ There is a need for further research on peer and gender relations in the context of ESL programs and classes that stereotype Latina/os.

School Climate

Few students negotiate the time from youth to adulthood without being taunted or faced with peer harassment at some point. Evidence suggests, however, that Latinas are more likely than Anglos to feel that their education is interrupted by other students, to feel unsafe, and to see fights between different racial/ethnic groups (Smith: 1995). Latinas are more likely to fear for their personal safety in school (7.7 percent) than White (2.5 percent) or African American girls (6.1 percent), and express more apprehension than their males peers (6.8 percent). Only African American boys expressed the same level of fear about going to school as Latinas (7.5 percent) (CDC: 1998).

According to 1996 national data from the Department of Education, Latina/os generally are the most likely to report feeling unsafe or very unsafe at school, more than African American or White students (13 percent to 9 percent and 8 percent, respectively). Other national data support this conclusion. Data in 1992 from a longitudinal study found that

Hispanics were more likely than White students to agree that they "don't feel safe at this school" (15 percent to 9 percent) and to report that "fights often occur between different racial/ethnic groups" (32 percent to 21 percent) (Educational Testing Service: 1998).

Recent research on Hispanic education extends the idea of "safety" to the idea of "social or psychological safety" in the classroom and the learning process. Students feel psychologically safe and comfortable in classrooms, in one student's terms, "when all of my other classmates respect me and they don't mess around. When you don't have side comments, like sometimes when I try to speak in front of a class because I'm afraid of what people are going to say" (Shivley: 2000, p. 3).

Compounding this issue is gender. Latinas are at double jeopardy even before we consider all the other touchstones for childhood insult (social class, language, physical traits, etc.). Recent qualitative research finds that Latinas more often than girls of other racial/ethnic groups say that they have been the targets of sexual slurs and, significantly, insults against their intelligence (Haag: 1999). Previous research indicates differences along ethnic lines among young children, where 10 percent of Latinas report sexual harassment before the 3rd grade (AAUW Educational Foundation: 1993). Girls who report being the target of sexual harassment are likely to experience a range of negative outcomes, such as not wanting to go to school, not wanting to talk as much in class, and not being able to pay attention (AAUW Educational Foundation: 1993).

While many are loath to use the word, students do report experiencing racism in their schools. At its most subtle, they report negative stereotyping by teachers and peers (Burke: 1995), while others report overt statements about inherent capabilities (or the lack thereof). For example, a "frustrated White teacher told [students] that 'we had no futures' cause we were Hispanic, that we'd never get out of Avila, that we'd work at McDonald's" (Cohen et al.: 1996, p. 58). In other cases, teachers and counselors assume that students who speak Spanish are gang members (Romo & Falbo: 1996). Urciuoli argues that such behavior flows from the racializing of Spanish speakers, a process by which people who "use languages other than English in public and in ways that are not . . . unequivocally middle class presentation . . . are seen as dangerously out of order" (Urciuoli: 1996, p. 38).

A 1989 San Diego school system study of high- and low-achieving Latinas gathered qualitative evidence of racist comments and tendencies in the schools. "Mexican students tend not to be included in activities here," one Latina writes. "Mexican girls aren't allowed to be cheerleaders and are not featured in the yearbook. Students . . . think Mexicans have no ability.

They walk away from us." Another person reports that her "10th grade English teacher was very prejudiced. She ignored me and other Hispanics when we raised our hands. Lots of students and parents complained." These comments cut across achievement levels, as did experiences with peers. "Some White girls tease and call me Chola and mimic Mexican accents in the bathroom," one writes. When asked what they didn't like about school, low and high achievers alike pointed most often to unpleasant or hostile incidents with peers and teachers, often involving racial tensions or insults (e.g., "people making fun of your clothes," "some White kids feel superior to Mexicans and Blacks," "some people are prejudiced, not used to Hispanics") (San Diego City Schools: 1989, p. 6).

For nearly 10 months of the year, most children spend six to eight hours a day in school. For children of color, school is often an environment immediately associated with tension: to fit in and be accepted by the dominant institution, they are pushed to distance themselves from their culture of origin. First-generation students have to learn a new language (both verbal and nonverbal), abide by cultural norms that may diverge from those they practice at home, and negotiate a system that was probably designed with a very different generic student in mind. The prototypical student has at least some cultural capital: educated parents, fluency with English (and no accent), access to financial support for educational and cultural activities, familiarity with the educational and cultural activities, familiarity with the educational "system," and few other responsibilities to detract from full-time attention to schooling and extracurricular activities. Children undoubtedly do their best to walk the line between acceptance in school and the maintenance of ties to their home culture. Yet many face a seemingly immovable system which neither they nor their parents are able to negotiate. By the time they reach high school they are set in adverse tracks of low-level or remedial classes that perpetuate boredom and mutual disinterest: the system doesn't care about them and, by then, many of them no longer care about the system (Valenzuela: 1999).

Transition to Work or College

Most educational research assumes that high school graduates will, or ideally should enroll in college immediately following high school. However, a large number of students choose to work or enter the military upon high school completion. For some of these young adults, college will come— but later. Still, the direct high-school-to-college transition is the path that leads to the greatest likelihood that a student will complete a college degree within 10 years of high school graduation (Adelman: 1999).

○

> Not every school does get [college] recruiters to come to a school. I
> think that would be a good thing because like something might inter-
> est them but they never really thought about it. If somebody would
> come and talk about it and not only talk about their occupations but
> college choices.
>
> —AAUW Educational Foundation, focus group with Latina
> high school students on education, Los Angeles, 1998

○

Aside from the educational experiences and outcomes already discussed, the economic needs of their families and the type of *financial aid*
packages available for their schools and programs of choice affect Latinas' college enrollment. At this transition point, Latinas' commitments to
academic success may be tempered by their *preparedness to leave home.*
To the extent that postsecondary schooling means leaving communities,
families, and friends, choosing school may feel like a slight of their family's and friends' priorities. These two factors are especially significant at
the moment of transition out of high school.

FINANCIAL AID Applications are notoriously difficult to read and understand—even for a parent for whom English is the first language. For
Latina/o parents, these forms may deter application for scholarships and
state aid—which in turn limits the number and types of schools a student
considers for postsecondary education. Latina/os are more likely to attend
less expensive community and state colleges, which offer fewer resources
for financial aid. One study suggests that of the three-quarters of Latina/o
parents eligible for aid, only half applied for it (So: 1984). Latina/o parents were severely undereducated about financial aid and less likely than
Anglo parents to seek information about financial aid through formal
channels (So: 1984). Furthermore, many forms of aid are applicable only
to certain schools or specific fields of study (Rendón & Amaury: 1987;
Mortenson: 2000). Therefore, students dependent on funding other than
from their families for their college education may find their options
severely constrained (So: 1984).

LEAVING HOME Young adults differ in their eagerness and preparation
to move away from home to attend school. For many, attachment to
friends and family make this separation nearly impossible—a factor that
may be particularly poignant for Latinas who come from a culture that

emphasizes familial ties, particularly for women. Some women's families support their college aspirations only if they attend schools near home (Guerra: 1996; Wycoff: 1996). Latinas from small Latino towns or rural areas may also fear the prospect of moving into a larger, bewildering, if not intimidating, world for which many students have had little preparation (Ginorio & Huston: 2000; Ginorio & Grignon: 2000). These apprehensions may result in individuals choosing to attend college—such as community college—close to home. For those who do move away, the pull to return home may cause them to leave school before completing their degrees. Even when leaving for school means relocating 40 or 50 miles away, there may be some family resistance to girls going away to college (Ginorio & Huston: 2000; Ginorio & Grignon: 2000; Guerra, 1996; Castro: 2000). This fascinating theme—which captures the dissonance between an individual Latina's educational goals and her other priorities and values in the family and community—certainly deserves further research and attention.

○

Why is higher education such a disappointing experience for us nowadays, particularly in private colleges? . . . Is the American Dream accessible only when one denies one's own past? Once again, the young people are pushed to the margins, their journey from the barrio to the classroom marked by depression. . . . When I was a graduate student at Columbia University from 1987 to 1990, not a single course was offered on Puerto Ricans on the mainland, although the school, on 116th St. and Broadway in New York, is surrounded by millions of Spanish-speaking Borinquens. . . . While society is already accepting Latinos as a major economic and political force, private colleges hesitate.

—(Stavans: 1995)

○

Many middle-class students are prepared for college classrooms by received wisdom and informal knowledge acquired from friends, siblings, and parents who have been there and share their experiences. Many are able to attend camps and campus activities that familiarize them with college environments. Furthermore, many high school teachers—particularly those responsible for teaching college-prep classes—help students engage in anticipatory socialization. They help young people learn how to ask questions in the classroom, how to approach a teacher during office hours, or how to argue a grade. Latinas do not have the same access to this "cultural capital," and the conflicts of leaving home may weigh more heavily on young women than men, although the issue invites further research.

Themes and Questions for Further Research:

○ How do concerns about leaving home at the high-school-to-college transition point influence Latinas' educational decisions?

○ Most young adults who leave school before receiving a diploma are *not* gang members or teen parents. Yet little is known about minors who are not in school. How do their experiences differ from young people who may be just as disengaged from school, yet remain in the system? Is "getting out" truly the best option? What alternative schooling opportunities might benefit those who leave the public school system before graduation?

REFERENCES

AAUW Educational Foundation. (1998). *Gender Gaps: Where Schools Still Fail Our Children*. Washington, DC.

AAUW Educational Foundation. (1993). *Hostile Hallways: The AAUW Survey on Sexual Harassment in America's Schools*. Washington, DC.

Adelman, C. (1999). *Answers in the Tool Box: Academic Intensity, Attendance Patterns and Bachelors Degree Attainment*. Washington, DC: U.S. Department of Education, Office of Educational Research and Improvement.

Aponte, R., & Siles, M. (1994). *Latinos in the Heartland: The Browning of the Midwest*. East Lansing, MI: Julian Samora Research Institute, Michigan State University. ERIC #ED414104.

Archer, J. (1996, March). Surge in Hispanic Enrollment Predicted. *Education Week [On-line serial]*, 15 (27). Available at *www.edweek.org/ew /vol-15/27census.h15*.

Arias, M. B. (1986). The Context of Education for Hispanic Students: An Overview. *The American Journal of Education*, 95, 26–57.

Azmitia, M., & Brown, J. R. (1999). *Continuity and Change in Latino Immigrant Parents' Beliefs About the "Path of Life."* Santa Cruz, CA: University of California.

Bressler, S. (1996). Voices of Latina Migrant Mothers in Rural Pennsylvania. In Judith Leblanc Flores (ed.), *Children of La Frontera: Binational Efforts to Service Mexican Migrant and Immigrant Students*. Washington, DC. ERIC #ED393647.

Brown, F., & Stent, M. D. (1977). *Minorities in U.S. Institutions of Higher Education.* New York: Praeger.

Bruno, J. E. (1983). Equal Education Opportunity and Declining Teacher Morale at Black, White, and Hispanic High Schools in a Large Urban School District. *The Urban Review,* 15 (1), 19–36.

Burke, D. J. (1995). Hispanic Youth and the Secondary School Culture. *The High School Journal,* 78, 185–194.

Cardoza, D. (1991). College Attendance and Persistence Among Hispanic Women: An Examination of Some Contributing Factors. *Sex Roles,* 7 (3/4), 147–165.

Castellanos, M., & Fujitsubo, L. C. (1997). Academic Success Among Mexican American Women in a Community College. *Community College Journal of Research and Practice,* 21 (8), 695–708.

Castillo-Speed, L. (ed.). (1995). *Latina: Women's Voices from the Borderlands.* New York: Simon & Schuster.

Castro, I. (2000). *Latinas/Latinos Achieving More Academically (LLAMA) Advocacy Program.* Paper presented at the "Urban Girls: Entering the New Millennium" conference, Buffalo, NY. April 14–15.

Centers for Disease Control and Prevention. (1998). Youth Risk Behavior Surveillance—United States, 1997, *MMWR,* 73.

Chacón, M. A., Cohen, E. G., Camarena, M. M., Gonzáles, J. T., & Strover, S. (1983, Winter). Chicanas in California Post Secondary Education. *La Red/The Net,* Supplement no. 65.

Chesney-Lind, M., & Hagedorn, J. K. (1999). Just Every Mother's Angel: An Analysis of Gender and Ethnic Variations in Youth Gang Membership. In M. Chesney-Lind & J. Hagedorn (eds.). *Female Gangs in America: Essays on Girls, Gangs, and Gender.* Chicago: Lake View Press.

Cohen, J., Blanc, S., with Christman, J., Brown, D., & Sims, M. (1996). *Girls in the Middle: Working to Succeed in School.* Washington, DC: American Association of University Women Educational Foundation.

College-Bound Hispanics: Marking the Path. (1998, February). *Hispanic Outlook in Higher Education,* 8 (11), 3.

Collins, W. A., Maccoby, E. E., Steinberg, L., Hetherington, E. M., & Bornstein, M. H. (2000). Contemporary Research on Parenting. *American Psychologist,* 55 (2), 218–232.

Commonwealth Fund. (1997). *The Commonwealth Fund Survey of the Health of Adolescent Girls.* New York.

Delgado-Gaitan, C. (1991). Involving Parents in Schools: A Process of Empowerment. *American Journal of Education,* 100 (1), 20–46.

Dietrich, L. C. (1998). *Chicana Adolescents. Bitches, 'Ho's,' and Schoolgirls.* Westport, CT: Praeger.

Durán, R. (2000). *Latino Immigrant Parents and Children Learning and Publishing Together in an After School Setting.* Paper presented at the Annual Meeting of the American Educational Research Association, New Orleans, LA. April 24–28.

Educational Testing Service. (1998). *Order in the Classroom. Violence, Discipline, and Student Achievement.* Princeton, NJ.

Erickson, P. (1998). *Latina Adolescent Childbearing in East Los Angeles.* Austin, TX: University of Texas Press.

Fairchild, H. (1989). School Size, Per Pupil Expenditure, and Academic Achievement. *Review of Public Data Use, 12,* 221–229.

Fine, M., & Weis, L. (eds.). (1998). *The Unknown City: The Lives of Poor and Working-Class Young Adults.* Boston: Beacon Press.

Flores-Niemann, Y., Romero, A., & Arbona, C. (2000, February). Effects of Cultural Orientation on the Perception of Conflict between Relationship and Education Goals for Mexican American College Students. *Hispanic Journal of Behavioral Sciences, 22* (1), 46–63.

Fordham, S. (1996). *Blacked Out: Dilemmas of Race, Identity, and Success at Capital High.* Chicago: University of Chicago Press.

Forste, R., & Tienda, M. (1992). Race and Ethnic Variation in the Schooling Consequences of Female Adolescent Sexual Activity. *Social Science Quarterly, 73* (1), 12–30.

Fuentes, L. (1994). Educating Puerto Ricans in the U.S.: The Struggle for Equity. *Equity and Excellence in Education, 27* (1), 16–19.

Fuller, B., Eggers-Piérola, C., Holloway, S. D., Liang, X., & Rambaud, M. F. (1996). Rich Culture, Poor Markets: Why Do Latino Parents Forgo Preschool? *Teachers College Record, 97* (3), 400–418.

Gándara, P. (1995). *Over the Ivy Walls: The Educational Mobility of Low-Income Chicanas.* Albany, NY: State University of New York Press.

García & Associates. (1998, February 27). Cited in "Why Hispanic American Women Succeed in Higher Education." *Hispanic Outlook in Higher Education, 12.*

Genesee, F. (1999). *Program Alternatives for Linguistically Diverse Students.* Educational Practices Report 1, Center for Research on Education, Diversity and Excellence, Santa Cruz, CA. Washington, DC: Office of Educational Research and Improvement.

Genesee, F., & Gándara, P. (1999, Winter). Bilingual Education Programs: A Cross-National Perspective. *Journal of Social Issues.*

Ginorio, A. B., & Grignon, J. (2000). The Transition to and from High School of Ethnic Minority Students. In G. Campbell, Jr., R. Denes, & C. Morrison (eds.). *Access Denied: Race, Ethnicity, and the Scientific Enterprise* (pp. 151–173). New York: Oxford University Press.

Ginorio, A. B., Gutiérrez, L., Cauce, A. M., & Acosta, M. (1995). Psychological Issues for Latinas. In H. Landrine (ed.). *Bringing Cultural Diversity to Feminist Psychology* (pp. 241–263). Washington, DC: American Psychological Association.

Ginorio, A. B., & Huston, M. (2000, Spring). Latina Focus Group. Unpublished raw data.

Ginorio, A. B., & Martínez, L. J. (1998). Where Are the Latinas? Ethno-Race and Gender in Psychology Courses. *Psychology of Women Quarterly,* 22, 53–68.

Gómez, M. J., & Fassinger, R. E. (1994). An Initial Model of Latina Achievement: Acculturation, Biculturalism, and Achieving Styles. *Journal of Counseling Psychology,* 41 (2), 205–215.

González, S. T. (1988). Dilemmas of the High-Achieving Chicana: The Double-Bind Factor in Male/Female Relationships. *Sex Roles,* 18, 367–380.

Guerra, J. C. (1996). "It Is As If My Story Repeats Itself." Life, Language, and Literacy in Chicago Communidad. *Education and Urban Society,* 29 (1), 35–53.

Haag, P. (1999). *Voices of a Generation: Teenage Girls on Sex, School, and Self.* Washington, DC: American Association of University Women Educational Foundation.

Harris, M. G. (1988). *Cholas: Latina Girls and Gangs.* New York: AMS Press.

Headden, S. (1997, October 20). The Hispanic Dropout Mystery. *U.S. News and World Report.* Available at *www.usnews.com/usnews/issue /971020/20hisp.htm.*

Hispanic Children Are Less Well-Educated and More Likely to Drop Out. (1985, November). *Phi Delta Kappan,* 67, 242.

Huston, M., Ginorio, A., Frevert, K., and Bierman, J. (1996). *Final Report to the Program for Women and Girls at the National Science Foundation.* Available from the National Science Foundation or Rural Girls in Science, Box 353180, University of Washington, Seattle, WA 98195.

Kahn, J., & Berkowitz, R. (1995). *Sources of Support for Young Latina Mothers.* Washington, DC: Urban Institute.

Kaplan, C. (1990). *Critical Factors Affecting School Dropout Among Mexican-American Women.* Los Angeles: University of California, Los Angeles.

Katz, S. R. (1996). Where the Streets Cross the Classroom: A Study of Latino Students' Perspectives on Cultural Identity in City Schools and Neighborhood Gangs. *Bilingual Research Journal,* 20, 603–631.

LaVelle, M. (1996). *The Importance of Learning English: A National Survey of Hispanic Parents.* Washington, DC: Center for Equal Opportunity. ERIC #ED405726.

Lindberg, L. D., Boggess, S., Porter, L., & Williams, S. (2000). *Teen Risk-Taking: A Statistical Report.* Washington, DC: Urban Institute.

Lockwood, A. T., & Secada, W. G. (2000). *Transforming Education for Hispanic Youth: Exemplary Practices, Programs, and Schools.* Washington, DC: National Clearinghouse for Bilingual Education.

Luker, K. (1997). Dubious Conceptions: The Politics of Teenage Pregnancy. Cambridge, MA: Harvard University Press.

Manlove, J. (1998). The Influence of High School Dropout and School Disengagement on the Risk of School-Age Pregnancy. *Journal of Research on Adolescence, 8* (2), 187–220.

Martínez, Y. G., Scott, J., Jr., Cranston-Gingras, A., & Platt, J. S. (1994, Winter). Voices from the Field: Interviews with Students from Migrant Farmworker Families. *The Journal of Educational Issues of Language Minority Students, 14,* 333–348.

Meek, A. (1998, February). America's Teachers: Much to Celebrate. *Educational Leadership, 55,* 12–16.

Monsivais, G. I. (1990). *Latino Teachers: Well Educated but Not Prepared: An Executive Summary.* Claremont, CA: Tomas Rivera Center.

Morse, S. (2000, Fall). A Foot in Two Worlds: Latinas in School Today. *AAUW Outlook, 94* (2), 36–39.

Mortenson, T. G. (2000). Financing Opportunity for Postsecondary Education. In G. Campbell, Jr., R. Denes, & C. Morrison (eds.). *Access Denied: Race, Ethnicity, and the Scientific Enterprise* (pp. 221–236). New York: Oxford University Press.

Oakes, J. (1990). *Lost Talent: The Underparticipation of Women, Minorities, and Disabled Persons in Science.* Santa Monica, CA: RAND Publications Series.

Office for Civil Rights. (1999). *1997 Elementary and Secondary School Civil Rights Compliance Report: National and State Projections.* Washington, DC.

O'Halloran, C. S. (1995). Mexican American Female Students Who Were Successful in High School Science Courses. *Equity & Excellence in Education, 28* (2), 57–64.

Ortiz, V. (1997). Family Economic Strategies Among Latinas. *Race, Gender and Class, 4* (2), 91–106.

Patthey-Chávez, G. G. (1993). High School as an Area for Cultural Conflict and Acculturation for Latino Angelinos. *Anthropology and Education Quarterly, 24* (1), 33–60.

Pérez, G. V. (2000). *The Challenge of Migrant Student Identification.* Paper presented at the Annual Meeting of the American Educational Research Association, New Orleans, LA. April 24–28.

Perna, L. W. (2000). *Racial/Ethnic Group Differences in the Realization of Educational Plans.* Paper presented at the Annual Meeting of the American Educational Research Association, New Orleans, LA. April 24–28.

Pomales, J., & Williams, V. (1989, January). Effects of Level of Acculturation and Counseling Style on Hispanic Students' Perceptions of Counselors. *Journal of Counseling Psychology, 36,* 79–83.

Portillow, E. L. (1999). The Social Construction of Gender in the Barrio. In M. Chesney-Lind & J. Hagedorn (eds.). *Female Gangs in America: Essays on Girls, Gangs, and Gender.* Chicago: Lake View Press.

Portner, J. (1998, February 25). Hispanic Teenagers Top Black, White Birthrates. *Education Week, 17,* 5.

President's Advisory Commission on Educational Excellence for Hispanic Americans. (1996). *Our Nation on the Fault Line: Hispanic American Education.* Washington, DC.

Rendón, L. I., & Amaury, N. (1987). Hispanic Students: Stopping the Leaks in the Pipeline. *Educational Record, 68/69,* 79–85.

Reyes, O., & Jason, L. A. (1993). Pilot Study Examining Factors Associated with Academic Success for Hispanic High School Students. *Journal of Youth and Adolescence, 22* (1), 57–71.

Rich, L., & Kim, S. (1999). Patterns of Later Life Education Among Teenage Mothers. *Gender and Society, 13* (6), 798–817.

Rodríguez, C. (1993). *Minorities in Science and Engineering: Patterns for Success.* Tucson, AZ: University of Arizona, Tucson.

Rodríguez, C. (2000, March). Personal communication.

Romo, H. D., & Falbo, T. (1996). *Latino High School Graduation.* Austin, TX: University of Texas Press.

San Diego City Schools, Planning, Research, and Evaluation Division. (1989). *Empowering the Hispanic Female in the Public School Setting, Part II.* San Diego, CA: City School District.

Scott, M. S., Perou, R., & Urbano, R. C. (1992, Summer). The Identification of Giftedness: A Comparison of White, Hispanic and Black Families. *Gifted Child Quarterly, 36,* 131–139.

Seymour, E., & Hewitt, N. M. (1997). *Talking About Leaving: Why Undergraduates Leave the Sciences.* Boulder, CO: Westview Press.

Shivley, T. E. (2000). *High Trust, High-Involvement Culture: To Act, To Give, To Risk—A Paradigm for Student Voice in Educational Reform.* Paper presented at the Annual Meeting of the American Educational Research Association, New Orleans, LA. April 24–28.

Smith, T. M. (1995). The Educational Progress of Hispanic Students. In A. Livingston & S. Miranda (eds.). *The Condition of Education 1995, 4.* Washington, DC: U.S. Department of Education, Office of Educational Research and Improvement, National Center for Education Statistics, Data Development Division.

So, A. Y. (1984, July). The Financing of College Education by Hispanic Parents. *Urban Education*, 19, 145–160.

So, A. Y. (1987b, October/November). Hispanic Teachers and the Labeling of Hispanic Students. *The High School Journal*, 71, 5–8.

Stavans, I. (1995). *The Hispanic Condition: Reflections on Culture and Identity in America*. New York: Harper Collins.

Stevenson, H. W., Chen, C., & Uttal, D. H. (1990). Beliefs and Achievements: A Study of Black, White and Hispanic Children. *Child Development*, 61, 508–523.

Stockwell, J. (2000, April 12). The Young Voice of the Family: When Adults Can Speak Little English, Children Take on Grown-Up Role. *The Washington Post*, B.3.

Thorne, Y. M. (1995, September). Achievement Motivation in High Achieving Latina Women. *Roeper Review*, 18, 44–49.

U.S. Census Bureau. (1993b). *We the American . . . Hispanics*. Washington, DC.

U.S. Department of Education, National Center for Education Statistics. (1995). *Findings from The Condition of Education 1995: The Educational Progress of Hispanic Students*. Washington, DC.

U.S. Department of Education, National Center for Education Statistics. (1996a). *Digest of Educational Statistics 1996*. Washington, DC.

U.S. Department of Education, National Center for Education Statistics. (1997). *Findings from The Condition of Education 1997: The Social Context of Education*. Washington, DC.

Vail, K. (1998, February). Keeping Fernando in School. *The American School Board Journal*, 185, 30–33.

Valdés, G. (1997). Dual-Language Immersion Programs: A Cautionary Note Concerning the Education of Language-Minority Students. *Harvard Educational Review*, 67 (3), 391–429.

Valenzuela, A. (1999). Subtractive Schooling: U.S. Mexican Youth and the Politics of Caring. Albany, NY: State University of New York Press.

Valverde, S. A. (1987). A Comparative Study of Hispanic High School Dropouts and Graduates: Why Do Some Leave School Early and Some Finish? *Education and Urban Society*, 19, 320–329.

Vásquez-Nuttall, E., & Romero-Garcia, I. (1989). From Home to School: Puerto Rican Girls Learn to be Students in the United States. In C. T. Garcia Coll & M. de Lourdes Mattei (eds.). *The Psychosocial Development of Puerto Rican Women*. New York: Praeger Publishers.

Why Hispanic-American Women Succeed in Higher Education. (1998, February 27). *Hispanic Outlook in Higher Education,* 8 (13), 12.

Wycoff, S.E.M. (1996). Academic Performance of Mexican American Women: Sources of Support. *Journal of Multicultural Counseling and Development,* 24 (3), 146–155.

Yawn, B., Yawn, R., Brindis, C. (1997). *Adolescent Pregnancy: A Preventable Consequence?* Eugene, OR: Integrated Research Services.

Yonezawa, S. (1998). *The Relational Nature of Tracking: Using Feminist Standpoint Theory and Network Theory to Examine the Course Placement Process of 19 Secondary School Students.* Paper presented at the Annual Meeting of the American Educational Research Association, San Diego, CA. April 13–17.

25

NAUGHTY BY NATURE

Ann Arnett Ferguson

What are little boys made of?
What are little boys made of?
Frogs and snails
And puppy-dogs' tails,
That's what little boys are made of.

—Oxford Dictionary of Nursery Rhymes

What makes the presence and control of the police tolerable for
the population, if not fear of the criminal?

—Michel Foucault, *Power/Knowledge*

In order for me to live, I decided very early that some mistake had
been made somewhere. I was not a "nigger" even though you called
me one. . . . I had to realize when I was very young that I was none of
those things that I was told I was. I was not, for example, happy. I
never touched a watermelon for all kinds of reasons. I had been

invented by white people, and I knew enough about life by this time
to understand that whatever you invent, whatever you project, that is
you! So where we are now is that a whole country of people believe
I'm a "nigger" and I don't.

—James Baldwin, "A Talk to Teachers"

TWO REPRESENTATIONS OF BLACK masculinity are widespread in society and school today. They are the images of the African American male
as a criminal and as an endangered species. These images are routinely
used as resources to interpret and explain behavior by teachers at Rosa
Parks School when they make punishment decisions. An ensemble of historical meanings and their social effects is contained within these images.

The image of the black male criminal is more familiar because of its
prevalence in the print and electronic media as well as in scholarly work.
The headlines of newspaper articles and magazines sound the alarm dramatically as the presence of black males in public spaces has come to sig-
nify danger and a threat to personal safety. But this is not just media hype.
Bleak statistics give substance to the figure of the criminal. Black males
are disproportionately in jails: they make up 6 percent of the population
of the United States, but 45 percent of the inmates in state and federal
prisons; they are imprisoned at six times the rate of whites.[1] In the state
of California, one-third of African American men in their twenties are in
prison, on parole, or on probation, in contrast to 5 percent of white males
in the same age group. This is nearly five times the number who attend
four-year colleges in the state.[2] The mortality rate for African American
boys fourteen years of age and under is approximately 50 percent higher
than for the comparable group of white male youth, with the leading
cause of death being homicide.[3]

The second image, that of the black male as an endangered species, is
one which has largely emanated from African American social scientists
and journalists who are deeply concerned about the criminalization and
high mortality rate among African American youth.[4] It represents him as
being marginalized to the point of oblivion. While this discourse emanates
from a sympathetic perspective, in the final analysis the focus is all too
often on individual maladaptive behavior and black mothering practices
as the problem rather than on the social structure in which this endan-
germent occurs.

These two cultural representations are rooted in actual material conditions and reflect existing social conditions and relations that they appear to

sum up for us. They are lodged in theories, in commonsense understandings of self in relation to others in the world as well as in popular culture and the media. But they are condensations, extrapolations, that emphasize certain elements and gloss over others. They represent a narrow selection from the multiplicity, the heterogeneity of actual relations in society.

Since both of these images come to be used for identifying, classification, and decision making by teachers at Rosa Parks School, it is necessary to analyze the manner in which these images, or cultural representations of difference, are produced through a racial discursive formation. Then we can explain how they are utilized by teachers in the exercise of school rules to produce a context in which African American boys become more visible, more culpable as "rule-breakers."

A central element of a racist discursive formation is the production of subjects as essentially different by virtue of their "race." Historically, the circulation of images that represent this difference has been a powerful technique in this production.[5] Specifically, blacks have been represented as essentially different from whites, as the constitutive Other that regulates and confirms "whiteness." Images of Africans as savage, animalistic, subhuman without history or culture—the diametric opposite of that of Europeans—rationalized and perpetuated a system of slavery. After slavery was abolished, images of people of African descent as hypersexual, shiftless, lazy, and of inferior intellect, legitimated a system that continued to deny rights of citizenship to blacks on the basis of race difference. This regime of truth about race was articulated through scientific experiments and "discoveries," law, social custom, popular culture, folklore, and common sense. And for three hundred years, from the seventeenth century to the middle of the twentieth century, this racial distinction was policed through open and unrestrained physical violence. The enforcement of race difference was conscious, overt, and institutionalized.

In the contemporary period, the production of a racial Other and the constitution and regulation of racial difference has worked increasingly through mass-produced images that are omnipresent in our lives. At this moment in time it is through culture—or culturalism[6]—that difference is primarily asserted. This modern-day form of reproducing racism specifically operates through symbolic violence and representations of Blackness that circulate through the mass media, cinematic images, and popular music, rather than through the legal forms of the past. The representational becomes a potent vehicle for the transmission of racial meanings that reproduce relations of difference, of division, and of power. These "controlling images" made "racism, sexism, and poverty appear to be natural, normal, and an inevitable part of everyday life."[7]

Cultural Representations of "Difference"

The behavior of African American boys in school is perceived by adults at Rosa Parks School through a filter of overlapping representations of three socially invented categories of "difference": age, gender, and race. These are grounded in the commonsense, taken-for-granted notion that existing social divisions reflect biological and natural dispositional differences among humans: so children are essentially different from adults, males from females, blacks from whites.[8] At the intersection of this complex of subject positions are African American boys who are doubly displaced: as black children, they are not seen as childlike but adultified; as black males, they are denied the masculine dispensation constituting white males as being "naturally naughty" and are discerned as willfully bad. Let us look more closely as this displacement.

The dominant cultural representation of childhood is as closer to nature, as less social, less human. Childhood is assumed to be a stage of development; culture, morality, sociability is written on children in an unfolding process by adults (who are seen as fully "developed," made by culture not nature) in institutions like family and school. On the one hand, children are assumed to be dissembling, devious, because they are more egocentric. On the other hand, there is an attribution of innocence to their wrongdoing. In both cases, this is understood to be a temporary condition, a stage prior to maturity. So they must be socialized to fully understand the meaning of their acts.

The language used to describe "children in general" by educators illustrates this paradox. At one districtwide workshop for adult school volunteers that I attended, children were described by the classroom teacher running the workshop as being "like little plants, they need attention, they gobble it up." Later in the session, the same presenter invoked the other dominant representation of children as devious, manipulative, and powerful. "They'll run a number on you. They're little lawyers, con artists, manipulators—and they usually win. They're good at it. Their strategy is to get you off task. They pull you into their whirlwind."

These two versions of childhood express the contradictory qualities that adults map onto their interactions with children in general. The first description of children as "little plants," childhood as identical with nature, is embedded in the ideology of childhood. The second version that presents children as powerful, as self-centered, with an agenda and purpose of their own, arises out of the experience adults have exercising authority over children. In actual relations of power, in a twist, as children become the objects of control, they become devious "con artists" and adults become innocent, pristine in relation to them. In both instances, childhood has been constructed as different in essence from adulthood, as a phase of biological, psychological, and social development with predictable attributes.

Even though we treat it this way, the category "child" does not describe and contain a homogeneous and naturally occurring group of individuals as a certain stage of human development. The social meaning of childhood has changed profoundly over time.[9] What it means to be a child varies dramatically by virtue of location in cross-cutting categories of class, gender, and race.[10]

Historically, the existence of African American children has been constituted differently through economic practices, the law, social policy, and visual imagery. This difference has been projected in an ensemble of images of black youth as not childlike. In the early decades of this century, representations of black children as pickaninnies depicted them as verminlike, voracious, dirty, grinning, animal-like savages. They were also depicted as the laugh-provoking butt of aggressive, predatory behavior; natural victims, therefore victimizable. An example of this was their depiction in popular lore as "alligator bait." Objects such as postcards, souvenir spoons, letter-openers, and cigar-box labels were decorated with figures of half-naked black children vainly attempting to escape the open toothy jaws of hungry alligators.[11]

Today's representations of black children still bear traces of these earlier depictions. The media demonization of very young black boys who are charged with committing serious crimes is one example. In these cases there is rarely the collective soul-searching for answers to the question of how "kids like this" could have committed these acts that occurs when white kids are involved. Rather, the answer to the question seems to be inherent in the disposition of the kids themselves.[12] The image of the young black male as an endangered species revitalizes the animalistic trope. Positioned as part of nature, his essence is described through language otherwise reserved for wildlife that has been decimated to the point of extinction. Characterized as a "species," they are cut off from other members of family and community and isolated as a form of prey.

There is continuity, but there is a significant new twist to the image. The endangered species and the criminal are mirror images. Either as criminal perpetrator or as endangered victim, contemporary imagery proclaims black males to be responsible for their fate. The discourse of individual choice and responsibility elides the social and economic context and locates predation as coming from within. It is their own maladaptive and inappropriate behavior that causes African Americans to self-destruct. As an endangered species, they are stuck in an obsolete stage of social evolution, unable to adapt to the present. As criminals, they are a threat to themselves, to each other, as well as to society in general.

As black children's behavior is refracted through the lens of these two cultural images, it is "adultified." By this I mean their transgressions are made to take on a sinister, intentional, fully conscious tone that is stripped of any element of childish naiveté. The discourse of childhood as an unfolding developmental stage in the life cycle is displaced in this mode of framing school trouble. Adultification is visible in the way African American elementary school pupils are talked about by school adults.

One of the teachers, a white woman who prided herself on the multicultural emphasis in her classroom, invoked the image of African American children as "looters" in lamenting the disappearance of books from the class library. This characterization is especially meaningful because her statement, which was made at the end of the school year that had included the riots in Los Angeles, invoked that event as a framework for making children's behavior intelligible.

> I've lost so many library books this term. There are quite a few kids who don't have any books at home, so I let them borrow them. I didn't sign them out because I thought I could trust the kids. I sent a letter home to parents asking them to look for them and turn them in. But none have come in. I just don't feel the same. *It's just like the looting in Los Angeles.*

By identifying those who don't have books at home as "looters," the teacher has excluded the white children in the class, who all come from more middle-class backgrounds so, it is assumed, "have books at home." In the case of the African American kids, what might be interpreted as the careless behavior of children is displaced by images of adult acts of theft that conjure up violence and mayhem. The African American children in this teacher's classroom and their families are seen not in relation to images of childhood, but in relation to the television images of crowds rampaging through South Central Los Angeles in the aftermath of the verdict of the police officers who beat Rodney King. Through this frame, the children embody a willful, destructive, and irrational disregard for property rather than simple carelessness. Racial difference is mediated through culturalism: blacks are understood as a group undifferentiated by age or status with the proclivity and values to disregard the rights and welfare of others.

Adultification is a central mechanism in the interpretive framing of gender roles. African American girls are constituted as different through this process. A notion of sexual passivity and innocence that prevails for white female children is displaced by the image of African American females as sexual beings: as immanent mothers, girlfriends, and sexual partners of the boys in the room.[13] Though these girls may be strong, assertive, or troublesome, teachers evaluate their potential in ways that attribute to them inevitable, potent sexuality that flares up early and that, according to one teacher, lets them permit men to run all over them, to take advantage of them. An incident in the Punishing Room that I recorded in my field notes made visible the way that adult perceptions of youthful behavior were filtered through racial representations. African American boys and girls who misbehaved were not just breaking a rule out of high spirits and needing to be chastised for the act, but were adultified, gendered figures whose futures were already inscribed and foreclosed within a racial order:

> Two girls, Adila and a friend, burst into the room followed by Miss Benton, a black sixth-grade teacher, and a group of five African American boys from her class. Miss Benton is yelling at the girls because they have been jumping in the hallway and one has knocked down part of a display on the bulletin board which she and her class put up the day before. She is yelling at the two girls about how they're wasting time. This is what she says: "You're doing exactly what they want you to do. You're playing into their hands. Look at me! Next year they're going to be tracking you."
>
> One of the girls asks her rather sullenly who "they" is.
>
> Miss Benton is furious. "Society, that's who. You should be leading the class, not fooling around jumping around in the hallway. Someone has to give pride to the community. All the black men are on drugs, or in jail, or killing each other. Someone has got to hold it together. And the women have to do it. And you're jumping up and down in the hallway."
>
> I wonder what the black boys who have followed in the wake of the drama make of this assessment of their future, seemingly already etched in stone. The teacher's words to the girls are supposed to inspire them to leadership. The message for the boys is a dispiriting one.

Tracks have already been laid down for sixth-grade girls toward a specifically feminized responsibility (and, what is more prevalent, blame) for the welfare of the community, while males are bound for jail as a consequence of their own socially and self-destructive acts.

There is a second displacement from the norm in the representation of black males. The hegemonic, cultural image of the essential "nature" of males is that they are different from females in the meaning of their acts.

Boys will be boys: they are mischievous, they get into trouble, they can stand up for themselves. This vision of masculinity is rooted in the notion of an essential sex difference based on biology, hormones, uncontrollable urges, true personalities. Boys are naturally more physical, more active. Boys are naughty by nature. There is something suspect about the boy who is "too docile," "like a girl." As a result, rule breaking on the part of boys is looked at as something-they-can't-help, a natural expression of masculinity in a civilizing process.

This incitement of boys to be "boylike" is deeply inscribed in our mainstream culture, winning hearts and stirring imaginations in the way that the pale counterpart, the obedient boy, does not. Fiedler, in an examination of textual representations of iconic childhood figures in U.S. literature, registers the "Good Bad Boy" and the "Good Good Boy" as cultural tropes of masculinities:

> What then is the difference between the Good Good Boy and the Good Bad Boy, between Sid Sawyer, let us say, and Tom? The Good Good Boy does what his mother must pretend that she wants him to do: obey, conform; the Good Bad Boy does what she really wants him to do: deceive, break her heart a little, be forgiven.[14]

An example of this celebration of Good Bad Boy behavior, even when at the risk of order, is the way that one of the student specialists at Rosa Parks School introduced a group of boys in his classroom to a new student:

TEACHER: Hey, they're thugs! Hoodlums! Hooligans! Gangsters! Stay away from these guys.

BOY *(acting tough):* Yeah, we're tough.

TEACHER *(really having fun):* You ain't as tough as a slice of wet white bread!

BOY *(sidling up to the teacher chest puffed out):* I'm tougher than you.

TEACHER: Okay! Go on! These are a bunch of great guys.

The newcomer looks at home.

African American boys are not accorded the masculine dispensation of being "naturally" naughty. Instead the school reads their expression and display of masculine naughtiness as a sign of an inherent vicious, insubordinate nature that as a threat to order must be controlled. Consequently, school adults view any display of masculine mettle on the part of these boys through body language or verbal rejoinders as a sign of insubordination. In confrontation with adults, what is required from them is a performance of absolute docility that goes against the grain of masculinity. Black boys are expected to internalize a ritual obeisance in such exchanges so that the performance of docility appears to come naturally. According to the vice principal, "These children have to learn not to talk back. They must know that if the adult says you're wrong, then you're wrong. They must not resist, must go along with it, and take their punishment," he says.

This is not a lesson that all children are required to learn, however. The disciplining of the body within school rules has specific race and gender overtones. For black boys, the enactment of docility is a preparation for adult racialized survival rituals of which the African American adults in the school are especially cognizant. For African American boys bodily forms of expressiveness have repercussions in the world outside the chain-link fence of the school. The body must be taught to endure humiliation in preparation for future enactments of submission. The vice principal articulated the racialized texture of decorum when he deplored one of the Troublemakers, Lamar's propensity to talk back and argue with teachers.

Lamar had been late getting into line at the end of recess, and the teacher had taken away his football. Lamar argued and so the teacher gave him detention. Mr. Russell spelled out what an African American male needed to learn about confrontations with power.

> Look, I've told him before about getting into these show-down situations—where he either has to show off to save face, then if he doesn't get his way then he goes wild. He won't get away with it in this school. Not with me, not with Mr. Harmon. But I know he's going to try it somewhere outside and it's going to get him in *real* trouble. He has to learn to ignore, to walk away, not to get into power struggles.

Mr. Russell's objective is to hammer into Lamar's head what he believes is the essential lesson for young black males to learn if they are to get anywhere in life: to act out obeisance is to survive. The specter of the Rodney King beating by the Los Angeles Police Department provided the backdrop for this conversation, as the trial of the police officers had just begun. The defense lawyer for the LAPD was arguing that Rodney King could have stopped the beating at any time if he had chosen.

This apprehension of black boys as inherently different both in terms of character and of their place in the social order is a crucial factor in teacher disciplinary practices.

Normalizing Judgments and Teacher Practices

Teacher enforcement of rules results in differential treatment for children in general. Teachers must weigh immediate practical considerations about classroom management as well as more abstract imperatives of imparting social values and standards of interaction as they define the actions of a child as rule breaking.

A teacher decides whether to "notice" the behavior at all. Each time a child breaks a written or unwritten rule, the teacher has to make a decision about whether to take the time for disciplinary action. Another important consideration is the larger effect that this action might have on spectators in the public arena of the school.[15]

Hargreaves, Hester, and Mellor, in a study of how teachers come to label some children as deviant, analyze the function that rules play in these labeling practices. They identify two principles of rules by which teachers decide to intervene.[16] The first is a "moral" principle grounded in the belief that rules teach children values. The second, a "pragmatic" principle, recognizes rules as an efficient and effective way for imposing order and affirming teacher authority. The researchers also found that when and whether these principles came into play were highly dependent on the perception that the teacher had of a pupil. Teachers not only ranked rules according to their significance, but ranked individual pupils according to an evaluation of their culpability: what was tolerated in some pupils might be punished in others.[17] Most significant for this study is that the researchers found that the criteria used for determining hierarchies of culpability were highly subjective, including elements such as facial appearance, physical size, likability, friends, and style of presentation of self.

Teacher perceptions of students are grounded in their own location in social categories of race, class, and gender. They make sense of their interactions with pupils and the conditions of their work from these social locations.[18] Teachers bring different experiences and knowledge of racial structures into school that provide a framework from which to interpret, to organize information, to act. These factor into the creation of hierarchies of culpability of rule-breakers.

In the case of African American boys, misbehavior is likely to be interpreted as symptomatic of ominous criminal proclivities. Because of this, teachers are more likely to pay attention to and punish rule breaking, as "moral" and "pragmatic" reasons for acting converge with criteria of culpability. On the basis of "moral" reasons, teachers use troublemakers as exemplars to mark boundaries of transgressive behavior; this also has practical effects on general classroom order.

Black teachers are especially likely to advocate and enforce ways of presenting self in the world, strategies of camouflage, that will allow African American children not only to blend into and become a part of the dominant culture, but have survival value in the real world. Black boys must learn to hide "attitude" and learn to exorcise defiance. Thus they argue for the importance of instilling fear and respect for authority.

There are real consequences in terms of the form and severity of punishment of these social fictions. The exemption of black males from the dispensations granted the "child" and the "boy" through the process of adultification justifies harsher, more punitive responses to rule-breaking behavior. As "not children," their behavior is understood not as something to be molded and shaped over time, but as the intentional, fully cognizant actions of an adult. This means there is already a dispositional pattern set, that their behavior is incorrigible, irremediable. Therefore, the treatment required for infractions is one that punishes through example and exclusion rather than through persuasion and edification, as is practiced with young white males in the school.

The point must be made here that the power of the images to affect teachers' beliefs and behavior is greatly exacerbated because of their lack of knowledge about the black children in their classrooms. None of the teachers at Rosa Parks School were part of the community in which they taught; only the custodians and the "Jailhouse Keeper" were resident in the neighborhood. Teachers rarely visited children and families in their homes. Though school adults had many stories to tell me about the families of the boys I was interviewing, these were typically horror stories. Sad, shocking tales of one family's situation would become emblematic of "those families."

As a result of these stories, I was at first anxious about going into homes that were described as "not safe." After visiting with several families, I began to realize that school people had never stepped into any of the children's homes and knew nothing about the real circumstances in which they lived. This distance, this absence of substantive knowledge, further contributed to their adultification of the children and the fear that tinged their interactions with them.

Let us examine now more closely some widespread modes of categorizing African American boys, the normalizing judgments that they circulate, and the consequences these have on disciplinary intervention and punishment.

Being "At-Risk": Identifying Practice

The range of normalizing judgments for African American males is bounded by the image of the ideal pupil at one end of the spectrum and the unsalvageable student who is criminally inclined at the other. The ideal type of student is characterized here by a white sixth-grade teacher:

> Well, it consists of, first of all, to be able to follow directions. Any direction that I give. Whether it's get this out, whether it's put this away, whether it's turn to this page or whatever, they follow it, and they come in and they're ready to work. It doesn't matter high skill or low skill, they're ready to work and they know that's what they're here for. Behaviorally, they're appropriate all day long. When it's time for them to listen, they listen. The way I see it, by sixth grade, the ideal student is one that can sit and listen and learn from me—work with their peers, and take responsibility on themselves and understand what is next, what is expected of them.

This teacher, however, drew on the image of the Good Bad Boy when she described the qualities of her "ideal" male student, a white boy in her class. Here the docility of the generic ideal student becomes the essentially naughty-by-nature male:

> He's not really Goody Two-shoes, you know. He's not quiet and perfect. He'll take risks. He'll say the wrong answer. He'll fool around and have to be reprimanded in class. There's a nice balance to him.

The model category for African American boys is "at-risk" of failure. The concept of "at-riskness" is central to a discourse about the contemporary crisis in urban schools in America that explains children's failure as largely the consequence of their attitudes and behaviors as well as those of their families. In early stages of schooling they are identified as "at-risk" of failing, as "at-risk" of being school drop-outs. The category has been invested with enormous power to identify, explain, and predict futures. For example, a white fifth-grade teacher told me with sincere concern that as she looked around at her class, she could feel certain that about only four out of the twenty-one students would eventually graduate from high school. Every year, she said, it seemed to get worse.

Images of family play a strong role in teacher assessments and decisions about at-risk children. These enter into the evaluative process to confirm an original judgment. Families of at-risk children are said to lack parental skills; they do not give their children the kind of support that would build "self-esteem" necessary for school achievement. But this knowledge of family is superficial, inflamed by cultural representations and distorted through a rumor mill.

The children themselves are supposed to betray the lack of love and attention at home through their own "needy" behavior in the classroom. According to the teachers, these are pupils who are always demanding attention and will work well only in one-to-one or small-group situations because of this neglect at home. They take up more than their share of time and space. Donel, one of the African American boys who has been identified as at-risk by the school, is described by his teacher:

> He's a boy with a lot of energy and usually uncontrolled energy. He's very loud in the classroom, very inappropriate in the class. He has a great sense of humor, but again it's inappropriate. I would say most of the time that his mouth is open, it's inappropriate, it's too loud, it's disrupting. But other than that (dry laugh) he's a great kid. You know if I didn't have to teach him, if it was a recreational setting, it would be fine.

So Donel is marked as "inappropriate" through the very configuration of self that school rules regulate: bodies, language, presentation of self. The stringent exercise of what is deemed appropriate as an instrument of assessment of at-riskness governs how the behavior of a child is understood. The notion of appropriate behavior in describing the ideal pupil earlier, and here as a way of characterizing a Troublemaker, reveals the broad latitude for interpretation and cultural framing of events. For one boy, "fooling around" behavior provides the balance between being a "real boy" and being a "goody-goody," while for the other, the conduct is seen through a different lens as "inappropriate," "loud," disruptive."

Once a child is labeled "at-risk," he becomes more visible within the classroom, more likely to be singled out and punished for rule-breaking activity. An outburst by an African American boy already labeled as "at-risk" was the occasion for him to be singled out and made an example of the consequences of bad behavior before an audience of his peers; this was an occasion for a teacher to (re)mark the identity of a boy as disruptive. It was also one of those moments, recorded in my field notes, in which I observed the rewards that children might actually gain from getting into trouble.

> This incident takes place in a second-grade classroom in another school which I am visiting in order to observe Gary, who has been

identified as "at-risk" by the school and eligible for a special after-noon school program. The teacher, Miss Lyew, is an Asian woman with a loud, forceful voice. Twenty-five children are sitting in groups of three or four at tables as she goes over the recipe for making "a volcano erupt"—they do this together—she on the blackboard, they on sheets of paper in front of them. Miss Lyew has said she will call on people who have their hands raised. Lots of hands waving in the air and children vying for the right answer. There are always several possible answers for the next step, but only one that is "right." Chil-dren are not supposed to shout out the answer, but must wait to be called on. Sometimes, however, a child says the answer before being called on. Sometimes Miss Lyew ignores this, at other times she scolds the student.

It soon becomes clear that Gary is one of those she notices when he calls out. He gets a warning. The next time, Gary raises his hand and simultaneously calls out. She stops the class discussion of volcanoes and for the first time a kind of democracy enters the room. She turns to Gary's peers and asks what punishment Gary should get the next time he calls out an answer.

Now children are waving hands held high to suggest various forms of punishment; send him to the office, take points away from him, call his mother, send him home, send him to stand outside the room, wash his mouth out. There is no end to the various forms of punishment the children can think of. Gary himself gets into the act, he proposes that they take all the points away from his table. This is a punishment that Miss Lyew herself has threatened to use earlier in the day.

Miss Lyew looks indignant, then asks the class if this would be fair. How would the other children at the table feel? They would be pun-ished for something they didn't do. The teacher then asks the children to vote on which one of the punishments they feel Gary should face if he should call out again. The voting begins. I notice that all the girls, but only a few boys, vote, as sympathy breaks down along gender lines. The teacher urges, "Everyone has a vote." It is an amazing and fascinating display because the classroom has suddenly for the first (and for the only time during my observation) taken on the semblance of a democratic operation with children actually getting to "choose" how something should be done.

Gary sits dispassionately calm, almost serene. He is the eye of the storm. He has shaped the direction of class activity in a powerful way. The teacher presses the issue so that everyone finally raises their hand in some kind of vote. Finally, it has been decided, if Gary answers out of

turn again he will be sent out of the room and the next time his mother
will be called. Gary does not look anxious, he does not look humiliated.

The class returns to the study of classifying inanimate objects. They
are working on shapes. The answers are supposed to be, "It is a cube.
It is a rectangular prism," etc. I notice that several other kids call out
of turn and Miss Lyew does not pay attention. Enough time has been
spent on *that* lesson. In fact, one of the children reminds her about the
punishment when someone else calls out of turn, but she does not refo-
cus on the misdeed.

Gary is positioned as an "at-risk" black male in the room. From the
teacher's perspective, this carries with it powerful received meanings of
who the "at-risk" child is and what he needs to learn in order to succeed.
She believes, for one, that boys like Gary need to learn impulse control;
that they need to learn respect for authority, self-discipline, to be appropriate, to keep their mouths shut. Gary is not only more visible because
of the label, but the recipient of a series of specific remedies and prescriptions about what he needs. That Gary knows the answer and is bursting with the excitement of this knowledge is not as significant here as the
fact that in his case conformity to the rule must be enforced.

Most important, moments of public punishment are powerful learning
experiences about social location and worthiness for everyone involved.
These cultural spectacles signal profound meanings of "racial" difference
through a performance that engages audience as well as actors in a reen-
actment of social roles within relations of power. In these spectacles, the
singling out, the naming, the displaying of that which is "bad" affirms the
institutional power to stigmatize. Gary becomes a lesson to other children
in the room about what it means to be caught in the spotlight of disciplinary power. The spectators learn that to get in trouble with authority is
to risk becoming the example, the spectacle for the consumption of others. It is to risk, not mere momentary humiliation, but the separation from
one's peers as different.

Gary is made the object of a lesson. But he uses different strategies to
recuperate his sense of self. He tries to reenter the group by proposing a
punishment that the teacher in fact uses herself—to punish the whole table
by taking away the group points—but he's pushed farther to the margins.
Now he is not just someone who is disrupting the order of the room but
would drag others down with him as well. For a second-grade boy like
Gary, already labeled, the classroom is potentially a place of shame and
humiliation in the marginalizing activity of the teacher.

However, the moment is a complex experience. For several minutes
Gary is the focus of the entire room. In this moment of trouble and pun-

ishment, he has become the counterauthority. The teacher occupies one leadership pole and he another. He proposes his own punishment and he does not protest when a decision is finally made. He is the epitome of grace under pressure.

I, the adult observer, am impressed by his fortitude, his presence. By the end of the confrontation, it is clear to all the children, including Gary, that he receives special treatment, is marked for special attention. His exposure of the arbitrary nature of punishment captivates me.

Getting a Reputation

Children are sorted into categories of "educability" as they get a reputation among the adults as troubled, troubling, or troublemakers. They are not only identified as problems, as "at-risk" by the classroom teacher, but gain schoolwide reputations as stories about their exploits are publicly shared by school adults in the staff room, at staff meetings, and at in-service training sessions. Horror stories circulate through the school adult network so that children's reputations precede them into classrooms and follow them from school to school.

Once a reputation has been established, the boy's behavior is usually refigured within a framework that is no longer about childish misdemeanors but comes to be an ominous portent of things to come. They are tagged with futures: "He's on the fast track to San Quentin Prison," and "That one has a jail-cell with his name on it." For several reasons, these boys are more likely to be singled out and punished than other children. They are more closely watched. They are more likely to be seen as intentionally doing wrong than a boy who is considered to be a Good Bad Boy. Teachers are more likely to use the "moral principle" in determining whether to call attention to misdemeanors because "at-risk" children need discipline, but also as an example to the group, especially to other African American boys who are "endangered." The possibility of contagion must be eliminated. Those with reputations must be isolated, kept away from the others. Kids are told to stay away from them: "You know what will happen if you go over there." In the case of boys with reputations, minor infractions are more likely to escalate into major punishments.

Unsalvageable Students

In the range of normalizing judgments, there is a group of African American boys identified by school personnel as, in the words of a teacher, "unsalvageable." This term and the condition it speaks to is specifically about masculinity. School personnel argue over whether these unsalvageable boys should be given access even to the special programs designed for those who are failing in school. Should resources, defined as scarce, be wasted on these boys for whom there is no hope? Should energy and money be put instead into children who can be saved? I have heard teachers argue on both sides of the question. These "boys for whom there is no hope" get caught up in the school's punishment system: surveillance, isolation, detention, and ever more severe punishment.

These are children who are not children. These are boys who are already men. So a discourse that positions masculinity as "naturally" naughty is reframed for African American boys around racialized representations of gendered subjects. They come to stand as if already adult, bearers of adult fates inscribed within a racial order.

NOTES

1. *New York Times,* September 13, 1994, 1.

2. *Los Angeles Times,* November 2, 1990, 3.

3. G. Jaynes and R. Williams Jr., eds., *A Common Destiny: Blacks in American Society* (Washington, D.C.: National Academic Press, 1989), 405, 498.

4. See, for example, Jewelle Taylor Gibbs, "Young Black Males in America: Endangered, Embittered, and Embattled," in Jewelle Taylor Gibbs et al., *Young, Black, and Male in America: An Endangered Species* (New York: Auburn House, 1988); Richard Majors and Janet Mancini Billson, *Cool Pose: The Dilemmas of Black Manhood in America* (New York: Lexington Press, 1972); Jawanza Kunjufu, *Countering the Conspiracy to Destroy Black Boys,* 2 vols. (Chicago: African American Images, 1985).

5. See, for example, W.E.B. Du Bois, *Souls of Black Folk* (1903; reprint, New York: Bantam, 1989); Frantz Fanon, *Black Skins, White Masks,* trans. Charles Lam Markmann (New York: Grove Press, 1967); Stuart Hall, "The Rediscovery of 'Ideology': Return of the Repressed in Media Studies," in *Culture, Society, and the Media,* ed. Michael Gurevich et al. (New York: Methuen, 1982); Leith Mullings, "Images, Ideology, and Women of Color," in *Women of Color in U.S. Society,* ed. Maxine Baca Zinn and Bonnie Thornton Dill (Philadelphia: Temple University Press, 1994); Edward Said, *Orientalism* (New York: Vintage, 1978).

6. Gilroy, *Small Acts,* 24, argues that "the culturalism of the new racism has gone hand in hand with a definition of race as a matter of difference rather than a question of hierarchy."

7. Collins, *Black Feminist Thought,* 68.

8. While many of the staff at Rosa Parks School would agree at an abstract level that social divisions of gender and race are culturally and historically produced, their actual talk about these social distinctions as well as their everyday expectations, perceptions, and interactions affirm the notion that these categories reflect intrinsic, *real* differences.

9. See, for example, Phillipe Ariès, *Centuries of Childhood: A Social History of Family Life* (New York: Vintage, 1962).

10. Thorne, *Gender Play;* and Valerie Polakow, *Lives on the Edge: Single Mothers and Their Children in the Other America* (Chicago: University of Chicago Press, 1993).

11. Patricia Turner, *Ceramic Uncles and Celluloid Mammies: Black Images and Their Influence on Culture* (New York: Anchor, 1994), 36.

12. A particularly racist and pernicious example of this was the statement by the administrator of the Alcohol, Drug Abuse, and Mental Health Administration, Dr. Frederick K. Goodwin, who stated without any qualms: "If you look for example, at male monkeys, especially in the wild, roughly half of them survive to adulthood. The other half die by violence. That is the natural way of it for males, to knock each other off and, in fact, there are some interesting evolutionary implications. . . . The same hyper aggressive monkeys who kill each other are also hyper sexual, so they copulate more and therefore they reproduce more to offset the fact that half of them are dying." He then drew an analogy with the "high impact (of) inner city areas with the loss of some of the civilizing evolutionary things that we have built up. . . . Maybe it isn't just the careless use of the word when people call certain areas of certain cities, jungles." Quoted in Jerome G. Miller, *Search and Destroy: African American Males in the Criminal Justice System* (New York: Cambridge University Press, 1996), 212–13.

13. The consensus among teachers in the school about educational inequity focuses on sexism. Many of the teachers speak seriously and openly about their concern that girls are being treated differently than boys in school: girls are neglected in the curriculum, overlooked in classrooms, underencouraged academically, and harassed by boys. A number of recent studies support the concern that even the well-intentioned teacher tends to spend less classroom time with girls because boys demand so much of their attention. These studies generally gloss over racial difference as well as make the assumption that *quantity* rather than *quality* of attention is the key factor in fostering positive sense of self in academic settings. See, for example, Myra Sadker and David Sadker, *Failing at Fairness: How America's Schools Cheat Girls* (New York: C. Scribner's Sons, 1994). Linda Grant looks at both race and gender as she examines the roles that first- and

second-grade African American girls play in desegregated classrooms. She finds that African American girls and white girls are positioned quite differently vis-à-vis teachers. In the classrooms she observed, white girls were called upon to play an academic role in comparison with African American girls, who were cast in the role of teacher's helpers, in monitoring and controlling other kids in the room, and as intermediaries between peers. She concluded that black girls were encouraged in stereotypical female adult roles that stress service and nurture, while white girls were encouraged to press toward high academic achievement. Most important for this study, Grant mentions in passing that black boys in the room receive the most consistent negative attention and were assessed as having a lower academic ability than any other group by teachers. See Linda Grant, "Helpers, Enforcers, and Go-Betweens: Black Females in Elementary School Classrooms," in *Women of Color in U.S. Society,* ed. Maxine Baca Zinn and Bonnie Thornton Dill (Philadelphia: Temple University Press, 1994).

14. Leslie A. Fiedler, *Love and Death in the American Novel* (New York: Criterion, 1960), 267.

15. Teachers are also held in the grip of rules. One important consideration is the teacher's own presentation of self as a competent teacher. Teachers are assessed according to how well they control children and keep classroom order. Teachers, as well as children, are expected to show a respect for the rules, to be consistent in enforcing them. Adult conformity to the rules, their allegiance to them, is never taken for granted, as unproblematic, but must be publicly affirmed over and over. Just to be an adult, to occupy that status, is not enough. At one of the in-service workshops dealing with school discipline, several teachers blamed school discipline problems on the fact that some teachers did not wholeheartedly support the rules: "It doesn't help when some people just let the kids do whatever, just ignore some of the rules when they don't agree with them. I've been making my kids keep their caps off in the classroom, then when we go to assembly there are other classes where the kids are wearing their caps, which makes it impossible for me. I end up looking like the bad guy. We've all got to agree to the rules and then we've all got to stick by them."

16. Hargreaves, Hester, and Mellor, *Deviance in Classrooms,* 222.

17. Ibid., 227.

18. A substantial body of studies on teacher expectations have demonstrated that gender, class, and race have considerable influence over assumptions teachers have about students. For examples of gender bias, see Sadker and Sadker, *Failing at Fairness;* for class and ethnicity, see Ursula Casanova, "Rashomon in the Classroom: Multiple Perspectives of Teachers, Parents, and Students," in

Children at Risk: Poverty, Minority Status, and Other Issues in Educational Equity, ed. Andres Barona and Eugene E. Garcia (Washington, D.C.: National Association of School Psychologists, 1990); for class, see Ray C. Rist, "Student Social Class and Teacher Expectations: The Self-Fulfilling Prophecy in Ghetto Education," *Harvard Educational Review* 40, no. 3 (1970).

REFERENCES

American Psychiatric Association. *Diagnostic and Statistical Manual of Mental Disorders.* 4th ed. Washington, D.C.: American Psychiatric Association, 1994.

Anderson, Elijah. *Streetwise.* Chicago: University of Chicago Press, 1990.

Ariès, Phillipe, *Centuries of Childhood: A Social History of Family Life.* New York: Vintage, 1962.

Aronowitz, Stanley, and Henry A. Giroux. *Education under Siege: The Conservative, Liberal, and Radical Debate over Schooling.* South Hadley, Mass.: Bergen and Garvey, 1985.

Barrett, Michele. *Women's Oppression Today: Problems in Marxist Feminist Analysis.* London: New Left Books, 1980.

Bernstein, Basil. "Social Class, Language, and Socialization." In *Power and Ideology in Education,* ed. Jerome Karabel and A. H. Halsey, 473–86. New York: Oxford University Press, 1977.

———. *Towards a Theory of Educational Transmission.* Vol. 3 of Class, Codes, and Control. London: Routledge and Kegan Paul, 1974.

Billingsley, Andres. *Climbing Jacob's Ladder: The Enduring Legacy of African-American Families.* New York: Simon and Schuster, 1992.

Bordieu, Pierre. "The Economics of Linguistic Exchanges." *Social Science Information* 26, no. 6 (1977): 645–68.

Bowles, Samuel, and Herbert Gintis. *Schooling in Capitalist America: Educational Reform and the Contradictions of Economic Life.* New York: Basic Books, 1976.

Brewer, Rose M. "Theorizing Race, Class and Gender: The New Scholarship of Black Feminist Intellectuals and Black Women's Labor." In *Theorizing Black Feminism: The Visionary Pragmatism of Black Women,* ed. Stanlie M. James and Abena P. A. Busia, 13–30. New York: Routledge, 1993.

Butler, Judith. *Bodies that Matter. On the Discursive Limits of "Sex."* New York: Routledge, 1993.

———. "Performative Acts and Gender Constitution: An Essay in Phenomenology and Feminist Theory." *Theatre Journal* 40, no. 4 (1988): 519–31.

Carmichael, Stokely, and Charles V. Hamilton. *Black Power: The Politics of Liberation in America.* New York: Vintage, 1967.

Casanova, Ursula. "Rashomon in the Classroom: Multiple Perspectives of Teachers, Parents, and Students." In *Children at Risk: Poverty, Minority Status, and Other Issues in Educational Equity,* ed. Andres Barona and Eugene E. Garcia, 315–49. Washington, D.C.: National Association of School Psychologists, 1990.

Cassidy, Frederic G., ed. *Dictionary of American Regional English.* Vol. 2. Cambridge: Harvard University Press, 1991.

Clark, Kenneth. *Dark Ghetto: Dilemmas of Social Power.* New York: Harper and Row, 1965.

Collins, Patricia Hill. *Black Feminist Thought: Knowledge, Consciousness, and the Politics of Empowerment.* Boston: Unwin Hyman, 1990.

Commission for Positive Change in the Oakland Public Schools. *Keeping Children in School: Sounding the Alarm on Suspensions.* Oakland, Calif.: The Commission, 1992.

Connell, R. W. "Teaching the Boys: New Research on Masculinity and Gender Strategies for Schools." *Teachers College Record* 98, no. 2 (1996): 206–35.

Connell, R. W., et al. *Making the Difference: Schools, Families, and Social Division.* London: George Allen and Unwin, 1982.

Crenshaw, Kimberle. "Beyond Racism and Misogyny: Black Feminism and 2 Live Crew." In *Words that Wound: Critical Race Theory, Assaultive Speech, and the First Amendment,* ed. Mari J. Matsuda et al., 111–32. Boulder, Colo.: Westview Press, 1993.

Dalla Costa, Mariarosa. "Women and the Subversion of the Community." In *The Power of Women and the Subversion of Community,* ed. Mariarosa Dalla Costa and Selma James, 19–54. Bristol, England: Falling Wall Press, 1973.

De Laurentis, Teresa. *Technologies of Gender: Essays on Theory, Film, and Fiction.* Bloomington: Indiana University Press, 1987.

Dillard, J. L. *Black English: Its History and Usage in the United States.* New York: Vintage, 1973.

Du Bois, W.E.B. *Souls of Black Folk.* 1903. Reprint, New York: Bantam, 1989.

Eder, Donna. "Ability Grouping and Students' Academic Self-Concepts: A Case Study." *Elementary School Journal* 84, no. 2 (1983): 149–61.

Eder, Donna, Catherine Colleen Evans, and Stephen Parker. *School Talk: Gender and Adolescent Culture.* New Brunswick, N.J.: Rutgers University Press, 1995.

Fanon, Frantz. *Black Skins, White Masks.* Trans. Charles Lam Markmann. New York: Grove Press, 1967.

Feagin, Joe, and Melvin Sikes. *Living with Racism: The Black Middle-Class Experience.* Boston: Beacon Press, 1994.

Fiedler, Leslie A. *Love and Death in the American Novel*. New York: Criterion, 1960.

Filby, N. N., and B. G. Barnett. "Student Perceptions of 'Better Readers' in Elementary Classrooms." *Elementary School Journal* 81, no. 5 (1982): 435–49.

Foley, Douglas E. *Learning Capitalist Culture: Deep in the Heart of Tejas*. Philadelphia: University of Pennsylvania Press, 1990.

Fordham, Signithia, and John U. Ogbu. "Black Students' School Success: Coping with the 'Burden of Acting White.' " *Urban Review* 18, no. 3 (1986): 176–206.

Foucault, Michel. *Discipline and Punish*. Trans. Alan Sheridan. New York: Vintage, 1979.

———. *Power/Knowledge: Selected Interviews and Other Writings, 1972–1977*. Ed. and trans. Colin Gordon. New York: Pantheon, 1980.

Gibbs, Jewelle Taylor. "Young Black Males in America: Endangered, Embittered, and Embattled." In *Young, Black, and Male in America: An Endangered Species*, ed. Jewelle Taylor Gibbs et al., 1–36, New York: Auburn House, 1988.

Gilmore, Perry. " 'Gimme Room': School Resistance, Attitude, and Access to Literacy." *Journal of Education* 167, no. 1 (1985): 111–28.

Gilroy, Paul. *Small Acts: Thoughts on the Politics of Black Culture*. New York: Serpent's Tail, 1993.

Gilyard, Keith. *Voices of the Self: A Study of Language Competence*. Detroit: Wayne State University Press, 1991.

Goodwin, Marjorie Harness. *He-Said-She-Said: Talk as a Social Organization among Black Children*. Bloomington: Indiana University Press, 1990.

Gouldner, Helen. *Teachers' Pets, Troublemakers, and Nobodies: Black Children in Elementary School*. Westport, Conn.: Greenwood Press, 1978.

Grant, Linda. "Helpers, Enforcers, and Go-Betweens: Black Females in Elementary School Classrooms." In *Women of Color in U.S. Society,* ed. Maxine Baca Zinn and Bonnie Thornton Dill, 43–63. Philadelphia: Temple University Press, 1994.

Hall, Stuart. "The Rediscovery of 'Ideology': Return of the Repressed in Media Studies." In *Culture, Society, and the Media,* ed. Michael Gurevitch et al., 56–90. New York: Methuen, 1982.

Hargreaves, David H., Stephen K. Hester, and Frank J. Mellor, eds. *Deviance in Classrooms*. London: Routledge and Kegan Paul, 1975.

Harper, Philip Brian. *Are We Not Men? Masculine Anxiety and the Problem of African-American Identity*. New York: Oxford University Press, 1996.

Hoberman, John M. *Darwin's Athletes: How Sport Has Damaged Black America and Preserved the Myth of Race*. Boston: Houghton Mifflin, 1997.

Hochschild, Arlie Russell. *The Managed Heart: Commercialization of Human Feeling*. Berkeley and Los Angeles: University of California Press, 1983.

———. *The Second Shift: Working Parents and the Revolution at Home*. New York: Viking, 1989.

Hochschild, Jennifer L. *The New American Dilemma: Liberal Democracy and School Desegregation*. New Haven: Yale University Press. 1984.

hooks, bell. *Yearning: Race, Gender, and Cultural Politics*. Boston: South End Press, 1990.

Hull, John D. "Do Teachers Punish According to Race?" *Time*, April 4, 1994, 30–31.

Jaynes, G., and R. Williams Jr., eds. *A Common Destiny: Blacks and American Society*. Washington D.C.: National Academy Press, 1989.

Jordan, June. *On Call: Political Essays*. Boston: South End Press, 1985.

Kelley, Robin. *Race Rebels: Culture, Politics, and the Black Working Class*. New York: Free Press, 1994.

Kotlowitz, Alex. *There Are No Children Here*. New York: Doubleday, 1991.

Kozol, Jonathan. *Savage Inequalities: Children in America's Schools*. New York: Harper-Collins, 1991.

Kunjufu, Jawanza. *Countering the Conspiracy to Destroy Black Boys*. 2 vols. Chicago: African American Images, 1985.

Labov, W. *Language in the Inner City: Studies in the Black English Vernacular*. Philadelphia: University of Pennsylvania Press, 1972.

Levine, Lawrence. *Black Culture and Black Consciousness: Afro-American Folk Thought from Slavery to Freedom*. New York: Oxford University Press, 1977.

Mac an Ghaill, Mairtin. *The Making of Men: Masculinities, Sexualities, and Schooling*. Buckingham, England: Open University Press, 1994.

MacKinnon, Catharine A. *Feminism Unmodified: Discourses on Life and Law*. Cambridge: Harvard University Press, 1987.

McLeod, Jay. *Ain't No Making It: Leveled Aspiration in a Low-Income Neighborhood*. Boulder, Colo.: Westview Press, 1987.

Majors, Richard, and Janet Mancini Billson. *Cool Pose: The Dilemmas of Black Manhood in America*. New York: Lexington, 1992.

Marsh, P., E. Rosser, and R. Harre. *The Rules of Disorder*. London: Routledge and Kegan Paul, 1978.

Massey, Douglas S., and Nancy A. Denton. *American Apartheid: Segregation and the Making of the Underclass*. Cambridge: Harvard University Press, 1993.

McKerrow, Raymie E., and Norinne H. Daly. "The Student Athlete." *National Forum* 71, no. 4 (1990): 42–44.

McNeil, Linda M. *Contradictions of Control: School Structure and School Knowledge*. New York: Routledge and Kegan Paul, 1986.

Mehan, Hugh, Alma Herrweck, and J. Lee Miehls. *Handicapping the Handicapped: Decision-Making in Student's Educational Careers.* Stanford: Stanford University Press, 1986.

Messerschmidt, James W. *Masculinities and Crime: Critique and Reconceptualization of Theory.* Lanham, Md.: Rowman and Littlefield, 1993.

Miller, Jerome G. *Search and Destroy: African American Males in the Criminal Justice System.* New York: Cambridge University Press, 1996.

Mils, C. Wright. *The Sociological Imagination.* New York: Oxford University Press, 1959.

Minnesota Department of Children, Families and Learning. *Student Suspension and Expulsion: Report to the Legislature.* St. Paul: Minnesota Department of Children, Families and Learning, 1996.

Mullings, Leith. "Images, Ideology, and Women of Color." In *Women of Color in U.S. Society,* ed. Maxine Baca Zinn and Bonnie Thornton Dill, 265–89. Philadelphia: Temple University Press, 1994.

Oakes, Jeannie. *Keeping Track: How Schools Structure Inequality.* New Haven: Yale University Press, 1985.

Ogbu, John U. "Class Stratification, Racial Stratification, and Schooling." In *Class, Race, and Gender in American Educational Research: Toward a Nonsynchronous Parallelist Position,* ed. Lois Weis, 163–82. Albany: State University of New York Press, 1988.

Omi, Michael, and Howard Winant. *Racial Formation in the United States: From the 1960s to the 1980s.* New York: Routledge and Kegan Paul, 1986.

Perkins, Useni Eugene. *Home Is a Dirty Street: The Social Oppression of Black Children.* Chicago: Third World Press, 1975.

Perry, Theresa, and Lisa Delpit, eds. *The Real Ebonics Debate: Power, Language, and the Education of African American Children.* Boston: Beacon Press, 1998.

Pettigrew, Thomas, ed. *Racial Discrimination in the United States.* New York: Harper and Row, 1975.

Polakow, Valerie. *Lives on the Edge: Single Mothers and Their Children in the Other America.* Chicago: University of Chicago Press, 1993.

Rist, Ray C. "Student Social Class and Teacher Expectations: The Self-Fulfilling Prophecy in Ghetto Education." *Harvard Educational Review* 40, no. 3 (1970): 411–51.

———. *The Urban School: A Factory for Failure, A Study of Education in American Society.* Cambridge: MIT Press, 1973.

Sadker, Myra, and David Sadker. *Failing at Fairness: How America's Schools Cheat Girls.* New York: C. Scribner's Sons, 1994.

Said, Edward. *Orientalism.* New York: Vintage, 1978.

Sailes, Gary A. "The Exploitation of the Black Athlete: Some Alternative Solutions." *Journal of Negro Education* 55, no. 4 (1986): 439–42.

Sellers, Robert M., and Gabriel P. Kuperminc. "Goal Discrepancy in African-American Male Student-Athletes' Unrealistic Expectations for Careers in Professional Sports." *Journal of Black Psychology* 23, no. 1 (1997): 6–23.

Sentencing Project. *Young Black Americans and the Criminal Justice System: Five Years Later.* Washington, D.C.: Sentencing Project, 1995.

Smitherman, Geneva. *Talkin and Testifyin: Language of Black America.* Detroit: Wayne State University Press, 1977.

Stack, Carol B. *All Our Kin: Strategies for Survival in a Black Community.* New York: Harper and Row, 1974.

Sudarkasa, Niara. "African American Families and Family Values." In *Black Families,* ed. Harriette Pipes McAdoo, 9–40. Thousand Oaks, Calif.: Sage, 1997.

Tattum, Delwyn P., ed. *Management of Disruptive Pupil Behavior in Schools.* New York: John Wiley and Sons, 1986.

Thorne, Barrie. *Gender Play: Girls and Boys in School.* New Brunswick, N.J.: Rutgers University Press, 1993.

Trudgill, P. *Sociolinguistics: An Introduction.* Harmondsworth: Penguin, 1974.

Turner, Patricia. *Ceramic Uncles and Celluloid Mammies: Black Images and Their Influence on Culture.* New York: Anchor, 1994.

United States Commission on Civil Rights. *Teachers and Students: Differences in Teacher Interaction with Mexican American and Anglo Students.* Washington, D.C.: U.S. Government Printing Office, 1973.

United States Department of Justice Statistics. *Profile of Jail Inmates.* Washington, D.C.: U.S. Government Printing Office, 1980.

Wolf, Alexander. "Impossible Dream." *Sports Illustrated,* June 2, 1997, 80–82.

Weinstein, Rhonda Strasberg, and Susan E. Middlestadt. "Student Perceptions of Teacher Interactions with Male High and Low Achievers." *Journal of Educational Psychology* 71, no. 1 (1979): 421–31.

West, Candace, and Don H. Zimmerman. "Doing Gender." *Gender and Society* 1, no. 2 (1987): 125–51.

Willis, Paul. *Learning to Labor: How Working Class Kids Get Working Class Jobs.* New York: Columbia University Press, 1977.

———. "Cultural Production Is Different from Cultural Reproduction Is Different from Social Reproduction Is Different from Reproduction." *Interchange* 12, nos. 2–3 (1981): 48–67.

26

EXAMINING WOMEN'S PROGRESS IN THE SCIENCES FROM THE PERSPECTIVE OF DIVERSITY

Beatriz Chu Clewell and Angela B. Ginorio

RESEARCH STUDIES OFTEN FAIL to address multiple equity areas, and their findings are prone to misinterpretation as a result. Campbell (1989), MacCorquodale (1988), McDowell (1990), and other observers have written eloquently about this problem. Grant and Sleeter (1986) reviewed a ten-year sample of education literature from four journals to determine the degree to which race, social class, and gender were considered. They found very few papers examining the interaction of these status groups, and they warned that attending only to racial status oversimplifies the conclusions and may help perpetuate gender and class biases. McDowell reviewed seventy-three papers published between 1980 and 1986 on educational research in science, cognition, and education and found that 68 percent did not consider race, class, or gender in their analysis. None of the studies included class alone or in combination with race or gender in their analyses. In a summary of research on sex and ethnic differences in mathematics and science for students in Grades 4 through 8, Lockheed, Thorpe, Brooks-Gunn, Casserly, and McAloon (1985) found thirty-one studies addressing gender and sixteen addressing ethnicity, but only six addressing the two factors simultaneously.

At the college level, there are so few ethnic minority science students that review by both ethnicity and gender is very rare. For example, even though the number of ethnic minority students planning graduate work has grown significantly, Grandy (1992) reported that of the 121,982 people taking the Graduate Record Examination (GRE) in December 1990, only 1,063 were ethnic minorities (.9 of 1 percent). Despite the size of this sample, a seventy-two-cell table of ethnicity (six categories) by gender (two categories) by field (six categories) winds up with forty-five cells filled with one-digit numbers—including five with zeroes (p. 8)! The problems reported with data on black college students by the Howard University Institute for the Study of Educational Policy in 1976 are still true today for all ethnic minority students.

This chapter's reference list is extensive, but had we cited only studies that address any two issues together (for example, ethnicity and gender or disability and gender) we would have had a very short list. It should also be noted that many of these papers are what have been viewed as nonmainstream sources: research reports and special issues or articles in journals on ethnic minorities and/or women. The authors have prepared a description of studies involving interaction among issues, and interested readers can obtain copies by writing to Angela B. Ginorio at the University of Washington.

This chapter focuses on populations underrepresented in SME fields. The K–12 section includes only reports with information on American Indians, African Americans, and Latino/as. The rest of the chapter also includes information on Asian Americans, disabled students, and lesbians. (The Asian-American pattern of participation in SME fields is different from that of other ethnic minorities, but at the college level it exhibits variations affected by gender.) Thus we report on a limited selection of studies, and we include references to other groups (for example, white women) only to provide a context for the experiences of women of color, women with disabilities, and lesbians. We discuss class issues when they were noted in the literature—which is to say, not as frequently as we suspect they were operating.

Only recently have SME programs begun to address the needs of the physically disabled. Disabled persons have not had full access to science in high school, higher education, or careers (Ricker, 1978; Lucky, 1989). Opening science to the physically disabled involved more than widening doors and providing alternatives to stairs; it also involves making a commitment to the basic right of disabled students to learn and to receive encouragement and opportunities that will lead to science-related careers (Ricker, 1978).

While studying the status of ethnic minorities, women, and the disabled may be difficult, it is far easier than studying populations not protected by antidiscrimination laws, such as lesbians and gays. In the latter case, no numbers are kept by any institution. We have only the results of a few specialized studies, plus some extrapolations from general surveys of the population. Lesbians face different issues from those confronted by heterosexual women of color or disabled women. There is evidence of homophobia in academic (Governor's Commission on Gay and Lesbian Youth, 1993) and scientific communities (Tinmouth & Hamwi, 1994). Because visible factors do not make lesbians' sexual minority status obvious, disclosure of their sexual orientation becomes an issue of prominence. Fear of the repercussions of coming out contributes to the difficulties faced by lesbian scientists, engineers, and mathematicians.

Although deep structural issues shape the experience of diverse populations in our society, we begin our review at the individual level, so as to understand and sort what we know about individuals before tackling the complexities of the sociocultural level. Our analysis follows the educational ladder, going from the early years (K–3) to middle school (4–8) and high school (9–12) and concluding with the undergraduate and graduate levels and a very brief overview of postgraduate employment. The chapter closes with a discussion of directions for further research.

Lower Ladder (Grades K–12)

As indicated earlier, the focus here is on racial/ethnic groups underrepresented in mathematics and science: African Americans, Latino/as, and American Indians. From this point on, the term *women and girls of color* will refer to members of these groups.

Early Years (K–3)

Few studies have analyzed education in early life. This is unfortunate, because the first years seem especially important. After third grade, data show great consistency in children's performance from one year to the next, leaving much less room for intervention (Entwisle, Alexander, Cadigan, & Pallas, 1986). Even less is known of the early antecedents of mathematics or science achievement for girls of color or girls with disabilities. Data from the National Assessment of Educational Progress (NAEP) begin to document results by race/ethnicity and gender at the fourth grade. (Except for recent mathematics and science assessment results, presented later in this chapter, the NAEP does not provide disaggregation of data by gender within racial/ethnic subgroups.)

However, we did identify a few studies for this age group that focus on race, social class, and sometimes gender differences in early mathematics education. Some looked at student perception of and preparation for mathematics up to the point of school entry. Another focused on how social factors shape the attainment of children as they begin their academic careers. Other studies examined student progress and achievement during the first years of schooling as well as factors influencing that progress.

Three studies investigated race, social class, and gender differences in mathematics readiness at the time of school entry, mostly concluding that differences are small (Entwisle & Alexander, 1990; Tizard, Blatchford, Burke, Farquhar, & Plewis, 1988). "Basic mathematical thought develops in a robust manner among lower- and middle-class children, black and white" (Ginsberg & Russell, 1981, p. 56). (Although not mentioned in the quote, Ginsberg and Russell found very few gender differences for any of the groups studied.) The Entwisle and Alexander study found that African-American and white students had equivalent scores in computational and verbal skills on the California Achievement Test at the start of first grade, but there was a significant difference of about one-quarter of a standard deviation favoring white students in mathematics concepts (reasoning skills). Tizard and her colleagues had similar findings in their 1988 study of black and white British preschoolers (Tizard, Blatchford, Burke, Farquhar, & Plewis). Black boys outperformed girls in mathematics reasoning but there was no significant difference between white boys and girls. Boys of the two races also performed similarly. Furthermore, the authors felt that the significant difference seen for black boys over girls was due to sampling fluctuations, as it did not show up in subsequent scores for this sample. Entwisle and Alexander also found that all groups scored higher if their parents expected them to do well, that unlike white parents, African-American parents did not have higher expectations of boys than girls or perceive boys as having more ability in mathematics, that socioeconomic factors were an important influence on mathematics skills for all groups, and that family configuration (mother-father, mother-other, and mother only) did not affect mathematics scores for children of either sex or race at this age.

Once students enter school, what influences their success in mathematics? Researchers have studied effects of student and parent expectations and of parent socialization on success in the early years of schooling. One tracing study was conducted in two Baltimore schools—one with white, middle-class enrollment and the other with mixed-race, lower-class enrollment—from the first through third grades (Entwisle & Baker, 1983). The study sought to answer the question of whether socializing forces that shape mathematical performance along stereotypic sex-role lines are present long before junior high. The researchers found that experience in these early grades does differ by gender. Although their arithmetic marks or general aptitude were not higher than those of girls, boys developed higher expectations for performing well in mathematics, apparently in response to differential expectations held by their parents. The link between parent and child expectations was considerably weaker in the lower-class school; also, parents whose children attended the lower-class school expected more from girls in arithmetic than they did from boys. Thus the tendency for boys to be overly optimistic or for girls to be overly pessimistic about their arithmetic performance was not as strong in the lower-class school as it was in the middle-class school.

Given that students of both genders and races start out with similar mathematics achievement, what accounts for their differential performance as they progress through school? One longitudinal study tracked a sample of black and white first graders for twenty-four months and found that by the end of the period, blacks—both girls and boys—were about half a standard deviation behind, despite roughly equal starting scores (Entwisle & Alexander, 1992). The most important factors affecting this change were differences in socioeconomic status, followed by segregation. Over the two-year period, students in integrated schools showed about the same gains in mathematics skills, while segregated schools tended to penalize blacks, especially poor ones. The overall difference between racial groups could be traced mainly to the performance of segregated youngsters. Once again, family configuration was not related to achievement levels. Poor children of both races and genders consistently lost ground in the summer, but tended to perform at similar levels or better than their wealthier peers in the winter when school was in session.

Another study of British working-class children traced their progress in infant school (Blatchford, Burke, Farquhar, Plewis, & Tizard, 1985). Results showed few differences in literacy and numeracy between black and white five-year-olds entering school, although girls had higher test scores than boys. Test score variation could be attributed mainly to teaching at home and mothers' educational achievement. By the end of the third grade, white boys had the highest scores, girls of both races performed at similar levels, and black boys scored the lowest. A follow-up study of this cohort (Plewis, 1991) noted that white children of both sexes had higher mathematics scores than black children by the end of junior high school, at age eleven.

In an attempt to relate income, gender, age, and level of cognitive development to selected domain-specific skills, Stokes (1990) tested African-American students ages five to eight. She found ability to solve mathematics problems correlated significantly with level of cognitive development, but not with gender. The study also suggested that age is more important to success in addition, subtraction, and algorithm problems and less important to success in measurement and word problems, while the opposite is true for cognitive level (which is relatively uncorrelated with age).

Middle School (Grades 4–8)

The middle school years have been identified as the most crucial for the mathematics/science talent pool. According to Berryman (1983), after eighth grade, more people leave the pool than enter it. It is in middle school that girls, especially girls of color, must develop skills and maintain attitudes to carry them through high school courses in mathematics and science. What do we know about the achievement and experiences of girls of color during the middle school period? What are some of the factors that influence their performance and persistence on the mathematics/science ladder?

Achievement and Performance

At this point in the research on girls of color, it is difficult to say which of their intersecting statuses is the most powerful influence on their performance and participation in mathematics and science. When we also consider class, socioeconomic status (SES), disability, language minority status, and sexual preference, the complexity of the problem becomes obvious and overwhelming.

MATHEMATICS   Research on white students suggests that mathematics performance diverges between girls and boys by eighth or ninth grade, almost always favoring boys (Armstrong, 1981; Fennema, 1980; Fennema & Carpenter, 1981; Fox, Brody & Tobin, 1985; Moore & Smith, 1987). Ethnic and racial differences on standardized tests are larger and appear much earlier than gender differences (Dossey, Mullis, Lindquist, & Chambers, 1988; Gross, 1988; Reyes & Stanic, 1988). NAEP mathematics scores have shown large differences favoring white students beginning at the fourth-grade level in 1972, 1978, 1982, 1986, 1990, and 1992 (Dossey et al., 1988; Mullis, Dossey, Owen, & Phillips, 1993).

In addition, Gross (1988, 1989) suggests that students who fall below standard performance for a grade level are unlikely to catch up; this is especially true for African-American and Latino students. By age nine, for example, African Americans performed well below the NAEP mathematics average, and the difference increased with age (Holmes, 1980; Matthews, 1983). In past NAEP mathematics assessments, students of color made greater gains than white students—though their scores were still well below the national average (Dossey et al., 1988; Matthews, Carpenter, Lindquist, & Silver, 1984). More recently, however, white students have gained more than most minorities, while still lagging behind gains of Asian-American/Pacific Islander students (Mullis et al., 1993).

There is less evidence of gender differences in mathematics performance among students of color. Jones (1987) found that both African-American and white women scored lower than men at all levels of mathematics. Moore and Smith (1987) reported that the largest differences in favor of boys were among white and Latino students, and the smallest were among African-American students. Nelson (1978) reported no gender differences in mathematics achievement among African-American fifth graders but she did find that eleventh-grade boys had higher scores than girls. This suggests achievement patterns for African-American males and females similar to those noted for white students. Results from the most recent NAEP mathematics assessments (1990 and 1992) for Grades 4, 8, and 12 (displayed in Table 26.1) again show similar patterns of achievement for white and African-American male and female students at each grade level, with males either equal to or slightly ahead of females. The results for Latino students in 1992, however, show females outperforming males at all three grade levels, in marked difference from the 1990 assessment. Although it is too early to tell, it might be interesting to follow this development to see if it is the beginning of a trend.

In a study of the relationship of race, class, and gender to mathematics achievement among fifth, eighth, and eleventh graders, Kohr and his colleagues (1989) observed differences across grade levels for SES and race, but not for gender, with white students scoring higher than African-American students. Achievement also varied directly with SES level, with higher-SES students having higher achievement than lower-SES students.

SCIENCE The performance gap between men and women, and between white and Asian-American students as compared to their African-American, Latino, and Native American counterparts, persists in the 1990 NAEP science assessment (Jones, Mullis, Raizen, Weiss, & Weston, 1992). As shown in Table 26.2, boys outperformed girls in all racial/ethnic groups, especially at higher ages and levels of proficiency. NAEP data show an advantage for boys in physical sciences at Grade 3 that increased at Grades 8 and 12, but data were not disaggregated by sex within racial/ethnic categories (Jones et al.).

Table 26.1. Average Mathematics Proficiency Levels by Race/Ethnicity and Gender, Grades 4, 8, and 12, 1990 and 1992.

	1990 Average proficiency	1992 Average proficiency
Grade 4		
White Male	221 (1.4)	228 (1.0)
White Female	220 (1.3)	225 (1.3)
Black Male	189 (2.1)	192 (1.6)
Black Female	190 (2.5)	191 (1.6)
Hispanic Male	198 (3.1)	200 (1.6)
Hispanic Female	198 (2.3)	201 (1.7)
Grade 8		
White Male	271 (1.2)	277 (1.2)
White Female	269 (1.3)	277 (1.1)
Black Male	238 (3.2)	237 (1.9)
Black Female	238 (3.3)	237 (1.5)
Hispanic Male	245 (2.6)	246 (1.7)
Hispanic Female	242 (3.4)	247 (1.9)
Grade 12		
White Male	303 (1.5)	307 (1.0)
White Female	298 (1.4)	303 (1.0)
Black Male	272 (2.4)	277 (2.3)
Black Female	264 (2.5)	273 (1.8)
Hispanic Male	280 (3.3)	281 (3.4)
Hispanic Female	272 (3.7)	285 (2.5)

Proficiency levels for grade 4 are as follows: Advanced, 280; Proficient, 248; Basic, 211. For grade 8: Advanced, 331; Proficient, 294; Basic, 256. For grade 12: Advanced, 366; Proficient, 334; Basic, 287.

Source: *Adapted from Mullis, Dossey, Owen, and Phillips, 1993.*

COURSE ENROLLMENT/PARTICIPATION Students in Grades 4 through 8 rarely have a choice about taking mathematics and science classes, as the general curriculum usually includes these subjects (Lockheed et al., 1985). Thus there is little variation due to gender or race/ethnicity at the middle school level, though schools show substantial differences in the amount and quality of mathematics and science instruction. However, participation in related activities does differ. By age nine, sex and ethnic differences in other science activities are already apparent (Kahle & Lakes, 1983). From 1976–77, NAEP data on science attitudes showed that nine-

Table 26.2. Distribution of Students and Average Science Proficiency by Race/Ethnicity and Gender.

	Percentage of students	Average proficiency
Grade 4		
White Male	36 (0.7)	243 (1.3)
White Female	34 (0.7)	241 (1.1)
Black Male	7 (0.3)	205 (1.8)
Black Female	8 (0.4)	206 (1.8)
Hispanic Male	6 (0.2)	213 (1.6)
Hispanic Female	5 (0.2)	211 (1.9)
Grade 8		
White Male	36 (0.8)	274 (1.8)
White Female	35 (0.7)	271 (1.4)
Black Male	7 (0.3)	232 (2.9)
Black Female	8 (0.3)	230 (2.1)
Hispanic Male	5 (0.2)	243 (3.0)
Hispanic Female	5 (0.2)	239 (2.5)
Grade 12		
White Male	36 (0.8)	307 (1.5)
White Female	37 (0.7)	298 (1.3)
Black Male	6 (0.4)	261 (2.7)
Black Female	8 (0.4)	253 (2.9)
Hispanic Male	4 (0.3)	2781 (3.1)
Hispanic Female	4 (0.3)	268 (3.5)

Levels of science proficiency are as follows: Level 200—Understands simple scientific principles; Level 250—Applies general scientific information; Level 300—Analyzes scientific procedures and data; Level 350—Integrates specialized scientific information.

Source: *Jones, Mullis, Raizen, Weiss, & Weston, 1992, p. 12.*

and thirteen-year-old girls consistently had less exposure than boys. Furthermore, the 1977–86 trend analysis of NAEP responses continued to reflect differential experiences based on gender. White students had more science experiences than African-American students, and the difference increased with age. Johnson (1981) studied the extent of extracurricular mathematics activities undertaken by a small sample of African-American youth in Grades 7 and 8. He found no sex differences; all reported low participation. A study of 1981–82 NAEP data nevertheless revealed that African-American girls at ages nine and thirteen had conducted the fewest science experiments (Hueftle, Rakow, & Welch, 1983), and the 1990

NAEP science assessment shows this trend continuing for thirteen-year-old African-American girls, who were the most likely to respond that they had never done a science experiment.

Factors Affecting Performance and Participation

It is clear that females and males in racial/ethnic categories are much more similar to each other than to students in other categories. Obviously, race/ethnicity is much more important than gender in this matter. A study of Chicano, white, and African-American adolescents by Creswell and Houston (1980) confirms that ethnicity was the primary source of variance in performance.

However, there are some differences in performance, achievement, and participation rates between girls of color and their male counterparts. There are also differences between girls of color and white girls. To study these factors, it is useful to classify them as *learner-related* and *environmental* variables.

Learner-Related Variables

Variables such as attitudes, perceptions, and learning styles depend on factors each student brings to the learning process.

ATTITUDES AND PERCEPTIONS Students' performance and participation in mathematics and science seem to depend on enjoyment of the subjects, perceptions of the subjects as useful to themselves and/or as the domain of white males, and confidence in their own abilities. Although this has been shown to be true for white girls and women (Fennema & Sherman, 1978; Jones et al., 1992; Sherman, 1980), it is unclear whether such a relationship exists between attitudes and achievement for girls and women of color. Research on white women and girls has also documented a decline in attitudes toward mathematics and science that begins in middle school and escalates through high school (Fennema & Sherman, 1978; Jones et al., 1992; Mullis & Jenkins, 1988; Schreiber, 1984). By high school, boys' attitudes toward mathematics are substantially more positive than girls' (Dossey et al., 1988; Fennema & Sherman, 1978) even though girls' attitudes are as positive as those of boys in elementary school (Dossey et al., 1988; Matthews, 1984). A similar trend occurs for science (Jones et al., 1992; Schreiber, 1984). Furthermore, males who report liking science demonstrate higher science proficiency than females who report liking science (Jones et al., 1992).

Interestingly, NAEP data on science preference show greater disparities between males and females age thirteen and older than among racial/ ethnic categories, although all students show declining preference for both mathematics and science after Grade 4 (Jones et al., 1992; Dossey et al., 1988). James and Smith (1985) attempted to find out when alienation from science occurs, and they concluded that the greatest decline was between Grades 6 and 7. This held true for the whole population as well as for female and African-American students. African Americans started out well ahead in science subject preference, but by the later grades were at or below the population; females ranked at or below the total population and the African-American population across all grade levels. This study did not disaggregate data by race and gender.

Yong (1992) found no gender differences in attitude toward mathematics and science among gifted African-American middle school students—but did find significant gender differences in attitudes toward success in mathematics and perception of the subject as a male domain. Girls tended to anticipate positive consequences as a result of success in mathematics more than boys did. Further, girls were less likely than boys to perceive mathematics as a male domain.

A study of African-American students in Grades 5 and 11 concluded that few sex differences existed in mathematics attitudes, but that those differences favored males (Nelson, 1978). Fifth graders showed no sex differences in achievement, but eleventh-grade males had higher achievement scores than females. The study also found significant relationships between mathematics achievement and attitudes for fifth-grade males and eleventh-grade females. Creswell and Exezidis (1982) reported that African-American and Mexican-American adolescent women had more positive attitudes toward mathematics than did their male counterparts and that the attitudes of African Americans were more positive than those of Mexican Americans. Data from the 1992 NAEP mathematics assessment show few sex differences among nine-year-olds in liking for mathematics.

In a study of attitudes toward science Rakow (1985) found that sex appeared to be a better predictor of the attitudes of nine-year-olds than ethnicity. Males of all the groups studied—whites, African Americans, and Latinos—had much more positive attitudes than did females, with Hispanic females having the least positive attitudes. For thirteen-year-olds, the pattern was repeated. This study was based on 1981–82 NAEP data. NAEP data from 1990 show that for nine-year-old white and African-American students, girls are less likely than boys to answer yes when asked, Do you like science? whereas Latina girls are more likely than boys to agree. For thirteen-year-olds, boys of all three groups are more likely to respond that they like science than are girls. The pattern reappears for seventeen-year-olds, but the percentages of white and African-American women liking science have declined, whereas those for white men and Latinos of both sexes have increased slightly.

Overall, students' liking of math and science declines from elementary to high school. Thirteen-year-olds show a sharp drop in preference for mathematics, and seventeen-year-olds show a further drop. Except for Latino nine-year-olds, boys of all groups like mathematics better than do girls. Latino and African-American students of both sexes surpass their white counterparts in mathematics preference. In science, the gap between boys and girls increases sharply after age thirteen, while preference for science, though declining, is fairly similar across racial/ethnic lines. For all three age levels, white boys show greater preference for science than white girls. However, African-American students show little gender difference for nine- and thirteen-year-olds; the gap increases sharply (favoring boys) at seventeen. Latina girls start out liking science more than boys at nine, but after thirteen, boys show a greater preference.

Stereotypes about mathematics and science are part of the middle school intellectual environment. Both girls and boys begin to view mathematics as masculine by Grade 6 or 7 (Erickson, 1987), but this view is more likely to be held by boys than by girls (Armstrong, 1981; Brush, 1980; Eccles (Parsons) et al., 1983; Fennema & Sherman, 1977, 1978; Fox 1981; Kahle & Lakes, 1983; Kelly, 1978; Sherman, 1980). Students of all groups also absorb racial stereotypes of mathematics and science as white fields (Hall, 1981: Kenschaft, 1981). It seems, however, that like white girls and women, girls and women of color are less likely than their male counterparts to consider science and mathematics as male domains. MacCorquodale (1980) found that white and Mexican-American women in her study were less biased than their male counterparts and thought that science was just as appropriate for women as for men. Yong (1992) concluded that the gifted African-American middle school girls in her study were less likely to perceive mathematics as a male domain than their gifted male counterparts.

The importance and usefulness students ascribe to science and mathematics, and the self-confidence they feel in working with these subjects, affect their attitudes. As they progress in high school, girls see mathematics as diminishing in usefulness to women and increasing in usefulness to men (Boswell & Katz, 1980; Fennema & Sherman, 1978). African-American students of both sexes have misperceptions about science, have fewer scientific experiences, find science less useful out of school, are less aware of scientific methods and how scientists work, and are less confident of the ability of science to solve problems (Kahle, 1982). MacCorquodale (1980) found that whereas white and Mexican-American women and men shared positive attitudes toward science, white women and Mexican-American men perceived it as most important for an understanding of the world. Mexican-American women rated science as less important than did either white women or white and Mexican-American men.

A study of African-American eighth graders in an inner-city school found that although there were no sex differences in mathematics and science achievement, boys scored higher than girls on science self-concept. Further, boys were significantly more likely than girls to choose a science-related occupation over a non-science-related occupation (Jacobowitz, 1983). Rhone (1989), on the other hand, found mathematical self-concept to be a significant predictor of adolescent African-American girls' and boys' mathematics achievement and problem-solving ability. In a study of achievement, self-efficacy, anxiety, and attributions in mathematics among African-American junior high school students, Lewellyn (1990) found females outperforming males in mathematics achievement but found no gender differences for mathematics anxiety, self-efficacy, or attributions. (This study also noted that greater self-efficacy for both boys and girls was achieved in the eighth grade, suggesting a possible developmental trend. Ninth graders in the same study also used ability attributions more than seventh or eighth graders.) Hart and Stanic (1989) found sex differences in mathematics self-confidence reversed for white and African-American seventh graders. Among whites in this study, boys scored higher than girls on the Fennema & Sherman confidence scale, but among African Americans, girls scored higher than boys. Furthermore, African-American girls showed more confidence than any of the other three groups.

Although most research has associated positive attitude with increased participation and performance, this may not be true for people of color. Several studies have shown that African-American and Latino students have positive attitudes toward mathematics and science equaling or exceeding those of white students, but still have lower achievement levels in these subjects (Gross, 1988; James & Smith, 1985; Kahle, 1982; Matthews, 1984; Rakow 1985; Walker & Rakow, 1985). The association does seem to apply to gender, however, as studies reveal that men have more positive attitudes and also achieve at higher levels (Kahle & Lakes, 1983; Mullis & Jenkins, 1988; Rakow, 1985; Schibeci, 1984; Schreiber, 1984; Simpson & Oliver, 1985; Walker and Rakow, 1985).

Marrett (1986) has suggested that for students of color the relationship between attitude, involvement, and achievement is complex and that, at least for African Americans, forces other than attitude shape participation in mathematics and science. The relationship may be even more complex for girls and women of color. The most recent NAEP assessments show that African-American and Latina girls and women differ from their white counterparts in preference for science (1992) and mathematics (1990). For all groups, males seem to surpass females in liking for mathematics. A larger percentage of African-American and Latino males and females responded that they liked mathematics than did their white counterparts of either sex. Science preference shows little gender difference among African Americans and Latinos; the difference between white males and females is much larger, favoring males. There is some evidence that African-American adolescent girls show more liking for science and greater mathematics self-confidence than do their white sisters or African-American and white males. A burning question is whether or not, for women and girls of each of the underrepresented groups, attitude toward mathematics and science is related to achievement. This is definitely an area where more research is needed.

Attitudes that influence course taking in high school are present at middle grades. Some girls are already avoiding science electives, and some African-American and Latino students say science is optional without recognizing the effect of this belief on their educational and occupational choices (MacCorquodale, 1980). Nevertheless, MacCorquodale found no significant sex or ethnic differences in attitudes toward science courses among Mexican-American and white eighth graders. In attempting to identify the determinants of middle school students' intentions to enroll in a high school science course, Crawley and Coe (1990) found that the relative contributions of attitudes and social pressures to the prediction of intention vary according to students' gender, race/ethnicity, general ability, and science ability, but the authors provide no data on race and gender interactions. They found that the major determinant of males' attitudes toward enrolling in science is the perceived difficulty of science vis-à-vis other elective subjects, whereas for females, the major determinant is interest in learning new information. Minority students value the opportunity to do "fun" experiments, and this is the major determinant for them.

LEARNING STYLES Researchers have begun to address female and male *learning styles*, that is, basic differences in the way people process knowledge (Belenky, Clinchy, Goldberger, & Tarule, 1986; Gilligan, 1982). Parallel research on people of color is grouped around various racial and ethnic groups, with most studies looking at African-American learning styles. Some studies have suggested that African-American culture is more affective and cognitively united than the prevailing European tradition of universal facts and knowledge (Hale-Benson, 1984; U.S. Congress, 1988). Ramirez and Castaneda (1974) examined the ways Mexican-American children's learning styles differed from those of white children by applying the psychological concepts of field dependence and field independence. There is, however, no research on the learning styles of girls of color and the ways in which sex and race or ethnicity interact to influence learning.

Research on learner characteristics and their relationship to mathematics and science focuses on locus of control/learned helplessness, cognitive skills, cognitive abilities, persistence and independence, language background, and spatial visualization skills. These factors have all been cited as influencing differential achievement in mathematics and science for women and people of color. For a review of research on these topics, see Clewell and Anderson, 1991.

Environmental Variables

Variables such as schools, teachers, parents, peers, and society as a whole also affect students' learning experiences.

SCHOOL-RELATED FACTORS   Teacher expectations and encouragement may affect student attitudes and achievement.

Matthews (1984) found that teachers may have strong positive effects on mathematics attitudes of students of color. Students of color indicated that they were encouraged and assisted by teachers who worked with them, gave them extra help, explained things carefully, and provided encouragement (Matthews, 1981; Treisman, 1982). Teachers' expectations of achievement potential were lower for students of color (Olstad, Juarez, Davenport, & Haury, 1981). Gross (1988) found that high-achieving African-American students must prove themselves to the teacher each time they enter a new math class. And Beane (1985) suggested that teachers tend to see students of color as low achievers and white students as high achievers even when performance is the same. Hall, Howe, Merkel, and Lederman (1986) support this finding, reporting that teachers in desegregated junior high school science classes rated the ability of whites higher than that of African Americans with similar achievement scores. In the same study, teachers also expressed the belief that African-American girls made the most effort and their male counterparts the least effort. Irvine (1985) found that a girl's race affected the amount of feedback she received from the teacher, with white girls receiving the least classroom feedback of any type, although girls overall received less feedback than boys.

Students of color developed the best mathematics attitudes and performance on reasoning tasks when teachers showed positive attitudes toward students, felt comfortable with the mathematics curriculum, and interacted positively with students during mathematics instruction (Pulos, Stage, & Karplus, 1982). Schools that raised African-American students' mathematics achievement on normative and criterion-referenced tests all offered a safe and orderly environment, a clear school mission, high expectations for students, time on task, and frequent monitoring of student progress (Engman, 1986).

Balanced and comprehensive illustrations in science and mathematics texts may help girls of color to develop positive attitudes toward these subjects and to see themselves as science professionals. Studies in the 1970s and early 1980s revealed that textbooks contained a stereotyped view of women and minorities and perpetuated the common view of mathematics and science as white male domains. More recent studies have found that contemporary texts are much less sexist and racist than those of two decades ago (García, Harrison, & Torres, 1990), although representation of women and people of color in careers requiring knowledge of advanced mathematics is less than adequate. Powell and García (1985) found that recent elementary textbooks do show students of color performing science activities, but that the majority of adults shown in science-related occupations are white. There is no research on the effect of textbooks on the mathematics and science attitudes of girls of color.

Instructional techniques and strategies may have differing success with various groups of students. Erickson, Gall, Gersten, and Grace (1987) looked at whether instruction differentially affected the achievement of boys and girls in basic algebra. They found that boys' achievement was most affected by classroom management and teacher presentation, whereas girls showed lower achievement with increased quizzing, more guided practice, and higher-level cognitive questions. This find suggests that girls may have greater difficulty performing under stress. Cooperative learning situations in this class enhanced girls' achievement. A very different pattern emerged in an intermediate algebra class, however, where active questioning, guided practice, and assistance resulted in greater gains for girls than for boys.

Mathematics is customarily taught in a manner inappropriate to the needs of many people of color, as shown by research on American Indians (Green, Brown, & Long, 1978), Latinos (Valverde, 1984), and African Americans (Beane, 1985). Among others, Lockheed and Gorman (1987) have suggested adjusting teaching strategies and curricula to the cultural milieu of students in a class. Cohen, Intili, and DeAvila (1982) studied the relationship of social status and cooperative interaction to learning in a hands-on experimental program for bilingual elementary classes. This study showed a clear relationship between status (social rankings in which it is usually believed that it is better to be in the high than in the low state) and peer interaction, with higher-status children interacting more. A higher degree of task-related peer interaction, in turn, led to higher achievement. There is also some evidence favoring inquiry learning over traditional approaches for middle school students generally and for girls in particular (see Clewell, Anderson, & Thorpe, 1992, for a review of these studies). While few studies have examined the relationship of instructional approach to the achievement of students of color, there is evidence that middle school African-American and Latino students experience positive effects from hands-on inquiry activities (Cohen & DeAvila, 1982). This study also reported higher achievement for a bilingual, mostly Hispanic group of students in a cooperative inquiry program, compared to control classes with a competitive structure.

Activity-based classroom science programs have been cited as successful with students of color. Reynolds (1991) studied the effects of an experiment-based physical science program on the content knowledge and process skills of African-American, Latino, and white urban fourth to eighth graders. Results showed significant impact on process skills but not on content skills. Further, white and Latino students benefited from the program, whereas African-American students did not. Girls did better than boys, net of other factors (such as race or grade level).

A partial explanation for the low performance of students of color in mathematics has been underrepresentation in high school mathematics courses, which results from the cumulative effects of years of education. By the time critical decisions are being made regarding high school class placement, as many as one-third to one-half of African-American and Latino students have fallen so far behind as to be ineligible to take higher-level mathematics courses in the future (Gross, 1988).

There are very few studies on the influences of peers on girls' attitude toward mathematics and science, and we found none on such peer influences among students of color, let alone girls of color. Talton and Simpson (1984) found that children's views become more and more homogeneous, with similarity reaching a peak at the ninth grade. Girls have a strong conflict between liking science and desiring popularity, especially with boys (Schreiber, 1984), which may explain why girls in single-sex schools express more positive attitudes toward science than those in mixed schools (Kelly, 1981). Kelly and Smail (1986) found that boys often show stronger sex-role stereotypes than girls, which tends to support this finding.

HOME AND SOCIETAL FACTORS Parents' expectations regarding children's success in certain subjects are a potent influence on performance and attitudes in those subjects. Parsons, Adler, and Kaczala (1982) found that parents' perceptions of their children's math aptitudes favored sons over daughters despite the similarity of boys' and girls' actual performance. (Andrews reported similar findings in 1989.) Additionally, these sex-stereotyped parental beliefs were critical to the children's own achievement self-concepts. Rhone (1989) found that parental expectation was a strong predictor of African-American seventh and eighth graders' mathematics achievement and problem-solving ability.

Kahle and Lakes (1983) and Schreiber (1984) reported that parents of middle school girls had low expectations of their performance in science. This did not hold true for African Americans, however, who were the most supportive of the four groups—Latino, Asian American, African American, and white—studied by Andrews (1989). Asian-American and Latino parents in this study were more likely to see mathematics as a male domain than either African-American or white parents. A more recent study found parental influences on African-American girls to be more similar to such influences on white boys than other groups (Maple & Stage, 1991).

Family background and parental influence affect both attitude and achievement of mathematics students (Tsai & Walberg, 1983). As MacCorquodale (1988) noted, Mexican-American parents were more supportive of children than were white parents but lacked the experience and information necessary to assist in children's education. NAEP data suggest a correlation between home support for and involvement in students' learning, parental education level, and proficiency in various science subject areas (Dossey et al., 1988; Mullis & Jenkins, 1988). This relationship was tested by items on the mathematics and science assessments that collected data on parental education, home assistance with homework and projects, participation in science-related projects, number and kinds of reading material in the home, and television viewing habits. Mullis and Jenkins interpret NAEP results as suggesting that African-American and Latino students from lower-SES homes are disadvantaged by differences in parental education levels and access to reading materials in the home.

The exposure of students to role models in science has been linked to a corresponding improvement in attitudes. Because few scientists are women of color, girls of color see much less of role models than other students. Smith and Erb (1986) demonstrated a connection between increasing exposure to female role models—by having women scientists visit classrooms to talk about their careers or by giving students information about women who have made important contributions to science, for example—and changes in early adolescents' attitudes toward women scientists. The study found that both boys' and girls' attitudes toward women scientists improved after exposure to the role models. Although this study did not disaggregate data by race, some researchers have suggested that the lack of diverse role models in science may lead students of color to view science as a white male domain (Beane, 1985; Malcom, 1990; Marrett, 1986).

High School (Grades 9–12)

This section discusses mathematics and science achievement of women of color in high school, including their course-taking patterns, intended undergraduate majors, and career plans.

Achievement and Performance in Mathematics and Science

On the 1992 NAEP mathematics assessment, African-American and Latina girls continue to show lower proficiency and achievement levels than white girls at Grade 12. African-American and white girls lag even further behind their male counterparts than in middle school. For Latino students, however, just the opposite is the case: Latina girls outperform boys, and their gender gap has also increased from that of middle school (Mullis et al., 1993).

The NAEP 1990 science assessment lists African-American and Latina girls at all grade levels with lower average proficiency than their white counterparts. In each racial/ethnic category, males outperform females, with the differences widening sharply at Grade 12 (Jones et al., 1992). Using data from the 1990 NAEP science assessment, Bruschi and Anderson (1994) found that by age seventeen, males consistently outperformed females in all racial/ethnic groups in all content areas except natural sciences. (White males outperformed white females in this area as well.)

School-Related Factors Affecting Achievement and Performance

Teachers are an important influence on students of color. In a study of role-model effects in high school, Evans (1992) did not find evidence of a gender-based effect. He did find, however, that African-American teachers induced a nearly 19 percent increase in the achievement of African-American students whose mothers lacked a college education; the effect appeared to be equally strong with male or female students or teachers.

Research shows that students of color have less exposure to mathematics and science activities and experiences in high school than whites, and there is some evidence of gender differences favoring males in exposure to these activities. Rakow and Walker (1985) found that seventeen-year-old white students reported more science participation than did African-American or Latino students. Of this group, Latina women reported the least science experience.

There is also some evidence that girls of color have less access to computers than their male counterparts. Grignon (1992) reported significant gender differences in the application of software and course taking among eighth and twelfth grade Menominee Indian students. In Grade 12, the differences occurred in the use of software; girls spent less time using games and graphics than did boys in the same grade. Girls also were enrolled at a significantly lesser rate in classes offering sophisticated graphics programs. Also, more boys than girls enrolled in computer science classes.

Two studies on at-risk girls of color reveal interesting findings. One was designed to determine the effectiveness of supplementary computer-assisted algebra materials on achievement levels and attitudes of urban minority students who had failed a semester of basic algebra (Mickens, 1991). This study found that students receiving computer-assisted instruction (CAI) had greater academic achievement than students in the control group and that the achievement level was greater for female students than for male students. Furthermore, students of both sexes in the experimental group indicated that they perceived their teachers to have a high expectation for their success. In another study of a remedial mathematics course for at-risk high school students using CAI and computer adaptive testing (CAT), Signer (1991) found that African-American female students exhibited greater self-confidence toward computer use than was found in other studies that examined gender.

Course Enrollment and Participation

Course enrollment also has an effect; students who have taken advanced mathematics and science courses tend to have higher achievement levels. Traditionally, females and students of color enroll in fewer optional or advanced courses in mathematics than white male students (Fennema, 1984; Marrett, 1981). Vanfossen (1984) investigated the gender gap between the sophomore and senior years and concluded that women took fewer mathematics courses than men and that differential performance was due to gender differences in enrollment in advanced mathematics courses. This echoes the general underrepresentation of students of color in high school mathematics courses (Gross, 1988). Davis (1986, 1989) found that regardless of race/ethnicity, higher levels of mathematics achievement correlated with enrollment in advanced mathematics courses. Anick, Carpenter, and Smith (1981) found that African-American students averaged about one year less high school mathematics than was the norm for all students. Sells (1980) studied high school course patterns and found that African-American women were the least prepared of all students in mathematics, while white men were the most prepared. A later study, however, found that African-American women took more advanced mathematics courses in high school than did African-American men (Matthews, 1984).

NAEP data from the 1982 mathematics assessment also revealed that course experiences varied not only between African-American and white students but also from school to school. African-American students in racially segregated schools took more mathematics courses than those in integrated schools, but achievement in segregated schools was lower (Davis, 1986, 1989).

Lee and Ware (1986) set out to identify the point at which high school students, especially girls, were most likely to leave the college prep mathematics sequence, and to find predictors of persistence. They found that girls tended to drop out of the less advanced courses in the college prep mathematics sequence at a greater rate than boys, but the proportion of girls making the transition to advanced levels was slightly higher than that of boys. The early leakage, however, diminished the pool of female advanced mathematics students. The study also found a direct positive relationship— stronger for boys than girls—between social class and persistence in mathematics. When SES was held constant, African-American females were more likely to persist in mathematics even though, in general, the proportion of minority students decreases with each increasingly advanced course.

African-American students enroll in fewer than three years of high school science and tend to avoid advanced science courses, and those who are college bound are much more likely than their white peers to report no courses in the biological or physical science areas (Anderson, 1989). In fact, Anderson and Pearson (1988) found that more than half of the high-ability African-American students who eventually left science had not completed an advanced mathematics or science course in high school.

Rakow and Walker (1985) suggest that the underrepresentation of Latino students in advanced high school science courses may be due to their absence from college prep programs. Data from the 1990 NAEP science assessment show a direct relationship between high school science course taking and average proficiency, with more course work in each content area being related to higher proficiency in that area and to higher overall proficiency (Jones et al., 1992). Data from this assessment show that more males than females had taken a year or more of physics, and more white and Asian-American/Pacific Islander students had taken one year or more of this subject than had their African-American, Latino, and American Indian counterparts (Jones et al., 1992).

There is some evidence that the gender gap in course taking has begun to narrow, though differences favoring boys persist for the more advanced courses. Data from the 1993 SAT Student Descriptive Questionnaire (SDQ) show few gender differences in years of study of mathematics and natural sciences for African-American, American Indian, Latin American, Mexican-American, and Puerto Rican students. What differences there were occurred for the last three racial/ethnic groups. In terms of course-taking patterns, a larger proportion of females consistently studied biology, chemistry, and space/earth science/geology. For physics, more males took courses than females, except among African Americans, where 56 percent of the course takers were female, and Latin Americans and Puerto Ricans, where there was an even split between males and females. Females surpassed males in all groups in science honors course participation.

For mathematics, the pattern is similar: females of almost all underrepresented groups surpass males in algebra, geometry, trigonometry, and precalculus. Among American Indians, slightly more males than females take trigonometry and precalculus. For calculus, American Indian, Latino, and Mexican-American males surpass their female counterparts in course taking. Puerto Ricans are evenly split, and African-American females surpass males 58 percent to 42 percent. With the exception of American Indians, females once again outnumber males in the taking of honors courses. For African Americans, the difference in favor of females is very large (63 percent versus 37 percent).

Comparison of 1988 and 1993 SDQ data confirmed that females of all underrepresented groups are taking more courses at all levels of mathematics and science. In 1988, the crucial filter in mathematics was precalculus; that is, more males than females in all groups except African Americans took precalculus. By 1993, females formed the majority of precalculus students among African Americans, Latin Americans, Mexican Americans, and Puerto Ricans. The critical filter is now calculus. The gap also narrowed in physics for all groups between 1988 and 1993.

Career Interests and Aspirations

Relatively few women of color are mathematical scientists, but among women of color, African Americans are most likely to have earned a bachelor's degree in mathematics (National Science Foundation [NSF], 1994).

Studies report that African-American interest in scientific careers is lower among women than among men of similar achievement levels (Jacobowitz, 1983), and African-American men and white women have a greater level of participation in hard science careers than African-American women (NSF, 1994).

In 1993, female SAT takers of all underrepresented groups surpassed male SAT takers of those groups in plans to major in the biological sciences. Here again, the difference for African Americans was very large— 63 percent versus 37 percent. For engineering, just the opposite was true for every group, with a much larger proportion of males than females among prospective majors. This was also true for physics, but the differences were not as large. For mathematics, American Indian, Latin American, and Mexican-American males outnumbered females, but female African-American and Puerto Rican students outnumbered males.

A number of studies have investigated influences on women's choices of majors and careers in scientific fields (Berryman, 1983; Ethington & Wolfle, 1988; Ware & Lee, 1988). Many girls forfeit the opportunity to pursue a mathematics career because by the time they enter junior high they have not developed adequate interest in mathematics and thus fail to enroll in the courses required for quantitative majors in college (Berryman, 1983). A study of factors affecting the attitudes of African-American and female middle school students toward science and science-related careers found that across both races and both sexes, the major factor affecting science-related career decisions appeared to be personal contact with a scientist (Hill, Pettus, & Hedin, 1990). The study also found that African-American females scored higher than white females on a self-image subscale. On a relevance-of-science subscale, African-American males who knew a scientist outscored their female counterparts, while the opposite was true for white students; on this subscale, African-American females who did not know scientists outscored their male counterparts, while the opposite was true for white students. These findings suggest differences between African-American and white females regarding traditional gender roles, with the African Americans being less influenced by tradition. The study concluded that sex differences in the pursuit of science careers are primarily based on interest in these careers established by the time children reach middle school.

Ethington and Wolfle (1988) found that the number of math and science courses taken in high school was the most important factor in determining women's choice of a quantitative major. Maple and Stage (1991) echoed this finding, concluding that number of math and science courses completed through the senior year of high school was one of three variables with significant direct effects on African-American females' choice of major field. (The other two were sophomore choice of major and math attitudes.) Steinkamp and Maehr (1984) found females' orientation toward these fields to be higher than males' in disadvantaged communities, but lower in upper-middle-class communities. Dunteman, Wisenbaker, and Taylor (1979) found that for African Americans, higher family SES increased the likelihood of selecting a science major; indeed, after background measures were controlled, African Americans revealed a higher probability of majoring in science than did whites. Berryman (1983) reported ethnic/socioeconomic interactive effects on the selection of a quantitative major. Ethington and Wolfle (1988) did not find interactive effects for race and SES but did find that both variables had significant effects. Their study revealed that for African-American and white women with equal measures on other variables, African-American women were more likely to select a quantitative field, supporting other research that found that sex rather than race is a major factor in the underrepresentation of minority women in the sciences.

Krist (1993), in one of the few studies to examine the motivation of high-ability African-American women making educational and career choices in mathematics and science, tested the utility of the academic choice model of achievement developed by Eccles-Parsons and her colleagues (1983; see also Meece, Parsons, Kaczala, Goff, & Futterman, 1982). The study supported the model, which is based on expectancy-value theory, and confirmed that achievement behavior for this population also involved choices made by the individual, influenced by cultural norms and socialization experiences. The study also found that gifted African-American women had higher self-esteem and confidence than their white counterparts and that they expected to succeed in traditionally male-dominant fields. Other findings included early interest in mathematics and science, with middle school a critical period for the decision. Extended families, particularly mothers and grandmothers, encouraged and helped the women in the study; friends, mentors, and the community affected their aspirations and expectations more strongly than did their school experiences; and they were affected more often by racial stereotyping than sex-role stereotyping.

Issues in Conducting Research on Girls and Women of Color, Lesbians, and Disabled Girls and Women

This chapter has discussed the dearth of studies integrating race, social class, and gender or considering disability status and sexual orientation and has urged the necessity of such research. At present, the collection and reporting of national data hinders this research. For example, NAEP math and science reports are disaggregated by sex within racial/ethnic categories only for data on proficiency levels. The NAEP collects the gender and racial/ethnic data needed to disaggregate all its reports, but it does not do so.

Social class or socioeconomic status are even more difficult to report. Proxy characteristics such as parents' education and occupation and family income can be used to determine SES, but such information is difficult to obtain and, when self-reported, of questionable reliability. Further, the greater the disaggregation by various characteristics, the smaller the sample size of the population being studied.

The failure of research studies and national data bases to disaggregate data by race/ethnicity and gender may be due to the tendency of researchers and policy makers to ignore people of color, but the sheer difficulty of working with such small numbers may also be a factor. When the numbers of people of color are too small for quantitative methods, qualitative data as well as case studies can provide different lenses to explore issues for groups with small populations in a given setting. Information about students contextualized by information on their institution, faculty, and peers could provide data useful in generating explanations or challenging established explanations.

It is reassuring, nevertheless, that there have been changes in data reporting to include disaggregation by race/ethnicity and gender within racial/ethnic categories. For an example of this, see the recent NSF publication *Women, Minorities, and Persons with Disabilities in Science and Engineering* (1994).

Doing research is one issue; publishing and disseminating it is another. Three factors make information on ethnic minorities hard to find: it is rarely gathered; when it is gathered, sample sizes are often too small for standard statistical analysis; and when it is analyzed, it tends to appear in research reports and not in official journals (Ginorio, 1993). The *Journal of Women and Minorities in Science and Engineering* provides an easily identifiable outlet for research on women of color. But science and education journals also need to include this information if it is to reach the audience that needs to find out about it.

Given projected demographic changes, an increasingly larger proportion of the population will belong to groups currently underrepresented in mathematics and science fields; half of the individuals in these groups will be women and girls. Given this dramatic shift, it is no longer feasible, appropriate, or just to conduct research solely on white subjects and use the findings of this research to make policy decisions for the entire populace.

REFERENCES

Anderson, B. T. (1989). Black participation and performance in high school science. In W. Pearson, Jr., & H. K. Bechtel (Eds.), *Blacks, science, and American education* (pp. 43–58). New Brunswick and London: Rutgers University Press.

Andrews, J. V. (1989, April). *Attitudes and beliefs about mathematics: Do parents, students, teachers, counselors and principals agree?* Paper presented at the annual meeting of the American Educational Research Association, San Francisco, CA.

Anick, C. M., Carpenter, T. P., & Smith, C. (1981). Minorities and mathematics: Results from the National Assessment of Educational Progress. *Mathematics Teacher, 74,* 560–566.

Armstrong, J. M. (1981). Achievement and participation of women in mathematics: Results of two national surveys. *Journal for Research in Mathematics Education, 12,* 356–372.

Beane, D. B. (1985). *Mathematics and science: Critical filters for the future of minority students.* Washington, DC: American University, Mid-Atlantic Center for Race Equity.

Belenky, M. F., Clinchy, B. M., Goldberger, N. R., & Tarule, J. M. (1986). *Women's ways of knowing: The development of self, voice, and mind.* New York: Basic Books.

Berryman, S. E. (1983). *Who will do science? Minority and female attainment of science and mathematics degrees.* New York: Rockefeller Foundation.

Blatchford, P., Burke, J., Farquhar, C., Plewis, I., & Tizard, B. (1985). Educational achievement in the infant school: The influence of ethnic origin, gender and home on entry skills. *Educational Research, 27*(1), 52–60.

Boswell, S. L., & Katz, P. A. (1980). *Nice girls don't study mathematics.* Washington, DC: National Institute of Education. (ERIC Document Reproduction Service No. ED 188 888).

Bruschi, B. A., & Anderson, B. T. (1994, February). *Gender and ethnic differences in science achievement of nine-, thirteen-, and seventeen-year old students.* Paper presented at the annual meeting of the Eastern Educational Research Association, Sarasota, FL.

Brush, L. (1980). *Encouraging girls in mathematics: The problem and the solution.* Cambridge, MA: Abt Books.

Campbell, P. B. (1989). So what do we do with the poor, non-white female? Issues of gender, race, and social class in mathematics and equity. *Peabody Journal of Education, 95,* 112.

Clewell, B. C., & Anderson, B. T. (1991). *Women of color in mathematics, science and engineering: A review of the literature.* Washington, DC: Center for Women Policy Studies.

Clewell, B. C., Anderson, B. T., & Thorpe, M. (1992). *Breaking the barriers: Helping female and minority students succeed in mathematics and science.* San Francisco: Jossey-Bass.

Cohen, E. G., & DeAvila, E. A. (1982). *Learning to think in math and science: Improving local education for minority children.* Final report to the Walter S. Johnson Foundation. Stanford, CA: Stanford University School of Education.

Cohen, E. G., Intili, J., & DeAvila, E. A. (1982). *Learning science in bilingual classrooms: Interaction and social status.* Stanford, CA: Stanford University Center for Educational Research.

Crawley, F. E., III, & Coe, A. S. (1990). Determinants of middle school students' intention to enroll in a high school science course: An application of the theory of reasoned action. *Journal of Research in Science Teaching, 27,* 461–476.

Creswell, J. L., & Exezidis, R. H. (1982). Research brief: Sex and ethnic differences in mathematics achievement of black and Mexican American adolescents. *Texas Tech Journal of Education, 9,* 219–222.

Creswell, J. L., & Houston, G. M. (1980). *Sex related differences in mathematics achievement in black, Chicano and Anglo adolescents.* Houston, TX: University of Houston. (ERIC Document Reproduction Service No. ED 198 079).

Davis, J. D. (1986). *The effect of mathematics course enrollment on racial/ ethnic differences in secondary school mathematics achievement* (NAEP Report 86-EMC). Princeton, NJ: Educational Testing Service.

Davis, J. D. (1989). The mathematics education of black high school students. In W. Pearson, Jr., & H. K. Bechtel (Eds.), *Blacks, science, and American education* (pp. 23–42). New Brunswick and London: Rutgers University Press.

Dossey, J. A., Mullis, I.V.S., Lindquist, M. M., & Chambers, D. L. (1988). *The mathematics report card: Are we measuring up? Trends and achievement based on the 1986 national assessment* (Report No. 17-M-01). Princeton, NJ: Educational Testing Service.

Dunteman, G. H., Wisenbaker, J., & Taylor, M. E. (1979). *Race and sex differences in college science program participation* (NSF No. SEC-7–18728). Arlington, VA: National Science Foundation.

Eccles (Parsons), J., Adler, T. F., Futterman, R., Goff, S., Kaczala, C., Meece, J. L., & Midgely, C. (1983). Expectancies, values and academic behaviors. In J. T. Spence (Ed.), *Achievement and achievement motives: Psychological and sociological motives* (pp. 75–146). New York: W. H. Freeman.

Engman, L. R. (1986). School effectiveness characteristics associated with minority student mathematics achievement. *Dissertation Abstracts International, 47,* sec. 3, 813A. (University Microfilms No. DA86–07170).

Entwisle, D. R., & Alexander, K. L. (1990). Beginning school math competence: Minority and majority comparisons. *Child Development, 61,* 454–471.

Entwisle, D. R., & Alexander, K. L. (1992). Summer setback: Race, poverty, school composition, and mathematics achievement in the first two years of school. *American Sociological Review, 57,* 72–84.

Entwisle, D. R., & Baker, D. P. (1983). Gender and young children's expectation for performance in arithmetic. *Developmental Psychology, 19,* 200–209.

Entwisle, D. R., Alexander, K. L., Cadigan, D., & Pallas, A. (1986). The schooling process in first grade: Two samples a decade apart. *American Educational Research Journal, 23* (4), 587–613.

Erickson, D. K. (1987). *A review of research on the effect of mathematics teachers' classroom behavior on girls' and boys' learning, attitudes, and participation in mathematics.* Paper presented at the American Education Research Association Special Interest Group on Research on Women in Education Conference, Portland, OR.

Erickson, D. K., Gall, M. D., Gersten, R., & Grace, D. P. (1987, April). *The differential effects of teacher behavior on girls' and boys' achievement, attitudes and future coursework plans in high school algebra classes.* Paper presented at the annual meeting of the American Educational Research Association, Washington, DC.

Ethington, C. A., & Wolfle, L. M. (1988). Women's selection of quantitative undergraduate fields of study: Direct and indirect influences. *American Educational Research Journal 25* (2), 157–175.

Evans, M. O. (1992, Summer). An estimate of race and gender role-model effects in teaching high school. *Journal of Economic Education,* 209–217.

Fennema, E. (1980). Sex-related differences in mathematics achievement: Where and why. In L. H. Fox, L. Brody, & D. Tobin (Eds.), *Women and the mathematical mystique* (pp. 76–93). Baltimore, MD: Johns Hopkins University Press.

Fennema, E. (1984). Girls, women, and mathematics: An overview. In E. Fennema & J. Ayer (Eds.), *Women and education: Equity or equality* (pp. 137–164). Berkeley, CA: McCutchan.

Fennema, E., & Carpenter, T. P. (1981). Sex-related differences in mathematics achievement, spatial visualization and affective factors. *American Educational Research Journal, 14* (1), 51–71.

Fennema, E., & Sherman, J. A. (1978). Sex-related differences in mathematics achievement and related factors: A further study. *Journal for Research in Mathematics Education, 9* (3), 189–203.

Fox, L. H. (1981). *The problem of women and mathematics.* New York: Ford Foundation.

Fox, L. H., Brody, L., & Tobin, D. (1985). The impact of early intervention programs upon course taking and attitudes in high school. In S. F. Chipman, L. R. Brush, & D. M. Wilson (Eds.), *Women and mathematics: Balancing the equation* (pp. 249–274). Hillsdale, NJ: Erlbaum.

García, J., Harrison, N. R., & Torres, J. L. (1990). The portrayal of females and minorities in selected elementary mathematics series. *School Science and Mathematics, 90* (1), 1–12.

Gilligan, C. (1982). *In a different voice: Psychological theory and women's development.* Cambridge, MA: Harvard University Press.

Ginorio, A. B. (1993). Feminism and ethnicity. *FOCUS: Newsletter of the Society for the Psychological Study of Ethnic Minority Issues, 7* (1), 3–4.

Ginsberg, H. P., & Russell, R. L. (1981). Social class and racial influences on early mathematical thinking. *Monographs of the Society for Research in Child Development, 46* (6 Serial No. 193).

Governor's Commission on Gay and Lesbian Youth. (1993, July). *Making colleges and universities safe for gay and lesbian students.* Boston, MA: Author.

Grandy, J. (1992). *Graduate enrollment decisions of undergraduate science and engineering majors: A survey of GRE test takers* (Research Rep. 92–51). Princeton, NJ: Educational Testing Service.

Grant, C. A., & Sleeter, C. E. (1986). Race, class, and gender in education research: An argument for integrative analysis. *Review of Educational Research, 56* (2), 195–211.

Green, R., Brown, J. W., & Long, R. (1978). *Report and recommendations: Conference on mathematics in American Indian education.* Washington, DC: Educational Foundation of America and American Association for the Advancement of Science.

Grignon, J. R. (1992). Computer experience of Menominee Indian students: Gender differences in coursework and use of software. *Journal of American Indian Education, 32,* 1–15.

Gross, S. (1988). *Participation and performance of women and minorities in mathematics: Vol. 1. Findings by gender and racial/ethnic group.* Rockville, MD: Montgomery County Public Schools, Carver Educational Services Center.

Gross, S. (1989, March). *Early mathematics performance and achievement: The beginning of a downward spiral for blacks and Hispanics.* Paper presented at the annual meeting of the American Educational Research Association, San Francisco, CA.

Hale-Benson, J. E. (1984). *Black children: Their roots, culture, and learning styles* (Rev. ed.). Baltimore, MD: Johns Hopkins University Press.

Hall, P. (1981). *Problems and solutions in education, employment and personal choice of minority women in science.* Washington, DC: American Association for the Advancement of Science.

Hall, V. C., Howe, A., Merkel, S., & Lederman, N. (1986). Behavior, motivation, and achievement in desegregated junior high school science classes. *Journal of Educational Psychology, 78* (2), 108–115.

Hart, L. E., & Stanic, G.M.A. (1989, March). *Attitudes and achievement-related behaviors of middle school mathematics students: Views through four lenses.* Paper presented at the annual meeting of the American Educational Research Association, San Francisco, CA.

Hill, O. W., Pettus, W. C., & Hedin, B. A. (1990). Three studies of factors affecting the attitudes of blacks and females toward the pursuit of science and science-related careers. *Journal of Research in Science Teaching, 27,* 289–314.

Holmes, B. J. (1980). *Black students' performance in the national assessments of science and mathematics* (No. SY-SM-50). Princeton, NJ: Educational Testing Service.

Hueftle, S. J., Rakow, S. J., & Welch, W. W. (1983). *Images of science: A summary of results from the 1981–82 national assessment in science.* Minneapolis: Minnesota Research and Evaluation Center.

Irvine, J. J. (1985). Teacher communication patterns are related to the race and sex of the student. *Journal of Educational Research, 78* (6), 338–345.

Jacobowitz, T. J. (1983). Relationship of sex, achievement, and science self-concept to the science career preferences of black students. *Journal of Research in Science Teaching, 20,* 621–628.

James, R. K., & Smith, S. (1985). Alienation of students from science in grades 4–12. *Science Education, 69* (1), 39–45.

Johnson, R. C. (1981). *Psychosocial influences on the math attitudes and interests of black junior high school students.* St. Louis, MO: Institute of Black Studies.

Jones, L. R., Mullis, I.V.S., Raizen, S. A., Weiss, I. R., & Weston, E. A. (1992). *The 1990 science report card: NAEP's assessment of fourth, eighth, and twelfth graders.* Washington, DC: National Center for Education Statistics.

Kahle, J. B. (1982). Can positive minority attitudes lead to achievement gains in science? Analysis of the 1977 National Assessment of Educational Progress, Attitudes Toward Science. *Science Education, 66,* 539–546.

Kahle, J. B. (1982). *The disadvantaged majority: Science education for women.* Burlington, NC: Carolina Biological Supply Company.

Kahle, J. B., & Lakes, M. K. (1983). The myth of equality in science classrooms. *Journal of Research in Science Teaching, 20* (2), 131–140.

Kelly, A. (1978). *Girls and science.* Stockholm: Almquist and Wilksell International.

Kelly, A. (Ed.). (1981). *The missing half: Girls and science education.* Manchester, England: Manchester University Press.

Kelly A., & Smail, B. (1986). Sex stereotypes and attitudes to science among eleven-year-old children. *British Journal of Educational Psychology, 56,* 158–168.

Kenschaft, P. C. (1981). Black women in mathematics. *American Mathematical Monthly, 88,* 592–604.

Kohr, R. L., Masters, J. R., Coldiron, J. F., Blust, R. S., & Skiffington, E. W. (1989). The relationship of race, class, and gender with mathematics achievement for fifth-, eighth-, and eleventh-grade students in Pennsylvania schools. *Peabody Journal of Education, 66* (2), 147–171.

Krist, P. S. (1993). *Educational and career choices in math and science for high ability African American women.* Unpublished doctoral dissertation, University of North Carolina, Chapel Hill.

Lee, V. E., & Ware, N. C. (1986, April). *When and why girls "leak" out of high school mathematics: A closer look.* Paper presented at the annual meeting of the American Educational Research Association, San Francisco, CA.

Lewellyn, R. J. (1990). Gender differences in achievement, self-efficacy, anxiety, and attributions in mathematics among primarily black junior high school students. *Dissertation Abstracts International, 50,* sec. 7, 1989A. (University Microfilms No. AAC89–22339).

Lockheed, M. E., & Gorman, K. S. (1987). Sociocultural factors affecting science learning and attitude. In A. B. Champagne & L. E. Hornig (Eds.), *This year in school science, 1987: Students and science learning* (pp. 41–66). Washington, DC: American Association for the Advancement of Science.

Lockheed, M. E., Thorpe, M., Brooks-Gunn, J., Caserly, P., & McAloon, A. (1985). *Sex and ethnic differences in middle school mathematics, science and computer science: What do we know?* Princeton, NJ: Educational Testing Service.

Lucky, L. F. (1989). Boosting science careers for the physically handicapped student. *Quarterly Journal of the Florida Academy of Sciences, 52* (3), 145–153.

MacCorquodale, P. (1980). *Psycho-social influences on the accomplishments of Mexican-American students.* Paper presented at the meeting of the American Association of School Administrators, Chicago, IL. (ERIC Document Reproduction Service No. ED 200 355).

MacCorquodale, P. (1988). Mexican-American women and mathematics: Participation, aspirations, and achievement. In R. R. Cocking & J. P. Mestre

(Eds.), *Linguistic and cultural influences on learning mathematics* (pp. 137–160). Hillsdale, NJ: Erlbaum.

McDowell, C. L. (1990). The unseen world: Race, class, and gender analysis in science education research. *The Journal of Negro Education, 59,* 273–291.

Malcom, S. M. (1990). Reclaiming our past. *The Journal of Negro Education, 59* (3), 246–259.

Maple, S. A., & Stage, F. K. (1991). Influences on the choice of math/science major by gender and ethnicity. *American Educational Research Journal, 28* (1), 37–60.

Marrett, C. B. (1981). *Patterns of enrollment in high school mathematics and science.* Madison: Wisconsin Research and Development Center.

Marrett, C. B. (1986, April). *Minority females in precollege mathematics: Towards a research agenda.* Paper presented at the annual meeting of the American Educational Research Association, San Francisco, CA.

Matthews, W. (1981). Black females and mathematics: Barricade or bridge? *Journal of Social and Behavioral Science, 27,* 88–92.

Matthews, W. (1983). *Influences on the learning and participation of minorities in mathematics.* Madison: Wisconsin Center for Education Research.

Matthews, W. (1984). Influences on the learning and participation of minorities in mathematics. *Journal for Research in Mathematics Education, 15* (2), 84–95.

Meece, J. L., Parsons, J. E., Kaczala, C. M., Goff, S. B., & Futterman, R. (1982). Sex differences in mathematics achievement: Toward a model of academic choice. *Psychological Bulletin, 91,* 324–348.

Mickens, M. (1991). Effects of supplementary computer-assisted instruction on basic algebra 1 and basic algebra 2 achievement levels of mathematics for at-risk minority students (low-achieving). *Dissertation Abstracts International, 53,* sec. 3, 704A. (University Microfilms No. AAD92–15127).

Moore, E.G.J., & Smith, A. W. (1987). Sex and ethnic group differences in mathematics achievement: Results from the national longitudinal study. *Journal for Research in Mathematics Education, 18* (1), 25–36.

Mullis, I.V.S., Dossey, J. A., Owen, E. H., & Phillips, G. W. (1993). *Mathematics report card for the nation and the states* (NAEP Report No. 23-STO2). Princeton, NJ: Educational Testing Service.

Mullis, I.V.S., & Jenkins, L. B. (1988). *The science report card: Trends and achievement based on the 1986 national assessment* (Report No. 17-S-01). Princeton, NJ: Educational Testing Service.

National Science Foundation. (1994). *Women, minorities, and persons with disabilities in science and engineering* (NSF Report No. 94–333). Arlington, VA: Author.

Nelson, R. E. (1978). *Sex differences in mathematics attitudes and related factors among Afro-American students*. Knoxville: University of Tennessee.

Olstad, R. G., Juarez, J. R., Davenport, L. J., & Haury, D. L. (1981). *Inhibitors to achievement in science and mathematics by ethnic minorities*. Seattle: University of Washington (ERIC Document Reproduction Service No. ED 233–404).

Parsons, J. E., Adler, T. F., & Kaczala, C. M. (1982). Socialization of achievement attitudes and beliefs: Parental influences. *Child Development, 53,* 310–321.

Plewis, I. (1991). Pupils' progress in reading and mathematics during primary school: Associations with ethnic group and sex. *Educational Research, 33* (2), 133–140.

Powell, R., & García, J. (1985). Portrayal of minorities and women in selected elementary science series. *Journal of Research in Science Teaching, 22,* 519–533.

Pulos, S., Stage, E. K., & Karplus, R. (1982). Setting effects in mathematical reasoning of early adolescents: Findings from three urban schools. *Journal of Early Adolescence, 2* (1), 39–59.

Rakow, S. J. (1985). Minority students in science. *Urban Education, 20* (1), 103–113.

Rakow, S. J., & Walker, C. L. (1985). The status of Hispanic American students in science: Achievement and exposure. *Science Education, 69,* 557–565.

Ramirez, M., & Casteneda, A. (1974). *Cultural democracy: Bicognitive development and education*. New York: Academic Press.

Reyes, L. H., & Stanic, G.M.A. (1988). Race, sex, socioeconomic status, and mathematics. *Journal for Research in Mathematics Education, 19* (1), 26–43.

Reynolds, A. J. (1991). Effects of an experiment-based physical science program on cognitive outcomes. *Journal of Educational Research, 84* (5), 296–302.

Rhone, L. M. (1989). Relations between parental expectation, mathematics ability, mathematics anxiety, achievement on mathematics word problems, and overall mathematics achievement in black adolescents. *Dissertation Abstracts International, 50,* sec. 12, 3902A. (University Microfilms No. AAD90–04317).

Ricker, K. S. (1978). Science and the physically handicapped. *Viewpoints in Teaching and Learning, 55,* 67–76.

Schibeci, R. A. (1984). Selecting appropriate attitudinal objectives for school science. *Science Education, 67,* 595–603.

Schreiber, D. A. (1984). *Factors affecting female attitude formation toward science: Specific reference to 12–14 year old female adolescents and their affective orientation toward middle school science.* Master's Thesis, University of Cincinnati, Cincinnati, OH. (ERIC Document Reproduction Service No. ED 256 617).

Sells, L. W. (1980). The mathematics filter and the education of women and minorities. In L. H. Fox & D. Tobin (Eds.), *Women and the mathematical mystique* (pp. 66–75). Baltimore, MD: Johns Hopkins University Press.

Sherman, J. (1980). *Women and mathematics: Summary of research from 1977–1979 NIE Grant.* Final report. Madison: Women's Research Institute of Wisconsin, Inc. (ERIC Document Reproduction Service No. ED 182 162).

Signer, B. R. (1991). CAI and at-risk minority urban high school students. *Journal of Research on Computing in Education, 24* (2), 189–203.

Simpson, R. D., & Oliver, J. S. (1985). Attitude toward science and achievement motivation profiles of male and female science students in grades six through ten. *Science Education, 69,* 511–526.

Smith, W. S., & Erb, T. O. (1986). Effect of women science career role models on early adolescents' attitudes toward scientists and women in science. *Journal of Research in Science Teaching, 23,* 667–676.

Steinkamp, M. W., & Maehr, M. L. (1984). Gender differences in motivational orientations toward achievement in school science: A quantitative synthesis. *American Educational Research Journal, 21,* 39–59.

Stokes, A. (1990). Relationships among level of cognitive development, gender, chronological age, and mathematics achievement. *Journal of Negro Education, 59,* 299–315.

Talton, E. L., & Simpson, R. D. (1984). Relationships between peer and individual attitudes toward science among adolescent students. *Science Education, 69* (1), 19–24.

Tinmouth, J., & Hamwi, G. (1994). The experience of gay and lesbian students in medical school. *Journal of the American Medical Association, 271,* 714–715.

Tizard, B., Blatchford, P., Burke, J., Farquhar, C., & Plewis, I. (1988). *Young children at school in the inner city.* Hillsdale, NJ: Erlbaum.

Treisman, P. U. (1982). *Helping minority students to excel in university-level mathematics and science courses.* Unpublished manuscript, University of California Professional Development Program, Berkeley.

Tsai, S., & Walberg, H. J. (1983). Mathematics achievement and attitude productivity in junior high school. *Journal of Educational Research, 76,* 267–272.

U.S. Congress. Office of Technology Assessment. (1988, December). *Elementary and secondary education for science and engineering: A technical memo-*

randum (OTA-TM-SET-41). Washington, DC: U.S. Government Printing Office.

Valverde, L. A. (1984). Underachievement and underrepresentation of Hispanics in mathematics and mathematics-related careers. *Journal for Research in Mathematics Education, 15* (2), 123–133.

Vanfossen, B. E. (1984, August). *Sex differences in mathematics performance: Continuing evidence.* Paper presented to Sociologists for Women in Society session. American Sociological Association.

Walker, C. L., & Rakow, S. J. (1985). The status of Hispanic American students in science: Attitudes. *Hispanic Journal of Behavioral Sciences, 7,* 225–245.

Ware, N. C., & Lee, V. E. (1988). Sex differences in choice of college science majors. *American Educational Research Journal, 25,* 593–614.

Yong, F. I. (1992). Mathematics and science attitudes of African-American middle grade students identified as gifted: Gender and grade differences. *Roeper Review, 14* (3), 136–140.

PART SIX

SINGLE SEX VERSUS COEDUCATION

IF BOYS AND GIRLS are so different in their educational styles and needs, if it is so difficult to create true gender equity in the classroom, does it make sense to separate the genders altogether? In this section, five authors address the advantages and disadvantages of educating girls and boys together and separately.

Pamela Haag takes a comprehensive look at the literature and research on single-sex education in her piece, "Single-Sex Education in Grades K–12: What Does the Research Tell Us?" Summarizing both quantitative and qualitative research, Haag offers insight into whether single-sex education truly benefits children. Valerie Lee addresses a similar issue in "Single-Sex Versus Coeducational Schools." Her thorough investigation into Catholic schools closely examines both boys' and girls' schools and the effects, if any, of separating the sexes. "Why Johnny Can't, Like, Read and Write" also looks at single-sex schooling. In her piece, Christina Hoff Sommers uses the British educational system as evidence to make the case that single-sex education is necessary to address the particular learning styles of boys.

Some researchers, however, wonder if single-sex schooling is truly the answer to gender equity problems in schools. In "What's Sex Got to Do with It? Simplistic Questions, Complex

Answers," Patricia B. Campbell and Ellen Wahl take a critical look at the questions that are being asked regarding education, suggesting that there are far more complex issues to be addressed than the simple dichotomy of single sex versus coeducation. Finally, Peggy Orenstein offers in her piece, "Anita Hill Is a Boy: Tales from a Gender Fair Classroom," a description of one teacher's novel approach to gender inequity in her class and the surprising results of her ingenuity.

As with almost all questions surrounding gender equity, the debate over the advantages and disadvantages of single sex and coeducation is not easily reduced to a few simple answers. With their variety of perspectives, these pieces illuminate the many facets of the discussion and the diverse responses available to students, parents, and educators.

SINGLE-SEX EDUCATION IN GRADES K–12

WHAT DOES THE RESEARCH TELL US?

Pamela Haag

INTEREST IN SINGLE-SEX CLASSES and schools has been reinvigorated by the educational reform movement and by skepticism that the coeducational environment is genuinely coeducational—that it fosters equitable treatment of boys and girls. When the U.S. Department of Education sponsored a roundtable on K–12 single-sex education in 1992, participants concurred that although "instructional ideas that emerge from single-sex schools have relevance for educators working in coeducational environments . . . the discussion about single-sex education frequently pits those in coeducational and single-sex schools against each other in a dichotomy that essentially falsifies their real interests and intent."[1]

This "pro" or "con" stance toward single-sex education still shapes much of the popular literature on the subject, but is misleading from a research perspective. First, single-sex learning has been inspired by several different—sometimes opposing—ideological and social contexts, especially in the last decade. Some feminists have advocated experimental single-sex environments because they may minimize the deleterious effects of gender stereotypes (for example, the notion that math is a masculine subject). On the other hand, advocates of African American "immersion schools" or academies[2] that have emerged in the last four years sometimes champion single-sex programs for the degree to which they reinforce students in normative—and traditional—gender roles.

Carol Ascher (1992), for example, summarizes the shared qualities of African American schools and programs by noting that "their content and structure . . . emanate from a belief in the importance of gender differences." The programs, according to Ascher, all include "appropriate role models of the same sex" and "female and male initiation rites." From another perspective, parents and students sometimes choose single-sex private schools for girls because of their more traditional mission statements. These schools, as Peter Carpenter (1987) asserts, to some extent certify *class* privileges. Each of these constituencies may advocate the same *practice*—single-sex education—but do so for notably different reasons and goals. As Lyn Yates (1993) notes, "sex mix . . . is not a physical variable that has a simple effect, but one whose effect is shaped non-uniformly in different types of school cultures." The structure of single-sex education, in other words, does not in and of itself ensure any particular outcomes, positive or negative, because it has multiple inspirations and forms.[3]

Assessments of single-sex education's "success" or "failure," therefore, are contingent on the goals of the stakeholders. The indicators by which research measures effects—and schools measure "success"—vary accordingly. For example, James Macfarlane's (1985) study of single-sex math classes asked, "Do segregated classes change the participation rates of male and female students?" He measured the success of the program, in part, by the extent to which it bolstered subsequent math participation for girls. In contrast, the Illinois Academy (1994) evaluated single-sex math classes by asking, among other questions, "Is a single-sex section an effective way to enhance the subsequent coeducational class achievements" of its participants? Here, the measure of success is math achievement for girls who persist, regardless of their number. As these examples show, researchers select different outcomes and indicators based on their hypotheses of what single-sex education can do for students.[4] If the primary concern is preventing dropouts or reducing teen pregnancy rates, single-sex programs may be judged successful even if they do not appreciably bolster academic performance. But if the primary concern is science uptake or college admission rates, then indicators of success or failure will be more closely tied to academic achievement.[5]

It is also difficult to compare research about the effectiveness of single-sex programs across historical contexts. In 1996 Cornelius Riordan observed, "The more that [single-sex] schools remain rare and special, the more effective they will be" for the minority of students who select them. His analysis suggests that the benefits of single-sex public schools may not persist if such schools become more prevalent; their advantages are related to their singularity. Likewise, coed schools' attention to gender equity since the early 1990s may diminish the relative advantages of single-sex education observed today, compared to those observed in the 1970s or early 1980s.[6]

The disparate contexts, programs, and school types grouped under single-sex education—as well as differing research conditions—complicate statistical analysis of single-sex education's effects, by any indicator. Perhaps the most troublesome obstacle in single-sex research is selection bias, which Valerie Lee and Marlaine Lockheed (1990) call a "social phenomenon and a statistical nuisance." Students for the most part cannot be assigned randomly to single- or mixed-sex environments, so researchers must carefully control for background variables such as socioeconomic status that would skew their results. The possibility of selection bias is especially profound in the United States, where single-sex schools are overwhelmingly private. Do students achieve because of a school's sex composition or because the schools draw from economically and educationally privileged populations? Several studies reviewed in this essay applied statistical controls for students' prior academic abilities as determined through standardized tests or grades; family and social background variables such as socioeconomic status, parents' education, and father's occupation; and school variables such as curriculum track and teacher training. Some studies that introduced no controls assert that the populations they compare are sufficiently homogeneous to mitigate selection bias.[7]

Cause and effect post a second major research challenge in single-sex education: When a single-sex school works, *why* does it work? Does a single-sex environment in and of itself produce certain outcomes or do these outcomes result from other factors *indirectly* associated with single-sex schools—such as class size, teacher preparation, and administration practices? The cause and effect question has particular relevance, of course, for policymakers or practitioners who hope to duplicate certain single-sex advantages for girls in the coeducational environment.

The variety of inspirations, desired outcomes, and sociocultural contexts for single-sex education, in summary, make it difficult to answer the question, "Does single-sex education work better for girls?" Instead, some researchers view single-sex contexts, in Lee's (1992) phrase, as "a source of pedagogical insight" or "laboratories" that may inform and improve the coeducational environment. Researchers like Emmanuel Jimenez ask, "What do single-sex and coeducational schools actually do that is different?" Others, including Valerie Lee, approach the research project with an eye to learning what properties contribute to the success or failure of the single-sex school.[8]

This essay will review the research[9] on K–12 single-sex schools and classes with particular attention to effects on girls.[10] Although researchers agree that findings on the subject have been inconsistent overall, exhibiting a "now-you-see-it-now-you-don't effect" that is both "tantalizing and frustrating," according to Judith Gill, this essay will emphasize findings on specific outcomes about which researchers share some agreement. The first section, summarizing research on single-sex education and attitudinal variables, looks at self-esteem, subject preference, sex stereotyping, and, finally, "environment" issues. The second section, which explores achievement variables, examines two groups of studies: those that show few or no effects by school type (coed or single sex), and those that interpret positive effects as a result of school type. Where possible, special emphasis will be placed on single-sex *classes*—particularly classes in math and science, the focus of many recent pilot programs aimed at boosting girls' performance in grades K–12.

Unfortunately, much of the literature here is anecdotal, with numerous "reports of individual experiences that are neither based on nor informed by qualitative research methodology," as Gaell Hildebrand notes. According to a 1996 review, single-sex classes have been proliferating "at a rate well ahead of the research evidence on which its success, or otherwise, could be determined." Because sound published research on single-sex classes is sparse, this review supplements articles on the topic with notable unpublished papers delivered at conferences.[11]

Finally, this review does not limit itself to U.S. studies because so much of the signal work on single-sex education has been conducted in countries like England, New Zealand, Australia, Thailand, Jamaica, and Nigeria that offer single-sex public schools. Although these studies frequently reflect a distinct cultural and economic context, their findings offer insights into the outcomes American educators might expect were they to institute public school forms of single-sex education. Since the United States has so few public single-sex schools or programs at present, research insights from countries rich in public single-sex schools may in some ways be more pertinent for comparison than evidence from private single-sex schools within the United States.

Section 1: Attitudinal and Environment Variables

Self-Esteem

Although many researchers question the inherent value of "self-esteem" as an independent outcome or educational goal, a few published studies have tested the popular wisdom that girls in single-sex schools have a higher self-concept. Interestingly, studies that found higher "self-esteem" for girls in the single-sex environment used a multidimensional measure comprising such subcategories as academic, athletic, and social esteem. Levels of esteem in specific domains (that is, academic achievement or physical appearance) may differ by school type, these studies concluded.

Cairns (1990) investigated self-esteem and locus of control (an individual's sense of how environment hinders or facilitates her/his goals) for 2,295 students in 76 secondary and academically oriented "grammar" schools in Northern Ireland. Departing from earlier studies by Foon (1988) and Lee and Bryk (1986), he applied a multidimensional measure of "self-esteem" comprising four subcategories—social, cognitive, athletic, and general—to create a subtler portrait of the interaction between school type and attitudes. After conducting an analysis of variance by gender and school type for each separate kind of school (secondary and grammar), Cairns concluded that "for the third time, and in a third culture . . . single-sex schools are associated with benefits in terms of self-esteem and locus of control." He cautioned, however, that his findings of higher esteem may be confined to the domain of cognitive self-concept and to the context of academically oriented single-sex grammar schools.[12]

Granleese and Joseph (1993), also investigating Northern Ireland, hypothesized that "gender intensification"—sex role rigidity—would be strongest in a mixed-sex social environment for adolescent girls. Like Cairns, Granleese and Joseph deployed a domain-specific self-concept measure in their study of 167 girls from two Belfast secondary schools— one single-sex and the other coed—matched for location and religious affiliation. The authors discovered that girls at the single-sex school were less critical of their own behavioral conduct—the single best predictor of "global" (overall) self-worth in the all-girls school—than were girls at the mixed-sex school, where physical appearance was the single best predictor of degree of global self-worth. They concluded that "although scores on global self-worth may not be any different between girls from single-sex and mixed-sex schools, the *determinants* of global self-worth are."[13]

Self-esteem studies that do not find positive effects on girls of single-sex education indirectly support Granleese and Joseph's conclusion: They tend to analyze general self-concept rather than its specific components, and find no overall benefit by school type. Foon (1988) surveyed 1,675 secondary students in 16 nongovernmental (private) coed and single-sex schools in Australia to gauge the effects of school type on general self-esteem, performance, and subject preferences. She found no significant differences in self-esteem between girls from mixed and single-sex schools, although she reported higher self-esteem for *boys* attending single-sex schools.[14]

Brutsaert and Bracke (1994) found little effect of school type in their study, which measured the "general well-being" of 2,095 sixth grade students in 60 private Belgian elementary schools. This study defined well-being as "adjustment to school life as reflected by affective outcomes" such as "self-esteem, sense of mastery, [and] sense of belonging." After controlling for students' socioeconomic status and size of school, and performing a stepwise multivariate regression analysis,[15] Brutsaert concluded that, at least on the elementary school level, "girls do not seem to be influenced in any way by the gender organization of the school." Boys, in contrast, are negatively affected not by the gender composition of the student population, but by a preponderance of female teachers on staff, which lowers boys' overall sense of well-being. This study underscores the importance of considering students' grade level and the sex composition of the *staff* in assessing the effects of sex organization on outcomes such as esteem.[16]

Smith (1996) conducted a longitudinal study over a 10-year period, investigating students' attitudes and achievement in one all-boys' and one all-girls' high school in Australia that had transitioned to coeducation (N = 1,300). Both girls' and boys' self-concept, measured by the Marsh Self-Description Questionnaire II, declined initially during the transition but after five years increased to a level above that which was measured when the students were in single-sex classrooms.[17]

Taken as a whole, studies of girls' self-esteem as affected by school type suggest that the sources of esteem for girls may differ in single-sex and coeducational schools. Two published studies that argue for self-esteem gains for girls in single-sex schools point to higher degrees of *cognitive* self-worth and freer *behavioral conduct*. Studies have not shown a significant interaction of school type and *general* or overall self-concept. In other words, neither school type has been shown in these studies to generate a greater quantity of overall esteem for girls, although a specific source of esteem—for example, appearance or athletic skill—may differ for girls in single-sex and coed schools.

Attitudes Toward Academic Subjects

There is something of a consensus that girls in single-sex schools tend to perceive subjects such as math and physics as less "masculine" and may have stronger preferences for them than their coeducated peers. The consistency of this finding in a variety of single-sex schools suggests that it may be a factor intrinsic to the single-sex environment rather than a characteristic of educational practices or policies indirectly associated with these schools. However, more research is needed to ascertain such cause-and-effect relationships. None of the attitude studies reviewed here comments on single-sex classes.

Published studies that use subject preferences and girls' attitudes toward math and science as indicators have concluded uniformly that single-sex environments have a positive effect for girls. Girls in these environments rate fields such as physics as less masculine than do their coeducational counterparts. Foon notes that students attending single-sex schools "seem to be less rigidly attached to traditional views about the appropriateness of subject areas by sex." Females, in particular, she found, were more likely to prefer science in single-sex than the coed schools. Vockell and Lobonc (1981), in one of the first studies of coeducation and subject preference, administered a questionnaire to 476 non-coed and 280 coed juniors and seniors in U.S. high schools. They found that "non-coed girls rated physical sciences as less masculine than the coed girls." No distinctions by school type were evident in the ratings of the biological sciences. Subsequent studies in other cultures have generated similar findings. Stables (1990) surveyed more than 2,300 British comprehensive (public) school students (ages 13–14), asking them to weigh the importance of school subjects and rank subjects by preference. Stables found no differences in the perception of subject importance by sex and school type, but consistent, significant sex differences on every attitude section. These differences were greater among coeducated students. Single-sex education, he concluded, "tends to reduce polarization of attitudes between the sexes generally, but especially regarding physics, where the polarization is particularly marked in the mixed-sex schools."[18]

Two more recent studies have found single-sex schools exerting a significant effect on girls' subject preferences, and have refined the factors that seem to influence positively girls' attitudes toward the sciences: Mallam (1993) found that students in all-girls Nigerian schools favored math more than girls in coed Nigerian public boarding schools. She found the highest percent of positive attitudes in all-girls' schools where mathematics was taught by female teachers. Finally, Colley et al. (1994) in Britain administered a survey asking students to rank their school subject preferences. Their database included 648 students aged 11–12 years, and 485 students aged 15–16 from three single-sex girls' schools, four single-sex boys' schools, and four public coeducational schools. In the younger age group, girls from single-sex schools showed much stronger preferences than their coed peers for such stereotypically "masculine" subjects as mathematics and science. Young boys from single-sex schools similarly showed stronger preferences for such stereotypically "feminine" subjects as music and art. Among older pupils, however, gender rather than school type accounted for most differences.[19]

Degree of "Sex Stereotyping"

Despite the fairly uniform findings showing girls' stronger preferences for less "traditional" subjects in single-sex schools, published research that examines sex roles and stereotyping more generally has found no consistent relationship between school type and degrees of sex stereotyping.

Two studies used the "Attitudes Toward Women" scale[20] to measure respondents' views of the sexes and gender-appropriate "social behavior." Harris (1986) surveyed 538 first-year students in an Australian university psychology class, two-thirds of which was female. Her findings, when analyzed by gender and school type, did "not support the hypothesis that either a single-sex or a coeducational school is more likely to foster traditional sex role stereotypes." Signorella and Frieze's (1996) longitudinal study of a U.S. private school transitioning to coeducation found a lessening of sex role clichés over time in all grades, but no indication that class type (single-sex or coed) influenced the degree of stereotyping. The findings, although based on a small sample, "show no consistent tendency for students in single-sex classrooms to display less gender stereotyping," conclude the authors.[21]

Lee and Marks (1994) found that sex stereotyping, albeit of different sorts, occurs with as much frequency in the single-sex context as in the coeducational. After analyzing data from surveys, school records, class observations, and interviews from 66 classrooms in 21 schools, the authors found that no school was entirely free of sexism. "Gender reinforcement and embedded discrimination" were evident in all three types of schools (girls', boys', and coeducational), yet were more common in single-sex schools. "Gender domination and active discrimination of females," which Lee notes "can only occur in environments in which both sexes are present," were common in coeducational schools. Surprisingly, 66 percent of all the sexist incidents in the coeducational classrooms occurred in chemistry classes, although those classes constituted only 20 percent of the observations. This "localization of sexism in coeducational schools to physical science classes," the study notes, "is striking," especially in comparison to the unremarkable nature of these classes in the girls' schools.[22]

Lee and Marks conclude that "strong policies [insisting] on the equitable treatment of male and female students make a difference" in the degree of sex stereotyping found in schools. But the mere separation of girls and boys appears not to diminish the extent to which gender roles are reinforced. Gill (1996), in an overview of single-sex environments in New Zealand, also submits that "teacher awareness is of much more significance than school gender context in producing or overcoming stereotypical gender limitations on students."[23]

Recent popular commentary on single-sex education sometimes informally assumes that single-sex environments by their nature diminish sex stereotyping. This assumption confuses "sex" and "gender."[24] Single-sex schools have either all-male or all-female student populations, yet the reproduction of gender roles—cultural norms of "masculine" and "feminine" behavior—can occur in a single-sex as well as a mixed-sex environment. Boys in an all-male school, for example, may assume the highly gendered role of the "sissy"; conversely, girls in all-female environments may nonetheless be "trained" or schooled in feminine norms just as surely as girls in coeducational environments, as Lee and Marks' work underscores. Sound teacher training seems to offer promise of reducing sex stereotyping in both the coed and single-sex environment.

The "Environment" Question

Three studies agree that single-sex environments are perceived by students to have higher levels of "order," control, and "organization." But the studies diverge in their assessments of whether students find single-sex settings to be more "affiliative," "involving," or pleasant than the coed environment.

Two of the formative early works on school type—Dale's multivolume *Mixed or Single-Sex School?* (1969) and Coleman's *The Adolescent Society* (1961)—examined coed and single-sex "environments" in terms of how well they satisfied students. Dale's work, which became a research basis for the shift toward coeducation in the late 1960s, administered a questionnaire to thousands of former British secondary school students. He found that students "preferred" a coed environment over single-sex schools, which in their perception overemphasized academic work and academic success. Arguing that schools should act as microcosms of society, Dale endorsed coeducation on the strength of its more "natural" environment for students. Coleman, in contrast, surveyed the American coeducational landscape and concluded that the schools constituted an "adolescent subculture," a contained world of social interactions governed by "cars and the cruel jungle of rating and dating" rather than interest in either academic achievement or social adjustment. Countering Dale's study, Coleman speculated that single-sex schools provided a more effective environment for education because they diminished somewhat the "competition for adolescent energies" apparent in the coed "subculture."[25]

Two published studies by Trickett et al. and Schneider and Coutts (1982) revisited the debate over the relative merits of school environment. Both studies agreed that students perceive the environments to be distinct. Trickett et al. used data from 456 randomly selected grade 10 and 12 students in 15 representative U.S. single-sex and coeducational boarding schools to gauge environmental differences between school type, as measured by a Classroom Environment Scale survey. Single-sex schools, Trickett concluded, enjoyed higher levels of student involvement, affiliation among students, task orientation, competition, organization, and teacher control than coed schools. Trickett did not analyze his data by sex. In the same year Schneider et al. surveyed 2,029 grade 10 and 12 students in 13 Canadian private coeducational and single-sex schools using the "High School Characteristics Index."[26] In contrast to Trickett, Schneider and Coutts concluded that students perceive "coeducational schools as placing greater emphasis than single-sex schools on affiliation and . . . nonacademic activities." Schneider and Coutts, who analyzed their data by school type, grade, and sex, found that girls and boys in single-sex schools both perceive single-sex schools to have greater "authority structure" and "order" (Trickett) and "greater emphasis on control and discipline" (Schneider and Coutts). In 1988 Schneider et al. revisited the school environment issues, using the same student population, in a study that gleaned through an "attitudes" questionnaire that "the majority of male *and female* students from both school types . . . reported a preference for coeducation."[27]

A study by Gierl (1994) that deployed the "Classroom Environment Scale" in an all-girls' classroom setting argues, contrary to Schneider (1988), that girls have more positive perceptions of—and preferences for—the single-sex classroom. Gierl sought the "intrinsic characteristics" of a single-sex 11th-grade physics class in a U.S. Catholic school. Comparing data from four groups—girls in an all-girls class and a mixed-sex class, and boys in an all-boys class and a mixed-sex class—he discovered negligible differences in final marks. Yet he found that "females in the single-sex class reported that Physics 20 was more involving than Physics 10 [the mixed-sex class] when compared to males in the single-sex class and males in the mixed-sex class." Females perceived the class to be more affiliative and to have higher levels of "order and organization," and "had a stronger preference" for the "gender-specific context."[28]

Further research might pinpoint the school or classroom-level characteristics that encourage the perception of a more orderly learning environment in the single-sex school These practices may prove adaptable to the coeducational classroom. In any event, there is no necessary relationship between *perceptions* of environment and achievement, as the next section will elaborate.

Section 2: Achievement Variables— Single-Sex Classes and Single-Sex Schools

Single-Sex Classes and Their Effect on Achievement Outcomes for Girls

There is very little research at this point on single-sex classes, and enthusiasm is high for implementing programs on an experimental basis and gathering evidence to move beyond anecdotal assessment. The fledgling body of research on single-sex classes has yielded relatively consistent findings: Whereas girls perceive the classrooms in many cases to be superior, and may register gains in confidence, these benefits have not translated into measured improvements in achievement. Some studies, in fact, report diminished achievement for girls in single-sex classrooms. A few studies that look more specifically at teacher training and peer interaction have identified these factors as more crucial to creating a positive learning environment than classroom sex composition.

Girls' documented preferences for single-sex classes have not yet translated into corresponding gains in achievement. Studies that attempt to assess the effects of single-sex schools and classes on achievement— whether through grades, test scores, or standardized aptitude tests—have so far found few correlations between the two. Although they often recommend the continuation of single-sex classes as an important experiment that has not produced negative effects, studies of single-sex classes to date have fairly consistently documented a paradox: Girls' higher estimations of single-sex math and science classes come in the absence of any accompanying achievement gains.

One of the early studies of single-sex classes by Macfarlane and Crawford (1985) illustrates the attitude/achievement paradox. Macfarlane analyzed data from the first year of a longitudinal study of sex-segregated mathematics classes in Ontario on several attitudinal and achievement measures. The sample included grade 10–13 students and a control group from a school of similar socioeconomic status. Macfarlane found that after the first year, "students' responses indicate . . . that while there were some changes in the attitudes of students [in the single-sex classes], they did not differ significantly from the changes in the attitudes of students at the comparison school. This would tend to suggest that the segregated classes had no significant effect on students' attitudes as measured by the Mathematics Attitudes Scales." Twenty-five percent of all students in the single-sex classes self-reported that the classes had "improved their attitudes, with females responding more positively than males." Achievement gains, however, were "not so much evident with respect to actual marks and test scores," despite students' perceptions of higher performance. In fact, marks of students in the single-sex classes fell significantly from grades 9 to 10 while those of students at the comparison school remained stable. There was no difference between the scores of the schools on the Canadian Achievement Test math portion. Generally, students reported more dramatic attitude changes than test scores or attitude scales otherwise indicated.[29]

In the same year Harvey (1985) evaluated science test results of 2,900 students in 17 secondary schools in England—two coed schools with single-sex science classes, six coed schools with coed science classes, six all-girls schools, and three all-boys schools. Harvey controlled for identical verbal reasoning scores on standardized tests. His results indicated that there was no advantage to teaching students in single-sex science groups, that girls in coed schools perform better in science than girls in single-sex schools, and that no difference was apparent between boys in coed and boys in single-sex schools.[30]

Rowe (1988) wanted to determine the "extent to which . . . establishing single-sex classes in a coeducational postprimary school [was] effective in improving students' mathematics achievement and confidence, as well as their subsequent participation" in math. Through a sample of 398 middle-school students randomly allocated to single-sex and mixed-sex classes at one Australian middle school, Rowe found that for the "intact groups"—those students who remained in either a coed or single-sex class—students in single-sex classes registered consistently higher gains in confidence than those in mixed-sex classes. Among the "shift group"— those students who, because of scheduling constraints, moved from single-sex to mixed-sex classes—Rowe found that confidence scores declined, "significantly so" for girls. Although higher confidence was associated statistically with achievement and greater rates of persistence in advanced mathematics classes for girls, Rowe reported no significant differences in mathematics achievement per se. The change in students' mathematics achievement over time, he discovered, "independent of confidence, was similar for all students, regardless of class type." Confidence gains observed in the single-sex classes for girls did not relate directly to achievement gains.[31]

Leder and Forgasz (1994) gathered both qualitative and quantitative data—attitudinal and performance measures—to better integrate into their study the many factors that influence achievement. Comparing performance data on roughly 160 Australian students—half of them, boys and half, girls—in grade 8 single-sex math classes (male and female) and two coed math classes, the study found no significant differences for females by class grouping, much as Macfarlane had shown earlier. The study also confirmed Forgasz's 1993 research on achievement, which found "gender differences" in the scores of 7th-grade boys and girls in coed schools, "irrespective of" the class type in which they learned. Furthermore, the differences in the scores of males in mixed and single-sex settings were greater than between corresponding groups of females. Leder and Forgasz echo other studies of single-sex schools in noting that some student beliefs and stereotypes about math persisted "or were more pronounced at the end of the year." However, both female students and their mothers were more "favorably inclined toward the single-sex mathematics program than were their male counterparts." The authors conclude that the study did not provide "unequivocal evidence" that single-sex math classes per se address gender differences in mathematics learning outcomes, but the study does confirm an overall preference among female students for the single-sex classroom environment.[32]

Of related interest are a few studies of sex ratios in the classroom and their effects. Webb (1984), interested in both interaction and achievement outcomes, administered tests in mathematical reasoning ability at the beginning and end of the school year to 77 students in two junior high schools. Over the course of the year, the students worked for a period of time in majority male, majority female, or equal male-female groups. She then analyzed transcripts of group work. Webb did not simply document the quantity of interactions by sex, but scrutinized their substance, classifying comments into six positive and negative categories. The categories are: asks for explanation and does not receive one, asks for explanation and receives one, asks for procedural information and receives it, and so on. "The major result in the patterns of same-sex and cross-sex interaction in majority female groups," she concluded, was that females asked the males for explanations much more often than would be predicted on the basis of the males' numbers in the group. "In groups with two females and two males, a striking result is that when females asked males for explanations, only 7 percent of their requests were granted. In contrast, females responded to 70 percent of the males' requests." Webb concludes that decreasing the number of males, ironically, results in a greater focus on the males in the group, and that girls amassed more "negative" interactions—

for example, they more frequently asked for information and did not receive it. Webb's study validates one of the rationales for single-sex classes for math and science: girls' perceived disadvantage in attracting classroom attention in a mixed-sex group.[33]

Workman's (1990) study of a 10-week experiment with single-sex groupings in two Northern California high school geometry classes found, again, no differences in performance between the single-sex and mixed-sex groups. Many students felt they learned less in the single-sex groups, although they did not elaborate why. Teachers noted that the groups that worked best together were those in which some members were friends and/or a member "was one of the brighter students in the class," regardless of the sex composition of the grouping.[34]

Parker and Rennie (1986), investigating single-sex groupings in Australia, similarly concluded that effects extrinsic to the sex composition of the class may account for girls' perceptions of an improved atmosphere and interactive environment in the single-sex class. They designed an inservice program involving 20 teachers to facilitate a nonsexist approach to teaching. All teachers were given special help to increase their confidence in teaching the subject unit on electricity, yet half of the teachers (the experimental group) were also exposed to a program to alert them to sexist patterns in the classroom. The authors found that in the experimental classes, "boys and girls in mixed-sex and single-sex groups exhibited the same pattern of activity, whereas the control classes showed behavior differences in the mixed-sex group." Hence, teacher training in nonsexist approaches seemed to foster the same positive results in the coed context as those observed in the single-sex control group. Parker and Rennie concluded that teachers can be made aware of sexism and trained to improve their classroom style but that, in areas where teachers have a "low level of awareness" or skills, single-sex groupings may benefit girls' science education.[35]

Gaell Hildebrand (1996), skeptical of single-sex initiatives in Australia, argues that single-sex classes often give the appearance that a school system is "doing something" about gender equity "without [changing] any of the . . . ways that gender is socially constructed in schools."[36] In a policy review, Parker and Rennie (1996) assert that the implementation of single-sex classes is not a "cost-neutral innovation. [Administrators] must be prepared . . . to resource the change, especially through the provision of professional development support." The placement of students in single-sex classes, they argue, "created environments in which teachers could address some of the apparent shortcomings of the students' previous education. . . . Where teachers had, or were prepared to develop, strategies . . . these shortcomings were addressed effectively."

Achievement in Single-Sex Schools: Studies That Do Not Show Differences Attributed to School Type

Research findings are more ambiguous concerning the effects of single-sex schools on girls' achievement. This section will review studies that have found limited or no positive effects for girls in single-sex schools. The next will examine studies that do attribute some positive outcomes to school type.

While most of the studies summarized here did find uncorrected or "raw" gaps favoring girls in single-sex schools, once findings were adjusted for socioeconomic or ability variables, these differences diminished. The studies suggest that the selectivity of most single-sex schools and/or the socioeconomic status of students who attend such schools account for most differences in achievement between single-sex and coeducational contexts.

Finn's (1980) descriptive study[37] of examination results in the United States, Sweden, and Britain confirmed that "patterns of sex differences are remarkably similar across the three countries, especially in coeducational schools." Yet he found "little if any correlation of school characteristics with distinctions between boys' and girls' achievement profiles." That is, none of the school characteristics selected or background features (Finn controlled for socioeconomic status, family size, and parents' education) mediated large discrepancies "between male and female students in terms of verbal and science achievement." In England's single-sex school population, Finn did discover a smaller gap between boys' and girls' performance, but did not feel confident in ascribing the trend to the effects of school type. A hypothesis for future research, he proposed, would be that female teachers and peers may facilitate girls' learning in British single-sex schools.[38]

Steedman (1985) also utilized a large database (those born in Great Britain in a particular week in 1958 who participated in the National Child Development Study) and performance on standardized general exams. She controlled for both parents' educational level, the father's occupation, and the selectivity of the school. She further controlled for pre-existing differences in academic achievement as indicated by primary school attainment at ages 7 and 11. Steedman found that with a few exceptions (French language scores), differences in examination results were not explained by school type once discrepancies at intake were considered.[39]

Bell (1989) hypothesized that the degree of competitiveness of single-sex schools—how elite they are—has been overlooked in analysis of their effectiveness. Working with an Assessment Performance Unit test for British students at ages 11, 13, and 15, Bell found no "evidence of difference between the two types of schools" once "selective schools" were removed from the sample. "When no allowance is made for the type of school"—meaning here, its degree of selectivity—"there are large differences between the subcategory performance between single-sex and mixed schools for each sex of pupil. However, these results do not indicate that single-sex schooling is more effective than mixed schooling but reflect the fact that a greater proportion of the single-sex schools are independent or grammar with pupil selection policies."[40]

It is difficult to identify or analyze the effects of school type because this macro variable interacts with population variables, such as an individual's socioeconomic status prior to enrolling in the school. Because students are "nested" within schools and communities, variables relevant to populations interact with school type level variables to influence outcomes. A more sophisticated statistical technique, Hierarchical Linear Modeling (HLM), allows researchers to control simultaneously for variables at both the school level (for example, school type) and student population level (for example, socioeconomic status or parental background).

Two recent studies that apply HLM to the single-sex education question have not found significant school type effects. Young and Fraser (1992) analyzed a stratified random sample of 4,917 students from 233 Australian schools. They used HLM to determine which factors account for differences—confirmed in the first stage of the analysis—between girls' and boys' physics achievement. The percentage of explained variance in physics achievement within schools was 88 percent and between schools was 12 percent. In other words, Young and Fraser found a great deal of "between-schools" (single-sex versus coed) variance that was not explained by factors such as a student's attitude toward science, the occupation of his or her parents, and the numbers of books in the student's home. Further investigations were then made into between-school variables. Sex composition—whether single-sex or mixed—of the school reduced between-school variance only marginally (by 7 percent); the addition of school type (Catholic, independent, government) caused a more substantial reduction in between-schools variance (15 percent). However, when the average socioeconomic level of the students within the school (an aggregate variable) was included in the model, the drop in unexplained between-school variance was more dramatic (41 percent). "This variable appeared to swamp the effects of sex composition of the school and school type, with the inclusion of the latter not significantly reducing the unexplained between-schools variance," Young and Fraser observe. They conclude that what influences student performance in physics is the average socioeconomic status of the students attending the school and not the school's sex composition.[41]

More recently, Harker and Nash (1997) used data gathered in a longitudinal study of more than 5,000 8th-grade equivalent students in New Zealand, and utilized HLM to control simultaneously for individual characteristics (for example, socioeconomic status) and school type characteristics. As with other studies, Harker confirmed statistically significant raw differences in favor of girls at single-sex schools in the data. Yet after applying controls for ability levels, social and ethnic backgrounds, and mix at the two types of school, he observed that "initial significant differences between them disappear." The "difference in average academic attainment of girls who attend single-sex as against coeducational schools is more apparent than real," he finds. "When it comes to policy options that might be seen as emerging from the data, it would seem that school type is not an important factor in . . . [improving] the performance level of girls in math and science."[42]

In another recent study, LePore and Warren (1997) used the National Educational Longitudinal Study of 1988 to test three hypotheses: first, that boys and girls who attend single-sex Catholic secondary schools score higher on tests of achievement and self-concept than their counterparts in Catholic mixed-sex schools; second, that any advantages are especially powerful for female students; and, third, that these advantages can be explained by pre-enrollment differences in learning between students. The researchers found that "boys in single-sex schools do not increase their test scores any more than boys in coeducational schools," although they may score higher on achievement tests. For girls, they conclude, "nowhere did we find statistically significant positive effects of single-sex school enrollment for girls. . . . We find no evidence that single-sex Catholic school boys or girls learn more than their coeducational Catholic school peers during high school."

LePore and Warren speculate that their findings differ from those of Lee and Bryk (1986) [see next section, "Achievement in Single-Sex Schools: Studies That Show Some Positive Effects"] in part because something about Catholic schools may have changed from the 1980 "High School and Beyond"[43] data utilized in the 1986 study. They further speculate that the "advantage" associated with enrollment in a single-sex secondary school may have dwindled after coed schools addressed gender bias issues spotlighted in the 1980s.[44]

Achievement in Single-Sex Schools: Studies That Show Some Positive Effects

Studies that have discovered positive achievement outcomes attributable to the single-sex environment have all dealt with single-sex schools rather than classes.

Hamilton's (1985) descriptive study of 1,146 boys and girls—representing 14 percent of the grade 11 high school population of Jamaica—used scores on the standardized general certificate exam to compare achievement across school type. Hamilton did not control for background variables, but drew from elite and non-elite schools to ensure a more representative sample. She found that boys *and* girls from single-sex institutions performed "significantly better" than their counterparts in coed schools.[45]

Jimenez and Lockheed's (1989) study of mathematics performance in Thailand asks, "Would a student, randomly chosen from the general population, do better in a coeducational or in a single-sex school, and are the effects similar for male and female students?" Jimenez, concerned about selection bias, ran a regression to identify the most common background variables associated with the selection of single-sex schools. For girls, these variables included maternal education, educational expectations, home language, and private school choice. Having established predictors for single-sex school choice, Jimenez applied a Heckman two-step methodology[46] to correct for student background and selection bias and therefore more accurately discern whether students in single-sex schools have an achievement advantage. Jimenez discovered that a Thai 8th-grade girl with the background of an average single-sex school student, chosen randomly from the population, would improve her achievement by about 40 percent in a single-sex context, whereas a boy would *reduce* his score by 20 percent. Jimenez then explored possible reasons for the performance difference. Finding no structural or administrative advantages to single-sex schools (the opposite, in fact), he ran a regression for average pre-test score, proportion of mothers with greater than primary education, and proportion of fathers with professional occupations. Jimenez found a high correlation between an average student's pre-test and post-test scores for both boys and girls in both single-sex and coed schools. The study concluded that "peer quality" effects seem to account for most of the difference between the two types of schools.[47]

In some respects Carpenter and Hayden's (1987) study of single-sex schools in Queensland and Victoria, Australia, confirms the importance of peer influence, social context, and socioeconomic status on positive outcomes for achievement. Questioning whether "type of secondary school attended affects girls' academic achievement net of other relevant factors," the authors compared the effects of school type with 12th-year students in Queensland (N = 460) and Victoria (N = 579). In Queensland all public secondary schools are coeducational, and all single-sex schools are private. Victoria, in contrast, contains many single-sex, public secondary schools. Carpenter and Hayden used multiple regression analysis to identify predictors of 12th-year success, and found that in both provinces, the mother's educational level affected achievement. In Victoria, however, school sex composition emerged as a factor that exposed girls to encouragement to attend college and mediated the effects of social structure. In Queensland, with a narrower range of schooling options, school sex composition was found to have no bearing on academic achievement. Carpenter's study implies that social context—including socioeconomic status and the variety of schooling available—may heighten or minimize the effects of school type.[48]

Riordan's extensive work on single-sex education in the United States similarly has found that school type benefits certain populations more than others. Riordan's 1985 study examined the various types of Catholic private schools used in comparisons with public schools, and concluded that only mixed-sex Catholic schools could be validly compared to coeducational public schools. Using a sample of white public and Catholic school students[49] from the full National Longitudinal Study of the High School Class of 1972, Riordan tested for differences between Catholic single-sex and public mixed-sex schools on several academic outcomes measures, including test scores in reading and math, 1972 verbal and math SAT scores, and a 1979 measure of educational attainment. Riordan found that Catholic single-sex schools scored consistently higher than coed public schools; attainments in Catholic mixed-sex schools differed little from those in public coed schools. Of all the populations tested, however, "females in Catholic single-sex schools [were] clearly the most favored group in any comparison with public school students." Riordan attributes some of the advantage to school context, and presents data to support the idea that Catholic single-sex schools heighten the academic atmosphere (requiring students, for example, to spend more time on homework), although he does not definitively attribute the differences in attainment to school context.[50]

A subsequent study in 1994 used the "High School and Beyond" longitudinal data to clarify further the effects of single-sex education on different populations and in specific curricular areas. Riordan conducted separate analyses for students by sex and race on academic and attitudinal outcomes. He discovered that among African American and Hispanic American students attending Catholic secondary schools, both males and females in single-sex schools scored higher on standardized cognitive tests than their same-sex peers in mixed-sex schools. To explain the one-year grade equivalent of difference in cognitive learning, Riordan applied a set of formal and informal school variables as controls. They included type of curriculum, amount of homework, discipline, parental interest, and number of successful role models. Policies in single-sex schools emphasize the academic side of these variables, he argues, which explain virtually all of the test score differences between the two types of schools. Both males and females in single-sex schools also gained on attitudinal variables such as leadership behavior and a "sense of environmental control," but much less of this difference was explained by school variables.[51]

Some of Lee's substantial research on single-sex education, like Riordan's, has used the longitudinal "High School and Beyond" data to gauge achievement and attitude effects—and sustained effects over time—of single-sex education. Lee and Bryk (1986) examined a random sample of 1,807 students in 75 Catholic high schools, drawn from the "High School and Beyond" survey, which included data for students' sophomore and senior years. The study controlled for several background variables, including socioeconomic status, race/ethnicity, and plans to attend college. Data were analyzed for numerous academic and attitudinal variables. The hypothesis that students in single-sex schools would "significantly outperform their counterparts in coeducational schools on a wide array of outcomes" was confirmed by the analysis. Girls' schools, Lee and Bryk found, evidenced "consistent and positive effects" on students' attitudes toward academics (a point borne out in other research on attitudes, discussed above), course enrollment patterns, achievement, and educational aspirations. While conceding the possibility of a "selection bias"—that parents choose single-sex schools for specific reasons that affect outcomes—Lee speculates that policies or conditions within single-sex schools—ranging from school resources, curriculum homogeneity, gender composition of the faculty or administration, to school teaching environment—may contribute to effects on achievement and attitudes.[52]

Marsh (1989) disputes Lee and Bryk's (1986) findings on methodological grounds, generating different conclusions from the same data. He criticizes Lee's use of a "one-tailed" significance test, which allows the discovery of "significant differences" only in the direction of single-sex education. (Hence, Marsh argues, Lee cannot find any positive effects in favor of coeducation.) He also faults Lee and Bryk's placement of significance at $p < 0.05$, rather than the stricter standard of $p < 0.01$. Marsh concludes that 9 of the 74 tests Lee found statistically significant (1986) would have been nonsignificant had a two-tailed test been used. Furthermore, at the $p < 0.01$ level, he contends, only 3 of the 74 tests were statistically significant. Marsh also argues that the controls for pre-existing differences in Lee's study failed to account for possible pre-existing differences in academic achievement. Marsh conducted four separate analyses to determine which differences in 1982 and 1984 outcomes "may (possibly) be interpretable" as school type effects. Although large differences by school type were ascertained before any controls were applied, the differences diminished in number as Marsh sequentially applied controls in the next stages. When he controlled for pre-enrollment differences in student achievement as represented in 1980 academic outcomes—the "most demanding test" of school type differences—he found only three significant effects by school type, on relatively unimportant variables.[53]

Lee has defended her methodological premises, and in 1990 Lee and Marks revisited the "High School and Beyond" survey to investigate the "sustained effects" of single-sex schools on attitudes, behaviors, and values. The 1990 study first discovered that those women who had attended single-sex schools had higher educational aspirations and were more likely than their coed counterparts to attend selective four-year colleges. However, after controls were applied for attendance at a selective college, the effects on young women's aspirations disappeared. This led Lee and Marks to conclude that single-sex education may be an indirect influence, in that it facilitated "entry into a select college in the first place," rather than a direct influence. The study found that single-sex girls continued to hold less stereotypic views of gender roles into the college experience, and that this constituted one of the sustained effects of single-sex secondary education. "Something of value appears to be going on" in single-sex secondary schools, Lee and Marks conclude.[54]

Lee has also researched single-sex education outside the United States, using data from the Second International Mathematics Study (SIMS) to investigate the effects of school type on Nigerian girls' math achievement. Nigeria, like Australia and New Zealand, presents unique opportunities to study school type effects because its public schools include single-sex schools.

Lee and Lockheed's 1990 study of 1,012 students in 9th-grade Nigerian public schools measured mathematics achievement and stereotypic views of mathematics. Analyzing data drawn from the Second International Association for the Evaluation of Educational Achievement, Lee and Lockheed found no significant "gender gap" between mathematics scores of Nigerian boys and girls, "once the other variables in the model are taken into account." But girls in single-sex schools outperformed other girls in mathematics, the study found, while boys in single-sex schools did the reverse, after the study adjusted for substantial differences in student background, school resources, and teacher attitudes. As in other studies, girls in single-sex schools had a less stereotypical view of math, while boys in single-sex schools had magnified stereotypes of the subject.[55]

Assessing some of her work on single-sex education in a recent review of "Gender Equity and the Organization of Schools" (1997), Lee mused on why advantages for girls found in single-sex Catholic schools did not translate to other independent single-sex schools. She tried to identify unique characteristics of Catholic single-sex schools that might account for their measured benefits, characteristics "simultaneously related to the effectiveness and equity parameters" that constitute "good" schools as Lee defines them. These characteristics include smaller school size, a constrained curriculum that is mostly academic, homogeneity in course selection, high order pedagogy, and teachers' belief in their students' ability to learn. "Single-sex schools for girls," she concludes, "often look this way."[56]

Lee cautions, in this spirit, that the extensive research on single-sex education "should not be interpreted as favoring gender separation in educational settings," an approach she sees as "misguided." Rather, the characteristics of schools that show advantages for girls might be incorporated into coeducational schools as they are restructured in the context of educational reform. "High schools should be smaller," she recommends, and "function as communities." These properties are commensurate with a certain type of single-sex school—Catholic and private—that has proven advantageous for girls.[57]

Summary

Studies that have discovered positive achievement effects attributable to school type share some characteristics. Several studies view their findings—and positive outcomes—as specific to certain contexts. Lee, for example, does not find the same positive outcomes for independent schools generally as she does for Catholic single-sex schools; Carpenter and Hayden document positive outcomes for single-sex schools in one context—Victoria, rich in single-sex public schools—and not in another—

Queensland, with no single-sex public schools; Jimenez similarly underscores that research on single-sex education must be "sector specific"; that is, it must adequately control for differences between and among private and public schools.

Second, many of these studies emphasize peer influence and peer group characteristics—including socioeconomic status—as strong factors that may affect performance and relate indirectly to school type. Jimenez and Lockheed conclude that "peer groups account for the bulk of the difference in achievement effects between coeducational and single-sex schools," particularly for girls, and Carpenter and Hayden similarly find that friends' college plans and academic achievement are positively correlated in single-sex schools. Lee and Bryk (1986) also note that association with academically oriented friends is more likely in single-sex schools. Incidentally, studies of single-sex schools that found no corrected positive effects also corroborate the importance of peer socioeconomic status and influence in determining outcomes. Such studies include those by Young, who found that the "average socioeconomic status" of peers most dramatically influenced student science performance; Bell, who attributed raw differences in performance to the "fact that a greater proportion of the single-sex schools . . . [have] pupil selection policies"; and Workman, who noted the positive influence of "bright" students on group learning outcomes.

Notwithstanding the socioeconomic contexts that may augment a single-sex environment's positive outcomes for girls, these studies also tend to recognize that the schools are "doing something different" or, in Lee's terms, that something of value is happening in them for girls, perhaps extrinsic to sex composition itself, that may be reproducible in the coeducational context. Consequently, these studies view policy and training interventions as particularly valuable. Jimenez concludes that "there are important managerial incentives, teacher practices, and social interactions in female single-sex settings . . . that result in enhanced achievement." Lee summons data from "effective" Catholic single-sex schools to profile how public, coeducational schools might be restructured and re-organized in ways conducive to higher achievement. Riordan speculates that Catholic schools "may be able to provide greater control and discipline," and a stronger academic program, which might inform coeducational practice.

Other studies have not claimed positive achievement effects for single-sex programs. Of particular interest is the paradox regarding single-sex classes: Although research finds that girls tend to view the single-sex classroom as more conducive to learning, and express greater confidence in this environment, research has also demonstrated consistently that girls' math and science achievement, measured by a variety of means, has not shown statistically significant gains in the single-sex classroom. Those studies that investigate girls' achievement in single-sex schools and conclude that school type does not affect outcomes typically ascribe the raw differences in scores to factors such as the selectivity of the school or the socioeconomic advantages of those parents opting for single-sex education.

Studies that concentrate on attitudinal variables have yielded some consistent findings. On self-esteem, an outcome of arguable value in educational research, studies that examine differences in specific domains of self-concept note that girls in single-sex schools may draw greater confidence from academic competence, whereas girls in mixed-sex contexts may draw more esteem from physical appearance. Studies have not documented overall differences in the level of self-esteem. Research on girls' subject preferences has documented almost uniformly that single-sex contexts foster less stereotypical views of subjects such as math, and may foster stronger preferences for these traditionally "male" fields. However, studies that investigated "sex stereotyping" more generally have not found that the single-sex environment minimized this practice to any significant degree. Finally, studies concur that students perceive the single-sex school environment to be more "orderly" and "controlled," but diverge somewhat in their assessments of which environment is "preferred" by students.

Although research findings often may be referenced as in support or opposition to single-sex education, the overview of literature presented here suggests that specific practices and characteristics of single-sex environments may contribute to their purported success, and that at least some of these practices may be translatable to coeducational environments. Furthermore, the research—while inconsistent in its overall assessments of whether or not single sex is "better" than coeducation for girls—does reveal some areas of consensus on specific indicators, which may serve as starting points for further research into how and why single-sex schools affect educational outcomes.

NOTES

1. U.S. Department of Education, Office of Educational Research and Improvement, "Single-Sex Schooling: Perspectives from Practices and Research," unpublished paper. December 1992: 71.

2. Much of the interest in single-sex education in the last two years has been stimulated by the establishment of all-male African American schools and pull-out programs or, as in the Baltimore example, coeducational Afrocen-

tric academies that have single-sex classes. Because this is a recent phenomenon, research on the single-sex aspects of these schools is limited.

3. Carol Ascher, "School Programs for African American Males . . . and Females," *Phi Delta Kappan* 73, no. 10 (June 1992): 779; Peter Carpenter and Martin Hayden, "Girls' Academic Achievement: Single-Sex Versus Co-educational Secondary Schools in Australia," *Sociology of Education* 60 (1987): 156; L. Yates, *The Education of Girls: Policy, Research and the Question of Gender* (Melbourne: Australia Council for Educational Research, 1993): 96.

4. James Macfarlane and Pat Crawford, "The Effect of Sex-Segregated Mathematics Classes on Student Attitudes, Achievement, and Enrollment in Mathematics," evaluation for the North York Board of Education, Willowdale, Ontario, September 1985: 2; Illinois Mathematics and Science Academy, "Calculus-Based Physics Exploratory Study," December 1994: 12.

5. Single-sex classes have of late been inspired by a desire to narrow the gap between girls' and boys' math achievement, and in other cases by social concerns.

6. Cornelius Riordan, cited in Scott Baldouf, "Merits, Demerits of Single-Sex Education Raised in Harlem," *Christian Science Monitor,* September 4, 1996.

7. Valerie E. Lee and Marlaine M. Lockheed, "The Effects of Single-Sex Schooling on Achievement and Attitudes in Nigeria," *Comparative Educational Review* 34, no. 2 (1990): 228.

8. Valerie E. Lee and Helen M. Marks, "Who Goes Where? Choice of Single-Sex and Co-educational Independent Secondary Schools," *Sociology of Education* 65 (1992): 229; U.S. Department of Education, Office of Research and Improvement, Gilbert Edes, "Girls' Schools: Laboratories in Progress," in "Single-Sex Schooling: Proponents Speak," December 1992: 5; Emanuel Jimenez and Marlaine Lockheed, "Enhancing Girls' Learning Through Single-Sex Education: Evidence and a Policy Conundrum," *Educational Evaluation and Policy Analysis* 11, no. 2 (1989): 118.

9. This review is based on more than 100 articles and essays from national and international contexts. It includes some unpublished work presented at conferences or available through ERIC in the case of single-sex classes, especially, but confines itself to a review of research conducted after 1980.

10. Partly for expediency, this review concentrates on research on the effects of single-sex programs on girls. Sorting through the findings as they apply to even one group of students—boys or girls—is a substantial project. Additionally, concern about girls' academic performance and opportunities has

inspired many of the studies on single-sex education in the first place. However, by no means are findings concerning girls' outcomes equally applicable to boys. Several studies have documented that boys may thrive in coeducational environments, for reasons that require more research, whereas girls may accrue some benefits in single-sex environments. The impossibility of providing theoretically optimal learning environments for both sexes by conducting coed programs for boys at the same time as single-sex programs for girls underscores the importance of extracting from the available research insights into how to improve the coeducational environment itself for all students.

11. Judith Gill, "Different Contexts, Similar Outcomes," paper presented at the American Educational Research Association annual meeting (New York, 1996); 7; Gaell Hildebrand, "Together or Apart? Organization, Policy and Practice in Co-educational and Single-Sex Education," paper presented at the American Educational Research Association annual meeting (New York, 1996): 3; Judith Gill, "Rephrasing the Question: Is Single-Sex Schooling a Solution to the Equity Equation?" *Curriculum Perspectives* 12, no. 4 (1992): 2.

12. Ed Cairns, "The Relationship Between Adolescent Perceived Self-Competence and Attendance at Single-Sex Secondary School," *British Journal of Educational Psychology* 60 (1990): 210.

13. Jacqueline Granleese and Stephen Joseph, "Self-perception Profile of Adolescent Girls at a Single-Sex and a Mixed-Sex School," *The Journal of Genetic Psychology* 60 (1993): 210.

14. Anne Foon, "The Relationship Between School Type and Adolescent Self-Esteem, Attribution Styles, and Affiliation Needs: Implications for Educational Outcome," *British Journal of Educational Psychology* 58 (1988): 44–54.

15. Many "inferential" statistical studies, which attempt to generalize about populations with some known probability of error from the database or study, utilize regression analysis to determine the relationship between variables hypothesized to be relevant to the outcome of interest—for example, girls' achievement in math. A "multivariate regression analysis" uses two or more independent variables (in this case, for example, the sex composition of the teaching staff, or the sex composition of the student body) to predict a dependent variable (in this case, affective outcomes such as a student's "sense of mastery" or self-esteem).

16. H. Brutsaert and P. Bracke, "Gender Context in Elementary School," *Educational Studies* 20, no. 1 (1994): 3, 10.

17. Ian Smith, "The Impact of Schooling on Student Self-Concepts and Achievement," paper presented at the Biennial Meeting of the International Society for the Study of Behavioral Development (August 1996).

18. Foon, "School Type and Adolescent Self-Esteem": 52; Edward Vockell and Susan Lobonc, "Sex Role Stereotyping by High School Females in Science," *Journal of Research in Science Teaching* 18, no. 3 (1981): 213; Andrew Stables, "Differences Between Pupils From Mixed and Single-Sex Secondary Schools in Their Enjoyment of School Subjects and their Attitudes to Science and to School," *Educational Review* 42, no. 3 (1990): 227.

19. Winifred Mallam, "Impact of School-Type and Sex of the Teacher on Female Students' Attitudes Toward Mathematics in Nigerian Secondary Schools," *Educational Studies in Mathematics* 24 (1993): 227; Ann Colley, "School Subject Preferences of Pupils in Single-Sex and Co-educational Secondary Schools," *Educational Studies* 20, no. 3 (1994): 381.

20. The "Attitudes Toward Women Scale for Adolescents" and its adaptation for children is used to assess attitudes about gender roles and in its standard form has 12 items with four responses, according to Signorella.

21. Mary Harris, "Co-education and Sex Roles," *Australian Journal of Education* 30, no. 2 (1986): 172; Margaret Signorella and Irene Frieze, "Single-Sex versus Mixed-Sex Classes and Gender Schemata in Children and Adolescents: A Longitudinal Comparison," *Psychology of Women Quarterly* 20 (1996): 606.

22. Valerie E. Lee and Helen M. Marks, "Sexism in Single-Sex and Co-educational Independent Secondary School Classrooms," *Sociology of Education* 67 (1994): 93, 104, 114.

23. Lee and Marks, "Sexism in Single-Sex": 115; Gill, "Different Contexts": 17.

24. In feminist theory, "sex" typically designates the biological status of being "male" or "female," whereas "gender" designates the characteristics that have been associated with being male or female—that is, masculine traits such as aggression or "feminine" traits such as nurturance. "Gender" would include, as well, physical appearances associated with maleness and femaleness. In this light, some of the research on single-sex education has confused sex and gender, as in references to "*single-gender*" schools. Schools with all girls are not necessarily single "gender" because they may include students with both "masculine" and "feminine" identities. The example of the "sissy" in an all-boys school captures the possibility that one might have both masculine and feminine "*gender*" roles in a single-sex context.

25. R. R. Dale, *Mixed or Single-Sex School?* (London: Routledge and Kegan Paul, 1969); J. S. Coleman, *The Adolescent Society* (New York: Free Press, 1961): 51, 231.

26. The "High School Characteristics" Index consists of 30 10-item scales in true-false format, Schneider and Coutts (1982): 900.

27. Edison Trickett et al., "The Independent School Experience: Aspects of the Normative Environments of Single-Sex and Coed Secondary Schools," *Journal*

of Educational Psychology 74, no. 3 (1982): 374; Frank W. Schneider and Larry M. Coutts, "The High School Environment: A Comparison of Coeducational and Single-Sex Schools," *Journal of Educational Psychology* 74, no. 6 (1982): 899, 904; Frank Schneider, "In Favour of Coeducation: The Educational Attitudes of Students from Coeducational and Single-Sex High Schools," *Canadian Journal of Education* 13, no. 4 (1988): 490.

28. Mark Gierl, "A Student's Perspective on the Intrinsic Characteristics of the Single-Sex Physics Class," paper delivered at the American Educational Research Association annual meeting (New Orleans, 1994): 15.

29. Macfarlane and Crawford, "The Effect of Sex Segregated Mathematics Classes": 11, 19, 28.

30. T. J. Harvey, "Science in Single-Sex and Mixed Teaching Groups," *Educational Research* 27, no. 3 (1985): 179–182.

31. Kenneth J. Rowe, "Single Sex and Mixed Sex Classes: The Effects of Class Type on Student Achievement, Confidence and Participation in Mathematics," *Australian Journal of Education* 32, no. 2 (1988): 183, 195.

32. Gilah Leder and Helen Forgasz, "Single-Sex Mathematics Classes in a Coeducational Setting: A Case Study," paper presented at the American Educational Research Association annual meeting (New Orleans, 1994): 20, 23.

33. Noreen Webb, "Sex Difference in Interaction and Achievement in Cooperative Small Groups," *Journal of Educational Psychology* 76, no. 1 (1984): 39.

34. Mary Burke Workman, "The Effects of Grouping Patterns in a Cooperative Learning Environment on Student Academic Achievement," thesis, Dominican College (May 1990): 36.

35. Lesley Parker and Leonie Rennie, "A Comparison of Mixed-Sex and Single-Sex Grouping in Year 5 Science Lessons," paper presented at the American Educational Research Association annual meeting (San Francisco, 1986): 1; Lesley Parker and Leonie Rennie, "Single-Sex Grouping: Issues for School Administrators," paper presented at the American Educational Research Association (New York, 1996): 15, 10.

36. Gaell Hildebrand, "Together or Apart? Organization, Policy and Practice in Co-educational and Single-Sex Education," paper presented at the 1996 American Educational Research Association annual meeting in New York: 17.

37. A "descriptive" study, as opposed to an inferential statistical study, is one that analyzes data but does not posit or test a hypothesis to predict future outcomes based on the data gathered.

38. Jeremy Finn, "Sex Differences in Educational Outcomes: A Cross National Study," *Sex Roles* 6, no. 1 (1980): 23.

39. Jane Steedman, "Examination Results in Mixed and Single-Sex Schools," in *Studying School Effectiveness,* ed. David Reynolds (London: Falmer, 1985).

40. John Bell, "A Comparison of Science Performance and Uptake by Fifteen-Year-Old Boys and Girls in Co-educational and Single-Sex Schools—APU Survey Findings," *Educational Studies* 15, no. 2 (1989): 201.

41. Deidra Young and Barry Fraser, "Sex Differences in Science Achievement," unpublished paper (1992): 7.

42. Richard Harker and Roy Nash, "School Type and the Education of Girls: Co-ed or Girls Only?" paper delivered at the American Educational Research Association annual meeting (Chicago, 1997): 17, 18.

43. "High School and Beyond" is a longitudinal study of secondary education conducted by the National Center for Educational Statistics in 1980. According to Lee, the original sample from which Lee and others draw smaller samples consisted of 1,015 schools and approximately 36 sophomores and 36 seniors within each school, for a total sample of more than 73,000 students. Private schools were deliberately oversampled.

44. Paul C. LePore and John Robert Warren, "A Comparison of Single-Sex and Coeducational Catholic Secondary Schooling: Evidence from the National Educational Longitudinal Study of 1988," *American Educational Research Journal* 34, no. 3 (Fall 1997): 492, 505–506.

45. Marlene Hamilton, "Performance Levels in Science and Other Subjects for Jamaican Adolescents Attending Single-Sex and Co-educational High Schools," *Science Education* 69, no. 4 (1985): 525–547.

46. Heckman's two-step methodology, as Jimenez describes, allows for the researcher to correct for sample selection bias by estimating what determines choice of school and then correcting for the selection bias on the basis of results achieved through the first step.

47. Jimenez and Lockheed, "Enhancing Girls' Learning": 125, 135.

48. Carpenter and Hayden, "Girls' Academic Achievement": 157.

49. Riordan excluded minorities from this study in order to better mitigate the effects of socioeconomic status on the findings.

50. Cornelius Riordan, "Public and Catholic Schooling: The Effects of Gender Context Policy," *American Journal of Education* 5 (1985): 533.

51. Cornelius Riordan, "Single Gender Schools: Outcomes for African and Hispanic Americans," *Sociology of Education and Socialization* 18 (1990): 177–205. I have drawn some of this summary from Riordan's description of his research in *Equality and Achievement: An Introduction to the Sociology of Education* (New York: Longman, 1997): 138–139.

52. Valerie E. Lee and Anthony Bryk, "Effects of Single-Sex Secondary Schools on Student Achievement and Attitudes," *Journal of Educational Psychology* 78, no. 5 (1986): 387.

53. Herbert Marsh, "Effects of Attending Single-Sex and Co-educational High Schools on Achievement, Attitudes, Behavior, and Sex Differences," *Journal of Educational Psychology* 81, no. 1 (1989): 78, 80.

54. Valerie E. Lee and Helen M. Marks, "Sustained Effects of the Single-Sex Secondary School Experience on Attitudes, Behaviors and Values in College," *Journal of Educational Psychology* 82, no. 3 (1990): 588.

55. Valerie E. Lee and Marlaine Lockheed, "The Effects of Single-Sex Schooling on Achievement and Attitudes in Nigeria," *Comparative Education Review* 34, no. 2 (1990): 225.

56. Valerie E. Lee, "Gender Equity and the Organization of Schools," in *Gender, Equity and Schooling: Policy and Practice* (New York: Garland Publishing, 1997): 152.

57. *Ibid.*, 152, 154, 156.

28

SINGLE-SEX VERSUS
COEDUCATIONAL SCHOOLS

Valerie Lee

WHEN SECONDARY SCHOOLING—both public and private—began, students were segregated by sex. The shift to coeducation by U.S. public schools occurred with relatively little controversy. Such developments were driven largely by efficiency concerns of local school boards rather than by any deliberate educational philosophy. The lack of debate over what Europeans considered a major educational shift is puzzling,[1] especially because the move to coeducation in public schools was not accompanied by any broad social changes in women's roles.

The early Catholic schools offered the sexes different types of preparation. The first Catholic boys' schools focused on preparing young men for the priesthood; the girls' schools taught those Christian graces believed most appropriate for marriage and motherhood. Around the turn of the twentieth century two forces began to change the nature of Catholic high schools: enrollments began to increase, reflecting increasing demand for education; and as more Catholic colleges opened, the function of Catholic secondary schools began to shift toward preparing students for passage to Catholic higher education. Slowly, training for boys became more broadly academic than the classical training appropriate for the priesthood. Related developments occurred in girls' schools.

Even though the mission of Catholic high schools broadened in the first half of this century, they remained almost entirely single-sex institutions until after World War II. It was widely argued that coeducation provided opportunities for young men and women to work in a more socially relaxed atmosphere and better prepared students for their future lives, but Catholic educators resisted such arguments. The Church's viewpoint on coeducation was stated forcefully by Pope Pius XI in 1929 in his encyclical *Christian Education of Youth:*

> False and also harmful to Christian education is the so-called method of "coeducation." This, too, by many of its supporters, is founded upon naturalism and the denial of original sin: but by all, upon a deplorable confusion of ideas that mistakes a leveling promiscuity and equality, for the legitimate association of the sexes. . . . These principles [denying the idea of coeducation], with due regard to time and place, must, in accordance with Christian prudence, be applied to all schools, particularly in the most delicate and decisive period of formation, that namely, of adolescence.[2]

Although in theory Catholic educators had to conform to the Pope's teaching on this issue, the financial hardship of providing separate schools for the sexes allowed for exceptions. A coeducational school could be tolerated, for example, when a community could afford only a single Catholic school. Even here, however, coeducation was frequently circumvented by an organizational call for "co-institution," which entailed the operation of essentially separate schools for the sexes within a common building, with shared library and laboratory facilities.[3]

Philosophical opposition to coeducation persisted through the 1950s. As late as 1957, the Sacred Congregation of Religious issued a detailed statement concluding that coeducation was naturally dangerous to high school youth. In the 1960s, however, as broad changes beset Catholic schools, a movement toward coeducation began to spread. New schools were often coeducational, and many existing single-sex schools began accepting students of the opposite sex. In a recent study of Catholic high schools, one-sixth of the schools indicated that they had changed from being single-sex to coed within the last two decades.[4]

For those high schools that remained single-sex, the renewal of American Catholic institutions spawned by Vatican II had substantial effects. At St. Madeline's, an emphasis on the development of women's full potential was melded to a traditional ethic of personal commitment to family and community. As a result, St. Madeline's of the 1980s was a very different institution from what it had been in the 1950s. We had ample reason to suspect that such schools might have a powerful influence on the young women whom they educated. Similarly, although the account is less dramatic, the boys' school that we visited, St. Edward's, was also a very strong institution that placed a distinctive mark on its students. These field observations encouraged us to examine the relative benefits of single-sex and coeducational Catholic secondary schools more systematically. Although now somewhat reduced in availability, the single-sex option remains prevalent and is still a major source of variability among Catholic high schools.

School Characteristics

In 1983, just over 20 percent of Catholic secondary schools were boys' schools and just over 25 percent were girls' schools, making the single-sex proportion 46 percent overall. Although more recent data are harder to establish, it appears that the proportion of boys' schools had declined by 2 or 3 percent by the late 1980s, with the proportion of girls' schools remaining constant.[5] Boys' schools enroll the most advantaged students and girls' schools the least. In terms of staff resources, student-faculty ratios are highest in boys' schools, lowest in girls' schools. Boys' school faculties are somewhat more educated and more stable (both in longevity of employment and in annual turnover rates). In terms of fiscal resources, starting salaries are highest in boys' schools and lowest in girls' schools. Tuition levels are also higher in single-sex than in coed schools. Per-pupil expenditures are highest in boys' schools, but lowest in girls' schools.

Boys' and girls' schools also deploy their human and fiscal resources differently. Boys' schools, for example, are considerably larger than girls' schools and operate larger classes. When combined with a relatively high per-pupil expenditure by Catholic school standards, these features allow boys' schools to pay teachers higher salaries. In comparison, girls' schools pay lower salaries. They are also smaller in size and have a more favorable student-teacher ratio. In essence, boys' schools strive for economic efficiency—larger schools focusing almost exclusively on delivering an academic program to students in relatively large groups. The girls' schools are smaller institutions with smaller classes and more intimate, personal environments.[6]

Past Evidence on Single-Sex Schooling

The 1960s and 1970s witnessed a rapid movement away from single-sex schooling, both within and outside the Catholic sector and at both secondary and postsecondary institutions. Single-sex education was increasingly viewed as a barrier to successful adolescent socialization. As the demand for single-sex education began to decline, institutions either closed or converted to coeducation in order to stabilize enrollments.[7]

Ironically, this trend occurred at precisely the time that research on post-secondary institutions was beginning to document positive effects for single-sex education, particularly for young women. Researchers have reported that graduates of women's colleges are more likely than their coed college counterparts to complete their bachelor's degrees, to advance to graduate school, and to attain leadership positions.[8] Several advantages of women's colleges have been cited: a more favorable climate for students, which supports the serious engagement of women in academic work;[9] more circumscribed heterosexual activity, which eliminates some distraction from schooling; a greater identification with the community on the part of both students and faculty; and female faculty who support and encourage women in a fashion rare in coeducational institutions, where male students typically receive more serious academic consideration.[10]

Because American single-sex education is now confined exclusively to the private sector, most research on single-sex secondary schools has been conducted outside of the United States.[11] Many of these studies are of modest research quality, due to small and nonrandom samples of schools and a lack of statistical controls for differing selectivity among schools. Many studies are also quite dated and thus do not reflect changing attitudes about sex roles in recent decades. Studies conducted in the 1960s and 1970s reflect the social context of that period, when schools were often seen as oppressive institutions and reformers argued for making students' lives more enjoyable. Coeducational schools were found to offer more opportunities for positive social contact across the sexes, whereas single-sex schools (especially for girls) emphasized control and discipline[12] and a more academic orientation.[13] Interestingly, order and discipline, which are now seen as characteristics of "good" schools, were interpreted as negative features within this research stream.[14] It is also noteworthy that studies reported that girls' school students evidenced less sex-stereotyped attitudes and behaviors.[15]

As we began our study, there was almost no research on the relative effectiveness of single-sex and coed schools in terms of students' academic achievement.[16] Fortunately, *High School and Beyond* provides excellent data for investigating this question; the school and student samples are relatively large and randomly selected compared with previous research on this topic.

The Effects of Catholic Single-Sex Schools

We learned in our field research that there is a small subset of Catholic high schools at which vocational training is a primary institutional purpose. In seeking to compare the relative effectiveness of different types of schools, it is important to ascertain that all schools in the sample are addressing similar instructional purposes. Because vocational schools are atypical of the Catholic sector as a whole, we have eliminated the few vocational schools and their students from the analysis reported in this chapter.[17] The resulting analytic sample of schools and students presents a nearly ideal natural experiment. We have a relatively large national sample of schools, with similar institutional purposes (traditional academic programs), and students whose characteristics are similar in most ways.

Background Differences

The four groups of students used in these analyses (boys and girls in single-sex and coed schools) are well matched (see Table 28.1). There are, however, some personal and family background differences worth noting. In general, boys are somewhat more likely to have repeated a grade in elementary school; girls in coed schools are particularly unlikely to have done this. Although plans for college attendance at entry into high school are quite similar across the four groups, students in boys' schools come from more advantaged families. The level of families' financial sacrifice (as represented by tuition as a proportion of discretionary family income) is slightly higher in single-sex schools than in coed schools, probably as a result of single-sex schools' higher tuitions. These students' families are making a somewhat greater sacrifice to send their children to a single-sex school, which suggests that such families may be placing a higher value on education for their children.

The proportion of non-Catholics is evenly distributed across the four groups. Students in coeducational schools, however, consider themselves more religious than those in either type of single-sex school. Students' religiousness parallels their elementary school experience, with those who attended Catholic elementary schools scoring considerably higher on this measure. Students who transfer from the public to the Catholic sector for high school are more likely to choose single-sex schools; those from Catholic elementary schools are more likely to be found in coeducational schools. Both of these trends are stronger for boys than for girls. Minority students, especially boys, are somewhat more likely to be in single-sex schools. Girls in coed schools are somewhat more likely to come from single-parent homes.

A picture thus emerges showing somewhat different types of students in the four groups in our analytic sample. Although boys' schools have the highest minority enrollment, their students are also more advantaged than their coed school counterparts in terms of social class. Girls' school students are less advantaged than those in boys' schools and generally are

Table 28.1. Characteristics of analytic sample.

Variables	Girls in coed schools	Girls in girls' schools	Boys in coed schools	Boys in boys' schools
Academic Tracks				
% Academic	78.2	76.7	72.0	80.5
% General	13.7	17.4	21.6	16.2
% Vocational	8.1	5.8	6.4	3.3
Personal and Family Background				
Social class[a]	0.09	0.12	0.19	0.23
% Black	4.6	2.7	3.3	7.1
% Hispanic	6.4	10.1	4.0	8.5
% Single-parent family	20.1	16.1	14.3	12.4
Financial sacrifice[a]	0.08	0.09	0.07	0.09
Religious Characteristics				
% Non-Catholic	8.1	9.9	8.5	7.8
Religiousness[a]	0.41	0.13	0.35	0.07
Elementary school experience				
% All-Catholic	62.3	55.6	64.5	54.2
% All-public	16.2	23.1	16.6	27.6
Academic Background				
% Repeated elementary grade	4.8	6.7	9.3	8.2
% College plans, gr. 8	76.6	76.4	68.0	77.4

Source: *Modified from Lee and Bryk (1986), 385.*
[a]*These are weighted standardized composite variables, with mean = 0, s.d. = 1.*

more similar to girls in coed schools. Overall, the degree of confounding between each gender in the two types of schools in this natural experiment is slight, although somewhat stronger for boys.

Analytic Approach

We report separate cross-sectional results at sophomore and senior year as well as sophomore-to-senior change. There are several reasons for presenting both types of analyses. First, some of the outcome variables of interest were measured only at either sophomore or senior year. Second, for certain outcomes, such as attitudes toward academics or the time spent on homework, it is reasonable to hypothesize that these attitudes and behaviors are formed early in the secondary school experience and then remain relatively constant throughout the secondary years. For these outcomes, the sophomore-year measures are especially important. Third, measures of sophomore-to-senior gain do not fully capture a school's effect on its students. Because Catholic secondary schools typically begin at grade 9, student status at the end of the sophomore year includes two years of a school-specific effect. The sophomore results are thus not pure "preprogram measures," and adjusting for sophomore year standing removes a substantial portion of the single-sex school effect that is now expected to accumulate between sophomore and senior year.[18] Hence there is good reason to believe that relying only on change analyses would underestimate the true school effects. It is also widely assumed, however, that the statistical adjustments employed with cross-sectional analyses underadjust for preexisting differences between groups. This implies a likely overestimation of the school effects if we consider only the sophomore- or senior-year results. The combination of cross-sectional and longitudinal analyses thus provides a degree of balance to these potentially competing biases.

Because there are some differences among the types of students who attend Catholic coeducational and single-sex schools, we have introduced a number of statistical adjustments. All effect estimates reported in the next section are adjusted for three sets of variables: student background, academic curriculum track, and school social context.[19] We also modify our reporting format, shifting from the positive/negative summaries to an accounting of "standardized effect sizes." Positive/negative summaries are quite adequate for largely descriptive and exploratory purposes, but they do not convey sufficient information to judge the substantive significance of any finding; nor do they facilitate a direct comparison of the relative size of effects among the various outcomes. The standardized effect sizes reported in Tables 28.2–28.4 represent the average difference (in standard deviation units) between students in single-sex and coed schools, after taking into account the influence of personal and family background, track placement, and school social context. Positive effects represent an advantage for single-sex schooling. Because previous research has demonstrated different effects for young men and women in the two types of schools, we present separate results for the two genders.

Effects on Attitudes, Behaviors, and Course Enrollment

Students in girls' schools are more likely to associate with academically oriented peers and to express positive interests in both mathematics and English (see Table 28.2). Although the boys' school effects on academic

Table 28.2. Estimated effects of attending a single-sex school
on student attitudes, behaviors, and course enrollment.

Variable	Females	Males
School-Related Attitudes		
Interest in mathematics	0.23*	0.12
Interest in English	0.26*	0.14
Association with academically oriented peers	0.23*	0.04
Attitude toward socially active peers	0.10	0.26*
Attitude toward student athletes	−0.18	0.30*
School-Related Behaviors		
Incidence of discipline problems	−0.03	−0.15
Unexcused absences	−0.11	−0.19
Homework, hrs./wk.	0.36***	0.23*
Television, hrs./day	−0.15	0.17
Course Enrollment		
Mathematics	0.16*	0.46***
Science	−0.02	0.40***
Vocational	0.11	−0.26*
Social studies	0.12	−0.05

Source: *Modified from Lee and Bryk (1986), 388.*

Note: *Effects were calculated with ordinary least squares regression, and include adjustments for personal and family background, religious characteristics, academic background, and academic curricular track. Group mean differences on these variables are described in Table 28.1. Additional adjustments were made for the social composition of the school (average school social class, percentage of black students, and percentage of Hispanic students). All effect sizes reported in this chapter are in standard deviation units, and were calculated by dividing the unstandardized regression coefficient for the single-sex dummy variable by the standard deviation of the appropriate dependent variable among students of that gender in coeducational schools.*

The asterisks indicate nominal statistical levels ($*p < .05$; $**p < .01$; $***p < .001$), using one-tailed tests of significance. A correction factor of 1.5 has been introduced for the design factor associated with the two-stage probability sampling plan (Coleman et al., 1982). These conventions apply to all significance tests reported in this chapter.

attitudes are also generally positive, they are not statistically significant. Students in boys' schools are more likely than their counterparts in coed schools to hold positive attitudes about socially active peers and athletes. These effects do not appear, however, for girls' schools.

With regard to school-related behaviors, students in single-sex schools spend significantly more time on homework, and this is especially true for girls. Students in boys' schools enroll in a larger number of mathematics and science courses, and they are less likely than their counterparts in coed schools to enroll in vocational courses. The course enrollment pattern for girls is more similar across the two school types. Girls in single-sex schools take more mathematics courses and take slightly more vocational offerings and social science courses than their coed school counterparts.

Effects on Academic Achievement

We examined single-sex school effects on achievement in reading, mathematics, science, and writing separately at sophomore and senior year, as well as gains in these areas over the last two years of high school (see Table 28.3). In general, attending single-sex schools positively affects academic achievement. Every one of the statistically significant effects on achievement favors single-sex schools.

Again, the pattern of effects is different for males and females. The estimated boys' school effects are largest at sophomore year, and though still positive, are somewhat diminished by senior year. Boys' school students do not display any statistically significant sophomore-to-senior gains in achievement. For students in girls' schools, however, the estimated effects increase in size from sophomore to senior year, with gains in reading and science achievement that are statistically significant. The girls' school effects on academic achievement are particularly salient in light of the fact that these students are not taking more academic courses than their coed school counterparts (except in mathematics, where no gain is seen; see Table 28.2). As a result, the effects cannot be attributed to more academic courses taken, which is the major explanatory factor for secondary school achievement. By discounting such alternative hypotheses, an explanation based on the environment and social organization of an all-girls' school appears more plausible.

Effects on Educational Aspirations and Affective Outcomes

For nonacademic outcomes—educational aspirations, locus of control, self-concept, and sex-role attitudes—the estimated effects generally favor single-

Table 28.3. Estimated effects of attending a single-sex
school on student achievement at sophomore and senior
year and on sophomore-to-senior achievement gains.

Variable	Females	Males
Reading Achievement		
Sophomore year	0.11	0.20*
Senior year	0.21*	0.18
Reading gain[a]	0.14*	0.05
Mathematics Achievement		
Sophomore year	−0.04	0.26**
Senior year	0.01	0.18*
Mathematics gain	0.04	0.00
Science Achievement		
Sophomore year	−0.05	0.01
Senior year	0.17	0.01
Science gain	0.20**	0.01
Writing Achievement		
Sophomore year	0.01	0.24*
Senior year	0.08	0.08
Writing gain	0.07	−0.05

Source: *Modified from Lee and Bryk (1986), 389.*

[a]*For gains, we employed a covariance model, with senior-year status as an outcome and sophomore status as a control variable in addition to the control variables listed in the note to Table 28.2.*

*$p < .05$. **$p < .01$. See also note to Table 28.2.*

sex schools, with larger effects accruing for students in girls' schools (see Table 28.4). The estimated girls' school effect on educational aspirations is statistically significant at sophomore and senior year, and for the sophomore-to-senior gain. Girls' schools also display a statistically significant positive effect in senior-year locus of control and sophomore-year self-concept. None of the estimated boys' school effects is statistically significant.

The final outcome, which measures students' views about women's roles, is a composite of attitudes about the compatibility of work and motherhood, the traditional role of men as achievers, and whether most women are satisfied with home and child care rather than careers. A pos-

Table 28.4. Estimated effects of attending a single-sex school on educational aspirations, locus of control, self-concept, and sex-role stereotyping.

Variable	Females	Males
Educational Aspirations		
Sophomore year	0.19*	0.13
Senior year	0.23**	0.11
Aspirations gain[a]	0.15*	0.07
Locus of Control		
Sophomore year	0.16	0.18
Senior year	0.21*	−0.04
Locus gain	0.14	−0.12
Self-Concept		
Sophomore year	0.18*	0.08
Senior year	0.10	0.12
Concept gain	0.02	0.09
Sex-Role Stereotyping[b]		
Sophomore year	−0.16	0.15
Senior year	−0.25*	−0.03
Stereotyping gain	−0.17*	−0.09

Source: *Lee and Bryk (1986), 390.*

[a]*For gains, we employed a covariance model, with senior-year status as an outcome and sophomore status as a control variable in addition to the control variables listed in the note to Table 28.2.*

[b]*This is the "traditional role of women" measure used in Chapter 8. The variable has been renamed here to be more informative in the context of the issues discussed in this chapter.*

*$p < .05$. **$p < .01$. See also note to Table 28.2.*

itive effect on this measure indicates a more stereotypic attitude about women's roles. We find that girls' school students are considerably less likely to evidence stereotyped sex-role attitudes than comparable girls in coed schools. Further, the attitudes among students in girls' schools show a significant decline in stereotyping from sophomore to senior year. Interestingly, although students in boys' schools hold slightly more sex-stereotypic views than their coed school counterparts at sophomore year, this difference disappears by senior year. Sex-stereotyped attitudes apparently are not an inevitable consequence of an all-male environment, at least as such environments are realized in Catholic schools.

We consider the results on sex-role stereotyping among our most interesting findings. Although the traditional purpose of girls' schools was to provide an appropriate finishing experience for Catholic women in their future roles as wives and mothers, this aim no longer dominates students' education in these schools. The former goal has been replaced by a proactive orientation toward gender equity. A more traditional view is still emphasized in some schools, as we observed at St. Frances, but the analyses suggest that the norms of St. Madeline's have become more commonplace. The 1980s portrait of St. Madeline's appears to capture broad and general features of contemporary Catholic girls' schools as empowering environments for young women.

Are These Effects Large or Small?

The reporting of research results in standardized effect sizes is becoming increasingly common, because it provides a convenient metric for comparing results across different outcomes and studies. Moreover, the substantive significance of these estimated effects can be assessed by reference to some external standards. In the current case, two standards are particularly appropriate.[20]

The first standard is based on the average amount of learning for public school students during a year of instruction. It has been shown that this gain is approximately equivalent to a standardized effect size of 0.10.[21] This standard provides us with a way to interpret any estimated effect in terms of an increment to student learning that is associated with attendance at a single-sex school. For example, recall from Table 28.3 that the girls' school effect on the gain in science achievement is 0.20. This means that attendance at a girls' school doubles the learning in science for Catholic school girls over the course of their junior and senior years. While girls in coed schools are making two years of progress, their single-sex counterparts are making four. By this standard, the reported effects would have to be judged as substantively very important.

A second approach to evaluating the significance of the estimated effects focuses on the fact that single-sex school organization is a school-level factor. This suggests that we consider the estimated effects relative to the amount of variation naturally occurring between schools. If the latter were large, it would indicate that the estimated single-sex school effects might be of limited importance relative to other school characteristics that might be studied.

For each of the statistically significant effects reported in Tables 28.2–28.4, we have estimated the amount of between-school variability on these outcomes and then recomputed the effect size estimates based on this standard. The results are presented in Table 28.5, along with the corresponding student-level effect sizes previously reported. Over half of the effect sizes based on the between-school variation are in excess of 1.0.[22] To put these numbers in some perspective, a 1.0 effect size added to a "typical" Catholic school would move its outcomes from the 50th percentile (half the schools are better and half are worse) to about the 83rd percentile (only 17 percent of the schools are better). A 1.65 effect size would move a "typical" school to the 95th percentile. When viewed against the total variation naturally occurring among schools, the estimated single-sex effects thus appear very substantial indeed.

Other Possible Explanations of the Observed Effects

When attempting to draw casual inferences from nonexperimental research, plausible alternative explanations might be offered for any set of results. The most frequently encountered objection is a selection hypothesis; that is, the individuals within the groups vary in important ways besides the exposure to a different program. In response to this concern, we have introduced in our analyses statistical adjustments for individual background and track placement and for school context differences—the sorts of factors usually cited in selection hypotheses.

In general, the pattern of results after adjustments is not substantially different from unadjusted mean differences on these outcomes. This holds true whether we consider the cross-sectional results at sophomore and senior year or the longitudinal analyses. Although it is always possible that students and parents are choosing single-sex schools for reasons other than those that we have already taken into account, the evidence assembled here, coupled with our field observations, provides strong support for the conclusion that there are significant outcome differences favoring attendance in single-sex over coed schools in the Catholic sector. The estimated effects are especially strong and pervasive for girls. Our analyses also suggest possible effects for boys' schools, although the evidence here is not as strong.

To what do we attribute the observed effects associated with attending single-sex Catholic schools? Are these advantages a result of factors intrinsic to this form of school organization? Could the effects be due to some other set of considerations, such as school resources and academic policies, which just happen to be associated with single-sex Catholic schools?

Table 28.5. Comparison of estimated effect sizes
in terms of student- versus school-level variability.

Variable	Effect size based on variability among students	Effect size based on variability among schools
Females		
Interest in mathematics	0.23*	1.35
Interest in English	0.26*	1.95
Association with academically oriented peers	0.23*	—
Homework, soph.	0.36***	0.96
Mathematics courses	0.16*	0.67
Reading achievement, senior	0.21*	0.84
Reading achievement gain	0.14*	0.81
Science achievement gain	0.20**	1.03
Educ. aspirations, soph.	0.19**	2.14
Educ. aspirations, senior	0.23*	—
Educ. aspirations gain	0.15*	1.44
Locus of control, senior	0.21*	1.14
Sex-role stereotyping, senior	−0.25*	−1.16
Sex-role stereotyping gain	−0.17*	−1.13
Males		
Attitude toward socially active peers	0.26**	—
Attitude toward student athletes	0.30*	1.82
Homework, soph.	0.23*	0.51
Mathematics courses	0.46***	1.31
Science courses	0.40***	1.15
Vocational courses	−0.26*	−1.39
Reading achievement, soph.	0.20*	0.84
Math achievement, soph.	0.26**	1.19
Writing achievement, soph.	0.24*	0.93
Mathematics achievement, senior	0.18*	0.75

Source: *Lee and Bryk (1986), 391.*

Note: *The effect sizes in column 1 are identical to those reported in Tables 28.2, 28.3, and 28.4. The statistical significance of these effects are taken from those tables. The effect sizes given in column 2 were calculated by dividing the unstandardized regression coefficient for the single-sex dummy variable by an estimate of the standard deviation between schools on the corresponding dependent variable. The latter were estimated using restricted maximum likelihood estimation. For some dependent measures, a point estimate of zero was obtained for between-school variance. These are marked by (—) in the table.*

*p < .05. **p < .01. ***p < .001. See also note to Table 28.2.

We have already mentioned a number of differences between single-sex and coed schools in terms of their structure and resources. Girls' schools are smaller and have smaller classes than coed schools. The boys' schools have more resources, as measured by the proportion of the faculty with advanced degrees, by lower teacher turnover, and by more stable faculties. The girls' schools, in contrast, are the least well positioned on these variables. A similar pattern emerges when we focus attention on fiscal resources. Boys' schools have the highest per-pupil expenditure, but the girls' schools have the lowest. In short, the distribution of resources among Catholic schools is complex, and neither single-sex nor coed schools have a clear and overwhelming advantage.

Further, although we know that there are important substantive relations involving tangible resources, their effects on academic outcomes are mostly indirect. As a result, there is no evidence that resources could account for the effects associated with single-sex schooling presented here. The most powerful factors affecting academic outcomes have been shown to be students' enrollment in academic courses. The most pervasive effects documented above, however, have been for girls' schools, and their students are not enrolling in more academic courses than their coed school counterparts.[23]

In both boys' and girls' schools, students rate their schools and the quality of teaching in them much more positively than do their counterparts in coed schools.[24] How to interpret these data, however, remains an open question. One explanation is that this set of schools, labeled "single-sex," just happens to have unusually effective staffs. It seems more likely, however, that single-sex schools produce not only positive environments for learning but also positive environments for teaching. From this vantage point, the positive reports about teaching and school quality provide just more evidence of single-sex school organization effects rather than a competing explanation for these effects.[25] We have even further support, then, that something important is occurring in Catholic single-sex schools.

A cursory examination of our findings indicates a broad base of positive effects for single-sex schools across a diverse array of educational outcomes. Whether considering academic achievement in specific curriculum areas at sophomore or senior year, gains in academic achievement over the two years, future educational plans, affective measures of locus of control or self-concept, sex-role stereotyping, or attitudes and behaviors related to academics, single-sex schools appear to deliver specific advantages to their students. Are these schools better, somehow, in ways that are unrelated to their single-sex organization? It is possible, although we have not been able to discern a set of factors that is not at least indirectly tied to the single-sex organizational form. On the basis of the empirical evidence assembled here, we conclude that a single-sex school organizational effect is the most plausible explanation for the observed results.

Although this book focuses on students' experiences in their high schools, our findings on single-sex schools prompted us to undertake some follow-up analyses as these students moved into college and beyond.[26] It was found that attending a single-sex high school had sustained, positive effects. Again, the effects were stronger for graduates of girls' schools. These students continued to have higher educational aspirations and attended more selective four-year colleges than their academic qualifications would lead one to expect. Students from all-girls' high schools also continued to hold less stereotypic attitudes, were more likely to be politically active in college, and were especially satisfied with their college experience. No differences were found on these outcomes for men from either coed or single-sex high schools. Both male and female students from single-sex high schools were especially likely to have plans for attending graduate school, especially in the field of law.

These results indicate that something positive is occurring in single-sex Catholic high schools. In general, the results appear stronger for girls than boys. Although some may question whether the observed boys' school effects are sufficiently large and pervasive to declare an overall organizational effect, the results for girls' schools are quite convincing.

As has been suggested about single-sex postsecondary education, single-sex secondary schooling may in fact serve to sensitize young women to their occupational and societal potential in an atmosphere free of some of the social pressures that adolescent females experience in the presence of the opposite sex. Adolescence is a critical period for the formation of attitudes about oneself. The results here support the contention that some separation of students' academic and social environments may remove distractions that can interfere with the academic development of students. Although the aims of schooling are varied, academic pursuits rightly belong at the top of the list. If the positive benefits of social contact, widely cited as an advantage of coeducational schooling, act to undermine the academic development of some students, particularly female students, then considerably more thought about the social organization of secondary education seems warranted.

Our results also raise questions about the appropriateness of "students' satisfaction with the school environment" as a major criterion for evaluating schools. This factor has been a primary focus in much of the previous research on single-sex schooling, and that students prefer to attend coeducational schools has been a central element in the argument for the adoption of a coeducational policy. Although student satisfaction is an important consideration (particularly in private schools, which depend on enrollment and tuition for their very existence), when uncoupled from concerns about academic attitudes, school behavior, and achievement, it offers only a partial and somewhat distorted view of schooling. In particular, if improving the social environment is accompanied by a general decline in academic behavior and performance, then a failure to recognize these unintended negative consequences is very troublesome.[27]

It is far from clear, however, that this presumed tension between social and academic purposes is valid. In particular, the results in this chapter indicate that stronger academic attitudes and behaviors, as well as higher achievement in Catholic single-sex schools, are accompanied by very positive reports from students about their schools. These results suggest that a positive social environment can accompany high academic achievement—the two are not contradictory.

In an era when single-sex secondary schools are often considered an anachronism and when these schools are often being merged with opposite-sex schools to create coeducational institutions thought to be more economically and socially viable, it is striking that there has been so little empirical investigation of this form of school organization. For this reason, the particularly strong and pervasive effects for students in Catholic girls' schools merit special attention. It would be one of the great ironies of educational reform if, in equalizing opportunities for young women by breaking down access barriers to the boys' schools with greater resources and more facilities, we are inadvertently destroying one of our great resources—a set of educational institutions especially conducive to young women's learning.

The results of this chapter ought at least to encourage educators to ask whether secondary education in the United States is being enriched or impoverished by the gradual disappearance of single-sex schooling. To be sure, the relevant policy consideration is not whether all secondary schools (or even all Catholic secondary schools) should be single-sex. Rather, public policy should focus on finding ways to preserve existing single-sex schools and to encourage their development in other contexts where the option does not currently exist.

NOTES

1. For a further discussion of this point, see Tyack and Hansot (1988).

2. Pius XI, "Christian Education of Youth," 26–27. Cited in Buetow (1970), 261.

3. Fison (1959). Cited in Buetow (1970), 262.

4. These data are taken from NCEA (1985). The data were collected in 1983 from the principals of all the nation's Catholic high schools.

5. Personal communication with Fred Brigham, based on an internal NCEA tabulation, July 28, 1988.

6. Bryk et al. (1984), 46. Also cited in NCEA (1985), 154–155.

7. This change has been best documented at the level of higher education, but the phenomenon has taken place within Catholic and independent secondary schools as well. See Hyde (1971); Astin (1977a, 1977b); Block (1984); and NCEA (1985), 152.

8. Astin (1977a).

9. Graham (1970, 1974); Tidball and Kistiakowsky (1976); Oates and Williamson (1978); Block (1984).

10. Graham (1974), 5.

11. Dale's three-volume work (1969, 1971, 1974) investigates pupil-teacher relationships, social aspects, and attainment and attitudes within single-sex and coeducational schools in the United Kingdom. Feather (1974) studies schools in Australia, and Finn (1980) compared U.S. and British schools of 1970. Jones, Shallcross, and Dennis (1972) compared schools in New Zealand. Schneider and Coutts (1982) investigated this issue in Canadian Catholic schools.

12. Dale (1969, 1971); Jones, Shallcross, and Dennis (1972); Feather (1974); Schneider and Coutts (1982).

13. Jones, Shallcross, and Dennis (1972) and Trickett et al. (1982) support the more academic environment of girls' schools. Dale (1969, 1971) and Feather (1974), however, found no relationship between single-sex schooling and academic orientation.

14. Coleman, Hoffer, and Kilgore (1982) stress this point.

15. See Winchel, Fenner, and Shaver (1974); Lockheed (1976); and Trickett et al. (1982).

16. Two older British studies (Dale, 1971, 1974) offered mixed results. Since the initiation of our research, several more recent reports on this topic have appeared. Two studies in developing countries have shown results that favor single-sex education for girls and coeducation for boys (Jimenez and Lockheed, 1989; Lee and Lockheed, 1990). For recent U.S. domestic research, see Riordan (1990). Riordan (1990), along with Lee and Bryk (1986) and Lee and Marks (1991), constitute the major evidence on the effects of single-sex schooling in the United States. For a critique of this evidence, see Marsh (1989) and a rejoinder by Lee and Bryk (1989).

17. We have excluded from the analysis 8 of the 83 Catholic high schools on the *HS&B* file—those which enroll more than 25 percent vocational track students. Of the excluded group, 5 are girls' schools, 3 are coeducational schools, and no boys' schools are excluded. Of the schools which remain in the sample, the average vocational enrollment is 6 percent.

18. For a discussion of the statistical details of this problem, see Anderson et al. (1980).

19. Specifically, we regressed each outcome variable against a model consisting of a dummy variable for single-sex versus coed schools, the list of personal, family, and academic and background variables from Table 28.1, two dummy variables for academic and general track membership, and three measures of school social context (average social class, percentage of black students, and percentage of Hispanic students). For the change analyses, we introduced sophomore status as another covariate in addition to the background, track, and school composition measures.

    The use of controls for school social context is based on findings from previous research using *HS&B*, which has shown that school social context is an important predictor of academic achievement above and beyond the effects of student-level social demographic characteristics. In research on private school effects, the inclusion of social context variables has resulted in substantially different effect estimates. See Hoffer, Greeley, and Coleman (1985) and Willms (1985).

20. There is a third standard, frequently used in interpreting effective sizes, that is based on the normal probability distribution. By this standard, an effect size of 0.20 means that the probability of the score of a randomly chosen student from a single-sex school exceeding the score of a randomly chosen counterpart from a coed school is approximately 0.54. From this point of view, the statistically significant results reported here might appear small.

    The use of this standard for research on high schools can be very misleading, however, for reasons detailed by Jencks (1985). In brief, a great deal of learning has occurred by sophomore year in high school. As a result, student performance is extraordinarily variable and comparing an estimated school effect against this standard will produce an artifactually small estimate.

21. Hoffer, Greeley, and Coleman (1985) show that a standardized effect size of 0.10 on the gain from sophomore to senior year on one of the *HS&B* academic achievement measures is equivalent to the amount of learning demonstrated by the average public school student during one full year of secondary school instruction.

22. The typical procedures for estimating variance components in nested models produce biased estimates when the data are unbalanced, as in the *HS&B*

sample employed in this investigation. As an alternative, we used a procedure known as restricted maximum likelihood estimation, which allows us
to compute the between-school variance component in the presence of
unbalanced nested data. The latter provides a consistent estimate of the variance between schools under the assumption that the outcome variables are
normally distributed. Our analytic model treated schools as a random factor
and adjusted for the same set of student-level covariates (specified as fixed
factors) that were employed in estimating the effects in Tables 28.2–28.4.
This is an example of a random intercept model in a hierarchical linear
model analysis. For further discussion, see Bryk and Raudenbush (1992).

23. Single-sex schools are much more likely to be sponsored by religious orders.
    For girls' schools, it is impossible to separate a single-sex organization
    effect from a religious order governance effect, because these two variables
    are almost totally confounded in that instance. The data on boys' schools,
    however, is sufficient to sustain further analysis. In particular, we recom-
    puted the boys' school effects reported in Tables 28.2–28.4 under an ana-
    lytic model that adjusted for that factor. That is, we added a control
    variable that distinguished boys' schools operated by religious orders from
    those run by other organizations, such as parishes and dioceses. The boys'
    school effects remained virtually unchanged. Although we cannot totally
    discount the possibility of a governance effect, we have no evidence that
    particularly favors this alternative explanation.

24. Using the same analytic sample, the average of student ratings of their
    schools is presented for the three types of schools:
    The "perceived quality of teaching" variable is an aggregate of two
    student-level factors: (1) student perceptions of the quality of instruction;
    and (2) the students' reports about the proportion of their instructors who
    have certain desirable characteristics (e.g., are patient, present materials
    clearly, treat students fairly, return graded work promptly). Variables are
    standardized (mean = 0, s.d. = 1) around the Catholic school mean. The
    "general school rating" variable is an aggregate of a student-level factor
    created from students' ratings of various aspects of their schools (e.g., con-
    dition of buildings, library facilities, the school's reputation in the commu-
    nity, fairness and effectiveness of discipline, faculty interest in students).

25. See Lee and Bryk (1986) for a more extended discussion of possible alterna-
    tive school-level explanations for the effects shown in this chapter.

26. Lee and Marks (1990) used *HS&B* data to follow these same students
    beyond high school. In particular, they examined the effects of attending a
    single-sex high school (again, separately for males and females) on attitudes
    and behaviors in college. Because 85 percent of the sample attended college,

the decision to go to college was not considered as an outcome. Less than 20 percent of the sample attended Catholic colleges, and very few (about 9 percent for women, 2 percent for men) attended single-sex colleges. Students who attended single-sex high schools were neither more nor less likely to select a single-sex college.

27. The decision that some schools have made to change from single-sex to coeducational organization was not made simply to improve the social environment. Such decisions are always multifaceted, usually involving questions of enrollment, scale, and cost. The assumption that today's adolescents are somehow more content in the presence of the opposite sex and that they will therefore desire to attend coeducational schools is quite prevalent among school personnel. The issue we address here is that decisions favoring coeducation may be made at some cost, and the cost may be in the important area of academics. Academic considerations (and costs) should be a factor in this important decision that educators face more and more frequently.

REFERENCES

Anderson, A., A. Auquier, W. W. Hauck, D. Oakes, W. Vandaele, and H. I. Weisberg. 1980. *Statistical methods for comparative studies: Techniques for bias reduction.* New York: Wiley.

Astin, A. W. 1977a. *Four critical years: Effects of college on beliefs, attitudes, and knowledge.* San Francisco: Jossey-Bass.

———. 1977b. On the failure of educational policy. *Change,* 9: 40–45.

Block, J. H. 1984. *Sex role identity and ego development.* San Francisco: Jossey-Bass.

Bryk, A. S., P. B. Holland, V. E. Lee, and R. A. Carriedo. 1984. *Effective Catholic schools: An exploration.* Washington, D.C.: National Catholic Educational Association.

Bryk, A. S., and S. W. Raudenbush. 1992. *Hierarchical linear models: Applications and data analyses methods.* Newbury, Calif.: Sage Publications.

Buetow, H. A. 1970. *Of singular benefit: The story of Catholic education in the United States.* New York: Macmillan.

Coleman, J. S., T. Hoffer, and S. B. Kilgore. 1982. *High school achievement: Public, Catholic, and private schools compared.* New York: Basic Books.

Dale, R. R. 1969. *Mixed or single-sex school? Vol. 1: A research study about pupil-teacher relationships.* London: Routledge & Kegan Paul.

———. 1971. *Mixed or single-sex school? Vol. 2: Some social aspects.* London: Routledge & Kegan Paul.

————. 1974. *Mixed or single-sex school?* Vol. 3: *Attainment, attitudes, and overview.* London: Routledge & Kegan Paul.

Feather, N. T. 1974. Coeducation, values, and satisfaction with school. *Journal of Educational Psychology,* 66: 9–15.

Finn, J. D. 1980. Sex differences in educational outcomes: A cross-national study. *Sex Roles,* 6: 9–25.

Graham, P. A. 1970. Women in academe. *Science,* 69: 1284–1290.

————. 1974. *Women in higher education: A biographical inquiry.* ERIC Document no. ED 095 742. New York: Barnard College, Columbia University.

Hoffer, T., A. M. Greeley, and J. S. Coleman. 1985. Achievement growth in public and Catholic schools. *Sociology of Education,* 58: 74–97.

Hyde, S. 1971. The case for coeducation. *Independent School Bulletin,* 31: 20–24.

Jencks, C. 1985. How much do high school students learn? *Sociology of Education,* 58(2): 128–135.

Jiminez, E., and M. E. Lockheed. 1989. Enhancing girls' learning through single-sex education: Evidence and a policy conundrum. *Educational Evaluation and Policy Analysis,* 11(2): 117–142.

Jones, J. C., J. Shallcross, and C. L. Dennis. 1972. Coeducation and adolescent values. *Journal of Educational Psychology,* 63: 334–341.

Lee, V. E., and A. S. Bryk. 1986. The effects of single-sex secondary schools on student achievement and attitudes. *Journal of Educational Psychology,* 78(5): 381–396.

————. 1989. A multilevel model of the social distribution of high school achievement. *Sociology of Education,* 62(3): 172–192.

Lee, V. E., and M. E. Lockheed. 1990. The effects of single-sex schooling on student achievement and attitudes in Nigeria. *Comparative Educational Review,* 43(2): 209–231.

Lee, V. E., and H. M. Marks. 1990. Sustained effects of the single-sex secondary school experience on attitudes, behaviors, and values in college. *Journal of Educational Psychology,* 82(3): 578–592.

————. 1991. Which works best? The relative effectiveness of single-sex and coeducational secondary schools. Paper presented at the annual meeting of the American Educational Research Association, Chicago.

Lockheed, M. E. 1976. *The modification of female leadership behavior in the presence of males.* Princeton, N.J.: Educational Testing Service.

Marsh, H. W. 1989. Effects of attending single-sex and coeducational high schools on achievement, attitudes, behaviors, and sex differences. *Journal of Educational Psychology,* 81: 70–85.

National Catholic Educational Association (NCEA). 1985. *The Catholic high school: A national portrait.* Washington, D.C.: National Catholic Educational Association.

Oates, M. J., and S. Williamson. 1978. Women's colleges and women achievers. *Journal of Women in Culture and Society*, 3: 795–806.

Riordan, C. 1990. *Girls and boys in school: Together or separate?* New York: Teachers College Press.

Schneider, F. W., and L. M. Coutts. 1982. The high school environment: A comparison of coeducational and single-sex schools. *Journal of Educational Psychology*, 74: 898–906.

Tidball, M. E., and V. Kistiakowsky. 1976. Baccalaureate origins of American scientists and scholars. *Science*, 193: 646–652.

Trickett, E. J., J. J. Castro, P. K. Trickett, and P. Shaffner. 1982. The independent school experience: Aspects of the normative environment of single-sex and coed secondary schools. *Journal of Educational Psychology*, 74: 374–381.

Tyack, D., and E. Hansot. 1988. Silence and policy talk: Historical puzzles about gender and education. *Educational Researcher*, 17(3): 33–41.

Willms, J. D. April. 1985. Catholic school effects on academic achievement: New evidence from High School and Beyond follow-up study. *Sociology of Education*, 58: 98–114.

Winchel, R., D. Fenner, and P. Shaver. 1974. Impact of coeducation on "fear of success" imagery expressed by male and female high school students. *Journal of Educational Psychology*, 66: 726–730.

29

WHY JOHNNY CAN'T, LIKE, READ AND WRITE

Christina Hoff Sommers

THERE IS A MUCH-TOLD STORY in education circles about a now-retired Chicago public school teacher, Mrs. Daugherty. She was a dedicated, highly respected sixth-grade teacher who could always be counted on to bring out the best in her students. One year she had a class she found impossible to control. The students were noisy, unmanageable, and seemingly unteachable. She began to worry that many of them had serious learning disabilities. When the principal was out of town, she did something teachers were not supposed to: she entered his office, and looked in a special file where students' IQs were recorded. To her amazement, she found that a majority of the students were way above average in intelligence. A quarter of the class had IQs in the high 120s—128, 127, 129; several in the 130s—and one of the worst classroom culprits was in fact brilliant: he had an IQ of 145.

Mrs. Daugherty was angry at herself. She had been feeling sorry for the children, giving them remedial work, and expecting little from them. Things soon changed. She immediately brought in challenging work, increased the homework load, and inflicted draconian punishments on any malefactor. She ran the class with uncompromising discipline. Slowly but perceptibly, the students' performance improved. By the end of the year, this class of former ne'er-do-wells was among the best behaved and highest performing of sixth-grade classes.

The principal was delighted. He knew about this class and its terrible reputation. So at the end of the year, he called Mrs. Daugherty into his office to ask her what she had done. She felt compelled to tell him the truth. The principal heard her out and forgave her. He congratulated her. But then he said, "I think you should know, Mrs. Daugherty, those numbers next to the children's names—those are not their IQ scores. Those are their locker numbers."[1]

The moral of the story is clear: Strict is good. Demanding and expecting excellence can only benefit the student. These were once truisms of education. Even today, setting and enforcing high standards for students surely is uncontroversial. Who would question the need for challenging work, high expectations, and strict discipline? The sad answer is that a lot of education theorists are skeptical about these things. Rousseauian romanticism, in the form of progressive education, has long been a powerful force in American schools. The shift away from structured classrooms, competition, strict discipline, and skill-and-fact-based learning has been harmful to all children—but especially to boys.

Don't Fill a Vase, Light a Fire

Progressive pedagogues pride themselves on fostering creativity and enhancing children's self-esteem. Exacting discipline and the old-fashioned "dry-knowledge" approach are said to accomplish the opposite; to inhibit creativity and leave many students with feelings of inadequacy. Progressives frown on teacher-led classrooms with fact-based learning, memorization, phonics, and drills. Trainees in schools of education are enjoined to "Teach the student, not the subject!" and are inspired by precepts such as "[Good teaching] is not vase-filling; rather it is fire-lighting."[2]

In this "child-centered" model, the teacher is supposed to remain in the background so that students have the chance to develop as "independent learners." Drill and rote have no place in a style of education focused on freeing "the creative potential of the child." One well-known proponent of progressivism, Alfie Kohn, author of *The Schools Our Children Deserve* and *Punished by Rewards,* suggests that the modern cooperative classroom should resemble a musical jam session: "Cooperative learning not only offers instruments to everyone in the room, but invites jazz improvisation."[3]

Child-centered education has been prevalent in American schools of education since the 1920s. According to University of Virginia education scholar E. D. Hirsch, Jr., the "knowledge-based approach currently employed in the most advanced nations [has been] eschewed in our own schools for more than half a century."[4] Except for a brief period in the late fifties and early sixties (when the Soviet Union's success with Sputnik generated fears that an inadequate math and science curriculum was a threat to national security), the fashion in American education has been to downplay basic skills, knowledge acquisition, competitive grading, and discipline. This fashion has opened a worrisome education gap that finds American students near the bottom among advanced countries.[5]

In recent years, a growing number of British educators have become convinced that progressive methods in education are a prime reason their male students are so far behind the girls. There is now a concerted movement in Britain to improve boys' educational prospects by going back to a traditional pedagogy. Many British educational leaders believe that the modern classroom fails boys by being too unstructured, too permissive, and too hostile to the spirit of competition that so often provides boys with the incentive to learn and excel. Added to this is the national concern over the economic consequences of male underachievement. Stephen Byers, the British schools standards minister, says, "Failure to raise the educational achievement of boys will mean that thousands of young men will face a bleak future in which a lack of qualifications and basic skills will mean unemployment and little hope of finding work."[6]

By contrast, the looming prospect of an underclass of badly educated—even barely literate—American boys has yet to become a cause for open concern among American educators, not to speak of politicians. Nevertheless, the day of reckoning cannot be far away. Massachusetts Institute of Technology economist Lester Thurow observes, "Within the developed world, the under-educated and under-skilled are going to be left out, or perhaps more accurately, thrown out of the global game."[7] There are some disquieting voices. In a 1995 article in *Science*, University of Chicago education researchers Larry Hedges and Amy Nowell warned about the bleak employment outlook for the "generally larger number of males who perform near the bottom . . . in reading and writing."[8]

Boys in the United Kingdom

Like American boys, boys in Great Britain and Australia are markedly behind girls academically, notably in reading and writing. They too get most of the failing grades, and more of them lose interest in school. The big difference is that British educators and politicians are ten years ahead of Americans in confronting and addressing the problem of male underachievement.

In 1988, a council of British headmasters organized a clearinghouse for information on effective classroom practices and programs for boys. Nearly a decade later, they published a booklet summarizing what they had learned. *Can Boys Do Better?* describes specific classroom activities and teaching styles that have been tried at British schools such as Moulsham High School in Chelmsford and Thirsk School in North Yorkshire.[9] Nearly every suggestion violates some hallowed progressive tenet. Here is a partial list of the approaches that these practitioners found work for boys:

○ More teacher-led work

○ A structured environment

○ High expectations

○ Strict homework checks

○ Consistently applied sanctions if work is not done

○ Greater emphasis on silent work

○ Frequent testing

○ One-sex classes

The British headmasters call for "silent" (solitary) reflection and study; they do not celebrate collaborative learning. The headmasters advise schools to avoid fanciful, "creative" assignment, noting, "Boys do not always see the intrinsic worth of 'Imagine you're a sock in a dustbin.' They want relevant work."[10] Nor are they concerned about the students' self-esteem. They know that boys do better than girls on self-esteem questionnaires, but that "gender gap" does not strike them as evidence that girls are being tragically shortchanged. As Peter Downes, former president of the Scottish Headmasters' Association Associates, dryly notes, "Boys swagger . . . while girls win the prizes."[11] He urges teachers to be brutally honest with boys about what life has in store for them if they continue to underperform academically.

Coed public schools throughout Great Britain are now experimenting with all-male classes. In 1996, Ray Bradbury, the head teacher of King's School in Winchester, was alarmed by the high failure rate of his male students. Seventy-eight percent of the girls were getting passing grades or better, but only 56 percent of the boys. Bradbury identified the thirty or so boys he thought to be at risk for failure and placed them together in a class. He chose an athletic young male teacher he thought the boys would find easy to like. The class was not "child-centered." The pedagogy was strict and old-fashioned. As Bradbury explained, "We consciously planned the teaching methodology. The class is didactic and teacher-fronted. It involves sharp questions and answers, and constantly checking understanding. Discipline is clear-cut—if homework isn't presented, it is completed in a detention. There is no discussion."[12]

Here is how one visiting journalist describes a typical class: "Ranks of boys in blazers face the front, giving full attention to the young teacher's instructions. His style is uncompromising and inspirational. 'People think that boys like you won't be able to understand writers such as the Romantic poets. Well, you're going to prove them wrong. Do you understand?' "[13]

The teacher finds that the boys in his single-sex class actively support one another with genuine team spirit: "When girls are present, boys are loath to express opinions for fear of appearing sissy." He chooses challenging but male-appropriate readings: "Members of my group are football mad and quite 'laddish.' In the mixed classes they would be turned off by *Jane Eyre*, whereas I can pick texts such as *Silas Marner* and The War Poets." The initial results have been promising. In 1996, the boys were far behind the girls. By 1997, after only a year in the special class, the boys had nearly closed the gap. As one of the boys said, "We are all working hard to show we can be just as successful as the other groups."[14]

The authors of *Can Boys Do Better?* are careful not to claim too much for their pedagogical practices: "It should be stressed that many of these strategies [to help boys do better] have only recently been implemented and it is too early in many cases fully to evaluate their effectiveness."[15] However, a follow-up study by the National Foundation for Education Research in 1999 (*Boys' Achievement, Progress, Motivation and Participation*) supported the headmasters' key propositions: "The following items all emerge as being important: highly structured lessons, more emphasis on teacher-led work, clear and firm deadlines, short-term targets."[16] The same report noted that all-male classes and all-male schools may be "singularly well-placed to raise achievement among boys, as they could tailor their strategies directly to the needs of boys."[17] More recently, the cautious optimism of the boy-focused educators who have been advocating and practicing a more traditional pedagogy for boys was spectacularly vindicated.

In the fall of 1998, the British government introduced into primary schools a compulsory back-to-basics program called the "Literacy Hour." Its explicit purpose was to narrow the achievement gap between boys and girls. The program incorporates practices that are antithetical to most of the hallowed precepts of progressivism: it is phonics-centered, whole-class, teacher-led, with old-fashioned emphasis on such things as grammar and punctuation. David Blunkett, the education secretary, also insisted that teachers find boy-friendly reading materials such as adventure, sport, or horror stories as well as nonfiction. "Boys like reading technical texts," Blunkett told a conference of school principals.[18]

The effects of the back-to-basics program on male literacy were immediate and dramatic. In the fall of 1999, British newspapers announced the
good tidings: "Boys Close Literacy Gender Gap";[19] "Boys Catching Up
with Girls Thanks to Literacy Hour."[20] According to the *Daily Mail*:

> While the girls are still ahead, the ability gap has dramatically nar-
> rowed. Education Secretary David Blunkett will see the new key state
> results as complete vindication of his back-to-basics policies in primary
> schools. . . . The figures suggest that the new regime is paying rich div-
> idends. Last year just 64 percent of 11-year-old boys were proficient
> in reading. Today's figure is 78 percent. The remarkable improvement
> has exceeded the wildest expectation of the government.[21]

To an American observer, the very fact that the plight of *boys* is making headlines is almost as remarkable as anything the British are doing to
help them. Just as remarkable is that the initiatives to solve the problem
of lagging boys are coming as much from the government as from the tra-
ditionalist forces in education. Success in helping boys has become a political imperative. The *Daily Telegraph* noted that Secretary Blunkett has
"Staked his political future" on the drive to narrow the gender gap: "Mr.
Blunkett has promised to resign if 80 percent did not reach [proficiency] in
the national curriculum English tests for 11-year-olds in 2002."[22]

Anyone who is aware of and concerned about the large number of outwardly confident but academically mediocre American boys will want to
pay close attention to the initiatives unfolding in Britain. The U.S. Department of Education reports that "the gap in reading proficiency between
males and females [favoring females] is roughly equivalent to about one
and a half years of schooling."[23] The gap shows up early, and it remains
large at every stage that children are tested. In 1998, for example, eighth-
grade boys were 13 points behind girls on the National Assessment of
Educational Progress. For twelfth-graders the gap was 15 points.[24] (The
NAEP scale scores range from 0 to 500.) The 1994 Department of Education "Reading Report Card for the Nation and the States" showed that
47 percent of the nation's fourth-grade boys were "below basic" in reading; for females the figure was 36 percent.[25] American education officials
know all about the problem of boys, but there is no visible effort to make
the problem known to the public at large, nor is anyone openly committed to addressing and solving it.

By the time they reach college age, many American young men are outside the culture of the written word. In an annual survey of college freshmen conducted by the Higher Education Research Institute at UCLA,

students are asked how many hours per week they spent reading for pleasure during the preceding year. The 1998 results were consistent with
other years: 35 percent of males answered "none." Reading for pleasure is
something these young men have never gotten used to. Among females,
the figure was 22 percent.[26]

The debate between traditionalists and progressives over how to teach
language skills is old. What is frustrating is that in the United States this
debate has been carried on for decades without anyone taking serious
notice of the fact that American boys were becoming significantly less literate than girls. Surely this fact is one to which attention must be paid;
surely the question of what is a "best practice" in the teaching of reading
and writing must consider how well it works for boys.

The federal government, state departments of education, and women's
groups have been expending millions of dollars addressing a surreal self-
esteem problem that allegedly afflicts girls more than boys. In the matter
of literacy, we have a real and genuinely alarming difference between
males and females. But this shows boys in trouble, and no one seems to
want to talk about that, much less take concerted action to correct it. For
while it is perfectly acceptable to say that boys are psychologically distressed and in need of rescue from the myths of boyhood, it is not popular to say that our educational system is shortchanging boys academically.
So at the present time, we in the United States are taking no constructive
action to aid the nation's underachieving boys.

The Wider Background

A frieze on the facade of the Horace Mann building of Columbia Teachers College celebrates nine great education pioneers. Among them are
Johann Heinrich Pestalozzi (1746–1827), Johann Friedrich Herbart
(1776–1841), and Friedrich Froebel (1782–1852). Few Americans know
much about the profound influence that these eighteenth-century German
and Swiss theorists have had on American education. Froebel, for example, is credited with inventing the concept of the kindergarten. The German word "Kindergarten" literally means a garden whose plants are
children. Froebel regarded children as fragile young plants and the ideal
teacher as a gentle gardener:

> To young plants and animals we give space, and time, and rest, know-
> ing that they will unfold to beauty by laws working in each. We avoid
> acting upon them by force, for we know that such intrusion upon their
> natural growth could injure their development. Yet man treats the

young human being as if it were a piece of wax, a lump of clay out of which he can mould what he will! . . . Education and instruction should from the very first be a passive, observant, protective, rather than prescribing, determining, interfering. . . . All training and instruction which prescribes and fixes, that is interferes with Nature, must tend to limit and injure.[27]

Froebel wrote these words almost two hundred years ago, but his plant/child metaphor continues to inspire American educators. In the most straightforward sense, the plant metaphor is profoundly antieducational; after all, you can't teach a plant; all you can do is help it develop. Progressive educators oppose "interference" with the child's nature and look for ways to release his or her creative forces. Teachers are urged to build on the "natural curiosity children bring to school and ask the kids what they want to learn."[28] All this is antithetical to classical education. A traditional teacher such as Mrs. Daugherty establishes a strict curriculum based on requirements and standards that all students are expected to satisfy. She knows what her students need to learn at each stage, and there is little likelihood that she will ask them to choose what they should take up next.

Best Practice: New Standards for Teaching and Learning in America's Schools is a 1998 summary of the "emerging standards of state-of-the-art teaching."[29] Its authors, three curriculum experts from National-Louis University in Evanston, Illinois, are themselves progressives, but they base their recommendations on what "good teachers do." Their list of "best practices" reflects what they say is the "unanimous" opinion of leading education experts. As the authors explain:

> Whether the recommendations come from the National Council of Teachers of Mathematics, the Center for the Study of Reading, the National Writing Project, the National Council for the Social Studies, the American Association for the Advancement of Science, the National Council of Teachers of English, the National Association for the Education of Young Children, or the International Reading Association, the fundamental insights into teaching and learning are remarkably congruent. Indeed, on many key issues the recommendations from these diverse organizations are unanimous.[30]

What are the specific recommendations of these leading education organizations? The authors of *Best Practice* draw up a list of the "new" standards and practices. The list, in fact, is not new. It is a compendium of the basic tenets of progressivism. It is also the exact opposite of what the British headmasters are recommending for boys. As the authors of *Best Practice* explain, our major teaching associations agree that our schools need:

○ LESS student passivity: sitting, listening, receiving, and absorbing information

○ LESS rote memorization of facts and details

○ LESS emphasis on competition and grades in school

○ MORE active learning in the classroom with all the attendant noise and movement of students doing, talking, and collaborating

○ MORE cooperative, collaborative activity; developing the classroom as an interdependent community.[31]

Many of these recommendations reflect views put forward by Harold Rugg and Ann Shumaker in *The Child-Centered School*, a classic of progressivism written back in 1928.[32] As the education scholar Diane Ravitch explains, Rugg and Shumaker believed that the primary focus of education should be "freedom, activity and creative self-expression."[33] These ideas were also present in the works of Rugg's famous and influential contemporary William Heard Kilpatrick of Columbia University. They would return again in the 1960s, when A. S. Neill's *Summerhill* became a best-seller, and again in the writings of the "angry young educators" such as John Holt, Herbert Kohl, and Jonathan Kozol. Here is a précis of their contribution from a recent historical retrospective by Lynn Olson in *Education Week*: "They derided the meaningless routines, dehumanizing discipline, and lock step schedules of many schools; denounced the unbridled authoritarianism and the school's role in perpetuating social inequities; and waxed eloquent over their own attempts at innovation."[34]

In 1986, an influential book, *Women's Ways of Knowing*, gave a feminist twist to the progressivist agenda. Its authors claimed that women learned best in a cooperative, collaborative classroom. They impugned competition and favored "connected learning"—a "warmer and fairer" teaching style that allows students to "empathetically enter into the subject they are studying."[35]

The authors of *Best Practice* boast that their recommendations are the expression of an "unrecognized consensus" stemming from a "remarkably consistent, harmonious vision of this 'best educational practice.' "[36] Altogether oblivious to the widening learning gap that is leaving American children far behind the children of other industrial countries, they celebrate the "potential transforming power" of progressivism's "harmonious vision." It is a vision that anyone concerned with the career prospects of American young people can no longer afford to trust. Treating children as plants unfolding "to beauty by laws working in each" has not succeeded. Basic intellectual skills such as reading and writing do not develop by way of laws working within. Literacy does not come naturally to human beings. It certainly does not come naturally to many little boys.

For some years now, British education officials have been complaining that the progressive approach to the teaching of language skills disadvantages boys. In 1995, School Standards Minister Stephen Byers said, "A return to more structured reading lessons will benefit both boys and girls, but the evidence shows that it is boys who have been most disadvantaged by the move away from phonics."[37]

Bonnie Macmillan, a British education scholar, has researched the decline in literacy in the primary grades. Her conclusion in *Why Schoolchildren Can't Read* is the same as Byers's: progressive education methods—especially whole language—put boys at special risk: "Boys are more likely than girls to have problems learning to read. . . . They may be more distracted by extraneous noise, particularly speech, during learning tasks, and may be more susceptible to picture effects, the wide range of bright and colorful illustrations in their readers distracting their attention from the decoding tasks."[38] And she concludes: "[S]ince . . . boys [are] more susceptible to developing reading problems than girls, it seems likely that the lack of appropriate instruction will take more of a toll on the reading attainment of boys."[39]

As far as I know, no one in the United States has considered the problem of language teaching in this light. The idea that some approaches are better for one sex than the other is not in itself politically incorrect, provided they favor girls. For the time being we cannot expect our public officials to suggest that teachers assign more boy-friendly materials.

Other Pedagogical Derailments

The British experience suggests that boys respond well to the older pedagogies. If that is right, it is boys who are paying the highest price for the current misguided fashions in education. Once such fashion is the celebration of "cooperative learning" and the denigration of competition. The London *Daily Telegraph*'s education writer, Janet Daley, who thinks as well as she writes, correctly points out that boys have been adversely affected by the current trend to de-emphasize the competitive elements in learning. "By rejecting the old-fashioned ladder of tests, measurable achievement and competition, incentives were lost that had once given school a comprehensible point to many pupils—particularly the male ones. [A] world in which no one can be called a winner and nothing counts as losing will have little call on the young male psyche."[40]

The movement to eliminate competitive rankings in American schools has made great headway in recent years. Pat Riordan, dean of admissions at George Mason University, researched class rankings for the National Association of Secondary Schools. She estimates that 60 percent of schools no longer use them.[41] At Community High, a public secondary school in Ann Arbor, Michigan, academic awards at graduation are kept a secret. There are no class rankings, no valedictorian. At graduation, everyone gets a turn to speak. As the guidance counselor explains, "Everybody is seen as an equal contributor to the class of '99."

WE HONOR ALL STUDENTS says a bumper sticker from Drew Elementary School in Arlington, Virginia. The implication is that schools with honor rolls dishonor those who do not qualify. Jim Mitchell, executive director of the Maryland Association of Elementary School Principals, explains the new hostility to the honor roll: "It flies in the face of the philosophy of not making it so competitive for those little kids. . . . We even frown on spelling bees."[42]

Throughout the country, battles are raging. Typically, school officials are seeking to eliminate competitive practices, and parents and school board members are fighting to reinstate them. After several schools in Prince William County, Virginia, tried to eliminate the honor roll, the school board intervened. In defending it, one board member, John Harper, Jr., expressed an opinion very much at odds with the spirit of progressivism but shared by many parents: "To me, competition is what America is all about. The more they compete, the better they become."[43]

Competition that provides incentives to excel is as natural to a successful classroom as it is to a successful sports team. Competition in matters of intellect is not harmful but essential to progress. The Talmudic sage who said, "The envy that scholars bear to one another increases the world's wisdom" had it right. Competitive learners have always been a driving force in the advancement of knowledge. Of course grades are competitive, but they "increase the world's wisdom." E. D. Hirsch, the educator and reformer from the University of Virginia, advises, "[I]nstead of trying fruitlessly to abolish competition as an element of human nature, we should try to guide it into educationally productive channels."[44]

A lot of what is now considered bad practice—an emphasis on skills and drills, a reliance on competitive motivations, a teacher-centered pedagogy—is unavailable in many of today's schools. Yet these practices may be especially effective in getting boys to learn and progress. American educators need to ask whether, in moving away from skills and drills, phonics, teacher-led discussions, competition, and same-sex classes, they have not inadvertently been moving away from what works for boys.

The War Against Single-Sex Education for Boys

As soon as they identified the gender education gap, British educators began seriously experimenting with same-sex classes in coed public schools as a way of helping to narrow it. This courted progressivist rancor. As the London *Times* pointed out in 1994, "The schools' proposal [for same-sex classes] challenges the progressive orthodoxy of the past 30 years that holds that single-sex is 'unnatural.' "[45] Marian Cox, headmistress at the Cotswold School, admitted that single-sex schools were an unorthodox measure, but, she said, "We have a national crisis with boys' under-achievement in English. Either we tackle it, or we put our heads in the sand and ignore it. We felt the time had come to bite the bullet."[46]

When American schools try to develop special programs for boys, they find groups such as the National Organization for Women and the American Civil Liberties Union poised to oppose them. In 1989, threats of lawsuits from both organizations prevented the Detroit public schools from proceeding with plans for all-male academies for at-risk urban youths. When schools in Dade County, Florida, were considering establishing two all-male classes for underachieving boys, the U.S. Department of Education's Office of Civil Rights blocked them.

In 1994, Senator John Danforth tried to address this impasse. He offered an amendment to an education bill proposing that ten school districts be permitted to experiment with same-sex classes without threat of lawsuit. The amendment passed the Senate but was rejected in conference with the House of Representatives. Says Danforth, "I was stunned at the organized opposition to the amendment. Opponents argued vehemently that the provision would result in injustice to young girls, despite the amendment's requirement that same-sex classes be offered to both boys and girls."[47]

The vehemence is supplied by girl partisan groups such as NOW, which argues that "segregation" by sex is as pernicious as that by race. Anne Connors, president of the New York City chapter of NOW, has stated the organization's official position: "Public money should not be used to fund institutions segregated on the basis of sex."[48] But at least NOW is consistent: it applies the principle that "segregated schools and classes are bad" to both all-male and all-female programs. NOW has joined the ACLU in challenging the legality of the highly successful Young Women's

Leadership School in East Harlem, a girls-only public school started in 1996.

Other women's groups, such as the National Women's Law Center, suggest that same-sex programs may be justifiable for girls, but not for boys. Deborah Brake, a senior counsel at NWLC, notes that the "considerable network" of federal, state, local, and private scholarships and programs for girls and women may be legitimate because of past inequities: "In light of the history of discrimination against women in education and the barriers that female students continue to face based on their gender, there [may be] a legitimate place for such programs."[49] Judith Shapiro, president of Barnard College, is less tentative. In a 1994 opinion piece in the *Baltimore Sun:* "In a society that favors men over women, men's institutions operate to preserve privilege, women's institutions challenge privilege and attempt to expand access to the good things of life."[50]

In fact, our society does not favor boys. It certainly does not favor the growing number of boys who are disengaged, barely literate, and without the prospects of going to college. These young men have very little access to "the good things of life." Unfortunately, elite educational leaders such as Shapiro and Brake, who oppose single-sex pedagogy for boys, have little interest in finding out whether all-male classes are useful for the many thousands of at-risk boys.

A School in Baltimore

Harford Heights Elementary School, the largest elementary school in Maryland, is in a poor section of Baltimore. No one at the school has read the report of the British headmasters; but Harford teachers and administrators, determined to find ways to help young males succeed academically, have found their own way to many of the practices recommended in *Can Boys Do Better?*

Since the mid-nineties the school has experimented with same-sex classes for both boys and girls. These classes are optional. Parents and teachers jointly decide who will most benefit. In selecting students for the all-male classes, school officials give boys with behavior problems and boys from fatherless homes priority. (These two groups often overlap.)

As in Great Britain, the all-boy classes are taught by male teachers, and the boys' natural competitiveness and high-spiritedness are not discouraged but channeled to good ends. As the former principal who initiated the program said, "The boys become competitive rather than combative."[51]

Walter Sallee, who has taught an all-boys class at Harford Heights for three years, uses many of the old-fashioned methods favored by the British headmasters. His classes are highly structured. He teaches phonics, grammar, and diction. He carefully monitors student progress. He uses a lot of boy-friendly materials; for example, he has developed math lessons based on Jackie Robinson's baseball statistics. His students, like boys everywhere, are fascinated by sports and sports stars, so these lessons are a great success. In gym class, his focus is character education through sportsmanship.

Sallee works hard to exploit the boys' natural competitiveness to promote academic achievement. He breaks his class (twenty-seven ten-year-old boys in 1998–99) down into "teams." He turns classroom activities into contests. There is an elaborate point system. There are prizes. School uniforms are optional at Harford, but most of the boys in Sallee's class choose to wear them. Teams get extra points when all members don the uniform.

The boys in his all-male classes are mostly poor and African-American. Sallee is concerned about their self-esteem and confidence; but he does not rely on gimmicks or therapeutic methods. The boys gain confidence by mastering skills, becoming good sports, being team players and young gentlemen. One of Sallee's primary aims is to help his students develop their social skills. They learn to express themselves with confidence, and they learn manners. Several times a year the all-boy and all-girl classes take part in shared events. One favorite occasion is a Thanksgiving banquet. The boys escort the girls to the table, help them into their chairs, and engage in polite conversation. The children love it—especially the girls.

Sallee's students are at risk for every kind of academic and behavioral problem. But in this all-male environment, such problems nearly vanish. Should a boy neglect to do his work or misbehave, he hurts his team and disappoints his teacher. School disengagement is a problem for many boys, but it is especially severe among young black males. The boys in Sallee's class are the very opposite of disengaged. They are enthralled. As Sallee told me, "They love the positive attention they get in the class. They look forward to it and hate to miss a single day."[52]

Harford Heights offers same-sex classes in grades three, four, and five. The classes are a great success with parents, who are asking for more of them. It is easy to see why. Millions of parents, rich and poor, from all ethnic backgrounds, would welcome an opportunity for their sons to attend a class like Mr. Sallee's. Boys everywhere need structure, phonics, diction, grammar, and a competitive environment. Mr. Sallee's deliberate efforts to teach ethics through sportsmanship and good manners could be the making of many boys. But the likelihood of many parents having such an opportunity is remote. The forces arrayed against public, same-sex education for boys are formidable indeed.

Some Private Boys' Schools

The Heights School is in the center of Potomac, Maryland, one of the wealthiest suburbs of Washington, D.C. In many ways, it could not be more unlike Harford. The students at Harford are mostly poor and black; at the Heights they are predominantly white and middle or upper middle class. Harford is in a run-down section of Baltimore. Heights sits on twenty wooded acres. Harford is a public elementary school. Heights is an independent all-male Catholic elementary and high school. But there are some striking similarities in the way the two schools educate boys.

The much-loved Heights headmaster (recently retired), Joseph McPherson, can sound very much like Sallee when talking about how boys learn. "Boys need games, and they thrive on competition," he explains. "Who can skip the rock the most number of times?" All twenty-seven teachers at the Heights are male. "Boys are much more docile to men," says McPherson. Yet the school is hardly macho. The younger boys (aged eight to ten) attend class in log cabins filled with collections of insects, plants, and flowers. They memorize poetry and take weekly classes in painting and drawing. The day I visited, I observed a class of well-behaved fifth-graders sitting in rows, wearing blue blazers, and taking turns performing scales on their recorders.

Competition is part of the everyday life of the school—there are lots of awards and prizes—but, as in Sallee's class, it is constrained by ethics. One favorite all-school game is "Capture the Flag": It's a war game, played with a great deal of team spirit and with an established tradition of the older boys protecting the younger ones.

For McPherson, the goal of educating children is not only to impart information and teach skills but to "provide them with a noble vision of life—to convey to them that they have to do something great with their lives." He believes that adult males are uniquely suited to impart this philosophy to boys. McPherson explains that male teachers can introduce boys to the world of ideas, of nature, art, poetry, and music, and generally "expand their range of interests without the boys feeling they are risking their masculinity."

Landon, another distinguished boys' school, is a few miles away from the Heights. The headmaster, Damon Bradley, explained to me that at all-male academies boys do things "they would never agree to do if girls were around." At Landon, 75 percent of the boys are involved in music and art. "Competition is something boys respond to," says the headmaster. But in a boys' school, competition takes place in unusual pursuits. One highly coveted honor at Landon is to be selected for the bell choir. Oddly enough, football players and other school athletes love the choir and vie for a place in it. It is hard to get into the choir, which is run like a team sport. Headmaster Bradley seems touched by all the burly choir members with their thick necks wearing white gloves. In his writings on boys' schools, Bradley dwells on the ancient view that manliness and virtue are intimately related:

> Our Latin teacher has explained to me that the Latin word for "man" (vir) can easily be recognized in the word *virtute,* as its root derivation, suggesting that "virtue" and "manliness" were integrally linked in the Roman mind. . . . [I]n the classical world—and arguably in boys' schools—manliness is defined more by virtue and less by might. . . . [T]he primary challenge of our schools is to help boys fuse "gentleness" with manliness.[53]

Why Single-Sex Classes Are Generally Unavailable

When the U.S. Supreme Court ruled in 1996 that the Virginia Military Institute was violating the Fourteenth Amendment to the Constitution by excluding women, it dealt an almost fatal blow to same-sex education *for boys.* In the majority opinion, written by Justice Ruth Bader Ginsburg, the Court retained full protection for any female-only programs that could be said to compensate for the disabilities women suffer: "Sex classifications may be used to compensate women 'for particular economic disabilities [they have] suffered,' to 'promote equal employment opportunity,' to advance the full development of the talent and capacities of our Nation's people. But such classifications may not be used, as they once were, to create or perpetuate the legal, social and economic inferiority of women."[54]

In light of this ruling, all-girls programs could still be seen as compensatory; all-boys programs, on the other hand, are regarded as discriminatory. The ruling puts a chill on all special initiatives for boys. However, while it discourages them, it does not strictly prohibit them. Programs that separate the sexes while offering each the same resources and opportunities remain permissible. At least, that is how the U.S. Office of Civil Rights seems to be interpreting the law. Programs in Maryland, Virginia, and California have so far survived legal challenges from the Office of Civil Rights because they cover both boys and girls and are voluntary.[55] In practice, however, single-sex education is an allowable option for girls, but rarely for boys.

In 1996, the California state legislature allocated $5 million toward the development of all-male and all-female "academies." These may be either separate school or special programs within existing coed schools.[56] Sean Walsh, a spokesman for then-Governor Pete Wilson, who initiated the program, justified it as a corrective against the laissez-faire progressivism that has seen literacy plunge in the primary grades: "The [same-sex] academies will allow a more structured, more disciplined environment where kids could get a core curriculum, a sense of right and wrong, a sense of personal responsibility, a sense of duty."[57] The program is in its early stages, but it is already quite popular with parents and students. There is anecdotal evidence that it is succeeding, but a formal analysis of the program will be submitted to the state legislature in 2000.

Women's groups remain uneasy, however. In 1998, the American Association of University Women released *Separated by Sex: A Critical Look at Single-Sex Education for Girls*. The report, a compilation of essays by several scholars, turned out to be inconclusive. Most of the contributors agreed that more careful and systematic long-term research was needed. But the AAUW press release was categorically negative. "What the report shows is that separating by sex is not the solution to gender inequity in education," wrote Maggie Ford, president of the AAUW Educational Foundation. Critics soon pointed out the disparity between the full report and the press summary.[58] One of the contributing scholars, Cornelius Riordan, was stunned by the negative spin in the press release. He told the *Los Angeles Times* that the releases were "slanted" and "off the deep end."[59]

The episode should stand as a warning. In their laudable efforts to evaluate the efficacy of same-sex programs objectively, California legislators would do well to take precautions not to be pulled into the acrimonious misandrist maelstrom that this issue currently generates in this country. Otherwise, they'll find themselves in the position of Professor Riordan and Senator Danforth before him. I spoke to California Governor Pete Wilson in June 1999 about the evaluation. He was pessimistic about the prospects of a fair review. He believed the entire process was being compromised by politics and special agendas.

Meanwhile, the British experiment with all-male pedagogy is proceeding, with promising initial results. On July 14, 1997, The *Times* of London carried a story under the headline "Boys Do Better in Single-Sex Schools": "Boys gain more from single-sex education than girls, according to research that will ignite the debate over the advantages of segregating sexes at school.

Boys in single-sex schools did about 20 percent better than those in mixed sex [classes]."[60]

This *Times* story reported the findings of a small study carried out by a research group commissioned by all-male British schools; its conclusions may not be relevant to American boys. At this time we simply don't know whether single-sex classes are the key to a better pedagogy for boys. Nor are we likely to find out in the near future so long as girl-partisan organizations effectively discourage research and debate on the same-sex solution to the problem of lagging boys.[61]

Coeducation is a strong tradition in the United States, and it is doubtful that we will ever adopt a single-sex system on a large scale. On the other hand, those who oppose it on ideological grounds should not be indulged. Single-sex classes do not cost substantially more than mixed classes. They seem to be working for privileged boys who attend private schools like Heights and Landon as well as for the disadvantaged boys in Mr. Sallee's class. The British headmasters believe in them. We need a national discussion of the merits of all-male classes. And we need to take care that groups such as NOW, the AAUW, and the National Women's Law Center do not control and shape that discussion.

Suppose the British headmasters and government officials are right in suggesting that boys would generally be much better off in a traditional learning environment. What are the chances that American schools will provide it? At present, the prospects for change do not look bright. To begin with, the academic plight of boys has not yet even been identified as a serious problem by either the government or the educational establishment. Boys are still not on the agenda. The media's interest in boys is focused not on their academic deficits but on their potential for violence. Then, too, the child-centered, therapeutic style of education under which boys do not do well appears deeply entrenched in many of our "best" school systems.

All the same, I am optimistic that change for the better will be coming rather quickly on the heels of a widespread public awareness that the future of our children, and especially of our sons, is in jeopardy. The onset of a galvanizing awareness (which the British already have) cannot be delayed here much longer.

NOTES

1. Story told by Dr. Carl Boyd, president and CEO of the Art of Positive Teaching, an educational foundation in Kansas City (keynote address, National Coalition for Sex Equity Experts, July 1998). For an interesting

(albeit controversial) discussion of the effects of teachers' expectations on students, see Robert Rosenthal and Lenore Jackson, *Pygmalion in the Classroom: Teacher Expectations and Pupils' Intellectual Development* (New York: Irvington, 1992) (originally published 1968).

2. Steven Zemelman, Harvey Daniels, and Arthur Hyde, *Best Practice: New Standards for Teaching and Learning in America's Schools* (Portsmouth, N.H.: Heineman, 1998), p. 51.

3. Alfie Kohn, *What to Look for in a Classroom* (San Francisco: Jossey-Bass, 1998), p. 51.

4. E. D. Hirsch, Jr., *The Schools We Need: And Why We Don't Have Them* (New York: Doubleday, 1996), p. 9.

5. Department of Education, *Pursuing Excellence: A Study of U.S. Twelfth-Grade Mathematics and Science Achievement in International Context* (Washington, D.C.: U.S. Government Printing Office, 1998). See also Harold Stevenson, *A TIMSS Primer* (Washington, D.C.: Thomas B. Fordham Foundation, 1998) (for full date report, see http://www.csteep.bd.edu /timss).

6. Liz Lightfoot, "Boys Left Behind by Modern Teaching," *Daily Telegraph,* January 5, 1998. Estelle Morris, MP, expressed similar sentiments in a 1996 Labour Party consultation paper, "Boys Will Be Boys?: Closing the Gender Gap." Morris: "Boys' underachievement not only represents a massive waste of talent and ability. It is also personally disastrous and socially destructive. If we do not act quickly we will reap a harvest of young men who are unemployable and face decades of social division."

7. Lester Thurow, "Players and Spectators," *Washington Post Book World,* April 18, 1999, p. 5.

8. Larry Hedges and Amy Nowell, "Sex Differences in Mental Test Scores, Variability, and Numbers of High-Scoring Individuals," *Science 269* (July 7, 1995), p. 45.

9. Robert Bray et al., *Can Boys Do Better?* (Bristol: Secondary Heads Association, 1997).

10. Ibid., p. 17.

11. Barclay Mcbain, "The Gender Gap That Threatens to Become a Chasm," *Herald* (Glasgow), September 17, 1996, p. 16.

12. "Top Marks to the Lads," *Daily Telegraph,* January 17, 1998.

13. Ibid.

14. Ibid.

15. Bray et al., *Can Boys Do Better?,* p. 1.

16. Annette MacDonald, Lesley Saunders, and Pauline Benefield, *Boys' Achievement, Progress, Motivation and Participation* (Slough, Berkshire, England: National Foundation for Educational Research, 1999), p. 18.

17. Ibid., p. 13.

18. Liz Lightfoot, "Boys Need a Ripping Yarn to Keep Up Interest," *Daily Telegraph,* April 24, 1999.

19. John O'Leary, "Boys Close Literary Gender Gap," *Times* (London), October 7, 1999.

20. David Hughes, "Boys Catching Up with Girls Thanks to Literary Hour," *Daily Mail,* October 6, 1999, p. 12.

21. Ibid.

22. John Clare, "Primary Schools Failing to Teach Reading Properly," *Daily Telegraph,* July 6, 1999, p. 12.

23. Department of Education, *The Condition of Education* (Washington, D.C.: U.S. Department of Education, 1995), p. 13.

24. National Center for Education Statistics, *NAEP [National Assessment of Educational Progress] 1998 Reading Report Card for the Nation and the States* (Washington, D.C.: U.S. Department of Education, 1999), p. 42.

25. Department of Education, *NAEP 1994 Reading Report Card for the Nation and the States* (Washington, D.C.: U.S. Department of Education, 1996), p. 138.

26. Higher Education Research Institute, *The American Freshman: National Norms for Fall 1998* (Los Angeles: Higher Education Research Institute, 1998), pp. 39, 57.

27. Friedrich Froebel, *The Student's Froebel,* ed. W. H. Herford (Boston: Heath, 1904), pp. 5–6. (The quotation is cited in Hirsch, *The Schools We Need.* See especially Hirsch's Chapter 4, "Critique of Thought World," for a thorough and astute analysis of the influence of romanticism on American education, pp. 69–126.)

28. Zemelman et al., *Best Practice,* p. 9.

29. Ibid., book summary on back cover. See Hirsch's Chapter 5, "Reality's Revenge," *The Schools We Need,* for his critique of *Best Practice* (pp. 127–76).

30. Ibid., p. 4.

31. Ibid., p. 5.

32. H. Rugg and Ann Shumaker, *The Child-Centered School* (Yonkers-on-Hudson, N.Y.: World Book, 1928).

33. Diane Ravitch, *The Troubled Crusade: American Education 1945–1980* (New York: Basic Books, 1983), p. 50.

34. Lynn Olson, "Lessons of a Century," *Education Week,* April 21, 1998.

35. Mary Field Belenky et al., *Women's Ways of Knowing* (New York: Basic Books, 1986). Quotations are from a summary of the book in the *American Association of University Women Report: How Schools Shortchange Girls* (Washington, D.C.: American Association of University Women Educational Foundation, 1992), p. 72.

36. Zemelman et al., *Best Practice,* p. 6.

37. Lightfoot, "Boys Left Behind by Modern Teaching."

38. Bonnie Macmillan, *Why Schoolchildren Can't Read* (London: Institute of Economic Affairs, 1997), p. 124.

39. Ibid., p. 125.

40. Janet Daley, "Progressive Education in Britain," *Ex Femina* (Washington, D.C.: Independent Women's Forum, October 1998), p. 13.

41. June Kronholz, "At Many U.S. Schools, the Valedictorian Is Now a Tricky Issue," *Wall Street Journal,* May 17, 1999, p. 1.

42. Ann O'Hanlon, "Ruckus Over the Honor Roll," *Washington Post,* April 8, 1997, p. D1.

43. Ibid.

44. Hirsch, *The Schools We Need,* p. 245.

45. Charles Hymas, "Boys Get Their Own Classes to Catch Up," *Times* (London), July 19, 1994, p. 1.

46. Ibid.

47. John Danforth, "Single-Sex Education vs. Woman at VMI," *Washington Times,* January 17, 1996, p. A15.

48. New York City, NOW, http://www.now.org.

49. Deborah Brake, "Single-Sex Education After VMI" posted on Internet at edequity@tristam.edc.org, April 20, 1998.

50. Judith Shapiro, "What Women Can Teach Men," *Baltimore Sun,* November 28, 1994, p. 11A.

51. Megan Rosenfeld, "All-Male Classes Raise Grades and Hackles," *Washington Post,* March 26, 1998, p. A16.

52. Author's interview with Walter Sallee.

53. Damon Bradley, "On Not Letting Georgette Do It: The Case for Single-Sex Boys' Education," *The Vincent/Curtis Educational Register* (Boston:

Vincent/Curtis, 1996), p. 5. Diane Hulse, director of the Collegiate Middle School, an all-boys academy in New York City, did a small study comparing the attitudes of 186 boys at Collegiate to 239 children at a comparable coed school. She found that the Collegiate boys were less vulnerable to pressure, felt they had greater control over their academic performance, and had more egalitarian attitudes toward women. See Diane Hulse, *Brad and Cory: A Study of Middle School Boys* (Hunting Valley, Ohio: University School Press, 1997).

54. *United States v. Virginia,* 116 S.Ct. 2264, June 26, 1996.

55. *New York Times,* October 9, 1997, p. A22.

56. Fact sheet: "Single Gender Academics Pilot Program" (http://www.cde.ca.gov), May 7, 1999.

57. Richard Lee Colvin, "Can Same-Sex Classes Aid Desperate Communities?" *Los Angeles Times,* January 10, 1996, p. 1.

58. See, for example, Rosemary Salomone, "Single-Sex Schooling: Law, Policy, and Research," in *Brookings Papers on Education Policy,* ed. Diane Ravitch (Washington, D.C.: Brookings Institution, 1999), p. 264; and "Schools for Girls," *Wall Street Journal,* March 13, 1998, p. A16.

59. Nick Anderson, "One-Sex Schools Don't Escape Bias, Study Says," *Los Angeles Times,* March 12, 1998, metro A1.

60. John O'Leary, "A-Level Analysis Finds Boys Do Better in Single-Sex Schools," *Times* (London), July 14, 1997.

61. See, for example, American Association of University Women, *Separated by Sex: A Critical Look at Single-Sex Education for Girls* (Washington, D.C.: American Association of University Women, 1998), p. 70.

30

WHAT'S SEX GOT
TO DO WITH IT?

SIMPLISTIC QUESTIONS, COMPLEX ANSWERS[1]

Patricia B. Campbell and Ellen Wahl

THE LINGUIST NOAM CHOMSKY uses the sentence "Colorless green ideas sleep furiously" to make the point that a sentence may be linguistically correct but still make no sense.[2] Similarly, while the question "Are single-sex classes better than coed classes?" sounds logical, it makes little sense when it doesn't include what goes on in the classes, the pedagogy and practices of the teachers, or anything about the students other than their sex. Yet the public, media, and even some researchers compare classes and attribute outcomes to this single factor of whether the class is all girls, all boys, or girls and boys together. We can assume that most parents would prefer that their child be in a good single-sex math class rather than a bad coed one. We can also assume that these same parents would prefer a good coed math class over a bad single-sex class.

In this paper, we look at the research on single-sex and coed classrooms and explore why such a simplistic question is being asked about such a complex topic. We examine why so many people have already decided what the answer is regardless of what the research says. Finally, we suggest ways to reframe the questions to acknowledge the interplay of factors involved in promoting high-quality education for girls and for boys, so that educators and the public can make considered decisions about policy and practice.

During the past five years, single-sex classes have been set up in public schools from Cocoa Beach, Florida, to Presque Isle, Maine, and from New Bedford, Massachusetts, to Ventura, California, with many more communities discussing their establishment. While there have been no surveys or formal counts of single-sex classes, anecdotal data indicate that the classes are overwhelmingly for girls, primarily at the middle school level and almost always in mathematics or the sciences. In general, these classes are seen as a way to address girls' lower levels of achievement and participation in advanced mathematics and physics courses, as well as women's much lower rates of employment in engineering and the physical sciences.[3] Whether these classes are legal within the context of public schooling is in question, and limitations on what is legal may affect how the developers of single-sex classes explain their purposes (for instance, using the notion of all-girls' classes for "remediation" or "compensation," which has standing in legal arguments as a way to equalize opportunity).

These are good faith efforts, attempts to remedy situations of inequity or promote higher-quality education for the students in question. They appear to have been influenced by the popularization of ideas about gender issues in education, such as the differential amount and quality of attention girls and boys receive in the classroom.[4] Myth and popular notions, however, seem to be mixed up with what is actually known from research about the efficacy of single-sex classes compared to coed ones.

The Problems with the Existing Research

In fact, the sheer size of the base of research comparing single-sex and coed classes in the United States and in other countries is quite small. Within that small body of research, results must be interpreted with caution. Most of the studies do not control for such important variables as the teacher, the curriculum, and student self-selection. If a single-sex class taught by one teacher is compared to a coed class taught by another teacher, there is no way of telling what proportion of any difference found is due to the teacher and how much is due to the sex breakdown of the class. On the positive side, since comparisons of single-sex and coed classes are usually made of classes within the same school, there are fewer differences in student socioeconomic status and available resources than there are in comparisons of single-sex and coed schools.

Within the research that does exist, results are not consistent. For example, in studies of achievement, one study found no differences in girls' subsequent math and science course taking[5] while another found short-term but not long-term gain.[6] No differences in grades or SAT scores between girls in single-sex math classes and girls in coed classes were reported by one group of researchers,[7] while other researchers found single-sex grouping has little effect on the achievement scores of either males or females,[8] and yet another[9] identified short-term but not long-term achievement gains for girls in single-sex classes.

In studies of attitudes, girls in single-sex classes have been found to have noticeably more favorable attitudes toward science and mathematics than girls in coed classes.[10] However, in one of those cases, the girls in the single-sex classes became more personally negative about mathematics at the same time that they became more positive about girls doing mathematics.[11] Still, teachers, researchers, and students all said that girls in coed classes participated less, were less extroverted, had less interaction with the teacher, and were subject to more harassment from other students than girls in single-sex classes.[12]

There is much that the research has not yet addressed. Few studies have explored qualitatively or quantitatively what in fact does take place with regard to content, pedagogy, interaction, social organization, or climate in differently constituted classrooms. We do not have research-based knowledge of what features, practices, or conditions of single-sex or coed classrooms promote better or different outcomes for girls or boys. The purposes and premises underlying different attempts at single-sex education are rarely included as part of the outcomes that are measured. There is a consequent lack of attention to what constitutes successful outcomes; for example, is success in achievement measured simply by greater gains, by gains that close the gap in achievement between groups, or by acquisition of skills and knowledge in relation to standards?

The results from the above studies are ambiguous at best, and indicate there is no clear evidence to support the claim that single-sex classes are better for girls. Yet interest in single-sex classes is growing as is an erroneous belief that research clearly supports this claim. Examples of this erroneous belief can be found in sources as diverse as the *New York Times* and the Ukiah (CA) local Point/Counterpoint website. For example, a September 27, 1997, *New York Times* editorial explained, "The impetus for the new school was studies showing that girls, particularly girls from poor neighborhoods, learn better when boys are not in class," with no references or data to support their claim. Similarly, again without references or data, a September 19, 1997, Point/Counterpoint questioned "why sexual segregation builds such self-confidence and provides the best education."[13]

Assumptions That Deserve Questioning

Why is there such a disconnect between what the research says and what people believe? To answer this question, we need to look at some assumptions that may be behind these inaccurate conclusions. Eliyahu Goldratt's comment about identifying the source of error may be illuminating here:

> When I was a physicist, people would come to me from time to time with problems in mathematics they could not solve. They wanted me to check their numbers for them. But after a while I learned not to waste time checking the numbers—the numbers were almost always right. However, if I checked the assumptions, they were almost always wrong.[14]

We suggest that there are at least four assumptions in need of questioning before we consider future directions for research and action:

QUESTIONABLE ASSUMPTION 1 Girls and boys are opposites with different skills, interests, and learning styles. Thus, one or both sexes are better served by single-sex classes.

QUESTIONABLE ASSUMPTION 2 Boys will be boys and little, if anything, can be done to stop boys from disrespecting girls and creating a difficult environment. Thus, girls are better served in single-sex classes.

QUESTIONABLE ASSUMPTION 3 Gender equity refers to fairness for girls. Thus, the focus should be on what works for girls, in whatever setting.

QUESTIONABLE ASSUMPTION 4 Our efforts to reduce the gender gaps in subjects such as math and science, or in promoting coed environments that serve both boys and girls, have not been successful. Thus, single-sex classes are the only option left for addressing the inequities.

As is so often the case, reality is much more complex than beliefs, especially beliefs about the opposing nature of females and males. While there are some differences between the average girl and the average boy, there are much greater differences among girls and among boys than there are between girls and boys. Just knowing if someone is a girl or a boy tells you nothing about the person's math skills, athletic interests, or even level of aggression. While the average boy is more aggressive than the average girl, there are many girls who are more aggressive than most boys.[15] Analyses of thousands of studies have found that gender differences in cognitive and affective areas are relatively small and becoming smaller.[16] For example, the degree of overlap in girls' and boys' math skills has been computed to be between 90 and 99 percent,[17] while in verbal skills the degree of overlap has been found to be 96 percent.[18]

The second assumption implies that negative behavior by boys is inevitable, tolerable, and impossible to change. Looking at the research, there is some indication that boys are more apt to cause disruption in classrooms than are girls, and that boys get more positive and negative attention in classes than do girls.[19] Indeed, one study found that teachers were surprised at the extent to which the dominant and harassing behavior of boys was impeding girls' educational progress.[20] Their surprise is revealing both of their tolerance of disrespectful behavior and their lack of awareness of how a hostile climate affects educational participation. But the research also indicated that girls were not the only ones whose education was negatively affected. The same study found that while girls in single-sex classes received the least amount of harassment from other students, boys in single-sex classes received the most.[21] From controlled research studies to newspaper articles, it has been found that many fewer boys than girls prefer single-sex classes.[22] Even teachers preferred coed over single-sex classes for boys.[23] This may just mean that girls, boys, and teachers tend not to like hostile classroom climates.

Clearly stereotypical gender expectations are a major concern in the construction of positive environments for learning for both girls and boys. The National Women's Law Center worries that "when the design of single-sex schools or programs is premised on fixed notions about what women as a group are like or what women as a group are capable of, it tends to reinforce limiting stereotypes that create barriers to women's advancement."[24] These fixed notions tend to ignore issues of sexual orientation as well. Indeed the adult assumption that single-sex education eliminates sexual tensions or distractions denies the existence of homosexual and bisexual youth.

The role of the teacher as leader, rule-maker, and shaper of the social organization is key to making education work. But teachers' roles and responsibilities have not been given the attention they deserve in the studies or in gender issues in education generally. Indeed, there have been only minimal attempts of any sort to develop, monitor, and evaluate truly equitable classroom environments, and to analyze how equity and excellence are linked with respect to opportunity, treatment, and outcome in these settings.

The third assumption is that gender equity is only about girls, that the problems of inequitable access and outcomes in education affect only girls, and that the benefits of the solutions accrue only to girls. This assumption derives in part from the gender equity field itself, which began with a focus on girls and women. In recent years, we have seen a gradual shift toward a definition that includes the condition of being male or female in this or any other society, and the resources, rights, and privileges, as well as the limitations and costs associated with that condition. Viewing the issue from only the perspective of effect on girls inevitably has an impact on both research design and conclusions. It also negatively affects public policy conversations, setting up the familiar and useless debate that begins with "What about the boys?" but more important, it runs counter to our efforts to transform the social organization of the classrooms, institutions, and society to promote high-quality outcomes for each and all.

The fourth assumption, that little has changed, taps into the understandable and admirable frustration of teachers and others at what appears to be the slow pace of change toward gender equity. In fact, there has been significant movement in the past years with regard to achievement and course enrollment, especially in mathematics and science. Girls are now taking mathematics through calculus in equal numbers to boys, and gender differences in general mathematics achievement have declined to almost nothing.[25] However, there is some indication that gender differences favoring boys are greater in more complex mathematical areas, such as problem solving, than they are in areas such as computation.[26] And after an initial surge, the numbers of young women going into mathematics-related careers such as engineering and computer science have plateaued and in some cases declined.[27] Yet there has been enough change that one research study of single-sex and coed schools concluded, "It would be naïve to suggest that schools have not responded to the recent focus on gender bias in schools and classrooms."[28]

A final assumption, often unstated, is that in this society higher status and privilege are associated with class (high socioeconomic status), race (white), and gender (male). The highest-status students in coed classes tend to be white, male, and upper-middle-class; they in turn reap the benefits in the form of higher achievement and participation. If girls and boys are in separate classes, then highest-status students in all-boys classes remain the same, and upper-middle-class white girls become the highest-status students in their classes. This, we argue, does not count as significant progress.

Measuring progress at the classroom level is confusing. Gains in participation and achievement are often observed at the classroom level, but can not necessarily be attributed to changes that were implemented at the classroom level. An increase in the number of girls electing to take the full sequence of higher level math classes is a good example. Consider the interventions that may have had an impact on that outcome, all of which are external to the classroom. They might include a change by the district requiring four years of mathematics for graduation; more messages to girls from parents and guidance counselors about the importance of these courses for their future career and educational options; or the success of reform efforts at the district, state, or national level to require rigorous standards for content and participation by all students.

Refining the Research Questions

What, then, are the implications for research and action? Our research agenda needs to focus on complexity rather than single variable analysis and attribution. In short, our recommendations for research are to recognize the complexity: Design for it and control for it or describe it, and communicate it. We suggest a number of areas and ways of posing questions that might begin to respect this complexity. For example:

1. Look at the outcomes in relation to premises and purposes. What is the rationale behind the establishment of the single-sex classroom within the context of the history of coeducation in this country? Is the single-sex classroom being established because of a belief that girls need more support and help (remediation) to achieve the same outcomes as boys? Is it to provide experience, skills, and confidence (compensation) that have been denied to girls because of inequitable opportunities and low expectations in ways that might be different from what boys receive in class? Is it to separate boys from girls and protect each from the distractions (raging heterosexual hormones) the other brings to the learning process? Each has implications for what outcomes are valued and measured, and how success is judged.

2. Look at content and pedagogy in relation to the sex makeup of the classroom. If the research question continues to be, "Is single sex better than coed?" then it is essential to control for the content of the curriculum and the pedagogy. We, of course, would recommend asking different questions, such as "Does making a class single sex or coed make a difference in the content and pedagogy?" in which case it is essential to control for the teacher and the resources provided; or asking "What is the impact of the sex of the students in the classroom on the pedagogy?" in which case we need to look at other possible influences on the choice of the pedagogy, such as

teacher style or teacher expectations about the students and their needs. When the same teacher teaches single-sex male, single-sex female, and coed classes, what happens? Does the teacher change in her or his behaviors, approaches, or expectations as the year progresses, or from year to year? Do those classes in turn have effects on achievement or participation? What is the causality chain here? Is it single sex versus coed, or is it what happens in the classroom? Can you factor out what happens in the classroom from the sex of the students in the classroom? This may be the place to raise questions about what constitutes "rigor" and "seriousness": Do these terms refer to the amount or quality of the content, the way that students are pushed to their level of intellectual challenge, or the level or quality of the outcomes that are expected?

3. Look at classroom climate in both single-sex and coed classrooms in relation to the norms and rules, and in relation to the role of the teacher as leader and shaper of the social organization. In the coed classes where there was little or no disrespect of girls or boys, teachers all had explicit rules about no put-downs.[29] What is the effect of rules on disrespect in the classroom? How are norms established and sustained within classrooms regarding respect, tolerance, and non-exclusion on the basis of gender or other characteristics? What is the relationship between respect and learning, not just from the negative side (no one learns well in an environment of distrust and disrespect) but from the positive (does/how does an equitable environment contribute to excellence in outcomes?).

We believe it is time to step back and focus attention on some of the questions that have not been asked in the discussions about single-sex education and coeducation. These are not all research questions, but are critical to shaping what we study, how we study, and why we study. First, what is a good education? Does it differ with respect to gender and equity? Can a good education be excellent if it isn't equitable, if it doesn't reach the vast majority of students—girls and boys of all colors and abilities? Does good education mean only the level and quality of the academic offerings? Does it refer also to socialization? Into whose culture, what norms, what kind of society? Does a good education differ for girls and boys? Do girls and boys need different things to get a good education? Does a good education differ if it's single-sex male, single-sex female, or coed? What is the differential education that girls and boys get, based on whether they're girls or boys, within classrooms of the same institution, or between institutions?

We are left with dilemmas. The first is a problem of building scientific theory on previous data. Conditions in the larger society around gender roles and expectations have changed dramatically since the research on gender was initiated in the early 1970s. What does that do to our earlier results, and what data and conclusions need to be reexamined and retested? At the very least, it suggests that we be very cautious in our use of older data and contextualize carefully our use of newer findings.

The second dilemma is more troubling. We have serious questions about the wisdom of proposing research about a strategy—single-sex classrooms in public education—that has questionable legality and questionable evidence of success. Devoting public dollars to this effort may not be an appropriate use of taxpayer funds.

In the end, our view is that the effort in both research and public policy needs to focus on what is needed to make the coeducational classroom fully equitable, promoting high-level outcomes for both girls and boys, in environments of high expectations, respect, participation, and civility. That needs to be the message to the research community, to the policy community, to parents, and to the public at large.

NOTES

1. Thanks are due to Kathryn Acerbo-Bachmann and Christina Boyer for their thoughtful review of early drafts of this paper.

2. Noam Chomsky, *Syntactic Structure* (The Hague: Mouton Pub., 1957), 15.

3. Patricia B. Campbell and Ellen Wahl, "Of Two Minds: Single Sex/Co-Education and the Search for Gender Equity," *New York Law School Journal of Human Rights* (In press).

4. *The AAUW Report: How Schools Shortchange Girls,* researched by the Wellesley College Center for Research on Women (Susan Bailey et al.) (Washington, DC: AAUW Educational Foundation, 1992).

5. Bonnie S. Wood and Lorrie A. Brown, "Participation in an All Female Algebra I Class: Effects on High School Math and Science Course Selection," *Journal of Women and Minorities in Science and Engineering* 3, no. 4 (1997): 265–278.

6. Gilah Leder and Helen Forgasz, "Single Sex Mathematics Classes in a Coeducational Setting," paper presented to the annual meeting of the American Educational Research Association, Chicago, 1994.

7. Wood and Brown, "Participation," 265–278. This study did find that girls in the single-sex classes increased their math standardized achievement test

scores between their 8th and 11th grades to a greater degree than did girls in the coed class. However, the use of *t* tests rather than analysis of variance with repeated measures in the analysis makes the results less reliable.

8. Leslie Parker, *A Strategy for Optimizing the Success of Girls in Mathematics. Report of a Project of National Significance* (Canberra, Australia: Commonwealth Schools Commission, 1985); Leder and Forgasz, "Single Sex Mathematics," 1994; K. Rowe, "Single Sex and Mixed Classes: The Effect of Class Type on Student Achievement, Confidence and Participation in Mathematics," *Australian Journal of Education* 32, no. 2: 180–202.

9. S. Smith, *Separate Tables? An Investigation into Single Sex Settings in Mathematics* (London: Her Majesty's Stationery Office, 1986).

10. Lesley H. Parker and Leonie J. Rennie, "Single Sex Grouping Issues for School Administrators," paper presented to the annual meeting of the American Educational Research Association, New York City, April 1995; Bonnie Wood, "NCTM Talk," presentation at the annual meeting of the National Council of Teachers of Mathematics, 1996.

11. Wood, "NCTM Talk," 1995.

12. Parker and Rennie, "Single Sex Grouping," 1995.

13. Point/Counterpoint, Rachel Mullis, ukiahlite website, 9/19/97.

14. Eliyahu Goldratt and Jeff Cox, *The Goat* (Great Barrington, Mass.: North River Press, 1984).

15. Alice Eagly and Valerie Steffin, "Gender and Aggressive Behavior: A Meta-Analytic Review of the Social Psychological Literature," *Psychological Bulletin* 100, no. 3 (1986): 309–330.

16. Janet S. Hyde, Elizabeth Fennema & Susan J. Lamon, "Gender Differences in Mathematics Performance: A Meta Analysis," *Psychological Bulletin* 107, no. 2 (1990): 139–155; Janet S. Hyde and Marcia Linn, "Gender Differences in Verbal Ability: A Meta-Analysis," *Psychological Bulletin* 104 (1988): 53–69; Eagly and Steffin, "Gender and Aggressive Behavior," 1986.

17. Hyde et al., "Gender Differences in Mathematics," 1990.

18. Hyde and Linn, "Gender Differences in Verbal Ability," 1988.

19. *The AAUW Report: How Schools Shortchange Girls.*

20. Parker and Rennie, "Single Sex Grouping," 1995.

21. Ibid.

22. Tamar Lewin, "In California, Wider Test of Same-Sex Schools," *The New York Times* (October 9, 1997); Section A, pp. 1, 12.

23. Parker and Rennie, "Single Sex Grouping," 1995.

24. National Women's Law Center, "Single Sex Education After the VMI Decision" (Washington, DC: National Women's Law Center, 1997): 6.

25. National Center for Education Statistics, *Findings from the Condition of Education 1997: Women in Mathematics and Science* (Washington, DC: National Center for Education Statistics (NCES 97–982). July 1997; Hyde et al., "Gender Differences in Mathematics," 1990.

26. Elizabeth Fennema et al., "Gender Differences in Mathematical Thinking: A New Study and Reflections from Different Perspectives," *Educational Researcher* (In press); Hyde et al., "Gender Differences in Mathematics," 1990.

27. National Science Foundation, *Women and Minorities and Persons with Disabilities in Science and Engineering 1994* (Washington, DC: National Science Foundation, 1994).

28. Paul C. LePore and John Robert Warren, "A Comparison of Single-Sex and Coeducational Catholic Secondary Schooling: Evidence from the National Educational Longitudinal Study of 1988," *American Educational Research Journal* 34, no. 3 (1997): 485–511.

29. Patricia B. Campbell and Jennifer Storo, "Making It Happen: Pizza Parties, Chemistry Goddesses & Other Strategies that Work for Girls and Others" (Newton, Mass.: Education Development Center, 1996).

REFERENCES

The AAUW Report: How Schools Shortchange Girls. Researched by the Wellesley College Center for Research on Women (Susan Bailey et al.). Washington, DC: AAUW Educational Foundation, 1992.

Campbell, Patricia B. and Jennifer Storo. "Making It Happen: Pizza Parties, Chemistry Goddesses and Other Strategies That Work for Girls and Others." Newton, Mass: Education Development Center, 1996.

Campbell, Patricia B. and Ellen Wahl. "Of Two Minds: Single Sex/Co-Education and the Search for Gender Equity." *New York Law School Journal of Human Rights* (In press).

Chomsky, Noam. *Syntactic Structure.* The Hague: Mouton Pub., 1957, 15.

Eagly, Alice and Valerie Steffin. "Gender and Aggressive Behavior: A Meta-Analytic Review of the Social Psychological Literature." *Psychological Bulletin 100*, no. 3 (1986): 309–330.

Fennema, Elizabeth, Thomas P. Carpenter, Linda Levi, Janet Hyde, and Sarah Jaffee. "Gender Differences in Mathematical Thinking: A New Study and Reflections from Different Perspectives. *Educational Researcher* (In press).

Goldratt, Eliyahu and Jeff Cox. *The Goal.* Great Barrington, Mass: North River Press, 1984.

Hyde, Janet S. and Marcia Linn. "Gender Differences in Verbal Ability: A Meta-Analysis." *Psychological Bulletin 104* (1988): 53–69.

LePore, Paul C. and John Robert Warren. "A Comparison of Single-Sex and Coeducational Catholic Secondary Schooling: Evidence from the National Educational Longitudinal Study of 1988." *American Educational Research Journal 34,* no. 3 (1997): 485–511.

Lewin, Tamar. "In California, Wider Test of Same-Sex Schools." *New York Times,* 9 October 1997. Section A, pp. 1, 12.

Mullis, Rachel. "Point/Counterpoint." *Ukiahilite:* September 29, 1996. Website http://www.ukiahilite /pcp1.html.

National Center for Educational Statistics. *Findings from the Condition of Education 1997: Women in Mathematics and Science.* Washington, DC: National Center for Education Statistics (NCES 97–982), July 1997.

National Science Foundation. *Women and Minorities and Persons with Disabilities in Science and Engineering 1994.* Washington, DC: National Science Foundation, 1994.

National Women's Law Center. *Single Sex Education After the VMI Decision.* Washington, DC: National Women's Law Center, 1997.

Parker, Leslie. *A Strategy for Optimizing the Success of Girls in Mathematics. Report of a Project of National Significance.* Canberra, Australia: Commonwealth Schools Commission, 1985.

Parker, Lesley H. and Leonie J. Rennie. "Single Sex Grouping Issues for School Administrators." Paper presented to the annual meeting of the American Educational Research Association, New York, April 1996.

Smith, S. *Separate Tables? An Investigation into Single Sex Setting in Mathematics.* London: Her Majesty's Stationary Office, 1986.

Wood, Bonnie. "NCTM Talk." Paper presented to the annual meeting of the National Council of Teachers of Mathematics, 1995.

Wood, Bonnie S. and Lorrie A. Brown. "Participation in an All Female Algebra I Class: Effects on High School Math and Science Course Selection." *Journal of Women and Minorities in Science and Engineering 3,* no. 4 (1997): 265–278.

ANITA HILL IS A BOY

TALES FROM A

GENDER-FAIR CLASSROOM

Peggy Orenstein

THERE IS NO SINGLE MAGIC FORMULA that will help girls retain their self-esteem. Scores of educators around the country are working to develop gender-fair curricula in all subjects and reexamining traditional assumptions about how children best learn. Some educators are developing strategies to break down gender and race hierarchies in cooperative learning groups.[1] Others are experimenting with the ways that computers, if used to their best advantage, can enhance equity in math and science courses.[2] Individually, teachers find that calling on students equitability, or simply waiting for a moment rather than recognizing the first child who raises his hand, encourages girls to participate more readily in class. On a national level, the Gender Equity in Education Act, which should be implemented in 1994, includes provisions for improved data gathering, for the development of teacher training programs, for programs to encourage girls in math and science, and for programs to better meet the needs of girls of color.

In trying to address the thornier issues of the hidden curriculum, some school districts have offered self-defense classes for girls, introduced aspects of sexuality education as early as kindergarten, or developed curricula that explicitly take on sexual harassment.[3] A few principals in embattled urban neighborhoods have recast their schools as round-the-clock community centers, offering recreational activities, adult education, medical care, and a flotilla of social services.[4] Others have begun mentoring programs or sponsored mother-daughter activities to help raise educational attainment rates and career aspirations among girls of color.[5]

Meanwhile, heated debate has arisen over whether mere reform—such as adding a few prominent women to existing texts or what has been called the "add women and stir" approach to gender equity[6]—is, indeed, adequate. In science, for instance, educators question the merits of a repackaged, "girl-friendly" curriculum versus a more radical examination of the very nature of objectivity and evidence collection.[7] Is it enough to simply call on girls more often or to introduce cooperative learning without changing the core of the male-dominated curriculum? Is it enough to change the substance of the curriculum but retain traditional classroom structures?

My own gender journey ends where it began, in the classroom of one teacher who is trying not only to practice equity but to teach it, to change both boys' and girls' perspectives on the female self. Judy Logan has been teaching for twenty-six years, twenty-two of them at San Francisco's Everett Middle School, where she currently coordinates the Gifted and Talented Education Program (GATE). Her students are an ethnically diverse lot, and although her classes have the highest proportion of white children in the school, about 40 percent of the pupils are Latino, Filipino, Asian American, or African American. As sixth graders, they spend three hours each morning with Ms. Logan learning language arts and social studies. Over the next two years, the students take quarter-long required and elective courses from all four GATE teachers which combine English and history. But whether she is teaching classes on Greek mythology or world cultures, American history or English literature, Ms. Logan has an agenda beyond the standard lesson plan: she aims to blast the hidden curriculum wide open.

Stepping into Ms. Logan's classroom from the drab hallways of Everett is somewhat of a shock. There are images of women everywhere: the faces of Abigail Adams, Rachel Carson, Faye Wattleton, and even a fanciful "Future Woman" smile out from three student-made quilts that are draped on the walls. Reading racks overflow with biographies of Lucretia Mott, Ida B. Wells, Emma Goldman, Sally Ride, and Rigoberta Menchú. There is a book on Jewish holidays and one on Muslim women. There is a section on Pele, the Hawaiian goddess of volcanoes, and a coffee table book on artist Judy Chicago's famed "Dinner Party." On the back wall there is a display of student submissions to this year's city-wide National Organization for Women (NOW) essay contest on "Women We Admire." For the eighth year in a row, Ms. Logan's students—an equal number of girls and boys—won first or second prizes in all three grades. A giant computer-paper banner spans the width of another wall proclaiming, "Women are one-half of the world's people; they do two-thirds of the world's work; they earn one-tenth of the world's income; they own one one-hundredth of the world's property."

It almost seems wrong. Looking around Ms. Logan's classroom, I find myself wondering, "Where are the men?" Then it dawns. This is a classroom that's gone through the gender looking glass. It is the mirror opposite of most classrooms that girls will enter, which are adorned with masculine role models, with male heroes, with books by and about men— classrooms in which the female self is, at best, an afterthought. This is what a classroom would look like if women were the dominant sex. Educator Emily Style has written that the curriculum should be both a window and a mirror for students, that they should be able to look into others' worlds, but also see the experiences of their own race, gender, and class reflected in what they learn.[8] In Ms. Logan's class, girls may be dazzled by the reflection of the women that surround them. And, perhaps for the first time, the boys are the ones looking in through the window.

When Boys Are Girls

Forty-one sixth graders crowd into Ms. Logan's classroom each morning, and when I visit on a mid-February day, there isn't an extra chair in the house. Normally, the students sit at long, low tables arranged in vertical rows, but today those have been pushed aside, and the sixth graders have turned their child-sized chairs toward the front of the classroom. Ms. Logan sits among them, a fiftyish woman, with a round, pleasant face made owlish by her red plastic-framed glasses. She is dressed casually in an oversized African print shirt, leggings, and knee-high boots.

Today is the culmination of their African American history class. As a final project, each student has researched the lives of two prominent African Americans (past or present) and must now perform brief dramatic monologues as those people. The students have gone to great lengths to fulfill their assignment: the room is awash with costumes, props, audiotapes, books, and athletic gear. Although they had the option to recite their piece alone for Ms. Logan, most have chosen the limelight, and the posterity of the video camera, which is positioned at the back of the room.

Before class began, Ms. Logan told me that the first year she introduced this project she assigned only one monologue, but she noticed that while girls opted to take on either male or female personae, the boys chose only men. "It disturbed me that although girls were willing to see men as heroes, none of the boys would see women that way," she said. This was no surprise: I recall observing the same phenomenon among the student-written myths from Weston's English classes. At the time I wondered how the boys, who could only see male experience as relevant, would ever learn to see girls as equals.

Faced with the same concern, Ms. Logan decided to add her own hidden curriculum to the assignment. She began requiring two reports, one from the perspective of a man and one presented as a woman. To ask a group of boys, most of whom are white, to take on the personae—to actually *become*—black women forces an unprecedented shift in their mindset. Yet Ms. Logan found they accepted the assignment without question.

"As long as it's required, they accept it," she explained. "But it wouldn't occur to them to choose it."

When the students have settled into their chairs or onto pillows on the floor, Ms. Logan asks for volunteers to begin. Jeremy is among the first to perform his female monologue. He saunters up to the stool that Ms. Logan has placed at the front of the room, a gangly white boy whose loose gait and rubbery features remind me of a Muppet. Like many of the boys, he has minimized the indignity of being required to "become" a woman by performing without a costume: he wears an orange baseball jacket, jeans, and untied sneakers.

He looks around uncomfortably. "To understand the blues," he begins, "you have to understand black history. When we were slaves, the only way we could express our pain was to sing, so we started singing about racism and about love. And that was the blues. To sing the blues, you have to live them, and I'm an example of that. My name is Etta James."

There is muffled tittering from the class.

James goes on to detail her life, starting with her discovery at age fifteen by R&B front man Johnny Otis, and including an incident in which she was threatened at gunpoint in a Texas restaurant for using a whites-only rest room. She touches on her heroin addiction and descent into petty crime, then finishes up with her recent triumphant comeback.

"It wasn't that we wanted to sing the blues," James concludes. "We women had to. And even though men owned the record companies, even though men were the deejays and they controlled the world, we had to sing and be heard. And we were so strong, we women singers—it was scary."

James walks to one side of the classroom, where she has stashed a small tape recorder. She presses a button, returns to center stage, and begins to lip-sync to a bluesy ballad. This is too much for the class to handle, and the disbelief they've so valiantly suspended for the past five minutes comes crashing down. A boy begins to laugh and more join in, as do some of the girls. James tries to keep a straight face, but even she knows that the image of an eleven-year-old white boy syncing the blues is ridiculous, and a struggle for control ensues: Etta briefly gives way to Jeremy, who starts to giggle. Then she regains the upper hand for a moment before losing out to the boy once more. The whole performance ends up more comedic than respectful, and although Jeremy receives a vigorous hand when it is over, he has opened the door for the boys to make a mockery out of the feminine part of their assignment.

"Ms. James," Ms. Logan says when the applause dies down, "did you apologize when the restaurant owner threatened to kill you?"

"Yes," James answers, hopping back onto the stool.

"And how did that feel?"

"I felt really bad about it," James says. "I guess I wasn't used to racism."

Ms. Logan nods her head, "I'd like to ask Ms. James to step aside now and let me ask Jeremy a question."

Jeremy jumps off the stool, takes a few steps and turns around, now himself.

"Was it hard for you when you got up here to sing because some of the people were laughing?" Ms. Logan asks.

Jeremy shrugs. "Sort of," he says.

"Was it different when you practiced it at home?"

"It was more serious at home," Jeremy answers, ducking his head. "I did it seriously."

"Class, I'd like you to understand the interaction between the audience and the performer," Ms. Logan says. "If you laugh, it's very hard for Jeremy to stay in character, but if you support him, he can take risks. How you respond has tremendous impact on what a performer can and can't do. Jeremy, you took some real risks up there and I thought that was great."

As Jeremy returns to his seat, one of the boys turns to another, who had instigated the laughter. "I didn't think it was funny until you had to go and laugh like that," he says. "I would give him an A if I was grading."

A third boy says, "Me, too," and slaps Jeremy five as he walks by.

As the reports proceed, it becomes clear that the subtexts of Ms. Logan's lessons are not just about gender, nor, in fact, are they about race. Muhammad Ali's monologue sparks a discussion about the price one pays for success. West Indian writer Jamaica Kincaid inspires comment about noninvasive tourism. And when Charles, a shy African American boy costumed in gym shorts and a sleeveless jersey, finishes his report as Michael

Jordan after a near-disastrous stumble partway through, Ms. Logan steps to the fore and puts a hand on his shoulder.

"I'd like to ask you as Charles," she says, "how did it feel for you to stand up here like this?"

"I didn't like it," he says, his voice trembling slightly. "It was hard for me. I didn't like it at all."

"And how could we, as your audience, have helped you out?"

"You were fine," he says. "You listened and didn't laugh when I messed up. It was me. I'm sorry."

Ms. Logan addressed the students. "How many of you have one thing in this class that's really, really hard for you?" she asks.

Most of the sixth graders raise their hands.

She turns to a small, alert-looking boy. "What's your hard thing?" she asks.

"I don't know," the boy replies, "but I'm sure there is one."

"Well, okay," Ms. Logan says, turning to a girl who has raised her hand. "What's yours?"

"Stage fright," the girl says, giving a mock shudder.

"How many of you have stage fright, a little bit or a lot?"

About a third of the students raise their hands.

"And what can we, as an audience do to help?"

"Don't laugh," says Charles.

"Listen," says a girl.

"Smile and look encouraging," says another girl.

"Yes," says Ms. Logan, "show expressions of support. Charles, it was really brave of you to get up here and do this when you had the option not to. You have nothing to apologize for. I know how hard it was, and it took a lot of courage."

Charles leaves the stage smiling. Although this mini-lesson on the value of supportiveness and appropriate risk taking was conducted surrounding a boy's experience, it seemed especially relevant for girls. I thought about the exaggerated fear of humiliation among the young women I have met, a fear so acute that they often silenced themselves in class. Like Weston's history teacher, Ms. Nellas, who stressed that " 'dumb' questions lead to learning," Ms. Logan has confronted her students' anxieties and taken the shame out of imperfection. Later, when a minute Asian American girl begins lip-syncing "What a Difference a Day Makes" as Dinah Washington, the class begins to giggle again and she falters.

"Remember what we learned about the audience and performers, class," Ms. Logan warns, and the students simmer down. By the end of the piece, the girl's performance is so precise that the class is mesmerized, and they finish out the last chorus along with her: "What a difference a day makes, and the difference is you!" (I'm surprised that they know the words, until I remember that the song is also the advertising jingle for the California state lottery.)

Over the course of the next few mornings the students are visited by nearly eighty-four prominent African Americans. Ida B. Wells talks at breakneck speed, reeling off an account of her life as a journalist, an activist, and co-founder of the National Association for the Advancement of Colored People (NAACP). Jackie Robinson discusses the difficulty and rewards of breaking the color barrier in baseball. The class is introduced to a fiery Angela Davis and a very nervous Frederick Douglass. Sculptor Richmond Barthé informs them, "You probably don't know me because certain people who write certain history books didn't put me in them because of my certain color," and poet Paul Laurence Dunbar recites his "Ode to Ethiopia." There are flashes of humor, as when Miles Davis' tape recorder goes on the fritz and Ms. Logan suggests that someone else step in until the trumpeter is ready.

"You know how temperamental these artists can be," she confides to the class.

There are also moments of true poignancy. Maya Angelou, for instance, in the guise of a freckle-faced white boy, discusses the trauma of being raped by a supposed family friend. When the man was subsequently murdered, she explains, looking sorrowfully at the class, "I didn't know whether to laugh or cry, whether to feel sorrow or joy." (Later, when recalling her first pregnancy, Ms. Angelou also asserts that "the pain of childbirth is overrated.")

After two hours of reports, the sixth graders take a fifteen-minute break, during which they have a snack and read to themselves. I join three girls in a corner who are chatting quietly over apples and boxes of juice. Holly wears glasses, has a precocious expression, and speaks in a clipped voice. I ask how she has enjoyed her year in Ms. Logan's class. "I like that Ms. Logan does things on women and women's rights," she answers. "She never, never discriminates against girls, and I'm glad that someone finally got that idea." She takes a bite of apple and chews thoughtfully. "But sometimes I think the boys don't like it."

Jill, a chubby-cheeked girl with dark eyebrows, who seems meek in Holly's presence, pipes up. "My older brother had Ms. Logan," she says. "And he said all she ever talked about was women, women, women. He didn't like her."

"I guess it's because all the other teachers ignore women," Holly says. "But sometimes I worry about the boys, that they get kind of ignored."

"Look at this room," complains Dana, who is Chinese American. The girls turn and scrutinize the walls. "There's all this stuff on women everywhere."

"That's true," says Holly. "But I'm still glad someone finally got the idea that we're all the same. I mean except for a few things, of course. That's good, I guess."

As the girls talk, I recall what a teacher at Weston once told me, that "boys perceive equality as a loss." Apparently, girls are uneasy with it, too. Even these girls, whose parents have placed them in this class in part because of Ms. Logan's sensitivity to gender issues, have already become used to taking up less space, to feeling less worthy of attention than boys.

I wander to the back of the room, where Mindy, who is an eighth grader, lolls near the video camera. Mindy is a model of grunge chic, dressed in a faded plaid shirt, battered jeans, and purple Converse sneakers. She has lank brown hair which hangs to her jaw, and a pair of oval granny glasses balanced on her snub nose. Mindy has been in Ms. Logan's class for three years, and is taping today's proceedings as a favor to her teacher. I ask her opinion, as a veteran of the class, about Ms. Logan's attempts at gender-fair teaching.

"The boys definitely resent it," she says matter-of-factly. "They think Ms. Logan is sexist. But you know what I think? I think that it's the resentment of losing their place. In our other classes, the teachers just focus on men, but the boys don't complain that *that's* sexist. They say, 'It's different in those classes because we're focusing on the important people in history, who just happen to be men.' "

Mindy rolls her eyes and adopts a long-suffering expression. "The girls like having all the women's history stuff, though," she continued, "unless they like some guy and worry about what *he* thinks about it. But I don't think that's so true by eighth grade. In sixth grade the girls are nervous about what the boys think because they're not used to it yet. But now I enjoy it, and a lot of the other girls do, too."

Of all the African American history monologues Nick's, which is performed just after the break, makes the strongest impression. Nick is a thin boy with carrot-colored hair, milky skin, and freckles. He performs as Anita Hill and, like many of the boys, has chosen to proceed without the aid of a costume. Unlike some of the other female monologues delivered by males, there is complete silence as Professor Hill relates her personal history and her now notorious encounters with her onetime boss, Clarence Thomas. The sixth graders are old enough to remember seeing Hill on television when she testified before the Senate Judiciary Committee, and they watch intently, recognizing the importance of her words. Hill declines to go into detail about what, precisely, Judge Thomas said to her, because, she explains, "in the end, no one will really know what happened between us, except us."

Hill ends her report by looking straight into the video camera. "I had to have the courage to speak out against sexual harassment for other women in this country," she says solemnly. "So they could speak out, too, and become strong."

When she is finished, Professor Hill blushes to the roots of her red hair.

"Dr. Hill, I'm a great admirer of yours," Ms. Logan says, "and I'd like to know whether, even though Judge Thomas was confirmed, you feel some good came out of the hearings?"

Hill nods her head. "I showed other women that they can come forward," she responds. "They don't have to take that kind of behavior from *anyone.*"

"Give her a hand, everyone," Ms. Logan says, and even though she is gesturing to a boy—who in most cases would undoubtedly be ashamed to be called "her" in front of forty peers—no one even flinches. Instead, the students burst into applause. And Nick, who has, if only for a few minutes, lived the experience of a sexually harassed woman, takes his seat.

Education That Includes Us All

After the bell rings, and the students leave for lunch, Ms. Logan and I sit across from each other at one of the low tables. "This is learning from the inside out," she explains enthusiastically. "They do the research, they connect into that other life, and they really *become* the person. People always ask me how you can get boys to stop being so totally male-oriented. I say, 'You just do it, and they'll pick it up as you go.' If you do a project like this, they really have to take on a female persona in a serious way, in a way that's respectful to the woman and her role in history. It's a thrill for me to hear the way boys stand up for women's rights in their monologues. And I think it's meaningful for them, too."

I tell Ms. Logan about my conversation with the sixth-grade girls, about how, in spite of their gratitude toward her for treating them fairly, they worry that equity excludes boys. Before I can even finish my thought, she begins to smile. This is a comment she's heard before.

"It's true," she says. "Sometimes the kids resist the idea of gender equity, and it isn't always the boys either. One year, during a quilt project, a sixth-grade girl said, 'Why do we always study women, Ms. Logan? I feel like I'm not learning anything about men and I don't think that's right.' But she waited to say that until we were in the library and the librarian *and* the principal were listening. Later, I took her aside and said, 'We've done the NOW essay contest and this quilt, and I don't think that's so much considering that women are half of humanity. This is your history we're talking about!' It turned out that she was concerned that the boys would feel left out by those lessons."

Ms. Logan explains that, in fact, only two of her sixth-grade projects focus exclusively on women. Others, such as the African American history reports, simply ensure that women are given equal time. "But because I do that," she explains, "because I *include* women, I'm seen as extreme. If I took those lessons out and concentrated only on men's experience for a whole year, *that* would be 'normal.' "

Ms. Logan can't pinpoint exactly when she began teaching what she calls an "inclusive curriculum." "I never had a moment of 'Aha!' " she says thoughtfully. "I wish I could say I did, that I knew exactly when I started to think this way or teach this way. I do know that if you grow as a person, you grow as a teacher. So, in the 1970s, when I took some classes and started learning more about women myself, women came into the classroom."

For years, Ms. Logan taught her unconventional curriculum gingerly, keeping, as she says, "my mouth and my classroom door shut," to avoid undue notice. Then, at a 1986 women's history conference she met Peggy McIntosh, a former middle school teacher. Now associate director of the Wellesley College Center for Research on Women, McIntosh had developed a five-phase curricular model based on the changes she's seen educators go through when trying to teach inclusively.[9] Using history as an example, McIntosh describes Phase One as "Womanless and All-White History," which most of us learned as children. In Phase Two, teachers notice that there are no white women or people of color in the curriculum, and they cast about for a few exceptional achievers to sprinkle in. During Phase Three, the politics of the curriculum are unmasked and the focus in on issues: sexism, racism, classism, and victimization. Phase Four heralds a new era, in which the daily lives of women and minority men are themselves considered worthwhile subjects of intellectual inquiry. Only when those four phases are combined does Phase Five become possible: "History Redefined and Reconstructed to Include Us All." In McIntosh's ideas, Ms. Logan found confirmation of her unorthodox approach to education. In Ms. Logan's teaching, McIntosh found her theories brought to life. The two quickly became friends and colleagues.

Inclusive education, as defined by both Ms. Logan and McIntosh, turns the conventional student-teacher relationship on its head. Students may become the "experts," producing their own curriculum, as in the African

American history class, and teachers become learners. Like many educational philosophers, McIntosh and Ms. Logan also question the grounding of classroom interactions in competition rather than cooperation, in individual "right" and "wrong" answers rather than a collective search for meaning. In her own book, *Teaching Stories,* Ms. Logan writes that, during lessons that explore gender roles, which can easily turn into opportunities to cast blame for inequities, emphasizing tolerance is especially important. "If my class seems anxious at the beginning of a 'woman's unit,' I reassure them that women's studies is not about 'ruling over,' it is about 'existing with,' " she writes. "It is important to be explicit with these reassurances right away. Feminist teaching is not about allowing a win/lose situation to develop between boys and girls."[10]

On the other hand, sitting in her classroom today, Ms. Logan admits that delicacy has its limits. "I present women's lives without apology," she says. When I question her again about occasional student resistance, she shrugs. "I usually find that boys only resist studying women when they're presented as 'lesser,' " she says. "And if they're presented as 'lesser,' girls don't want to study women either. And I can't blame them."

If You Start with Sexual Harassment, You'll Get to Susan B. Anthony

In late April, several weeks after the African American history monologues, I visit Ms. Logan's afternoon elective for seventh and eighth graders entitled American Women Making History. This is the second week of the course, which meets every other day. There are thirty-five students in the class, and nearly half of them are boys. Some are even boys whom I've heard deride Ms. Logan's classes as too woman-oriented. They are here, nonetheless, either because their friends have chosen the class or simply because they think Ms. Logan is a good teacher. "I was absent the day they passed out the descriptions of the class," explains one boy whom I've heard make sexist jokes. "So I didn't even know what it was called when I signed up, but I figured whatever Ms. Logan was teaching would probably be okay."

Ms. Logan kicked off the first week of the course by explaining Peggy McIntosh's phase theory, the remnants of which are still on the board. She explained that she wanted the class to be a combination of Phases Two, Three, and Four: they would look at women who had achieved great things, they would study the struggles of women to attain equal rights, and they would culminate with individual or group reports that could cover famous, nonfamous, or infamous women.

At their second meeting, the class read a short story by Jamaica Kincaid entitled "Girl." Written in the voice of a short-tempered mother, the piece is a fast-paced, single-sentence list of the messages about gender that an unnamed protagonist received as a child, such as " . . . on Sundays try to walk like a lady and not like the slut you are so bent on becoming . . ."[11] As a homework assignment, Ms. Logan asked the students to write their own "girl" or "boy" pieces. Today, they are reading them aloud to one another. In many ways, this exercise echoes the "gender journey" that I saw some of the same students undertake last spring as sixth graders. That earlier assignment allowed them to explore the ways that gender shaped their perceptions of one another. This assignment asks that they look at how stereotypes affect themselves.

After winning the toss of a coin, the boys begin, but their pieces are a mere litany of parental nagging, a series of "don'ts" that would apply to any child. It is almost as if they did not understand the assignment, or, perhaps, as boys, cannot imagine that their experience is mediated by gender. On the other hand, their very neutrality may reveal that, at times, silence can affect boys as profoundly as girls. I peek over the shoulder of Andrew, a frail, bespectacled boy, who opted to pass when his turn came. He has written "Boys don't cry" in his essay. Ms. Logan has told me that Andrew is often mocked by other boys because of his small size and gentle nature. He may be, then, in the best position among his peers to understand the limitations of conventional masculinity, yet he also has too much to lose by articulating them.

The assignment proves much easier for the girls. Although a number of their essays are tributes to their parents, who urge them to "be myself no matter what" and have helped them navigate the messages of sexism that they are bombarded with at school and in the media, they still amass an impressive catalogue of the ways they feel diminished as girls. By now, the list is all too familiar: the despised frilly dresses, the expectation that they will be tidy, the curtailed freedom in comparison to their brothers, the assumptions that they are emotionally fragile or bad at sports, the fear of being branded a slut. But unlike other, similar conversations about femininity which I have both overheard and instigated, this discussion is taking place in the presence of boys, as part of the overt school curriculum.

After the first burst of energy subsides, the girls turned to a topic that has come up at every school I have visited this year: sexual harassment on campus.

"Sexual harassment in school is the worst," says Mindy, who is in this class, too. "It's like if you wear a tight shirt, you're asking for it."

"I feel safer if I wear big clothes," says Alissa, a curvy girl with wild blond hair that she pushes from her face every few minutes. "I buy my clothes three sizes too big. It's the fashion, but it makes me feel better. My mom says I look like a freak, and I say, 'Mom, dude, it's because I don't want people commenting on my body. I *have* to dress like this.' As a girl, you can't be accepted unless you wear big clothes. Then it's like, 'Oh, a girl,' not like, 'Oh, a body.' "

"I managed the boys' basketball team this year," says Shannon, who tries to make her freckled face look more mature by wearing lipstick, mascara, and eyeliner. "And this boy, Fred, walked up during practice and he just reached out"—she extends both arms—"and he grabbed both of my tits. And this other boy standing there said, 'Did he just touch you?' I said, 'Yeah,' and he said, 'Fred, you shouldn't do that.' Fred said, 'I didn't do anything!' and walked away. Then this guy turns to me and says, 'Next time you should really watch yourself.' Like it was my fault!"

"How long would a girl last in this school if she went up and grabbed guys you know where?" Mindy asks rhetorically. "Not long. She'd be out of here."

"But it's not just boys," says another girl. "When I'm shopping, I think, 'Would people think I'm a ho' if I wear this?' Girls, too. Would Shannon think I was a ho'? Would Alissa? I think about that."

Alissa glances away, brushing her hair from her face yet again. Shannon looks down.

When the girls have talked for over ten minutes, Ms. Logan interrupts. "I want to stop and check with the boys," she says. "They've been very patient and I'd like to hear what this experience of listening to this has been like. But I want to tell the girls, I'm not leaving it at this. There are places we can go from here. This is a very important, scary, and profound conversation you're having."

"It's true that some guys are assholes in school," says a small, pale boy in a paisley shirt. "But there are nice people, too. And there are things that are harder for boys. When it comes to gay and lesbian issues, it's much harder for boys. You can't, like, hold hands with another boy."

"Has it been easy or hard for you boys to hear this?" Ms. Logan asks. "Can you separate yourself from it, or do you hear the girls and feel persecuted or defensive?"

"I can separate myself," the same boy continues, "but I feel angry at the boys who do that."

"Boys who do that to girls learn it from their families," says another boy, who is tall and athletic with a rattail haircut.

"I think it's also a lot of peer pressure from other guys," says Alissa.

"Of course it is," says Luis, a Latino boy who has pulled his 49ers jacket up over his mouth and nose.

"It's like how boys learn to see girls," says one of the girls. "I mean, you turn on *MTV Spring Break* and there's these stupid girls with huge breasts and the tiniest bathing suits dancing around like pieces of meat, and all these boys going crazy in the audience. It makes me feel, like, totally degraded."

"But if you're a guy," says Luis, "you see all those great bodies, and you think you want a girl like that. You think you *should* have a girl like that."

"I didn't really know it was this bad," says another boy. "This has kind of changed the way I think. You hear all these girls talk at once and you realize it's kind of a big deal. I'll try to treat girls better. And I think other boys need to learn how to talk to girls, too."

"I'd like to point out that today you girls heard many voices that had experienced what you had," says Ms. Logan, "but you also had allies among the boys. We have to be careful not to assume that all boys engage in this behavior. And we have to be careful that boys feel that they can take an active part in changing this kind of behavior, in changing the behavior of others. Because it's not just a female job to change it, but a male job as well. Many men have been involved in the feminist movement since suffrage, and that's very important in making change. Part of talking about history is talking about the things that are handed down to us over the years in terms of gender. Maybe one idea for a class project for some of you might be to collect the stories and the experiences with gender in this school and make them into a book."

"Boy, I'd like to do that!" says one of the boys.

"Maybe people need more education and we can provide some of that," Ms. Logan says.

When the bell rings, signaling the end of the day, the students stand up as usual and place their chairs on top of the tables, but they don't leave the room. Instead, they cluster together to continue their conversation about today's lesson.

"Some of the boys," Alissa says to me, "the ones that talked? I thought, how *totally* cool that they're saying something about this!"

Fifteen minutes later, there are still a handful of students loitering near the chalkboard. They are reluctant to leave, even when Ms. Logan shoos them out the door.

"Okay you guys," the teacher says, laughing. "Get out of here! Go home!"

When the last student has finally gone, Ms. Logan moves about the room, picking up books and straightening tables. I ask her whether pursuing a project on sexual harassment will really allow her students to learn about women's history, about such things as suffrage, abolitionism, and temperance. "Peggy McIntosh always says that if you start your Civil War class with *Diary of a Slave Girl* you'll get to Abraham Lincoln," Ms. Logan says. "But if you start with Lincoln, you'll never get to *Slave Girl*. Well, if you start a course on women's history with sexual harassment, with something that connects to the students' experience, you'll get to Susan B. Anthony eventually. And it will mean more to them, because they can relate it to their own experience. But if you start with Susan B. Anthony, you may never get to sexual harassment, and you lose that important connection to their lives."

When the American Women Making History class convenes again two days later, the students continue their discussion on sexual harassment. But one of the boys asks Ms. Logan if, instead of calling out their comments, they can proceed more formally, by raising hands. That way, he says, the boys won't be trampled by the girls who continually interrupted them during the last class. Ms. Logan shoots me a look. But this turn of the tables comes with a difference: the girls openly concede that they have been unfair, and they apologize.

"It was good to get our feelings out the other day," says Mindy, "but they were so forceful that we excluded the boys, so they didn't get to talk. I hope they can talk more today."

Although they try to comply with the boys' request, the girls simply have too much to say to be patient, and, once again, they begin blurting out their thoughts. The boys, meanwhile, continue to raise their hands whenever they'd like to speak. Eventually, the students begin to wrestle over what, exactly, constitutes sexual harassment, an issue that the United States judicial system has not yet fully resolved.

"If you say a girl is beautiful, it's not sexual harassment," advises one girl. "If you say she's got big boobs and she's a slut, it is."

"Is it sexual harassment if you write a note to someone, but the girl doesn't see it?" asks an intensely serious African American boy.

"It could be sexism if you write a note," Shannon says, "but not harassment. I mean, don't you have to *harass* them, like say it out loud and bother them?"

"It's not sexual harassment to write notes," says another boy, whose blond bangs fall nearly to his nose, "but it can start sexual harassment because it gets around and everyone starts believing it and saying it to the girl. The note can *lead* to sexual harassment."

"I think we have a double standard," a Latina girl says. "Sexual harassment happens to girls more, but we go up and feel on guys, too. Maybe some of them like it, but maybe some don't and they don't want to say anything."

"That's a good point," Ms. Logan says. "It's how the person feels about it, not if the person is a boy or a girl."

But it's Alissa who brings up the most complex issue for young women who, although steeped in the ethos of desirability, are struggling to come to terms with harassment: the conflicting feelings of shame and pleasure that boys' remarks can evoke. "Sometimes," she says slowly, "it's like you're almost flattered that the guy is paying attention to you. So you say it bothers you, but deep inside, you kind of think it's flirting. But it's not really flirting, it's something else. And when you realize it's something else, you feel really bad, like you can't believe you thought there was anything good about this. It's totally confusing."

The girls nod their heads and the boys look thoughtful. I consider the myriad articles I have read discussing sexual harassment, all of the television reports devoted to the topic. These children have helped each other puzzle through the most salient controversies in less than a quarter of an hour.

"I want to stop the discussion here," Ms. Logan says after a few more minutes. "We've gotten a lot done on this and it's very important, but the class isn't about sexual harassment. It's American Women Making History. Next time we'll see a video called "How Women Got the Vote" that ties in with what you're talking about today, in terms of how women and men can change history when they feel discriminated against. The women and men of the suffrage movement worked long and hard and some of them didn't see change in their lifetimes. They developed many strategies about how to change their environment and change history. Those lessons should not have to be reinvented today. You have many, many lessons to learn from the men and women who came before you and changed history."

The class takes a break, and I go over to talk to Luis, who during today's discussion pulled his chair into a corner apart from the rest of the class.

"I'm one of the guys that talks that crap about girls" he says, by way of explanation. "I always tell them I don't mean it. But if I said that here, I'd get blamed for all the things I've said and I couldn't really defend myself, because it's true."

He looks away from me as if he's embarrassed. "Men are pigs, you know?" he says.

"Do you think so?" I ask.

"Well, I guess we don't have to be," he admits, "but I'm just trying to have fun before I get old. I don't know, maybe I'll do it less now, though."

Luis tells me that he chose to take this class because he was interested in the topic. "But I don't tell my friends," he says. "If I told them I was interested in women's history, they'd call me a fag. So I just take it and don't talk about it."

By early June, the seventh and eighth graders have learned about Susan B. Anthony as well as Rosie the Riveter. They've heard speakers from the city's Latina community and studied the internment of Japanese Americans from the female perspective. They've analyzed images of women in the media and visited a feminist bookstore. They have learned as individuals as well as cooperatively, utilized the creative as well as the cognitive, thought in the concrete and in the abstract. The students have also researched their individual or group reports, which they are scheduled to present today.

About a third of the class has participated in some aspect of the sexual harassment project. When their turn comes, the first team, comprised of two boys and two girls, steps to the front of the class. They have chronicled the instances of harassment that they have witnessed over the past several weeks in classes, on the schoolyard, and in the hallways. The slurs are, essentially, identical to the ones leveled at Weston and at Audubon, but some—especially "suck my burrito"—inspire bursts of laughter, which the teacher does not ignore.

"I want to point out," says Ms. Logan, "that laughing releases tension, but it's disparaging to laugh at things that are serious. Sexual words are uncomfortable, and sometimes that makes us laugh, but I see laughter as partly participating in it."

The second group of students, who call themselves "the policy committee," offers up the legal definition of sexual harassment as well as the school's official punishment for it, which is outlined in the district's student handbook. One of the girls, who interviewed the school counselor, proclaims, "She says she has and will enforce the rules."

"But," a boy in the committee adds, "she had no approximate number of how many times sexual harassment has been reported or how many times she's actually done anything. Only one person has ever been suspended for sexual harassment, for one day, for actually holding a person against a wall and touching her."

The team that undertook a teacher survey reports discouraging results: only six out of seventy-two teachers cared enough to fill out the several page questionnaire. One girl on the committee says that she saw a teacher use the back of his survey to write out a hall pass. Meanwhile, the group that surveyed students about their attitudes was also disappointed. Of seventy-five surveys handed out to boys, only twelve were returned. Among those, the responses were often facetious, such as "I harassed her because she deserved it," or "because her butt's too big," or "because she has big tits."

"So what they're saying," Ms. Logan points out, "is that the responsibility for the harassment rests with the female."

The students on the committee nod, considering this.

The female students were the only segment of the school's population that promptly completed and returned their surveys. Like the girls in Ms. Logan's class, they reported that they were harassed frequently—sometimes daily—and felt that harsher penalties should be enforced against their tormentors. Most of the girls said that they tell no one when they are harassed, and they often blamed themselves or their choice of clothing for provoking unwanted attention.

"Most girls thought there was no point in telling the counselors because they wouldn't do anything," concludes Alissa, who helped administer the survey.

"Well," says Ms. Logan, "there seems to be little awareness by the girls that they have the right not to be treated that way. Girls can only ask the counselor to do something if they know they have that right."

Ms. Logan pauses and looks around the class. Then she does something unique among the teachers I've observed: she defines the hidden curriculum. "Class," she says, "there's something you need to know about, called the hidden curriculum. The hidden curriculum is all the things teachers don't say, but that you learn in class anyway. Sometimes, the hidden curriculum is what you learn the most. Sexual harassment is part of the hidden curriculum for girls, and for boys, too, because they learn whether it has anything to do with them or not. The girls in these surveys are trying to be inconspicuous so they won't be harassed. They're trying not to be in the wrong place at the wrong time, trying not to dress a certain way. They learn to become silent, careful, not active or assertive in life. That's what the hidden curriculum teaches girls."

The students listen with solemn expressions.

"So what should we do about it?" Ms. Logan asks. "Reporting to each other is good, but what else can we do?"

"Let's make a booklet," says one girl. "Maybe we could hand it out with the student handbook to all the students and teachers."

"And there should be guidelines," a second girl offers.

"There should be an assembly," says a third.

"We have to work on getting girls not to be ashamed," Mindy says fiercely.

Ms. Logan nods her head in agreement. "This year is over," she says, "but this topic is not. I'll be home this summer so if anyone wants to work on a booklet for next year, we can do it." Several students eagerly raise their hands.

After class, I ask Luis what he thought about the reports. Over the last few weeks, he has had it pretty rough. Shortly after their first discussion of sexual harassment, he made an obscene comment to one of the girls in the class. All of the girls immediately banded together and stopped speaking to him, even though he subsequently apologized. "He talks like that all the time," one girl told me angrily. "He always apologizes, but then he does it again. We don't have to take that anymore."

"I know they look at me when they talk about guys who do this," Luis tells me now. "It's embarrassing, but I guess they want me to learn. And I guess I've got to learn sometime."

Luis still averts his gaze and smiles nervously when he talks to me, so it's hard to tell if he means what he says. But at least he's been in the room this quarter, at least he hears it. And if the girls do, indeed, decide that they will not socialize with boys who mistreat them, he may yet have to learn his lesson.

Stitching It All Together

For the last four years, as a final, unifying project, Ms. Logan's sixth-grade class makes a quilt with a women's history theme. Like the essays for the NOW competition, most of the quilts feature "Women We Admire." The students each pick a woman—who may be fictional or actual, past or present, famous or anonymous—and create a muslin quilt square in her honor. Some of the students draw faces, others draw symbols of their honorees' achievements: a gorilla for Dian Fossey, a double helix for Rosalind Franklin, a family tree commemorating a loved great-grandmother. An adult volunteer (usually someone's mother) then sews the squares together and the children help by ironing the seams and knotting the back of the quilt to the front through the cotton-batting center. They also compose essays about the women they have honored. Last year, Ms. Logan, who is adding science to her sixth-grade curriculum, asked her students to make a quilt entitled "Some Women in Science." In the center of the piece there is a large muslin square, painted blue and decorated with the phases of the moon. It bears a quote by nineteenth-century astronomer Maria Mitchell which encapsulates Ms. Logan's educational philosophy: "In my younger days," it reads, "when I was pained by the half-educated, loose and inaccurate ways that we [women] had, I used to say, 'How much women need exact science.' But since I have known some workers in science who were not always true to the teachings of nature, who have loved self more than science, I have now said, 'How much science needs women.' "

When I visit them during the last week of the school year, the sixth graders are busily finishing their quilt squares. Ms. Logan is engaged in a discussion with one of the boys, Jimmy, who has represented tennis star Monica Seles by drawing a bloody knife lying across a tennis racket.

"What do you admire about Monica Seles?" she asks.

Jimmy shrugs. "She was in the paper," he says. "She got stabbed."

"This quilt is about honoring women we admire," Ms. Logan responds. "It's okay to choose her because you admire her, but it's not okay to do a square on her because she was stabbed."

Jimmy begins to sulk. "But without being stabbed she's just another tennis player!" he complains.

"This quilt is not about violence toward women," Ms. Logan says firmly. "You can make a square with tennis rackets if you want to."

I've noticed that, during each of the projects I've observed—the African American history monologues, the American Women Making History class, and the quilt project—the boys who are most resistant to studying the female experience choose to focus on women in sports, especially tennis or track. When I mention this to Ms. Logan, she nods. "That's what they can best relate to," she says. "When boys feel like they're being forced to admire women they try to pick one that they think behaves sort of like a man. It's a step in the right direction. If they don't go beyond that at any point, I guess I'd see it as a failure, but sometimes you have to meet children where they're ready to learn."

I continue walking around the room, glancing at the students' work. Holly has chosen Kristi Yamaguchi, while her friend Dana has chosen Polly Bemis, the Chinese American heroine of the book *A Thousand Pieces of Gold*. Several students have decided to honor the subjects of their African American history monologues and still others have chosen to honor relatives. One Latino boy is drawing a picture of his aunt. "She's a single mom," he explains, "and her baby is in the hospital and she has two other kids at home. She has to work really hard, so I admire that."

A number of Ms. Logan's students are focusing on women in the arts. One of the boys tells me that Frieda Kahlo is a big inspiration to him. One of the girls, a redhead named Kristi, has chosen the Japanese artist Mayumi Oda. Oda's paintings depict women as goddesses, as founts of power. They are described in one collection as "a feminine view of the positive self." Kristi tells me she just thinks they're "neat."

Jimmy stares despondently at his new square, which looks rather stark with just a tennis racket. "I've decided to do Billie Jean King instead of Monica Seles," he says. "But I thought it was kind of important, a tennis player getting stabbed just so she wouldn't win. I don't know why that's not appropriate."

Jeremy is sitting on the floor near the door, putting the finishing touches on a square commemorating Rosa Parks, whom he first learned about in elementary school. His journey this year has taken him from Anita Hill, whom he wrote about in the NOW essay contest, to Etta James, to Parks. He shrugs when I mention this, more intent on the fact that one of the girls is laughing at his rendition of Ms. Parks's face—the eyes seem, somehow, to have gotten slightly crossed. When I press him further, Jeremy turns to me in exasperation.

"I don't see what the big deal is about women," he says, and I prepare to hear him say that he's tired of Ms. Logan's unfair focus on the female sex. But I've judged Jeremy too quickly. "I mean, as long as they're interesting, what's the difference if they're women? Women are people, too, you know."

Jeremy completes his square and brings it to Ms. Logan. She places it with several others that will be sewn together later and smiles. "This is how you teach about gender," Ms. Logan says to me as Jeremy sifts through the finished squares. "You do it one stitch at a time."

NOTES

1. Elizabeth G. Cohen, *Designing Groupwork: Strategies of the Heterogeneous Classroom,* 2nd ed., with a foreword by John J. Godlad, New York: Teachers College Press, 1994.

2. Marcia C. Linn, "Gender Differences in Educational Achievement," in *Sex Equity in Educational Opportunity, Achievement, and Testing,* Princeton, NJ: Proceedings of the 1991 Invitational Conference of the Educational Testing Service, 1992; "MMAP: Middle-School Mathematics Through Applications Project," Palo Alto, CA: Documentation from the Institute for Research on Learning, 1993.

3. Suzanne Alexander, "New Grade-School Sexuality Classes Go Beyond Birds and Bees to Explicit Basics," *The Wall Street Journal,* April 2, 1993, p. B1; [Susan Strauss], *Sexual Harassment to Teenagers: It's Not Fun/It's Illegal— A Curriculum for Identification and Prevention of Sexual Harassment for Use with Junior and Senior High School Students,* St. Paul, MN: Minnesota Department of Education Equal Educational Opportunities Section, 1988.

4. Michael Winerip. "Public School Offers a Social-Service Model," New York *Times*, December 8, 1993, p. A1; Michael Winerip, "In School: A Public School in Harlem That Takes the Time, and the Trouble, to Be a Family," New York *Times*, January 26, 1994, p. A19. For more on integrating values of home and community into the school setting, see Jane Roland Martin, *The Schoolhome: Rethinking Schools for Changing Families*, Cambridge, MA: Harvard University Press, 1992.

5. Josefina Villamil Tinajero, Maria Louisa Gonzalez, and Florence Dick, *Raising Career Aspirations of Hispanic Girls*, Bloomington, IN: Phi Delta Kappa Educational Foundation, 1991; "Facts and Figures on Hispanic Americans, Women, and Education," in *The Broken Web: The Educational Experience of Hispanic American Women*, Teresa McKenna and Flora Ida Ortiz, eds., Berkeley, CA: Floricanto Press, 1988, pp. 195–209.

6. Judy Logan, *Teaching Stories*, with a forward by Peggy McIntosh, St. Paul, MN: Minnesota Inclusiveness Program, 1993, p. x. Logan wrote *Teaching Stories* with the aid of an American Association of University Women Eleanor Roosevelt grant.

7. Di Bentley and Mike Watts, "Courting the Positive Virtues: A Case for Feminist Science," *European Journal of Science Education*, 8 (1986), pp. 121–23. See also Sue Rosser, *Biology & Feminism: A Dynamic Interaction*, New York: Twayne Publishers, 1992; Evelyn Fox Keller, *Reflections on Gender and Science*, New Haven: Yale University Press, 1985; Ruth Bleier, *Science and Gender: A Critique of Biology and Its Theories on Women*, New York: Pergamon Press, 1984; Evelyn Fox Keller, *A Feeling for the Organism: The Life and Work of Barbara McClintock*, San Francisco: W. H. Freeman and Co., 1983.

8. Emily Style, "Curriculum as Window and Mirror," in *Listening for All Voices: Gender Balancing the School Curriculum*, proceedings of a conference held at Oak Knoll School, Summit, NJ, June, 1988, p. 6.

9. Peggy McIntosh, "Interactive Phases of Curricular Re-Vision: A Feminist Perspective," Working Paper No. 124, Wellesley, MA: Wellesley College Center for Research on Women, 1983; Peggy McIntosh, "Interactive Phases of Curricular and Personal Re-Vision with Regard to Race," Working Paper No. 219, Wellesley, MA: Wellesley College Center for Research on Women, 1990. McIntosh's phases are meant to be applied across the curriculum.

10. Logan, *Teaching Stories*, p. 44.

11. Jamaica Kincaid, "Girl," in *At the Bottom of the River*, New York: Plume Contemporary Fiction, 1992, p. 3.

Grateful acknowledgment is made for permission to reprint the following:

From Bernice Resnick Sandler, "Too Strong for a Woman: The Five Words that Created Title IX," with edits by Bernice Resnick Sandler. Originally published in *Equity & Excellence in Education*, Vol. 33, No. 1, April 2000, pp. 9–13. Used by permission of the author.

From David Tyack and Elisabeth Hansot, "Feminists Discover the Hidden Injuries of Coeducation" in *Learning Together*. © 1992 Russell Sage Foundation, New York, New York, pp. 243–270. Used by permission of the Russell Sage Foundation.

From Carol Gilligan, "Images of Relationship" in *In a Different Voice*, pp. 24–63, Cambridge, Mass.: Harvard University Press, pp. 24–63. Copyright © 1982, 1983 by Carol Gilligan. Reprinted by permission of the publisher.

From William Pollack, "Real Boys: The Truths Behind the Myths" in *Real Boys*. Copyright © 1998, 2000 by William Pollack. Used by permission of Random House, Inc., Scribe Publishing, and Zachary Shuster Harmsworth.

From Michael Gurian, "Where It All Begins: The Biology of Boyhood" in *The Wonder of Boys*. Copyright © 1996 by Michael Gurian. Used by permission of Jeremy P. Tarcher, a division of Penguin Putnam.

From Barrie Thorne "Do Girls and Boys Have Different Cultures?" in *Gender Play*. Copyright © 1993 by Barrie Thorne. Reprinted by permission of Rutgers University Press.

From Dan Kindlon and Michael Thompson, "Thorns Among Roses: The Struggle of Young Boys in Early Education" in *Raising Cain*. Copyright © 1999 by Dan Kindlon, Ph.D. and Michael Thompson, Ph.D. Used by permission of Ballantine Books, a division of Random House, Inc., and Penguin Books, Ltd.

From Myra M. Sadker and David Sadker, "The Miseducation of Boys" in *Failing at Fairness*. Copyright © 1994 by Myra Sadker and David Sadker. Used with the permission of Scribner, a Division of Simon & Schuster, Inc., and Leap First.

From Lyn Mikel Brown, "The Madgirl in the Classroom" in *Raising Their Voices*, Lyn Mikel Brown, Cambridge, Mass.: Harvard University Press,